Library of
Davidson College

Also in the Variorum Collected Studies Series:

ROBERT FOX
Science, Industry and the Social Order in
Post-Revolutionary France

ROBERT FOX
The Culture of Science in France, 1700–1900

MAURICE CROSLAND
Studies in the Culture of Science in France and Britain
since the Enlightenment

JOHN HARRIS
Essays in Industry and Technology in the 18th Century:
England and France

JOHN RUSSELL MAJOR
The Monarchy, the Estates and the Aristocracy in
Renaissance France

ALFRED SOMAN
Sorcellerie et justice criminelle:
Le Parlement de Paris (16e–18e siècles)

ANDRÉ-E. SAYOUS
Structure et évolution du capitalisme européen,
XVIe–XVIIe siècles

BRIAN PULLAN
Poverty and Charity:
Europe, Italy and Venice, 1400–1700

PAUL F. GRENDLER
Culture and Censorship in Late Renaissance Italy and France

R.W. HOME
Electricity and Experimental Physics in 18th-Century Europe

ALLEN G. DEBUS
Chemistry, Alchemy and the New Philosophy, 1550–1700

E. WILLIAM MONTER
Enforcing Morality in Early Modern Europe

JOHN W. O'MALLEY
Religious Culture in the 16th Century:
Preaching, Rhetoric, Spirituality and Reform

COLLECTED STUDIES SERIES

The Limits of Absolutism
in *ancien régime* France

Professor Richard Bonney

Richard Bonney

The Limits of Absolutism
in *ancien régime* France

VARIORUM
1995

This edition copyright © 1995 by Richard Bonney.

Published by VARIORUM
    Ashgate Publishing Limited
    Gower House, Croft Road,
    Aldershot, Hampshire GU11 3HR
    Great Britain

    Ashgate Publishing Company
    Old Post Road,
    Brookfield, Vermont 05036
    USA

ISBN 0-86078-482-7

British Library CIP Data
    Bonney, Richard
    Limits of Absolutism in *ancien régime* France.
    (Variorum Collected Studies Series; CS 491)
    I. Title II. Series
    944

US Library of Congress CIP Data
    Bonney, Richard
    The Limits of Absolutism in *ancien régime* France/Richard Bonney.
    p. cm. — (Collected Studies Series: CS491)
    Includes index.   ISBN 0-86078-482-7
    1. Monarchy—France—History. 2. Despotism—France—History.
    3. Taxation—France—History. 4. France—Politics and
    government—17th century. 5. France—History—17th century.
    I. Title. II. Series: Collected Studies: CS491.
    JN2358.B66 1995   94–37035
    320.444'09'03—dc20   CIP

The paper used in this publication meets the minimum requirements of the American National Standard for Information Sciences - Permanence of Paper for Printed Library Materials, ANSI Z39.48-1984. ∞ ™

Printed by Galliard (Printers) Ltd
    Great Yarmouth, Norfolk, Great Britain

COLLECTED STUDIES SERIES CS491

CONTENTS

Introduction — vii–xi

THE DEVELOPMENT OF THE MONARCHICAL SYSTEM

I   Absolutism: what's in a name? — 93–117
French History 1. Oxford University Press, 1987

II   Bodin and the development of the French monarchy — 43–61
*Transactions of the Royal Historical Society,
5th series 40. London: Royal Historical Society, 1990*

III   Was there a Bourbon style of government? — 161–177
*From Valois to Bourbon: Dynasty, State & Society
in Early Modern France, ed. K. Cameron. Exeter, 1989*

RESISTANCE TO THE DEVELOPMENT OF THE MONARCHICAL SYSTEM:
MAZARIN AND THE FRONDE

IV   The French Civil War, 1649–53 — 71–100
*European Studies Review 8.
London: Sage Publications, 1978*

V   The English and French Civil Wars — 365–382
History 65. London: Historical Association, 1980

VI   Cardinal Mazarin and his critics: the remonstrances
of 1652 — 15–31
*Journal of European Studies 10. Chalfont St Giles,
Bucks: Science History Publications Ltd, 1980*

VII   Cardinal Mazarin and the great nobility during
the Fronde — 818–833
*English Historical Review 96.
London: Longmans, 1981*

VIII   La Fronde des officiers: mouvement réformiste ou
rébellion corporatiste? — 323–340
XVIIe Siècle 145. Paris, 1984

IX	Mazarin et la Fronde: la question de responsibilité *La Fronde en Questions*, ed. R. Duchêne and P. Ronzeaud. Aix-en-Provence: Université de Provence, 1989	329–338

THE DEVELOPMENT OF ROYAL FINANCE

X	The secret expenses of Richelieu and Mazarin, 1624–61 *English Historical Review 91*. London: Longmans, 1976	825–836
XI	The failure of the French revenue farms, 1600–60 *Economic History Review*, 2nd series 32. Oxford: Basil Blackwell, 1979	11–32
XII	The state and its revenues in *ancien régime* France *Historical Research 65*. Oxford: Basil Blackwell, 1992	150–176
XIII	Louis XIII, Richelieu, and the royal finances *Richlieu and his Age*, ed. J.A. Bergin and L. Brockliss. Oxford: Clarendon Press, 1992	99–133
XIV	'Le secret de leurs familles': the fiscal and social limits of Louis XIV's *dixième* *French History 7*. Oxford University Press, 1993	383–416
XV	Comparative fiscal systems on the eve of modernity: the French enquiry of 1763 *La genèse de l'État moderne et le cas ottoman*, Table-ronde d'Istanbul, 1991, ed. J.-Ph. Genet and E. Eldhem, Varia Turcica, E.S.F. et I.F.E.A. Istanbul, 1994	61–81
Additional notes		1–3
Index		1–13

This volume contains xii + 338 pages

INTRODUCTION

There is probably never an optimum time for a working historian to collect together his papers for republication. Perspectives change. A new paper given here or there might replace one in an existing collection, to its benefit. The shape of the collection as a whole would be somewhat affected, but would much change? There has been an underlying pattern to the research interests and associated publications of this historian's career. These have been encompassed here under three broad categories – the nature of the governing system, which for want of a better term is called 'absolutism'; the political crisis of the mid-seventeenth century which, again for lack of an acceptable alternative is called the Fronde (this author has never accepted that *la Fronde* should become 'the Frondes' in English, even if it is a more accurate view of what actually happened in a series of revolts); and the development of royal finance. It becomes immediately apparent that one aspect of the author's work – the provincial intendants of Richelieu and Mazarin, the subject of his first book,[1] and those of Louis XIV, the subject of a projected book, are largely conspicuous by their absence. They are briefly considered in chapter II, in relation to the theoretical underpinning of the monarchy and the power accorded to their subordinate officials (the *subdélégués*); again in chapter III, which addresses the question as to whether there was a Bourbon style of monarchy to compare with the Valois; and finally, in chapter XIV, which discusses their role in helping to establish the new tax called the *dixième*. The explanation is simple if curious: the occasion for giving a paper on the intendants has never presented itself. Articles and book chapters are inevitably *pièces de circonstances*, to some extent, where the subject matter is suggested by the context of the occasion. Although some published material is excluded from this volume,[2] it is hoped that there nevertheless remains a degree of coherence to the subject matter of almost twenty years' worth of publications.

---

1 Cf. R. J. Bonney, *Political Change in France under Richelieu and Mazarin, 1624-1661* (Oxford, 1978).
2 The following papers (in chronological order) have been excluded: 'The paradox of Mazarin', *History Today* 32 (1982), 18–24; 'France's war by diversion', *The Thirty Years' War*, ed. N. G. Parker (Routledge and Kegan Paul, 1985), 144–53 [trans. as 'La France et la guerre de diversion', *La Guerre de Trente Ans*, ed. N. G. Parker (Paris, Aubier, 1987), 226–38]; 'Guerre, fiscalité et activité d'État en France, 1500–1660: quelques remarques préliminaires sur les possibilités de recherche', *Genèse de l'État moderne: Prélèvement et redistribution*, ed. J-Ph. Genet and M. Le Mené (Paris, 1987), 193–201; 'Precursors of the modern state', *French History* 3 (1989), 466–78; 'Jean-Roland Malet: historian of the

The driving force behind all the various publications has been consideration of the growth of the French state, on the one hand in its ideological and institutional aspects (part I) and on the other in its fiscal aspects (part III). Another central interest has been the opposition such developments provoked in the crisis of the mid-seventeenth century (part II). Chapter I discusses the historiography of absolutism, a theme developed elsewhere.[3] One aspect of Bodin's contribution towards the ideological development of the French monarchy is considered in chapter II, though it should be stressed that Bodin's arguments were used by later commentators for their own purposes. The third paper in part I evaluates the change that occurred in one province – the small and distant province of Béarn – in the century following the Bourbon succession (chapter III). The story has significant implications for the speed of the process of assimilation of the newly acquired provinces, as well as for the nature of Henri IV's régime. Political and institutional change was brought about in the wake of the Bourbon dynasty, under Louis XIII and Louis XIV if not under Henri IV, and intendants were crucial to the success of these developments, even in Béarn. Chapter III serves as a reminder of a point made only in passing elsewhere – that religious uniformity was an objective of the Bourbon dynasty, if not immediately after the conversion of Henri IV in 1593 then at least from the time that Louis XIII struck out against Concini and asserted his own control of power in the *coup d'état* of April 1617.

Magnate and office-holder resistance to the institutional and fiscal strengthening of the French monarchy are considered in two separate chapters (chapters VII and VIII respectively). Should the Fronde be called a revolution? The question has recently been posed once again.[4] In two articles republished here (chapters IV and V), the author argued that there was a case for calling the Fronde a civil war, a depiction which certainly rests on contemporary evidence. Although it conveys no immediately obvious resonance in English, there is equally strong evidence for calling the Fronde by one of the terms used by contemporaries – *la Fronde*, a fight with slings: the first recorded figure to deploy the sling to devastating effect was David when he overwhelmed Goliath

---

finances of the French monarchy', *French History* 5 (1991), 180–233; 'The sinews of power: the finances of the French monarchy from Henri IV to Louis XIV', *History Review* 12 (1992), 7–12. Currently two papers – 'State competition for resources and fiscal innovation under Louis XIV' and 'Taxation and the problem of European regions' – remain unpublished. There are two introductions and four forthcoming chapters in *Economic Systems and State Finance* and *The Rise of the Fiscal State in Europe, c.1200 – c.1815*, both edited by the author.
3 *L'absolutisme* (Paris, 1989); Portuguese translation by M. do Anjo Figueiredo: *O absolutismo* (Lisbon, 1991).
4 O. A. Ranum, *The Fronde. A French Revolution, 1648–1653* (New York and London, 1993).

(1 Sam. 17:49).[5] On such an historical precedent might the corrupt and overmighty political system of Mazarin be brought down by the lowly, or so it might seem to the popular readership of the political pamphlets known as the *Mazarinades*. But though it threatened to become a revolution, the Fronde was singularly short on lasting achievement. This historian finds it difficult to accept 'the fact that millions of peasants and city-dwellers paid substantially lower taxes, or no taxes at all for two or three years' must be considered an 'important revolutionary accomplishment'.[6] There is rather more substance to the depiction of the Fronde as a *révolution manquée*, a revolution which failed or misfired. Above all, it was a crisis provoked in some measure by Mazarin, the chief minister from 1643 to 1661 (chapter IX) and directed against him personally by the leaders of the opposition, since he provided a much-needed focus for unity (chapter VI).

The 'fiscal imperative', the increased requirements posed by the costs of war, and the long-term consequences of fiscal growth may be seen as the *primum mobile* for the development of the state. However, the periodization is necessarily a longer one than the crisis of the mid-seventeenth century. For this reason, the papers which discuss the finances of the French monarchy have been placed together in part III. It is hoped that they represent a not unimportant contribution towards what has been called the 'new fiscal history'.[7] The author's first published article was on the secret expenses under Richelieu and Mazarin (chapter X). The original argument was important and remains unaffected by a marginal revision of the figures:[8] very high interest rates could be paid to financiers by means of the *comptants*, without effective scrutiny by the *Chambre des Comptes*. Corruption was an omnipresent feature of government by a chief minister and his clients, a consequence of lax ethical standards in contemporary perceptions and practice.[9] But there were also institutional aspects of secrecy and unaccountability, which made these corrupt practices much more dangerous. There was a mid-century failure of institutional control which combined with the assertion of executive independ-

---

5 Depicted in the engraving by Abraham Brosse (1651), with text commencing 'La Fronde en cet endroit fit un coup...': H. Carrier, *La presse et la Fronde, 1648–1653: Les Mazarinades...* (2 vols., Geneva, 1989–91), ii, 251.
6 Ranum, *The Fronde*, 345.
7 P. T. Hoffman and K. Norberg (eds.), 'Introduction', *Fiscal Crises, Liberty, and Representative Government, 1450–1789* (Stanford, 1994), 2; J. D. Tracy, 'Taxation and state debt', *Handbook of European History, 1400–1600. Late Middle Ages, Renaissance and Reformation. I. Structures and Assertions*, ed. T. A. Brady, Jr., H. A. Oberman and J. D. Tracy (Leiden, New York, Cologne, 1994), 563.
8 Bonney, *The King's Debts. Finance and Politics in France, 1589–1661* (Oxford, 1981), 173 n. 4, 308–9.
9 On this, see particularly Bonney, 'Ethics and Politics in Seventeenth-Century France: the Foucquet-Colbert Rivalry and the "Revolution" of 1661', for the Derek Watts *Festschrift* (University of Exeter Press, 1995).

ence to produce something approaching financial chaos at the centre. The intractability of managing one aspect of the fiscal system, the revenue farms, is the subject of chapter XI. Here it is demonstrated that the key purpose of revenue farming, which was to secure a settled, regular, income was vitiated by the increasing need in wartime to compensate revenue farmers for their losses: the farmers could not be refused compensation because they provided short-term loans which were vital for the war effort. The evolution of the French revenue system in its entirety over the longer term is considered in chapter XII: the eighteenth century saw a much greater reliance on indirect revenues than was the case under Richelieu and Mazarin. The relationship of political planning to state finance, and the difficulties of implementing fiscal reform under Richelieu are the subject of chapter XIII. The great Cardinal statesman is shown to have had a reform plan of sorts, but one which would have turned back the clock with regard to the development of the state.

Finally, the last two papers reach the eighteenth century. Towards the end of Louis XIV's reign, the long-term financial consequences of nearly a century of continuous warfare were assuming national significance in terms of the costs of debt servicing.[10] The intellectual argument surrounding the establishment of a new direct tax in wartime (the *dixième* of Louis XIV) and the difficulties of its enforcement are discussed in chapter XIV. The final chapter moves on to the later years of Louis XV's reign to assess the chances of reform in time of peace. How could a reform of direct taxation best be secured? Bertin was a proponent of introducing a national land register (*cadastre*). Since the scheme met with opposition in 1763, one way to progress appeared to be to examine in detail how other states had introduced comparable measures of reform, to ascertain the extent to which these reforms had proved beneficial, and to establish what difficulties and obstacles had to be overcome (chapter XV). An earlier paper had compared English and French developments around the time of the crisis of the mid-seventeenth century (chapter V). Such national comparisons need to be extended over a longer timescale, but they are notoriously difficult to achieve. There is a lack of contemporary evidence on which to base such comparison, apart from diplomatic reports. One of the great interests of the enquiry launched by Bertin in 1763 and continued by L'Averdy, his successor as controller-general of finance, was precisely that it attempted to make systematic comparisons based on a common questionnaire. We have not arrived at a prototype of the European Union, with its directives to ensure harmony and conformity to a set of rules; instead we are in the era of sovereign states, with multiple institutional structures and diverse fiscal traditions. The reports arising from the enquiry are revealing precisely because

---

10 M. M. and R. J. Bonney, *Jean-Roland Malet: premier historien des finances de la monarchie française* (Comité pour l'histoire économique et financière de la France, Paris, 1993), 70–4, 82–8.

they emphasise diversity, and because some of them (for example, the Spanish one) were written, or edited, by financial experts close to the centre of power.

The author is grateful to Variorum for this opportunity to place together a set of papers, some old, others quite recent, which have appeared in different locations and are inevitably difficult to track down. Working on the material anew, he is very conscious of the gaps; but it is hoped that what emerges is rather greater than the sum of the parts. The history of the state is now back on the agenda as the publications from the European Science Foundation Project on the Origins of the Modern State in Europe begin to emerge.[11]

The author thanks several Editors and publishers for permission to reproduce the articles which appear in this volume: the Editor of *French History* (Chapters I and XIV); the Honorary Secretary, on behalf of the Council of the Royal Historical Society (Chapter II); the Secretary to the University of Exeter Press (Chapter III); the Editor of *European History Quarterly* (Chapter IV); the Association Secretary on behalf of the Historical Association as publishers of *History* (Chapter V); the Editor of *Journal of European Studies* (Chapter VI); the *Editor of English Historical Review* (Chapters VII and X); the translator, Professor Yves-Marie Bercé, and the Editor, Monsieur Georges Molinié, *XVIIe Siècle* (Chapter VIII); Professor Roger Duchêne, Président du C.M.R.-17 (Chapter IX); the Editor of Economic Historical Review (Chapter XI); Professor P. K. O'Brien, Director of the Institute of Historical Research and Editor of *Historical Research* (Chapter XII); Drs Joseph Bergin and Laurence Brockliss and Oxford University Press (Chapter XIII); and Monsieur Jacques Thobie, Directeur de l'Institut Français d'Études Anatoliennes, Editor of *Varia Turcica* (Chapter XV).

RICHARD BONNEY

Leicester
November, 1994

PUBLISHER'S NOTE
The articles in this volume, as in all others in the Collected Studies Series, have not been given a new, continuous pagination. In oreder to avoid confusion, and to facilitate their use where these same studies have been referred to elsewhere, the original pagination has been maintained wherever possible.

Each article has been given a Roman number in order of appearance, as listed in the Contents. This number is repeated on each page and quoted in the index entries.

References in the Additional Notes are indicated with an asterisk in the margin next to the relevant part of the text.

---

[11] The author's edited volume, *Economic Systems and State Finance* (Oxford, 1995), is the first of seven volumes from the European Science Foundation project to appear.

This book is dedicated to my wife, Margaret, and my children, Alexander, Katherine, Sarah and Christine.

I

ABSOLUTISM: WHAT'S IN A NAME?

The last decade has witnessed such a proliferation of writing on the theme of absolutism that a review is not inappropriate. In the English-speaking world, interest in the subject arises naturally from the traditions of political theory and constitutional history. It is self-evident that considerations of power must be one of the main areas of enquiry of the historian. In France, too, there are signs of a reawakening of interest in the history of the state, as is shown by the organization of conferences on the theme and in the current research projects of certain prominent scholars. In some respects, however, this historical outpouring is surprising, since it runs counter to the emphasis in recent French historiography on socio-economic history, especially history 'from the bottom up'. Whatever the current fashion, it is difficult for the historian of early modern France to ignore the preoccupations of his twentieth-century colleagues following two world wars precipitated by authoritarian regimes and the disease of totalitarianism that infects much of the world.

It is a statement of the obvious that rulers throughout the ages have possessed authoritarian ambitions. Yet it is surprising to read an account of the general characteristics of absolutism that commences as late as the fifth century, and concludes that the 'perfection' of absolutism was the work not of Louis XIV but of Napoleon Bonaparte.[1] It was in the late Roman Empire that an early statement of absolutist intentions, if not a fully-fledged absolutist theory, first emerged. Seneca advocated that Nero use mercy because 'in a position of unlimited power this is the truest self-control'; an all-embracing love of the human race, even as of oneself, dulled 'the edge of supreme power'. Ulpian's third-century dictum *quod principi placuit legis habet vigorem* ('what has pleased the Emperor has the force of a *lex*', that is, a law passed in assembly by the Roman *populus*) was of great importance for future political argument derived from Roman law. A crude sixteenth-century formulation by Loisel ('qui veut le roi, si veut la loi') is merely a repetition of the statement. Medieval lawyers had also discussed at length the Roman legal maxim *princeps legibus solutus* (*est*) ('the prince is freed from (absolved, or above) the laws'), perhaps the

---

[1] R. É. Mousnier, *La monarchie absolue en Europe du ve siècle à nos jours*. Presses Universitaires de France, 1982. 245 pp. The vicissitudes of absolutism in the middle ages have been discussed by J. A. Burns, 'Absolutism: the history of an idea', Creighton Lecture, University of London (10 November 1986).

© Oxford University Press 1987

origin of the term *pouvoir absolu*. The idea that the king was 'Emperor in his kingdom' was a specific application of Roman law principles to the conditions in fifteenth-century France. Thus though the term 'absolutism' is a neologism dating from the French Revolution, the term 'absolute power' was certainly used in the middle ages and early modern period.

What does absolute power mean to the historian of early modern France? The simplest definition is 'freedom of the monarch in practice from institutional checks on his power', in short, a regime where the ruler is not limited by institutions outside the kingship itself. There is no historical inevitability that power will be concentrated in this way. Indeed, the history of medieval kingship is in part concerned with the fragmentation of power into 'estate states' (*Ständestaat*), only gradually corrected by the so-called 'royal mechanism' (*Königsmechanismus*), the tendency of the monarchy to absorb functions and increase its power by balancing the different interest groups within the country against each other and gaining increasing control over them. Among modern sociologists it is Norbert Elias who has stressed this tension most clearly, between what modern political commentators would be inclined to call pluralism and a unitary state or centralization.[2]

The term 'centralization' is best avoided by the historian of early modern France, however, since it was first coined in 1794 during the Terror and after Louis XVI had been guillotined. It was alien to sixteenth- and seventeenth-century political theory. Instead, contemporaries stressed the distinction between the king's delegated and his retained justice. As Mousnier points out in a useful chapter on the state in his monumental study of French institutions,[3] in the 'public and political affairs of our kingdom' the king was sovereign and therefore absolute, but in his subjects' affairs liberties and privileges were protected though they might be infringed on a temporary basis during an emergency.[4] Mousnier concludes that the French monarchical state possessed extensive political powers but only feeble resources;[5] this might be seen as a reason for the failure of absolutism. Others have argued that absolutism was in any case a logical impossibility and that all that could be achieved was a strengthening of monarchical institutions ('*relative* absolutism').[6] Though the 'drive to absolutism' occurred under successive French kings between, say, 1500 and 1789, 'absolutism was always in the making but never made'.[7]

---

[2] Norbert Elias, *The civilizing process. I. The history of manners. II. State formation and civilization,* trans. Edmund Jephcott. Basil Blackwell, 1978 and 1982. xviii + 314 pp. and viii + 376 pp. Idem, *The court society,* trans. Edmund Jephcott. Basil Blackwell, 1983. 301 pp. For the royal mechanism: *State formation,* p. 161.

[3] R. É. Mousnier, *The institutions of France under the absolute monarchy, 1598-1789,* trans. Brian Pearce. Chicago University Press, 1980 and 1984. 2 vols, xix + 783 pp. and xix + 695 pp. Original French edition at Presses Universitaires de France, 1974 and 1980.

[4] Ibid. i. 665.

[5] Ibid. i. 740.

[6] Perez Zagorin, *Rebels and rulers, 1500-1660* (2 vols, Cambridge, 1982), i. 91.

[7] David Parker, *The making of French absolutism.* Edward Arnold, 1983. xvi + 160 pp.

I ABSOLUTISM IN THEORY

Absolutism may be perceived as no more than a conservative philosophy – in David Parker's formulation, 'a pragmatic, frequently *ad hoc* and contradictory attempt to *restore* royal authority in the context of a rapidly changing world'.[8] In any case, as several perceptive commentators have observed, absolutism is an essentially negative term, telling us less about what absolutism was than about what it was not.[9]

Absolutist theory has been addressed in two general studies, by Herbert Rowen and Nannerl Keohane. Whether or not Louis XIV actually used the words 'l'état c'est (à) moi' has been endlessly contested. Rowen concludes that he 'probably did not'. Such a comment, however, 'would have been quite in character' since, as his attitude to the transfer of territory in foreign policy matters shows, the king thought the state belonged to him.[10] Clearly, 'proprietary dynasticism' – defined by Rowen as the king acting as the owner of public power – was more than an aberration. However, there was also an alternative view of kingship as an office, which was the one which triumphed. Louis XIV recognized that there were indeed two views when he accepted the will of Carlos II. Philip V, he said, had been called to the crowns of Spain by 'birth . . . as well as the late king's testament'.[11] Rowen discusses the writings of political theorists, but rightly stresses that discussion of proprietary issues was very much a response to events, such as when a debate over the succession to a state occurred. The negotiations at the end of the War of the Spanish Succession were delayed by conflicting ideologies, the Allies favouring the view of kingship as a transferable office (and by this means removing the rights of Philip V to the French throne), while Louis XIV remained firm to his upbringing, his promises to Philip and to the fundamental laws of the French monarchy – that is, until the Peace of Utrecht was reluctantly conceded.

Political thought might thus shift under the impact of events. The relationship between ideas and the ordering of society is one of the most complex historical problems. Men make ideas; they put ideas into action; they may also take actions which break with accepted ideas and consciously or unconsciously mould the thoughts of future generations. Nannerl Keohane's study of French political thought from Seyssel (1519) to Rousseau (1762) is welcome as an almost unique attempt to span the period from the Renaissance to the Enlightenment;[12] but while it provides many insights, it also demonstrates in an acute form some of the problems arising from the attempt to view political thought as the 'history of

---

[8] Ibid. p. 90.
[9] Pierre Goubert and Daniel Roche, *Les français et l'ancien régime*. Armand Colin, 1984. 2 vols, 384 pp. + 394 pp. See i. 221. See also R. M. Jackson (below, n. 18), p. 208. Jackson uses the expression 'striving towards absolutism'.
[10] Herbert H. Rowen, *The king's state. Proprietary dynasticism in early modern France*. Rutgers University Press, 1980. 232 pp. See pp. 70, 76.
[11] Ibid. p. 114.
[12] Nannerl O. Keohane, *Philosophy and the state in France: The Renaissance to the Enlightenment*. Princeton University Press, 1980. xii + 501 pp.

ideologies'. The author's aim is to show how the arguments of Montesquieu and Rousseau are rooted in earlier French thought, but this poses the question of discontinuity. For example, in Rousseau's *Social Contract* absolute sovereignty is exercised not by the monarchy but by a collective entity. Keohane stresses the interplay between an emphasis on the indivisibility of sovereignty and the gradual emergence of a concept of 'interests' meaning rather more than self-interest but rather less than 'public interest', the second development occurring later than the first.

The traditional place assigned to the jurists in the period 1515-1661, and their subsequent decline, is missing in Keohane's account. The two jurists who have received most of the recent attention are Bodin and Loyseau.[13] Of the two, Bodin has caused more disagreement among commentators, reflecting the contradictions in his statements about sovereign power. The 'principal point of sovereign majesty and absolute power' was considered by Bodin 'to consist principally in giving laws unto the subjects in general, without their consent'. Sovereignty was 'absolute and perpetual power' in relation to the subject. However, Bodin argued that although the king was, in theory, absolute he ought to refrain from exercising his full power: for example, he should not violate the goods and property of his subjects whose welfare was the supreme law. Even in a monarchical state, the right of levying taxes depended upon the consent of the estates.[14] Bodin's vision was of a commonweal ordered in proper harmonic proportion, in which 'one sovereign prince' was necessary, and on whom all others depended.[15] Such moral philosophy is absent from Loyseau's political thought. In Loyseau's view, France was 'possibly today the most pure and perfect monarchy in the world', in which the king levied taxes without the consent of the estates. However, such levies must either be voluntarily agreed by the people or else necessary as, for example, when the prince had to save his subjects from danger.[16]

Like all legal theorists, Bodin and Loyseau present a rather artificial, perhaps even a one-dimensional view of historical development. The excessive reliance of historians on such writings results, it has been said, in a static picture of society and institutions, a description of how the structure was supposed to have operated rather than how it actually did.[17] The French monarchy evolved in response to both theoretical standpoints and political imperatives. Richard Jackson's study of the French coronation from 1364 to 1825 throws much light on the process, and on the role of

---

[13] Howell A. Lloyd, *The state, France and the sixteenth century*. Allen & Unwin, 1980. xx + 233 pp. Idem, 'The political thought of Charles Loyseau (1564-1627)', *Eur Stud R*, 11 (1981), 53-82. David Parker, 'Law, society and the state in the thought of Jean Bodin', *Hist Pol Th*, 2 (1981), 253-85.

[14] Parker, *The making of French absolutism*, pp. 271-2. Lloyd, *The state, France and the sixteenth century*, pp. 158, 160.

[15] Parker, pp. 277-8. Lloyd, p. 161.

[16] Lloyd, pp. 163-6 and 'The political thought of Charles Loyseau', p. 69.

[17] Roger Mettam, 'Two-dimensional history: Mousnier and the ancien régime', *History*, 66 (1981), 221-32. See p. 221.

the coronation oath in particular.[18] The French king swore two oaths in Latin, one concerning the bishops and the church, the other the so-called 'oath of the kingdom'. Though it is often claimed that the coronation oath included a clause prohibiting alienation of the demesne, there is no contemporary proof of this; the law of inalienability was a matter of custom, which was enshrined by edict in 1566 and 1579. Rights of pardon were accorded to the new king; but even when used most extensively (by Louis XIV), the right never extended to individuals regardless of crime.

The most significant threat to the future of absolute monarchy in France before the Revolution itself came in 1593 with the League's attempt to elect a Catholic king, which would have had the effect of replacing the laws of succession by a prior law of Catholicity. The Estates General failed to agree, and Henri IV timed his abjuration with consummate skill. Though the subsequent success of the Bourbon dynasty could not have been foreseen in 1593, these events ensured that it would be a Catholic dynasty committed to the vision of a single faith in the realm. This had been the viewpoint of the Gallican clergy without whose support the coronation at Chartres could not have been mounted.[19] The establishment of a single religion in France was also the essential condition of papal assent in 1595 to Henri's abjuration two years earlier.[20]

The practical implications of absolutist theory are investigated by Sarah Hanley in her study of the forty-seven royal visits to the *Parlement* of Paris between 1315 and 1713 which qualify under her criteria for the designation of *lit de justice*.[21] This procedure, a special assembly for political purposes, is depicted in many accounts as an 'absolutist' link between the reigns of Francis I and Louis XIV, the special sessions of the *Parlement* being held to deal with opposition, particularly the presentation of remonstrances which held up the registration of legislation. Hanley demonstrates that after the posthumous publication of Jean du Tillet's *Recueil des roys de France* (1580; it first appeared under a different title in 1577), a myth about the origins of the *lit de justice* grew, suggesting that it had been a constitutional forum in the middle ages. This was far from the case: the first two *lits de justice* held by Francis I in 1527 stand out as an innovation, and were required to deal with the aftermath of the rebellion of the Constable of Bourbon and the king's repudiation of the treaty signed while he was in captivity at Madrid. The apparent link between reigns provided by the *lit de justice* is in fact no link at all, since the term had dif-

[18] Richard A. Jackson, *Vive le roi! A history of the French coronation from Charles V to Charles X*. University of North Carolina Press, 1984. xvi + 310 pp. French edition at Strasbourg, 1984.

[19] René Pillorget, 'Le sacre d'Henri IV roi de France et de Navarre à Chartres le 27 février 1594', *Herrscherweihe und Königskrönung im frühneuzeitlichen Europa*, ed. H. Duchhardt (Weisbaden, 1983), 103-17. J. P. K. Powis, 'Gallican liberties and the politics of later sixteenth-century France', *Hist J*, 26 (1983), 515-30.

[20] David Parker, *La Rochelle and the French monarchy. Conflict and order in seventeenth-century France*. Royal Historical Society, 1980. xiv + 234 pp. See pp. 130-1.

[21] Sarah Hanley, *The lit de justice of the kings of France. Constitutional ideology in legend, ritual and discourse*. Princeton University Press, 1983. xiii + 389 pp.

ferent meanings, and the assembly was used for different purposes, between 1527 and 1673. There were relatively few of them in the sixteenth century, whereas Louis XIII held twenty (all but three at Paris), most of which were designed to secure the registration of fiscal edicts against the opposition of the *Parlement:* they at least seem to fit the description of the textbooks. In contrast, Louis XIV held only nineteen in his much longer reign, all before 1673. Five were held during his minority and raised constitutional issues. The *lit de justice* of October 1652 is seen as particularly important, since it was held at the Louvre, thus humiliating the *Parlement* of Paris at the end of the Fronde. The ceremonial rituals and prepared discourses for these sessions demonstrate the interplay of forces – in Hanley's definition, juristic, dynastic and absolutist – that shaped the customary constitution.

Popular attitudes to this customary constitution are not easily discerned, since most people were illiterate or only semi-literate. The historian therefore has to look for indirect evidence, and this is to be found in the tradition of popular revolt in the late sixteenth and earlier seventeenth centuries. There have been several books on this subject,[22] but Yves-Marie Bercé's study of revolts in south-western France, now reissued in abridged form, provides the most effective typology of revolt (detailed, yet not so complex as to create unnecessary categories), and, above all, the most challenging analysis of the mentality of the rebels.[23] Rumours played a crucial role in spreading popular rebellion. These rumours might be fuelled by talk of the malevolence of a traditional stereotype, the *gabeleur cannibale,* by the revival of traditional fears such as the *impôt sur la vie,* and by the resurgence of traditional hopes such as the *impôt remis* by a peace treaty or the death of the king. What is particularly striking, however, is the political naïvety of the seventeenth-century rebels. The absolute monarch was above reproach as an individual. The epithet *père du peuple* had real force, despite the fact that the king presided over the detested increase in taxes which provoked rebellion. The king was not culpable: he was misled by his ministers, 'Messieurs de Paris ou du Conseil se mocquans de leurs souffrances, augmentant de nouvelles charges et impositions tous les ans, soubz ce beau pretexte des nécessitez de l'estat . . . '[24] Rebellious peasants did not merely address themselves to members of the central government as the origin of their misfortune, but to the local office-holders and agents of financiers. They wanted local officials, accountable to the locality: 'otez-nous ces officiers de finance, rendez cette province pays d'Estat . . . donnez leur un syndic'.[25]

[22] Among others, Foisil (below, n. 84). R. Pillorget, *Les mouvements insurrectionnels de Provence entre 1596 et 1715* (1975).

[23] Yves-Marie Bercé, *Histoire des croquants.* Seuil, 1986. 411 pp. Abridged edition of idem, *Histoire des croquants. Étude des soulèvements populaires au xviie siècle dans le sud-ouest de la France* (2 vols, Paris/Geneva, 1974).

[24] Bercé, *Histoire des croquants,* i. 391, ii. 736. The chapter and the text are omitted from the revised edition.

[25] Bercé, i. 418–19 and ii. 754. Abridged edn, p. 144.

Notwithstanding Yves-Marie Bercé's remarkable attempt to depict popular attitudes to the crown, the ideological success of the proponents of absolutism is difficult to gauge. Except at periods of crisis such as the wars of religion, the Fronde and the outbreak of the Revolution, it was rarely safe and invariably unwise for one's career prospects to publish opposing views. Nevertheless, one of the most interesting periods is the crisis provoked by the Maupeou 'revolution' of 1770-4, which led to a flood of writings studied by Durand Echeverria.[26] This is an examination of the thought of a brief historical period, not the study of the development of ideas over a long time-scale. The author works from the assumption that the central issue dominating politics in these years was whether France was to be ruled by a form of absolute monarchy or by aristocratic corporations (that is, the *Parlements*). This central political concern spread to an awareness of, and reflections upon, virtually every aspect of French society. Later, the popular enthusiasm for the American Revolution became symptomatic of this widespread preoccupation with political and social problems. But during the Maupeou 'revolution' and its aftermath, this consciousness was evident only among members of the literary elite. 'Patriots', royalists and 'independents' alike shared a belief that some sort of political 'revolution' – by which was meant a non-violent coup or fundamental change by rational agreement – was both inevitable and necessary. The practical difficulty was that there was no consensus on what the nature of this revolution should be.

The independents, who sought to avoid the aristocratic and absolutist extremes, failed to make headway during the aristocratic resurgence of 1774-88. Thus in 1788 the ministers accused their opponents of seeking an 'aristocracy of magistrates', while they in turn were charged with seeking despotism. Echeverria argues that the paralysis caused by these two conflicting standpoints in the crisis of 1788-9 in turn led to a radicalization of the so-called 'independents', whose views were to triumph in the Revolution. Within this ferment of ideas, the heightened religious disputes of the eighteenth century aroused by the Jansenist controversy clearly have a place. However, Dale Van Kley is not altogether successful in linking the issues in his study of the circumstances surrounding the trial of Robert-François Damiens for his assassination attempt on Louis XV in 1757.[27]

II ABSOLUTISM IN PRACTICE: THE ROLE OF KINGS AND REGENTS

A Kings

To be effective, the power of the monarch had to be exercised personally. A series of recent biographies of monarchs and regents provide many

---

[26] Durand Echeverria, *The Maupeou revolution. A study in the history of libertarianism. France, 1770-1774.* Louisiana State University Press, 1985. 347 pp.

[27] Dale K. Van Kley, *The Damiens affair and the unravelling of the ancien régime,*

illustrations of what absolutism meant in practice. No one can doubt that in foreign policy the king's decision was supreme. The fateful decision to invade Italy was taken by Charles VIII 'contre la volonté des princes et des grands' in 1493-4, at an age of only 22 or 23.[28] Francis I was 20 at the time of his accession on New Year's Day 1515. He could have brought about a change of policy, since Louis XII's intervention in Italy had led to disaster. Instead, he chose to avenge the grave defeats from the previous reign. The die was cast for an aggressive foreign policy, and the early victory at Marignano simply served to encourage Francis's ambitions. If territorial expansion is the only criterion by which his reign is to be judged, then Francis achieved little. He annexed parts of Savoy, but failed in his lifetime bid to extend his dominion beyond the Alps.[29] The problems of foreign policy remained unresolved for his successor in 1547: Henri II has been a rather neglected monarch until the recent study by Ivan Cloulas,[30] but his relatively short twelve-year reign is of considerable interest. It was a period of administrative innovation, which saw the creation of offices that were to last for the rest of the *ancien régime,* such as those of the *présidiaux* and the intendants of finance. The costs of war were the driving force behind such innovation, and it was Henri's personal decision to renew the conflict with the emperor which has to be seen as the primary cause.

As to the king's personal exercise of power in terms of domestic policy, it is clear that his subjects expected to see their ruler. To this end Francis I's court was peripatetic, as Knecht shows.[31] To what extent did the king consult his subjects? Professor Major considers that Francis 'accepted the existence of the provincial and local estates, recognized their right to give consent to taxation and generally respected their privileges'.[32] In contrast, Knecht notes that the effectiveness of the estates was limited to matters of secondary importance to the crown; where its financial interest was at stake, they were virtually powerless. The king's official pronouncements about wishing to consult his subjects cannot always be taken at their face value. Prince Philip, writing to Charles V in 1547, stated that Francis ruled like a despot rather than a natural overlord, following his whim rather than his reason, and that the French people were willing to put up with anything.[33] An overstatement from a hostile witness, no doubt. However,

1750-1770. Princeton University Press, 1984. 373 pp. Damiens seems to have been an anticlerical and to have condemned even Jansenist priests: ibid. pp. 49-50.

[28] Y. Labande-Mailfert, *Charles VIII et son milieu, 1470-1498. La jeunesse au pouvoir* (1975), p. 219.

[29] R. J. Knecht, *Francis I.* Cambridge University Press, 1982. xv + 480 pp. See pp. 37, 429. For an account of the reign which is particularly strong on social and economic questions: Jean Jacquart, *François Ier*. Fayard, 1981. 440 pp.

[30] Ivan Cloulas, *Henri II.* Fayard, 1985. 691 pp.

[31] Knecht, *Francis I,* pp. 93-5.

[32] J. Russell Major, *Representative government in early modern France.* Yale University Press, 1980. xiv + 731 pp. See p. 55.

[33] Knecht, *Francis I,* p. 356. The Venetian ambassador stressed in 1535 that 'whatever burden he places on them, they pay without restriction'. His successor in 1546 commented

Chancellor Poyet perhaps best summed up the king's political philosophy in 1540. 'The king is not asking for advice as to whether or not [his laws] are to be observed', he said. 'Once the king has decreed them, one must proceed; no one has the right to interpret, adjust or diminish them.'[34] This reads like a statement of undivided legislative sovereignty before Bodin conceived of it in conceptual terms. In the promulgation of laws, Francis I certainly does not seem to have adopted the consultative standpoint depicted by Professor Major.

A superficial contrast between the reigns of Henri III and Henri IV might suggest that the former demonstrated weakness because he consulted his subjects, while the latter demonstrated strength because he did not. Rather surprisingly, Henri III emerges with his reputation enhanced by his most recent biographer, Pierre Chevallier.[35] Circumstances required a military leader who shared the nobleman's pursuits. Instead, France was ruled by a king who preferred oratory and bureaucratic administration on the model of Philip II. Nevertheless, the king had a defiant wish to defend his sovereignty, as revealed in the crises of 1576–7 and 1585–9. On the first occasion, he placed himself at the head of the Catholic League, and at the Estates General of Blois announced that the implementation of the Peace of Monsieur, which established legal rights for Huguenots, would contravene his coronation oath. Catherine de Médicis privately disapproved of his policy: 'jamais il n'aurait dû se prononcer d'une manière si absolue', she remarked.[36] In the aftermath, the king became his own master for perhaps the first time in the reign, abolishing all leagues in his kingdom but guaranteeing limited rights to the Huguenots.

In the second crisis during the last years of the reign, the issue of the succession dominated all else. Henri's reputation with contemporaries suffered because he deployed his oratorical skills in support of the Bourbon succession. He never wavered from his view that Henri of Navarre must abjure – to this extent he envisaged what proved to be the only viable solution to France's misfortunes.[37] If Henri III seemed to capitulate to Guise in the edict of union, it was because the edict stipulated that leagues without the permission of the monarch were acts of *lèse majesté* in 'toute monarchie bien ordonnée'.[38] The execution of the Guises resulted from a trial held in secret under the king's presidency. On his death-bed, the king stated that he had been forced to 'user de l'autorité souveraine qu'il avait plu à la divine Providence de me donner sur eux'.[39] The League regarded

that 'his subjects pay extraordinary sums, as much as he wants': Elias, *State formation*, pp. 219–20.
[34] Ibid. p. 361.
[35] P. Chevallier, *Henri III. Roi Shakespearien*. Fayard, 1985. 751 pp.
[36] Ivan Cloulas, *Catherine de Médicis* (1979), p. 402. Chevallier, *Henri III*, p. 348.
[37] Chevallier, pp. 392–3, 706.
[38] Ibid. p. 657.
[39] Ibid. p. 703. After the murder of the Guises on his orders, Henri III told his mother 'je commence de nouveau à être roi et maître', having been held 'prisonnier et esclave' since the Day of the Barricades: ibid. p. 672.

this as a tyrannical act, and set out along the path of deposition. For Henri III, in control only of Tours, Blois and Beaugency (less territory than Charles VII had held as the maligned 'roi de Bourges'), the options narrowed down to the defence of the laws of succession against the wishes of the Catholic League. The stage was set for the alliance with Henri of Navarre and assassination by Jacques Clément.[40]

Henri IV thus had to fight for his kingdom in the so-called 'war of the Bourbon succession'. His reign has been the subject of four recent studies.[41] His political biographers have experienced difficulty in handling his life, since while he lived for fifty-six years, the reign lasted only for twenty-one, of which a mere twelve were years of civil peace. Both Babelon and Garrisson thus devote more space to the earlier years of Henri's career, as prince of the blood and governor of Guyenne, but because of the paucity of direct source material their accounts tend to become a narration of events. Buisseret's study, too, is essentially a life and times. He takes us blow by blow (literally, battle by battle) through the first Bourbon king's career before and after 1589. In contrast, Greengrass concentrates on the Catholic League and the threat it posed to Henri IV.[42] The focus is on the king's political achievement in restoring stability. 'There was nothing natural or automatic about it', he comments; 'it was a deliberate, in some senses artificial creation, which could have been easily overturned and which was constantly being tested, but which became stronger the longer it lasted.'[43] Recovery under Henri IV paved the way for the achievements of Richelieu and Mazarin.

However, it seems somewhat perverse to call the period of the cardinal ministers 'the first generation of French absolutism'.[44] To do so implies that changes over a long period reached their culmination at a precise moment in history. A similarly misleading impression is given by the argument that specific events, such as the establishment of the *droit annuel* in 1604 or the alleged failure of the Estates General of 1614–15, marked the introduction of absolutism in France.[45] Developments occurred much more gradually. Historians are divided as to whether the key periods for the development of absolutism were the reigns of a strong monarch or the periods of royal minority when the regent tried to hold on to the gains of previous generations. In Knecht's view 'Francis [I] never became as

---

[40] Ibid. pp. 687, 706.

[41] Jean-Pierre Babelon, *Henri IV*. Fayard, 1982. 1103 pp. Mark Greengrass, *France in the age of Henri IV: The struggle for stability*. Longman, 1984. xiii + 237 pp. David Buisseret, *Henry IV*. Allen & Unwin, 1984. 249 pp. Janine Garrisson, *Henry IV*. Seuil, 1984. 347 pp.

[42] For the League, see also the review article by M. Greengrass, 'The sixteen, radical politics in Paris during the League', *History*, 69 (1984), 432–9.

[43] Greengrass, *France in the age of Henry IV*, pp. xi–xii.

[44] Ibid. p. 207.

[45] 'Par l'institution du droit annuel, Henri IV n'en avait pas moins choisi entre deux politiques; il tentait de renforcer l'absolutisme . . . ': R. É. Mousnier, *La vénalité des offices sous Henri IV et Louis XIII*, 2nd edn (1970), p. 600. 'Par ses délégués aux Etats généraux de 1614 et 1615, la France s'est abandonné à l'absolutisme royal': idem, *L'assassinat de Henri IV. 14 mai 1610* (1964), p. 266.

absolute as Louis XIV', though his reign 'marked the beginning of a new, more "absolute" form of government'.[46] Janine Garrisson appears to subscribe to the view that Henri IV was 'le premier souverain aux visées absolutistes'. She concludes that the war against Spain of 1595-8 was 'un facteur puissant de ciment national et donc de consensus monarchique'.[47]

Louis XIII has attracted both a modern political biography and an essay in 'psychoanalytic-history' based on the diaries of his personal physician, Jean Héroard.[48] In contrast, the king with the longest reign in modern European history has aroused surprisingly little recent attention. J. H. Shennan's pamphlet introduces some of the key issues of Louis XIV's reign and endorses the conventional view of his absolute power.[49] Shennan quotes Louis XIV's comment that the Bourbon kings could boast that 'there isn't a better house, nor greater power, nor more absolute monarchy than theirs anywhere else in the world'.[50] However, in a useful historiographical essay on the *ancien régime,* William Doyle comments that 'even Louis XIV, the bureaucrat-king whom conscientious monarchs were to copy for over a century, looks less like a royal revolutionary than the prisoner of routines elaborated under the great cardinals who governed France between 1624 and 1661. His chief innovation was simply to take over the personal power that was lawfully his when he was old enough to do so. The rest was propaganda, although brilliant propaganda.'[51] David Parker subscribes to the view that 'the deification of the king was an ideological illusion perpetrated by those who sensed that it was necessary for the stability of the regime. Yet it was not imposed in any crude fashion on an unwilling or hostile public . . . the upper classes were predisposed to accept the ethos of the absolute state.'[52] This 'fabrication' of Louis XIV's image will be the subject of a forthcoming study by Peter Burke.

Central to the development of an absolutist ethos was an institution which has become the subject of serious study only relatively recently: the court. Le Roy Ladurie has provided an analysis of court factions in 1709 based on Saint-Simon's memoirs, which includes a diagram of the alliances.[53] The work that has received the most publicity, however, is Norbert Elias's study of court society. He comments that Louis XIV, 'who

---

[46] Knecht, *Francis I,* p. 429.
[47] Garrisson, *Henri IV,* pp. 282-3. She also (p. 267) uses the term 'la centralisation politique'.
[48] Pierre Chevallier, *Louis XIII, roi cornélien.* Fayard, 1979. 694 pp. Elizabeth Wirth Marvick, *Louis XIII. The making of a king.* Yale University Press, 1986. 278 pp.
[49] J. H. Shennan, *Louis XIV.* Methuen: Lancaster pamphlets, 1986. 50 pp. See p. 4: 'he remained the absolute ruler of his kingdom, which meant that no individual or institution could challenge his supreme power, but he was also expected to uphold the authority of the laws which he had inherited with his kingdom as well as to amend outmoded legislation and create new laws when necessary'.
[50] Ibid. p. 7.
[51] William Doyle, *The ancien regime.* Macmillan: Studies in European History, 1986. 62 pp.
[52] Parker, *The making of French absolutism,* pp. 150-1.
[53] Emmanuel Le Roy Ladurie. *The mind and method of the historian,* trans. Siân and Ben Reynolds. Harvester Press, 1981. 310 pp. See p. 153.

is often taken as the supreme example of the omnipotent absolute monarch, proves on closer scrutiny to be an individual who was enmeshed through his position as king in a specific network of interdependences'.[54] The king used his most private acts, such as ceremonial in the bedchamber, to establish differences of rank and to distribute distinctions, favours, or proofs of displeasure.[55] Under Louis XIV a stable balance of privileges emerged, and this 'court mechanism' proved enduring: 'no-one could break out without laying hands on these privileges, the basis of his whole personal and social existence'.[56] In Elias's view, Louis XIV was not an innovator 'and did not need to be'. His task was not to conquer and create, but to secure and consolidate the existing structure. Absolute monarchy antedated his reign: 'he had to supervise and keep alive the tensions between the different estates and classes. An innovating genius might well have foundered on this task . . .'[57] The danger for his successors, however, was that 'the privileged monopoly elites were frozen in the equilibrium consolidated by Louis XIV'.[58]

The design of Versailles itself has been seen as reinforcing visually the structure of the French monarchy. In a new study of Versailles, Guy Walton comments that the needs of the king and his family, rather than of the French government, had the greatest influence on the design.[59] The location of the king's bedroom, only one room away from the Hall of Mirrors, demonstrated the openness of the state apartments. Versailles was a source of ideas throughout Europe. Blenheim was modelled on it, for example, although its architect, Sir John Vanbrugh, had expressed the view that greater architecture could be built under a constitutional monarchy and Whig liberty than under an absolutist French king.[60]

No review article on such a broad theme as absolutism can claim to have encompassed the entirety of recent publications on the subject. It is clear, however, that there are some significant omissions. There is surprisingly little of quality on the personal rule of Louis XIV, while nothing at all has been published recently on Louis XV. This leaves Evelyne Lever's recent biography of Louis XVI in splendid, but unnecessary, isolation.[61] The demise of absolutism may tell us something about its nature, and Mme Lever's thesis is that while Louis XVI was eager to introduce changes, such as a more equitable system of taxation, he was unwilling to relinquish power or to preside over the destruction of the *ancien régime*. If the king achieved the opposite of his intentions, it was because of his, and his ministers', vacillation and irresolution. Thereafter, Louis XVI and Marie Antoinette were left with only the threadbare hopes of a plan of escape,

[54] Elias, *Court society*, p. 3.
[55] Ibid. p. 84.
[56] Ibid. p. 88.
[57] Ibid. p. 127.
[58] Ibid. p. 273.
[59] Guy Walton, *Louis XIV's Versailles*. Viking, 1986. 256 pp. See p. 38.
[60] Ibid. p. 219.
[61] Evelyne Lever, *Louis XVI*. Fayard, 1985. 695 pp.

and after its failure at Varennes, of armed intervention from abroad. The remarkable fact about the monarchy, however, is that it survived until September 1792, long after the abolition of the absolutist structure itself.

B Regents

If a king such as Louis XIV was able to enjoy the full exercise of personal rule from 1661, it was in part because a determined regent had hung on to the vestiges of power during the Fronde. The role of the four regents who exercised personal power in the early modern period[62] is clearly of some significance. Nicola Sutherland considered that Catherine de Médicis was the 'first [to begin] to move towards the later conception of absolutism',[63] evidenced by her attempt to enforce religious toleration on the warring Catholic and Protestant factions, an attempt that was fatally weakened by her later implication in the St Bartholomew Massacres. In contrast, the regent's most recent biographer, Ivan Cloulas, sees the period after 1559 essentially as that of the collapse of absolutism, with the consultation of Frenchmen in four meetings of the Estates General as 'la grande nouveauté'.[64] Although there have been attempts to re-establish Marie de Médicis' reputation as a stateswoman[65] her regency essentially saw an attempt to placate the great nobility, while her revolts against Luynes in 1619 and 1620 have not enhanced her standing in the view of most later scholars. If Marie's Habsburg preferences were too obvious for comfort, Anne of Austria suffered the disadvantage of being born the daughter of Philip IV.[66] The Spanish government hoped that her heart would be, from their point of view, in the right place; but their hopes were dashed. The interests of her elder son were paramount. Louis XIII's foreign policy had to be brought to fruition; at home the power of the monarchy had to be handed on without restriction to Louis XIV at his majority. For the most part Anne of Austria was successful in implementing these policies. The extent to which she could have achieved them without the guidance of Mazarin as chief minister is open to question. It was this, perhaps most of all, which made her achievement more permanent than that of Marie de Médicis, even if the obduracy of regent and chief minister was a significant factor in precipitating the Fronde. Anne's willingness to stand aside from politics after the end of her formal power in 1651 was in marked contrast to the precedent set by Marie de Médicis.

[62] The power exercised by Anne de Beaujeu in 1483 was not strictly speaking that of a regent, since Charles VIII was legally of age to rule.
[63] 'Without her conservative achievements the later monarchy would have had no foundations upon which to build . . . ': N. M. Sutherland, 'Catherine de Medici and the ancien régime', *Historical Association Pamphlet* (1966), p. 34. See also p. 27. Idem, *The Huguenot struggle for recognition.* Yale University Press, 1980. 394 pp.
[64] Ivan Cloulas, *Catherine de Médicis.* Fayard, 1979. 704 pp. See p. 610.
[65] 'She deserved more from France . . . She had preserved the throne and the power of her husband and had given her son a solid foundation to build on. She had served France well': J. Michael Hayden, *France and the Estates General of 1614* (Cambridge, 1974), pp. 172–3.
[66] Ruth Kleinman, *Anne of Austria. Queen of France.* Ohio State University Press, 1985. xiii + 350 pp.

The decimation of the royal family through illness and premature death in 1711-14 brought Philippe d'Orléans to the regency on 2 September 1715.[67] His dealings with the *Parlement* of Paris are particularly interesting, for he achieved what Marie de Médicis dared not attempt, and Anne of Austria failed to enforce: the exile of the *Parlement* to Pontoise, which occurred in the second half of 1720. This coup is the more remarkable because Orléans had made concessions not accorded when the earlier regencies were established in 1610 and 1643. By emphasizing his legislative powers against the *Parlement,* the regent continued Louis XIV's policy and effectively annulled his earlier concessions. 1720 was a clearcut victory without a shot being fired, underlining 'the success, viewed retrospectively, of Louis XIV's regime'.[68] In 1723 the regency came to an end. Louis XV was left a secure throne and the opportunity to govern as he wished – ultimately with Cardinal de Fleury as chief minister. This was the positive achievement. There was also a negative side: the regent 'by temperament . . . was closer to Law than Dubois'[69] and his personal commitment to Law's System, and thus responsibility for its failure, needs to be stressed. One might even argue, as had Samuel Bernard in the last years of Louis XIV's reign, that the System was incompatible in an absolute monarchy, 'there being no foundation for the bank he proposes in a country where everything depends on the king's pleasure'.[70]

It may be suggested that two of the four regencies – those of Catherine de Médicis and Philippe d'Orléans – were periods of innovation, respectively in the attempt to enforce religious toleration and to secure a new funding arrangement for the troubled royal finances. In contrast, the 'absolute' power enjoyed by some French kings – such as Louis XV before the Maupeou 'revolution' – appears more like the straitjacket of hidebound traditions.

III ABSOLUTISM IN PRACTICE: THE POWER OF MINISTERS

'Absolutism' was not merely good for the king; it presented unrivalled opportunities for his ministers. The earliest ministers of the French crown have not been greatly studied, the exceptions in recent times being Bellièvre and Sully. It is with Richelieu that studies of ministers really come into their own, the recent contribution of Joseph Bergin being the most distinguished example.[71] Anyone expecting from the title a full-scale political biography will be disappointed. Instead, what we find is the most thorough-going description of the creation of a ministerial fortune in any

---

[67] J. H. Shennan, *Philippe, duke of Orléans. Regent of France, 1715-1723.* Thames & Hudson, 1979, 191 pp.
[68] Ibid. p. 139.
[69] Ibid. p. 141.
[70] Claude-Frédéric Lévy, *Capitalistes et pouvoir au siècle des lumières. II. La révolution libérale* (Paris/The Hague/New York, 1979), p. 155 n. 108.
[71] J. A. Bergin, *Cardinal Richelieu. Power and the pursuit of wealth.* Yale University Press, 1985. ix + 341 pp. French translation forthcoming at Robert Laffont.

period of the *ancien régime*. The new fortune was built up by a network of agents such as the archbishops of Bordeaux and Reims, personal intendants and special councils. Though there was heavy reliance on the leasing of revenues, and much of the income was managed by a consortium of Protestant financiers, Richelieu's personal supervision of the fortune seems clear. The cardinal took care not to borrow from his financiers, thus avoiding the problems encountered by the French monarchy. The importance of the patronage of Marie de Médicis in Richelieu's rise to power emerges even more clearly than in earlier accounts. So, too, does the impressive collection of provincial governorships, which makes it difficult to view Richelieu as an opponent of the governors. (Similarly, his vast landed estates make it impossible to see him as an opponent of the nobility.) Just as Richelieu elbowed out political opponents to acquire governorships, he disposed ruthlessly of social competitors in his native Poitou and consolidated his position with a dukedom in 1631. Though Richelieu's income from land increased tenfold between 1620 and 1642, this was a result of the growth of his possessions. He was a benign absentee landlord, not a rack-renter.

Bergin suggests a grand design in the creation of a fortune of some 22 million net when what we are witnessing is perhaps simple opportunism. He uses the expression 'complex investment strategy' to describe the private policy of a chief minister who professed (as a ploy?) to the *surintendants* his ignorance of public finance. Bergin emphasizes the 'conscious and perfectly realistic ordering of priorities' by Richelieu, in both his public and private business affairs.[72] As with his conduct of public business, so with his private affairs: 'routine matters of administration he left to those employed for that purpose, but the decisions which shaped the history of his wealth were his alone'.[73] This study prompts the comment that the architect of Louis XIII's power, who stressed his disinterested pursuit of matters that were of concern to the crown, ruthlessly exploited the fruits of office. It is also arguable that the growth in the personal power of the chief minister might act as a threat to absolutism: this was the criticism in turn of Concini, Luynes, Richelieu and Mazarin.[74]

Another minister who exploited the fruits of office, though on a smaller scale, was Colbert, the dedicated opponent of Foucquet's alleged ministerial corruption. The tercentenary of Colbert's death in 1683 prompted a three-day conference, the collected papers for which have appeared as a wide-ranging volume, appropriate to that minister's extensive portfolio.[75] Were his powers compatible with absolute monarchy? Jean Meyer depicts Colbert as the most important of a small band of ministers

---

[72] Bergin, *Cardinal Richelieu*, p. 67.
[73] Ibid. p. 68.
[74] R. J. Bonney, *The king's debts. Finance and politics in France, 1589-1661* (Oxford, 1981), pp. 86, 94, 100, 156-8, 212, 234-5.
[75] *Un nouveau Colbert. Actes du Colloque pour le tricentenaire de la mort de Colbert...*, ed. R. Mousnier. CDU-Sedes, 1985. 338 pp.

who advised Louis XIV, but who prudently left the king the freedom to form his own judgement. However, the only Russian participant at the colloquim, Vladimir Malov, demonstrates from the correspondence of the papal nuncio Roberti that in January 1667 Colbert was the driving force behind an ultimately unsuccessful attempt to reduce the age for taking monastic vows. Guy Antonetti provides a fundamental reassessment of the *caisse des emprunts* of 1674. Far from marking a far-sighted new departure in French finance to remedy the deficit, Colbert's scheme is shown conclusively to have been no more than a traditional, short-term, credit operation. By closing it down in 1684, Le Peletier recognized that Colbert's scheme had become a threat to financial stability. What emerges from this collection of papers is less a 'new Colbert' than an appropriate revival of interest in the minister, though one which had been foreshadowed in two recent biographies.[76] For a 'new Colbert' to be delineated his financial administration needs to be studied with much greater attention, as does his correspondence. The real Colbert remains as elusive as ever.

The career of Colbert's great rival, Louvois, was spectacular by almost any standards and is fully revealed in Corvisier's biography.[77] The rivalry with Colbert remains a complex matter. Conflict seems inevitable, since the men were similar in temperament but different in social origins, and above all in generation. Louvois' career was punctuated by triumphs and set-backs largely relating to Colbert and his family. The dynastic aspect of the conflict is undeniable. Corvisier also views it as a struggle for control of policy. The fundamental issue was whether to fight the war on the continent (Louvois' preference) or at sea (the special concern, and thus preference, of Colbert and Seignelay). Ultimately, Louvois' reputation rests on his achievements for the French Army. Despite the inaccuracy of contemporary statistics, there can be no doubt that the army increased dramatically in size (to 300,000 men or so) at a time when the population was no longer expanding. Corvisier views Louvois as the minister who created for Louis XIV the most powerful army in contemporary Europe and initiated reforms which proved to be 'une étape décisive dans la formation de l'armée moderne'. The strengthening of the state was undoubtedly in part a consequence of the growth of royal military power. Louvois was one of the best informed of all Louis XIV's servants and perhaps of all war ministers in the *ancien régime*. Though at his death in 1691 the kingdom was imperilled by the War of the League of Augsburg, it was a sign of Louis XIVs esteem for Louvois that his son was entrusted with the secretaryship of state at 23. The decision proved disastrous and Barbezieux never became a minister of state. The policy of direct administration by ministers was vulnerable to the choice of personalities made by the king.

---

[76] Inès Murat, *Colbert* (1980). Jean Meyer, *Colbert* (1981).
[77] André Corvisier, *Louvois*. Fayard, 1983. 558 pp.

IV ABSOLUTISM IN PRACTICE: FINANCIAL INSTITUTIONS AND PATRONAGE

It has been said that 'absolutist states . . . were machines built overwhelmingly for the battlefield'.[78] The financing of war required credit and brought about a state of perpetual reliance on financiers. Their profits were notorious. Contemporaries almost universally agreed that the financiers (often termed contemptuously *maltôtiers*) were social upstarts with 'an insatiable avidity to get rich quick'. They were seen as spectacularly wealthy, a view the financiers themselves encouraged to assist their creditworthiness. Such wealth, it was thought by the public at large, arose as a result of the huge profits in royal financial transactions, and was encouraged by ministerial corruption. Much of this myth of the *laquais-financier* is dispelled by Daniel Dessert's monumental thesis on 534 financiers who participated in the king's financial affairs between 1653 and 1720.[79]

The rise of new men in such a rigidly hierarchical society was problematic. Training was necessary before one could become a financier; business and social connections were also indispensable. As with so much else in *ancien régime* France, the acquisition of office held primary importance: 255 members of the group held the position of *secrétaire du roi*, which conferred first-degree nobility; 201 held the office of *receveur-général des finances*. Dessert also underscores the extent of aristocratic participation in financial dealings and illuminates the nature of aristocratic investment in the financiers' ventures. Colbert's financial group might displace Foucquet's, but Dessert concludes that 'la composition sociale du petit monde des protagonistes du système, par essence, n'évolue jamais'.[80]

The foundation of the financiers' wealth was clearly less secure than contemporaries assumed: ninety-eight financiers in the group ended their careers in ruin. Dessert is commendably frank about the difficulties of determining accurately the size of financiers' fortunes. These were subject to wild fluctuation since they contained a very high proportion of paper credits. A great nobleman whose wealth was in property and land might seem to have the same amount of money; but invariably he was richer in real terms – the basis of his wealth was secure. The calling of a *chambre de justice* by the crown could, and did, ruin financiers whose fortunes had seemed secure only a few months before. Elaborate procedures might be taken to conceal assets through arrangements with one's wife, one's children, fictitious transfers of property, and so on; but financiers were speculators, and as in any form of speculation some made remarkable gains, while others did not. Good management was important, but so too were social connections and luck. Quite apart from the new evidence which Dessert presents on the extent of ministerial profiteering, his study is particularly valuable for the insight it provides into the practice of ab-

---

[78] Perry Anderson, *Lineages of the absolutist state* (1974), p. 32.
[79] Daniel Dessert, *Argent, pouvoir et société au Grand Siècle*. Fayard, 1984. 824 pp.
[80] Ibid. p. 365.

solutism from the viewpoint of a significant vested interest group. Financiers were essential to the French monarchy, but the crown was unable to devise a satisfactory system of moderate, guaranteed profits. As a result, absolutism engendered the worst of all possible worlds. It rationalized default on repayment to its creditors. It was an irresponsible political power whose contractual word was not its bond. High interest rates prevailed, in Colbert's words, because 'le roy n'a aucun crédit . . . on ne traite avec luy que dans la croyance qu'il doit faire banqueroute'.[81]

Such managerial problems in central finance had arisen because of the fiscal imperatives of war: an army could not be paid if the tax revenues did not arrive promptly. The inexorable rise of taxation under absolutism is an important issue in its own right, and one which is only beginning to be investigated.[82] It prompts the question whether a so-called absolute monarchy inevitably, and in all periods, taxed its subjects more heavily than – for example – monarchy limited by parliamentary grant which developed in England.[83]

Yet absolute monarchy did not distribute the fiscal burden equally between the provinces. It was assumed, for example, that Normandy carried 25 per cent of the country's burden in direct taxes, much more than its fair share, and that however desirable it was to reduce regional inequity it was in practice difficult to do so.[84] Each province had a unique set of difficulties and problems. The case for tax reform was argued in Dauphiné for almost a century from 1540 to 1640, as Daniel Hickey has shown.[85] There, the fiscal system permitted taxable holdings acquired by exempt and privileged individuals to be removed permanently from taxation. The fiscal burden on the third estate increased inexorably with the rise in taxation and intensified land acquisition by privileged individuals. A sustained offensive was launched against the inequities of the fiscal system. In the 1580s leadership in the campaign was taken up by the towns, where it seems that lawyers, merchants and *bourgeois* were most heavily taxed. The result was that the urban elite had a fiscal interest in opposing the privileged orders at the meetings of the estates in the 1590s, which were paralysed by the confrontation.

[81] Bonney, *The king's debts,* p. 274.
[82] Examples of the new interest are A. Guéry, 'Les finances de la monarchie française sous l'ancien régime', *Annales ESC,* 23 (1978), 216–39. J. B. Collins, 'Sur l'histoire fiscale du xviie siècle: les impôts directs en Champagne entre 1595 et 1635', ibid. 34 (1979), 325–47.
[83] P. Mathias and P. K. O'Brien, 'Taxation in Britain and France, 1715–1810. A comparison of the social and economic incidence of taxes collected for the central governments', *J Eur Econ Hist,* 5 (1976), 601–50. This article has produced a debate: D. N. McCloskey, 'A mismeasurement of taxation in Britain and France, 1715–1810', ibid. 7 (1978), 209–10; Mathias and O'Brien, 'The incidence of taxes and the burden of proof', ibid. 7 (1978), 211–13. The revenues of Louis XIII were never less than five times those of Charles I, but when the king's extraordinary income is taken into account the differences become much greater: R. J. Bonney, 'The English and French civil wars', *History,* 65 (1980), 366–7.
[84] M. Foisil, *La révolte des Nu-Pieds et les révoltes normandes de 1639* (1970), p. 62. For ministerial views on the impossibility of reform: Bonney, *The king's debts,* p. 13.
[85] Daniel Hickey, *The coming of French absolutism: The struggle for tax reform in the province of Dauphiné, 1540–1640.* University of Toronto Press, 1986. 273 pp.

These divisions over the tax system help explain the inability of the three orders in Dauphiné to present a common front against the royal edict in 1628, which undermined the provincial estates by establishing *élections*. In Hickey's view, it is 'clear . . . that the move by the crown in 1628 was occasioned by essentially fiscal motives'. The crown 'was interested in increasing its revenues from Dauphiné without provoking the protests and contestation that had marked . . . the 1540s, the 1570s and the 1590s'.[86] Since the government wanted to increase taxation, but the third estate lacked the capacity to pay and refused to do so without reform, there seemed no alternative but to change the fiscal system to one of land tax. An alliance of interests was thus formed between the crown and the third estate. Absolutism was not simply imposed from the top down; in the case of Dauphiné, social groups which were anxious for tax reform actively encouraged royal intervention.

The demise of the estates of Dauphiné under Richelieu introduces the whole problem of local representation within an absolute form of government. Professor Major has made this subject very much his own.[87] Louis XIV, according to the author, 'was not as blindly opposed to representative assemblies as one might think'. He accepted, indeed strengthened, the 'society of orders' and controlled the 'remnants of the once vibrant, popular institutions'. But he based his authority on personal relations with his leading subjects rather than on an administrative revolution. Major does not tell us what this form of absolutism is to be called, but let us assume that he would accept the term 'personal absolutism'. There was an alternative, in his view, which he terms 'an institutional form of absolutism', and which he considers to have been propounded first by Sully, the finance minister of Henri IV, and later by Marillac as Keeper of the Seals under Louis XIII. If they had had their way, 'public officials who served at the king's pleasure [that is, a reformed system of *élus*] would have been less able to oppose reforms, popular institutions would have been so completely suppressed that they could not have risen again, and the society of orders would have been so weakened that the privileged would have been less able to prevent change',[88]

These are large claims, and it is a matter of dispute whether either Sully or Marillac had any such intention. In any case, it is by no means certain that the creation of *élections* (whether determined primarily by fiscal necessity or by some absolutist grand design) necessarily and inevitably meant the destruction of the provincial estates. Sully is alleged to have sought the creation of such offices because as a result he would 'obtain control of the tax-collecting machinery'. Marillac is supposed to have had such motives too, for Richelieu abandoned his attempt to 'construct a centralized, absolutist state administered by a loyal, non-hereditary, and

[86] Ibid. pp. 166, 174.
[87] Major, *Representative government in early modern France*.
[88] Ibid. p. 672.

probably non-venal, bureaucracy . . . '⁸⁹ Yet the prerequisites for 'institutional absolutism' – tax officials who did not own their offices, firmly under royal control – are not shown by Professor Major to have existed. He does not postulate at what point, if ever, the crown could have bought out the *élus* and thus created the sort of officials he considers necessary: with the rise in office prices in the early seventeenth century, it was almost certainly too late by the time of Marillac's ministry. Although office prices fluctuated according to market conditions, there was a general tendency for them to rise with inflation, which remained true throughout the *ancien régime* as Professor Doyle reminds us.[90] It thus became progressively more difficult to compensate whole sections of office-holders given the financial problems of the French monarchy.

Because of the grave problems involved, and the risk of alienating the population in outlying provinces, it seems unlikely that the early Bourbon kings were committed to any blueprint for absolutism such as Professor Major suggests. If Henri IV's 'approach to government was pragmatic rather than theoretical',[91] why should that of his successors have been different? A distinction needs to be drawn between Marillac's own views (about which relatively little is known)[92] and the policy to which Louis XIII was irrevocably committed. The crucial point is that estates in one form or another survived in the four great outlying provinces (Brittany, Burgundy, Provence and, above all, Languedoc), and their continued existence was in itself a limitation on the absolute power of the king. There is not a great deal of evidence to support the contention that the estates genuinely *governed* the localities where they remained, let alone that they were genuinely representative. Leaving aside the narrow basis of the franchise within those provinces with surviving estates – twenty-two baronies represented the nobility of Languedoc! – there were still alternative instruments of government available to the crown in each locality. It is true that the estates had often originally sought the creation of provincial sovereign courts. By the seventeenth century, however, there was much more rivalry – for example, in Brittany and Languedoc – between the *Parlement* and the local estates than Professor Major suggests.

Institutional rivalry and other power relationships within the province are the concern of William Beik in his study of Languedoc between 1620 and 1690.[93] In a lengthy introduction on absolutism, his personal preference emerges for a mix between the *étatiste* viewpoint of French

---

[89] Ibid. pp. 377, 619.

[90] William Doyle, 'The price of offices in pre-revolutionary France', *Hist J*, 27 (1984), 831–60.

[91] Major, *Representative government*, p. 261.

[92] Much rests on a letter to Richelieu dated 27 January 1630, concerning the refusal of an offer of 1.8 million *livres* from the deputies of Burgundy for the revocation of *élections*: 'l'uniformité que le Roy désire establir dans son roy[au]me luy fait refuser ces offres et persévérer à l'establissement des eslections . . . ' *Les papiers de Richelieu*, ed. P. Grillon (1975–), v. 51. Was Marillac simply expressing a personal opinion?

[93] William Beik, *Absolutism and society in seventeenth-century France. State power and provincial aristocracy in Languedoc.* Cambridge University Press, 1985. 375 pp.

historians such as Mousnier and the view of a social pact between the crown and the upper classes propounded by Marxist commentors such as Perry Anderson. 'Absolute monarchs and their ministers did improve the state apparatus in significant ways', Beik comments, 'but their modernity has been over-emphasised by historians.' 'It is necessary to stress the influence of the traditional social climate in which such innovations took place.'[94] One of his most original contributions is a chapter called 'Tax flows and society'. He calculates that in 1677 65.6 per cent of Languedoc's taxes went to the monarchy, but that virtually the whole of the remainder went to the provincial notables. He concludes that 'the rulers of Languedoc had a strong vested interest in the provincial tax revenues, and that in most cases the income they shared with the king at the expense of the taxpayers came to them by virtue of their position, not as recompense for services rendered'.[95] Moreover, this favourable position seems to have strengthened with the passing of time, while that of the crown deteriorated. Taxation was one of the most important forms of ready wealth in the province. One reason why Louis XIV's power was greater than that of his predecessors was that it was accepted positively, rather than resisted: his regime 'must have served the needs of the rulers of Languedoc and met their expectations'.[96]

Beik concludes that there was no real possibility of a provincial alliance against the crown. The structure of provincial government precluded it, and the social interests of the rulers lay with the national monarchy, not the provincial population. It is a verdict with which few historians would disagree. No claim is advanced that Languedoc is representative of national developments. Indeed, the depth of the institutional rivalry (between estates, *Parlement* and *Cour des Comptes*) appears to have been greater than that of other provinces. There seems to have been a long-term shift in authority from the *Parlement* of Toulouse to the provincial estates. Ultimately, it seems, the crown made a choice of its preferred institution, though the tax system of Languedoc, and the crucial role of the estates in voting taxes, probably made the outcome inevitable. Once the lines of authority were clear, and the attempt of the *Parlement* to intervene in the area of taxation had been firmly rejected, institutional rivalry in any case died out. What happened in other provinces is not so clear. A new generation of political historians of the French regions would do well to follow William Beik's model of investigation.

There remains the vexed question of the relationship of the provinces to the centre. It is now almost a decade since the appearance of studies on the provincial governors and intendants in early modern France.[97] This specialist research on institutions remains to be integrated into an overall

[94] Ibid. p. 339.
[95] Ibid. p. 261.
[96] Ibid. p. 281.
[97] R. R. Harding, *Anatomy of a power elite. The provincial governors of early modern France* (New Haven, Conn., and London, 1978). R. J. Bonney, *Political change in France under Richelieu and Mazarin, 1624–1661* (Oxford, 1978).

114   ABSOLUTISM: WHAT'S IN A NAME?

view of the development of power relationships within the state. This ambitious objective has been set by Sharon Kettering in her latest book.[98] She begins with the verdict that in the sixteenth and seventeenth centuries the French provinces were only partially under royal control. New institutions such as the intendants were an insufficient governing mechanism for the king and his ministers: the crown had to supplement its authority with ties of patronage and clientage which functioned both within the institutional framework and outside it. Kettering introduces the provincial power broker as 'a new type of state-builder in seventeenth-century France'. He was not a great noble or a provincial governor as in the sixteenth century. Instead he was a regional notable, usually a member of the lesser nobility, who gained increased status by collaborating with the government in return for royal patronage.[99] Kettering argues that brokerage was widely used as a means of integrating the peripheral provinces.

Kettering's analysis incorporates some of the recent approaches of sociologists, but historians may not all be willing to follow this approach, and may argue that difficulties emerge in its application to the intractable evidence of early modern France. It is easier to identify categories such as 'intendant-clients' or 'broker-clients' than to apply them with confidence to particular individuals. It remains to be demonstrated that the evolution of patronage relationships was itself the determinant of political change: the impact of new institutions resulting from the fiscal necessities of war may yet prove to have led to political change in early modern France; and that these new institutions in turn led to adjustments in the nature of patronage relationships. (How otherwise does one explain the greater acceptability of intendants after 1660 in comparison to their predecessors during the Thirty Years' War?) Whether or not one agrees with all aspects of the interpretation advanced by Kettering, there can be little doubt that her book focuses much more clearly than hitherto the debate on the significance of patronage relationships as an aspect of (in her expression) 'statebuilding'.

V CONCLUSION

It is clear from this survey of recent writing on the subject that there is little agreement among historians on the nature of absolutism. It is variously depicted as a conservative political philosophy and a form of political system; it is also used as a synonym for the entire *ancien régime*. Some historians adhere to the view that an absolute king in some meaningful sense enjoyed absolute power; others are equally convinced that absolutism might as well be described as a system of limited monarchy, though different in kind from that which developed in England.[100] All this

[98] Sharon Kettering, *Patrons, brokers and clients in seventeenth-century France*. Oxford University Press, 1986. x + 322 pp. See also Sharon Kettering, 'Patronage and politics during the Fronde', *Fr Hist Stu,* 14 (1986), 409–41.
[99] Kettering, *Patrons,* p. 7.
[100] J. S. Morrill, 'French absolutism as limited monarchy', *Hist J,* 21 (1978), 961–72.

suggests that, as in any complex historical question, there is no single, simple answer.

How, then, will study of the subject advance? Traditional historical skills such as political biography and the editing of state papers will remain important. In this context, the remarkable edition of Richelieu's papers in progress under Pierre Grillon's careful guidance should be noted as the paradigm.[101] Yet in all these state papers the key texts for the historian of absolutism are few in number. Ministers such as Richelieu and Mazarin were not high-minded 'absolutists' seeking to apply some blueprint for stronger monarchy on a docile population. They were first and foremost pragmatic politicians, seeking to cling to power, not above exploiting the fruits of office, above all desperate for success. Marillac seems to have been something of an exception, and his comment to Richelieu on Louis XIII's alleged desire to establish uniformity in his kingdom was noted above; but Marillac was a failure in office whose career ended in arrest. Other key texts are tantalizingly scarce: the fact that records of council debates were not kept is a considerable impediment to the historian. Foucquet's brief comment that the purpose of introducing intendants was to check the power of the provincial governors is an exception to the rule.[102] The private correspondence of kings and ministers is a source of crucial importance to the historian. Investigation of this evidence has scarcely begun in France, though it must be said that access to private archives is sometimes difficult to obtain, while the survival of such material is somewhat patchy. It is thus difficult to envisage that traditional skills such as the writing of political biography and the editing of primary sources will produce a definitive reassessment of absolutism. What is needed is a new approach.

It is premature to state with confidence what form this new approach will take. On the other hand, some aspects of it are already visible in current historical writing, even if a synthesis has not yet emerged. There will need to be comparative study, a modern version of Bodin's three types of government, monarchical, tyrannical and 'seigneurial'. A preliminary comparison between absolute monarchy in France and China has already been attempted.[103] Is it fanciful to suppose that the contrasting of Louis XIV with his almost exact contemporary K'ang-hsi, emperor of China (1661–1722),[104] might reveal new insights about each ruler? The contrasts between (the albeit political rivals) Richelieu and Olivares, so ably highlighted by John Elliott, have shown the value of such an approach.[105] Such contrasts might also be considered not merely in space but also time: the difference

[101] *Les papiers de Richelieu. Section politique intérieure. Correspondance et papiers d'état*, ed. P. Grillon. Pedone, in progress since 1975. The most recent volume to appear is volume *VI. 1631*. 1985. 811 pp.

[102] 'On avoit coustume de choisir [as intendants] les plus opposez aux intérests des gouverneurs . . . ': Archives du Ministère des Affaires Etrangères, Mémoires et Documents, France 905 fo. 519/2v, 10 Dec. 1658.

[103] R. E. Mousnier, 'Quelques remarques pour une comparaison des monarchies absolues en Europe et en Asie', *Rev Hist,* 272 (1984), 29–44.

[104] J. D. Spence, *Emperor of China. Self-portrait of K'ang-hsi* (1974).

[105] J. H. Elliott, *Richelieu and Olivares.* Cambridge University Press, 1984. 189 pp.

between the power of the emperor in the Roman world and that of the absolute ruler of early modern France might merit scholarly investigation.[106] The time-scale need not necessarily be backward: is there a 'modern absolutism'? The view has certainly been expressed,[107] and comparison between the nature of power enjoyed by so-called 'monocrats' and traditional absolute rulers is at least worth consideration. Underlying these comments is a simple truth, already recognized by economic historians,[108] that the study of one country's history in isolation carries the risks of tunnel vision. To understand the pace of industrialization – and one might infer, to understand the pace of absolutist or constitutional development – comparative study is necessary. It follows from this that to appreciate the impact of one aspect of absolutist development – such as the increase in fiscal power, or the growth in size and complexity of the army – comparative study, too, is necessary. It is self-evident that comparative study will provide one of the keys to unlock the dynamic of change, and it is likely that one paramount influence on the growth of the state will emerge from this historical reassessment. It is too early to conclude what this will be, but most scholars at the present time would probably lay odds that it will be the fiscal and organizational imperatives of war.

A second aspect of the new approach will be the adoption of a more complex methodoloy for the investigation. Again, the new synthesis has not emerged, but certain features can be discerned. The notarial archives are not the exclusive preserve of historians of demography or family history. Such records can be used systematically for assessing the impact of a political system on society as a whole. Jean-Paul Poisson's pioneering articles on the impact of the Fronde, the War of the Spanish Succession and Law's System, which have recently been reprinted, are good examples.[109] It has also been demonstrated by Daniel Dessert, among others, that the notarial archives are one of the crucial sources for prosopography. No serious assessment of absolutism can be achieved without a knowledge of how the functionaries made the system operate. If it is true that there were relatively few of them, and that the Revolution 'made' red tape,[110] this only serves to demonstrate how much greater should be our knowledge of their role. Absolutism has yet to produce its Sir Lewis Namier, French history its Namierite school. When the evidence permits, full-scale studies of dynasties of royal servants, such as that of David Sturdy on the d'Aligre family, will clearly add to the picture.[111] These detailed studies still need to be integrated into a more general interpretative framework. A new

[106] Fergus Millar, *The emperor in the Roman world (31 B.C.–A.D. 337)* (1977).
[107] Hugh Thomas, *An unfinished history of the world* (1979 and repr.), ch. 42.
[108] François Crouzet, *De la supériorité de l'Angleterre sur la France. L'économique et l'imaginaire, xviie-xxe siècle* (1985).
[109] Jean-Paul Poisson, *Notaires et société. Travaux d'histoire et de sociologie notariales.* Economica, 1985. 736 pp.
[110] Clive H. Church, *Revolution and red tape. The French ministerial bureaucracy, 1770-1850.* Clarendon Press, 1981. 425 pp. See graph 1 at p. 73.
[111] D. J. Sturdy, 'The formation of a "robe" dynasty: Étienne d'Aligre II (1560–1635),

methodology is required so that patronage studies (an adaptation of the techniques of prosopography) can be something more than the accumulation of detail about group connections, whether or not they are presented in tabular form. Can computerization handle the sophisticated data of patronage relationships, thus permitting the historian of absolutism to reach new conclusions? It remains to be seen. If all this amounts to a formidably challenging programme, then this suggests that the study of absolutism will remain alive and well, and that the next decade will witness as many publications on the subject as did the last.[112]

chancellor of France', *English His,* 95 (1980), 48-73. Idem, *The d'Aligres de la Rivière: Servants of the Bourbon state in the seventeenth century.* Royal Historical Society Studies in History, 48. 1986. 254 pp.

[112] The following titles were announced or appeared too late to be considered in this article: J. H. Shennan, *Liberty and order in early modern Europe. The subject and the state, 1650-1800.* Longman, 1986. 144 pp. *La monarchie absolutiste et l'histoire en France. Théories du pouvoir, propagandes monarchiques et mythologies nationales.* [Colloque tenu en Sorbonne les 26 et 27 mai 1986.] Presses Universitaires de France, 1986. M. Antoine, *Le dur métier de roi. Études sur la civilisation politique de la France d'ancien régime.* Presses Universitaires de France, 1986. 343 pp.

II

BODIN AND THE DEVELOPMENT OF THE FRENCH MONARCHY

THE 'history of ideologies' is now very much the vogue since Professor Quentin Skinner's fine study on *The foundations of modern political thought*.[1] Whether or not one agrees with all aspects of his interpretation of Bodin—and Dr Parker might argue that it fails to draw out sufficiently the moral philosopher inside the jurist,[2] while Professor Rose might prefer to stress the Judaizing tendencies of the theorist as a central preoccupation[3]—it is a testament to the decisive impact made by Skinner on the history of political thought that no-one has challenged his new and radical approach. It is no part of the purpose of this paper to do so. Indeed, an understanding both of Bodin's predecessors and of the ideological conflict of the 1570s which influenced the drafting of the *Six bookes of a commonweale* (the title given to the *République* by its first English translator, Richard Knolles) is fundamental before any appreciation of the theorist can be made free from distortion. It is no use at all asserting that Bodin started from scratch, even on the issue of sovereignty, where he made his most original contribution.[4] Bodin himself minimized his originality, basing his commentary on the powers historically enjoyed by French kings. The French king had traditionally regarded his authority as that of *princeps legibus solutus*, as an absolute ruler above the law. If the French king had been unable to do those things described by Bodin, in the view of that author, 'il n'estoit pas Prince souverain'.[5] Bodin also

---

[1] For his discussion of Bodin, Skinner, *The foundations of modern political thought. II. The Age of Reformation* (Cambridge, 1978), 284–301. A recent study of French political thought consciously adopts at least a history of ideologies veneer, but is disappointing on Bodin: N.O. Keohane, *Philosophy and the state in France. The Renaissance to the enlightenment* (Princeton, NJ 1980), 67–82.

[2] D. Parker, 'Law, society and the state in the thought of Jean Bodin,' *History of political thought*, ii (1981), 253–85.

[3] P. L. Rose, *Bodin and the great God of nature* (Geneva, 1980). Also idem, 'Bodin's universe and its paradoxes: some problems in the intellectual biography of Jean Bodin', *Politics and society in Reformation Europe*, ed. E. I. Kouri and T. Scott (1987), 266–88.

[4] See R. J. Bonney, *L'absolutisme* (Paris, 1989), chapter one.

[5] J. Bodin, *Les six livres de la république* ... (Paris, 1583, repr. Darmstadt, 1977), 154. Idem, *The six bookes of a commonweale*, trans. R. Knolles (1606), ed. K. D. McRae (Harvard, Mass., 1962), 107. A. Esmein, 'La maxime *princeps legibus solutus est* dans

noted the contribution of the canon lawyers of the Middle Ages to the development of his political theory and remarked that Pope Innocent IV was he who best understood the nature of sovereignty.[6]

The history of ideologies, therefore, helps us to place a political thinker of the stature of Bodin in his context. The reservation that one might have about this approach, however, is whether it necessarily helps us to understand or to estimate the significance of a thinker such as Bodin in the longer term. It is not merely that there is a difficulty with the 'snapshot' presentation of a particular political theorist in his historical context, which arises when he is divorced from his followers: the significance of Bodin in the seventeenth century cannot be assessed without a full study of Loyseau, Le Bret and Domat in France, which is still awaited. The differences between Bodin's influence on them and on other thinkers such as Grotius and Hobbes[7] has never been analyzed systematically and needs to be taken into account. A second and more important difficulty is that we cannot assume that the 'true' historical legacy of a theorist such as Bodin will appear simply by studying the debt owed by subsequent political theorists to Bodin in the context of their times. This paper seeks to argue that one or two central ideas of a key political thinker are so seminal that they prove decisive in the political arena itself, and not just in the relatively abstract world of political thought. The nature of politics in a given country can become consciously and unconsciously moulded as a result of the gradual, insidious, long-term impact of a seminal idea.

Such, it will be contended, is the significance of Bodin's discussion of the role of the commissioner and the distinction he makes between the commission and the office for the later development of the French monarchy and what, for want of a better term, is frequently referred to as 'absolutism' in France. It used to be assumed by virtually all historians that Bodin's new conception of sovereignty was crucial to this development. However, what one might call the 'revisionist' school of French historians is now beginning to question the significance of Bodin's theory *tout court*. The most recent exponent of this line of reasoning suggests that 'the notion of legislative sovereignty had much less significance both in theoretical discourse and in legal practice than has frequently been supposed; nor was the influence of

---

l'ancien droit public français', *Essays in legal history* . . ., ed. P. Vinogradov [Vinogradoff] (Oxford, 1913), 205.

[6] Bodin, *République*, 132–133. Idem, *Commonweale*, ed. McRae, 92. The Papal origins of the theory and practice of absolute sovereignty have recently been stressed by Professor Prodi: P. Prodi, *The Papal prince. One body and two souls: the Papal monarchy in early modern Europe*, trans. S. Haskins (Cambridge, 1988).

[7] Although King has made a start in considering Bodin's influence on Hobbes: P. King, *The ideology of order. A comparative analysis of Jean Bodin and Thomas Hobbes* (1974).

Roman law on monarchical absolutism as clear-cut as some authorities suggest'.[8] Dr Parker maintains that 'as one expression of the need to create stability out of instability or as a means of legitimizing the regime, the concept of legislative sovereignty is comprehensible; but as an explanation of how the system really worked, and on whose behalf, it is inadequate'.[9] Taking the examples of the post-Bodin jurist Cardin Le Bret and Jean Domat, it is argued that in the seventeenth century 'the concept of legislative sovereignty effectively disappeared or, at least, was subsumed within an essentially traditional world-view'.[10] Dr Parker's reading of Cardin Le Bret is clearly at variance with that presented later in this paper; but the fundamental difficulty with the 'revisionist' viewpoint is that it is much more effective in its depiction of the limitations on royal freedom of action—for example, in the crown's dealing with the *Parlements*—than it is in its analysis of the strength of (in English constitutional terminology) the royal prerogative, notably in the powers accorded to provincial intendants and other royal commissioners. On this latter point, either the explanation provided by the 'revisionists' is impressionistic[11] or silence prevails.[12] To remedy this unjustified neglect, the principal discussion in this paper will not be concerned with the arguments of the 'revisionists', but rather to re-examine the traditionalists' line, which stresses the importance of Bodin's new conception of sovereignty for the development of French absolute monarchy.

These historians have almost invariably argued their case without explaining the process by which such sovereignty might be exercised.[13]

---

[8] D. Parker, 'Sovereignty, absolutism and the function of the law in seventeenth-century France', *Past and Present* cxxii (1989), 36–74, at p. 71.

[9] *Ibid.*, 72.

[10] *Ibid.*, 48.

[11] Relatively short shift is given to the intendants of Louis XIV in R. C. Mettam, *Power and faction in Louis XIV's France* (Oxford, 1988), 211–17. Something of the flavour of this account is provided by the opening remark to this section of the book at p. 211: 'There are a number of reasons why the *intendants* could not have been the cornerstones of "absolutism" that some old-fashioned historians have maintained them to be.' The present author is embarked on a detailed study of the intendants during the personal rule of Louis XIV.

[12] There is no mention of the provincial intendants in Parker, 'Sovereignty, absolutism and the law'. At p. 65, in the context of the *grands jours* of Auvergne, he comments that 'justice by commission of this sort, cutting across all vested interests, was perhaps as near to absolutism in the popular sense as the crown ever got'.

[13] There have been some exceptions, notably at the Munich conference on Bodin: R. Polin, 'L'idée de République selon Jean Bodin', *Jean Bodin. Proceedings of the international conference on Bodin in Munich*, ed. H. Denzer (Munich, 1973), p. 349; also *ibid.*, p. 469: in the discussion, Freund asserted that the development of the commission was 'fondamental pour toute pensée politique postérieure', while Derathé noted that the distinction between *officier* and *souverain* was 'plus importante, plus développée dans la littérature postérieure que chez Bodin'.

But it will be argued that the importance of Bodin's discussion lay as much in the process of issuing royal commissions as in the concept of sovereignty. As early as 1919, Otto Hintze had drawn attention to Bodin as offering 'the first theoretical discussion' of royal commissions; 'it apparently became as basic to the French administrative law of the *ancien régime*', Hintze wrote, 'as was his theory of sovereignty to constitutional law ...'—a distinction between administrative and constitutional law with which few historians would now agree.[14] However, apart from an oblique reference to 'magistrates and commissioners',[15] Professor Skinner does not discuss royal commissions at all; neither does Professor Keohane, who nevertheless argues that Bodin's ideas 'were crucial for the development of absolutism in France'.[16] Professor Franklin did mention commissions in 1973, it is true, and noted that Bodin was apparently 'oblivious' to the idea that 'it would be technically legitimate for a king to circumvent the courts by attributing functions to commissioners'[17]—but even this would seem to be rather less than a complete discussion of the significance of Bodin's theory.

It is a curious omission on the part of modern commentators, because if we compare Bodin with his two most important predecessors in the sixteenth century, Claude de Seyssel[18] and Guillaume Budé,[19] this issue provides one of the most striking contrasts in their writings. The earlier theorists were silent on the powers of royal commissioners; Bodin not only discusses them, but characteristically provides a definition:[20]

> An Officer therefore is a publike person, who hath an ordinarie charge by law limitted vnto him. A Commissioner is a publike person, but with an extraordinaire charge limited vnto him, without law, by vertu of commissi[on] onely.

Richard Knolles's translation is not as elegant as the French original; nor is it entirely accurate. Under the office-holder's powers, he substitutes 'law' for *édit*, while in the original French there is no mention of law at all in the context of the commissioner. We must therefore

---

[14] O. Hintze, 'The commissary and his significance in general administrative history: a comparative study', *The historical essays of Otto Hintze*, ed. F. Gilbert (New York, 1975), 281–2.

[15] Skinner, 300.

[16] Keohane, 81.

[17] J. H. Franklin, *Jean Bodin and the rise of absolutist theory* (Cambridge, 1973), 99–100.

[18] C. de Seyssel, *La monarchie de France* [1515], ed. J. Poujol (1961).

[19] G. Budé, *De l'institution du prince* [1518] (repr. 1547; facsimile repr., Farnborough, 1966).

[20] Bodin, *République*, 372. Idem, *Commonweale*, ed. McRae, A77, 278.

necessarily quote the French original and then the translation which we would propose:

> L'Officier est la personne publique qui a charge ordinaire limitée par edict [sic]. Commissaire, est la personne publique qui a charge extraordinaire, limitée par simple commission.
>
> The office-holder is a public person who has an ordinary function limited by edict. The commissioner is a public person who has an extraordinary function, limited by a simple commission.

In Book III, chapter 2 of the *République*, ('Des Officiers & Commissaires'), Bodin proceeded to distinguish different types of commissions, citing examples from ancient Rome, and noting that commissions tended to develop into offices. However, for our purposes his two most important comments concerned the nature of the commissioner's powers and the distinction between them and the powers of the office-holder. Commissions were almost invariably addressed to office-holders, but Bodin argued (to quote Knolles) that 'an officer in the qualitie of an officer, cannot be also a commissioner, for the self same charge limited vnto him by his office'.[21] In his view, 'the ordinary hearing of the cause is to be preferred before the commission, even as the qualitie of the officer is to be preferred before the qualitie of the Commissioner; and the acts of the officers [are] more assured than the acts of the Commissioners.'[22] Commissions might be issued in different forms, but whatever type of commission was issued, it 'is directed with power and authoritie to heare and proceed in the cause; either without appeal, or else with appeal reserved vnto the sovereign prince ... as sometime [a] commission is given out for the instruction of the affaires, or proceedings, vnto the definitive sentence exclusively or inclusively, saving the execution thereof, if appeal be made'.[23] In Bodin's view, the essential elements of the commission were the right to hear cases without appeal (or with appeal reserved to the sovereign), periodicity and revocability; offices, on the contrary had 'a continuance perpetuall [sic]'. It therefore followed:[24]

> the power of an officer besides that it is ordinarie, it is also better authorised, and larger than is a commissioner's, & that is it for which the Edicts and lawes leave many things to the consciences and discretions of the Magistrats [sic]: who indifferently applie and interpret the lawes according to the occurrents & exigence of the causes presented: Whereas Commissioners are otherwise bound,

[21] Bodin, *République*, 380. *Idem, Commonweale*, ed. McRae, 284.
[22] *Ibid.*
[23] Bodin, *République*, 381. *Idem, Commonweale*, ed. McRae, 285.
[24] Bodin, *République*, 387–8. *Idem, Commonweale*, ed. McRae, 289.

and as it were tyed vnto the verie words of their commission, and especially where question is of the affaires of state ...

It is clear from Bodin's discussion of the powers of the commissioner that he was indulging in an historical survey: 'orderly proceeding required that wee should before speake of Commissioners, then of officers; for that they were before any lawyers or Officers established ...'[25] Bodin was clearly influenced by Louis XI's so-called 'law of irremovability' (*loi d'inamovibilité*), promulgated in 1467: '... ordinary offices and charges by the prince once lawfully bestowed', runs Knolles's translation, 'cannot from them on whom they are so bestowed be againe taken, except they have committed some criminall cause ...'[26] Since office-holders were permanently established, in Bodin's view their authority was likely to be 'more assured'. Bodin as we have seen also had a high opinion of Pope Innocent IV as 'hee that of others best knew the lawes of maiestie or soveraigntie' and of the canon lawyers who stated that 'the Pope can neuer bind his owne handes'.[27] He was thus almost certainly aware of a distinction made by the canon law between *officium* and *dignitas*, and of papal practice which had distinguished between a commission of a delegate judge who was named (*facta personae*) and one who was not (*facta dignitati*): the canon law dictum had been that 'a delegation made to the Dignity without expressing a proper name passes on to the successor'; in contrast, a named delegation was necessarily temporary and lapsed with the death of the appointee.[28] Bodin clearly thought in terms of the named delegation which lapsed with the death or revocation of the appointee.

Subsequent theorists, notably Charles Loyseau, writing in *Cinq Livres du Droit des Offices* (1609), echoed Bodin's arguments that the office-holder's powers were ordinary ones and thus capable of extension, whereas a commissioner had extraordinary powers which were limited.[29] The fact that the commissioner had 'no assured rank' ('point de rang asseuré') in the social hierarchy was of great importance to

---

[25] Bodin, *République*, 392–3. *Idem, Commonweale*, ed. McRae, 293.

[26] Bodin, *République*, 393. *Idem, Commonweale*, ed. McRae, 293. The ordinance of 21 October 1467 stated that 'désormais nous ne donnerons aucun de noz offices, s'il n'est vaquant par mort ou par résignation faicte de bon gré et consentement du résignant, dont il apperre [*sic*] duement, ou par forfaicture préalablement jugée et déclarée judiciairement et selon les terms de justice, par juge compétent ...': *Ordonnances des rois de France de la troisième race*, ed. C. E. J. P. Pastouret et al. (1820), xvii. 26.

[27] Bodin, *République*, 132–3. *Idem, Commonweale*, ed. McRae, 92.

[28] E. H. Kantorowicz, *The king's two bodies. A study in medieval political theology* (Princeton NJ, 1957), 384–6.

[29] C. Loyseau, *Cinq livres du droit des offices* (1613 edn.), 570. For Loyseau's importance as a theorist: H. A. Lloyd, 'The political thought of Charles Loyseau, 1564–1627', *European Studies Review*, xi (1981), 53–82.

Loyseau, who was preoccupied with questions of honour and status.[30] Thus if an office-holder and a commissioner found themselves both with powers to judge the same case, the commissioner should be the one to give way.[31] This was a significant and far-reaching attempt to limit the independence of the government from its permanent officials. But Loyseau went still further, and argued that the commissioner should publish his commission in the locality. If he did not do so, then no-one was obliged to recognise or obey him because his powers were unknown.[32] Acceptance of the principle of publicity would have given the local law court the opportunity to criticize the powers contained in the commission and to make representations to the king's council. But it was not generally accepted.

The most important French theorist of the next generation was Cardin Le Bret, whose treatise *De la souveraineté du roy* (1632) marked a decisive change in the prevailing theory about the nature of the powers of the royal commissioner. (Le Bret was a former intendant, and was half-way through a distinguished career as a councillor of state when he published his *magnum opus*.)[33] He reversed the priorities of Bodin and Loyseau. The power to grant commissions was 'a right of sovereignty' ('un droit de souveraineté');[34] indeed, 'to confer commissions to whomseover they wish[ed was] one of the principal rights of the sovereign authority of kings'.[35] The commissioner had supremacy over the local office-holders because he represented 'more particularly the person of the prince'—in this respect, Le Bret cited the canon law maxim *omnis delegatus maior est ordinario in re delegata*.[36] Finally, since the person chosen as commissioner would often be a councillor of state, he would bring to his commission 'the prerogatives of the rank and precedence which is owed to this status (qualité) ...'[37] By the third decade of the seventeenth century, therefore, Le Bret had overturned the arguments of Bodin and Loyseau, without losing or altering their central preoccupation with sovereignty. Le Bret continued to stress that the power to issue royal commissions was an emanation of the king's undivided legislative sovereignty. Thus during the Fronde, at a time when Le Bret himself was the *doyen* of the council

---

[30] For Loyseau: H. A. Lloyd, 'The political thought of Charles Loyseau, 1564–1627', *European Studies Review* xi (1981), 53–82. *Idem, The state, France and the sixteenth century* (1980).
[31] *Ibid.*, 571.
[32] *Ibid.*, 569.
[33] G. Picot, *Cardin Le Bret, 1558–1655, et la doctrine de la souveraineté* (Nancy, 1948).
[34] C. Le Bret, *De la souveraineté du roy* (1632), 149.
[35] *Ibid.*, 160.
[36] *Ibid.*, 151.
[37] *Ibid.*, 160.

of state, a decree was issued on 18 February 1652 which annulled the commission conferred by Gaston d'Orléans on Talon and Le Secq, *trésoriers de France* at Caen 'to carry out the function of intendants'—such powers could be granted only by the king himself and the *trésoriers* were warned that if they attempted to usurp such authority as intendants they would be guilty of treason.[38]

While the extension of the concept of treason during Richelieu's ministry was one of Le Bret's more notorious achievements,[39] the idea that the power to issue commissions emanated from the king's undivided legislative sovereignty although voiced by Le Bret seems to have originated with Bodin. Bodin, of course, was drawing on the medieval distinction between the king's 'retained' and his 'delegated' justice; there had undoubtedly been royal commissioners of various types, including *maîtres des requêtes* on circuit-tour, in the later Middle Ages.[40] However, the extant evidence suggests that royal commissions of *intendant* or *surintendant de justice*, the true precursors of the intendants of the seventeenth century, were few and far between before the publication of Bodin's *Six bookes of a commonweale* in 1576: perhaps a dozen commissions survive from the period before 1577, the earliest being the power of Pierre de Panisse as intendant of justice in Corsica, which was issued on 24 August 1556.[41] In other words, Bodin is unlikely to have had much knowledge of the practical difficulties facing royal commissioners before he advanced his theory.

It is thus a curious irony that the influence of Bodin extended into an area which it would have been virtually impossible for him to have envisaged. There was no 'system' of intendants—provincial officials empowered by royal commissions—prior to the late 1630s and it was not until the ruling of 22 August 1642 that the principle of one

---

[38] *Arrêts du conseil du roi. Règne de Louis XIV. Inventaire analytique des arrêts en commandement. I. 20 mai 1643–8 mars 1661*, ed. M. Le Pesant (1976), no. 1630. A[rchives] N[ationales] E 1698 no. 35 and E 1700 no. 26, 18 Feb. 1652.

[39] R. E. Giesey, L. Haldy, J. Millhorn, 'Cardin Le Bret and lese majesty', *Law and history review*, iv (1986), 23–54.

[40] G. Dupont-Ferrier, 'Le rôle des commissaires royaux dans le gouvernement de la France, spécialement du xive au xvie siècle', *Mélanges Paul Fournier* (1929), 171–84; Bonney, *Political change in France under Richelieu and Mazarin*, 102.

[41] It has long been established that this was the earliest commission: G. Hanotaux, *Origines de l'institution des intendants des provinces* (1884), 10. More recently: M. Antoine, 'Institutions françaises en Italie sous le règne de Henri II: gouverneurs et intendants, 1547–1559', *Mélanges de L'école française de Rome* xciv (1982), 815–18. For the 1560s: Bonney, *Political change*, 140. For Sade de Mazan in 1577: D.J. Buisseret, 'Les précurseurs des intendants du Languedoc', *Annales du Midi*, lxxx (1968), 87–88. Professor Antoine has discovered a number of new commissions from the period before 1577. However, most of these are not of *intendants de justice*, although the individuals appointed may be regarded as their functional precursors: M. Antoine, 'Genèse de l'institution des intendants', *Journal des savants* (1982), 283–317, especially 291–7.

intendant de la justice, police et finances per *généralité* (or fiscal district) was established. It was the powers conferred by their commissions and the supplementary decrees and rulings of the council on these powers which completely altered the nature of royal administration in France and gave Bodin's discussion, with the subsequent interpretation of Le Bret, a posthumous significance. What had started as an historical argument had now become a matter of great contemporary relevance, due to the progressive extension of the intendants' powers by royal commission and the refusal of the king's council to permit registration of these powers in the sovereign courts.[42] As the number of tasks assigned to the intendants increased, so it was recognized that their capacity for fulfilling them was hindered by the enormous geographical areas over which some had responsibility; it was even suggested that 'to keep a province properly controlled by this method ... it would be necessary to have as many intendants as there are *élections* (that is to say, lesser fiscal districts)'—that 170-odd intendants were needed rather than 22 to keep France effectively administered.[43]

There was never any prospect of such expansion; but it is clear that relatively early on the intendants were relying increasingly on subordinate officials whom they had appointed (*subdélégués*). Sometimes the power of *subdélégation*, a crucial development in the French monarchy of the *ancien régime*,[44] had been conferred on the intendant by his commission[45] or by a specific decree of the council;[46] but this was certainly not always the case, and there is at least a suggestion that the intendant sometimes exceeded his powers in this matter, even under Richelieu and Mazarin, by, for example, allowing his subdelegates to carry out judicial prosecutions.[47] Some of the subdelegates served successive intendants for long periods of time and provided continuity in provincial administration—thus Jean Anoul, a *juge royal* at Uzès, was a faithful servant of the intendants of Languedoc from 1630 to 1661. By the 1660s, significant powers were being conferred by the intendants on their *subdélégués* in certain areas of responsibility, for example in the general investigation into titles of nobility (*recherche de noblesse*). Following a decree of the council on 25 February 1666, Claude Pellot, the intendant of Guyenne, drew up

---

[42] R. J. Bonney, *Political change in France under Richelieu and Mazarin, 1624–1661* (Oxford, 1978), 135–59, 244–5.
[43] Bonney, *Political change in France under Richelieu and Mazarin*, 46–7, 72–4, 237, 453–5.
[44] M. Antoine, *Le dur métier du roi. Études sur la civilisation politique de la France d'ancien régime* (1986), 61–80.
[45] Bonney, *Political change in France under Richelieu and Mazarin*, 146, 149, 155, 275.
[46] *Ibid.*, 272.
[47] *Ibid.*, 249–50.

general instructions for his subdelegates, which emphasised the political sensitivity of the investigation and outlined the procedure to be adopted in the hearings. It is perfectly clear from the extant documentary evidence that it was the subdelegates, and not the intendant himself, who dealt with these cases. They provided him with a dossier on each nobleman and advised the intendant on whether the claim to nobility should be accepted or rejected. The intendant simply acted upon their advice, either by signing an *ordonnance de maintenu de noblesse*, or, in the case of a false claim to nobility, a standard ordinance which was printed with blank spaces for the names of the subdelegate and the name of the *roturier* who had sought fiscal exemption to be filled in by hand.[48]

Given the growing amount of business imposed by the central government on the intendants, it is not surprising that such methods were adopted. By the end of Louis XIV's reign, an intendant such as Basville in Languedoc had used his thirty-three years in office to build up a network of some twenty-two subdelegates.[49] This was certainly one of the more elaborate examples, but it merely serves to illustrate a problem of which Colbert was well aware. The Roman law principle was perfectly clear: *delegatus non potest subdelegare*; a commissioner could not empower a subdelegate without having been given prior authorisation by a royal commission.[50] In 1645, the king's council confirmed this principle in a case concerning the intendancy of Poitou. René I Voyer d'Argenson, the intendant, obtained a decree of the council empowering his son, René II, to act as subdelegate for the recovery of the king's taxes in the *élections* of Saintes and Cognac. However, René I had not been able to confer on his son the power to investigate crimes of tax rebellion 'since this authority derived solely from His Majesty's power'. This power was granted in a subsequent decree of the council.[51]

This was an unusual case of subdelegation, and d'Argenson was no doubt particularly careful to clear the lines of authority, since the powers were being attributed to his own son. Colbert contended that later intendants had been much less scrupulous,[52] and in the penultimate year of his ministry (1682), he demanded details of the

---

[48] A[rchives] D[épartementales du] Gers (Auch) C 362, printed ordinance of Pellot, 15 Apr. 1666; his instructions to subdelegates, 12 June 1666; his undated printed ordinance concerning Barthélémé Carrère, drawn up on the report of his subdelegate, Pierre Chadebert, an *avocat* in the *Parlement* of Toulouse.

[49] Bonney, *Political change in France under Richelieu and Mazarin*, 428.

[50] Antoine, *Le dur métier du roi*, 69.

[51] AN E 199^b, fo. 146, 15 Feb. 1645.

[52] For Colbert's hostility to subdelegates: J. Ricommard, 'Les subdélégués des intendants au xviie et xviiie siècles', *L'information historique* xxiv (1962–3), 144–5.

extent of delegated responsibilities in each of the intendancies. One of the clearest answers was given by Poncet de la Rivière, intendant at Bourges. He did not use the word sovereignty, but there can be no doubt that it was what he was talking about:[53]

> ... you order me to assume jurisdiction only in those matters where the king has given me the power, and not to appoint permanent subdelegates, merely using them for specific matters when I cannot be present in person. You will permit me to inform you, Monsieur, that I have always acted in this way, that I have given no judgement in matters beyond my competence, and that I have never issued a commission of subdelegate. I only empower people to hold preliminary hearings in specific cases (*pour l'instruction de chaque affaire particulière*) when I cannot be present in person. As a result, I have no subdelegate who judges without appeal in matters concerning my authority. They can scarcely in truth be called subdelegates, since they are only empowered for particular cases when I send them to hold preliminary hearings, or to obtain further information on matters where I have received a complaint. But since people empowered in this way sometimes increase their authority, as I have observed on more than one occasion, you will kindly favour me, Monsieur, with the jurisdiction over any judgements which may follow ... Since I have had the honour to serve in the provinces [as intendant], I have made it a cardinal principle to carry out all my functions without the help of others, so that I have always been in a position to give account of what it was that I had done ...

A similar denial of any generalized power of subdelegation was made by Marle, the intendant at Riom,[54] while at Pau, duBois du Baillet was reluctant even to use his predecessor's subdelegate without official approval.[55] Whatever the actual practice in the provinces, the intendants knew their Bodin and Le Bret and, as we might expect, in their answers to Colbert they studiously avoided any statement which might be interpreted as undermining royal sovereignty.

The question is whether or not later ministers undermined this balance, firstly by the creation of permanent offices for *subdélégués* during the war of the Spanish Succession, and secondly by the establishment in certain provinces of permanent general subdelegations (*subdélégués-généraux*). The first matter is usually dismissed as a temporary fiscal expedient resulting from the war: the *subdélégués* were established as office-holders in April 1704, and the measure was

---

[53] AN G⁷ 124, 20 June 1682.
[54] AN G⁷ 101, 19 July 1682.
[55] AN G⁷ 112, 18 Aug. 1682.

revoked in August 1715; thereafter, there was no further attempt to repeat the experiment in the *ancien régime*.[56] The edict of creation made it clear:[57]

> ... the ministry of these officials has become so important and their functions so extensive, that we have judged it necessary to invest those who henceforth exercise them with a character which gives them the prominence and authority necessary for the good functioning of their duties with more honour and impartiality ...

The government appeared to have swung full circle by accepting the argument of Bodin and Loyseau that office-holders had more permanency and a higher social status than temporary commissioners. However, if the comments of the intendant of Amiens are at all representative, even the windfall that the government expected from the sale of these offices was not as great as it might have hoped—by 1710 the subdelegates were declared to be in greater need of revenues than to be burdened with new taxes: they were not the wealthy local office-holders the government had sought to appoint.[58] The long-term political disadvantages of the introduction of venality must have been clear and, as has been seen, the decision was reversed with the coming of peace in 1715.

The general subdelegation is more interesting, because it became a permanent feature of the *ancien régime*.[59] The first commission as *subdélégué-général* was issued on 14 January 1702 to the sieur Basset in Dauphiné;[60] two others were issued before 8 November 1704, when a similar commission was issued to Saint-Macary in Béarn: the Dauphiné and Béarn examples are alike in that both conferred an acting intendancy on an individual during the absence abroad of the previously commissioned provincial intendant. Méliand, who had been appointed intendant of Béarn in April 1704, served simultaneously for five years as intendant there and in Catalonia; but this was a device to permit him to hold two salaries, the salary as intendant of the army being insufficient to cover his real costs.[61] At the provincial estates of 1706, St-Macary, the *subdélégué-général* or acting intendant, ran into conflict because he had appointed as his *subdélégué* the syndic

---

[56] Antoine, *Le dur métier du roi*, p. 76 and the articles by J. Ricommard there cited, notably, 'L'édit d'avril 1704 et l'érection en titre d'office des subdélégués des intendants', *Revue historique*, 195 (1945), 24–35, 123–39.

[57] C. V. E. Boyer de Sainte-Suzanne, *L'administration sous l'ancien régime. Les intendants de la généralité d'Amiens (Picardie et Artois)* (1865), 583.

[58] AN G⁷ 92, 8 Sept. 1710. There had been difficulty in finding purchasers in Béarn as late as 1706: AN G⁷ 117, 5 Oct. 1706.

[59] Antoine, *Le dur métier du roi*, 125–79.

[60] *Ibid.*, 130, 169–70.

[61] AN G⁷ 116, 24, 25 Nov. 1704. AN G⁷ 118, 20 Jan. 1710. AN G⁷ 119, 8 Mar. 1711.

of the province. The acting intendant alleged that the two posts were not incompatible, and the controller-general agreed; but this was clearly not the view of the province's representatives. Although called a subdelegate-general, St-Macary as acting intendant had appointed his own subdelegate despite the Roman law maxim *delegatus non potest subdelegare*. However, the controller-general did not take St-Macary to task for having done so.[62] Nevertheless, with the possible exception of this incident, St-Macary seems to have been scrupulous in the exercise of his powers. On Méliand's return as intendant in 1709, St-Macary's authority should have come to an end: but did it do so if the intendant did not return to the province itself, but went straight to Versailles? St-Macary asked the ministers to settle the issue.[63] Despite the apparent oddity of the general subdelegation, which became increasingly common in the eighteenth century as a device to permit the absence of the intendant from the province, it led to no undermining of the notion of sovereignty, as the creation of offices for subdelegates in 1704 had done, albeit potentially.

Indeed, contrary to Colbert's fears, the evidence suggests that the intendants and acting intendants (*subdélégués-généraux*) of Louis XIV never became possessed of sovereign powers in their own right except in specific instances where the crown had given prior authorisation. Much has been written about the development of French absolutism, and even about the drafting of decrees of the council,[64] but few commentators have focused attention on the intendants' own drafting of decrees (*projets d'arrêts*), empowering them to deal with a specific case often without appeal. The draft decree was sent to the minister, often the controller-general, for approval, together with the various documents justifying the need for such a specific additional power.[65] In one sense, this process may be seen as the monarchy relying more than hitherto on the local initiative of the intendant; but in an equally important sense, the procedure enshrined Bodin's principle of undivided legislative sovereignty residing in the king, even if it was exercised on his behalf by the ministers, and the council in this case. The king's sovereignty remained undivided: the intendant was merely his agent in specific delegated matters. Furthermore, authorization by these decrees of the council was personal to the intendant: if a change of intendants occurred before the final sentence was pronounced by the tribunal over which he presided, the new appointee was careful to

---

[62] AN G⁷ 117, 5 Oct. 1706: 'luy ayant donné cette commission ...'.

[63] AN G⁷ 118, 20 Aug. 1709.

[64] Most recently, a distinguished study by A. N. Hamscher, *The conseil privé and the Parlements in the age of Louis XIV: a study in French absolutism* (Transactions of the American Philosophical Society, lxxvii, 1987).

[65] AN G⁷ 92, 22 Dec. 1710. This carton has several examples.

obtain a decree transferring authority in the case to him (*arrêt de subrogation*).[66] This was the Bourbon monarchy's equivalent to the Papacy's *facta personae* which we encountered earlier.

Moreover, the evidence suggests that most intendants were prudent, and took care to obtain the requisite prior authorisation for their actions. When they did not seek it, their judgements might be called into question by the minister. Carré de Montgeron received a commission on 16 September 1705 as intendant of Berry which empowered him, among other duties, to 'investigate carefully any exactions, misappropriation, violence and malversation which may have been carried out in financial matters in the said province, and to proceed against the offenders by judgement of last resort and without appeal'. Although the intendant recognised that normally he should have requested a specific decree of attribution in a case involving financial corruption in the *brigade des gabelles* at Épineuil, the intendant warned the accused that the case was being heard without appeal and commenced procedures against them. He did so not because he wished to arrogate sovereignty for himself, but because he had only one witness in the case, who lived thirty leagues away and wanted to return home. If the witness had left the province, then the case would have fallen. The minister nevertheless denounced Montgeron's actions and warned him that the accused in the case might have grounds for a civil action against him. In a reply couched in diplomatic language, the intendant remained quite unrepentant. He enclosed a copy of the appropriate passage from his commission, cited above, and commented that the council had in any case chosen to support his action by subsequently granting an *arrêt d'attribution*. His words are significant for our purposes:[67]

> I well know that it is common practice to request specific decrees each time some matter arises which requires investigation, and which will result in a prosecution. But these do not render null and void legal procedures which have been begun by the intendant as a result of the powers confered by his commission, unless these decrees mention the fact ...

Thus as late as 1707 Bodin—as reintepreted by Le Bret—was alive and kicking in Berry, with an assertion by the intendant of the fundamental right of the commissioner to adjudge without appeal, notwithstanding all the practical constraints of political prudence

---

[66] AN G⁷ 127, 19 Jan. 1709. Foullé de Montargis, the new intendant, sent a draft decree with the appropriate power based on those granted to Montgeron, his predecessor, in the case, but with a simple substitution of names.

[67] AN G⁷ 127, 18 May 1707.

during the war of the Spanish Succession, and above all the desire not to offend the superior courts which were helping to contribute towards the war effort. Although Montgeron was replaced as intendant in the late summer of the following year, there is no evidence that he was recalled in disgrace. On the contrary, he was transferred to the intendancy of Limousin—neither promotion nor demotion. The intendant, not the minister, had won the argument. However, what the intendant could not do was to overrule the decision of the majority of judges in such cases without appeal, even when he felt that the sentence was too lenient or, as happened in Berry in 1714, too severe.[68]

The case has been argued in this paper that Bodin left a posthumous legacy to the French monarchy, in a concept of the royal commission that in turn permitted the development of the idea of subdelegation. The distinction between the commission and the office, which was first made by Bodin, was fundamental for the later development of the French monarchy and made it, if not unique, distinctive in comparison with its European counterparts, where no such definition had been made. If we take the example of the Spanish Habsburg union of crowns, in 1581 and 1592 Philip II swore to uphold the privileges respectively of Portugal and Aragon and in 1652 Philip IV did so with regard to Catalonia, notwithstanding previous acts of rebellion within these kingdoms. Not until after the establishment of the new Bourbon dynasty were the privileges of the outlying Iberian kingdoms revoked (in 1707), while in 1713 the Catalans still demanded the confirmation of their privileges even though they were in rebellion. They received a stony reply from Philip V's representatives, who echoed Bodin's words that it was not for a king's subjects to treat with their prince.[69] Contractual monarchy was finally dead, and it is symptomatic of Philip V's government that intendants on the French model were introduced after 1711.[70] But the earlier concessions to rebels had served to emphasise the Habsburgs' conception of a contractual monarchy.

However, although the formal introductions of intendants was not made until 1711, there had been precursors in Castile under Habsburg rule. Officials with powers resembling those of the later intendants (*jueces de comisión*) may have been appointed already in the fifteenth century to deal with particular cases. They seem to have been used rather more frequently in the 1590s, although as yet no commission has been found. Their first extensive employment, however, was during

---

[68] AN G⁷ 128/130, 16 Aug. 1714.
[69] AN G⁷ 508, 21 June 1713.
[70] H. Kamen, *The war of succession in Spain, 1700–15* (1969), 115 and references at n. 104, and 390.

58

Olivares's ministry (1622–43), but even so the powers of the commissioners were restricted in crucial respects,[71] while those of the existing law courts in the localities actually grew in the course of the seventeenth century: 'centralized justice collapsed', it has been said, 'and the settlement of disputes reverted to the community.'[72] An example of the restricted powers accorded to royal commissioners in Castile is provided by the 60-day commission granted by Philip IV on 11 July 1627 to Juan de Morales to serve in Jerez de la Frontera, with appeals from his decision to be heard only by the council of finance (*Consejo de Hacienda*).[73] What a curious document it is from the perspective of a French historian! It was issued only six years before some of the most wide-ranging French commissions of intendant, which included considerable powers of prosecution; if there was a time limit on the French intendants, by the 1630s and 1640s it was a three-year and not a 60-day rule.[74] The Spanish commission was, in contrast, an exceptional delegation of closely circumscribed powers—it was desirable that Morales should carry out his delegated tasks in less than 60 days if possible. His commission illustrates Bodin's argument that commissioners were 'tyed vnto the verie words of their commission': Morales was empowered to act in a specific case concerning the tax arrears of Jerez de la Frontera for the years 1611 to 1625. In so far as he had any jurisdiction in Cadiz, Sanlucar de Barrameda and Puerto de Santa Maria, it was merely with respect to this specfic case. In contrast, French commissions, even as early as that of Pierre de Panisse in 1556, were not tied to a specific lawsuit or fiscal problem, but contained general powers as *intendant de la justice*, and later *intendant de la justice, police et finances*; as has been seen, specific attributions of authority were granted separately by decrees of the council.

How are we to explain this discrepancy between Bourbon and Habsburg governing practice in the late 1620s and early 1630s? Clearly, the highly developed conciliar structure in Castile, which was considerably in advance of its French equivalent in the sixteenth century, was an important reason. At its inception, the Habsburg system had been more sophisticated than its counterparts elsewhere,

[71] The author is grateful to Professor Juan Gelabert of the University of Cantabria (Santander) for communicating this information in a letter of 25 November 1988, and for commenting on this article in draft form.

[72] I. A. A. Thompson, 'The rule of the law in early modern Castile', *European history quarterly*, xiv (1984), 221–34, esp. at p. 222. R. L. Kagan, *Lawsuits and litigants in Castile, 1500–1700* (Chapel Hill, NC, 1981).

[73] The author is grateful to Professor Gelabert for sending a copy of this commission in a letter of 20 November 1987. The source is Archivo General de Simancas (Valladolid), Consejo y Juntas de Hacienda, legajo 671.

[74] Bonney, *Political change in France under Richelieu and Mazarin*, 49, 146.

BODIN AND THE DEVELOPMENT OF THE FRENCH MONARCHY   59

and this may have served to impede subsequent administrative innovation; however, the system failed to evolve and to address itself in the seventeenth century to a new fundamental requirement, the mechanism of contact between the periphery and the centre.[75] Habsburg Spain was stable, it has been said, 'because it was largely self-governing, not because it was governed by an absolute monarchy'.[76] Indeed, in Spain the conciliar structure itself was part and parcel of the contractual nature of monarchy, and served as a limitation on the absolute power of the king[77]—this helps explain the opposition to Olivares's reforming plans and his use of *juntas* composed of his supporters. Doubtless also Philip IV was anxious to avoid alienating the *Cortes* of Castile, which until 1664 enjoyed significant fiscal powers.[78]

Nevertheless, one suspects that the crucial reason for the lack of Castilian intendants on the French model in the lifetime of Philip IV is the absence in Spanish political thought of any real theoretical discussion of the nature and extent of the commission itself. Bodin's ideas failed to make an impact in Spain, except in the diluted form of Botero's *Reason of state*[79] and Justus Lipsius's *Six bookes of politickes or civil doctrine*,[80] which did not discuss the commission. Spanish political thought after Bodin remained contractualist, and free from his central preoccupation with the issue of unlimited legislative sovereignty.[81] It is true that one of its leading theoreticians, Francisco Suárez, categorically dismissed the view that it was possible for the community 'to retain essential power itself', and 'merely to delegate this power to its prince'. On the contrary, he argued, the ruler was not the delegate but the 'proper owner' of his powers; ultimately, the prince was *legibus solutus*, free from the coercive power of the positive laws. On the other hand, according to Suárez, it was lawful for the community to resist its prince, even to kill him, if it had no other means

---

[75] Kamen, *op. cit.*, 37.

[76] H. Kamen, *Spain in the later seventeenth century, 1665–1700* (1980), 17.

[77] B. Cárceles, 'The constitutional conflict in Castile between the council and the Count-Duke of Olivares', *Parliaments, estates and representation*, vii (1987), 51–9.

[78] C. Jago, 'Habsburg absolutism and the Cortes of Castile', *American historical review*, lxxxvi (1981), 307–26. I. A. A. Thompson, 'Crown and Cortes in Castile, 1590–1665', *Parliaments, estates and representation*, ii (1982), 29–45. Idem, 'The end of the Cortes of Castile', *Parliaments, estates and representation*, iv (1984), 125–33.

[79] G. Botero, *The reason of state* [1589], ed. and trans. P. J. and D. Waley (1956).

[80] J. Lipsius, *Six bookes of politickes or civil doctrine* [1589], trans. W. Jones [1594] in *The English experience*, 287 (Amsterdam/New York 1970).

[81] B. Hamilton, *Political thought in sixteenth-century Spain. A study of the political ideas of Vitoria, De Soto, Suárez and Molina* (Oxford, 1963). G. Lewy, *Constitutionalism and statecraft during the golden age of Spain: a study of the political philosophy of Juan de Mariana, SJ* (Geneva, 1960).

of preserving itself. The right of self-preservation could 'by no covenant be relinquished'.[82]

There was a considerable difference between a relatively cautious absolutism in theory and a much more cautious exercise of power in practice in Spain. In 1622, the president of the council of Castile reminded the king that 'the origin of monarchies was derived from the common approval and election by the people, giving the sovereign power to [one person as a result of an agreement and under conditions], ... in order for him to undertake to maintain [a just power], which is the origin and foundation of peace.'[83] Not surprisingly, the Habsburg monarchs reflected this tradition. It was Philip II who had stated that 'the community was not created for the prince, but rather ... the prince was created for the community'.[84] His successors did not depart greatly from this dictum. Philip IV was reminded by the count of Peñaranda that 'it is the people who raise up and give power to kings for their own defence and preservation ... God did not create kingdoms for the defence of kings but kings for the good of kingdoms'.[85] As Dr Thompson has demonstrated, not only had the king of Castile customarily taken an oath in the *Cortes* to maintain the royal patrimony and to confirm the customs, privileges and liberties of the cities—Philip II, Philip III and Philip IV all did so soon after their accession[86]—but also they had agreed to 'mutual, reciprocal and obligatory' contracts with the *Cortes* which went far beyond petitions of subjects to their king and made the grant of additional taxation conditional on the fulfilment of the contract. In 1642, it was recognised that the *Cortes* had been offered by the crown certain conditions as a 'pact and obligation' and that if these were not honoured then the towns would be freed from contributing to the agreed increases in taxation; on another occasion, it was judged 'very dangerous ... to break with the cities and the ancient custom of these kingdoms'.[87] This was an ascending theory of sovereignty, and a practice of government, which was light years away from Jean Bodin's descending theory, that 'the principall point of soveraigne maiestie, and absolute power, ... consist[s] in giving laws vnto the subiects in generall, without their consent ...'[88]

---

[82] Skinner, vol. ii., 177–8, 182–4.
[83] Cárceles, *op. cit.*, 56.
[84] H. G. Koenigsberger, 'The statecraft of Philip II', *European studies review*, i (1971), 3.
[85] R. A. Stradling, *Philip IV and the government of Spain, 1621–1665* (Cambridge, 1988), 301.
[86] Thompson, 'The end of the Cortes of Castile', 126.
[87] Thompson,' Crown and Cortes in Castile', 34–5, 42.
[88] Bodin, *Republique*, 142. Idem, *Commonweale*, ed. McRae, 98.

II

When writing his *Foundations of modern political thought*, Professor Skinner expressed the hope that by situating the work of the leading political thinkers in 'the more general social and intellectual matrix out of which their works arose' a history of political theory 'with a genuinely historical character' might arise. This would then provide 'a clearer understanding of the links between political theory and practice'.[89] This paper has suggested that the methodology which Professor Skinner advocates, 'the history of ideologies', can at best provide only one half of the answer. A better understanding of the ideas and the ideologists, in his words, 'on what questions they were addressing and trying to answer, and how far they were accepting and endorsing, or questioning and repudiating, or perhaps even polemically ignoring, the prevailing assumptions and conventions of political debate'[90] is certainly necessary. But it is not enough in itself. To achieve the ultimate objective, 'a clearer understanding of the links between political theory and practice', something else is necessary. This is not merely to establish when the foundations were completed for a new concept of the state as 'an omnipotent yet impersonal power'[91] but to ascertain precisely how such a new concept might have been translated into practice. In other words, so far there has perhaps been too great a concentration on the ideology and the ideologists and not enough on the mechanisms by which their ideas were put into effect. Hence the emphasis in this paper, which has been less about Bodin and more concerned with the development of the French monarchy. It remains to be seen whether this methodology will meet with general approval, or be considered an anachronistic exercise of viewing that which the beholder wishes to view. If the legitimacy of the exercise is accepted, then clearly the methodology will have to be refined, although it is by no means clear that a single methodology would be appropriate to the possible impact of all types of political ideas. But what is clear is that political thought can no longer be regarded as a sacrosanct and isolated activity, followed by a few historians with a minority specialist interest, but which is devoid of any importance or relevance to the scholarly pursuits of the majority. And if the history of ideologies has been criticised as insufficient, we may nevertheless be grateful to its leading exponent for having laid the ghost of a narrow, and ultimately sterile, textualist approach which the majority of historians could ignore with impunity.

[89] Skinner, vol. i., x, xi, xiii.
[90] *Ibid.*, vol. i., xiii.
[91] *Ibid.*, vol. ii, 355–6, 358. For the application of this development to France: H. A. Lloyd, *The state, France and the sixteenth century* (1980).

III

Was there a Bourbon style of government?

A conference devoted to the theme of 'From Valois to Bourbon' must address itself to many fundamental questions, not least of which is did it matter that the dynasty changed, or as Bodin might have put it, was there a consequential change in the 'estate' (*estat*)?[1] This in turn raises the hoary old chestnut of continuity and change. Although the relatively recent study of French institutions by Mousnier[2] takes 1598 as its starting point, very few institutional historians in the past have seen the Bourbon dynasty as a new departure. One needs to think only of Hanotaux's study of the origins of the intendants[3]; while the most recent work by Michel Antoine has sought to reinforce this historiographical tradition by stressing the Valois origins of several institutions which we have sometimes viewed as decidedly

---

[1] J. Bodin, *Les six livres de la république...*, Paris, 1583; repr. Darmstadt, 1977, p. 509. Idem, *The six bookes of a commonweale*, trans. R. Knolles (1606), ed. K. D. McRae, Harvard, Mass., 1962, p. 410.

[2] R. E. Mousnier, *The institutions of France under the absolute monarchy, 1598–1789*, Chicago, 1980, 1984. Original French edn. respectively 1974 and 1980.

[3] G. Hanotaux, *Origines de l'institution des intendants des provinces* (1884).

Bourbon in character⁴. Of course, such an approach must be closely related to the contemporary events — the same institution could be used for quite different purposes in a changed political context.

The transition from a Valois to a Bourbon government, whether it involved a change of style or not, therefore raises some of the most important issues for the historian. Although some may raise a semantic objection to the application of the term 'government' in this period⁵, if the historian is to explain political realities, the substance and not just the form of political power, without inhibition, he should not necessarily restrict himself to contemporary terminology. Thus this paper assumes that in this context the use of the term 'Bourbon style of government' is not anachronistic. There is no established methodology for analysing the character of Bourbon government, although there is, of course, Saint-Simon's famous comparison of the first three Bourbon kings⁶. However, a modern assessment of the 'state of the kingdom' at the end of each of these reigns, respectively in 1610, 1643 and 1715 might seem rather trite. An alternative methodology is to leave any long-term changes in the central government out of the reckoning altogether, and to concentrate instead on the state of one particular province at about 1710, a hundred years after Henri IV's assassination. Clearly by that date, if a Bourbon 'style of government' cannot be detected, then there is no purpose in prolonging the discussion. And which province could be better suited to such detailed investigation than the vicomté de Béarn, the Bourbon heartland before the accession of Henri IV in 1589? To what extent had this autonomous province been incorporated into the kingdom by 1710; on what discernible principles, if any, was it governed; and were these different from elsewhere in France? These, then, are the questions that will be addressed in what follows, and in the conclusion we will attempt to establish how far Béarn can be taken as an exemplar, and the differences between the Valois and Bourbon styles of government in France as a whole.

This is not the place to repeat in full the story of the incorporation of Béarn and Navarre into the kingdom of France, but certain crucial steps must be recalled. At the end of 1596, Henri IV had determined that

---

⁴ M. Antoine, *Le dur métier du roi. Etudes sur la civilisation politique de France d'ancien régime* (1986).

⁵ Cf. M. Antoine, 'La monarchie absolue', *The political culture of the old regime*, ed. K. M. Baker, Oxford-New York, 1987, pp. 11–12.

⁶ Louis de Rouvroy, duc de Saint-Simon Vermandois, 'Parallèle des trois premiers rois bourbons' [May 1746], *Ecrits inédits de Saint-Simon*, ed. P. Faugère, 3 vols., 1880, i.

163   WAS THERE A BOURBON STYLE OF GOVERNMENT?

his *domaine ancien*, including these two provinces, would remain separate from *nostre maison de France* 'sans y pouvoir estre aucunement compris ny meslé'[7]. The Edict of Fontainebleau of 15 April 1599 permitted Catholic worship in Béarn[8]; but this measure was criticized elsewhere in France as being insufficiently robust to deal with what was effectively a Protestant state. Moreover, had Henri IV produced a legitimate daughter, she could have inherited Béarn but not France because of the Salic Law debarring female succession. The twin needs to restore Catholic supremacy and to exclude the possibility of a female succession, which could have broken the personal union with France, were powerful factors in leading to the formal incorporation of Béarn and Navarre. Despite a new ruling in July 1607, they retained their independence in Henri IV's lifetime, although the first Bourbon king made some significant progress towards incorporation, not least by appointing Brûlart de Sillery as Chancellor simultaneously of France and Navarre[9].

However, the vital decisions were made during the majority of Louis XIII, at the end of 1616 and in June 1617: first, that Béarn should be incorporated into France, and second that Catholicism should be re-established without restriction there[10]. But it took Louis XIII's invasion in 1620 to implement these decisions, and then only by force, which specifically abrogated the privileges (*fors*) of Béarn 'en tant qu'il seroit besoin pour l'effet de ces présentes'[11]. The estates of Béarn refused to discuss the Edict of Union until a later meeting, when they were no longer under coercion; and when they did so in June 1622 they demanded its abrogation, and resolved to continue to use Béarnais as their language. They never retracted their demand for abrogation or registered the Edict of Union[12]. Meanwhile, on at least four occasions, the estates of Basse Navarre demanded that Louis XIII visit their province and take the oath of loyalty to their constitution; but although the king had promised this in the Edict of Union of 1620,

---

[7] P. Tucoo-Chala, *La vicomté de Béarn et le problème de sa souveraineté des origines à 1620*, Bordeaux, 1961, pp. 126, 194–5.

[8] C. Desplat, 'Edit de Fontainebleau du 15 avril 1599 en faveur des catholiques du Béarn', *Réformes et Révocation en Béarn, XVIIe — XXe siècles*, Pau, 1986, 223–246.

[9] Tucoo-Chala, pp. 127, 195–6. A. D'Estrée, *La Basse Navarre et ses institutions de 1620 à la Révolution*, Paris-Saragossa, 1955, p. 29.

[10] Tucoo-Chala, pp. 130–1, 196–8.

[11] *Ibid.*, pp. 132, 198–9.

[12] *Ibid.*, pp. 133, 199–200.

he did not in fact do so[13]. At the accession of Louis XIV in 1643, they renewed this demand; and despite the fact that apparently neither Henri IV nor Louis XIII had taken such an oath, the Regency government committed the new king to do so at his majority. In 1660, Louis XIV swore the oath before the deputies of the estates at St-Jean-de-Luz, shortly before his marriage to Maria Teresa. However, he resisted subsequent pressure, made on at least five occasions in the later seventeenth century, to repeat the oath in person on the territory of Navarre[14]. The king of France continued to call himself also king of Navarre, thus recognizing that it was not an 'annexe de la France, mais un royaume séparé', while the customs of Basque Navarre were sufficiently different from those of Béarn so that it remained under a separate administration[15].

It is not surprising, given this chequered history of the moves towards incorporation with France, that the privileges of the Pyrenean provinces were always regarded with suspicion by the crown after 1620, and that unsuccessful attempts were made to subvert them[16]. Colbert instructed Faucon de Ris, the intendant of Guyenne, to draw up a secret memorandum on the means to reduce the provinces of Bigorre, Marsan, Tarsan, Gabardan, Labourd and Soule into *pays d'élections* by suppressing their estates; but Béarn was recognized as being too difficult to deal with in this way. The three memoranda sent by Faucon de Ris in 1682 in reply to this instruction provide fascinating insights into the privileges of these *pays francs*[17] and the thinking of governmental officials about regional autonomy in the later seventeenth century. The intendant ruled out *élections* in Labourd, Soule and Marsan because the land was too infertile to produce sufficient tax revenue. There was also the consideration of 'l'humeur volage et impatiente des Basques' which meant that they would not support such an innovation; moreover, in the case of war with Spain 'ce pays seroit à mesnager'. However, the intendant felt that Marsan, Tarsan and Gabardan ('un même pays qui estoit anciennement joint à celuy de Béarn') could be joined to the *élection* of Les Lannes, an area of *taille réelle*[18]. As for Bigorre, an *élection* had been established in 1632, but subsequently revoked

---

[13] Estrée, *op. cit.* p. 38.
[14] *Ibid.*, pp. 38–9.
[15] *Ibid.*, pp. 36, 39.
[16] There are references to various attempts at subversion of provincial privilege in J. R. Major, *Representative government in early modern France*, New Haven and London, 1980, pp. 598, 632–3, 650–1.
[17] For this term used in relation to Labourd: AN G7 131, 5 Nov. 1680.
[18] AN G7 132, 17 Aug. 1682.

165   WAS THERE A BOURBON STYLE OF GOVERNMENT?

the following year[19]. The crown received only 20,000 *livres* per annum from the province, whereas de Ris considered that it could easily pay ten times the amount and the people be less oppressed than at present. The mountain people were 'farouches et indisciplinables' and needed the stamp of justice. Before taxes could be increased, however, the community debts would have to be liquidated — but in the meantime there was no difficulty, in the intendant's view, in suspending the estates[20]. But did it happen? As late as 1691, a subsequent intendant of Guyenne, Bazin de Bezons, hesitated even to extend the rights of the tobacco monopoly to Soule, Labourd and Bayonne while there was a war with Spain, given that these were frontier provinces 'habités par des Basques qui sont gens legers'[21].

Béarn had to be handled even more carefully for two reasons. It had a central place in the falsification of coinage, which was regarded as vital for bringing Spanish gold and silver into the kingdom: any attempt to eliminate this traditional activity would not only be against French interests but would risk the wholesale desertion of the population across the frontier[22]. Secondly, the population was predominantly Protestant. From 1685 the intendant's role was to supervise a population of 8000 'new' Catholics who had taken up their new faith after massive forced abjurations — as late as 1714 there were fears that Béarn could yet revert to its pre-1620 status as a Protestant state[23]. Of course, such possibilities seem in retrospect to have been illusory, but the intendant's difficulties in policing a large Protestant population seem to have been reason enough for not attempting to abolish its estates. In short, the motives of the government in attempting to establish *élections* in this part of France seem to have resulted less from a desire for administrative uniformity, though in principle, no doubt, the ministers would have considered uniformity a worthwhile long-term objective, than from a pragmatic response to perceived local realities. There was no great wish to confront distant provinces on this issue for fear of over-commitment: the crown had many problems to deal with at the same time; the province had only one — to defend its privileges to the death. Those passionate emotions that could bring a *petit pays* such as Labourd close to civil war in 1679[24] would then be directed outside the province and

---

[19] Cf. Estrée, *op. cit.*, p. 156. R. J. Bonney, *Political change in France under Richelieu and Mazarin, 1624–1661*, Oxford, 1978, p. 349, n. 4.
[20] AN G7 132, 13 Aug. 1682.
[21] AN G7 135, 20 Jan. 1691.
[22] AN G7 131, 2 Mar. and 22 July 1680.
[23] '...voir tout le Béarn comme il a esté autrefois': AN G7 120, 14 Apr. 1714.
[24] AN G7 131, 18 Mar. 1679.

exclusively against the government. Faucon de Ris was correct in his belief that Colbert favoured a gradualist policy, a piecemeal process of attrition, with regard to the privileges of Béarn and Navarre.

The result was that instead of converting them into *pays d'élections*, a new intendancy was created for Béarn and Navarre in 1682. It was small, and administrative rearrangement was always on the cards — indeed, it was actively canvassed by the intendant in 1691[25] — prior to the definitive reorganization in 1716 resulting from the establishment of the *généralité* of Auch. The first intendant, du Bois de Baillet, was contemptuous of the estates of Béarn[26]:

> ...c'est plustost une cohue qu'une assemblée réglée. Toutes choses s'y resoluent par caballes et on y consomme le temps en des disputes inutiles et pour des bagatelles qui ne valent pas la peine d'estre agitées.

The intendant told the estates that they must increase the size of their money grant to the crown forthwith; he considered that they could pay four times their present contribution without difficulty. However, when it came to the first financial crisis of Louis XIV's reign, the war of the League of Augsburg, it proved difficult to levy *affaires extraordinaires* in Béarn. Without careful wording of the fiscal edict or decree, the Béarnais considered such measures 'comme faicts pour toute autre province que pour le leur...' Feydeau, a later intendant, commented that the application of French legislation to Béarn was not as straightforward as elsewhere 'à cause de leur for'[27]. The intendants sometimes fell into the trap of referring to Béarn as 'le royaume', alluding to its former status as an independent vicomté linked to the kingdom of Navarre in the person of its prince who happened to have become the king of France in 1589; such comments gave at least some legitimacy to its claims of privileged status. Until 1710 the intendants even tacitly accepted that business at the estates of Béarn should be conducted in Béarnais: it took approximately 170 years for the Valois policy which was enshrined in the ordinance of Villers-Cotterêts of 1539 to be applied strictly to the Bourbon patrimony of Béarn[28].

---

[25] AN G7 113, 7 Aug. 1691.
[26] AN G7 112, 22 Sept. 1682.
[27] AN G7 113, 7 Feb. 1690.
[28] R. J. Knecht, *Francis I*, Cambridge, 1982, p. 359. The deliberations of the estates in 1709 were still in Béarnais, especially in the third estate: A[rchives]

167   WAS THERE A BOURBON STYLE OF GOVERNMENT?

Incontestably, the two most controversial fiscal measures of Louis XIV's reign were the *capitation* of 1695 and the *dixième* of 1710. The first caused little difficulty in Béarn, except that the province sought an *abonnement* on favourable terms such as those obtained by Languedoc and Brittany, while the nobles considered their quarter share of the final assessment excessive. Pinon, the intendant, acted as their mediator with the Controller-General at Paris, and used the argument that it was dangerous to alienate a frontier province at a time of war with Spain. There was little or no sign of social antagonism between the second and third estates over this issue[29]. In contrast, the discussion of the *dixième* provoked a fierce constitutional conflict within the estates of Béarn. The estates offered 50,000 *livres* for an *abonnement* (10,000 more than they had offered for the *capitation* in 1696), but this was rejected by Desmaretz, the Controller-General, as 'modicque... et... peu proportionnée au secours que le Roy a lieu d'attendre...' The crown would accept the offer for the *abonnement des terres* alone. The third estate was prepared to accept the crown's offer, but the second estate, led by the baron d'Arros, refused. The town of Morlàas proposed, and the estates eventually accepted on the casting vote of the president (the vote was 39–39), that the *partage* between the estates should be taken to the ministers for resolution[30]. The demise of the estates of Dauphiné in 1628 had revealed the dangers to a province of social divisions between the second and third estates resulting from fiscal grievances[31]. But the conflict between the estates of Béarn petered out. Why was this? Clearly, the crown held effective disciplinary control: the baron d'Arros was at first debarred from entering the estates for four years as a result of his opposition to the *dixième*; subsequently, the intendant persuaded the ministers that news of his exclusion was sufficient punishment and he could safely be readmitted subject to good conduct. The baron was clearly humiliated and had to thank the estates for helping him convince the king that his conduct had been innocent and in effect misinterpreted[32]. The constitutional crisis in Béarn in 1711 did not

---

D[épartementales des] P[yrénées]-A[tlantiques] (Pau), C 752. St-Macary, the *subdélégué-général* (acting intendant) was himself a Béarnais and spoke to the estates in the local dialect. However, by 1711 there was an intendant from the north (Barillon) and this important session was reported (and presumably conducted) in French.

[29] AD P-A C 744 fos. 354^v-356^r, 426, 447^v-448^r.
[30] AD P-A C 753, fos. 452^r, 457^v, 473, 478, 482, 487.
[31] Bonney, *Political change*, p. 354. D. Hickey, *The coming of French absolutism: the struggle for tax reform in the province of Dauphiné, 1540–1640*, Toronto, 1986.
[32] AD P-A C 2, 29 Aug. 1711, 19 Feb., 9 May 1712. C 754, fos. 126, 184^v.

develop into a sustained campaign between the two orders as had happened in Dauphiné a century earlier; but as in Dauphiné, the crown exploited its opportunity. In this case it did not suspend the estates indefinitely (as in Dauphiné), but it modified its rights.

The first move was made by Barillon, the intendant, who by an ordinance of 1 August 1711 required local communities to have the tax rolls for the *taille, taillon* and *capitation* countersigned by his *subdélégués* before the sums could be levied. This was denounced at the estates of 1712 as undermining the privileges of the *pays*. The intendant denied any such purpose; the form in which taxes were levied was not part of the estates' powers, he contended, and in any case his was a reforming measure which placed the communities under a similar regime to that of the estates themselves: as a result of a decree of the council of state of 19 June 1688, the crown required all levies resulting from the deliberations of the estates to be countersigned by the intendant. The communities should not be exempted from a procedure to which the estates were subject (although whether this decree had been enforced was questioned even by the intendant, who blamed the provincial *syndic* for not reading out the 1688 decree at the beginning of each session, as he was required to do). The king had no intention of damaging the estates' privileges, but 'il est de première règle' the intendant contended, 'que le Roy n'accorde point de privilège contre loy même'[33]. This may have been a fair reflection of royal and ministerial attitudes, but it was a tactless statement to make to the provincial estates. The intendant made matters far worse, and ultimately secured his own transfer from Béarn to Roussillon, a less controversial posting, by alleging that the resistance to his ordinance (and indeed, the controversy over the *dixième* the previous year) had been caused by the influence of the Parlement of Pau on members of the estates. At this point, the estates declared that they 'ne peuvent trouver la seureté en la conservation de leurs droits et de leurs privilèges que par un arrêt du conseil'[34]. The estates sought the protection of the king's council against the principal royal agent in the province, the intendant, and the session of 1712 broke up in acrimony.

What was the response of the government to this opportunity to deliver 'province-requested absolutism'? No comfort was given to the estates

---

[33] AD P-A C 754, fos. 68, 145, 177.
[34] AD P-A C 754, fol. 300. The allegation that the Parlement was responsible for resistance to the *dixième* was made in a letter to the Controller-General: AN G7 119, 31 May 1712: '...c'est le Parlement seul aux Etats derniers dont la brigue avoit emporté au corps de la noblesse...'

III

169 WAS THERE A BOURBON STYLE OF GOVERNMENT?

of Béarn and Navarre. The sessions of the estates were henceforth reduced from six weeks, the rule that had prevailed since 1670, to four weeks; not surprisingly, this provoked remonstrances from the 1713 estates[35]. Moreover, a decree of the council of state of 13 September 1712 reiterated and strengthened the earlier decree of 19 June 1688 concerning the intendant's powers at the estates of Béarn and Navarre. The estates were no longer allowed to send deputies to Paris or to the court (at Versailles) for any reason without prior written permission of the king, countersigned by a secretary of state. No deliberations of the interim meeting of estates' representatives (the *abrégé*) could take place except in the presence of the intendant on penalty of nullity. The new rules were to be read out at each session of the estates[36]. However much Barillon had foolishly provoked the estates, they had ended up weaker rather than stronger; by 1715 the third estate, led by the town of Morlàas, recognized its almost complete dependence on the good offices of a subsequent intendant, Harlay, for winning fiscal concessions from the government[37].

But the conflict of 1711–12 in Béarn had another protagonist, the Parlement of Pau, as Barillon had indicated. This institution was a creation of the Bourbon dynasty in 1624, and unlike the estates, its business was conducted in French. Originally largely Protestant in composition, the Parlement had been gradually purged of its Huguenot membership so that it sought full implementation of the restrictive religious legislation which culminated with the revocation of the Edict of Nantes in 1685. Indeed, one of its councillors, St-Macary, was given the responsibility of supervising this task as *commissaire pour les contraventions*[38]; he it was who was later entrusted by the crown with the acting intendancy (*subdélégation générale*) during the long absence of Méliand as intendant of Catalonia as well as Béarn after 1704. However, in view of the traditional hostility between the Parlement and the intendant in Béarn[39], the crown made a serious error in 1685 in appointing the first president of the Parlement as caretaker-intendant: he immediately told the Parlement that 'l'execution de lad[ite] commission depend[ai]t naturellement de la juridiction de la cour' and that

---

[35] AD P-A C 755, fol. 4.
[36] AD P-A C 755, fol. 218.
[37] AD P-A C 756, fol. 44^v-45^r.
[38] AD P-A B 4539, fol. 14, 16 July 1685.
[39] F. Loirette, 'L'administration royale en Béarn de l'union à l'intendance, 1620–1682. Essai sur le rattachement à la France d'une province frontière au XVIIe siècle', *XVIIe Siècle*, 45, 1964, 77–81. Bonney, *Political change*, p. 404.

he would refer all matters other than secret ones to its judgement[40]. Thus it was that the crown unwittingly assisted the Parlement of Pau in its belief that it, and not the intendant, should be 'seul maître de la province'[41]. Compliments paid by new intendants to the Parlement early on in their period of office could not prevent later structural conflict, which was limited only by the fact that several of the intendants were already members of the Parlement — this was true of St-Macary (the acting intendant) and des Chiens de Launeville; the latter was rewarded with the intendancy because he had acted as the Parlement's agent at Paris and had negotiated the loans to help discharge the successive fiscal demands of the government on the lawcourt[42]. By 1701, the Parlement was becoming restless at these fiscal demands, and it demanded in return an increased jurisdictional area (*ressort*) by the addition of Bigorre[43]; however, the administrative rearrangement of 1716, which created the *généralité* of Auch, specifically rejected any alteration to the respective jurisdictions of the Parlements of Bordeaux, Pau and Toulouse[44].

The Parlement of Pau was thus destined to remain a small and relatively unimportant 'superior court' in the kingdom. This did not make it any the less aggressive in response to the intendant Barillon's ordinance of 1 August 1711, which it claimed overturned the traditional system in the province for the levy of taxation and would result in increased costs and perpetual conflict[45]. Accordingly, it issued a decree on 19 February 1712, which sought to suspend the intendant's ordinance. The constitutional conflict rapidly became acrimonious, and the Parlement drew up a memorandum on the 'entreprises de Mr de Barillon sur la jurisdiction du Parlement'[46], while the intendant sent his own account of the conflict to the ministers[47]. Matters came to a head when the lawcourt discovered that the intendant had sought to blacken its reputation with the ministers by

---

[40] AD P-A B 4539, fol. 18, 30 Aug. 1685.
[41] Cf. the comment of the intendant Harlay de Cély as late as 1713: '...que cette compagnie souffre impatiam[men]t [*sic*] l'intendance, et que quelque contens qu'ils soient de l'intendant, ils voudroient anéantir absolument ses fonctions et être seuls maîtres de la province...': AN G7 120, 7 Mar. 1713.
[42] AD P-A B 4542, fol. 80^v-81^r, 19 Jan. 1693. B 4545, fol. 113^v, 15 Dec. 1702. B 4546, fol. 121^v, 3 June 1707.
[43] AD P-A B 4545, fol. 43^v, 13 Sept. 1701.
[44] A[rchives] D[épartementales du] Gers (Auch) C 430, fol. 1^v.
[45] AD P-A B 4547, fol. 201^v, 15 Feb. 1712.
[46] AD P-A B 4547, fos. 214, 222, 21 and 25 Apr. 1712.
[47] AN G7 119, 10 Mar., 22 Apr. 1712.

III

171   Was there a Bourbon style of government?

accusing it of interference with the deliberations of the estates of Béarn[48]. The Chancellor attempted to mediate, arguing rather disingenuously that Barillon was a *galant homme* who was incapable of doing such a thing[49]; but the Parlement was not satisfied with this, and took its protest directly to the king, separating this issue from the jurisdictional conflict with Barillon and receiving in the end a special assurance that the king had not gained any unfavourable impression of the Parlement from the intendant's dispatches[50]. The lawcourt undoubtedly had its revenge, since Barillon was unceremoniously moved on to another province; a later intendant, Harlay, recalled the intrigue in 1715 and feared a similar fate because of his own conflict with the Parlement over the administration of the grain supply in time of famine[51].

The constitutional conflict between the Parlement and the intendant was settled by a ruling drawn up by a commission of the council, which was subsequently registered by the Parlement[52]. The essential point was won by the intendant — he alone signed the general levy for the province and the parish tax rolls, the issue which had been at the heart of the conflict; moreover, the council declared it 'd'une conséquence essentielle pour le bien des communautés' that the intendant should advise the crown on any extraordinary levies that might be necessary. However, the *juridiction contentieuse* in these and most other matters rested with the Parlement. It was an administrative fudge, and not surprisingly a later intendant, Harlay, denounced the ruling as an inadequate compromise full of inner contradictions. If the intendant followed the letter of the ruling, he would always find himself in conflict with the Parlement, whose essential aim was to destroy the intendancy and remain in sole charge of the province[53]. Within three years, Louis XIV was dead and the regency government had removed the restrictions on the rights of the superior courts to issue remonstrances[54], thus freeing the hands of the Parlement of Pau to continue its struggle for provincial ascendancy into the reign of Louis XV.

---

[48] AD P-A B 4547, fos. 232ᵛ-234ᵛ, 25 June 1712.
[49] AD P-A B 4547, fol. 240ᵛ, 18 July 1712.
[50] AD P-A B 4547, fos. 241ᵛ, 245ᵛ-246ʳ, 15 Aug. and after 28 Nov. 1712.
[51] AN G7 120, 28 July, 27 Aug. 1715. Harlay made it clear that he feared the hand of the duc de Gramont, the governor, in the attempt to dismiss him.
[52] AN G7 119, Oct. 1712. AD P-A B 4547, fol. 244ᵛ, 15 Nov. 1712. B 4548, fos. 154-156ᵛ, Oct. 1712.
[53] AN G7 120, 7 Mar. 1713.
[54] AD P-A B 4548, fol. 87, 14 Nov. 1715.

III

At first sight this lengthy digression into the later years of Louis XIV's reign in one of the smallest provinces of France might seem no more than of purely regional interest, and irrelevant to the broader consideration of the consequences of the transition from Valois to Bourbon dynasties. Yet if we ask what significance the provincial conflicts of 1711–12 in Béarn have for the historian, it is surely that they demonstrate that the veneer of Bourbon 'absolutism' was wearing very thin by the last years of Louis XIV's reign. But on one essential point, the Bourbon dynasty had won the argument where the last of the Valois had clearly lost. Everything was now referred to the king's council for arbitration. In its conflict with the intendant, the provincial estates saw the king's council as being neutral — the council alone could guarantee provincial privilege. Similarly, in a more serious and even more acrimonious conflict, the Parlement sought from the king's council a guarantee of its jurisdiction against the alleged encroachment of the intendant. The central government helped safeguard Béarnais privileges; and in the case of the Parlement it doubtless did so in recognition of the considerable financial sacrifice that individual *parlementaires* and the lawcourt as a collective entity had made during the wars of the League of Augsburg and the Spanish Succession.

If, in contrast, we consider the last years of Henri III's reign, clearly his conflicts with provincial institutions such as the governors and the Parlements were serious to a quite different degree: there was no sustained armed rebellion in the later years of Louis XIV's reign comparable to that of the League. But why was there armed rebellion in later sixteenth-century France? It was, in part, because religious conflict and factional rivalry had deprived the king's council of its capacity to act as the neutral arbitrator. There can be no doubt of Henri III's intention, affirmed by Richard Cook in 1584–5, to use his absolute powers 'either by his owne expresse commandment or by his Counsaile of Estate'[55]. What was lacking was any willingness on the part of significant sections of French society to accept the council's decisions. The council was prone to faction, and it was partisan in religious matters; at crucial points in the reigns of Charles IX and Henri III, the Parlements would not accept (and therefore, enforce) the royal Edicts of Pacification. No more, of course, would certain key provincial governors accept either the religious or the patronage policies of the central government. In the great crisis of Henri III's reign, the Parlements themselves fragmented on the question of whether their primary loyalty lay

---

[55] D. Potter and P. R. Roberts, 'An Englishman's view of the court of Henri III, 1584–1585: Richard Cook's "Description of the Court of France"', *French History*, 2, 1988, 328.

III

173   WAS THERE A BOURBON STYLE OF GOVERNMENT?

with a Catholic king or with the principle of hereditary succession.

Subsequently, the crucial developments were the settlement of Nantes, Henri IV's exclusion of the great nobility from the council, and the systematization of the sale of offices through the introduction of the *droit annuel* in 1604. None of these was inevitable; each formed part of that 'struggle for stability' — Mark Greengrass's phrase — which is so crucial to an understanding of Henri IV's political achievement. The unspoken clause in the settlement of Nantes was that while concessions were granted to the Huguenots in order to ensure peace, the king's council, the institution that ultimately would enforce the peace, would remain a Catholic body. Sully, of course, was the great exception — but one has only to think of the resurgence of the *barbons*, the greybearded former League supporters (Brûlart de Sillery, Villeroy and Jeannin), in the regency of Marie de Médicis to appreciate that his was an isolated role. The collapse of Huguenot support within the upper nobility has rightly been stressed as one reason for the failure of the Protestant cause in the seventeenth century; but the tame acceptance of a Catholic-dominated royal council has perhaps not been emphasised sufficiently. Of course, there was not much that could be done. The significance of the abjuration of Henri IV was that the Bourbon dynasty would remain Catholic; a Catholic king pledged to extirpate heresy by his coronation oath was unlikely to summon many Protestants to serve as his trusted councillors.

But the move towards the establishment of a Catholic-dominated royal council was greatly intensified by the exclusion of the great nobility from the council *before* the wave of abjurations symbolized by Lesdiguières's acceptance of the Constableship in 1622. The Estates General of 1588 had explicitly called for a noble majority in council membership[56]. On 25 November 1594, when the *surintendance des finances* was replaced by a finance commission, the number of great nobles exactly equalled the number of *robins* in the commission, with the Chancellor holding the balance[57]. However, arrangements suitable for a kingdom at war were no longer appropriate in time of peace. By 1598 the baron de Rosny, later known as the duc de Sully, as *grand maître de l'artillerie* and *surintendant des finances*, was almost the sole *noble d'épée* left in the council. After the Chancellor,

---

[56] B[ritish] L[ibrary] Egerton 1668, fol. 132.
[57] Bonney, *The king's debts*, p. 44 n. 6. AN 120 ap 29 fol. 1, 25 Nov. 1594. The *robins* were (besides the Chancellor, Cheverny) Bellièvre, Sancy, Forget de Fresnes and La Grange-le-Roy.

Sully may have enjoyed something close to precedence in the council[58]; but what he made up for in terms of seniority could not hide the numerical weakness of his class — Sully lost the argument over the need to retain *nobles d'épée* in the council even in peacetime[59], and not long after the death of his great mentor, Henri IV, he lost his own place in the council. With the departure from government of Sully in January 1611, the aristocratic presence, too, was gone.

How far this change was a result of latent aristocratic discontent, which came to a head with the Biron conspiracy of 1602[60], and how far it was simply a response to peace and the growing technical complexity of government[61] might at first seem an open question. But at the assembly of notables of 1617, the crown had given its answer[62]. A great number of nobles in attendance at the council meant that 'le secret aux affaires ne pouvoit estre gardé et la multitude des advis apportoit de la longueur aux advis [et] de la confusion.' There were likely to be arguments between the nobles over precedence within the council. In many instances the interests of the great nobility would be discussed within the council, while their offices — especially provincial governorships — required them frequently to be absent from the council: 'pour ces raisons Sa Ma[jes]té a esté jusques à présent contrainte de laisser le maniement secret de ses affaires aux ministres qui en avoient eu charge sous le Roy son père...'

The assembly of notables of 1626–7 considered that 'c'est chose digne de la justice du Roy de donner part aux honneurs, dignités et emplois à ceux de sa noblesse'[63] but it is clear that there were very few nobles employed during the majority of Louis XIII. Schomberg, la Vieuville and d'Effiat were the exceptions — rather surprisingly, an aristocratic background was regarded as a qualification for the *surintendance des finances*. But with the regency of Anne of Austria, the great nobility came back in force: Gaston

---

[58] B. L. Egerton 1680, fos. 57, 63.

[59] If he indeed argued for this systematically: cf. R. E. Mousnier, 'Sully et le conseil d'état et des finances', *Revue historique*, 192, 1941, 82–83. Idem, *La vénalité des offices sous Henri IV et Louis XIII*, 2nd. edn., 1971, pp. 603–5.

[60] Bonney, *The King's debts*, p. 66.

[61] M. Greengrass, *France in the age of Henri IV: the struggle for stability* (1984), p. 111.

[62] C. J. Mayer, *Des Etats Généraux et autres assemblées nationales*, 18 vols., The Hague, 1788–9, XVIII, 54–5. B. L. Egerton 1666, fos. 56^v-57^v. B. L. Add. Mss. 30555, fos. 195^v-196^r.

[63] B. L. Egerton 1666, fol. 176^v.

175 WAS THERE A BOURBON STYLE OF GOVERNMENT?

d'Orléans and Condé were named as members of the regency council in the testament of Louis XIII, but were outnumbered by Mazarin and the three *robins*[64]. Once the crisis of 1648 had broken, the council of state varied in number, but the aristocratic presence was certainly proportionately increased[65]. However, this advance was abruptly halted by the defeat of the Fronde, which settled the question of aristocratic participation. Under Louis XIV it appears that only two members of the old nobility were allowed into the *ministériat* (the maréchal de Villeroy in 1661, his childhood guardian, who continued in the position he had held since 1649; and the duc de Beauvillier after 1691). Although the great noble families returned in profusion in the eighteenth century (from 1714 to 1789 there were only three ministers who were *not* titled aristocrats)[66], in the short term, however, the exclusion of the great nobility from the council in the period from the reign of Henri IV to the Regency of Philippe d'Orléans was of profound importance. It was a Bourbon style of government quite different from that of the Valois: although it is clear that the role of the *robins* had been growing under Henri III, their preponderance was not assured. It may be suggested that the exclusion of the great nobility from the council and the ascendancy of the *robins* which filled the resulting vacuum were crucial processes in allowing the king's council to be recognized as the neutral arbitrator.

Paradoxically, the systematization of the sale of offices resulting from the establishment of the *droit annuel* in 1604 undoubtedly facilitated and consolidated the *robin* dominance of the king's council. Paradoxically, because there was a growing distinction between membership of the council and membership of the sovereign courts. The position of king's councillor was not an office, but an appointment by letters patent which was regarded increasingly as incompatible with office in the sovereign courts. On the other hand, in terms of earlier careers, by the seventeenth century king's councillors had almost to a man previously passed through the sovereign

---

[64] Bonney, *The king's debts*, p. 191. The *robins* were Séguier, Bouthillier and Chavigny.

[65] At the council of 4 Oct. 1648, five out of seven, Gaston, Condé, Conty, Longueville and La Meilleraye being balanced only by Mazarin and Séguier: *ibid.*, p. 208. At the council of 15 October, the proportion had reverted to four (Gaston, Condé, Conty, Villeroy) out of ten: Bibliothèque Nationale Clairambault 651, fol. 342ᵛ.

[66] A. Goodwin, 'The social structure and economic and political attitudes of the French nobility in the eighteenth century', *XIIth International Congress of Historical Sciences* Rapports, 1965, I., Vienne, 1966, p. 361.

courts. The ideology of the office-holders was conservative, not revolutionary. It was they, of course, who provided the juristic defence of absolutism, while their legal training, certainly in the seventeenth century, if not in the sixteenth, had imbued them with a profoundly absolutist view of monarchical sovereignty[67]. Thus it was that Louis XIV could rename the sovereign courts superior courts in 1665, and could curtail the Parlements' right of remonstrances in 1673 virtually without a protest. The arbitration of the king's council was accepted under Louis XIV, and it was only the Regency government's disastrous blunder in removing the limitations on the right of remonstrance that reopened the issue once more and paved the way for the constitutional conflicts of the eighteenth century.

The events after 1715, however, should not mislead us about the nature of the Bourbon style of monarchy and the great contrast it made with that of the last Valois kings. There is a degree of continuity in the policies of the first three Bourbon monarchs; but we could not, and should not, expect that in 1610 there would be the full implementation or acceptance of a style of government which reached its apotheosis only in the period between 1673 and 1715[68]. Nor can the historian state with confidence that had the Valois dynasty survived it might not have pursued comparable policies to those of the first Bourbon kings. The historian must content himself with the verdict that, given the assassination of Henri III without a direct male heir in 1589, the assessment of the Valois dynasty must rest on its achievements within a given historical context — the crisis of the League. The style of government pursued by the Bourbon dynasty was shaped and forged by the crisis of the war of succession, the challenge to Henri IV and the political necessity of his abjuration in 1593.

Thereafter, what becomes of crucial importance is the capacity of the Bourbon dynasty for survival. Not only was assassination a real threat in the case of Henri IV; the matrimonial problems of the Bourbons were an important destabilizing factor. The second generation was not entirely secure until the birth of Henri IV's second son Gaston in 1608, the third generation not until the birth of Louis XIII's second son Philippe in 1640. The crisis of the dynasty in the fourth generation is well known, following the decimation of the royal family in 1710–11. The effective period of

---

[67] L. W. B. Brockliss, *French higher education in the seventeenth and eighteenth centuries. A cultural history*, Oxford, 1987, pp. 449–450.

[68] Whether there was any significant development at all would seem to be questioned by R. C. Mettam, *Power and faction in Louis XIV's France*, Oxford, 1988.

177 WAS THERE A BOURBON STYLE OF GOVERNMENT?

royal minority was much longer than the legal minorities of 1610–14 and 1643–51. Twenty-nine years out of the seventy-two years of early Bourbon monarchy were years in which the king did not rule personally[69]. However, personal rule did not necessarily mean strong government, as the reign of Henri III had shown. Developments such as the rise of royal favourites and chief ministers, and other institutional factors, may have papered over the difficulties. But there was little prospect of an end to armed aristocratic faction as long as a king did not rule personally, while the danger abroad was very evident. The Spanish Habsburg enemies of the Bourbon dynasty had not lost sight of their ambition to establish an elective monarchy in France, and to partition the kingdom among hereditary (and preferably subservient) provincial governorships. Unlike the new Bourbon dynasty, which suffered two minorities within two generations, the Spanish Habsburgs had no royal minority between 1516 and 1665. It was therefore not at all inevitable that the new Bourbon dynasty would prevail against its foreign and domestic enemies and that any coherent Bourbon 'style of government' would have the opportunity to emerge. That it did so was due perhaps as much to accident as to design, just as the accidents of Alençon's death in 1584, Henri III's assassination without a direct heir, and the fact that the rival candidate to Henri IV was an ageing Cardinal who was also held in captivity had brought the first Bourbon to the throne in 1589.

---

[69] If we take the early Bourbon monarchy for this purpose to mean the years 1589–1661, the periods in question were the years 1610–21 and 1643–61.

IV

The French Civil War, 1649-53

Professor A. Lloyd Moote's *The Revolt of the Judges* is the first scholarly study of the Fronde in English for 35 years, and as such it has commanded a wide audience since it appeared in 1971.[1] Moote's view of the Fronde is oriented almost exclusively towards Paris and the *Parlement* of Paris in particular. He considers that the *Parlement* of Paris played a moderating role during the Fronde as a result of almost accidental compromises between conservative and less conservative members of that court. The history of the Fronde, in Moote's view, was in large measure the history of political reforms obtained under duress in 1648 and the defence of those measures by the office-holders. He believes that the Fronde was a 'victory-in-defeat' for moderate opposition and that 'nothing was done' by the government in 1652-3, at the end of the Fronde, to undo the measures enacted under duress four years earlier. It is thus evident that the political crisis of 1648 largely overshadows Moote's account of the Fronde, and it is essential to be clear about the issues at stake. In Moote's interpretation, Mazarin and D'Hémery, his finance minister, blundered into the crisis largely by their own folly: once they had brought about the crisis, they should have accepted proposals of the office-holders which in no way threatened the king's sovereignty. Moote blames Anne of Austria, the Regent, and Mazarin for the first civil war, which began in January 1649: 'the burden of guilt for the violence of 1649 has to be laid on [their] shoulders', he asserts. Mazarin is considered by Moote to have been 'unbalanced' and 'emotional' in his attitude to the concessions extracted from the crown by the office-holders in the summer of 1648, and in any case Mazarin, he believes, was 'unable to grasp [their] technical legal details. . . .'[2]

Moote has thus provided an account of the years 1648-9 which differes substantially from previous interpretations, such as those of Doolin and Kossman.[3] However, it is difficult to agree that the rebellion of the office-holders arose *simply* from miscalculations by the government, or that Mazarin's was the reaction of ignorance or paranoia. The crown had been fighting an expensive foreign war since 1635. By December 1647, the financial situation of the French crown was desperate. Massive new revenues were needed to stave off bankruptcy. Without new revenues, loans from the financiers would not be forthcoming. Without such loans, the war could not be continued. Mazarin and D'Hémery in 1645 had gambled on a quick settlement in the peace negotiations with the Spanish and Austrian Habsburgs at Münster: thus they had anticipated the revenues of the crown up to the end of the fiscal year 1647, and secured loans of 115 million *livres* on this security.[4] By January 1648, however, Mazarin's foreign policy appeared to have failed. The Dutch Republic, formerly allied with France, made a separate peace with Spain at a time when the prospect of peace between France and the Habsburgs appeared to have receded.[5] In these circumstances, the office-holders were not prepared to accept a prolongation of the war to 1650 or beyond. The rebellion of the office-holders did not arise simply from miscalculations by the government, but from a political impasse. Mazarin could not make concessions to the office-holders, however desirable these might be in political terms, because concessions cost money — the commodity which above all the government did not have at its disposal. The office-holders objected to the creation of offices to provide a new source of revenue for the crown. They objected to the anticipation of revenues up to the end of the fiscal year 1650. They objected to the use of extraordinary powers to force through fiscal measures (for example by the *lit de justice* of 15 January 1648). They also protested against an increase in the price of the renewal of the *droit annuel,* the annual payment for the privilege of resigning one's office to one's heir (this measure led to the *arrêt d'union* of 13 May 1648). Certainly, the government was responsible for the crisis of 1648 to the extent that Mazarin had made a political gamble for a quick peace settlement in the negotiations at Münster, a gamble which proved unsuccessful. Once the gamble had failed, and had been seen to fail, the government was at the mercy of its domestic critics and was no longer in control of events. The political confrontation operated in favour of

IV

The French Civil War, 1649-53

the office-holders. The financiers refused to make further loans to the government until the struggle between the crown and its office-holders was resolved. The government thus capitulated, and delegates from the Parisian sovereign courts met at the *Chambre St Louis* on 30 June 1648. Once the proposals of this assembly were made known, they brought about a collapse of financial confidence, and the situation was made worse by the dismissal of D'Hémery on 9 July. Bankruptcy followed later in the month, and with it effective government collapsed.

What was the significance of the proposals of the *Chambre St Louis* which were later enacted (in part) by the government in the declarations of 18 July and 22 October 1648? The *Chambre St Louis* did not say so directly, but what it wanted in effect was a return to peacetime forms of government. The intendants had been the provincial administrators of France since 1642 — yet the members of the *Chambre St Louis* demanded their recall. The lesser financial office-holders (the *trésoriers* and the *élus*) had not administered the *taille* (the chief direct tax) independently since 1642 — yet they were to be reinstated. The government had anticipated revenues in the form of loans from financiers regularly since 1639 — such loans, it was proposed, should be declared illegal. The cash expenses of the French crown had risen dramatically during the war — a limit was to be placed on such expenditure. The *taille* had been increased three-fold to help pay for the war — a reduction of 25 per cent, equivalent to the alleged interest rate charged by the financiers, was demanded. An extraordinary financial investigation *(chambre de justice)* was to be set up with the purpose of eliminating alleged corruption by the financiers. The members of the *Chambre St Louis* wanted a return to peacetime forms of administration not merely because they felt that this was good for France, but because it was also good for the office-holders. The sovereign courts were to regain their former powers, following the abolition of the intendants. The power of the crown to issue commissions was also to be curtailed. The effect of the other proposals would have been drastically to reduce the profitability of the sale of offices as a fiscal instrument of the crown.

Moote accepts that the proposals of the *Chambre St Louis* were 'the product of extraordinary circumstances' but considers them a 'serious attempt to deal with an institutional malaise'. The basic strength of the office-holders, in his view, was their ' [ambiguous] treatment of sovereignty'. They did not present a threat to the crown. What Moote calls the 'politics of duplicity' of Anne of Austria and Mazarin — that is to say, their determination to undermine the proposals although they were forced to enact certain of them — was thus, in Moote's view, unnecessary and self-defeating. He questions Mazarin's basic assumption that 'the prosecution of the foreign war necessitated certain risks'.[6] However, the proposals of the *Chambre St Louis* cannot be viewed in isolation from their context and their likely consequences. There is little doubt that the office-holders sought to restrict the king's fiscal powers by dismantling the system of war finance that had operated since 1635. Yet without independent powers of finance, the king could not conduct an independent foreign policy. There were strong arguments, from the ministerial standpoint, that the proposals of the *Chambre St Louis* meant fundamental limitations on the king's sovereignty, restricting his fiscal powers, his power to vary the unwritten constitution (for example, by conferring fiscal powers on the intendants), and above all his ability to wage a foreign war. Anne of Austria must also have considered that the proposals would prevent her son, Louis XIV, from governing in the way that his father had done between 1635 and 1642.

Without such a reasoned basis for their opposition to the proposals, the conduct of Anne of Austria and Mazarin during the Fronde would be inexplicable. Viewed from the ministerial standpoint, the anti-Habsburg foreign policy, and its supremacy over all domestic considerations, was not a new departure of the Regency government after 1643: it was a decision urged on Louis XIII by Richelieu in 1630, a decision which had nearly led to the cardinal's downfall on the Day of Dupes (10 November 1630). Peace was concluded with the Emperor on 24 October 1648, but the war with Spain dragged on. The attitude of the office-holders allowed only two courses of action for Anne of Austria and Mazarin. Either they could accept the demands, dismantle the system of war finance and recall the intendants permanently, thus risking the prospect of a humiliating peace with Spain; or else, the existing foreign policy must be brought to fruition, entailing a commitment to the system of war finance, the reintroduction of the intendants and the defeat of the office-holders. Since vital aspects of the king's sovereignty appeared to be threatened, the defeat of the office-holders was certain to be the course of action chosen by Anne of Austria and Mazarin. They did not regard the declarations

IV

The French Civil War, 1649-53

of 1648 as great reforming ordinances: rather, they regarded them as temporary expedients, aimed at retrieving the loss of political control by the government. The declarations would be annulled retrospectively once the king's sovereignty was no longer undermined and the king could act in *plenitudo potestatis*. This in fact happened: Moote's account of the end of the Fronde does not stand up to scrutiny. The declaration of 22 October 1652 disallowed criticism of the ministers by the *Parlement* of Paris, forbidding its interference in affairs of state and financial questions and annulling its previous interventions in this area. By the end of 1652, the government could pay for a foreign war once again, since the limit on secret expenditure was removed, the taxes supressed in 1648 were restored and the investigation of the financiers was halted. Chancellor Séguier made it clear that it was not necessary to revoke each item of unpalatable legislation passed during the Fronde. All that was needed was that the king's intention on a particular issue should be made clear: this was how those bêtes-noires of the *Frondeurs,* the intendants, were reintroduced in 1653.[7]

There is an imbalance in Moote's view of the Fronde. He does not examine the views of the provincial office-holders, not all of whom supported the stand adopted by their Parisian colleagues. Noble clientage and support for the factions within the *Parlements* is given only cursory treatment. There is no serious investigation of urban politics outside the capital; such popular support for the factions as is evidenced by riots, whether organized or not, is not examined.[8] When he does stray into the provinces, Moote does not appear always on a very sure footing: it is simply not possible, for example, to compress the events of the Fronde in Guyenne and Provence into a Parisian time-scale. Moote appears to perceive formal and static party alliances, coalitions and 'ministerial teams' almost in the way that Professor Namier saw these in the much more stable conditions of eighteenth-century British parliamentary politics. It is questionable whether these alliances existed in quite the way he suggests, for example in a provincial sovereign court[9] or a provincial town. It is virtually certain that the alliances were not static and that many of the *Frondeur* rebels of 1649 were royalists and supporters of Mazarin in 1652.

The most serious flaw, however, is in the relative treatment accorded to the office-holders (chiefly the *parlementaires* of Paris) and the nobles. Moote sees the nobles as essentially an anarchic force, without a programme of their own. For this reason, the noble Fronde is a confusion of which 'even the greatest historians have failed to make sense . . .'.[10] His account of the motives of the *Frondeur* nobles in 1649 and of the objectives of the groups he terms *Frondeur* and *Condéen* after·March 1649 leaves many questions unanswered. In a general way, Moote repeats unconsciously the nineteenth-century interpretations of Augustin Thierry and Chéruel, who argued that only the office-holders could be taken seriously during the Fronde: self-interest, intrigue for its own sake and treason were the exclusive prerogative of the French nobles.[11] In turn, this tradition derives from a royalist interpretation of the Fronde. In a deliberate attempt to discredit the nobles, Mazarin and Molé, the *premier président* of the *Parlement* of Paris, published only their *demandes particulières*. For reasons of political prudence, they kept secret their *demandes générales*.[12] Many of the nobles who participated in one or other stage of the *Fronde* were indeed *Malcontents:* but it should not be assumed that they were motivated exclusively by self-interest. Moote does not allow for the fact that some of the lesser nobles, and a significant number of magnates, supported the proposals of the *Chambre St Louis* and the political measures of 1648. The evidence of the *cahiers* of the provincial nobles to the abortive Estates-Generals of 1649 and 1651[13] and of the political pamphlets issued during each revolt of the nobles[14] suggests, indeed, that the nobles wanted to go further than the office-holders in the implementation of these measures: they wanted to put teeth into the declarations of 18 July 1648 and 22 October 1648. A substantial body of opinion among the nobles wanted to reverse the political changes which had occurred under Richelieu and Mazarin and to mitigate the domestic consequences of the war. They wanted to remove Mazarin from power and sign an immediate peace with Spain. Without peace, they assumed that there could be no end to administrative change imposed by the government. Without Mazarin's removal from office, it was assumed that there could be no peace with Spain. Since personalities and policies were inseparable, the demands of the nobles were in a sense realistic (although unconstitutional); moreover, there is evidence to suggest that these views commanded a measure of public support until the summer of 1652. The nobles wanted a reduction of taxes because this issue was popular and for reasons of self-interest, too. Most of the nobles were exempt from the *taille,* but their peasant farmers and tenants were not: the *seigneur* could not expect his peasant farmers to pay both higher rents and higher taxes to the crown. A reduction of taxation would mean that existing rents could be paid, perhaps even that they could be raised.[15] The nobles would thus stand to benefit economically from the policies they advocated: they recognized that the 1630s and 1640s had seen a rise in rents which was not offset by a rise in prices of foodstuffs to increase the income of the peasant producer.[16] If the *laboureurs* were pressed too hard, all but the wealthiest would go under, as indeed happened in the Hurepoix during the Fronde.[17]

If the nobles did indeed have political objectives, which were held with some consistency, then why have these not been observed and analyzed? One reason is the failure to perceive that the political changes imposed by Louis XIII and Richelieu — and continued by Anne of Austria and Mazarin during the minority of Louis XIV - did not merely affect the office-holders. To a greater or lesser extent, the privileges and raison d'être of almost every institution, corporate or sectional group and almost every region of France were affected by those changes, and no group was more affected than the *noblesse d'épée*. The general rise in taxation had affected the income of many nobles from their peasant farmers. Moreover, a remarkable number of provincial governors were removed from their posts, disgraced, exiled or imprisoned during Richelieu's ministry. Richelieu distrusted certain noble families, those whom he suspected of excessive independence, criticism of himself, or opposition to royal policy. Moote is silent on the clear connection, in terms of personalities and issues, between the aristocratic conspiracies and revolts before 1648 and those of the Fronde. Virtually all the aristocratic conspiracies after the Day of Dupes (10 November 1630) saw the establishment of peace between France and Spain as indispensable: peace had been prevented by the chief minister, whether Richelieu or Mazarin, who must therefore be ousted from power. This was the attitude of the *dévots* on the Day of Dupes,[18] of the Soissons conspirators in 1641,[19] of the Cinq-Mars conspirators in 1642[20] and of the *Importants* in 1643.[21] The participating individuals were frequently the same: Gaston d'Orléans was involved in conspiracies and revolts in 1626, 1629-30, 1631-4, 1641-2 and 1652. Louis d'Astarac, marquis de

IV

Fontrailles, was a *Frondeur* noble in 1649-50 and one of Mazarin's enemies whom the chief minister termed a 'republican'. Fontrailles's attitude was perfectly consistent, since he had taken the Cinq-Mars treaty to Spain for Philip IV's signature in 1642.[22] Frédéric-Maurice de la Tour d'Auvergne, duc de Bouillon, was in revolt in 1641-2 and 1649-50. In 1642, Richelieu forced him to hand over his principality of Sedan because of alleged participation in the Cinq-Mars conspiracy.[23] In his protestation of innocence, signed before notaries and dated 10 January 1643, Bouillon accused Richelieu shortly before his death of having held ambitions similar to those which were later attributed to Mazarin during the Fronde. If Louis XIII had died on his journey south to Perpignan, Bouillon asserted that Richelieu would have seized the Regency, arrested Louis XIV and Philippe d'Orléans, the two princes, and held them at the Château de Vincennes. Richelieu would probably have succeeded, Bouillon thought, because he held captive Gaston d'Orléans and Anne of Austria, possessed all the wealth in the kingdom, and the fortresses and military commands were in the hands of his relatives and clients.[24]

Two issues formed a link between the opposition of the nobles to Richelieu and their opposition to Mazarin. The first was the amnesty granted to political prisoners and exiles by the Regency government in 1643. Richelieu had proscribed so many nobles that all their demands could not possibly later be met on their return; yet a number of nobles were restored to their former governorships by Mazarin with the result that some of Richelieu's appointees feared for their positions and moved increasingly towards a policy of opposition to Mazarin. The second issue was the failure of Mazarin's peace negotiations with Spain in 1647-8. Moote asserts categorically that Mazarin 'threw away the chance for an honourable peace in his quest for more substantial territorial gains.'[25] This was certainly the belief of Mazarin's critics during the Fronde. They pointed to Mazarin's alleged 'obstinate aversion . . . to peace'; they asserted that Mazarin had prolonged the war in order to make himself indispensable to the Regent and to have a pretext for levying vast sums in taxes for personal advancement and family fortune. Above all, they pointed to the secret conduct of foreign policy between Mazarin at Paris and Servien at Münster and to the recall of the duc de Longueville (who was a *Frondeur* in 1649) and the comte d'Avaux, the two French plenipotentiaries, who, it was thought, had worked sincerely for peace between France and

The French Civil War, 1649-53

Spain. This was, however, only one interpretation and it was certainly not accepted by Mazarin. The first minister disclaimed all personal interest in the continuation of the war, but argued that after considerable loss of life and expenditure peace should at least be concluded on satisfactory terms.[26] Mazarin argued that he was merely continuing the foreign policy of Louis XIII and Richelieu, while the Spanish always became less flexible in their negotiating position when they suspected that France was weak. Mazarin believed that the comte de Peñaranda, the Spanish plenipotentiary at Münster, was instructed by his government to break off negotiations in 1648 in the expectation that the disappointed hopes of peace would lead to civil disorder in France.[27] Before the constitutional breakdown of 1648, Mazarin argued that if the *Parlement* of Paris registered new fiscal edicts to pay for ten more years' of war, then Spain would cease hoping for a political upheaval in France and would make peace within a few months.[28] After the breakdown, Mazarin argued that Philip IV would never make peace until the Fronde was defeated.[29] Bearing in mind that Philip IV wanted to reconquer Catalonia, civil war in France was obviously preferable from his point of view to an early peace treaty before the reconquest had been achieved. Accordingly, Mazarin's interpretation of the options in foreign policy must at least be treated with cautious respect.[30]

The outbreak of civil war thus presentd the *Frondeur* nobles — who flocked to Paris and signed an alliance among themselves on 18 January 1649[31] — with an opportunity to oust Mazarin, take over the government and reverse its foreign and domestic policies. On 3 February, Conty, the generalissimo of the *Frondeurs,* instructed his envoy to archduke Leopold William of the Spanish Netherlands to seek an immediate invasion of northern France. Already by this date, the archduke had proposed that the *Parlement* of Paris should be appointed as the mediator between France and Spain: Conty set in motion the dealings which resulted in the archduke presenting a letter to the *Parlement* of Paris on 19 February.[32] Moote is correct to argue that this offer was 'a trap' for the *parlementaires*. Pride and the desire to bring about international peace might have led them to accept the offer, but there is no doubt that they would have played the minor role of ratifying an agreement already reached by the archduke and Conty.[23] Of course, the peace negotiations with Spain were abortive because the *Parlement* of Paris made its peace with Mazarin. Moote is correct in viewing the Rueil settlement as 'a crushing defeat for the nobles'.[34] Conty called it a 'disastrous event' *('ce malheureux événement')*. He had made it clear as late as 25 March 1649 that the chief objectives of the *Frondeur* nobles were the exile of Mazarin and immediate peace negotiations with Spain. The grievances of the nobles, he asserted, were merely secondary considerations, their 'security' *(leurs sûretés)* if Mazarin could not be forced from office. Rather than agree to such a compromise, the nobles were prepared to continue the struggle.[35] In effect, the broad outlines of the Rueil settlement were made without their participation.

The gradual acceptance by Louis de Bourbon, prince de Condé, of the viewpoint of Conty, his younger brother, forms the link between the civil wars of 1649 and the following year. Condé had certainly criticized Mazarin's conduct of foreign policy after the Rueil settlement.[36] In the autumn of 1649, his supporters were talking of ousting Mazarin and replacing him with a Regency council drawn from the nobility; they talked also of setting up an investigation of financial administration since 1642 and an investigation of those who had allegedly 'prevented' peace with Spain since 1646.[37] On 2 October 1649, Condé had virtually made himself chief minister,[38] but Mazarin had escaped his control in the aftermath of the so-called Guy Joly 'double assassination plot' in December. However, on 16 January 1650, two days before his arrest, Condé reaffirmed his objective of subordinating Mazarin to himself.[39] The supporters of the princes went into revolt following the arrest of Condé, Conty and Longueville on 18 January 1650. Negotiations with Spain began in February 1650. The duchesse de Longueville and the vicomte de Turenne, Bouillon's younger brother (who were based on Stenay on the north-east frontier of France), signed a treaty with the archduke on 30 April 1650.[40] The princesse de Condé, Bouillon, La Rochefoucault, Sauveboeuf and Lusignan (who were based at Bordeaux) signed a treaty with Philip IV on 26 June 1650.[41] Both treaties were essentially similar, although the Bordelais rebels hoped for greater financial assistance from Philip IV since they were to be given less military support. Both treaties interpreted Mazarin's hostility to peace with Spain as the reason for his having arrested the princes: both treaties envisaged a joint effort to secure the release of the princes and immediate peace negotiations between France and Spain. This, too, was the policy on which the so-called 'union of the two Frondes' was signed on 30 January 1651. This was an agreement between

The French Civil War, 1649-53

Condé's supporters and certain *Frondeur* nobles of 1649, notably Beaufort, Retz and Fosseuse. Gaston d'Orléans signed the agreement, too.[42] Gaston's decision to turn against Mazarin resulted from his own attempts at negotiations for peace with Spain[43] and peace in Guyenne in the autumn of 1650. Gaston blamed Mazarin for the failure of peace negotiations with Spain and for the deterioration of his relations with the Regent; he determined that the king's council should be reorganized on Mazarin's downfall.[44] Gaston's position was strengthened, and Mazarin was forced into exile, by a large number of lesser nobles who had flocked to Paris on behalf of the princes and held a special assembly of their own between 6 February and 25 March 1651. The lesser nobles wanted the release of the princes, the exile of Mazarin and the re-establishment of noble privileges which allegedly had been undermined by the misgovernment of the state. In a speech to this assembly on 15 March 1651 the comte de Fiesque, a *Frondeur* noble in 1649, came out openly in favour of peace negotiations with Spain and a meeting of the Estates-General to further this purpose.[45] Gaston, and Condé after his release, agreed to both proposals. Foucquet de Croissy, one of Condé's clients and a signatory of the so-called 'union of the two Frondes', was sent to Stenay to negotiate with a representative of the archduke. The negotiations broke down on 27 April 1651, however. This in turn led to Turenne's breaking his treaty with Spain and his return to France.[46]

Condé wanted to control the government, and break once and for all the secret influence on the Regent exercised by Mazarin from his place of exile at Brühl in Germany. When Condé failed in his objective, he went into revolt and immediately recommenced negotiations with Spain, resulting in a treaty on 6 November 1651 on similar terms to those agreed in 1650 and proposed in 1649, that is to say, a subsidy alliance and the provision for immediate peace negotiations between France and Spain.[47] Mazarin regarded the military position as so serious in view of Condé prestige in the army and his enormous patronage connections that he felt obliged to return to France with a force of 6,000 German mercenaries.[48] When Condé invited Gaston to join his rebellion on 4 January 1652, in view of Mazarin's return from exile, he stated categorically that peace with Spain was one of his objectives.[49] On 24 January, the two princes signed an agreement which envisaged no cessation of the civil war until Mazarin had been exiled once more, an Estates-

General summoned, and peace negotiations with Spain undertaken.[50] The negotiations between the nobles and the government in 1652 were protracted because Condé refused to break his treaty with Spain.[51] The government sought to make this the quid pro quo for Mazarin's second exile, which began in August 1652 — but Condé did not fulfil his side of the bargain. As late as 3 October 1652, Gaston was proposing on his and Condé's part that the government should agree to immediate peace negotiations between France and Spain with Duke Charles IV of Lorraine as mediator. This proposal was rejected by the French government after two days.[52] While Condé concentrated on securing control in north-east France, however, a royalist coup occurred in Paris (14 October). Gaston made peace with the government on 28 October on terms which did not mention the issue of peace negotiations with Spain.[53] Condé continued to fight on for immediate peace negotiations between France and Spain, but as he himself admitted in December 1652, his cause was hopeless.[54] Turenne, the French military commander, had foreseen that neither the forces of Spain nor Lorraine would seek winter quarters in France and Turenne's forces were superior in number to those of Condé acting on his own.[55] Although Condé was a general in the Spanish army from November 1652, and although he was declared guilty of treason by the *Parlement* of Paris in March 1654, it should not be imagined that support for his cause vanished overnight. There is evidence to suggest that many lesser nobles supported Condé's stand against Mazarin. In 1652, certain of the lesser nobles called for a meeting of the Estates-General and immediate peace negotiations with Spain.[56] Between 1657 and 1659 there were further assemblies of lesser nobles on the same issues.[57] In 1655, a supporter of Mazarin confided to the chief minister that if Condé headed an invasion force in Normandy he would receive considerable popular support ('il seroit à craindre que le peuple n'y prestast la main . . .')[58] Nevertheless, Condé was unable to harness assemblies of the lesser nobles as a means of overthrowing Mazarin, who had returned from his second exile in February 1653. When Condé returned to France, it was after peace with Spain had been signed at the Pyrenees on 7 November 1659, and on Mazarin's terms: Condé had to abandon his alliance with Spain as a prior condition of his restoration.[59]

The French Civil War, 1649-53

The issue of peace negotiations with Spain, and Mazarin's apparent opposition to this objective, thus forms one link between all stages of the Fronde once the fighting began in January 1649. In Mazarin's view, the alliances between Spain and the nobles demonstrated that the nobles were unfit to participate in government and to make proposals for political change. He regarded the agreements between Philip IV and the nobles as partition treaties: 'one does not use the help of the devil to get to Heaven', he commented.[60] Technically, the agreements between Philip IV of Spain and the French nobles were not partition treaties since any gains by the Spanish troops were provisional only — they were to be held in trust *(en dépôt)* until a permanent peace settlement was arranged. However, the reliance on Spanish troops and subsidies clearly placed the French nobles in an ambivalent position. The nobles were in some senses politically naive and they certainly fell into the trap of believing their own propaganda. They assumed that once Mazarin was ousted from power, Spain would be willing to come to peace with a reconstituted French government. This argument rested on a further assumption that Mazarin was *persona non grata* in Spain and that Don Luis de Haro, the chief minister of Philip IV, had acted in better faith. None of these assumptions was correct. Philip IV and his ministers did not want a successful coup d'état in France leading to a just peace. They wanted anarchy in France leading to a settlement that was favourable to Spain.[61] If Mazarin was indeed *persona non grata,* why was it that Fuensaldaña, the representative of Philip IV, continued to negotiate with him during the Fronde?[62] In reality, the French nobles were powerless to bring about a realistic peace settlement, because Philip IV and his representatives had the whip-hand in the relationship.[63] Mercenary troops were used both by the French nobles in rebellion and by the French government in its attempts to suppress rebellion. The difference was that whereas the French government was the paymaster of its forces, the nobles in rebellion were not. Anne of Austria and her chosen first minister, whether in exile or not, were thus more credible negotiators with Spain than their noble opponents could ever hope to be.

Nevertheless, once Gaston and Condé assumed the leadership, the French nobles had a reasonable chance of success. Much depended on their unity and their political will. Were they prepared to coerce the Regent in 1651, even depose her, and impose a formal regency council drawn from leading members of the nobility?[64]

IV

After the declaration of Louis XIV's majority (7 September 1651), were they prepared to state openly that the king was not yet old enough to govern, and that Anne of Austria's influence must be removed because she had Mazarin's interests at heart?[65] More important, were they prepared to transform their words into deeds and seek an outright political and military victory? Condé, perhaps, was: but it seems doubtful whether Gaston was capable of such resolute action.[66] However, the dangers were real enough: Mazarin would scarcely have risked the adverse political reaction to his sudden return from exile at the end of 1651 had he not appreciated the dangers of a military takeover.[67] The one commander in France capable of opposing Condé was Turenne, the erstwhile commander of the French forces in Germany. In 1651, Bouillon and Turenne, his younger brother, had at long last received compensation for the loss of Sedan: but although reconciled with the court, Turenne did not turn up at a meeting of the military commanders and governors loyal to the government held on 2 January 1652. He did not seek a military command until March 1652.[68] Until the spring of 1652, therefore, Mazarin's presence in France was essential to resist the joint rebellion of Gaston and Condé. It was, after all, these two magnates on whom Mazarin had relied chiefly throughout 1648 and the first half of 1649;[69] without Gaston's agreement, Condé could not have been arrested in 1650; it was Gaston's decision to turn against Mazarin that had precipitated his first exile and the release of the princes. Gaston had refused stubbornly to support the government which had been reconstituted on 8 September 1651, the day after Louis XIV's majority was proclaimed.

The weakness of the nobles was more philosphical than practical, basically a contradiction between means and ends. The nobles wanted peace with Spain, yet they had no clear idea how to achieve this objective. They wanted to replace the rule of a chief minister by a formal regency council, perhaps as a temporary measure until the king reached the age of sixteen.[70] They asserted that such formal regency councils had indeed existed in the past.[71] It is certainly true that the proclamation of the king's majority at the age of fourteen (actually, in the case of Louis XIV, at the age of thirteen) was a legal fiction, resulting from an ordinance of Charles V dated 1374.[72] The king could not participate in government in any real sense until he was fifteen or sixteen. To oppose the proclamation of the king's majority at thirteen, however, the nobles, too, had to

The French Civil War, 1649-53

resort to a legal fiction: the formal regency councils envisaged in ordinances of the later Middle Ages.[73] However, the immediate precedents were the Regencies exercised by the Queen Mothers in 1561 and 1610 without any such formal councils. Indeed, recent absolutist theories tended to reinforce the position of the Regent, making her the bastion against a *monarchie aristocratique* during a royal minority.[74]

In any case, what evidence was there that greater participation of the nobles in government would solve the ills from which France was suffering? The nobles did not co-operate well during the Fronde. Their reconstituted council at Paris, comprising Chancellor Séguier, Gaston, Condé, Châteauneuf, Chavigny, certain other nobles, two *présidents* of the *Parlement* and Broussel, the illegally elected mayor of Paris, did not operate effectively in the summer of 1652. The duc de Beaufort shot the duc de Nemours in a duel arising from disagreements in the council![75] There were insuperable obstacles to effective noble participation in government, as had been recognized at the Assembly of Notables in 1617.[76] The first difficulty was the size of the nobility: how could government secrecy be maintained, and prompt action taken, if a large number of nobles participated in decision-making? Then there was an enormous problem with regard to the order of precedence in any governing council. There was no Table of Ranks in seventeenth-century France, and it would have been politically dangerous to have attempted to draw one up. There was, moreover, the probability that government business would frequently impinge on the private interests of members of the nobility. In such circumstances, could it be assumed that an impartial solution would be reached in the governing council? Finally, there was the problem of regularity of attendance. The magnates had provincial governorships, military commands, and moreover, large estates to manage. They usually had administrators for their estates, but they could not neglect their governorships and military commands for any length of time. How could continuity of policy be assured if there was a problem of noble absenteeism? Such considerations, rather than inherent factiousness and lack of talent among the nobles, had led the ministers to abandon any attempt to include them in the process of government after 1617. The exceptions to this rule were Gaston and Condé's father, who were included in the government on a personal basis after 1643 (Condé inherited his father's position in the king's council on 1 February 1647, shortly after the latter's death).[77] Over a generation, the exclusion of the nobility from government was a self-fulfilling prophecy: it reinforced tendencies towards political naivety and above all, faction.

If it was unlikely, for these reasons, that the nobles would succeed in their aim of participating directly in government, it was equally certain that within the existing constitution they lacked a central institution or forum in which their views could be expressed. Their hopes of the Estates-General during the Fronde were probably misguided:[78] effective political control of this institution would have had to have been wrested from the crown. Moreover, the Estates-General would have had to have played a wholly unprecedented role to serve the purpose of the nobles. The sovereign courts were not an effective susbtitute, quite apart from their unwillingness to be used by the nobles for their own ends.[79] In particular, the opposition of the *Parlement* of Paris to the Estates-General was used by Anne of Austria as a means of circumventing the nobles' hops for the postponement of the king's majority and a Regency council imposed at the assembly of the Estates.[80] Certainly, the sovereign courts could sometimes be coerced: the *Parlement* of Bordeaux was forced to join an alliance with Condé's supporters on 11 July 1650,[81] and with Condé himself on 3 January 1652.[82] Although the *Parlement* of Paris had kept recognition of its noble allies to a minimum in 1649 and had rejected an alliance with Gaston and Condé on 25 January 1652,[83] it was forced in effect to agree to such an alliance on 20 July 1652.[84] However, coercion was not indicative of genuine support. An *épuration* of the sovereign courts, which was proposed by the duc de Bouillon in 1649, and in a sense was put into practice by Gaston and Condé in the massacre at the *hôtel de ville* on 4 July 1652[85] was essentially counter-productive: it marked a clear break between the nobles on the one hand and the office-holders and *bons bourgeois* on the other and was, in Madame de Motteville's words, 'one of the principal causes of the ruin of the noble Fronde'.[86] The nobles had to coerce others to follow their lead. They had to call upon armed support from Spain in 1649, 1650 and 1652 and armed support from Lorraine, too, in 1652. They had to levy troops and war taxes of their own. They had to seek billets and munitions for their troops. Quite apart from the questionable legitimacy of such resistance, there was the practical consideration that such coercion might well prevent the objectives of the nobles from being achieved. The nobles claimed

The French Civil War, 1649-53

that they wanted to re-establish peace and peace-time forms of administration — in effect the *status quo ante* 1635, perhaps *ante* 1630 or even 1624. What they succeeded in doing was worsening the effects of war-time government since 1635. Civil war thus destroyed their ideal, the essential justification for their resistance. If a war government was what was needed, there was no reason why Mazarin should not continue in office and no reason why war-time forms of government, abolished in 1648, should not be restored.[87]

Were the nobles genuine in their aims? Mazarin, and supporters of the government, argued of course that they were not, and that the negotiation of peace with Spain was a spurious issue raised by *Malcontents* who sought to prevent a compromise solution to the political crisis in France.[88] The nobles, Mazarin argued, could not claim to be the 'restorers of the state' since they were the self-interested leaders of sedition and revolt. The existence of *demandes particulières* at each stage of the noble Fronde lends some credence to Mazarin's viewpoint. Madame de Motteville quoted with approval Philippe de Commynes's comment on the treaties of Conflans and St Maur-des-Fossés (October 1465) which ended the revolt of the nobles known as the war of the public weal: 'the public weal', Commynes wrote, 'had been turned into the private interest'.[89] Madame de Motteville judged the Rueil settlement of March 1649 in the same light in so far as the nobles were concerned. She argued that the Fronde lasted for as long as it did because the crown was forced to grant concessions which in turn encouraged new claims and demands from the nobles. She considered that Gaston and Condé were dragged into the conflict by the defence of the quarrels and claims of their clients among the lesser nobles.[90] The nobles were certainly as divided as the office-holders. There were great differences in terms of wealth, political power and social prestige between an office-holder who was a member of a sovereign court and one who was not. Similarly, there was a vast gulf between the provincial governor or magnate and the lesser noble. The lesser nobles might hope for pensions or relatively unimportant military commands: but they could scarcely hope for provincial governorships, unless the rules were changed.[91] The lesser nobles might criticize the conduct of a governor. One year they might take to arms to support his cause (as in Normandy in 1649); the next year they might not (as in Normandy in 1650).[92] The lesser nobles were sometimes divided — as in Brittany in 1651, when a large number followed Rohan and the *Parlement* of Rennes, while others supported La Meilleraye, the lieutenant-general, and the provincial Estates.[93] They might side with the lieutenants-general, the intendant and the provincial Estates in a peaceful confrontation with the local *Parlement* — as in Languedoc in 1651-2.[94] Alternatively, they might unite with the provincial governor in an armed conflict with the local *Parlement* — as in Guyenne and Provence in 1649.[95]

The attitude of the lesser nobles was thus unpredictable. The magnates hoped that the lesser nobles could be mobilized to serve their interests. Since their interests were so different such blind support was unlikely and did not in fact occur. Most of the magnates wanted to enjoy political power, whether in the provinces or the central government. In 1649, Conty wanted a place in the council of state and a fortress in Champagne (where he was governor). Longueville wanted a major position appertaining to the crown (for example, the Admiralty), a fortress in Normandy (where *he* was governor), and the right to resign his positions to his sons. The *Frondeurs* of 1649 were the claimants to the governorships, those who had not been satisfied by Mazarin after 1643. The duc de Beaufort wanted Brittany for Vendôme, his father, who had been disgraced in 1626; Bouillon wanted the Auvergne; Turenne wanted Alsace; Luynes wanted Touraine; La Trémouille was later to set his sights on Anjou, although in March 1649 he was claiming Roussillon and Cerdagne.[96] After his release in 1651, Condé sought and obtained the governorship of Guyenne, a much more dangerous power base than his former province of Burgundy. He sought the governorship of Provence for Conty, his younger brother. Mazarin, who viewed the governorships in strategic terms, appreciated the dangers of the situation and tried to limit the concessions[97] — but Mazarin was not always in command of events. The settlement of the Fronde was in large measure a settlement of the governorships, which rewarded those nobles who had come to terms with the government. Gaston, Longueville and La Rochefoucauld retained their governorships respectively in Languedoc, Normandy and Poitou. Conty was given Guyenne, Turenne the Limousin and Mercoeur (the younger son of Vendôme, who had married one of Mazarin's nieces) Provence. When Condé made his peace in 1659, he received his former province of Burgundy, thus necessitating a rearrangement of the governorships.

These competing claims for provincial governorships were certainly self-interested: but they were political in implication. A loyal magnate had to be rewarded in order to forestall rebellion; a rebellious magnate had to be bought off with concessions. Yet the nobles acted no differently from other privileged groups in society, except that they could back up their claims with armed force. Politics in seventeenth-century France operated in terms of the alliance of public issues with private grievances. The office-holders had to be paid their salaries and their *rentes,* and their investment in offices had to be guaranteed. Without such payments (which Mallet calculated cost the government over 45 million *livres* in 1640)[98] and without such security, the office-holders would withdraw their support from the government, as they did in 1648. In that year, the office-holders felt that they had nothing to gain by supporting Mazarin; by 1652 they had everything to lose if they did not do so. The Fronde had seen something which had not happened since the days of the League: the establishment of rival courts and rival claims to office. The civil war threatened to have a disastrous effect on the stability of office-holding. As the *Parlement* of Bordeaux discovered with the *Ormée,* if popular feeling was given any chance to express itself, there might be a demand for the abolition of offices altogether. The one certainty was that the crown, even if it had the political will to abolish offices, would never have been able to do so without paying compensation. The state of the royal finances precluded payment of the enormous amount of compensation that would have been necessary.[99] Even Mazarin might be acceptable if he paid the office-holders their salaries and their *rentes,* and allowed them the *droit annuel.* In securing the royalist coup at Paris in October 1652, the government made it clear that these concessions would indeed be forthcoming. Similarly, the settlement of the Fronde of the nobles took into account the basic social and economic interests of the magnates. The magnates were required to abandon their attempt to control the actions of the central government and their claim to participate in the king's council. Yet they retained considerable political and social power in the provinces: far from their wealth declining, it was greatly enhanced by a further round of pensions and land transfers and by the fact that their debts incurred during the Fronde were paid off by the government, and thus ultimately by the French tax-payer.[100] The interests of the lesser nobles, of course, were sacrificed.

IV

In both this paper and *The Revolt of the Judges* the Fronde is seen as the most serious political crisis of the French monarchy, certainly under Richelieu and Mazarin, and probably in the seventeenth century. There is agreement also that the outcome of the Fronde was not predetermined: once the political breakdown had occurred, almost any outcome was possible since the crisis had a dynamism and a momentum of its own. There is agreement on a negative aspect, too. There was no revolution in the sense of a powerful social movement with the participation of a broad spectrum of the people. In contrast to Porchnev's view,[101] there is little evidence of major *soulèvements populaires* in the countryside, or sustained urban insurrections. The *Ormistes* of Bordeaux[102] and the *Loricards* of Angers[103] were the exceptions not the rule. Although there was a power struggle in many of the towns in France, the established order was not overturned as a matter of course, while the refusal of the peasants to pay their taxes was a consequence, not a proximate cause, of the political upheaval.

Thereafter, the interpretations diverge. Professor Moote, starting from the basis of his research on the *Parlement* of Paris, argues that this institution had a central, determining role and that the events of the Fronde were in large measure decided at Paris. The Fronde, in his view, was a moderate, constitutional movement of reform led by men who for the most part did not want to participate in, let alone seize control of, the government. It commenced in June 1648, with the meeting of the *Chambre St Louis* and the proposals that were drawn up at that meeting and later enacted by the government. The movement was blown off-course somewhat by the events of 1649-52, when the nobles exploited the crisis for their own ends. Moote denies that a polarization of political society took place in France. It was of crucial importance, he argues, that the moderate Fronde should remain critical of the government yet disassociate itself from the nobles (as happened at Rueil in March 1649): 'the estrangement between the robe and the sword helped to keep the Fronde's reformist movement alive', he asserts. Thus Mazarin was prevented from an outright victory at the end of the office-holders' resistance in October 1652. The Fronde, in Moote's view, was a *révolution manquée* — a movement which was strong enough to prevent a clear-cut victory for absolutism but 'too narrowly concerned with obstructing royal power to think of seizing it and wielding it'. The success of the Fronde — in the sense of a 'mild victory-in-defeat' —

is explicable therefore only in terms of the failure of the political changes introduced by Richelieu and Mazarin. Nevertheless, 'if the Fronde had not checked this trend [towards political change], the progression from Henry IV to Louis XIV would have resulted in a much more powerful monarchy.'[104]

The interpretation in this paper starts from a different basis, namely an investigation of the reactions of French society to the political and fiscal changes introduced by Richelieu and Mazarin.[105] From this standpoint, the primary role accorded by Moote to the *Parlement* of Paris, his virtual disregard of the provincial courts and the regional basis of French politics, appear highly questionable. Far from any one institution or group of individuals controlling events, the breakdown was such that crucially important fighting occured in different areas at different times after January 1649.[106] Contemporaries had little difficulty in viewing the Fronde as a period of civil war even though some provinces were spared from the fighting.[107] It is also true that the fighting was not continuous and that both sides employed mercenary troops — but most civil wars in the early modern period were fought in this way. Above all, the view of the Fronde as a period of civil war emphasizes the issue of coercion, which came into the open only in January 1649, and the role of the nobles, who led the fighting. The end of the Fronde is seen as August 1653, the date of the fall of Bordeaux, the last bastion of resistance.

In this interpretation, the Fronde is viewed as a *révolution manquée* only in the sense that it failed, or more accurately, was defeated. The nobles were monarchists to a man,[108] and the monarchy was never seriously threatened. Moreover, since Louis XIV was only fourteen years old in 1652, he could scarcely be said to be responsible for the troubles.[109] The critics of the government therefore had to fall back on the traditional doctrine of the king's evil counsellors, and to argue that Louis XIV was 'held in captivity' by Mazarin.[110] If the nobles had won, that is, seized power by a coup d'état, they might well have carried out a conservative 'revolution' — a return to the forms of government before political changes were introduced by Richelieu and Mazarin as a result of the war. They would have sought immediate peace negotiations with Spain and in the unlikely event of these negotiations succeeding, they might well have cut government expenditure and taxation. There would have been no reintroduction of strong government and certainly no government by decree of the king's council with intendants enforcing these decrees.

That the nobles failed was due in part to their own organizational problems, to a failure of military strategy and political will. The nobles were divided socially and politically: the crown always had a body of support among the nobles, and there were certain nobles whose financial interests required a return to high levels of government expenditure and taxation.[111] Above all, however, the nobles could not command support from the sovereign courts when the polarization of attitudes occurred in 1652. Rather than follow the nobles to the brink, most of the office-holders were prepared, however reluctantly, to abandon the objectives of 1648-9 and support Anne of Austria and Mazarin. The war-weariness that was such a serious danger to Mazarin's position in 1648-9 came to be directed against the nobles, especially in northern France in the autumn of 1652. If there had to be a war, it was preferable to fight a foreign war against Spain on Spanish soil than a civil war outside the gates of Paris as it had been fought in the summer of 1652.[112] Unlike Charles I of England, Anne of Austria and Mazarin did not have to wait very long for a royalist party to form: in almost every town and law-court of France there was a strong royalist party, often with direct government encouragement and subsidies, working for the defeat of the Fronde.[113] There were financiers, too, who were willing to lend the government money at favourable rates of interest in the hope of securing compensation for their losses in the bankruptcy of 1648.[114] The strength of these local royalist parties, and the relative ease with which the government slipped back onto the course of high expenditure, loans from financiers and the administration of the *taille* by the intendants in 1653 suggests the strength, not the weakness, of the political changes introduced by Richelieu and continued by Mazarin. Far from the Fronde temporarily halting or weakening those political changes, it consolidated them and made them irreversible. The Fronde was important because it witnessed the last, desperate opposition of the French nobles to political change by means of armed rebellion. The nobles failed, or more accurately, they exchanged an illusory political power in the central government for a much greater local political, and especially economic and social power. As a result, at the end of the civil war, the crown was left considerably stronger than before in domestic political terms. The 'absolutism' of Louis XIV was possible only because of the achievements of Richelieu and Mazarin.[115]

The French Civil War, 1649-53

Notes

N.B. All printed works in English are published in London unless otherwise stated. All printed works in French are published in Paris unless otherwise stated.

1. A.L. Moote, *The revolt of the judges. The Parlement of Paris and the Fronde, 1643-1652* (Princeton, 1971) [hereafter abbreviated to Moote, *Revolt*]. An introduction to older interpretations of the Fronde is provided by R.J. Knecht, 'The Fronde', *Historical Association. Appreciations in History*, v (1975).
2. Moote, *Revolt*, 168-72, 180, and 354.
3. P.R. Doolir *The Fronde* (Cambridge, Mass., 1935). E.H. Kossmann, *La Fronde* (Leiden, 1954).
4. Archives Nationales, Paris (hereafter cited as AN) E 198a-206c, passim. The precise total was 115,676,265 *livres* from 107 contracts.
5. The Dutch feared the growing French power in the Spanish Netherlands and the prospect of a separate Franco-Spanish treaty: G. Parker, 'Why did the Dutch revolt last eighty years?', *Transactions of the Royal Historical Society*, 5th. ser., Vol. xxvi (1976), 69-70.
6. Moote, *Revolt*, 172, 180, 279.
7. Declaration of 22 October 1652: AN U 30, fo. 356. [For the aftermath of the Fronde with regard to the *Parlement* of Paris, cf. A.N. Hamscher, *The Parlement of Paris after the Fronde, 1653-1673* (Pittsburgh, 1976)]. Removal of the limitation on the secret expenses: AN E 1698, fo. 183, 16 November 1652. *Arrêts du conseil du roi. Règne de Louis XIV. Inventaire analytique des arrêts en commandement. I. 20 mai 1643-8 mars 1661* M. Le Pesant (ed., 1976), no. 1800. Restoration of the taxes abolished in 1648: AN X1b 8857, 31 December 1652. Abolition of the financial investigation inaugurated in 1648: AN P 2373, pp. 535-47, December 1652. For Séguier's view: Archives des Affaires Étrangères, Mémoires et Documents (hereafter cited as AAE), France 898, fo. 202v., 17 July 1656.
8. A recent study of the relationship between urban politics and urban riots is R. Pillorget, *Les mouvements insurrectionnels de Provence entre 1596 et 1715* (1975), 567-705.
9. See, for example, the analysis of seven groupings in the *Parlement* of Toulouse: AAE France 1636, fo. 48, 8 May 1652. Analysis of voting intentions at the *Parlement* of Paris in 1643: AAE France 848, fo. 105.
10. Moote, *Revolt*, 223.
11. Moote considers that the nobles had 'no programme of their own' (*Revolt*, 376). Cf. A. Thierry, 'Essai sur l'histoire de la formation et des progrès du Tiers État', *Recueil des monuments inédits sur l'histoire de France* (3 vols., 1850), Vol. i, ccviii. P.A. Chéruel, *Histoire de France pendant la minorité de Louis XIV* (4 vols., 1879-80), Vol. iii, 287.
12. For example, Molé's release of the *demandes particulières* of the *Frondeur* nobles in 1649: Omer Talon, *Mémoires* (J.E. Michaud and J.J.F. Poujoulat, 3rd. ser., Vol. vi, 1839), 350. *Oeuvres de Retz* (ed. A. Feillet et al., 10 vols., 1870-96), Vol. ii, 454. *Choix de Mazarinades* (ed. C. Moreau, 2 vols., 1853), Vol. i. 431-6. Cf. also Mazarin's comment to Le Tellier on 11 September 1652: *Lettres du Cardinal Mazarin pendant son ministère* (ed. P.A. Chéruel et al., 9 vols., 1872-1906), Vol. v. 228.

13. R. Mousnier, J.P. Labatut, Y. Durand, *Problèmes de stratification sociale. Deux cahiers de la noblesse por les États-Généraux de 1649-1651* (1965). Of course, futher research is required to determine whether other *cahiers* of the lesser nobles followed the line of Troyes and the Angoumois.

14. 'Contrat du mariage du Parlement avec la ville de Paris' (1649), *Choix de Mazarinades* (ed. Moreau), Vol. i, 39-50. *Oeuvres de Retz* (ed. Feillet et al.), Vol. v, 438-50. The document may have been written by Retz, one of the *Frondeur* nobles in January 1649, but neither the authorship, nor the precise dating, are certain. It was clearly the source for 'l'union ou l'association des princes sur l'injuste détention des princes de Condé, Conty et duc de Longeuville' of 1650: *Choix de Mazarinades* (ed. Moreau), Vol. ii. 63-8. For the ideas of Condé's supporters: 'Concordat de l'union faite entre le Parlement et la ville de Bordeaux avec nosseigneurs les princes contre les ennemis de l'estat', Archives Départementales (hereafter cited as AD) Gironde 4J 127, 3 January 1652. [Excerpts from this document in *Histoire de l'Aquitaine. Documents* (ed. C. Higounet, Toulouse, 1973), p. 219.] For the ideas of supporters of Gaston and Condé: 'Les articles de la dernière délibération de Messieurs les princes avec les bourgeois de la ville de Paris faite en Parlement et en la maison de ville les 6 et 8 juillet 1652', Bibliothèque Nationale, Paris (hereafter cited as BN) Lb 37, 2756 in 4°. Further research is required to determine whether these mainfestoes were drawn up by the magnates themselves or on their orders, and the relationship between these manifestoes and the mass of the Mazarinades.

15. Mousnier, Labatut, Durand, op. cit., 88,151. Cf. R. Mousnier, *La plume, la faucille et le marteau. Institutions et société en France du moyen âge à la Révolution* (1970), 380.

16. E. Leroy-Ladurie, *Les paysans de Languedoc* (2 vols., 1966), Vol. i, 465-71. B. Veyrassat-Herren and E. Leroy-Ladurie, 'La rente foncière autour de Paris au xviie siècle', *Annales E.S.C.*, Vol. xxiii (1968), 546, 554-5. E. Leroy-Ladurie, 'Dîmes et produit net agricole, xve-xviiie siècles', *Annales E.S.C.*, Vol. xxiv (1969), 830. *Les fluctuations du produit de la dîme. Conjoncture décimale et domaniale de la fin du moyen âge au xviiie siècle* (ed. E. Leroy-Ladurie and J. Goy, Paris and the Hague, 1972), 22, 76, 210, 261-2, 284, and 358 — the exception (page 95) being Alsace, which was devasted by the Swedish invasion. J. Jacquart, *La crise rurale en Ile-de-France, 1550-1670* (1974), 692-3. J. Jacquart, 'Immobilisme et catastrophes, 1560-1660', *Histoire de la France rurale. II. L'âge clasique des paysans, 1340-1789* (ed. E. Leroy-Ladurie, 1975), 252. J. Jacquart, 'La rente foncière, indice conjoncturel?', *Revue Historique*, Vol. ccliii (1975), 365-6.

17. Jacquart, *La crise rurale*, 692, 708-10.

18. G. Pagès, 'Autour du "Grand Orage." Richelieu et Marillac. Deux politiques', *Revue Historique*, Vol. clxxix (1937), 63-97. G. Mongrédien, *La journée des Dupes. 10 novembre 1630* (1961).

19. R. Mousnier, *Fureurs paysannes. Les paysans dans les révoltes du xviie siècle. France, Russie, Chine* (1967), 47. BN Ms. fr. 17331, fo. 46, n.d. (1641).

20. M. Faucheux, 'Le procès de Cinq-Mars', *Quelques procès criminels aux xviie et xviiie siècles* (ed. J. Imbert, 1964), 82. BN Ms. fr. 17331, fo. 97, 3 March 1642.

21. Chéruel, *Minorité*, Vol. i, 160-2.

22. *Lettres du Cardinal Mazarin à la reine, à la princesse palatine . . .* (ed. J. Ravenel, 1836), 26. G. Dethan, *Gaston d'Orléans. Conspirateur et prince charmant* (1959), 268. Talon, *Mémoires* (ed. Michaud and Poujoulat), 389-90. BN MS. fr.

The French Civil War, 1649-53

18431, fo. 724, 23 May 1650.

23. BN Ms. fr. 17331, fo. 105, 'Abolition du duc de Bouillon', September 1642. Bouillon was probably saved from execution only by the intervention of Frederick-Henry of Nassau, his uncle — and a vital ally of France — on his behalf: BN Ms. fr. 17331, fos. 111v.-112v.

24. AN 114b, no. 42/12 [AN Musée AE II 835], 10 January 1643. Bouillon was a *Frondeur* in 1649 largely over the unresolved issue of compensation for the loss of Sedan: BN 500 Colbert 3, fo. 177. The Regency government maintained that compensation could not be granted until Louis XIV's majority was proclaimed: *Acta pacis Westphalicae. Serie I. Instruktionen. Frankreich, Schweden, Kaiser* (ed. F. Dickmann et al., Münster, 1962), 149. AAE France 852, fo. 191, 17 November 1645. AAE France 854, fo. 83, 27 April 1646.

25. Moote, *Revolt*, 73.

26. BN Dupuy 775, fo. 83. For (somewhat disingenuous) Spanish claims that Mazarin opposed peace for reasons of self-interest: *Correspondance de la cour d'Espagne sur les affaires des Pays-Bas au xviie siècle. IV, 1647-1665* (ed. J. Cuvelier and J. Lefèvre, Brussels, 1933) nos. 215, 370, 594.

27. *Lettres du Cardinal Mazarin* (ed. Chéruel), Vol. iii, 112, 141. *Correspondance* (ed. Cuvelier and Lefèvre), nos. 105, 215. The French negotiators at Münster on 15 March 1647 accused the Spanish of bad faith. If the Spanish were forced to conclude a treaty, 'leur dessein est de le concevoir de sorte qu'ils le puissent rompre aisément . . .' British Library, Harleian 4459, fo. 130v.

28. Talon, *Mémoires* (ed. Michaud and Poujoulat), 204.

29. BN 500 Colbert 3, fo. 66, 25 February 1649. For the hardening of the Spanish negotiating position and Spanish support to the weakest faction in France in order to prolong the French political crisis: *Correspondance* (ed. Cuvelier and Lefèvre), nos. 123, 223, 250, 299, 321, 331, 428, 432, 434, and 599.

30. Chéruel, *Minorité*, op. cit., Vol. ii, 465-89, gives a reasoned defence of Mazarin's foreign policy from evidence. Gaston and Condé supported Mazarin's policy in 1647-8. For Spanish concentration on reconquests, rather than invasion of France: *Correspondance* (ed. Cuvelier and Lefèvre), nos. 303, 325, and 326.

31. *Oeuvres de Retz* (ed. Feillet et al.), Vol. ii. 636-7. BN Ms. fr. 3854, fo. 1. BN 500 Colbert 3, fo. 44.

32. BN Ms. fr. 3854, fo. 10. Instructions of Conty to Laigue, 3 February 1649.

33. Moote, *Revolt*, 198-9. BN Ms. fr. 3854, fos. 15, 65, 10 February and n.d., 1649. In the second document, Conty suggested Longueville as plenipotentiary and refused to accept any proposal for peace 'qui allast contre sa naissance et contre ce qu'il doibt à l'estat.'

34. Moote, *Revolt*, 217.

35. Talon, *Mémoires* (ed. Michaud and Poujoulat), 348. BN 500 Colbert 3, fo. 207, 20 March 1649. BN Ms. fr. 3854, fos. 73, 77, 109, 25 March and 2 April 1649.

36. Moote, *Revolt*, 243.

37. Guy Patin, *Lettres du temps de la Fronde* (ed. A. Thérive, 1921), 156-7. Patin noted that Gaston 'tient encore le parti du Mazarin, c'est ce qui retarde et affaiblit le parti de M. le prince . . .'

38. Moote, loc. cit. AN K 118a, no. 17 [AN Musée II 843].

39. BN Dupuy 775, fo. 122. Mazarin was forced to agree to 'ne départ[ir] jamais de ses intérests' and to beg Condé to treat him as his 'très humble serviteur . . .'

40. BN Ms. fr. 3855 fo. 1.

41. BN Dupuy 775, fo. 114. Cf. AN E 1696 fo. 258, 30 August 1650. *Arrêts du Conseil du roi* (ed. Le Pesant), no. 1246.

42. *Oeuvres de Retz* (ed. Feillet et al.), iii. 549-556. V. Cousin, *Madame de Longueville pendant la Fronde, 1651-1653* (1859), 373-84.

43. Talon, *Mémoires* (ed. Michaud and Poujoulat), 398. *Recueil des instructions données aux ambassadeurs . . . XI. Espagne* (ed. A. Morel-Fatio, 1894), 29-38. J. Lefèvre, 'Une tractation de l'archiduc Léopold-Guillaume avec le duc d'Orléans en 1650', *Bulletin de la commission royale de l'histoire,* Vol. ci (Brussels, 1936), 107-35. Kossmann, *La Fronde,* 178.

44. Talon, *Mémoires,* (ed. Michaud and Poujoulat), 399.

45. AN K 118a, no. 24/10. 'Journal de l'assemblée de la noblesse tenue à Paris en l'année 1651', especially 73-6 and 152.

46. *Mémoires de Turenne* (ed. P. Marichal, 2 vols., 1909-14), Vol. i, 167. *Recueil* (ed. Morel-Fatio), 45-55. BN Ms. fr. 3855 fos. 83, 87.

47. H.E.P.L. d'Orléans, duc d'Aumale, *Histoire des princes de Condé pendant les xvie et xviie siècles* (8 vols., 1863-96), Vol. vi. 101-3. F. DesRobert, *Charles IV et Mazarin, 1643-1661* (Nancy and Paris, 1899), 415. Cousin, *Madame de Longueville,* 389-401. *Correspondance* (ed. Cuvelier and Lefèvre), no. 724.

48. DesRobert, op. cit., 407, 422. BN Dupuy 775, fo. 143, 23 December 1651. Mazarin wrote to Lefèvre de la Barre, the *prévôt des marchands* at Paris, and expressed his hope that his forces would be sufficient in quality and number to 'faire pencher plus promptement la balance du costé de la justice' and thus bring about a just peace with Spain.

49. BN Dupuy 775, fo. 194.

50. They also wanted the exclusion of La Vieuville, the finance minister. DesRobert, *Charles IV et Mazarin,* 422, 428. C. Moreau, *Bibliographie des Mazarinades* (3 vols., 1850-1), no. 424. AAE France 881, fo. 161, 28 January 1652.

51. BN Dupuy 775, fo. 179, 15 July 1652.

52. BN Dupuy 775, fo. 197.

53. BN Dupuy 775, fo. 202, ratified at Paris on 31 October 1652.

54. BN Ms. fr. 18431, fo. 665. Condé to Don Luis de Haro, 25 December 1652. This letter is printed — the original had been intercepted by the French government, which published it as a propaganda piece.

55. DesRobert, *Charles IV et Mazarin,* 564.

56. A. Feillet, *La misère au temps de la Fronde et Saint Vincent de Paul* (5th. edition, 1886), 365-6. BN 500 Colbert 3, fo. 423. 'Requeste de la noblesse environ 1653.' The nobles referred in this document to the projected meeting of the Estates-General at Tours on 1 November 1652. They also referred to an *outrage* at Chartres 'impuni . . . depuis sept mois passyé'. For this incident on 17 August 1651, cf. AN E 1697, no. 251, 22 November 1651. *Arrêts du conseil du roi* (ed. Le Pesant), no. 1579.

57. They recalled the promise of Gaston that a meeting of the Estates-General would be held: A. Legrelle, 'Les assemblées de la noblesse de Normandie (1658-9)', *Société de l'histoire de Normandie. Mélanges.* 4th. ser. Vol. iv (1898), 326, 333, 345. They also negotiated with Condé, who was in exile: L. Jarry, *La guerre des Sabotiers de Sologne et les assemblées de la noblesse, 1653-1660* (Orléans, 1880), 132, 157.

58. P. Le Cacheux, 'Documents concernant les États de Normandie de février 1655', *Société de l'histoire de Normandie. Mélanges,* 5th. ser (1898 — published 1901), 140-1. Bishop of Sées to Mazarin, February 1655.

59. AN J 930, nos. 2, 4, 5 [AN Musée AE II 852]. Treaty of the Pyrenees, articles 79-87. Secret treaty, article 7.
60. *Lettres du Cardinal Mazarin* . . . (ed. Ravenel), 26. For the French government's view of the treaties as partition treaties: AN E 1698, no. 120, 23 July 1652. *Arrêts du conseil du roi* (ed. Le Pesant), no. 1736.
61. For Philip IV's hopes for the partition of France, as late as 1 March 1651: *Correspondance* (ed. Cuvelier and Lefèvre), no. 600.
62. *Recueil* (ed. Morel-Fatio), 1-19. Talon, *Mémoires* (ed. Michaud and Poujoulat), 452. *Lettres du Cardinal Mazarin* . . . (ed. Ravenel), 237-8.
63. As *Frondeurs* such as Retz observed: *Oeuvres de Retz* (ed. Feillet et al.), Vol. ii, 359, 428.
64. Mazarin was informed on 7 August 1651 that Gaston and Condé had this intention: AAE France 876, fo. 239. The Regent made the same accusation against Condé: *Oeuvres de Retz* (ed. Feillet et al.), Vol. iii, 340.
65. A phrase used by Retz: ibid., Vol. iii, 311.
66. Gaston's irresolution and timidity were proverbial: Talon, *Mémoires* (ed. Michaud and Poujoulat), 399, 407. *Oeuvres de Retz* (ed. Feillet et al.), Vol. iii, 82, 103.
67. Talon, *Mémoires* (ed. Michaud and Poujoulat), 305, emphasizes Condé's prestige and clientage network resulting from his recent military commands. Condé had been viceroy and lieutenant-general in Catalonia in 1647 and commander of the army of Flanders in 1648: AN K 117b, nos. 30, 34, 1 March 1647 and 17 March 1648.
68. Turenne, *Mémoires* (ed. Marichal), Vol. i. 176-8. DesRobert, *Charles IV et Mazarin*, 407, 421, 426.
69. Mazarin regarded their support as his trump card against the *Frondeur* nobles and the *Parlement* of Paris in 1649: BN Dupuy 775, fo. 83.
70. The postponement of the king's majority and the establishment of a Regency council were two reasons behind the pressure for a meeting of the Estates-General in 1651: Talon, *Mémoires* (ed. Michaud and Poujoulat), 423. AAE France 874, fo. 286v. Le Tellier to Mazarin, 21 April 1651.
71. For example, 'Les articles de la demière délibération . . .' (cited supra, n.14), article four.
72. *Ordonnances de roys de France de la Troisième race* (ed. H. Secousse et al., 21 vols., 1723-1849), Vol. vi, 26-30. Translated into French in 1892: ibid.,Vol. vii, 518-22.
73. Ordinances of Philip III (1271), Charles V (1374), and Charles VI (1392, 1403, 1407): ibid., Vols. vi. 45-54; vii. 530-8; viii. 581-3; ix. 267-9; xi. 349-50.
74. For example, Bertier de Montrave, 'La régence ou de l'autorité des reynes régentes' (12 November 1649): AAE France 1632, fos. 459-74. It should be noted that Bertier de Montrave was *premier président* of the *Parlement* of Toulouse, and not a member of the government.
75. Madame de Motteville, *Mémoires* (ed. Michaud and Poujoulat, ser. ii., Vol. x, 1838), 439-40.
76. C.J. Mayer, *Des États-Généraux et autres assemblées nationales* (18 vols., The Hague, 1788-9), Vol. xviii. 54-5. British Library, Egerton MSS. 1666 fos. 56v.-57v. British Library, Add. MSS. 30555 fos. 195v-196r.
77. AN K 117b no. 27. For this reason alone, Gaston and Condé lacked consistency in opposing Mazarin and his policies during the Fronde.

78. The failure of noble attempts to influence the elections in 1614 is emphasized by J.M. Hayden, *France and the Estates-General of 1614* (Cambridge, 1974), 77-80. Nevertheless, they did attempt to influence the elections in 1651: AAE France 875, fo. 132, 2 June 1651. Several cases of election disputes came before the *conseil d'en haut*.

79. For example, Molé's refusal to register the association of the *Frondeur* nobles (18 January 1649) in the *Parlement* of Paris: Molé, *Mémoires* (ed. A. Champollion-Figeac, 4 vols., 1855-7), Vol. iii, 337.

80. Motteville, *Mémoires* (ed. Michaud and Poujoulat), 390. For the opposition of the *Parlement* : Moote, *Revolt*, 295.

81. La Rochefoucault, *Mémoires* (ed. Michaud and Poujoulat, 3rd. ser., Vol. v, 1838), 439-40. *Oeuvres de Retz* (ed. Feillet et al.), Vol. iii. 60-1.

82. 'Concordat de l'union . . .' (cited supra, n. 14).

83. 'Un journal inédit du Parlement de Paris pendant la Fronde (1 déc. 1651-12 avril 1652)' (ed. H. Courteault), *Annuaire-bulletin de la société de l'histoire de France* (1916), 251. *Oeuvres de Retz* (ed. Feillet et al.), Vol. iv. 91-2. Talon, *Mémoires* (ed. Michaud and Poujoulat), 463.

84. Moote, *Revolt*, 344. AN U 30, fos. 165v.-166v.

85. H. Mailfait, *Un magistrat de l'ancien régime. Omer Talon, sa vie et ses oeuvres, 1595-1652* (1902), 356-7. AN E 1698, nos. 108, 120, 18 July and 23 July 1652. *Arrêts du conseil du roi* (ed. Le Pesant), nos. 1731, 1736. BN Colbert 3, fos. 409-13, 5 July 1652.

86. Motteville, *Mémoires* (ed. Michaud and Poujoulat), 438.

87. The argument was used in royalist propaganda: University of London, Add. MSS. 247, fo. 7.

88. Talon, *Mémoires* (ed. Michaud and Poujoulat), 357-8. BN 500 Colbert 3, fo. 66, 25 February 1649.

89. Philippe de Commynes, *Memoirs. The reign of Louis XI, 1461-1483* (trans. M. Jones, 1972), 104. Motteville, *Mémoires* (ed. Michaud and Poujoulat), 176.

90. Mottville, 239, 269, 301.

91. The lesser nobles in the *bailliage* of Troyes in 1651 wanted triennial governorships as a means of opening up appointments to themselves: Mousnier, Labatut, Durand, *Problèmes de stratification sociale*, 142.

92. P. Logié, *La Fronde en Normandie* (3 vols., Amiens, 1951-2), Vols. ii. 130; iii. 20, 48, 57.

93. B. Pocquet, *Histoire de Bretagne. La Bretagne province, 1515-1715* (Rennes, 1913), 428-33. AAE France 1508, fos. 76, 92, 28 and 29 September 1651. AN E 1697, nos. 229, 231, 249, 6 November 1651. *Arrêts du conseil du roi* (ed. Le Pesant), nos. 1568, 1569 and 1575.

94. BN Ms. fr. 18830 fos. 141-69. AAE France 1634, fos. 508v.-509v., 22 November 1650. AN E 1696, passim.

95. *Lettres et mémoires adressés au Chancelier Séguier, 1633-1649* (ed. R. Mousnier, 2 vols., 1964), Vol. ii. passim, anno 1649. Pillorget, *Les mouvements insurrectionnels*, 610-29.

96. BN 500 Colbert 3, fos. 157-9.

97. *Lettres du Cardinal Mazarin* . . . (ed. Ravenel), 70.

98. J.R. Mallet, *Comptes-rendus de l'administration des finances du royaume de France* . . . (London, 1789), 94.

99. According to Colbert's figures in the 1660s, 419.6 million *livres* in

The French Civil War, 1649-53

compensation would have been necessary: BN 500 Colbert 259, fo. 1.

100. For the growth of magnate revenues: D. Roche, 'Aperçus sur la fortune et les revenus des princes de Condé à l'aube du xviiie siècle', *Revue d'histoire moderne et contemporaine,* Vol. xiv (1967), 217-43. F.C. Mougel, 'La fortune des princes de Bourbon-Conty: revenus et gestion, 1655-1791', ibid., xviii (1971). For Gaston's expenses of 2.6 million *livres* at the end of the Fronde: Dethan, *Gaston d'Orléans,* 441.

101. B.F. Porchnev, *Les soulèvements populaires en France de 1623 à 1648* (1963), part three.

102. The most recent study is S.A. Westrich, *The Ormée of Bordeaux. A revolution during the Fronde* (Baltimore, 1972).

103. A. Débidour, *La Fronde angevine. Tableau de la vie muncipale au xviie siècle* (1877). British Library, Harleian MSS. 4468, fo. 183, 'relation du siège d'Angers'.

104. Moote, *Revolt,* 52, 219, 369, 375-6.

105. R.J. Bonney, 'The secret expenses of Richelieu and Mazarin, 1624-1661', *English Historical Review,* xci (1976), 825-36. Bonney, *Political change in France under Richelieu and Mazarin, 1624-1661 (forthcoming from Oxford University Press in 1978).*

106. There is no reliable account of all stages of the fighting. However, there is material in commandant de Piépape, *Turenne et l'invasion de la Champagne, 1649-1650* (1889) and DesRobert, *Charles IV et Mazarin.*

107. In September 1652, Mazarin, Le Tellier and Servien considered that the civil war had to be ended so that France could concentrate on the foreign war against Spain: *Lettres du Cardinal Mazarin* (ed. Chéruel et al.), Vol. v. 251. AAE France 884, fo. 341, 14 September 1652. Several fiscal documents refer to the difficulties of the tax-farmers becuase of 'la guerre civile'. For example: AN E 254b, fo. 326, 27 January 1653.

108. This point is difficult to document simply because it alludes to contemporary assumptions, and assumptions are not necessarily written down. Both Mazarin and Le Tellier called their magnate opponents 'republicans', but it is clear that what they meant by this term was opposition to the *ministériat: Lettres du Cardinal Mazarin . . .* (ed. Ravenel), 26. AAE France 875, fo. 202, 16 June 1651: 'ceux qui ont eu l'intention de réduire le ministériat en république ont réussy . . .' Opposition to the *ministériat* was not necessarily synonymous with republicanism, however, and Mazarin's use of language was notoriously immoderate during the Fronde. With regard to the future of the monarchy as an institution, the English Civil War 'restrained rather than encouraged extremist republican talk among the *Frondeurs,* and by reaction, caused them to stress the legitimacy of their demands': P.A. Knachel, *England and the Fronde. The impact of the English Civil War and Revolution on France* (Ithaca, 1967), 273. With regard to the person of the young king, the manifestoes which possibly emanated from the magnates purported to fear an assassination plot. Such an eventuality, they suggested, might best be prevented by the establishment of a formal regency council. (Cf. supra, n. 14). One of Condé's supporters did claim in November 1651 that 'sans feu ny poison il pouvoit faire périr le Roy' hoping that 'quand Monsieur le prince seroit roy qu'il auroit soing de sa fortune.' [British Library Harleian 4466, fo. 515, 20 November 1651.] Yet there is no evidence that this madman was acting on Condé's orders.

109. It is doubtful whether many Frenchmen believed *La Mercuriale,* a radical

pamphlet of 1652, which argued that Louis XIV was 'maître de ses volontés' and thus 'la véritable cause de cette guerre civile.' Quoted by Kossmann, *La Fronde,* 230-1.

110. This argument was used, for example, by the *Parlement* of Paris in its remonstrances of 21 January 1649 and in its decree of 20 July 1652.

111. Some nobles made loans to the government. For example, the duchesse d'Orléans lent 33,400 *livres* on 13 July 1651: AN E 248a, fo. 268. The duc d'Épernon lent 108,000 *livres* on 12 August 1651: AN E 248b, fo. 278. Other nobles made proposals *(avis)* to the council of finance for the establishment of new taxes and were to receive part of the proceeds if the tax were established. For example, Louise Elisabeth des Tempes de Valencay, widow of the maréchal de la Châtre: AN E 249c, fo. 360, 16 December 1651. The duchesse de Guise and Joyeuse: AN E 249c, fo. 506, 20 December 1651. Direct noble participation in the fiscal process is difficult to document because of the use of *prête-noms* and financiers as intermediaries.

112. Royalist propaganda emphasized the point: University of London, Add. MSS 247, fos. 4v.-7. For an example of the social and economic consequences of civil war: J. Jacquart, 'La Fronde des princes dans la région parisienne et ses conséquences matérielles', *Revue d'histoire moderne et contemporaine,* Vol. vii (1960), 259-60 and Jacquart, *La crise rurale,* 650-76. For the fall in urban rents at Paris during the Fronde: E. Leroy-Ladurie and P. Couperie, 'Le mouvement des loyers parisiens de la fin du moyen âge au xviiie siècle', *Annales E.S.C.,* Vol. xv (1970), 1019. See also J-P. Poisson, 'L'activité notariale comme indicateur socio-économique: l'exemple de la Fronde', *Annales E.S.C.,* Vol. xxxi (1976), 996-1,009.

113. For the royalist 'conspiracies' at Paris and Bordeaux: University of London, Add. MSS., 247. BN Dupuy 775, fo. 196, permission of Louis XIV for his loyal inhabitants of Paris to take to arms, 17 September 1652.

114. For example, the great financier Thomas Bonneau: cf. AN E 263b, fo. 620, 25 February 1654.

115. This paper was delivered at Sheffield University on 18 February 1976. A short version was delivered at the twenty-third annual conference of the Society for French Historical Studies at the University of California, Berkeley, on 1 April 1977. I am indebted to the Twenty-Seven Foundation, without whose generosity the research that went into this paper could not have been undertaken.

V

THE ENGLISH AND FRENCH CIVIL WARS

The political upheaval in France between 1648 and 1652–3 known as the Fronde has long attracted the interest of historians.[1] Verdicts upon its importance have varied greatly. Many nineteenth-century historians, for example, followed the judgements of certain contemporary memoirs and minimized its significance. More recently, however, historians have been looking beyond the memoirs written during the personal rule of Louis XIV, and making comparisons between the Fronde and the political upheavals in other countries in the 1640s. To the committed Marxist historian, England was a more advanced society and economy which in 1649 necessarily experienced a more advanced form of revolution led by the bourgeoisie. In contrast, France was a more backward economy and society in which the bourgeoisie was unable or unwilling to play its historical role in leading the first phase of revolution: France thus had to wait until 1789 for a 'bourgeois' revolution comparable to England in 1649.[2] While this line of argument serves usefully to highlight the difficulty of comparison, it is ultimately unconvincing to the historian without ideological commitment or belief in Marxist determinism.[3] Most historians would prefer to adopt the approach of direct comparison of political upheavals within the same chronological time-span. And some at least would agree with Trevor-Roper's dictum, in a justly famous if highly controversial article, that 'France . . . was certainly not immune from the general crisis (of the 1640s), and in the Fronde . . . it had a revolution, if a relatively small revolution.'[4] In this article, a comparison will be made between the origins and early course of the English Civil War and the Fronde in France. If the conclusion is that the contrasts are greater than the similarities, it is hoped

---

[1] The best short introduction to the Fronde remains R. J. Knecht, 'The Fronde', *Historical Association. Appreciations in History,* v (1975). The three standard accounts (none of which is entirely satisfactory) are: P. R. Doolin, *The Fronde* (Cambridge, Mass., 1935); E. H. Kossmann, *La Fronde* (Leiden, 1954); A. L. Moote, *The Revolt of the Judges: The Parlement of Paris and the Fronde, 1643–1652* (Princeton, N. J., 1971). The study by P. A. Knachel, *England and the Fronde: The Impact of the English Civil War and Revolution on France* (Ithaca, N.Y., 1967), is primarily a description of the course of Anglo-French relations during the Fronde and its aftermath.

[2] For the failure of the French 'bourgeois' revolution in 1648–53 according to one Marxist historian: B. F. Porchnev, *Les soulèvements populaires en France de 1623 à 1648* (1963), pp. 505–82. A restatement of the Marxist case is P. Anderson, *Lineages of the Absolutist State* (1974), who talks of 'the chain of great bourgeois revolutions from the revolt of the Netherlands to the unification of Germany' (p. 11) and refers to a 'bourgeois revolution' in England after 1640 (p. 142).

[3] An effective rebuttal of the Marxist thesis, and much else besides, is provided by R. Ashton, *The English Civil War: Conservatism and Revolution, 1603–1649* (1978).

[4] H. R. Trevor-Roper, 'The general crisis of the seventeenth century', *Past and Present,* xvi (1959), reprinted in *Crisis in Europe, 1560–1660. Essays from Past and Present,* ed. T. H. Aston (1965), p. 88. Mousnier's criticisms are to be found *ibid.,* pp. 97–104. Cf. also R. É. Mousnier, 'The Fronde', *Preconditions of revolution in early modern Europe,* ed. R. Forster and J. P. Greene (Baltimore, Md., 1970), pp. 131–59.

that the highlighting of these contrasts may place a new perspective on the separate historical development of the two countries in the seventeenth century.

I

In England, the issue of conflict after 1640 was the 11 years of so-called 'tyranny' or non-parliamentary rule between 1629 and 1640: years in which Charles I had arguably either attempted to regain ground lost to parliament in the 1620s or else create an effective monarchy, perhaps on the French model.[5] The greatest single constitutional issue in the 1630s was the levy of Ship Money: yet it was not until the summer of 1639, when Charles for the first time in his personal rule was fighting a war, that opposition to its collection became effective.[6] In renouncing parliament in 1629, Charles had in effect renounced his right to an active foreign policy. Such a policy might mean war, and an army required a certain minimum outlay by the king, depending on its size and other factors such as the difficulty of mobilization and supply. In the 1620s it was estimated that £1 million per annum would be needed for an English expedition to the Palatinate, without including any other military or naval expenses.[7] During Charles I's personal rule, it appears that the ordinary revenue of the crown rose from an annual average of £618,376 in the years 1631-5 to the 'immense figure' of £899,482 in 1636-41.[8] Yet, contrary to the views of some historians, this income does not appear 'immense' at all in comparison with Charles's needs in 1639-41. The Scots army of occupation in northern England had to be paid £850 a day after the treaty of Ripon (26 October 1640). The Irish rebellion in October 1641 required a second army and thus more expense. Charles *might* just have succeeded in avoiding financial disaster during the Scots war had he won a quick (and thus cheap) victory in the first few weeks. That he did not, forced the king to summon parliament for financial assistance. This, in turn, forced him to seek new political support, which had to be bought at the price of concessions. Bedford and some of Charles's other critics in parliament had a

---

[5] Ashton *op. cit.,* p. 15. For the 1620s: C. S. R. Russell, 'Parliamentary history in perspective, 1604-1629', *History,* lxi (1976); 1-27. *Parliaments and English politics, 1621-1629* (Oxford, 1979.) *Faction and parliament: Essays in early Stuart history,* ed. K. M. Sharpe (Oxford, 1978). (The author wishes to express his appreciation to Dr. Sharpe, who kindly commented on this paper when in draft form.)

[6] J. S. Morrill, *The Revolt of the Provinces. Conservatives and Radicals in the English Civil War, 1630-1650* (1976), pp. 24-9.

[7] S. L. Adams, 'Foreign policy and the parliaments of 1621 and 1624', *Faction and Parliament,* ed. Sharpe, p. 150 n. 38.

[8] The evidence is usefully summarized in G. E. Aylmer, *The King's Servants: The Civil Service of Charles I, 1625-1642* (1961), pp. 64-5. The phrase 'immense figure' is from C. S. R. Russell, *The Crisis of Parliaments: English History, 1509-1660* (Oxford, 1971), p. 319. For a more pessimistic picture of Charles I's financial position: R. Ashton, *The Crown and the Money Market, 1603-1640* (Oxford, 1960), pp. 41-6.

financial programme,⁹ but it was heavily dependent for success on the parliamentary leadership finding support in the House of Commons, and on the king accepting the restrictions on his prerogative that the programme entailed.

Charles I failed dismally at his first test of foreign war during the personal rule. In contrast, France was able to fight a prolonged foreign war against Spain from 1635 to 1659, a period which spanned the last years of Louis XIII's reign (he died in May 1643), the minority of his son Louis XIV (May 1643–September 1651) and a period when Louis XIV was legally declared of age to rule but was in practice too young to govern personally. One of the most important reasons why the French kings were able to sustain this long period of foreign warfare was that their revenues were never less than five times the size of Charles I's. Calculated at the current rate of exchange, the ordinary revenue of Louis XIII rose from an annual average equivalent to £4,383,991 in 1631–5 to £4,564,243 in 1636–41. However, when the king's 'extraordinary' income is taken into account, the differences become even greater, Louis XIII's total revenues being over 11 times Charles I's in 1631–5 and over six times in 1636–41.¹⁰ The pound sterling was a much more stable currency than the *livre tournois*, and fluctuations in the rate of exchange explain the relatively slower growth of Louis XIII's revenues in comparison with Charles I's during the last years of personal rule. The French taxpayers were clearly paying proportionately more in taxes, even allowing for the fact that the population of France was probably four times that of England. However, calculations of exactly how much more the French taxpayer paid should be tempered with caution, since they are heavily dependent on population estimates which are unreliable for the seventeenth century.¹¹

There was a substantial, and very unpopular, increase in taxes in France to pay for the war effort after 1635. The French crown had at its disposal a much wider range of financial resources than in England, and its independent control of these resources was jealously guarded. Neither Louis XIII nor Louis XIV summoned the national representative institution, the Estates-General, to approve taxes. The last meeting of the Estates-General before the Revolution of 1789 was in 1614–15, and it did not vote taxes. Although the Estates-General was summoned twice during the

⁹ C. S. R. Russell, 'Parliament and the king's finances', *The Origins of the English Civil War*, ed. Russell (1973), pp. 110–15. C. Roberts, 'The Earl of Bedford and the coming of the English revolution', *Journal of Modern History*, xlix (1977), 600–16.

¹⁰ The figures for Louis XIII's income are tabulated in R. J. Bonney, *The King's Debts: Finance and Politics in France, 1589–1661* (forthcoming from OUP in 1981), appendix two, tables 1 and 4. It should be noted that there were considerable differences between the definition of ordinary and extraordinary income in England and France. The rate of exchange is calculated on the basis of evidence in J. J. McCusker, *Money and Exchange in Europe and America, 1600–1775* . . . (Chapel Hill, N. C., 1978), p. 306. Earlier discussion of the relative income of Charles I and Louis XIII is based on incomplete information and an inaccurate rate of exchange: cf. J. U. Nef, *Industry and Government in France and England, 1540–1640* (original ed., 1940; 5th. ed., 1969), pp. 128–9. Charles I's total revenues are estimated at a maximum of £750,000 per annum in 1631–5 and £1,150,000 in 1636–41: Aylmer, *op. cit.*, p. 65. The respective figures for Louis XIII were £8,774,209 and £7,429,924.

¹¹ The crucial importance of population estimates in the calculation of *per capita* tax burdens emerges clearly from the debate on the eighteenth-century statistics: P. Mathias and P. K. O'Brien, 'Taxation in Britain and France, 1715–1810 . . .', *Journal of European Economic History*, v (1976), 601–50.

Fronde, and elections took place in 1649 and 1651, it did not actually meet. It is true that representative institutions had survived in certain *pays d'états* such as Brittany, Burgundy and Languedoc, to name the most important. In these provinces, the estates retained control over the chief direct tax, the *taille*, or its equivalent, although there was less effective control of the various indirect taxes. However, representative institutions had not survived in most of the French provinces. In these areas, the *pays d'élections*,[12] the *taille* had become a permanent direct tax after 1439, levied annually by royal decree. The *taille* could thus be increased dramatically in the 1630s to pay for the war against Spain, without the consent of the French propertied classes being sought or given. It is very doubtful whether these new and heavier taxes could have been levied without a profound change in French administrative procedures. The traditional way in which direct taxes were levied in France was by certain types of office-holder (the *trésoriers de France* and the *élus*) who as local property-owners had an interest in preventing increases in taxation. In the 1630s, however, the crown sent out royal commissioners into the provinces, men who did not have local property interests in the provinces in which they served. After 1642, these commissioners, the provincial *intendants,* had been given control of the levy of the *taille.* They were also empowered to raise special brigades to force the collection of taxes from recalcitrant parishes.

There is a profound contrast between the administrative structures in England and France before the political upheaval. The measures of Charles I's personal rule may have been enforced reasonably effectively until 1639–40, but they were heavily dependent on the good will of the Justices of the Peace and other administrators with local interests. These men may have done their best to enforce the personal rule, but once they met an unprecedented, articulate opposition in the localities in 1640, the system collapsed.[13] Not until the experiment of the Major-Generals in 1655–7 was the existing local administration circumvented in England in a comparable way to France, although the French *intendants* were civilian lawyers, not military commanders. The experiment of the Major-Generals took place only during the Protectorate, and left the country with a lasting dislike of Puritanism and military rule. Though Catholic to a man, and thus conforming to the religious convictions of the majority of the population, the French *intendants* were no better loved. After the death of Louis XIII in 1643, the *Parlements* and the other sovereign tribunals[14] tried to impose a time limit on administrative innovation, by specifying that once the war ended the new fiscal powers granted to the intendants should be revoked. By the summer of 1648, the crown had to give way to pressure for the abolition of the *intendants* in most of the provinces, although the war against Spain had not ended. They were later reintroduced into the provinces in 1652–3, at the end of the Fronde.

[12] Strictly speaking, areas with *élections*: these were lesser financial tribunals. Their functions, and the gradual introduction of the provincial intendants are discussed in R. J. Bonney, *Political Change in France under Richelieu and Mazarin, 1624–1661* (Oxford, 1978), pp. 163–90.

[13] A good local study of the attempt to enforce the personal rule is T. G. Barnes, *Somerset, 1625–1640 : a county's government during the 'personal rule'* (Oxford, 1961).

[14] The attitude of the sovereign tribunals to the provincial *intendants* is discussed in Bonney, *op. cit.*, pp. 238–58. The relationship between the various tribunals is suggested *ibid.,* p. 7.

In comparison with Louis XIII's government, Charles I's personal rule was a model of constitutional propriety: he at least had not circumvented the local administration, but tried to make it more effective. Strong government was needed in the localities in France, because the residual administrative problems were much greater: 'the monarchy was both more powerful, and more hamstrung by an administrative system of which it was at once the beneficiary and the victim.'[15] Office-holders were far more numerous than in England, where the sale of offices was illegal although it took place. Unlike England, the tenure of French office-holders was virtually absolute, and the majority of offices could be inherited. Grouped together in local tribunals, the political importance of the French office-holders was greater than that of the representative institution since they were permanent features of the political scene whereas the Estates-General had not met after 1615. It should not be assumed that big government in France was necessarily more successful in the long term than small government in England. Every year the king of France and his government had to cope with a complex administrative system rendered inefficient by the proliferation of offices; they also had to pay enormous salaries to office-holders which the king of England did not. Charles I paid on average about £350,000 per annum in salaries to office-holders.[16] Louis XIII was supposed to pay the equivalent of £1,882,007 in 1640 at the current rate of exchange, over five times the English figure. When, in the 1640s, the French crown defaulted on its obligations to pay salaries, it created enormous resentment among powerful vested interests who were already affronted by their loss of administrative power to the provincial *intendants*.

On 29 April 1648, d'Hémery, the French finance minister, precipitated the political crisis by suspending the salaries of all tribunals for four years, with the exception of the *Parlement* of Paris. The defence of a vital private economic interest of the office-holders forced them into the arena of high politics. The result was the decree of union (*arrêt d'union*) issued on 13 May, by which the Parisian sovereign tribunals declared their intention of meeting in the *Chambre Saint-Louis* to discuss their grievances, and implicitly to criticize royal policy. Just as Charles I had had to summon parliament, Anne of Austria, the Regent of France, had to allow the meeting at the *Chambre Saint-Louis* to take place. By 1647–8, the French government was effectively bankrupt. Despite the massive increase in taxes in the 1630s, revenues were no longer keeping pace with expenditure in the 1640s, and after 1643 the French monarchy had had to borrow on a scale which made the loans contracted by Charles I seem small beer. It is very difficult for a government to borrow in a climate of political instability: Charles I found this to his cost in 1640; so did Anne of Austria in 1648. Without new loans, both rulers had to make concessions to their critics. A

---

[15] G. E. Aylmer, 'Office-holding as a factor in English history, 1625–42', *History*, xliv (1959), p. 240. For France, the standard account is R. É. Mousnier, *La Vénalité des Offices sous Henri IV et Louis XIII* (2nd. ed., 1971).

[16] Aylmer, *The King's Servants*, p. 249. The French figure in 1640 is given in J. R. Mallet, *Comptes Rendus de l'Administration des Finances du Royaume de France* . . . (London, 1789), p. 94.

370   THE ENGLISH AND FRENCH CIVIL WARS

detailed consideration of the proposals of the *Chambre Saint-Louis* is beyond the scope of this survey. Their most important effect, however, was to make it very difficult for the government to exploit the system of office-holding for fiscal purposes, or to finance the war effort at all.[17] It has been seen that the success of Bedford's financial programme in 1641 depended on Charles I accepting restrictions on his prerogative. Cardinal Mazarin, the chief minister of Louis XIV, appears to have been better informed than some other foreign commentators and recognized that in financial matters Charles I's hands had been tied, which he saw as a structural weakness of the English Constitution.[18] His reaction to comparable restrictions on the French government in 1648 was predictable. A full implementation of the proposals of the *Chambre Saint-Louis* would, in his view, have abolished 'the most considerable parts of royal authority' ('la meilleure partie de la monarchie').[19] His attitude explains in large measure the breakdown of negotiations between the French government and its domestic critics in the last months of 1648.

II

The crisis broke in England in 1640 and France in 1648 because temporarily the crown had lost its way, and to escape from the impasse it had to find new political support. A consensus of MPs in the Long Parliament agreed on measures to destroy or neutralize the personnel and machinery of Charles I's personal rule and to condemn the measures and policies associated with what was now regarded as arbitrary government. However, between October and December 1641 this consensus began to disintegrate and tension between the king and his more committed critics in parliament had grown at an alarming rate. The passing of the Grand Remonstrance by the House of Commons on 22 November by only 11 votes was the single most controversial issue, since this measure recommended further radical reform. The political temperature was also heightened by other crucial questions such as the reform of the church, the political role of the bishops and the (Catholic) Queen, the provision of armed guards for Parliament and control of the Tower of London. (Control of the Bastille in Paris was an equally sensitive issue during the Fronde.) All these difficulties have to be viewed against the crisis of the rebellion in Ireland.[20] The single most decisive event, however, was Charles I's ill-conceived attempt on 4 January 1642 to arrest Lord Kimbolton and the five Members (Pym, Hampden, Haselrige, Holles and Strode) who were considered the leaders of the parliamentary opposition. The attempt failed, and as a result Pym was provided with powerful arguments to back his view that further constitutional advances were needed as a guarantee of the achievements of the

[17] '. . . Qu'il étoit impossible que le roi pût dorénavant soutenir la guerre': *Mémoires . . . de Montglat*, ed. J. F. Michaud and J. J. F. Poujoulat, 3rd. ser., v (1838), p. 200.

[18] Knachel, *England and the Fronde*, p. 28.

[19] P. A. Chéruel, 'Les carnets de Mazarin pendant la Fronde (septembre–octobre 1648)', *Revue Historique*, iv (1877), p. 135.

[20] The trend towards breakdown has been re-examined by D. H. Pennington, 'The making of war, 1640–1642', *Puritans and Revolutionaries: Essays in seventeenth-century history presented to Christopher Hill*, ed. Pennington and K. V. Thomas (Oxford, 1978), pp. 161–85.

Long Parliament in 1640-1. The Militia Ordinance was introduced shortly afterwards, on 31 January. Pym was also prepared to manipulate the London mob to secure his political ends, and the riots in the capital which were already a serious problem before the attempted arrest of the five Members were undoubtedly made worse by this event.

There is a curious parallel between these events and the situation in France six years later. After making substantial political concessions, the Regency government had forced the *Chambre Saint-Louis* to close its discussions at the end of July 1648. The provincial *intendants* were recalled from all but six frontier provinces, the crown's ability to borrow money was severely curtailed, and an extraordinary tribunal (*chambre de justice*) was established to investigate alleged corruption in financial administration. A reduction in direct taxes was also ordered. As in England in 1642, the issue was whether the new image of a government desiring to preserve the reforms was convincing. Might not Anne of Austria claim that her consent had been obtained under duress? Without a clearer statement of intent, or new institutional procedures, there was a strong possibility that once the crisis had passed the ministers would return to their old ways. The personnel of the Regency government had scarcely altered, although d'Hémery, the finance minister, had been replaced. The fears of the critics of the regime were confirmed by the ill-judged arrest of Broussel, Blancmesnil and Charton, and the exile of three other members of the *Parlement* of Paris who were considered leaders of the opposition, on 26 August 1648. The arrests were carried out successfully, but they provoked a storm of protest: the mob of the Île de la Cité set up barricades on 26-28 August. By its ineptitude, the Regency government, for the first time in the crisis, had created a temporary alliance of different social groups[21] against royal fiscal policy and perhaps the government itself. A deputation of the *Parlement* refused to co-operate with the government, arguing that it was impossible to contain the riot without releasing Broussel. The ministers reluctantly had to concede the point. In England, civil war was a further seven months in gestation after Charles I's attempted arrest of the five members. In France, civil war followed only four months after the arrest and subsequent release of Broussel. Within a few days, it became clear that Mazarin was prepared to evacuate the court from Paris and blockade the capital in order to coerce the *Parlement,* although the trial of strength was delayed by the voicing of the first criticism of the chief minister in the *Parlement,* the fears that the nobles would be drawn into the conflict on the side of the Parisian sovereign tribunals, and above all, by the crucial stage reached in the negotiations at Münster for a settlement of the Thirty Years' War.

Once civil war had broken out in England in August 1642 and France in January 1649, the similarity between the two conflicts becomes much less marked. Two examples will suffice to illustrate this, control of the army and

---

[21] Mousnier's argument (R. È. Mousnier, *La Plume, la Faucille et le Marteau. Institutions et Société en France du Moyen Âge à la Révolution* (1970), p. 287) that the barricades were the work of the lower classes acting on their own has been contested by J. L. Bourgeon, 'L'Île de la Cité pendant la Fronde: structure sociale', *Paris et Île de France. Mémoires*, xiii (1962), 127-44. Bourgeon's case (pp. 129-30) that an official version of events was fabricated to obscure the political isolation of the Regent appears to be borne out by A[rchives des] A[ffaires] É[trangères, Mémoires et Documents,] France 860, fo. 164, 26 Sept. 1648.

the military course of the war. In England, the Long Parliament's military position had been strengthened considerably by the passing of the Militia Ordinance, however controversial its provisions. Conversely, Charles I's position was weakened by his need to levy troops under the Commission of Array, the legality of which was open to question since the statute of 1405 on which it was based had lapsed and its terms were ambiguous.[22] In France in 1649, by contrast, troops could be levied legally only by letters patent issued by the king and countersigned by a secretary of state. The secretaries of state had followed the court to Saint-Germain-en-Laye, and the legality of decrees of the Parisian sovereign tribunals authorizing the levy of troops was at best doubtful. The Parisian tribunals thus had to rely on measures that were primarily defensive in character and had a recent precedent in the crisis year of 1636, the celebrated *année de Corbie* when for a time it had seemed that there was nothing to prevent Spanish troops marching on the capital. Above all, however, they relied on defections from the upper nobility and the army. Here, they were rather unlucky. The great defections in the French army came not during the first round of fighting between January and March 1649, but later in the Fronde, particularly after Condé went into revolt in September 1651. In the spring of 1649, however, Condé sided with the Regent and Mazarin. The enormous military prestige resulting from his recent commands and his two great victories at Rocroi and Lens, respectively in May 1643 and August 1648, was brought to bear on the side of the government. The other great general, Turenne, who was a commander of the so-called French 'army of Germany' based in Alsace, defected in March 1649, but Mazarin's agents had bought off his secondary commanders and their troops. During Condé's revolt in 1651–2, Turenne at first remained neutral and later threw in his lot with Mazarin and the government.[23]

It is also the case that the fighting in the French civil war was less protracted and less severe than in England, where the rival forces were much more evenly matched until the end of 1643. Whereas in England the fighting lasted for nearly six years (1642–6, 1648), in France it was sporadic in 1649 and 1650, when the fighting lasted for only a few months in each case, and reached a peak only in 1651–2 during Condé's revolt. The long duration of the fighting in England led to the creation of new institutions to fight the war which have no parallel in France, institutions such as the Committee of Both Kingdoms, the Committee for Taking the Accounts of the Kingdom, and local committees such as those established by the first Assessments Ordinance of February 1643 and the Sequestration Ordinance. The peers of the realm who had sided with the Commons tended to be defeatist almost from the outset. This defeatism within the high command, and their lack of military success, necessitated further great changes in 1644–5, the Self-Denying Ordinance and the creation of the New Model Army. Matters never reached this pass in France. The rebellion of 1649 was led by the Parisian sovereign tribunals who took the vital decision on 9 January to set up a fund for the levy of troops. A number of

[22] Morrill, *The Revolt of the Provinces*, pp. 39–40, 156–8.
[23] Mazarin's tortuous dealings with the upper nobility including Turenne and his elder brother, Bouillon, are discussed more fully in R. J. Bonney 'Cardinal Mazarin and the great nobility during the Fronde', forthcoming in *English Historical Review*.

discontented nobles arrived at Paris and on 18 January signed an alliance among themselves which pledged support to the *Parlement*. While the *Parlement* appointed Conty, the most important of these nobles, as its supreme commander or generalissimo, it never formally recognized the alliance of 18 January. When the *Parlement* of Paris made its peace with the government in March 1649, the demands of the nobles were not discussed and their interests were never properly taken into account.[24] On 20 July 1652, during Condé's rebellion, the *Parlement* of Paris declared Gaston d'Orléans lieutenant-general of the kingdom and Condé commander of the army, but the king's council replied on 23 July with a decree declaring anyone who obeyed their orders guilty of treason (*lèse-majesté*).[25] Only at Bordeaux during the dictatorship of a radical party known as the *Ormée* in 1652–3, was there properly speaking a period of institutional innovation to conduct a war effort against the crown.[26] Since the fighting was of shorter duration in France than England, there was not the same tendency towards radicalization in the army. There is no French parallel to the Leveller movement, no trend towards the promotion of 'base and mean fellows' in the military command, even if the extent of the transformation within the New Model Army has sometimes been exaggerated.[27]

The military course of the French civil war requires further investigation, since little is known of the fighting in the provinces,[28] pre-emptive military manoeuvres,[29] or the political and military role of neutralism particularly within specific regions.[30] Neutralism is likely to have been a factor playing ultimately into the hands of the government, just as it did at the end of the Catholic League in 1594–6. Moreover, the fighting was probably contained both by the recent example of England—which had pointed to the dangerous consequences of a protracted civil war—and recollection of the horrors of nearly 40 years of intermittent civil war during the late sixteenth-century wars of religion. Nevertheless, it is obvious that good fortune played a part in the government's survival in France: had Turenne's troops not deserted in 1649, had Turenne not suffered one of only two defeats in his long career at Rethel in December 1650, had Condé's army not been badly mauled at the Faubourg Saint-Antoine in July 1652, the outcome might have been very different. Moreover, the Spanish played the role of *deus ex machina* much less effectively than the Scots in the English civil war. Spain

---

[24] R. J. Bonney, 'The French civil war, 1649–53', *European Studies Review*, viii (1978), pp. 79–80.

[25] *Arrêts du conseil du roi. Règne de Louis XIV. Inventaire analytique des arrêts en commandement. I . . .* ed. M. Le Pesant (1976), no. 1736.

[26] S. A Westrich, *The Ormée of Bordeaux: a Revolution during the Fronde* (Baltimore, Md., 1972), pp. 60–72.

[27] M. A. Kishlansky, 'The case of the army truly stated: the creation of the New Model Army', *Past and Present*, lxxxi (1978), 51–74.

[28] An idea of the fighting in Guyenne is provided by Westrich, *op. cit.*, and in Provence by R. Pillorget, *Les Mouvements insurrectionnels de Provence entre 1596 et 1715* (1975).

[29] François de Baradat, a former favourite of Louis XIII and supporter of the government during the Fronde, had a key bridge over the river Marne in Champagne broken three times and rebuilt twice as the military situation dictated: cf. A[rchives] N[ationales] E 326b, fo. 406, 23 July 1659.

[30] Although the duc de Longueville had successfully raised his province Normandy in revolt in 1649, in 1652 he resisted the efforts of Gaston and Condé to encourage him to join their rebellion: cf. A. A. E. France 889, fo. 127. Draft treaty of February 1652 to bring Longueville into the treaty of 24 Jan. 1652 between Gaston and Condé.

hoped to profit from the French civil war in order to reconquer territories lost in the struggle between the two powers after 1635. If the Spanish military position had been stronger to take advantage of the French weakness, if their policies had been less self-interested, and above all if there had not been such resentment of their previous interventions in French politics—notably in the wars of religion and the political conspiracies earlier in the seventeenth century—the fighting during the Fronde would have been much more serious. The Scots wielded a two-edged sword, since they allied with Charles I in the Engagement signed on 26 December 1647 and invaded England the following year. The earlier Scots intervention in English politics had been self-interested to the extent that they had wanted to see an English church settlement on the Scottish Presbyterian model. In military terms, however, it had been much more important than the Spanish assistance to the *Frondeurs* and in the Committee of Both Kingdoms a degree of political co-operation was achieved for a time in the English civil war[31] which finds no parallel in France. What the Spanish wanted was simply to convert the *Frondeurs* into an additional Habsburg army, and this is what they achieved when they appointed Condé their generalissimo on 25 November 1652. By this time it was clear that the Fronde had collapsed. Condé spent the years from 1652 to 1660 in exile commanding Spanish troops and the remnants of the *Frondeur* force.

III

Professor Moote has argued that 'both geographically and socially, the Fronde was the most widespread of all the rebellions in mid-seventeenth-century Europe. Logically, it should have resulted in some sort of revolution or political transformation far more fundamental than the republican achievements of the Long Parliament in England . . .'[32] The conclusion of this survey is the reverse. The Fronde was geographically and socially more significant than the English civil war only because France was a bigger country with a larger population than England. There was no comparison between the intensity of the revolutionary experience in England and France. At no time during the Fronde did the opposition seriously consider committing the supreme revolutionary act, not merely of deposing but executing the king. The uncomfortable fact of civil war in England was left deliberately obscure by the argument that parliament was not fighting Charles I at all, but evil councillors who were the real architects of royal policy. However, already by the time of the Militia Ordinance (6 June 1642) there was a significant addition that 'the king's supreme and royal pleasure is exercised and declared in this High Court of law and council (i.e. parliament), after a more eminent and obligatory manner than it can

---

[31] Although relations between the English and Scots members soon broke down: L. Mulligan, 'Peace negotiations, politics and the Committee of Both Kingdoms, 1644–6', *Historical Journal*, xii (1969), 3–22.

[32] Moote, *The revolt of the judges*, p. 368. Moote's views on the general crisis are expressed in A. L. Moote, 'The preconditions of revolution in early modern Europe: did they really exist?', *The General Crisis of the seventeenth century*, ed. N. G. Parker and L. M. Smith (1978), pp. 134–64.

be by personal act or resolution of his own.'[33] The removal of the advisers during the personal rule and evidence of Charles I's duplicity eventually forced the leaders of the army in England to lay blame at the door of the king rather than his ministers. Nevertheless, those holding republican views in England even in 1649 were a tiny and uninfluential minority. The execution of the king was a pragmatic decision, an act of political necessity which overcame ideological objections.[34]

Mazarin feared the spread of republicanism as a form of plague from England after January 1649. However, the label 'republican' is not an objective description or valid historical category in France during the Fronde. It was a term of abuse, used by the ministers and supporters of the government against political opponents regardless of their actual views.[35] Louis XIV reached his majority only in September 1651, and at 13 he was still too young to rule personally. The king was a good king because he was still an untrained youth.[36] He had not been implicated in what were regarded as the abuses of government in the 1630s and 1640s. Indeed, one could argue that the troubles after 1643 arose from the fact that Louis XIV had not yet reached the age to rule. The government had been controlled by Anne of Austria, the Regent. On 18 May 1643, the *Parlement* of Paris had annulled the last will and testament of Louis XIII, which had imposed restrictions on the Regent's power, and had nominated members of a regency council. The *Parlement* freed Anne of Austria from these constraints, and she had appointed Cardinal Mazarin chief minister. For a long time, the *Parlement* was unwilling to take decisive action against the government because of constitutional propriety and its instinctive loyalty towards the Regent. Indeed, it seems that few members of the political classes in France were prepared to consider the possibility of deposing the Regent. Thus when the *Parlement* of Paris issued its remonstrances on 21 January 1649, which formed the ideological justification for the first civil war, it claimed to have taken to arms against Mazarin, the 'tyrannical' chief minister, and not against the king or the Regent. The resort to arms was not an act of rebellion, but one of duty since Mazarin should be brought to justice: the *Parlement* was the last bulwark in the defence of monarchical authority in France. In both 1649 and 1652 it was claimed that the war was directed not against the person of Louis XIV, but to rescue him from the 'captivity' in which he was held by Mazarin, who had usurped the king's sovereignty.[37]

[33] S. R. Gardiner, *Constitutional Documents of the Puritan Revolution, 1625–1660* (repr., Oxford 1979), p. 257.

[34] A. B. Worden, *The Rump Parliament, 1648–1653* (Cambridge, 1974), pp. 33–60.

[35] The arch-conspirator Cardinal de Retz, for example, was depicted as a republican in the letters patent justifying his arrest in December 1652: A. A. E. France 891, fo. 121, March 1653. Although Retz's political ideas were ambiguous it is doubtful if the allegation was justified: D. A. Watts, *Cardinal de Retz: the ambiguities of a seventeenth-century mind* (Oxford, 1980).

[36] Guy Patin, letters of 20 July 1658 and 26 August 1660 quoted by G. Lacour-Gayet, *L'Éducation politique de Louis XIV* (2nd. ed., 1923), p. 206. Guy Patin was a severe critic of Mazarin during the Fronde and the fact that he entertained such high hopes of Louis XIV even well after Mazarin's restoration to power is significant.

[37] Omer Talon, *Mémoires*, ed. J. F. Michaud and J. J. F. Poujoulat, 3rd. ser., vi (1839), pp. 323–8. The idea was also expressed in the remonstrances issued by the *Parlement* of Paris on 23 March 1652, and in its decree of 20 July 1652.

Mazarin's critics argued that without the removal of the chief minister there could be no permanent reversal of his unacceptable policies. He had replied by comparing his position with that of Strafford in England in 1641. If he were ousted from power, a reversal of royal policy would be forced on the government. Once Charles I had sacrificed Strafford, the monarchy itself did not long survive.[38] Of course, this view antedates by several years the ultimate failure of negotiation in England. By personalizing the issue, it suggests that the similarity between the English and French civil wars was greater than was in fact the case. The processes of impeachment in the 1620s and attainder as against Strafford in 1641 required the king's consent, however reluctant.[39] In the end, however, Charles I failed to defend the chief architect of 'Thorough' from the wrath of the Long Parliament. There was no parallel in recent French history to this execution. When ministers were placed on trial, as were La Vieuville in 1624 and Foucquet in 1661, it was before a special royal commission rather than the *Parlement* of Paris, and neither was executed. It is true that Léonora Galigaï, the widow of the Italian adventurer Concino Concini, had been executed in 1617 after a trial in the *Parlement*: but the trial took place on the orders of the king. It set no precedent for the Fronde because Mazarin's position at court was successfully defended by the Regent. When the *Parlement* took evidence against Mazarin in 1651–2, the trial did not proceed very far because it lacked support from Anne of Austria. In May 1652, Mazarin was placed under a royal safeguard and after the collapse of the Fronde in Paris a royal declaration was registered by the *Parlement* on 22 October which implicitly defended the chief minister from past and future criticism.[40] After Mazarin's return to the capital in February 1653 his position was unchallenged.

Mazarin was bitterly attacked during the Fronde, as nearly 5,000 political pamphlets or *mazarinades*, most of which were written to destroy his reputation, demonstrate. He was forced into temporary exile on two occasions, but his political position was greatly strengthened by the fact that he was a Cardinal of the church. What was missing in the Fronde was the peculiar intensity given to the English civil war by the religious threat, real or imagined. The French Protestants did not rebel, and if they took sides at all it was with the government.[41] It is sometimes said that Jansenism provided a Catholic opposition movement to Mazarin and the government. However, the so-called 'religious Fronde' followed upon, and had as its

---

[38] Knachel, *England and the Fronde*, pp. 32, 47. A. A. E. France 884, fo. 60v., 12 Aug. 1652.

[39] Russell, *Parliaments and English Politics*, pp. 15, 104. C. S. R. Russell, 'The theory of treason in the trial of Strafford', *English Historical Review*, lxxx (1965), 30–50. Gardiner commented that 'in after years Charles bitterly repented his compliance': *History of England*...ix (1894), p. 367.

[40] For the attempts to prosecute Mazarin during the Fronde: R. J. Bonney, 'Cardinal Mazarin and his critics: the remonstrances of 1652', *Journal of European Studies*, x (1980), 15–31. Information on the trials of 1617, 1624 and 1661 in Bonney, *The king's debts*... (forthcoming from OUP in 1981).

[41] S. Deyon, *Du loyalisme au refus: les Protestants français et leur député général entre la Fronde et la révocation* (Lille, 1976), pp. 35–41. However, there were fears of a Huguenot third party during the Fronde: *Journal des guerres civiles de Dubuisson-Aubenay, 1648–52*, ed. G. Saige (2 vols., 1883, 1885), i. 135. There is the hint of a Protestant connection with the Ormée: Westrich, *op. cit.*, pp. 33, 90, 94.

chief cause, the arrest of Cardinal de Retz in December 1652 and his elevation to the archbishopric of Paris in March 1654. It remains to be shown that there was any comparable Jansenist agitation during the years between 1648 and 1653, or that other radical religious movements had any real following or political importance in France in these years.[42] For a parallel with the situation in England in 1641, one has to go back in French history to 1587–9, when Henri III suffered the consequences of his failure to defend the country from foreign invasion in support of Protestant rebellion. The Catholic League provided a much more serious threat both to Henri III and Henri IV than did the Fronde to Louis XIV. The English civil war may not have been quite as straightforward a Puritan revolution as Gardiner's description might suggest. However, few would deny that opposition to Laud's ecclesiastical policies and the imposition of the new Prayer Book in Scotland, desire for 'root and branch' church reform among some sections of political opinion, and above all fear of 'popery' figured prominently among the causes of breakdown in 1640–2. One of the decisive charges against Strafford was that he had counselled Charles I to bring in an Irish — and, it was feared, Catholic — army to 'reduce this kingdom... of England'.[43] The English civil war was in large measure the product of a panic reaction in parliament to the Irish rebellion in October 1641. Charles I could not be trusted to meet this crisis, because of fear of popery which was compounded by his ill-fated attempt to arrest the five Members. What was needed was the passing of the Militia Ordinance, the prelude to civil war. The Fronde also arose from a crisis abroad: Mazarin's failure to secure peace with Spain, which meant the continuation of a foreign war during a royal minority. This situation was unparalleled in French history: in 1561 the Regent had not inherited a foreign war; in 1610, a full-scale European war was narrowly averted. The continuation of war implied the continuation of heavy taxes, which accounts in large measure for the unpopularity of the government. However, there was no panic, no fear for the future of Catholicism which had led to the taking of oaths of allegiance to the Catholic League in 1588–9. There was certainly fear of *mazarinisme* during the Fronde, but it was much less tangible than the earlier fear of a Protestant succession.

There were also important social and institutional factors working in France towards a more limited conflict than in England. There was greater social cohesion between gentry, office-holders and merchants in the House of Commons than was possible in France even at times when the Estates-General met. England had no agents of the central government in the localities comparable to the *intendants* who might challenge the primacy of the gentry exercised through the office of Justice of the Peace. It is true that

---

[42] But cf. R. M. Golden, 'The mentality of opposition: the Jansenism of the Parisian *curés* during the religious Fronde', *Catholic Historical Review*, lxiv (1978), 565–80. (However, the small extent of support for Jansenism within the *Parlement* of Paris is emphasised by A. N. Hamscher, 'The *Parlement* of Paris and the social interpretation of early French Jansenism', *ibid.*, lxiii (1977), 392–410; idem, *The Parlement of Paris after the Fronde, 1653–1673* (Pittsburgh, Pa., 1976), pp. 109–17.) Radical sects, especially the Illuminist movement which led to some extreme political pamphlets during the Fronde, are examined in Golden, 'Religious extremism in the mid-seventeenth century: the Parisian *Illuminés*', *European Studies Review*, ix (1979), 195–210.

[43] Russell, 'The theory of treason', p. 49.

378   THE ENGLISH AND FRENCH CIVIL WARS

in normal circumstances, members of the House of Commons were happy to leave high matters of state to the court of the king and the House of Lords. Clientage, which was an important factor in France during the Fronde,[44] also existed in parliament: many members of the Commons in the 1620s owed their seats to the nomination of peers and to some extent did their bidding. However, in the 1640s times were not normal and the pattern of deference and clientage broke down.[45] The attack on the political power of the bishops was the first sign of this. The Self-Denying Ordinance was another.[46] The proposal to try the king, which proved too much for the handful of peers who were all that remained of the House of Lords by 1649, proved to be the death warrant of the upper chamber. After the execution of the king, the House of Lords was abolished along with the monarchy. It is perhaps above all this attack on the Lords which has given rise to the myth of the 'bourgeois revolution' in England, although it should be noted that while the peers lost their legal privileges and immunities they did not lose their actual titles. Nevertheless, there is a world of difference between the rebellion of an Essex or Manchester in the 1640s and that of a Condé or Turenne in the Fronde. The Essex revolt in 1601 and the Main Plot two years later were the last occasions on which a disgruntled nobleman took up arms in England 'for no higher purpose than to secure what he judged to be his due.'[47] Already in Tudor England, the strength of the nobility lay more in influence than in power: 'it rested upon traditional allegiances, the tie of fee, office and retainer, the bonds between landlord and tenant, but not . . . upon regalian powers of jurisdiction or upon military service.'[48]

---

[44] In January 1650, Jean Perrault, a *président* in the *Chambre des Comptes* of Paris, was arrested essentially because he was a client of Condé and 'vraysemblablement [sic] [a eu] part aux secrets de Mr. le prince': *Histoire de la Maison de Nicolay. Pièces justificatives. II. Chambre des Comptes*, ed. A. M. de Bioslisle (Nogent-le-Rotrou, 1873), p. 438. P. Lefebvre, 'Aspects de la "fidelité" en France au xviie siècle: le cas des agents des princes de Condé', *Revue Historique*, ccl (1973), p. 101. Perrault was released in February 1651 along with Condé and joined his master in exile abroad in the 1650s. This sort of clientage was outlawed by the royal declaration of 22 Oct. 1652: Moote, *The revolt of the judges*, p. 352.

[45] For example, the Earl of Manchester followed traditional clientage procedures with regard to civilian appointments in the Eastern Association, but not with regard to military appointments: C. Holmes, *The Eastern Association in the English Civil War* (Cambridge, 1974), pp. 125–9, 172–7.

[46] The most recent account of the New Model Army downgrades the importance of the Self-Denying Ordinance. Its author, Kishlansky, does however argue that 'it struck hard at the peerage, as an order and as individuals, denying them their ancient military rights and implicitly censuring the conduct of the aristocratic generals': Kishlansky, 'The case of the army truly stated . . .', p. 58. Idem, *The Rise of the New Model Army* (Cambridge, 1979). Cf. A. N. B. Cotton, 'Cromwell and the Self-Denying Ordinance', *History*, 62 (1977), 211–31.

[47] L. Stone, *The crisis of the aristocracy, 1558–1641* (Oxford, 1965), p. 255.

[48] P. Williams, *The Tudor regime* (Oxford, 1979), p. 5.

In some respects social distinctions were more rigid in France than in England.[49] The fiscal privileges enjoyed by the clergy and nobility were also much more substantial. Offices had proliferated in France on a much greater scale than in England, and heredity of office had created a distinctive social group. Many French office-holders aspired to, or had attained nobility, but they were *noblesse de robe* who were not regarded as true nobles by the court nobility or the provincial gentry (the *noblesse d'épée* or *noblesse d'ancienne extraction*).[50] When the Estates-General met, the *noblesse d'épée* was represented in the second estate, the order of the nobility; but office-holders, whether *noblesse de robe* or not, sat in the third estate which they naturally thought demeaning.[51] There is evidence of conflict between these two groups during the Fronde, and in a sense the split between the conservative leadership in the *Parlement* of Paris and its supporters among the upper nobility in March 1649 may be viewed as a reflection of the distrust between robe and sword.[52] The failure of the *noblesse d'épée* and the office-holders to co-operate during the Fronde, and the divisions within their ranks — between court nobility and provincial gentry on the one hand, and office-holders in the sovereign and lesser tribunals on the other — was an important factor in weakening resistance to the crown. The French civil wars between 1649 and 1653 became a series of rebellions by the upper nobility, who looked to the office-holders for support, but failed to achieve any lasting political alliance. Thus in France there is even less sign of social change following in the wake of political upheaval than in England.[53] The rebellion of Condé in 1651–2 was not in essence different from that of his father in 1614. Although both the upper nobility and the office-holders lost their (separate) political struggles with the crown during the Fronde, their social and economic privileges were undiminished and arguably were reinforced.

[49] The importance of primogeniture and the absence of legal prohibitions on gentlemen entering trade are factors in social mobility in England that, on the whole, did not exist in France: R. Grassby, 'Social mobility and business enterprise in seventeenth-century England', *Puritans and Revolutionaries*, ed. Pennington and Thomas, pp. 359–61. In France the partible inheritance was the norm and equal legal rights of partible inheritance no doubt through participation in trade: D. Bitton, *The French Nobility in Crisis, 1560–1640* (Stanford, Ca., 1969). G. Huppert, *Les Bourgeois gentilshommes; an Essay on the Definition of Elites in Renaissance France* (Chicago, Ill., 1977). A Devyver, *Le Sang épuré; les Préjugés de Race chez les Gentilshommes français de l'Ancien Régime, 1560–1720* (Brussels, 1973). The late J. P. Cooper argued that 'the existence of customs and legal rights of partible inheritance are not necessarily reliable evidence of what families actually did' in France, but more evidence is needed: Cooper, 'Patterns of inheritance and settlement by great landowners from the 15th to the 18th centuries', *Family and inheritance . . .*, ed. J. Goody, J. Thirsk and E. P. Thompson (Cambridge, 1976), p. 254.

[50] The edict of January 1645 confirming the noble privileges enjoyed by members of the *Chambre des Comptes* of Paris distinguished 'nobles d'extraction et par leur naissance' from those ennobled through the tenure of office: *Chambre des Comptes*, ed. Boislisle, p. 417.

[51] Madame de Motteville commented on the *Parlement* of Paris that 'cette compagnie est toujours opposée aux États à cause qu'ils offusquent son pouvoir et que le mot de tiers état ne lui plaît pas . . .': Motteville, *Mémoires*, ed. J. M. Michaud and J. J. F. Poujoulat, 2nd. ser., x (1838), p. 390.

[52] Moote, *The revolt of the judges*, p. 219, talks of 'the estrangement between robe and sword' in March 1649. However, because of noble clientage this break was not as clear-cut as Moote suggests.

[53] Though there clearly was a degree of temporary social displacement at Bordeaux following the seizure of power by the *Ormée*: Westrich, *op cit.*, pp. 96–116.

The French monarchy was in a much stronger position to fight a civil war to a successful conclusion than its English counterpart, for reasons which were basically those which had enabled it to fight its foreign wars more successfully. The kings of France had superior financial resources, even taking into account the reduction in taxes ordered in 1648. There was a permanent standing army which if necessary could live off the land and become self-financing during the Fronde. Even in the crisis year of 1652, the crown was able to borrow money because of the expectation among the public at large, and among the financiers in particular, that the conflict would result ultimately in a royalist victory. In 1651–2 the provincial *intendants* were gradually reintroduced under the guise of *intendants* of the army serving with the troops in the provinces: these officials were given financial powers which extended beyond the army and encompassed the province in which the troops were operating.[54] Legislation in France had always been an essential aspect of the king's sovereignty: what most struck English observers of the Estates-General was that it lacked legislative power, possessing only the right to submit petitions which the king might 'approve, disallow or mitigate' at his pleasure.[55] It is clear that the proposals emanating from the *Chambre Saint-Louis* in 1648 lacked even the authority of the *cahiers* of an Estates-General and were no more than an interim statement of grievances. Preliminary petitions were drawn up in some localities in 1649 and again in 1651,[56] but the final *cahiers* were never established since the Estates-General did not actually meet. It is not surprising, therefore, that the legislative achievement of the Fronde was slight. The crown made certain concessions in 1648 which were not fully implemented and were in the end withdrawn after the collapse of the Fronde.

Parliament in England was both a forum for making complaints and a place where complaints were remedied by legislation. In the absence of the Estates-General, the French clergy met from time to time in their own assembly.[57] The French nobility did not enjoy a regularized right of assembly, although they did meet on their own initiative during the Fronde.[58] There was no single French institution, however, which could claim, as did parliament in England, to be the 'representative of the people'.[59] The

---

[54] Bonney, *Political Change in France under Richelieu and Mazarin*, pp. 63–4, 153–4, 279–80.

[55] Russell, *Parliaments and English Politics*, p. 56 n. 2.

[56] Two of these petitions are printed in *Problèmes de Stratification sociale; Deux Cahiers de la Noblesse pour les États Généraux de 1649–1651*, ed. R. É. Mousnier, J. P. Labatut, Y. Durand (1965).

[57] P. Blet, *Le Clergé de France et la Monarchie. Étude sur les Assemblées générales du Clergé de 1615 à 1666* (2 vols., Rome, 1959). L. Cans, 'Le rôle politique de l'assemblée du clergé pendant la Fronde (1650–1)', *Revue Historique*, cxiv (1913), 1–60.

[58] J. D. Lassaigne, *Les Assemblées de la Noblesse de France au xviie et xviiie siècles* (1965–6).

[59] D. M. Hirst, *The Representative of the People? Voters and Voting in England under the early Stuarts* (Cambridge, 1975).

failure of the Estates-General[60] left a power vacuum which could not be filled by the sovereign tribunals. There were three reasons for this. The competence of each tribunal was restricted by its rivals: the *Parlements* claimed an authority over financial questions denied by the *cours des aides* and *chambres des comptes*. None could lay claim to the totality of jurisdiction, let alone untrammelled legislative sovereignty. In normal circumstances, they did not legislate on their own initiative but simply amended legislation drawn up by the government which had been passed on to them for registration. A second reason why the sovereign tribunals could not fill the vacuum left by the Estates-General is that they represented none but office-holders who had gained entry into their respective courts through purchase. From the outset of the Fronde in 1648, there was no broad consensus in France about the measures to be taken to deal with the crisis, because the definition of the crisis was made from a narrowly sectional viewpoint. The *Parlement* of Paris made some attempt to overcome its own limitations;[61] but the standing of the office-holders in the community could not be tested objectively, and the attitude of landowners as a whole was a matter of mere speculation.

A third reason why the sovereign tribunals could not fill the vacuum left by the failure of the Estates-General is that each tribunal had a clearly defined *ressort* or geographical area. With the exception of the *grand conseil,* whose competence was limited, none extended throughout the kingdom. Although the *Parlement* of Paris was the most important lawcourt in the land, its jurisdiction extended over less than half of France. The decision of kings in the fifteenth and early sixteenth centuries to establish regional *Parlements*[62] — a trend followed with regard to the *cours des aides* and *chambres des comptes* rather later and to a lesser extent — is of crucial importance to the structure of local government in the seventeenth century. This limitation of a tribunal's geographical area is quite different from the situation in England, where the writ of parliament ran throughout the realm at least in periods of civil peace. Thus measures taken by the Long Parliament applied to the whole of England and when in 1648–9 a determined group seized control of the Commons and expelled its opponents, it could carry through a revolutionary course of action which affected the entire realm. 1649 in England was a political *coup* at the centre, a defeat

[60] This does not necessarily imply an adverse judgement on the Estates-General of 1614–15, though as Richelieu later commented it was not enough to know all the abuses of the system if one lacked the will to remedy them: *Mémoires du Cardinal de Richelieu*, ed. R. Lavollée *et al.* (10 vols., 1907–31), i. 368. J. M. Hayden, *France and the Estates-General of 1614* (Cambridge, 1974), p. 165. The Estates-General had nevertheless failed to vote taxes, or to insist on the redress of grievances before supply, although these failures were already apparent in the fifteenth century. The crown thus had no need to summon the Estates-General.

[61] A classic example of the sectional viewpoint is the fate of the original proposal at the *Chambre Saint-Louis* for a French version of *habeas corpus*. This was rapidly toned down, however, to freedom for office-holders from arbitrary arrest: Moote, *The Revolt of the Judges*, pp. 162–3; Talon, *Mémoires*, ed. Michaud and Poujoulat, pp. 244 note (proposal of 17 July 1648), 296 (article 15 of royal declaration of 22 Oct. 1648; this clause was not amended by the office-holders).

[62] Regional *Parlements* were established at the following dates: Toulouse (1443); Grenoble (1453); Bordeaux (1462); Dijon (incorporated into the kingdom of France in 1477); Rouen (1499); Aix (1501); Rennes (1553): cf. A. N. E 57, fo. 365, 3 Dec. 1617. Pau was added in 1620 and Metz in 1633. Louis XIV later added to the number.

for localism. The majority of those who had fought for Charles I perhaps did so more in reaction against parliament and central control than positively for the king.[63] The Commonwealth and Protectorate never succeeded in re-establishing firm ties of loyalty with the localities. When a local *Parlement* took to arms during the Fronde, the outcome of the struggle did not necessarily affect those parts of France outside the *ressort* of the tribunal. There were really four separate conflicts in 1649 based on the *Parlements* of Paris, Rouen, Aix and Bordeaux. Each was quite different in character. Events in one area proceeded at a different pace from the others. The settlements were also quite different. The crown was always likely to win the struggle with any one tribunal in France. Without joint resistance by several *Parlements,* which was not in fact achieved during the Fronde, it was always likely that regionalism would aid an eventual royalist victory. The government sought to exploit the regional and social differences of France in order to defeat the Fronde and by October 1652 it had largely succeeded in its aim.

---

[63] D. E. Underdown, *Pride's Purge: Politics during the Puritan Revolution* (Oxford, 1971), pp. 146–50. Morrill, *The Revolt of the Provinces*, p. 126.

VI

Cardinal Mazarin and his Critics: The Remonstrances of 1652

Few politicians in French history have aroused such intense opposition, personal and political, as Cardinal Jules Mazarin, chief minister of Louis XIV from 1643 to 1661. He was the only chief minister of the Bourbon kings with the dubious claim to have been exiled twice and *officially*[1] dismissed from office once. These events occurred in the great political upheaval of the Fronde between 1648 and 1652, during the later years of which Mazarin lived under threat of assassination.[2] Unlike Richelieu, his predecessor, his name became so notorious that for a time it entered the French language, as a verb—*se mazariner*,[3] to work for the victory of the chief minister over his enemies—and as more than one noun: a *mazarin*[4] was a supporter of the chief minister; *mazarinisme*[5] was the term used to describe his system of government, and the *mazarinades* were the scurrilous political pamphlets written to destroy his reputation. There can be little doubt that although in origin the political crisis was about other, wider issues, gradually the Fronde developed into a struggle for power. Once this had happened, personal criticism of Mazarin came to the fore so that by 1652 it may be said that opposition to his continuance in office was one of the few common bonds linking together a very diverse and ill-organized group of opponents to the regime. It is therefore worth examining the reasons why Mazarin was so unpopular and assessing whether the arguments and charges levelled against him were spurious or otherwise: for on this verdict rests not only his historical reputation but also our understanding of the Fronde itself, and the aims and aspirations of its participants.

Nearly 5000 political pamphlets were written during the Fronde. A few of these were written in support of the regime, and were paid for by the chief minister or his supporters, but the majority were distinctly hostile—so much so that even the *Parlement* of Paris (which was not noted for its support of the government during the Fronde) considered taking action against the authors and printers.[6] However, censorship failed during the Fronde. There were too many printing presses in Paris to police effectively (176 in 1644,[7] perhaps more by 1649–52) and they found a ready market not only among the Parisian poor—who could afford to buy the pamphlets since they were relatively cheap[8]—but also among the upper classes, who collected them avidly.[9] Strong-arm measures against the printers tended to backfire: at the attempted execution in July 1649 of Morlot, the printer of *La Custode du lit de la Reine*—a broadsheet which had speculated on the nature of the relationship between Anne of Austria and Mazarin—there was a riot and the printer escaped.[10] Nevertheless, although censorship was not particularly effective, common prudence dictated that authorship of the most controversial *mazarinades* remained in doubt. The activities of Dubosc-Montandré as Condé's polemicist are well known;[11] Claude Joly did not conceal that he had written the attack on Mazarin's *fausse et pernicieuse politique*;[12] but they were exceptions. The famous *Requête des trois Etats* of 1648,[13] which anticipated most of the later attacks on Mazarin, remains anonymous, and this anonymity is a serious obstacle to the historian. Contemporaries were in no doubt that there were great differences in the quality of the *mazarinades*. As early as 23 February, 1649, Guy Patin remarked on "cette effroyable quantité de libelles" but thought only one-third of sufficient quality to have been worth printing at all.[14] Cardinal de Retz, in a characteristic half-truth, observed that "il y a plus de soixante volumes de pièces composées dans le cours de la guerre civile ... Il n'y a pas cent feuillets qui méritent que l'on les lise."[15] Yet if a certain number of *mazarinades* are given prominence over the others, the questions of authorship and of the sections of opinion represented by the author, become crucial. Contemporaries recognized the difficulty: one could say that someone had *not* written one of the clever *mazarinades*—"n'étant pas assez habile homme pour cela"[16]—but it was much more difficult to prove authenticity if the author wanted to preserve the cloak of anonymity. The historian cannot state with confidence whose views were represented, say by the *Requête des trois Etats*, and whether the pamphleteer's claim to voice the opinion of thirteen provinces was anything more than literary flourish.

Thus the *mazarinades*, while they undoubtedly attest to the unpopularity of Mazarin and voice many of the different criticisms levelled against him, are inconclusive on the key issues to the historian, namely which criticisms were considered most important and by whom.[17] The remonstrances of the *Parlement* of Paris, the leading law-court in the land, are of a different standing. Those of 21 January, 1649,[18] contained one of the earliest direct attacks on Mazarin, which anticipated later criticisms. Yet in a sense these remonstrances were unrepresentative of opinion in that court, since they were the product of a crisis—the order sent by the government for the *Parlement* to leave Paris and the threatened blockade of the capital after it had refused to comply. In March, 1649, the *parlementaires* were prepared to allow Mazarin to participate in the peace negotiations at Rueil and when peace was signed they submitted once more to his authority as chief minister. The remonstrances of 23 March 1652,[19] which have largely escaped the attention of previous historians, [20] are not so obviously a *pièce de circonstance*. Unlike 1649, the crisis had arisen not three weeks but three months previously, with Mazarin's return from exile at the head of a force of 6000 German mercenaries. The *Parlement* had responded to the crisis on 29 December, 1651, by declaring Mazarin guilty of *lèse-majesté* and placing a price on his head—a decision that has been called "the most partisan and intemperate *arrêt* of the entire Fronde".[21] By March, 1652, the *Parlement* had had time to reflect on the wisdom of its earlier decision, which it claimed was justified by a previous royal declaration issued on 6 September, 1651, sanctioning Mazarin's exile. Yet most commentators agree that the *Parlement* had not yet fallen under the sway of the princes as it was to do in the summer of 1652: and alliance with Gaston and Condé, which had to be conceded in effect on 20 July, had been rejected on 25 January.[22] The *Parlement's* attitude to Mazarin in March, 1652, is all the more interesting, therefore, since it appeared to be neutral, occupying the middle ground while it lasted. The attitude of the court was personified by Omer Talon, its famous *avocat-général*. There was no fiercer critic of the regime than Talon, whose celebrated speech of 15 January, 1648, was regarded by some hardline supporters of Mazarin as the true origin of the Fronde.[23] Yet there was no member of the court more independent and more alarmed by the activities of the princes than Talon.[24] It is therefore of particular importance that he acted as a severe critic of the chief minister in March, 1652, at exactly the time when the remonstrances were being drawn up,[25] for the remonstrances show that the majority in the *Parlement* blamed Mazarin for the civil war and argued that the actions of the princes in opposing him were legitimate, if unfortunate for France. Thus the arguments contained in the remonstrances of 23 March are worth examination, not least because of the gravity of the charges levelled against Mazarin, and the role of the *Parlement* in challenging the position of the chief minister. Their status as a *pièce authentique* as against the amorphous mass of *mazarinades* was recognized at the time, and particularly by Gabriel Naudé, Mazarin's famous librarian and pamphleteer. On 8 April, Naudé advised the chief minister that a careful reply should be formulated, meeting each specific criticism by the *Parlement*. "L'avantage que Vostre Emin[ence] en pourroit tirer ne seroit pas moins grand que si elle avoit gaigné une bataille . . .", he wrote.[26] Since many of the counter-arguments survive in draft form among Mazarin's papers, for the first time both sides of the debate in 1652 may be perceived.

The remonstrances of 23 March, 1652, justified the earlier royal and *parlementaire* decisions of September and December, 1651, the first as a voluntary and irreversible act of the crown, the second as a necessary decision taken in the emergency of a foreign invasion. Mazarin, of course, accepted neither decision. He had bitterly resented the royal declaration of 6 September, 1651, sanctioning his exile,[27] even though it had been drafted in fairly bland terms. Once Mazarin returned to France he had it explained officially that the measure had been conceded by the Regent to prevent any attempt to postpone the king's majority.[28] The ministers were divided on what to do about the decree of 29 December, 1651, but Anne of Austria, Châteauneuf and Villeroy were set on having it annulled, and the Queen Mother had her way on 18 January, 1652.[29] The *Parlement* had ordered the sale of Mazarin's great library to pay the price they had placed on his head: the Cardinal, a man of culture, could not understand the depths of hostility that had led to such an extraordinary act of vandalism, and had the sale declared illegal by the same royal decree.[30] For their part, the *parlementaires* found it difficult to accept Anne of Austria's duplicity in publicly exiling her chief minister yet secretly requesting his recall. They thus contended that Mazarin's sudden arrival at the head of a force of mercenaries must have been a consequence of his "despair" at remaining in exile, and that he had a direct interest in the continuation of civil war in France. Indeed, they concluded that it was Mazarin who had prevented domestic peace and the ending of war with Spain (a view also put forward by the nobles[31]) and thus reasoned that his dismissal was imperative. Broadly speaking, they formulated seven areas of criticism of Mazarin, covering his personality, the nature of his power, his financial, patronage and foreign policies, the military conduct of the war against Spain, and finally his role in the origins and course of the Fronde.

Mazarin, it was claimed, was unworthy of holding ministerial office in France since he was an inveterate liar who wanted to "establir la perfidie par des maximes abominables". What were these maxims, which if allowed free rein would have destroyed the bonds of civil society? The remonstrances were not explicit on this point, but from the general tenor of the document, and the fact that its author was Mathieu de Morgues,[32] it may be gauged that the maxims were those of Machiavelli. In *The Prince*, Machiavelli had argued that "contemporary experience shows that princes who have achieved great things have been those who have given their word lightly"; conversely, the remonstrances declared that "un prince sans foy ne règne plus" and denounced the general tendency of royal favourites to encourage duplicity in their masters. More damaging still, certain statements of Mazarin were quoted against him, and above all the claim, made in letters of 23 December, 1651, to Louis XIV and Anne of Austria, that he would not seek to regain high office in France.[33] Of course, diatribes against the influence of Machiavelli had been commonplace at the time of Richelieu, of whom it had been said that he kept his breviary and his copy of *The Prince* on the same table.[34] Yet there were obvious reasons why the charge of Machiavellianism would tend to stick to Mazarin rather than his predecessor: by birth he was Giulio Mazarini, and by definition Italians were born under the influence of the great sixteenth-century political theorist.[35] Linked to geography was the question of Mazarin's social origins. To Guy Patin, he was "le bourgeois de Trinacrie" in Sicily,[36] and both the *Requête des trois Etats*[37] and the remonstrances accepted the myth of Mazarin's humble Sicilian origins. To be Italian was bad enough: to be Sicilian was worse. Had not the "Sicilian Vespers" (30 March, 1282) been a massacre of Frenchmen? Fear of a comparable act of vengeance by the chief minister was voiced,[38] although particularly unfair to Mazarin: by comparison with Richelieu, he was a paragon of moderation; others accused him of timidity and irresolution.[39] It is true that his uncle (or great-uncle), Giulio Mazarini (1544–1621), a Jesuit, had been born at Palermo: but Giulio II was born at the abbey of Pescina in the Abruzzi, the son of Pietro Mazarini (1576–1654), a client of the powerful Colonna family and a papal administrator.[40] Mazarin had entered papal service, too, and since he did not decide to switch masters until 1639, it could be objected that he was ignorant of French customs and laws.[41] Nevertheless, he was a Cardinal of the Church, appointed on 16 December, 1641, as a result of political pressure by Richelieu on Pope Urban VIII.[42] He was a naturalized Frenchman as well as a French Cardinal,[43] and in 1652 at the very time when the remonstrances were being debated, François de Harlay-Chanvalon, Archbishop of Rouen, led a deputation of the French clergy to protest against the attitude of the *Parlement*.[44] The attack on Mazarin was seen as an attack on the privileges of the French clergy in general—and this was a great source of strength to the chief minister in the dark days of 1652.

Mazarin was considered by his critics to be unfit to hold office in France: but should his particular office exist at all? The remonstrances of 1649 had focused criticism on the *ministériat* and had made "the strongest official statement on this subject"[45] during the Fronde, to the point of declaring the position of chief minister illegal. Those of 1652 did not go so far, but warned the king that Mazarin wanted to "se rendre maistre de vostre estat en s'emparant de vostre personne", and castigated his assumption of the title of *Surintendant de l'éducation du Roi*, "une qualité innouye en France". Here in essence was the doctrine of the king's evil counsellor, holding the king in captivity, which became the official theory of resistance on 20 July, 1652.[46] It had a certain validity in that Mazarin had arrived at Poitiers with a force of German mercenaries: but then his presence had been requested by Anne of Austria, the Queen Mother, to tilt the military balance against Condé, who was in rebellion.[47] When both sides in a conflict declared that they fought for the king, who had the better claim?

In 1649 it had been argued that the legitimate party was the one comprising the person of the king, the Regent and the first princes of the blood.[48] By January, 1652, however, Gaston and Condé had broken with Anne of Austria, declaring that Mazarin had always "gouverné en effet quoyqu'il fust banny en apparence ..." and that they could have no security while he was "maistre des affaires".[49] In the meantime, on 7 September, 1651, Louis XIV's majority had been proclaimed in the *Parlement* of Paris. Had Mazarin the same need of the "union of the royal family" which had existed in the first half of 1649? In theory, the king had entered his *plenitudo potestatis:* if he declared Mazarin to be his chief minister and under the royal safeguard,[50] then unless the declaration of majority itself was contested, Mazarin was always likely to survive and his opponents be declared guilty of *lèse-majesté*.[51] The critics of Mazarin had delayed their attack too long; the arguments contained in the remonstrances "ran counter to the will of a fully empowered king rather than a mere regent".[52] If the *Parlement* persisted, then this would be tantamount to its seizing the initiative in ministerial appointments: "... sommes-nous en quelque république, et le roy n'est-il plus que nostre doge?", asked one of the pamphlets of 1652.[53]

Apart from the practical difficulties in ousting Mazarin from power, there were a number of arguments in the Cardinal's favour on which the remonstrances were silent. The title of *Surintendant de l'éducation du Roi* had been granted by Anne of Austria in 1645 while Regent—but no-one could deny that in his lifetime Louis XIII had singled out Mazarin for special favour, and marked him out to play a key role in the upbringing of his son. Mazarin was Louis XIV's godfather at his baptism on 21 April, 1643.[54] Moreover, it was Louis XIII who had summoned Mazarin to enter the King's Council on 5 December, 1642, after the death of Richelieu, and who had confirmed his position in the regency council to be set up after his own death.[55] (It should be noted that Louis XIII envisaged no changes to the council except through forfeiture—that is to say, if a member committed treason—or died in office.[56]) He had not appointed Mazarin as his chief minister, it is true: but the action of the *Parlement* of Paris, on 18 May, 1643, in annulling the section of the king's testament which limited the Regent's powers, had made Mazarin's elevation virtually inevitable. The dying king may well have asked his wife to ensure Mazarin's continuance in office as the "plus sûr garant de l'autorité de son fils" during the royal minority.[57]

The remonstrances of 1652 objected not just to the nature of Mazarin's power, but the uses to which it was put, and especially to his financial policy. Mazarin, it was contended, had created a personal fortune on the back of the French tax-payer. He had become reliant on the financiers, "ses tributaires", who charged excessively high rates of interest for their services, and who had made such gains during his ministry that they were "les plus ardentz solliciteurs du retour de leur protecteur". Mazarin, it was alleged, was guilty of peculation on an enormous scale and there was a pressing need to examine the accounts of Thomas Cantarini who had handled some 36 million *livres* destined to pay for the war in Italy. Moreover, Mazarin's financial policy had not worked. The chief minister had not paid sufficient attention to the maxim that "les finances . . . sont les nerfz de la guerre" without which the army could not be paid nor the war continued: a royal bankruptcy, a repeat of 1648, could happen again. Already, the funds which should have been allocated to the payment of *rentes*, a principal investment for poor and rich alike, had been diverted, and the great fear was that the army would be forced to live off the land: "vos provinces seroient exposées à la licence des soldatz, qui les ont traitez depuis trois ans avec toute sorte d'hostilitez et de barbarie." The remonstrances thus followed the *Requête des trois Etats*[58] and other *Mazarinades* in castigating Mazarin's financial policy. Even supporters of the chief minister conceded the need for "un peu de modération et d'oeconomie dans l'administra[ti]on des finances" and admitted that the sins of successive finance ministers had come to rest on Mazarin himself.[59]

When Mazarin died in 1661, he left an enormous personal fortune of some 37 million *livres*: but in 1652 his personal fortune, created in his earlier years as chief minister, was threatened. He had undoubtedly lent the crown considerable sums of money during the Fronde,[60] yet once he had departed in exile to Brühl in 1651, the income from his benefices had been stopped and the *syndicat* of his creditors had obtained the backing of Pierre Broussel and the *Parlement* of Paris.[61] Effectively, Mazarin was bankrupt: it needed all the industry of Colbert, his *intendant de la maison*, the appointment of La Vieuville, a finance minister who was favourably disposed towards the Cardinal, and Mazarin's return from exile to sort out his personal affairs. Nevertheless, if the remonstrances were incorrect in detail, they were sound on the substantial issue: once Mazarin had secured his political position, he would regain his personal fortune. Apart from the fact that Italian banking associates such as Cantarini and Serantoni claimed to be Mazarin's creditors in 1651-52,[62] it seems doubtful whether the charge of peculation could ever have been proven against the chief minister. It would have been very difficult to elucidate the issues in the financial chaos of the Fronde;[63] besides, while Mazarin continued to enjoy royal favour he had nothing to fear from a financial enquiry— ultimately all monies which he had received could be said to have been voluntary gifts from the king to his most loyal servant. The remonstrances were probably correct in asserting that Mazarin's financial policy was over-optimistic and failed to pay sufficient attention to the danger of bankruptcy. The massive anticipation of revenues in 1645 could not easily be repeated. What would happen if the war continued after 1648, as it did against Spain? Moreover, borrowing on the scale undertaken by Mazarin and d'Hémery certainly forced up the interest rates charged by the financiers for their services. The argument in the remonstrances that the financiers were committed to a restoration of Mazarin in 1651-52 was true. At the end of the Fronde, the financiers recalled how they had "travaillé pour le retour de celuy qui a sauvé la France",[64] and this policy was hardly surprising in view of the hostility shown towards them by the critics of the regime. Indeed, there were common interests shared by Mazarin and the financiers in the later stages of the Fronde. Mazarin wanted the appointment of La Vieuville, because the former had received a *pot de vin* of 400,000 *livres*[65] and the new *surintendant* would work towards paying off Mazarin's debts. The financiers, led by Jean Doublet, wanted La Vieuville as the man to restore financial confidence and settle the royal debts outstanding from the bankruptcy of 1648.[66] The coincidence of interests became complete when, as the financiers recalled, Mazarin wrote to La Vieuville from Brühl advocating the repayment of principal to the financiers or at least current interest on outstanding royal debts.[67]

If the conduct of financial policy was a source of contention, the uses to which the money raised was put—namely patronage—also met with opposition. The remonstrances attacked Mazarin's control of patronage, his poor choice of recipients and the partisan nature of his appointments. Omer Talon made a rather different criticism,[68] but recognized that the situation facing the Regency government in 1643 had been peculiarly difficult. Richelieu had "élevé sa fortune sur la ruine de tous ceux qui l'ont attaqué", thought Talon, but at the end of Louis XIII's reign the exiles had returned and demanded compensation for their rough treatment. Money alone could not settle the disputes between the recent appointees and the proscribed, and serious disagreements between the factions remained which came to the fore in the Fronde.[69] It is difficult to see how Mazarin could have handled the situation much better; but the crucial error was to channel so much patronage to Condé, whose demands became exorbitant in the second half of 1649. Moreover, there were fundamental issues between Mazarin and rebellious magnates such as Condé and Harcourt during the Fronde. The nobles wanted to determine appointments to the provincial governorships for themselves, regardless of the strategic implications, and to secure control of the fortresses within their governorships, which ministers since the time of Henri IV had tried to wrest from their grasp.[70] Criticism of Mazarin's patronage system was inevitable, and followed from his position as chief minister: "c'est la querelle qui de tout temps a esté faitte aux favoris", it was argued in 1652, " ... parce qu'ils sont les canaux par lesquels les Roys font découler leurs grâces ...".[71] It could also be argued that there would have been no collapse of control over the patronage system, and no political intervention by the magnates, but for the bankruptcy of 1648 and the resulting power vacuum. For money kept the wheels of patronage turning, although by 1651 it appeared that the system built up by Mazarin might be turned against its master and prevent his return from exile.[72] Increasingly, the chief minister had to rely on a restricted group of his most loyal followers, men such as himself who in the dark days of the Fronde had not been prepared to come to private agreements with the King of Spain.[73] Only once the struggle between the crown and the princes had been resolved in 1652 could the patronage system be rebuilt and extended.

The remonstrances of 1652 came out strongly against Mazarin's foreign policy, although strictly speaking this area was outside the competence of the *Parlement* of Paris. Mazarin, it was argued, had lost the opportunity to conclude a favourable peace with Spain at the Westphalian peace negotiations, a charge which stuck during the Fronde and was one of the underlying causes of the civil war.[74] In 1651, during his exile at Brühl, Mazarin wrote a long memorandum to Brienne justifying his foreign policy. He contended that the Spanish had acted in bad faith at Münster, seeking to split the allies by making a separate peace with the Dutch in order to continue the war against France. As an example of Spanish malevolence, Mazarin pointed to their attempt to block peace between France and the Emperor, which was signed on 24 October, 1648. Mazarin claimed that he was merely continuing the foreign policy of Louis XIII and Richelieu, a task imposed on the Regency government by the testament of the late king. He said he was prepared to allow publication of the diplomatic correspondence to prove that he had not indulged in secret diplomacy to prevent peace, and indeed paid Jean de Silhon, his propagandist, to write a pamphlet on the subject.[75] He also said he was prepared to stand trial to clear the charge of delaying or preventing peace with Spain, a fate which the continuation of royal favour meant he never had to endure. It is true that the Regency government had had to show caution in its dealings with the Habsburgs: Anne of Austria was the sister of Philip IV of Spain and Mazarin was a foreigner by birth. For these reasons, it would have been political suicide to sign a peace with Spain that could later be criticized as detrimental to French interests.[76] The acid test of Spanish intentions was the negotiations in 1651, when Mazarin—the alleged cause of the previous breakdown—was safely in exile. Had the Spanish really been acting in good faith, presumably they could have come to a speedy arrangement with the reconstituted French government. However, before the Spanish were prepared to sit down to serious negotiations they insisted on the return of Lorraine to Duke Charles IV, Catalonia to Philip IV and the halting of French assistance to Portugal,[77] thus justifying Lionne's doubts the previous year about "la qualité de cette paix forcée".[78] Philip IV was not interested in a just peace, only one that was favourable to Spanish interests; accordingly some credence must be lent to Mazarin's view that the Spanish had broken off negotiations at Münster in the expectation that disappointed hopes of peace would lead to civil disorder in France.

It was not just the broad outlines of foreign policy which were criticized by the remonstrances of 1652. The whole conduct of the war was also attacked, and Mazarin was accused of assuming "tout seul la direction de la guerre" but frittering away the conquests of Louis XIII and the victories of Gaston and Condé in the early years of the Regency. There was particular criticism of the opening of the Italian front, where it was claimed that instead of pursuing French interests Mazarin had sought to establish an Italian fief for himself as place of exile if he were ousted from power in France. However, Mazarin's reluctance to go to Italy in 1651, even with the title of *Surintendant des affaires en Italie*,[79] belies the ambition of an independent fief. The general point, that Mazarin sought overall direction of the war effort, both at home and abroad, is substantially true. In December, 1651, he had to be discouraged from marching straight at the army of the princes,[80] and in the autumn of the following year it was Mazarin who won the prestige of having chased the Spanish beyond the French border,[81] and having reduced Condé, the most dangerous of his opponents, to the status of a Spanish generalissimo.[82] The charge that Mazarin had frittered away the hard-won gains of Louis XIII, Gaston and Condé, is more dubious. In the heady days after the great victory of Rocroi in 1643, total defeat of the Habsburgs must have seemed possible; but the deterioration of the French position after 1646 balanced the scales again, the war being essentially a struggle of resources with neither side able to drive home a short-term advantage on the battlefield. The Spanish hoped to profit from the weakness of France in order to complete the reconquest of Catalonia: by 1652, not only had this been achieved, but conquests in Italy and the Low Countries had also been made. The *Parlement* of Paris tried to have the best of both worlds: it prevented the registration of new fiscal edicts to pay for the war, yet criticized the government when it was unable to mobilize the army, and thus defend its conquests, because of a shortage of funds. The surprizing fact is not that there were strategic losses during the Fronde, but that Spain was so weak as to be unable to exploit further the breakdown in France.

The final criticism of Mazarin in the remonstrances of 1652 centred on his role in the origins and course of the Fronde. Mazarin's evil hand, it was alleged, was to be seen behind almost every unpopular or unsuccessful decision of the Regency government. He had ordered the arrest of the duc de Beaufort, one of the conspirators in the *Cabale des Importants* in 1643; the arrest and trial of the maréchal de La Mothe-Houdancourt, formerly Viceroy of Catalonia, in 1644–45; the arrest of Barillon, a *président* in the *Parlement* of Paris in 1645 (Barillon had died while imprisoned at Pinerolo and had consequently become the martyr of the officeholders); the attempted arrest of Broussel in 1648, which had led to the Days of the Barricades in Paris; finally, the arrest of Condé, Conti and Longueville in 1650, and subsequently their transfer to Le Havre, "lieu incommode à leur santé et dont ils pouvoient estre aisément envoyez hors du Royaume". To the oppression of individuals was added the charge that Mazarin had persecuted towns and lawcourts—particularly the capital, Paris, in 1649 when allegedly two million inhabitants (an inexcusable exaggeration when the total pre-siege population was probably less than a quarter of a million) had died from starvation during the blockade, and Bordeaux, which had been besieged in 1650. Mazarin was accused of responsibility for the breakdown of normal economic life during the civil unrest, and his alleged participation in privateering off the coast of Normandy and Brittany (in fact an English sideline) was said to have reduced 20,000 families to poverty.[83] These allegations cannot be investigated in detail without reviewing the whole origins and course of the Fronde: but it is clear that assigning responsibility for all these actions to the chief minister alone was tantamount to making Mazarin the scapegoat for all the misfortunes that had befallen the Regency government. Perhaps the regime had been somewhat accident-prone; but to link the events of 1643–51 in this way was to give a false unity, and imply an underlying tyrannical purpose, where in fact there were only a number of decisions taken separately on their merit. Such allegations against Mazarin lack any sense of balance: Beaufort would not have been arrested had he not been involved in intrigue, La Mothe had he been a more effective commander, Barillon and Broussel had they been less outspoken critics of the government. The arrest of the princes was a consequence of their intransigence, and had the blessing of Gaston, who wanted to impose conditions on their release. The blockade of Paris was a measure decided on jointly by Mazarin, Gaston and Condé, and when he went south to besiege Bordeaux in 1650, Mazarin had left Gaston in charge of the government at Paris. Chief minister of the Regent he had been: but Mazarin had not made every decision on his own. He had needed supporters, and chief among these had been Gaston and Condé, the first until late 1650, the second until mid-1649. Gaston had shown some recognition of this, and some sense of responsibility for the past, by removing all "faulcetez" concerning the sieges of Paris and Bordeaux in the declaration against Mazarin of September, 1651.[84]

Although the remonstrances of 23 March, 1652, represent the official position of the *Parlement* of *Paris* at the time, when they were first read out to the court they were received in stony silence. It is not difficult to per-

VI

ceive reasons for the hestiation of the *parlementaires:* although satisfyingly critical of Mazarin, the remonstrances were too long, too repetitive and too diffuse.[85] By broadening the scope of the attack against Mazarin, the remonstrances cast their net too wide, so that the king could declare that he found no "accusation précise contre luy", and that the remonstrances contained merely "un discours remply de passion, de hayne, de menaces, de désir de la vengeance et de [la] cruauté contre luy".[86] If necessary, the king was prepared to see Mazarin stand trial, but there had to be serious charges made against him: the remonstrances, and other investigations by the *Parlement* "ne contiennent rien sur quoy l'on puisse fonder une condamnation...".[87] If the diffuse nature of the charges levelled against Mazarin was a source of weakness, an even more serious objection to the remonstrances was that they were written in the tone of the *mazarinades.* Since the government was already predisposed to condemn the "fausses maximes que les libelles de la faction ont semées...",[88] its response to the remonstrances was therefore predictable. The *Parlement* had made a serious error in handing over the compilation of the remonstrances to Pierre Broussel, one of its most senior members and the fiercest critic of the government since 1648. Vigorous in debate, Broussel was not fluent with pen and ink, and had turned to Mathieu de Morgues for assistance. Morgues had been one of the chief propagandists against Richelieu and had followed the Queen Mother into exile in the Spanish Netherlands after 1631, where he had written many of his *dévot* pamphlets.[89] When the government learnt of the authorship of the remonstrances, it had the final weapon in its hands: the remonstrances came from the pen of a man who had sold himself to the Spanish cause,[90] and by implication it was that cause which was now being served. Despite Gaston's denial that there were Spanish troops in the army of the princes,[91] it was public knowledge that Condé had signed a treaty with Philip IV of Spain.

The government rejected the arguments contained in the remonstrances, but in order to clear his reputation permanently, Mazarin had to defeat the Fronde. The reasons why he won are complex, but three factors working in his favour are worth recalling. He never lost the favour of Anne of Austria (who while no longer Regent still exercised the decisive influence over Louis XIV),[92] and Mazarin had convinced Anne of the parallel between his own cause and that of Strafford in England. Once Charles I had sacrificed Strafford, the monarchy itself did not long survive.[93] Concessions could not be made to the opposition, because this merely served to encourage faction. The crown must retain its prerogative of choosing and dismissing ministers at will,[94] and this was the crucial issue regardless of the qualities—or faults—of the chief minister. The argument contained a certain internal logic, and since Anne of Austria wanted to retain Mazarin, she convinced the young Louis XIV of the need for stability. A second factor easing Mazarin's continuance in power was the basic weakness of the *Parlement* of Paris by the summer of 1652. Coerced by the princes on 20 July, the *parlementaires* saw Mazarin retaliate by establishing a rival court at Pontoise on 31 July. This "grand coup de partye" recalled the creation of Navarrist *parlements* by Henri IV in his struggle against the Catholic League, and the *parlementaires* were inclined to view Mazarin as a lesser evil than the princes provided that the rival court at Pontoise was abolished.[95] A third factor working in Mazarin's favour was the collapse of opposition during his second exile after August 1652. There were a number of reasons for this collapse—disagreements among the princes, the deterioration of their military position and war-weariness among the population at large being some of the most important. Above all, however, time worked on Mazarin's side: after a respectable absence from France, his return to Paris could be orchestrated by the ministers and "doucement insinué dans les espritz . . .".[96] Like all successful politicians, Mazarin was lucky. Two of his more credible rivals for the position of chief minister—Chavigny and Châteauneuf—died in 1652–53.[97] A third, the notorious Cardinal de Retz, was arrested after elaborate precautions and planning;[98] although he escaped in 1654, he was forced to remain in exile. Mazarin thus emerged victorious over the Fronde, his critics were dismissed as "republicans", and his innocence declared proven for all time. Strong government brought a return of censorship; the great flood of *mazarinades* was reduced to a harmless trickle. The remonstrances of 23 March, 1652, were forgotten—except, perhaps, by Cardinal Mazarin himself who, on his death-bed, advised Louis XIV to honour the magistrates but "les obliger de se tenir dans les bornes de leur devoir . . .".[99]

REFERENCES

N.B.: All printed works in French are published in Paris unless otherwise stated.

1. He was never dismissed in the sense of losing the confidence of Anne of Austria, the Queen Mother and Regent (1643–51). For the status of the royal declaration of 6 September 1651, endorsing his first exile, see below.
2. *Cf.* A[rchives des] A[ffaires] É[trangères, Mémoires et Documents,] France 881, f70v, 11 Jan. 1652. Mazarin had been allowed a company of guards for his personal security since 25 Feb. 1648: A.A.E. France 860, f40.
3. A.A.E. France 882, f168v, 5 Apr. 1652: "on se mazarine aussy bien fort. . . ."
4. A.A.E. France 879, f190, 23 Dec. 1651. Mazarin wrote to Louis XIV: "il est vray, Sire, que je ne puis pas nier que tous mes amys et ceux qui . . . m'accompagnent ne soient mazarins, et ne portent avec plaisir un nom qu'on a travaillé à rendre si odieux. . . ."
5. *Lettres, instructions et mémoires de Colbert* . . . , ed. by P. Clément (10 vols, 1861–82), i, 158: "[les Frondeurs] sont plus sur leurs gardes et prennent plus de précautions que jamais contre le mazarinisme."
6. A[rchives] N[ationales] X1b 8856, no. 51, 18 May 1649; X1b 8856, no. 2, 29 Jan. 1650.

VI

7. M.N. Grand-Mesnil, *Mazarin, la Fronde et la presse, 1647–9* (1967), 299.
8. *Ibid.*, 184–5.
9. Guy Patin commented that censorship would not be effective while the printers, *colporteurs* and *crieurs de gazettes* "trouveront des gens curieux de toutes ces nouveautés": Guy Patin, *Lettres au temps de la Fronde*, ed. by A. Thérive (1921), 74.
10. *Ibid.*, 123. A.A.E. France 865, f333, 27 July 1649.
11. *Œuvres de Retz*, ed. by A. Feillet *et al.* (10 vols, 1870–96), iii, 327–8. E. H. Kossmann, *La Fronde* (Leiden, 1954), 100–1, 108–10, 218.
12. C. Joly, *Recueil des maximes véritables et importantes pour l'institution du roy contre la fausse et pernicieuse politique du Cardinal Mazarin* (1st ed., 1652). *Cf.* A.A.E. France 886, f18v, 18 Nov. 1652: Le Tellier warned Mazarin that this book "n'est rien du tout qui vaille". Of course, the *Recueil* was no ordinary *mazarinade*: the first edition contains 512 pages, and Joly attempted to define a political doctrine of opposition.
13. *Choix de Mazarinades*, ed. by C. Moreau (3 vols, 1853), i, 28–34. Omer Talon, *Mémoires*, ed. by J. F. Michaud and J. J. F. Poujoulat (3rd ser., vi, 1839), 316–18.
14. Patin, *op. cit.* (ref. 9), 74.
15. *Œuvres de Retz*, ed. by Feillet *et al.*, iii, 334.
16. Patin, *op. cit.*, 100, with reference to Bertrand Bautru.
17. Thus they are inconclusive for different reasons than those suggested by Doolin, who thought them "of no direct value ... consisting of invectives against Mazarin" and lacking a consistent constitutional standpoint: P. R. Doolin, *The Fronde* (Cambridge, Mass., 1935), 152.
18. Talon, *Mémoires*, ed. by Michaud and Poujoulat, 323–8. B[ibliothèque] N[ationale] Ms. fr. 3854, ff 20–32. Commentary by Doolin, *op. cit.*, 73–77.
19. A. A. E. France 882, ff 98–108. The remonstrances are not to be found in the manuscripts of the *Parlement* of Paris because of Louis xiv's decision, on 18 Jan. 1668, to have all serious references to the Fronde torn from the registers. Instead, the manuscript copy is preserved in Mazarin's papers—the chief minister, after all, was directly affected.
20. A. L. Moote, *The Revolt of the Judges. The Parlement of Paris and the Fronde, 1643-1652* (Princeton, N.J., 1971), 330, summarizes the critique in seven lines.
21. *Ibid.*, 329.
22. R. J. Bonney, "The French Civil War, 1649–53", *European Studies Review*, viii (1978), 86.
23. Talon, *Mémoires*, ed. by Michaud and Poujoulat, 209–12. A. A. E. France 882, ff 348v–349v, 21 May 1652.
24. H. Mailfait, *Un magistrat de l'ancien régime. Omer Talon, sa vie et ses oeuvres, 1595–1652* (1902), 359–60.
25. Talon, *Mémoires*, ed. by Michaud and Poujoulat, 472. Moote, *op. cit.* (ref. 20), 329 n.33, sees an inconsistency in Talon's position.
26. A. A. E. France 882, f179v, 8 Apr. 1652: "maintenant que Vostre Émin[ence] a les remonstrances du Parlement escrites, il faudroit s'y attacher, comme à une pièce autentique [*sic*] ...."
27. Mazarin called it "un coup mortel" in a letter of 26 Sept. 1651 to Anne of Austria: *Lettres du Cardinal Mazarin à la Reine, à la Princesse Palatine ...* , ed. by J. Ravenel (1836), 291–2. On 30 Sept. 1651, Mazarin lamented to Colbert that the declaration was "un acte authentique" and said that he could not understand how the Regent had "donné les mains à une chose si infamante contre [luy]": *Lettres du Cardinal Mazarin pendant son ministère*, ed. by P. A. Chéruel and G. d'Avenel

28. (9 vols, 1872–1906), iv, 452, 454. M. Laurain-Portemer, "Le statut de Mazarin dans l'Église. Aperçus sur le haut clergé de la Contre-Réforme: Part 2", *Bibliothèque de l'École des Chartes*, cxxviii (1970), 5–80, p. 64.
28. A. A. E. France 884, ff 59v–60r, 12 Aug. 1652.
29. A. A. E. France 881, f74, 11 Jan. 1652. Le Tellier wrote to Mazarin that "la Reyne ayant persisté à vouloir que l'arrest du 29 [décembre] fust cassé...". For the decree: *Arrêts du conseil du roi. Règne de Louis XIV. Inventaire analytique des arrêts en commandment.* I. *20 mai 1643–8 mars 1661*, ed. by M. Le Pesant (1976), no. 1609.
30. *Cf. Lettres du Cardinal Mazarin* ..., ed. by Chéruel and d'Avenel, v, 20. A. A. E. France 887, f23v, 18 Jan. 1652.
31. Bonney, "The French Civil War", 78–9.
32. *Journal des guerres civiles de Dubuisson-Aubenay, 1648–52*, ed. by G. Saige (2 vols, 1883, 1885), ii, 186. On the question of authorship, see below.
33. A. A. E. France 879, ff190v, 194v, 23 Dec. 1651.
34. *Mémoires de l'abbé de Choisy*, ed. by J. F. Michaud and J. J. F. Poujoulat (3rd. ser., vi, 1839), 562: "Richelieu... avoit sur la même table son bréviaire et Machiavel".
35. E. Thuau, *Raison d'état et pensée politique à l'époque de Richelieu* (1966), 59.
36. Patin, *op. cit.* (ref. 9), 148.
37. Talon, *Mémoires*, ed. by Michaud and Poujoulat, 316.
38. *Cf. ibid.*, 300. For the Sicilian Vespers: S. Runciman, *The Sicilian Vespers. A history of the medieval world in the later thirteenth century* (Cambridge, 1958).
39. A. A. E. France 882, f159v. A. A. E. France 883, f249, July 1652. *Cf.* Talon, *Mémoires*, ed. by Michaud and Poujoulat, 272, 397.
40. G. Dethan, "Mazarin avant le ministère", *Revue historique*, ccxxvii (1962), 33–66, p. 35. Laurain-Portemer, "Le statut de Mazarin dans l'Église ... : Part 1", *Bibliothèque de l'École des Chartes*, cxxvii (1969), 355–419, p. 369.
41. *Cf.* Talon, *Mémoires*, ed. by Michaud and Poujoulat, 272.
42. P. Blet, "Richelieu et les débuts de Mazarin", *Revue d'histoire moderne et contemporaine*, vi (1959), 241-68.
43. A. A. E. France 881, f190: "Monseigneur le Cardinal Ma[z]arin aiant esté naturalisé françois et comme tel nommé par le feu Roy pour estre Cardinal national françois et le Pape Urbain l'aiant accepté en cette qualité. ..." Mazarin was naturalized by letters patent of April 1639, because he had acquired the abbey of Saint-Médard at Soissons. (Without letters of naturalization, a foreigner could not hold an ecclesiastical benefice in France.) Even before becoming naturalized, however, Mazarin called himself French "by gratitude and by temperament": G. Dethan, *The Young Mazarin*, translated by S. Baron (London, 1977), 113–14. Dethan's earlier view that Mazarin "devint premier ministre de Louis XIV sans avoir jamais été français" ["Mazarin avant le ministère", 56–57] is erroneous.
44. *Cf.* A. A. E. France 882, f315v, 14 May 1652. A. A. E. France 888, f158, n.d. [1652].
45. Doolin, *op. cit.* (ref. 17), 73.
46. Bonney, "The French Civil War", 91. A.N. U 30, ff165v–166v.
47. A. A. E. France 877, f337, 2 Dec. 1651.
48. Quoted by P. Logié, *La Fronde en Normandie* (3 vols, Amiens, 1951), ii, 63–64.
49. A. A. E. France 881, f136, 24 Jan. 1652.
50. For the need for "un acte autentique et un tesmoignage public" of royal confidence in Mazarin: A. A. E. France 881, f312, 19 Feb. 1652. For the placing of Mazarin under the royal safeguard: A. A. E. France 882, f312, 14 May 1652.
51. *Inventaire des arrêts*, ed. by Le Pesant, no. 1736. This conciliar decree referred to the decree of the *Parlement* of Paris of 20 July 1652 which had declared the king to be held in captivity by Mazarin.

VI

52. Moote, *op. cit.* (ref. 20), 330.
53. A. A. E. France 884, f299.
54. *Cf.* A. A. E. France 882, ff313v–314r, 14 May 1652.
55. *Cf.* A. A. E. France 882, f314, 14 May 1652. A. A. E. France 884, f57v, 12 Aug. 1652.
56. A. A. E. France 846, ff153–62, [20] Apr. 1643.
57. Laurain-Portemer, "Le statut de Mazarin dans l'Église", *Bibliothèque de l'Ecole des Chartes*, cxxviii (1970), 75–76.
58. Talon, *Mémoires*, ed. by Michaud and Poujoulat, 317.
59. A. A. E. France 881, ff30, 221, 313v, 8 Jan., 5 Feb. and 19 Feb. 1652.
60. For Mazarin's wealth in 1661: D. Dessert, "Pouvoir et finance au xviie siècle: la fortune de Mazarin", *Revue d'histoire moderne et contemporaine*, xxiii (1976), 161–81. For his position at the time of the Fronde: *Lettres . . . de Colbert*, ed. by Clément, i, 176–7. A. A. E. France 879, f187v, 23 Dec. 1651. A. A. E. France 886, f136v, 3 Dec. 1652.
61. *Lettres . . . de Colbert*, ed. by Clément, i, 69–74, 128.
62. *Ibid.*, i, 73. A. A. E. France 886, f136v, 3 Dec. 1652.
63. A. A. E. France 883, f248v, July 1652: ". . . quelque ressort que l'on ait fait jouer pour convaincre Monsr. le Cardinal Mazarin du crime de péculat, on n'a pas seullement trouvé le moindre jour à cette accusation." The preliminary trial papers drawn up by the *Parlement* of Paris are in B.N. Ms. fr. 6888. The financial problems of the crown during the Fronde are examined in detail in R. J. Bonney, *The King's Debts: Finance and Politics in France, 1589–1661* (Oxford, forthcoming), chap. 5.
64. A. A. E. France 893/2, f419v, *c.* 1654.
65. A. A. E. France 876, f182, 28 July 1651.
66. A. A. E. France 875, ff16, 115v, 6 May and [?] 1651.
67. A. A. E. France 890, f240, *c.* Feb. 1653.
68. Talon, *Mémoires*, ed. by Michaud and Poujoulat, 270–2.
69. R. J. Bonney, *Political Change in France under Richelieu and Mazarin, 1624–1661* (Oxford, 1978), 292–5.
70. For Bellièvre's opposition to the holding of fortresses by provincial governors or their clients at the time of Henri iv: A. A. E. France 764, f188, n.d., *c.* 1594.
71. A. A. E. France 883, f248, July 1652.
72. A. A. E. France 877, f278, 18 Nov. 1651.
73. A. A. E. France 879, f188, 23 Dec. 1651. Mazarin told Louis xiv that his love for France was so great that "aucun mauvais traictement n'est capable de l'esbranler . . .". His loyalty was recalled in 1652, when it was said that he was a minister "qui en sçavoit tous les secretz et qui eust pu facilement se vanger en les découvrant aux ennemis . . .": A. A. E. France 888, f116v.
74. A. A. E. France 885, f336, n.d. [1651]. Silhon wrote to Mazarin: "ce qui a causé les troubles de l'estat et fait naistre la guerre civile en France a esté le seul et le véritable empeschement de la paix générale"; but Silhon thought (f335v) that "les Espagnols ne vouloient point de paix . . .".
75. A. A. E. France 875, ff93–94, 26 May 1651. A. A. E. France 877, f45v, 30 Sept. 1651.
76. A. A. E. France 874, ff185–9, n.d. [1651].
77. A. A. E. France 875, f107, 28 May 1651. The same basic requirements were contained in the Spanish peace proposals of 21 March 1646: British Library Harleian Ms. 4458, f43.
78. A. A. E. France 870, f199, March 1650.
79. A. A. E. France 876, ff429v–430r, 15 Sept. 1651.

80. A. A. E. France 877, f379, 9 Dec. 1651.
81. A. A. E. France 885, f387, n.d. [1652].
82. A. A. E. France 886, f20, 18 Nov. 1652. Le Tellier wrote to Mazarin of the hope to "rédui[re] M. le prince à estre seulement le général des Espagnolz...".
83. For English privateering: *Lettres... de Colbert*, ed. by Clément, i, 489–90 and A. A. E. France 892, f428, 29 Oct. 1653.
84. A. A. E. France 876, f395, 8 Sept. 1651.
85. "Un journal inédit du Parlement de Paris pendant la Fronde (1 déc. 1651 – 12 avril 1652)", ed. by H. Courteault, *Annuaire-Bulletin de la Société de l'histoire de France* [année 1916] (1917), 304.
86. A. A. E. France 884, f58, 12 Aug. 1652.
87. A. A. E. France 888, f159, 1652. The *parlementaires* were "juges passionnez, suspects et incompétents...": A. A. E. France 889, f330, 17 Aug. 1652.
88. A. A. E. France 884, ff58, 60, 12 Aug. 1652. The remonstrances were written "en un stile... esloigné de la gravité du caractère de la justice...".
89. Thuau, *Raison d'état et pensée politique*..., 120–9.
90. A. A. E. France 884, f58v, 12 Aug. 1652.
91. A. A. E. France 881, f308, 18 Feb. 1652.
92. A. A. E. France 886, f114, 1652.
93. P. A. Knachel, *England and the Fronde. The Impact of the English Civil War and Revolution on France* (Ithaca, N.Y., 1967), 32, 47. A. A. E. France 884, f60v, 12 Aug. 1652.
94. A. A. E. France 884, f226v, 4 Sept. 1652.
95. A. A. E. France 884, f246, 4 Sept. 1652.
96. A. A. E. France 885, f388, 1652.
97. A. A. E. France 885, f165, 13 Oct. 1652: "la mort de Mr. de Chavigny est considéré de beaucoup de gens comme un jugement de Dieu." Before his death, Châteauneuf was exiled from Paris: A. A. E. France 886, f18, 18 Nov. 1652.
98. A. A. E. France 886, ff99, 233–235v, 252v–253r, 30 Nov., 18 and 19 Dec. 1652.
99. *Lettres... de Colbert*, ed. by Clément, i, 535. I would like to express my gratitude to the Twenty-seven Foundation, without whose generosity the research that went into this article could not have been undertaken.

VII

Cardinal Mazarin and the great nobility during the Fronde

THE relationship between the crown and the great nobility is one of the touchstones for an understanding of the political process in France and other European monarchies during the early modern period. When kings were strong, they tended to impose their will on the magnates. During royal minorities, or when kings were otherwise weak, the nobility tended to come back into the political arena with a vengeance. A short-sighted king, such as Henri II, stored up trouble for the future by channelling excessive patronage to two noble families, the Guise and the Montmorency. A weak and foolish king, such as Henri III, compounded his problems by raising Joyeuse and d'Épernon to a status above all other peers of the realm and second only to the princes of the blood. Problems with the nobility did not suddenly disappear in the seventeenth century after the end of the wars of religion: there was a long line of aristocratic conspiracies and rebellions from Biron in 1602 to Rohan in 1674.

It is remarkable how little has been written on these conspiracies in general,[1] or on the subject of the *Fronde nobiliaire* in particular – the most important of all the crises between the crown and the French aristocracy between the wars of the Catholic League and the end of the *ancien régime*. For 'the revolt of the nobles' is at least as good a description of the Fronde as 'the revolt of the judges'.[2] Indeed, one might argue that it is a better description since it encompasses all stages of the fighting between 1649 and 1653 even if it does not explain the collapse of the government in 1648.[3] Clearly, Mazarin's policy towards the great nobility merits attention. Difficulty with the nobles was commonplace; the complete breakdown of the relationship requires explanation.

As an Italian by birth, Mazarin was bound to encounter difficulties when chief minister of France after 1643. As Omer Talon remarked, he was vulnerable to 'toute sorte de mauvaises impressions que les peuples lui vouloient imposer . . .'.[4] The vast outpouring of political

---

1. The conspiracies and rebellions of the seventeenth century figure scarcely at all in a recent study of the provincial governors between 1515 and 1650: R. R. Harding, *Anatomy of a power elite. The provincial governors of early modern France* (New Haven and London, 1978). Those under Richelieu receive cursory treatment in O. A. Ranum, 'Richelieu and the great nobility. Some aspects of early modern political motives', *French historical studies*, iii (1963), 184–204.

2. Cf. A. L. Moote, *The revolt of the judges. The Parlement of Paris and the Fronde, 1643–1652* (Princeton, N.J., 1971).

3. R. J. Bonney, 'The French civil war, 1649–53', *European studies review*, viii (1978), 71–100.

4. Omer Talon, *Mémoires*, ed. J. F. Michaud and J. F. Poujoulat, 3rd ser., vi (1839), 300.

pamphlets, the *Mazarinades*, are evidence of a fairly conclusive kind on the extent of his unpopularity. Even that most respectable of institutions, the *Parlement* of Paris, in its remonstrances of 23 March 1652, blamed virtually all the evils of the body politic on Mazarin who as an Italian was regarded *ipso facto* as a disciple of Machiavelli.[1] There was much ignorance and xenophobia underlying these fears and accusations. Denunciation of the role of foreigners in government, moreover, was nothing new. In 1574 Henri de Montmorency-Damville had issued a propaganda piece of considerable importance which had castigated the influence of Chancellor Birague and Retz, the lieutenant-general in Provence, both of whom were Italian in origin.[2] There were other, more recent, precedents which were recalled by the diarist Guy Patin on 20 August 1649 when he considered Mazarin to be 'l'objet de la haine publique et ... en chemin de devenir aussi malheureux qu'ait jamais été le marquis d'Ancre'.[3] Patin was alluding to the fate of Concino Concini and his wife Léonora Galigaï, the favourites of Marie de Médicis, who had attempted to control royal patronage between 1610 and 1617, during which time there were three rebellions of the upper nobility directed chiefly against their influence. It is true that they had been toppled less by rebellious nobles than by a *coup d'état* organized by the king and Luynes, his new favourite, which had resulted in the death of Concini. After the 'palace revolution',[4] however, the revolt of the nobles was amnestied by the crown and all the blame for the civil disturbance was placed on the Italian. Mazarin had much less to fear from a palace revolution, because Louis XIV at the end of the Fronde was younger than his father at the time of the *coup d'état* against Concini. However, the precedent of assassination haunted Mazarin throughout the Fronde,[5] and he was equally concerned about the possible reissue by the *Parlement* of Paris of its decree of 8 August 1617 which had declared Concini and his wife guilty of treason and prohibited foreigners from holding offices and governorships in France.[6] One

1. R. J. Bonney, 'Cardinal Mazarin and his critics: the remonstrances of 1652', *Journal of European Studies*, x (1980), 15–31.
2. A. Devyver, *Le sang épuré. Les préjugés de race chez les gentilshommes français de l'ancien régime, 1560–1720* (Brussels, 1973), p. 50, n. 36. M. Greengrass, 'War, politics and religion during the government of Henri de Montmorency-Damville, 1574–1610' (Oxford D.Phil., 1979), p. 169.
3. Guy Patin, *Lettres pendant la Fronde*, ed. A. Thérive (1921), p. 139.
4. L. Batiffol, 'Le coup d'état du 24 avril 1617', *Revue Historique*, xcv (1907), 292–308; xcvii (1908), 27–77, 264–86.
5. There was a pertinent comment by Patin on 3 Sept. 1649: *ibid.* p. 141. *Cf.* A[rchives des] A[ffaires] E[trangères, Mémoires et Documents,] France 881, fo. 70^v, 11 Jan. 1652. After 25 Feb. 1648 Mazarin had a company of guards for his personal security.
6. The decree was read out by Viole in the *Parlement* of Paris on 22 Sept. 1648: *Journal d'Olivier Lefèvre d'Ormesson et extrait des mémoires d'André Lefèvre d'Ormesson*, ed. P. A. Chéruel (1860–1), i. 577. The decree was in effect reissued on 7 February 1651, and confirmed in a somewhat modified form by a royal declaration on 1 March 1651.

VII

of the legacies of Concini was that Frenchmen who disliked royal favourites in general had a particular loathing for the Italian version of the genre.

Mazarin's difficulties during the Fronde parallel the downfall of Concini in an important respect. In May 1616 the French government had been forced to sign a treaty with the rebellious nobles led by Henri II de Bourbon, prince de Condé. Condé gained enormous authority as a result of the arrangements in the peace of Loudun,[1] and to protect his own position Concini had to have him arrested the following September. The arrest of Condé was seen by his followers as an abrogation of the treaty, a prelude to a new trial of strength between the government and the nobility, and a justification for their rebellion.[2] The parallel is with the events of 1649–50. The government signed the peace of Rueil with the *Parlement* of Paris and its supporters on 11 March 1649.[3] It is true that Louis II de Bourbon, prince de Condé, had supported Mazarin in the first civil war. However, Armand de Bourbon, prince de Conty, his younger brother, had been the generalissimo of the *Frondeurs*, while another great noble, the duc de Longueville, had led the revolt in Normandy which coincided with the Parisian movement. All three princes were arrested by Mazarin on 18 January 1650.[4] With this *coup d'état* Mazarin crossed his Rubicon. Afterwards, political events rapidly got out of hand. The incarceration of the princes was an acid in the body politic. There would be continual revolts by their supporters until they were released – an event delayed by Mazarin until February 1651 and which forced him into exile. Why did Mazarin arrest the princes when the precedent was the collapse of Concini's regime after a similar decision? The answer can only be that Mazarin had no alternative if he wished to remain chief minister. On 2 October 1649 and again on 16 January 1650, just two days before the *coup*, Mazarin was forced to sign documents which in effect relinquished control of the government to Condé. Like father, like son: Mazarin had to ask the first prince of the blood to regard him as his 'très humble serviteur' and to be 'favoris[é] de sa protection . . .'. For his part, the Cardinal undertook to support Condé's interests in all matters.[5] Mazarin

---

1. *Négociations, lettres et pièces relatives à la conférence de Loudun*, ed. L. F. H. Bouchitté (1862).
2. A. A. E. France 771, fos. 1, 4, 26–29, 6 Jan., 30 Jan., 4 Feb. 1617.
3. However, the relationship between the *Parlement* of Paris and the *Frondeur* nobles was an uneasy one, and the nobles had tried to prevent the signing of the peace.
4. Condé at the moment of his arrest commented that 'il ne s'étonnoit pas de la prison des deux autres qui avoient porté les armes contre le service du roi; mais que pour lui . . . il avouoit qu'il ne s'attendoit pas à un tel traitement . . .': *Mémoires de François de Paule de Clermont, marquis de Montglat*, ed. J. F. Michaud and J. F. Poujoulat, 3rd ser., v (1838), p. 227.
5. B[ibliothèque] N[ationale] Dupuy 775, fo. 122, 16 Jan. 1650. *Cf.* the earlier submission of Mazarin: A[rchives] N[ationales] K 118a, no. 17 [Musée AE II 843], 2 Oct. 1649.

signed these documents not because he intended to hand over the government to Condé, but as a tactical ploy, to *reculer pour mieux sauter*. He could not keep to the agreement because he was obliged to follow the king's interests, his own interests, but not Condé's – this was the essence of his position as chief minister and favourite of the Regent. Thus in January 1650 he sought new political allies and then struck out against the princes.[1]

Throughout the political career of the Cardinal there is a central paradox: was he a great French statesman, who consolidated the achievements of Richelieu and brought his foreign policy to fruition, or was he simply – as most contemporaries and all his critics thought – an Italian adventurer whose luck never ran out? On his death in 1661, Mazarin left a fortune of some 37 million *livres*, perhaps the largest bequest under the *ancien régime* and considerably larger than that left by Richelieu.[2] At 9 million *livres*, his was the largest cash bequest under the *ancien régime*, more than the famous public store deposited by Sully in the Bastille in the years before 1611.[3] There were few outright gifts from the king. Indeed, almost all the allegations of corruption later levelled against Foucquet, the former finance minister, in 1661–4 could be made with equal, if not greater validity against the chief minister.[4] Of course, it may be argued that in building up this fortune in the 1650s, Mazarin was simply responding to his ordeal during the Fronde: he kept his cash deposits near his place of residence or else prudently stored near the border in case of another enforced departure from the kingdom as in 1651. It is true that not much detailed information is available on Mazarin's private finances between 1643 and 1651, when exile abroad led to his virtual bankruptcy. It is clear, however, that he became extremely wealthy. His fortune attracted public attention,[5] and in particular the covetous eyes of the French aristocracy.

    1. Vendôme was among the new allies, as is mentioned below. Apparently Mazarin also intended to arrest the ducs de Bouillon and de la Rochefoucauld and the maréchaux de Gramont and Turenne, but they escaped: *Mémoires . . . de Montglat*, pp. 226–7.
    2. D. Dessert, 'Pouvoir et finance au xviie siècle: la fortune de Mazarin', *Revue d'histoire moderne et contemporaine*, xxiii (1976), 161–81. By the time of his death in 1642, it was said that Richelieu had built up a fortune of 22·4 million *livres*, although debts of 6·5 million reduced the total to under 16 million. The subject merits a more satisfactory examination, but this was the claim of Hilaire, *avocat* of the duchesse d'Aiguillon: L. Batiffol, 'La fortune du Cardinal de Richelieu', *Revue des deux-mondes*, 8th ser., xxvii (1935), 896.
    3. *Cf.* L. Batiffol, 'Le trésor de la Bastille de 1605 à 1611', *Revue Henri IV*, iii (1909–12), 200–9.
    4. Denis Talon, the *procureur-général* of the *chambre de justice* in charge of the prosecution of Foucquet argued that 'le seul excès des biens qu'il possède et des profusions qu'il a faictes le rendent criminel': A.N. 144 a.p. 68, Dr. 1 [156 mi. 18], fo. 67. Mazarin's wealth was greater than Foucquet's, however, and the chief minister was criticized by Foucquet who denounced the activities of 'un estranger seul [qui] met des millions à couvert dedans et dehors le royaume abusant de son autorité absolue . . .': 144 a.p. 66, Dr. 1 [156 mi. 15], fo. 5.
    5. Dubuisson-Aubenay reported allegations in February 1649 that Mazarin had

There is a convincing parallel between attitudes to Mazarin's fortune and that of Concini and his wife, of whom it was said they had come to France 'destituez de tous moiens' but had acquired a vast fortune by 'voyes extraordinaires et illicites'. What must particularly have infuriated the judges at the trial of Léonora Galigaï in 1617 was that some of the wealth acquired by the favourites had been transferred abroad and placed in state loans at Florence and Rome. The wealth of Concini and his wife was confiscated to the crown and granted out almost immediately to Luynes, the new favourite.[1] In 1651, when the *Parlement* of Paris placed Mazarin on trial *in absentia*, one of the charges against him was that he had transferred money abroad, especially to Italy. The case did not proceed very far, because it lacked support from the Regent. The judges were unable to prove the allegations in the financial chaos of the Fronde. Nevertheless, it was said that Mazarin had misused the secret expenses (*comptants*) of the French monarchy for his private purposes,[2] and as late as 23 March 1652 the *Parlement* was still calling for an investigation of the accounts of Thomas Cantarini, who had handled some 36 million *livres* destined to pay for the war in Italy in the 1640s but which allegedly had been misappropriated by Mazarin.[3]

Whether Mazarin had acquired his wealth legally or illegally, most Frenchmen during the Fronde considered that he had a vast personal fortune. His critics wanted to confiscate it; his supporters wanted to share it by the more traditional methods of marriage and inheritance. As a Cardinal of the church, Mazarin of course had no wife or son; but as a good Italian he never forgot his family. He had brought a nephew, Paolo Mancini, to France; he also had five Mancini and two Martinozzi nieces – the celebrated *mazarinettes* as they came to be known in France – for whom he sought honourable suitors and to whom he could provide large dowries. (Nor should his brother, Michele Mazarini, be forgotten. He had the misfortune to die in 1648, but not before he had been made archbishop of Aix-en-Provence, viceroy in Catalonia and ambassador extraordinary to Rome.)[4] Royal favourites always tended to consolidate their position by marriage into the French nobility. It was said that Concini had wanted to

---

diverted funds to his private coffers which had been sent out in the 1640s for the war effort in Italy and Germany: *Journal des guerres civiles de Dubuisson-Aubenay, 1648–1652*, ed. G. Saige (1883, 1885), i. 171. The same was said in the most important pamphlet of 1648, the *Requête des Trois États...: Choix de Mazarinades*, ed. C. Moreau (1853), i. 31–32.

  1. For the accusation against Concini and his wife: F. Hayem, *Le maréchal d'Ancre et Léonora Galigaï* (1910), p. 235. B.N. 500 Colbert 221, fo. 27. For the grant to Luynes: R. de Crèvecoeur, *Un document nouveau sur la succession des Concini* (1891), p. 16. A.N. P 2349, p. 435, August 1617.
  2. BN MS fr. 6888, fo. 257, 25 May 1651.
  3. A.A.E. France 882, fo. 106.
  4. S. Kettering, *Judicial politics and urban revolt in seventeenth-century France. The Parlement of Aix, 1629–1659* (Princeton, N.J., 1978), p. 70.

repudiate his wife and marry Mlle de Vendôme.¹ In 1641, Richelieu married his niece to Condé then known as the duc d'Enghien.² In 1649, the duc de Vendôme proposed the idea of a marriage alliance to Mazarin. Vendôme was Henri IV's bastard by Gabrielle d'Estrées. In 1626 he had been removed by Richelieu from his governorship of Brittany and from this date he had a long history of conspiracy behind him. As late as September 1648 the Spanish considered Vendôme an irreconcilable enemy of Mazarin:³ yet the marriage was to be between his second son, the duc de Mercoeur, and Laura Mancini. It finally took place in 1651, while Mazarin was in exile. In September 1649, however, Condé was furious at the mere idea of such a marriage. Guy Patin commented on Condé's motives: 'cela fait penser que ce prince a quelque dessein contre le mazarin et sa fortune. . . .'⁴ This background explains the clause in the written submission of 2 October 1649, whereby Mazarin undertook not to marry off his nephew or any of his nieces without Condé's prior consent. At the same time, Condé was planning a marriage between the duc de Richelieu and Anne Poussart du Vigean which would place the duke under his, and Longueville's, influence and secure control of Le Havre, the most important fortress in France.⁵ It was to secure one marriage at a later date, and prevent the consequences of another that Mazarin had Condé arrested. Le Havre remained firmly in Mazarin's control, indeed the princes were transferred there later in 1650. With the first

1. A.A.E. France 771, fo. 93ᵛ, n.d. [1617].
2. A.A.E. France 838, fo. 46 and A.N. K 558 [Musée AE II 827], 7 Feb. 1641. Montglat commented that Richelieu was 'dans une telle élévation de fortune que les plus grands se tenoient heureux et honorés d'entrer dans son alliance . . .': *Mémoires . . . de Montglat*, p. 103.
3. For the Spanish view of Vendôme on 11 Sept. 1648: *Correspondance de la cour d'Espagne sur les affaires des Pays-Bas au xviiᵉ siècle. IV. 1647–1655*, ed. H. Lonchay, J. Cuvelier and J. Lefèvre (Brussels, 1933), no. 223. The reinstatement of Vendôme as governor of Brittany, the post from which he had been removed by Richelieu because of his participation in the Chalais conspiracy, was one of the demands of the duc de Beaufort, Vendôme's elder son, who rebelled in 1649: BN 500 Colbert 3, fo. 178. Both Vendôme and Beaufort had participated in the *Cabale des Importants*, the first conspiracy against Mazarin in 1643. Beaufort was arrested: BN MS fr. 17331, fo. 113, 11 Sept. 1643. Vendôme published a manifesto for Beaufort's release and went into exile: A.A.E. France 848, fo. 230.
4. Patin, *op. cit.*, ed. Thérive, p. 146 (17 Sept. 1649). *Cf. ibid.* p. 153 (24 Sept. 1649). However, it is possible to see Condé's opposition to the marriage as simply a reflection of his hostility to the Vendôme family. Condé allegedly stated 'que la maison de Vendôme étoit ennemie de la sienne': *Mémoires . . . de Montglat*, p. 216.
5. Montglat commented (*ibid.* p. 222) that 'le prince de Condé voulut favoriser le dessein du duc de Longueville pour s'emparer du Havre' and describes the marriage plan. Cardinal de Richelieu had obtained the fortress of Le Havre on 18 Oct. 1626. It had cost 345,000 *livres*, but the chief minister was probably reimbursed by the king: *Mémoires du Cardinal de Richelieu*, ed. R. Lavollée *et al.*, (1907–31), ix. 48. *Lettres, instructions diplomatiques et papiers d'état du Cardinal de Richelieu*, ed. D. L. M. Avenel (1853–77), ii. 275; iii. 205. Ironically, Louis XIII had altered Richelieu's last will and testament to ensure that Le Havre went to the young duke (the duc de Richelieu was aged only 18 in 1649) rather than the more formidable Brézé, Richelieu's other nephew: *Mémoires . . . de Montglat*, p. 135.

prince of the blood out of the way, the personal alliance with the duc de Vendôme could be consolidated by making him Admiral, head of French navigation and commerce, and governor of Burgundy, Condé's province.[1]

The story of Le Havre and the career of the duc de Mercoeur, whom Mazarin made governor of Provence in 1652, illustrate another aspect of relations between the royal favourite and the great nobility: the control of provincial governorships and fortresses within the provinces. Earlier royal favourites such as Joyeuse and d'Épernon had incurred the wrath of the French nobility by securing provincial governorships which, rightly or wrongly, other families regarded as their own.[2] Concini's power as lieutenant-general, first in Picardy, later in Normandy, and control of vital fortresses – first Amiens, Roye, Montdidier and Péronne, later Caen and Pont de l'Arche – had been bitterly resented by Condé and his supporters.[3] After 1631, Richelieu had been governor of Brittany and, though he had no time to visit the province, his power had been secured by the lieutenant-general: Charles de la Porte, duc de La Meilleraye, Richelieu's cousin.[4] Mazarin had kept La Meilleraye in that position once Anne of Austria became governor in 1647, and he kept Brittany loyal during the Fronde. Indeed, La Meilleraye was an important figure since he held two other great offices – the post of *surintendant des finances* in 1648–9 after the dismissal of d'Hémery, and that of *grand maître de l'artillerie*, which he resigned to his son in 1648.[5] The loyalty

1. For Vendôme as Admiral, the post promised him by Henri IV: BN Dupuy 775, fo. 110, 12 March 1650. For the promise of Henri IV: Sir George Carew, 'A relation of the state of France', *An historical view of the negotiations between the courts of England, France and Brussels, 1592–1617*, ed. T. Birch (1749), p. 429. For Vendôme as *grand maître, chef et surintendant de la navigation et commerce de France*, with his son the duc de Beaufort *en survivance*: A.A.E. France 868, fo. 181, 12 May 1650. The post had been created for Richelieu and held subsequently by Brézé and Anne of Austria: A.A.E. France 855, fo. 220, 4 July 1646. For Vendôme as governor of Burgundy: *Mémoires . . . de Montglat*, p. 229. Moote, *op. cit.* pp. 260, 262, 266.

2. The manifesto of the Catholic League (23 May 1588) had denounced d'Épernon's purchase of 'les places fortes d[u] . . . royaume': *Registres des délibérations du bureau de la ville de Paris . . . IX, 1586–1590*, ed. F. Bonnardot (1902), p. 133. Opposition to d'Épernon was intensified because instead of returning Joyeuse's offices and governorships to the Guises or their supporters on his death, Henri III transferred them to his chief favourite on 7 Nov. 1587: Girard, *Histoire de la vie du duc d'Espernon* (1655), p. 62.

3. Hayem, *op. cit.* pp. 132, 201–2. Condé had insisted on the removal of Concini from the lieutenant-generalship of Picardy and the governorship of Amiens during the Loudun negotiations: Bouchitté, *op. cit.* pp. 461, 480, 556–7, 655, 677.

4. La Meilleraye was not elevated to the status of duke and peer until 1663. During the Fronde he was invariably known as the maréchal de la Meilleraye. Richelieu had appointed him *maréchal de France* in 1639: *Mémoires . . . de Montglat*, pp. 76–77.

5. La Meilleraye was lieutenant-general in Brittany after 18 March 1632 by commission, and bought the position in 1637 from Brissac, its former holder, when he married his daughter. Brissac received 400,000 *livres*: A.A.E. France 827, fo. 116, 17 June 1637. Between 1642 and 1647, La Meilleraye was governor of Brittany, not lieutenant-general as Harding asserts (*op. cit.* n. 4 to appendix one at p. 288): A.A.E. France 844, fo. 165, 9 Dec. 1642. However, he agreed to abandon the title

of the effective head of the French artillery (La Meilleraye's son was aged only sixteen at the outbreak of the troubles) was worth having during the siege warfare of the Fronde. In 1650 La Meilleraye commanded the royalist army in Guyenne; two years later he was in command in Anjou.[1]

The loyalty of the other provincial governors was worth having too, for they enjoyed considerable political and military power. Mazarin had his own province, the Auvergne, which he held as governor after 1650 and refused to give up when forced into exile the following year.[2] The chief minister obviously could not hold all the provincial governorships in person, however. He had to find supporters and clients, which was no easy task. The provincial governors of eleven important provinces, including all the frontier provinces with the exception of Poitou, have recently been listed for the first two years of the Fronde.[3] Of the eleven, only four – Brittany, the province held by the Regent, the Dauphiné, Île-de-France and Lyonnais – caused Mazarin no real difficulty during the Fronde. In two others, Guyenne and Provence, he had supporters who were so independent that they were a thorn in his flesh. D'Épernon had to be moved from Guyenne to Burgundy in 1651, where he could start afresh: Mazarin's search for a marriage alliance probably weakened his negotiating position with a notoriously intractable character.[4] The comte d'Alais had to be arrested the following year to induce him to give up the governorship of Provence.[5] The governors of the

---

of governor quite early on in the Regency: A.A.E. France 1506, fo. 73, 25 Feb. 1644. For his appointment as *surintendant*: BN MS fr. 4222, fo. 206, 9 July 1648. For the post of *grand maître*: A.N. P 2365, pp. 233–42, 26 Sept. 1634. P 2373, pp. 407–21, 26 Apr. 1648. It is significant that the *Chambre des Comptes* registered his resignation of this post only on 16 Dec. 1652, at the end of the Fronde.

1. *Mémoires . . . de Montglat*, pp. 234, 262.
2. A.A.E. France 870, fo. 423, 15 April 1650. *Lettres du Cardinal Mazarin à la Reine, à la princesse palatine . . .*, ed. J. Ravenel (1836), p. 63.
3. Harding, *op. cit.* pp. 221–7. The loyal governors apart from Anne of Austria (no. 11) were Lesdiguères in the Dauphiné (no. 48), d'Estrées in the Île-de-France (no 71) who participated in loan contracts to the government, and Villeroy in the Lyonnais (no. 94). Villeroy was governor to Louis XIV, and was talked of as a possible successor to La Meilleraye as *surintendant*: *Journal des guerres civiles de Dubuisson Aubenay . . .*, ed. Saige, i. 97. A.A.E. 864, fo. 2ᵛ, 1 Jan. 1649. He was one of the leading voices in the government during Mazarin's exile in 1651: *Mémoires . . . de Montglat*, pp. 247, 256.
4. Montglat recorded the possibility of a marriage between one of Mazarin's Martinozzi nieces and d'Épernon's son: *Mémoires . . . de Montglat*, pp. 219–20. Louis-Charles-Gaston Nogaret de La Valette, duc de Candale, eventually obtained Mazarin's governorship of the Auvergne which he held until his death on 28 Jan. 1658. The province was then awarded to Mazarin on 26 Feb. 1658: R. E. Mousnier, *La plume, la faucille et le marteau. Institutions et société en France du moyen âge à la Révolution* (1970), pp. 210–12.
5. Kettering, *op. cit.* p. 141. On 10 Sept. 1653 Mazarin was made governor of Provence and paid 400,000 *livres* to the comte d'Alais. He was allowed to sell the post for 600,000 *livres* and presumably gave it to his son-in-law, Mercoeur: A.A.E. France 890, fos. 289, 297, 10 and 15 Sept. 1653.

remaining five provinces all rebelled against Mazarin at some time during the Fronde.

The nature of the threat provided by these governors varied from province to province. Gaston d'Orléans was an absentee governor of Languedoc and his control over the province was relatively weak and counter-balanced by lieutenants-general and a provincial intendant. In Champagne and Picardy there were also lieutenants-general to counter the power of Conty and d'Elbeuf: La Vieuville, the lieutenant-general of Champagne, was promoted to the post of *surintendant des finances* and created a duke and peer in 1651 as a reward for his loyalty.[1] His counterpart in Picardy, the duc de Chaulnes, rebelled once the governor returned to allegiance to the crown: theirs was a personal and family rivalry.[2] In Burgundy and Normandy,[3] however, there was no effective counterweight to the power of Condé and Longueville: this was an important factor in their arrest in 1650. Once other provinces which have not been listed, such as Poitou and Alsace, are brought into the picture then Mazarin's problems became even more serious. La Rochefoucauld, who as prince de Marsillac held the *survivance* on the governorship of Poitou, was a willing *Frondeur* in 1649 and as the new governor he was a signatory of the rebels' treaty with Philip IV of Spain on 26 June 1650.[4] Harcourt led the royalist armies in Normandy in 1649 and Guyenne in 1652. He expected great rewards from Mazarin, as he put it 'l'établissement de sa fortune'.[5] Instead he received the relatively modest governorship of Alsace, much less than his expectation. In the summer of 1652 he abruptly left his command and withdrew to Alsace.[6] Later, he signed two

---

1. P. de Guibours, le Père Anselme de Sainte-Marie, *Histoire généalogique et chronologique de la maison royale de France, des pairs, grands officiers de la couronne* . . . (3rd ed., 1726–33), v. 867–70. The *brevet* was issued at Poitiers on 26 Dec. 1651, after La Vieuville's appointment as *surintendant* (8 Sept.) Anselme included La Vieuville's letters patent among the 'duchez non enregistrez' by the sovereign courts. *Cf.* J. P. Labatut, *Les ducs et pairs de France au xvii*ᵉ *siècle. Étude sociale* (1972), p. 77 (where the elevation is misdated 1650) and pp. 95–96 (where it is correctly dated). La Vieuville was attacked by the mob at Reims in the spring of 1649 because of his loyalty to Mazarin: *Mémoires . . . de Montglat*, p. 211.

2. P. Deyon, *Amiens. Capitale provinciale. Étude sur la société urbaine au xvii*ᵉ *siècle* (Paris and The Hague, 1967), pp. 452–60.

3. Longueville was the greatest landed proprietor in Normandy. He was also the longest-serving governor in office in 1649 at the time of his revolt, since he had been appointed thirty years earlier. Already in 1636 Louis XIII had admitted that 'plusieurs vous suivront (to the army) qui ne voudront pas marcher soubz un autre . . .': BN MS fr. 3843, fo. 60, 25 July 1636. Thus although there were lieutenants-general in Normandy, they were unable to counter Longueville's power. One of them, the marquis de Beuvron, in any case rebelled in his cause in 1649 and 1650. Longueville's claim to the Admiralty, which would have prevented Mazarin's reconciliation with Vendôme and thus the Mercoeur–Mancini marriage, was probably an important factor in his arrest: *cf.* P. Logié, *La Fronde en Normandie* (Amiens, 1951).

4. BN Dupuy 775, fo. 114. His participation in the treaty is rather glossed over in the various apologia: Labatut, *op. cit.* p. 203. *Mémoires de La Rochefoucauld*, ed. J. F. Michaud and J. J. F. Poujoulat, 3rd ser., v (1838), 439–40.

5. Quoted by Logié, *op. cit.* ii. 131.

6. For Harcourt's grievances: A.A.E. France 875, fo. 314, n.d. [June 1651]. For

treaties with Philip IV under which Alsace would have been transferred to Spanish control.[1]

Harcourt's *volte-face* in 1652 was particularly ironic, since his appointment as governor of Alsace on 26 April 1649 had hindered Mazarin's chances of reconciliation with another powerful family. The governorship of Alsace had been promised to the vicomte de Turenne, the commander of the so-called French army in Germany based in that province. His elder brother, the duc de Bouillon, wanted the governorship of the Auvergne in March 1649, the province Mazarin appropriated for himself the following year. He also demanded the restitution of, or appropriate compensation for, his principality of Sedan which he had been forced to hand over to the government in September 1642.[2] Bouillon had been accused of complicity in the Cinq-Mars conspiracy in that year and his life had been spared only after the intervention of Frederick-Henry of Nassau, his uncle and a vital French ally, and on condition that this *place de sûreté* for potential rebels be placed firmly under royal control.[3] Bouillon protested innocence,[4] despite his record of conspiracy and rebellion under Louis XIII which was second to none. The issue of compensation for Sedan dragged on throughout the Regency and was complicated by Anne of Austria's insistence that a law passed by Louis XIII could not be amended until Louis XIV's majority was proclaimed.[5] Bouillon and Turenne claimed the right to be treated as sovereign princes despite the loss of their patrimony of Sedan,[6] and relations with Mazarin were soured by Bouillon's financial difficulties: by October 1647 his debts exceeded a million *livres*.[7]

The search for compensation led Bouillon and Turenne to participate in the first two rebellions of the Fronde in 1649 and 1650. Mazarin's enforced exile in 1651 provided a new impetus towards reconciliation, and it was during the chief minister's period abroad

---

his motives in going to Alsace: A.A.E. France 884, fo. 70, 16 Aug. 1652. In 1653 Mazarin offered Harcourt the more important governorship of Burgundy, provided that d'Épernon agreed to move. Harcourt rejected the offer because he considered the province rightfully to belong to Condé 'qu(i) . . . ne peut estre dépouillé': BN Dupuy 775, fo. 206. Harcourt was proven correct, since by the secret articles of the Peace of the Pyrenees Condé was restored as governor of Burgundy.

1. G. Livet, *L'intendance d'Alsace sous Louis XIV, 1648–1715* (Strasbourg-Paris, 1956), pp. 142–3, 171–2.

2. B.N. 500 Colbert 3, fo. 177, unsigned and undated requests of Bouillon and Turenne, March 1649. Cardinal Mazarin had negotiated the transfer of Sedan before he became chief minister: BN MS fr. 17331, fo. 106^v, 17 Sept. 1642.

3. BN MS fr. 17331, fos. 105, 111^v–112^v.

4. A.N. K 114b, no. 42/12 [Musée AE II 835], 10 Jan. 1643.

5. *Acta Pacis Westphalicae. Serie I. Instruktionen. Frankreich, Schweden, Kaiser*, ed. F. Dickmann *et al.* (Münster, 1962), p. 149. A.A.E. France 852, fo. 191, 17 Nov. 1645. A.A.E. France 854, fo. 83, 27 Apr. 1646.

6. Labatut, *op. cit.* pp. 352–3. They were accorded *brevets* to this effect on 20 March 1647 [A.A.E. France 856, fo. 290], 2 April and 26 October 1649 [A.N. K 118a, nos 9/1 and 9/2].

7. A.A.E. France 859, fos. 37–38.

that a preliminary settlement was drawn up. This conferred the status of sovereign prince on both Bouillon and Turenne and envisaged a royal gift of the duchies of Albret and Château-Thierry and the counties of Auvergne and Evreux (20 March 1651).[1] These were the preliminary terms, which preceded Bouillon and Turenne's disenchantment with Condé in the summer of 1651.[2] The declaration of Louis XIV's majority followed in September and Mazarin returned from exile in January 1652. The preliminary terms were then ratified by the government on 15 February 1652 with the provision that payment of the revenues from the duchies would be backdated to the previous year; there was also arrangement for compensation for lost revenues from Sedan and Raucourt. The capital value of the duchies and counties acquired by Bouillon exceeded six million *livres* out of his total assets of seven million.[3] It was scarcely surprising that the brothers' loyalty never flinched from this moment on, indeed the reconciliation could not have been more complete. In July 1652, shortly before his death, Bouillon was talked of as a possible *surintendant des finances* and had 'plus de part qu'aucun dans le gouvernement de l'état'.[4] Turenne was given command of the royalist army, perhaps the single most important factor in the defeat of the princes and the end of the civil war. In 1653 he was appointed governor of the Limousin. The final seal of the reconciliation came in 1662, the year after Mazarin's death, when Bouillon's son married the Cardinal's niece Anna-Maria Mancini and was rewarded with the chief minister's governorship of the Auvergne. The family of La Tour d'Auvergne had reached its apogee: the empty title of comte d'Auvergne conferred in 1651 was now backed up with the real power of a provincial governorship.[5]

The loyalty of some nobles, such as Bouillon and Turenne, could be bought. Others supported Mazarin through all trials and tribulations. The governors of Sedan and Lorraine – respectively the maréchaux de Fabert and La Ferté-Sénectère – were models of loyalty. It was with their assistance that Mazarin was able to return from exile, in what amounted to an invasion of France at the head of a force of 6,000 German mercenaries in January 1652.[6] It is also the case that

1. Labatut, *op. cit.* p. 197. *Arrêts du conseil du roi. Règne de Louis XIV. Inventaire analytique des arrêts en commandement. I. 20 mai 1643–8 mars 1661*, ed. M. Le Pesant (1976), no. 1378.
2. *Mémoires . . . de Montglat*, p. 255: '(ils) n'étoient pas conten(t)s de lui (i.e. Condé) sur ce qu'après les services qu'ils lui avoient rendus, il ne leur avoit fait aucune part de ses secrets. . . .'
3. Labatut, *op. cit.* p. 262 (who does not specify the value of the comté d'Auvergne). For the backdating of payments to 1 Jan. 1651: Le Pesant, *op. cit.* no. 1448. For the ratification of the agreement: A.A.E. France 889, fos. 92, 132, 15 Feb. and [?] Feb. 1652. For *nonjouissance* of revenues of Sedan and Raucourt: A.N. E 250a, fo. 73, 24 Jan. 1652.
4. *Mémoires . . . de Montglat*, p. 273.
5. Labatut, *op. cit.* pp. 197, 251.
6. Mazarin wrote several letters to Fabert and La Ferté shortly before his return,

the rebellion of a provincial governor did not necessarily bring about the revolt of his province. With Condé and Longueville safely locked up in 1650, the rebellion of their supporters in Burgundy and Normandy was suppressed with comparative ease. The population of Alsace was not consulted, nor did it participate in Harcourt's dealings with the Spanish in 1654: yet this was a province recently acquired by France whose loyalty might be thought suspect. The provinces where civil war was most acute – Guyenne and Provence – were those with the greatest internal divisions, not those where the governor chose to rebel. The timing of the rebellions was also a factor working in Mazarin's favour. Turenne's troops failed to follow their commander in his planned march on Paris in the spring of 1649. When Turenne finally invaded France in December 1650, the princes were incarcerated and could be moved to Le Havre, safely out of the reach of his army. The alliance of Gaston and Condé was not signed until 24 January 1652, after the declaration of the king's majority. If they had co-operated in a rebellion against Mazarin earlier, they would have presented a much more serious threat. Indeed, Gaston's more or less consistent support of the Regent despite his objections to the Cardinal by the autumn of 1650 was crucial: Gaston supported Anne of Austria, and she ensured that Mazarin was safe from a 'palace revolution' of the type which had destroyed Concini.

The failure of co-ordinated rebellion becomes clear if the Fronde is contrasted with two earlier aristocratic revolts, the war of the Catholic League in the 1590s and the disturbances of 1614–17. On both occasions, the nobles in rebellion had presented a fairly unified front. It is true that Henri IV after 1594 had succeeded in splitting the supporters of the Catholic League, but this serves to demonstrate their earlier unity. Moreover, as Sir George Carew remarked, Henri IV had been 'forced ... to compound with all those who had been in the League to leave them in those governments which they then held ...'.[1] Similarly the revolts led by Condé had resulted in two settlements – the treaties of Sainte-Menehould and Loudun – and the amnesty of May 1617. If the nobles had not been given all they wanted, they were certainly no worse off. The rebellions which

---

and was at Sedan on 26 Dec. 1651: *Lettres du Cardinal Mazarin pendant son ministère*, ed. P. A. Chéruel and G. d'Avenel (1872–1906), iv. 575. For La Ferté: E. Duvernoy, 'Gouverneurs et intendants de la Lorraine au xviie siècle', *Annuaire de la société d'histoire et d'archéologie de Lorraine*, xxxviii (1929), 14. Mazarin's presence at Sedan and the assistance accorded by the governors of the frontier fortresses were noted by Gaston and others in the *Parlement* of Paris: Talon, *Mémoires*, ed. Michaud and Poujoulat, p. 453. 'Un journal inédit du Parlement de Paris pendant la Fronde (1 déc. 1651–12 avril 1652)', *Annuaire-Bulletin de la société de l'histoire de France* [*année 1916*], ed. H. Courteault (1917), p. 212.

1. Carew, *op. cit.* pp. 458–9. In fact, Carew's verdict is substantially more accurate with regard to the secondary commanders than the leaders of the Catholic League. Mayenne was replaced by Biron as governor of Burgundy. Vendôme replaced Mercoeur as governor of Brittany, with Brissac as lieutenant-general.

failed were those in 1619–20, 1632 and 1641, which were badly co-ordinated, whose leadership and motives were unclear, or which suffered military defeat.[1] The first Fronde in January–March 1649 had a clear noble leadership.[2] Conty was its generalissimo, and he ensured that the demands of the nobles were presented in one document, much as in the early 1590s, 1614 and 1616. The great difficulty was the relationship between the *Frondeur* nobles and the *Parlement* of Paris. The *Parlement* made its peace with the government first, before the demands of the nobles were discussed and their interests were never properly taken into account.[3] Thereafter, the Fronde of the nobles saw no concerted leadership until 1652, and then the leadership divided. Gaston made his peace on 28 October 1652.[4] Condé became a Spanish generalissimo on 25 November 1652[5] and refused to make peace until the secret treaty was signed at the Pyrenees on 7 November 1659. Significantly, the projected marriage between Condé's son and Gaston's daughter could not take place during the Fronde because the children were too young,[6] and without this cement, the alliance between the two princes lacked durability.

The Fronde was not simply a struggle for royal patronage with Mazarin exclusively concerned with the defence of his position as chief minister and royal favourite. What made the Fronde so dangerous was that it was also the opposite. It was a struggle in which great issues were involved, which are largely outside the scope of this study, issues such as whether there was to be war or peace with Spain, the composition of the *ministériat*, the power of the government to levy taxes at will during a royal minority, and the administrative and fiscal consequences of a long war on the French office-holders and tax-payers. However, to understand the Fronde of the nobles, the way in which the political process operated has to be seen in perspective – against the background and issues of previous aristocratic revolts such as those against Concini, and through an appraisal of noble aspirations in which there was no convenient dividing-line between issues of principle and matters of self-interest. One need think back only to the self-interested attitude of the duc de Guise during the rebellions of the Catholic League, or that of the duc de Sully during the Protestant rebellions of 1615–16 and 1621–2 to see

1. It is significant that the only important military defeat inflicted on the government by the forces of rebellion was at La Marfée in 1641, but the death of the comte de Soissons, the leader of the revolt 'renversa tous les desseins...': *Mémoires... de Montglat*, p. 108.
2. There is a suggestion that the alliance between the *Frondeur* nobles was falling apart before the registration of the peace of Rueil, a rumour which they tried to dispel: BN MS fr. 3854, fo. 77, 25 March 1649.
3. Bonney, 'The French civil war', pp. 76, 79–80.
4. BN Dupuy 775, fo. 202.
5. H. E. P. L. d'Orléans, duc d'Aumale, *Histoire des princes de Condé pendant les xvie et xviie siècles* (1863–96), vi. 257.
6. *Ibid.* vi. 67. Gaston's daughter was under three at the time of the betrothal to the eight-year-old duc d'Enghien in 1651.

that principles and private interests had never been clearly separated. The Fronde was not a distinctive revolt in the sense that the nobles were unusually self-interested. Nor for that matter were dealings with Spain unusual. If rebellious Protestants could sign an alliance with Philip IV in 1629,[1] there was no difficulty at all in rebellious Catholic nobles doing so in 1650 and 1651.[2] Mazarin was unusual in that he did not sign an alliance with Spain during his exile in 1651, and he made a point of it in his propaganda.[3] On the other hand, the Cardinal recruited mercenary troops from the elector of Brandenburg: when Concini had recruited mercenary troops from Liège in 1617, this had been regarded as an act of treason.[4]

There is no denying that for the most part the Fronde was an inglorious rebellion. Yet if the nobles were often self-interested, Mazarin was not simply concerned with national survival during a war against Spain as his nineteenth-century biographer would have had us believe.[5] He was constantly preoccupied with family aggrandizement through marriage and the appropriation of governorships. It has been seen that this was a vital element in the confrontation with Condé in 1649. The same concerns were ever-present in Mazarin's career. In the last days of the Cardinal's life, his niece Hortensia Mancini married Charles-Armand de la Porte, La Meilleraye's son and Richelieu's second-cousin. Mazarin, with no son of his own, secured the survival of his name by stipulating as a condition of the marriage that La Porte be called the duc Mazarin. The aggrieved Nicolas Foucquet[6] provides an excellent witness of the chief minister's preoccupation with the marriage and succession question over a period of four or five years and the alternative ways of making La Meilleraye's son 'très puissant' and thus a fit husband for his niece. La Meilleraye's Breton estates and the lieutenant-generalship were

1. British Library, Add. MS. 30599, fos. 254–62, 3 May 1629.
2. The treaties were dated 30 Apr. 1650, 26 June 1650 and 6 Nov. 1651, the third of which was Condé's treaty with the Spanish: Bonney, 'The French civil war', pp. 80–81.
3. A.A.E. France 879, fo. 188, 23 Dec. 1651. Mazarin told Louis XIV that his love of France was so great that 'aucun mauvais traictement n'est capable de l'esbranler', which he contrasted with his opponents whom he called 'le party des Espagnolz'. The document, which was intended as a manifesto, includes an interesting justification of family aggrandizement: his was a family 'à qui l'aage n'a pas permis encore de pouvoir estre autre qu'innocente . . .'.
4. For Mazarin's recruitment of mercenaries under the comte de Waldeck: F. desRobert, *Charles IV et Mazarin, 1643–1661* (Nancy–Paris, 1899), p. 407. For Concini's recruitment of mercenaries as an act of treason: Hayem, *op. cit.* p. 231. BN 500 Colbert 221, fo. 23ᵛ.
5. Chéruel was not quite a biographer, but his account of the Fronde is centred on Mazarin and is flattering to him: P. A. Chéruel, *Histoire de France pendant la minorité de Louis XIV* (1879–80). Idem, *Histoire de France pendant le ministère de Mazarin, 1651–1661* (1882).
6. Apart from all his other grievances against Mazarin, Foucquet claimed that he had bought the fortresses of Belle-Île and Concarneau as a temporary service to the chief minister who intended them ultimately to form part of the inheritance of the duc Mazarin.

VII

deemed insufficient. The duc Mazarin must have a provincial governorship of his own. What better province to grant him than Alsace, bearing in mind all the difficulties the Cardinal had suffered with the comte d'Harcourt?[1] If Mazarin's difficulties with the great nobility arose in part because he was a foreigner, they were also a consequence of his ambition. In the words of Omer Talon, 'M. le Cardinal Mazarin . . . quoiqu'il fût f(a)ible, il ét(a)it glorieux . . . présumant beaucoup de sa conduite, et ne déférant aux sentimen(t)s de personne . . .'.[2]

It was the misfortune of France during the Fronde to suffer from the rival ambitions of a Condé,[3] who was aged only twenty-eight at the time of the breakdown in relations with the chief minister in 1649, and a Mazarin. This surely was a recipe for civil war if ever there was one – a civil war not ended until Condé accepted exile abroad and service to a foreign power, the fate Mazarin escaped by the skin of his teeth in 1651. Unlike his younger brother, Condé would never accept second place to Mazarin,[4] and it is surely no coincidence that it was not until January 1660, almost at the end of the Cardinal's life, that the first prince of the blood returned to France. On the other hand Conty followed a pattern which was much more typical of the French nobility. He ended his rebellion in 1653 and married Anna-Maria Martinozzi, another of Mazarin's nieces with a handsome dowry, the following year.[5] He was rewarded with important military commands and governorships culminating with the province of Languedoc on the death of Gaston d'Orléans in 1660. Conty's was certainly the easier path to the same objective.

If the Fronde was in part a personal rivalry between Mazarin and Condé it was also an expression of aristocratic opposition to the establishment of a *parvenu*, as the *Mazarinades* called him 'un étranger . . . de très sordide naissance'.[6] Mazarin established his position through the 'dispensation des bienfaictz'[7] so inevitably there was

---

1. *Les oeuvres de Mr Foucquet, ministre d'estat, contenant son accusation, son procez et ses défenses contre Louis XIV, roy de France*, (1696), xi. 12, 20. A.N. 144 a.p. 68, Dr. 2 [156 mi. 19], fos. 208, 216. The marriage contract was dated 28 Feb. 1661: G. Livet, *Le duc Mazarin. Gouverneur d'Alsace, 1661–1713* (Strasbourg-Paris, 1954), p. 15.
2. Talon, *Mémoires*, ed. Michaud and Poujoulat, p. 397.
3. For Condé's estimated fortune of 14·6 million *livres* in 1651: Labatut, *op. cit.* pp. 258–9. *Cf.* D. Roche, 'Aperçus sur la fortune et les revenus des princes de Condé à l'aube du xviiie siècle', *Revue d'histoire moderne et contemporaine*, xiv (1967), 217–43.
4. *Mémoires . . . de Montglat*, pp. 278–9: Condé 'avoit le coeur si grand, qu'il ne put jamais se resoudre à dépendre du cardinal Mazarin . . .'.
5. The dowry was 600,000 *livres*: Labatut, *op. cit.* p. 253.
6. As early as the *Requête des Trois États . . .* (1648): *Choix de Mazarinades*, ed. Moreau, i. 28–29. *Cf.* Retz's view: D. A. Watts, *Cardinal de Retz. The ambiguities of a seventeenth-century mind* (Oxford, 1980), p. 116. Retz was one of the signatories of the aristocratic union of 18 Jan. 1649.
7. Mazarin's 'choix . . . des personnes de toutes conditions qu'il a avancées au préjudice de ceux qui le méritent' was criticized by the *Parlement* of Paris: A.A.E. France 882, fo. 102, 23 March 1652.

criticism from established peers of the realm or claimants whose ambitions had not been realized.[1] The consistent support of Anne of Austria to her chief minister was of vital importance to Mazarin: it was with the Regent's assistance that he was able to raise the status of seventeen great noble families to peers of the realm between 1648 and 1652, a proliferation of titles that was unprecedented in the sixteenth and seventeenth centuries.[2] At first sight, this 'inflation of honours' appears to have been Mazarin's response to political difficulty. The chief minister tried to buy his way out of trouble. He obtained new titles for the great nobility and in return he expected consistent political support. Matters are rarely quite so simple. The status of duke was conferred on Chancellor Séguier in 1650, but the seals were removed from his custody twice during the Fronde, he participated in the council of the princes at Paris in the summer of 1652, and his son-in-law, the duc de Sully, opened the gates of Mantes to the rebel army.[3] The duchy of Rohan was re-established in 1648 for Henri Chabot, yet as governor of Anjou Rohan-Chabot joined Condé's rebellion in 1652.[4] On the other hand, for Bouillon, Conty, La Meilleraye and others the advantages of alliance with the chief minister were real enough, particularly after Mazarin achieved the status of duke and peer in his own right after the Fronde. Ironically, Mazarin's letters patent praised his 'douceur et . . . humanité sans exemple (à) concilier les intérêts des princes, des principales personnes et tout le corps de notre état . . .'.[5] A rather different story would have been told during the Fronde.

1. Labatut, *op. cit.* pp. 372-4. J. D. Lassaigne, *Les assemblées de la noblesse de France au xviie et xviiie siècles* (1965-6).
2. Labatut, *op. cit.* p. 81.
3. Labatut, *op. cit.* p. 96. *Journal des guerres civiles de Dubuisson-Aubenay* . . . , ed. Saige, ii. 274-5. Foucquet referred to this incident during his trial, rather unwisely since Chancellor Séguier was one of his judges: *Archives de la Bastille. Documents inédits. Règne de Louis XIV*, ed. F. Ravaisson-Mollien (1866, repr. Geneva, 1975), ii. 377-8.
4. Labatut, *op. cit.* p. 74. A. Débidour. *La Fronde angevine. Tableau de la vie municipale au xviie siècle* (1877), pp. 273-95.
5. Labatut, *op. cit.* p. 95. Mazarin purchased the duchy of Nevers from Charles III de Gonzague in 1659 (*ibid.* p. 75) and the letters patent were issued the following year. Mazarin purchased the duchy of Mayenne for 756,000 *livres* from the same duke of Mantua on 29 May 1654: Dessert, 'Pouvoir et finance', p. 166.

VIII

LA FRONDE DES OFFICIERS : MOUVEMENT RÉFORMISTE OU RÉBELLION CORPORATISTE ?

Selon Kossmann, la Fronde serait « une période d'imprudence et d'exagération sans signification et sans but. Elle n'est rien, car elle est tout en même temps ». Pour lui, les propositions de la Chambre Saint-Louis sont « simplistes, naïves, encombrantes mais foncièrement inoffensives ». Tout cela, conclue-t-il, « n'est pas une réforme du royaume. Cette réglementation est beaucoup trop partielle, trop superficielle... La révolution n'est pas venue »[1].

Tout au contraire, L. Moote présente la Fronde comme « une révolte des juges », une réaction des officiers contre la véritable révolution que Louis XIII avait apportée dans le gouvernement. Les propositions de la Chambre Saint-Louis, affirme-t-il, étaient « une tentative sérieuse de dissiper le malaise institutionnel ». Ces juges n'étaient pas des révolutionnaires : ils évitaient « les enjeux contitutionnels fondamentaux qui sont d'ordinaire l'avant-garde des révolutions réussies ». Ils étaient des réformateurs. « Leur attention aux réformes fiscales n'était pas le signe d'une entreprise superficielle, elle témoignait de la volonté d'affronter le problème immédiatement à l'ordre du jour »[2]. Plus récemment, un autre auteur, P. Zagorin, a parlé de la Fronde comme d'une « guerre civile révolutionnaire », mais il se range *grosso modo* aux opinions de L. Moote. « Les officiers étaient, note-t-il, les partisans d'une restauration, c'est-à-dire fidèles à la tradition, la coutume, condamnant l'innovation. » Il est vrai qu'un élan conservateur se retrouve souvent derrière les changements révolutionnaires survenus au cours des premiers âges de l'Europe moderne. Dans le contexte de 1648, un projet de restauration pouvait acquérir, chemin faisant, une signification originale. Selon la conclusion de Zagorin, les réformes proposées par les officiers venaient heurter les fondements même de l'absolutisme et du gouvernement monarchique[3].

Les oppositions historiographiques sont claires. Les uns, comme Moote et Zagorin, voient dans la Fronde des officiers un mouvement de réforme modéré, qui publie des propositions adaptées à l'état de la France en 1648. A l'inverse, d'autres, comme Kossmann, pensent qu'il s'agit « simplement d'une attaque contre les partisans, doublée d'une tentative de contrôler à l'avenir plus étroitement la gestion des finances par le gouvernement ». Ce fut un essai pour « résoudre l'inextricable chaos d'expédients fiscaux, sans pouvoir ni vouloir proposer les moyens de réorganiser le système des impôts d'une manière plus efficace »[4]. Le mouvement ne fut donc ni réformiste ni même adapté à l'état de la France en 1648.

Il y a trop d'écart entre les deux points de vue pour envisager de les concilier. Une fois de plus donc, il faut enquêter sur la Fronde, en s'interrogeant moins sur l'évolution du conflit avec le gouvernement que sur les buts premiers des officiers. Dans cette enquête, on évitera le mot de réforme qui implique un jugement de valeur, on parlera plutôt de propositions, vocable neutre qui ne préjuge pas des conclusions. Juger de la pertinence de ces propositions suppose une analyse de la politique royale avant la Fronde[5]. On se demandera aussi comment les contre-propositions des officiers, parisiens ou provinciaux, répondaient aux besoins du royaume, si leurs auteurs agissaient dans l'intérêt de la France ou dans la seule perspective de leurs intérêts corporatifs. Enfin, l'on étudiera le sort de ces propositions.

Ce réexamen devrait conduire à une perspective différente sur la Fronde. Celle-ci ne saurait, bien sûr, tout expliquer, car le rôle de la noblesse demanderait lui aussi une étude. Du moins toutes les thèses sur la Fronde confirment-elles le caractère primordial du mouvement des officiers en 1648-1649 sans lequel les agitations consécutives des Grands n'auraient jamais pu avoir lieu[6]. Les diverses étapes de la rébellion de 1648 à 1653 ont certes leur importance, mais l'examen des propositions financières et fiscales des officiers conditionne tout le reste.

*
* *

Pour Moote, si les propositions des officiers en 1648 souffraient d'une faiblesse particulière, c'est qu'elles étaient le produit de circonstances extraordinaires[7]. Il y avait d'abord et surtout une crise diplomatique. Les Hollandais avaient signé une paix séparée avec l'Espagne en janvier 1648, tandis que les négociations entre la France et l'Espagne avaient échoué. La paix avec l'Empereur ne semblait pas proche. Il y avait un grave risque que la Suède, l'autre grand allié de la France, ne suive l'exemple hollandais. Certes, la critique de la diplomatie royale n'apparaît pas dans la crise de l'été 1648, mais il n'y a aucun doute que la lassitude de la guerre était un aspect essentiel de la crise, de même que l'impatience en face de l'énorme charge fiscale résultant de treize années de guerre, et la certitude que les finances royales étaient mal gérées aussi bien dans les opérations de recette que dans les dépenses.

On ne peut dire si ce mécontentement aurait explosé sans les erreurs de tactique du gouvernement. Du fait des pratiques financières de Mazarin et d'Hémery, la couronne était acculée à la banqueroute dès la fin de 1647. Pouvait-on trouver des revenus neufs pour conjurer la banqueroute ? Cela aurait été bien difficile si l'on en juge

La Fronde des officiers

par l'opposition aux sept édits fiscaux imposés par le Lit de Justice du 15 janvier 1648. Le pouvoir avait aussi la possibilité de publier la banqueroute et de tenter de tourner l'affaire à son avantage ; cette solution avait été discutée et rejetée en août 1647 ; on y recourut en juillet 1648, trop tard. En définitive, on s'acheminait vers une banqueroute involontaire, provoquée par la perte de confiance des financiers. C'est ce qui arriva entre le 13 mai et le 30 juin 1648, pendant le débat sur la réunion de la Chambre Saint-Louis. Les ministres ne cachaient pas leur désarroi : « Il y a six semaines que le commerce d'argent a cessé. » La grande peur des gens de finances était que la Chambre Saint-Louis ne se limite pas aux plaintes des officiers mais envisage la politique royale dans son ensemble. La réunion serait devenue « une occasion de plainte et douleur générale pour décrier le gouvernement de l'Etat » ; les conséquences sur le gouvernement et sur les finances seraient imprévisibles.

Au cours du printemps et du début de l'été, le pouvoir commit deux graves erreurs tactiques. La première aboutit à souder l'opposition des officiers. Le 29 avril, Hémery avait suspendu les gages de tous les tribunaux, à l'exception de ceux du Parlement de Paris, cet expédient devant remplacer le manque à gagner du droit annuel. Certes, dans le passé, le Parlement avait reçu des traitements privilégiés, mais l'astuce cette fois était trop visible. En outre, nombre de conseillers avaient des parents dans les autres cours souveraines, qui leur demandaient de maintenir leur opposition. Le résultat fut l'arrêt d'union du 13 mai, annonçant qu'une réunion se tiendrait à la chambre Saint-Louis pour débattre des doléances des officiers. Ayant compris son erreur, Hémery voulut battre en retraite, d'autant plus qu'il redoutait une enquête sur sa gestion financière. Son avis fut repoussé par les autres ministres qui dénonçaient le scandale inouï de l'arrêt d'union et les conséquences à venir si des assemblées politiques telles que la Chambre Saint-Louis voyaient le jour. Leur fermeté entraîna une impasse de six semaines et l'effondrement de la confiance des financiers.

La seconde erreur tactique fut, le 27 juin, d'autoriser, pour trois jours après, la réunion de la Chambre. Cette capitulation prouvait que le gouvernement ne tarderait pas à s'incliner devant au moins plusieurs requêtes des officiers. De plus, rien n'assurait que les discussions de la Chambre se limiteraient à ces requêtes. Si des déclarations royales devaient en résulter, quel serait leur statut ? Les officiers voulaient qu'elles devinssent des textes solennels comparables aux grandes ordonnances réformatrices du XVIe siècle. Les ministres, au contraire, ne les envisageaient pas comme des réformes légales et définitives, mais comme des expédients qui permettraient au gouvernement de regagner un peu de crédit. Une fois les difficultés passées, les déclarations seraient annulées et réputées « extorquées par la violence des peuples ». Ce malentendu fondamental portait en germe les guerres civiles de l'année suivante.

Dans sa première proposition rédigée le 30 juin, la Chambre demandait la révocation immédiate des intendants de justice et de « toutes les autres commissions extraordinaires non vérifiées ès cours souveraines ». Des arrêts du Parlement, le 4 juillet, et de la Cour des aides, le 7 juillet, suivirent. Les intendants avaient été établis en 1642 dans chaque généralité des pays d'élections. Ils avaient pour charge la répartition des tailles selon le règlement du 22 août 1642 modifié par la déclaration du 16 avril 1643. Bien que les parlements aient tenté d'obliger les intendants à soumettre leurs commissions à un enregistrement, bien peu de commissaires s'étaient pliés à cette formalité. Le 10 juillet, le gouvernement consentit à révoquer les intendants envoyés dans le ressort du Parlement de Paris. Au cours de juillet, cependant, les ministres avancèrent qu'un certain nombre d'intendants étaient indispensables, ce nombre restant à négocier.

Au bout du compte, une déclaration royale du 18 juillet admit l'emploi d'intendants en Champagne, Picardie, Lyonnais, Provence, Bourgogne et Languedoc. Contrairement à ce qu'avaient réclamé les officiers, les intendants n'étaient pas cités nommément, il n'y avait pas non plus trace d'un enregistrement obligé devant les cours souveraines. Le chancelier Séguier avait tenté de sauver les pouvoirs fiscaux des intendants. Il avait agité le spectre d'une débâcle des recouvrements, et les arrérages qui s'accumulèrent pendant les années de Fronde lui donnèrent raison ; mais, là dessus, les opposants de ce mois de juillet avaient été intraitables. A titre de compromis, Séguier suggérait que les intendants maintenus puissent assister les gouverneurs des provinces dans leurs tâches militaires, sans posséder toutefois de prérogatives contentieuses ou financières, puisque cette juridiction revenait aux trésoriers et aux élus qui en avaient été dépouillés par le règlement du 22 août 1642. Cette disposition n'était pas négligeable, car à cette époque les pouvoirs fiscaux et militaires n'étaient pas séparables. Les six intendants demeurés en place furent chargés de payer la subsistance des troupes de leur province. Lorsque l'impôt des subsistances pouvait être levé, comme en Bourgogne en décembre 1648, l'intendant avait à y procéder selon les termes de la déclaration du 16 avril 1643. Dans les provinces où ils avaient été retirés, on put les faire revenir en les appelant intendants d'armée, puisque ceux-ci détenaient les pouvoirs financiers dans les territoires d'opération de leur armée.

Les critiques envers les intendants émanaient spécialement des officiers spoliés, trésoriers et élus. Les élus proclamaient que « le Roy est mal servi et le peuple ruiné par les traitants, leurs intendants et autres gens à leur dévotion qui font toutes leurs vexations impunément ». Les trésoriers avaient envoyé une députation auprès du Parlement pour dénoncer les « concussions, péculats, rançonnements

La Fronde des officiers

et autres violences ». « Ces intendants et partisans, déclaraient-ils, ont travaillé non seulement pour la ruine desdits trésoriers de France mais de tous les autres officiers des provinces. »

Les officiers auraient voulu une déclaration royale commençant par ces mots : « Le Roy ayant été informé des abus qui se commettoient dans les provinces par les intendants de justice au fait des tailles. » Le chancelier s'y opposa avec véhémence : « Il se pouvait, dit-il, que quelques-uns eussent malversé, mais il ne falloit pas les condamner tous, mais épargner leur honneur. » On lui répliqua que « c'étoit gens qui n'en avoient point ». Pourtant, si les parlementaires parisiens étaient prêts à défendre les pouvoirs de juridiction des trésoriers et des élus, ils ne voulaient pas humilier les anciens intendants. De la sorte, l'introduction de la déclaration du 18 juillet, vérifiée au Parlement le même jour, fut édulcorée ; elle suggéra que les abus avaient été involontaires et que le principal grief était la spoliation des officiers : « Le défunt roi ayant commis dans les généralités du royaume quelques-uns de nos officiers, avec pouvoir de faire l'imposition de nos deniers, en quoi il s'est *insensiblement* glissé plusieurs abus, outre l'intérêt notable qu'ont les officiers ordinaires créés et institués à cette fin, qui se trouvoient par ce moyen privés de la principale fonction de leur charge »[8].

Certes, le Parlement avait déjà présenté des remontrances contre les intendants les 1er février 1645, 10 avril 1647, et 29 août 1647, mais les conseillers ne souhaitaient pas accabler individuellement les intendants, soit en les excluant des fonctions publiques, soit en les condamnant à des restitutions pécuniaires pour leurs détournements prétendus. Cette modération résultait d'une solidarité sociale : presque tous les 128 intendants nommés par Richelieu et Mazarin étaient maîtres des requêtes et 56 d'entre eux avaient commencé leur carrière au Parlement.

La seconde proposition de la Chambre était de révoquer les baux des fermiers des tailles, taillon et subsistances, qui devaient désormais être levés « en la forme ancienne et comme auparavant ». A partir de 1642, le Conseil avait parfois nommé des receveurs généraux pour aider les intendants au département des tailles. Les intendants avaient pouvoir d'examiner les registres des receveurs et de poursuivre les cas de négligence ou de péculat. Ils pouvaient aussi démettre les receveurs et les remplacer par des commis proposés par les financiers. En ce qui concerne les personnes, ce changement avait pu être sans grande conséquence, puisque les associations de financiers prêtant au roi comprenaient souvent des receveurs de généralité. Mais au regard des institutions, le changement était d'importance, puisque, à la différence des receveurs, les commis offraient une garantie supplémentaire au profit des financiers. La mesure avait pour but d'empêcher les trop lourds arrérages et, après 1643, ce but fut à peu près atteint.

Les recettes de tous les impôts, y compris les tailles, avaient été systématiquement anticipées durant les dernières années de Louis XIII. La responsabilité ne peut pas en être attribuée — comme beaucoup d'historiens l'ont fait [9] — à Mazarin et Hémery. En 1642, les recettes des tailles avaient été anticipées d'un an par le moyen des emprunts contractés auprès des financiers. Hémery ne fit qu'aggraver le procédé au point de faire un peu figure de précurseur de John Law. En 1645, il avait engagé les revenus de la monarchie jusqu'en 1647. En 1648, il aliénait ceux de 1650 et 1651. Sous le gouvernement de la Régence, de 1643 à 1648, les emprunts royaux s'étaient élevés à la moyenne annuelle de 63 millions de livres, avec le record de 123 millions en 1645.

Les objections à la politique d'emprunts étaient nombreuses, mais la principale était l'inefficacité du procédé, du fait du poids croissant dans les impôts des intérêts à verser aux financiers. La seconde proposition de la Chambre dénonçait ce système et réclamait la libération des prisonniers détenus pour les restes des tailles. Elle demandait la remise des restes de 1646, puis, pour la suite, un rabais d'un quart, « beaucoup moindre que ce qu'en profitent les traitants ». Le conseiller Broussel se tailla un moment de gloire en justifiant le rabais du quart, « puisque les traitants avaient pareille remise » [10]. Cette remise ne résultait pas d'une intention polémique : l'intérêt des emprunts se limitait à 16,6 % dans la généralité de Paris, mais montait à 25 % partout ailleurs [11]. Le succès de la proposition dépendait de la capacité de la couronne à se passer des emprunts et de la valeur d'un budget amputé d'un quart des recettes directes.

Kossmann qualifie de naïve cette proposition de la Chambre. Dans le cas d'une paix à tout prix, la proposition était raisonnable. Mais il était rien moins que certain que Philippe IV ou Ferdinand III aient la même bonne foi, et plus vraisemblable qu'ils y verraient un signe de faiblesse, une promesse de capitulation. Gaston d'Orléans développa cette opinion devant la Chambre qu'il tentait de renvoyer. « Les ennemis, dit-il, se prévalloient, supposant que le royaume estoit divisé et qu'il penchoit à un soulèvement général. »

L'exemple des années 1635-1642 montrait que le gouvernement ne pourrait survivre à la fois à une réduction des impôts et à un retour aux levées « en la forme ancienne ». Les recettes n'étaient pas arrivées à Paris assez régulièrement ni assez vite pour soutenir l'effort de guerre ; les arrérages de certaines provinces avaient été gigantesques en 1642-43. Les intendants avec leurs brigades employées aux recouvrements avaient empêché l'effondrement du système fiscal. Mais en 1648, le rappel des intendants et le renvoi de leurs brigades laissaient les trésoriers et les élus impuissants en face des paroisses récalcitrantes. En janvier 1653, les élus reconnurent 30 millions d'arrérages pour seulement quatre années de taxes très réduites.

La Fronde des officiers

La déclaration du 18 juillet 1648 confirma le rappel des intendants — à l'exception de six —, la réduction des impôts d'un huitième, le retour en charge des receveurs généraux, « excepté ceux qui seront notoirement insolvables, accusés d'omissions de recettes et autres malversations ». Les prisonniers des tailles seraient libérés et les restes de 1646 remis. Ces concessions devaient être encore étendues par la suite. La déclaration du 20 octobre porta la réduction au cinquième des impôts directs des pays d'élections (soit 10 millions de livres, la charge étant estimée à 50 millions).

La troisième proposition renforçait la précédente, en demandant qu'après le paiement des charges ordinaires, toutes les assignations au profit des financiers fussent annulées et employées « à l'entretènement des maisons royales et affaires de la guerre ». Elle fut mise en œuvre par un arrêt du Conseil du 18 juillet. Le pouvoir n'y renonçait pas complètement aux emprunts ; Mazarin espérait seulement anticiper une nouvelle fois les revenus de 1649, 1650 et 1651 à un taux d'intérêt réduit. Quelques financiers, par crainte du pire, acceptaient de renégocier leurs contrats, mais il était peu probable que la majorité d'entre eux souhaitassent ou pussent le faire. La banqueroute fut générale à l'été 1648, elle touchait des douzaines de financiers. Puisqu'ils s'avéraient incapables d'emprunter sur le marché pour reprêter au roi, les financiers devaient solliciter du Conseil des arrêts de surséance pour se préserver de leurs créanciers. Tout au long de la Fronde, le premier souci des surintendants successifs fut de restaurer le crédit. Ceci n'était possible que si l'on reconnaissait que la révocation de 1648 était une rupture de contrat. « Bien loin d'apporter de l'argent dans l'Epargne, dit-on, plus tard, cette révocation tarissait toutes les sources d'où l'on en pouvoit espérer. » Les créances révoquées furent estimées de 80 à 120 millions de livres. Si le gouvernement voulait vraiment rétablir le crédit, il lui fallait alors dégager des fonds suffisants pour payer aux financiers les intérêts de leurs baux révoqués. Cette perspective était, bien sûr, regardée par les officiers comme inadmissible.

La quatrième proposition développait l'opinion frondeuse sur ce dernier point. Elle réclamait une Chambre de justice qui serait composée de conseillers députés par les quatre cours souveraines parisiennes. Elle enquêterait sur les « abus et malversations », et elle ne pourrait pas être renvoyée après paiement de compositions pécuniaires consenties par les financiers. Des lettres patentes du 12 juillet, enregistrées au Parlement le 18, annoncèrent effectivement la formation de cette Chambre de justice [12]. Il n'était pas précisé qui en nommerait les membres, réservant par là leur nomination à la couronne ; ils seraient choisis parmi les conseillers des cours souveraines, parisiennes ou non. La compétence était étendue non seulement aux abus et malversations, selon la formule consacrée, mais aussi aux « exactions et violences commises dans les provinces ». La Chambre pouvait ainsi enquêter sur la gestion des intendants avant 1648, mais, à vrai dire, rien n'annonçait que le gouvernement fût décidé à agir avec vigueur.

Au Lit de Justice du 31 juillet, Molé, premier président du Parlement, dénonça les prêts usuraires des gens d'affaires. Il imaginait que la couronne trouverait dans la confiscation des biens des financiers des « trésors immenses »[13] permettant de couvrir les dépenses de la guerre. Dans un mémoire, de ton plus modéré, Molé répétait : « Il est temps, Sire, de presser ces éponges et leur faire rendre ce que si injustement elles retiennent il y a si longtemps. Si Votre Majesté le commande, elle trouvera en un moment de quoi satisfaire à la dépense de plusieurs années. » Molé parlait de « justice publique »[14], mais le terme de revanche aurait été plus exact. Les officiers avaient souffert la perte de leurs gages et ne plaindraient pas les financiers qui seraient ruinés par la Chambre : « Encore leur restera-t-il beaucoup plus qu'ils n'ont eu par le partage de leurs pères. » Comme ils l'avaient dit le 9 juillet : « Puisque le roi avait déjà fait banqueroute aux gens d'honneur (c'est-à-dire aux officiers), il la pouvait bien faire à quatre ou cinq partisans »[15].

La suspension des gages des officiers par Hémery le 29 avril mettait le comble à une politique déjà ancienne. Les officiers étaient atteints dans les revenus du capital placé dans l'achat de leur office. Depuis 1645, Hémery révoquait systématiquement les gages et rentes qui avaient été assignés sur les recettes locales des tailles ou d'autres taxes. Il avait retranché un quart des gages des cours souveraines, la moitié des gages des autres officiers et les retranchements étaient encore plus sévères chaque année. Ces mesures étaient d'autant plus impopulaires que l'économie prétendue était presque annulée par les conditions des emprunts gagés là-dessus, anticipés et chargés d'intérêts. Comme l'écrivait Omer Talon dans ses *Mémoires* : « Hémery ne faisoit plus subsister l'Etat que des retranchements qu'il faisoit sur les officiers et sur les rentes... Ces retranchements furent mis en parti à des gens qui en fournissoient l'argent et auxquels le roi bailloit quinze pour cent d'intérêts »[16]. La sixième proposition de la Chambre Saint-Louis exigeait l'abrogation de tous les emprunts, y compris ceux faits sur les retranchements de gages ou de rentes. Les financiers dénoncés par le Parlement le 22 août étaient ceux-là mêmes qui avaient formé « le parti du retranchement des gages des officiers »[17]. C'est cette offensive d'août qui conduisit le Conseil à tenter l'arrestation de Broussel et des principaux opposants.

Officiers et rentiers se confondaient. Plus des trois-quarts des Parlementaires étaient rentiers, selon les fermiers des aides (1652)[18]. La huitième proposition, qui soumettait les retranchements de gages ou de rentes à une vérification des cours souveraines, « avec liberté des suffrages », était donc l'expression d'un intérêt corporatif.

La Fronde des officiers

A court terme, la neuvième proposition envisageait pour 1648 le paiement des rentes selon des proportions de 40, 50 ou 62,5 %, suivant leur revenu d'assignation. Elles seraient payées « par préférence à toutes charges, même de la partie de l'Epargne ». La déclaration du 22 octobre 1648 porta pour la durée de la guerre le taux de paiement jusqu'à 50 et même 62,5 % pour les rentes assignées sur les gabelles, le clergé et les aides. Le gouvernement ne tint pas parole ; il y eut cessation des paiements en janvier 1649, puis en janvier et en août 1652. Malgré tout, Mazarin pouvait encore à son second retour d'exil être accueilli comme le champion des rentiers parisiens.

La treizième proposition concernait l'usage des « comptants par certifications ». C'était, en théorie, des paiements devant rester secrets pour raison d'Etat. En pratique, il s'agissait d'affaires politiques sans publicité et sans examen de la Chambre des comptes [19]. La Chambre Saint-Louis notait que « l'administration serait toujours suspecte au public jusqu'à ce que l'on ait remédié à l'excès desdits comptants ». Pendant les années de paix de Henri IV, les comptants étaient montés à trois millions annuels. Ils dépassaient 49 millions par an entre 1643 et 1648. Cette croissance était le produit de taux d'intérêts supérieurs au denier légal 18 (5,55 %) fixé par la Chambre des comptes. Dans un discours du 3 août, Nicolay, premier président des Comptes, voyait là la première réforme nécessaire dans les finances, même pour les paiements à des alliés étrangers : « Il n'y [avait] rien à craindre que le monde en fût instruit » [20]. Pour les ministres, bien sûr, le secret devait être gardé, ne fût-ce que pour rassurer les financiers. Aucune concession dans ce sens n'apparut dans les déclarations des 31 juillet et 22 octobre [21]. Par un arrêt de vérification (27 novembre), la Chambre des comptes imposa la limite annuelle de trois millions [22]. En fait, de 1649 à 1652, la moyenne annuelle monta à cinq millions. Tous les surintendants, de La Meilleraye à La Vieuville, avouaient que les dépenses secrètes devaient fatalement dépasser le seuil des trois millions. Les ministres firent annuler le seuil qu'avait voulu imposer la Chambre des comptes par un arrêt du Conseil (16 novembre 1652), moins d'un mois après le retour à Paris.

Les autres propositions de la Chambre Saint-Louis touchaient soit la gestion des finances, soit les intérêts corporatifs des officiers. Par exemple, la quatorzième proposition soumettait les créations d'offices à une vérification par les cours souveraines. Elle visait particulièrement la création en janvier 1648 de douze maîtres des requêtes, création révoquée le 31 juillet. Elle condamnait aussi la création de parlements semestres, c'est-à-dire une seconde chambre alternant tous les six mois avec la première, citant le cas d'Aix, mais pas celui de Rouen. La déclaration du 22 octobre consentit à la suspension des créations pendant quatre ans et à leur vérification par les cours.

Les dix-neuvième et vingtième propositions tentaient de préserver la compétence des cours souveraines entamée par la juridiction des maîtres des requêtes ; la déclaration royale les entérina. L'esprit de réforme des officiers se confondait souvent avec leurs intérêts de corps ; ainsi que l'exprimait Talon : « Les officiers ont abandonné *en apparence* leurs intérêts pour travailler à ceux du public, mais dans les considérations publiques ils ont trouvé ce qu'ils désiraient » [23].

Est-ce que cette convergence d'intérêts divers pourrait durer longtemps ? Voyons la vingt-et-unième proposition qui constituait une espèce de version française de l'*habeas corpus*. La déclaration du 22 octobre limita significativement la condamnation des arrestations arbitaires, par lettres de cachet, aux seuls officiers. Il en fut de même pour les retranchements de gages, que refusaient les huitième, quatorzième et dix-septième propositions. La déclaration se contenta de renouveler le droit annuel selon les dispositions de 1637, soit sans emprunt forcé [24]. Les gages seraient versés pendant la durée de la guerre aux trois-quarts pour les cours souveraines et seulement à moitié pour les élus. Le renouvellement du droit annuel était pareillement soumis à des modulations. Cette tactique de division réussit et des parlementaires le reconnurent plus tard [25]. Les cours souveraines acceptèrent les termes du gouvernement et abandonnèrent la fragile « cause commune » de tous les officiers.

*
* *

Séguier, commentant les propositions fiscales de 1648, notait que « sur toutes les affaires, on parloit comme si on eût été en pleine paix » [26]. Les officiers semblaient croire la paix imminente, accessible avec un peu de bonne foi de la part des ministres. Le temps était donc venu, à leurs yeux, de restaurer le gouvernement du royaume et d'envisager des mesures à longue échéance en ignorant les difficultés les plus immédiates. Le Parlement réclamait donc des réformes de base : « Il suffiroit de penser au plus pressé et à ce qui étoit de plus de conséquence » [27].

Les concessions arrachées au pouvoir portaient le manque à gagner à trente millions de livres par an ; on estimait, d'autre part, en juillet 1649, que les remises de taxes, le rétablissement de gages et rentes et les résistances antifiscales des provinces ne laissaient plus au roi que vingt millions de revenu net. « Les finances étoient ainsi réglées et le pouvoir de lever des deniers si limité qu'il étoit impossible que le roi pût dorénavant soutenir la guerre » [28].

A ces problèmes financiers, les officiers proposaient des solutions explicitées par les remontrances présentées par les Comptes le 14 octobre 1648 [29]. Trop tardives pour être envisagées par la déclaration du 22 octobre, bousculées ensuite par les événements du blocus de Paris, ces remontrances tombèrent dans l'oubli. Elles réfutent pourtant l'accusation de simplisme avancée par Kossmann. Elles confirment l'opinion de Moote qui voit dans l'arrêt de vérification du 27 novembre la volonté de la Chambre des comptes de préserver les acquis de la Fronde parlementaire [30].

Plus qu'une simple Chambre de justice, les Comptes voulaient une enquête exhaustive sur la gestion des finances depuis 1630, sur les abus des comptants, des traités et des emprunts. Les rachats de rentes auraient coûté à la couronne trente millions et quinze autres millions auraient été perdus dans les aliénations du domaine royal. La gestion des fermes était sévèrement critiquée [31], ainsi que le marché du crédit, les buts des fermiers et le secret des transactions. Les Comptes dénonçaient la facilité donnée par le Conseil aux financiers de contracter des réemprunts au lieu de fournir une consignation en numéraire, la permission de jouir des baux avant leur enregistrement et leur examen par les Comptes. Le principe même des affaires extraordinaires était refusé. Le rôle des donneurs d'avis était condamné comme « tendant à la subversion [des lois] du royaume ». Les Comptes s'engageaient à d'autres contributions après le retour de la paix. Les remontrances n'expliquaient pas au bout de quel délai le roi tirerait profit d'une telle politique. La Chambre de justice de 1661 durerait cinq années de pleine activité. Dans l'immédiat, aucune nouvelle recette n'était imaginée, de sorte que le roi allait dépendre entièrement du succès des enquêtes sur la mauvaise gestion ancienne ou des économies promises dans le fonctionnement des impôts.

La réalité était cruelle. Entre 1643 et 1648, les dépenses de guerre à elles seules étaient montées à 41 millions de livres par an, plus du double du revenu net de vingt millions trouvé en 1649. La paix avait été signée avec l'Empereur en octobre 1648, mais il n'y avait rien de conclu avec l'Espagne et il fallait préparer la campagne de 1649 qui allait aboutir finalement au siège de Cambrai. Les dépenses militaires se présentaient dès les premiers mois de 1649 alors que les recettes n'arriveraient pas avant mai [32]. Dans une déclaration du 9 décembre, La Meilleraye avait fixé à 15 % les intérêts des emprunts anticipant sur les tailles. Cette déclaration fut retirée le 2 janvier après protestation du Parlement et des Comptes, mais elle demeura la référence politique pendant le blocus de Paris et le séjour de la Cour à Saint-Germain. A la paix de Rueil (11 mars), Molé et les Frondeurs modérés acceptèrent le denier 12 (8,33 %) pour les exercices de 1649 et 1650, mais le Parlement, en définitive, refusa son accord [33]. Si l'on considère que le taux de La Meilleraye était jugé insuffisant par les financiers, on mesure l'abîme entre les positions. Les opinions des officiers et celles du Conseil s'étaient encore éloignées pendant le siège de Paris. Lorsque le versement d'intérêts par la couronne reprendrait, les taux versés seraient bien plus proches des 25 % qui avaient provoqué la Fronde que des 8 % proposés au traité de Rueil.

Les officiers n'avaient pas réussi à convaincre les ministres de la sagesse ni de l'opportunité de leurs propositions [34]. Il leur fallait chercher d'autres alliés dans les cours souveraines provinciales [35] ou dans la grande noblesse, mais leur programme risquait d'y être oublié. Les cours provinciales, par exemple le Parlement d'Aix, n'insistaient pas pareillement sur les problèmes financiers et s'intéressaient surtout à des enjeux provinciaux comme l'hostilité au gouverneur, le comte d'Alais. Ces intérêts locaux éloignaient les corps provinciaux de la cause parisienne [36].

Les Parlements de Paris, Rouen, Aix et Bordeaux avaient chacun leurs enjeux particuliers. En dépit de leurs communs parrainages aristocratiques, les révoltes de Paris et de Rouen divergeaient bientôt. Longueville avait compris que, pour rallier à lui la cour de Rouen, il lui fallait à son tour réclamer la révocation du semestre. Après cet engagement, la venue d'un nouveau gouverneur nommé par Mazarin, le comte d'Harcourt, suffit à faire basculer la province dans la révolte. En Provence aussi la source des troubles fut la création d'un semestre, mais le comte d'Alais ne donna pas le signal de la révolte. Ce fut l'affaire d'une faction parlementaire résolue à obtenir la révocation du semestre et le rappel du comte d'Alais ; la première tâche s'avéra la plus facile. En Guyenne, il n'y avait pas de problème de semestre, mais un conflit aigu entre le Parlement et le gouverneur, le duc d'Epernon, appuyé par Mazarin. Ce conflit culmina entre mars 1649 et janvier 1650, alors qu'à ce moment les troubles parisiens avaient cessé. Certes, pendant les négociations de Rueil, Molé avait soutenu les révocations des semestres de Rouen et d'Aix, mais l'engagement n'alla pas plus loin [37]. Les motifs d'opposition étaient, en 1649, plus nombreux et plus puissants que les motifs de loyauté au Conseil, mais les motifs différaient considérablement d'un parlement à un autre [38]. Paris voulait « conserver l'avantage de sa primogéniture et sa dignité », et en septembre 1650 il refusa une union politique avec la cour de Toulouse [39].

Les grands nobles étaient plus difficiles encore à contrôler. Durant le blocus de Paris, une troupe bigarrée de gentilshommes mécontents avait rejoint la capitale et signé entre eux, le 18 janvier 1649, une alliance aux côtés du Parlement et contre Mazarin. Le Parlement ne reconnut jamais formellement cette alliance, mais accepta son concours et nomma Conty généralissime de l'armée de la Fronde. Molé et les Frondeurs modérés eurent bien de la peine à imposer la paix de Rueil contre les violentes objections de Conty et d'autres gentilshommes. Par des négociations séparées, Conty tenta de contraindre le Conseil à renvoyer Mazarin et à négocier avec l'Espagne. Le parti de Conty connut toutefois un grave revers lorsque Molé rendit publiques les exigences individuelles du prince et de ses

La Fronde des officiers

partisans en les coupant de leur contexte politique général. La paix de Rueil était un échec des Frondeurs nobles et un relatif succès pour le Parlement.

Cet « estrangement » entre la robe et l'épée aurait, selon Moote, donné un nouvel élan au mouvement réformiste [40]. A vrai dire, après Rueil, les cours souveraines parlèrent bien peu des problèmes financiers et la nouvelle tentative de réunion de la Chambre Saint-Louis en mars 1652 fut un échec. Sans doute le Parlement avait-il commis une erreur dans ses remontrances du 21 janvier 1649 mettant en cause Mazarin. Le tyran Mazarin aurait été responsable de la paix manquée avec l'Espagne et de la banqueroute ; les deux faits étaient liés : Mazarin voulait la guerre « afin de se rendre plus nécessaire et avoir plus de prétexte de lever de grandes sommes pour s'enrichir ». L'opinion populaire était persuadée que Mazarin avait envoyé le produit de ses pillages en Italie et en Allemagne pour continuer la guerre. Les remontrances du 23 mars 1652, plus virulentes encore, reprenaient ce thème [41].

En fait, il n'était pas évident de représenter Mazarin en tyran. Il n'avait pas ordonné une seule exécution durant son ministère ; il était cardinal, parrain du roi, il jouissait de l'appui de la plus grande part du clergé français. En le poursuivant, la Fronde risquait de ne plus ressembler qu'à une lutte pour le pouvoir. Molé l'avait compris et avait tenu à ce que Mazarin fût un des signataires de la paix de Rueil. Lorsque Mazarin eut fait arrêter Condé, Conty et Longueville (janvier 1650), sa prétendue haine contre la paix fut regardée comme la cause de l'arrestation des princes. La propagande aristocratique se focalisa sur la paix avec l'Espagne donnée comme le prélude nécessaire aux réformes du royaume. Ainsi le programme des officiers avait disparu du cœur du conflit.

Avec le premier exil de Mazarin et la libération des princes (13 février 1651), les intentions de Condé devinrent éclatantes. Le premier prince du sang espérait « se rendre maître du roi en éloignant les ministres qui ne sont pas dans ses intérêts » [42]. Par la menace, il obtint le renvoi de Servien, Le Tellier et Lionne. Il accordait dans ses manifestes une certaine place aux affaires de finances ; leur désordre, disait-il, était dû « à ce nombre innombrable de comptants que le Parlement se peut faire rapporter pour savoir qui en a profité » [43]. Mais on peut se demander s'il avait de réelles intentions de réforme. En septembre 1651, Condé était un rebelle, en novembre il était devenu l'allié de l'Espagne. Quand Gaston le rejoignit, le 24 janvier 1652, les princes publièrent que « Mazarin a toujours gouverné en effet, quoy qu'il fût banni en apparence ». Ils dénoncèrent la nomination de La Vieuville à la surintendance, mais ne prononcèrent rien sur les réformes à venir. Ils cherchaient l'alliance des cours souveraines en promettant de renouveler la déclaration du 22 octobre 1648 et de donner toute satisfaction aux officiers [44]. Néanmoins, le

Parlement de Paris refusa l'alliance (25 janvier 1652) et n'y consentit pour finir (20 juillet) qu'après un vote très serré. En dépit des craintes des ministres reflétées dans la déclaration du 22 octobre 1652, les clientèles et les fidélités nobiliaires n'avaient pas suffi à attirer assez de parlementaires dans le parti des Princes [45].

Comme le dit Moote, la Fronde était trop divisée pour prendre le pouvoir et trop engagée dans l'opposition au pouvoir pour penser efficacement à s'en emparer [46]. Ce fut ironiquement à l'été 1652, alors que la guerre civile avait discrédité la cause frondeuse, que des efforts sérieux pour s'emparer du pouvoir furent mis en œuvre. On envisagea alors un Conseil des finances, contrôlé par les Grands, chargé de réformer les finances royales. Etablir un tel conseil aurait donné aux Princes « tout ce qu'on leur a osté..., tout ce qu'ils ont perdu » [47]. Et pourtant ce conseil aurait pu être le vrai moyen de réaliser les propositions théoriques que la Chambre Saint-Louis avait rédigées en 1648.

***

Dans la version de la Fronde donnée par Moote, les officiers auraient remporté une victoire en dépit de leur défaite. Certes, Moote convient avec Kossmann qu'il n'y eut ni révolution, ni révolution manquée, mais le bilan ne lui semble pas entièrement négatif. Il y aurait un legs historique : « Si la Fronde n'avait pas entravé le courant vers l'absolutisme, l'évolution de Henri IV à Louis XIV aurait abouti à une monarchie bien plus puissante ». Les lendemains furent ambigus car le Lit de Justice du 22 octobre 1652 significativement ne faisait rien pour annuler les réformes annoncées quatre ans plus tôt [48].

L'humiliation du Parlement fut pourtant plus sévère que ne le suggère Moote : en effet, le Lit de Justice eut pour théâtre non pas la Grand-Chambre du Palais, mais le Louvre, ce que les magistrats avaient toujours pu éviter depuis 1527 [49]. Ils avaient pu écarter cet affront en 1649, alors qu'un article du traité de Rueil avait prévu un Lit de Justice à Saint-Germain. D'autre part, la déclaration d'octobre 1652 condamnait radicalement les arrêts rendus par le Parlement au cours de la Fronde. En interdisant aux conseillers de connaître des « affaires générales de l'Etat et de la direction des finances », le gouvernement cherchait à préserver les juridictions des cours rivales, les Comptes et les Aides. En interdisant les poursuites contre « ceux à qui le roi avait confié l'administration », le gouvernement cherchait à mettre Mazarin et les ministres hors d'atteinte des attaques comparables à celles de janvier 1649 ou mars 1652. La déclaration annulait également « tout ce qui a esté cy devant ou qui pourrait estre cy après résolu sur ce subject » [50] ; si cette clause avait un sens, c'était bien la condamnation de toute la législation frondeuse qu'on ne se donnait pas la peine de révoquer ouvertement [51]. Cette attitude a

La Fronde des officiers

pu être interprêtée comme un signe de faiblesse et il est vrai que le pouvoir évitait de relancer le débat politique [52]. Mais il n'y eut pas pour autant de victoire cachée des officiers, puisque le Conseil de 1653 à 1661 renoua simplement avec les pratiques antérieures à 1648. Les intendants provinciaux furent rétablis en 1653-54 dans tous les pays d'élections. Ils étaient appelés « commissaires départis pour l'exécution des ordres de Sa Majesté » plutôt qu'intendants de justice, police et finances, mais les titres étaient regardés comme synonymes et les fonctions étaient les mêmes. Leurs prérogatives sur les tailles des pays d'élections étaient les mêmes que celles de 1642 à 1648. La déclaration du 16 avril 1643, qui avait fondé leurs pouvoirs fiscaux, demeurait valide et les officiers spoliés, trésoriers et élus, n'avaient aucun doute à ce sujet [53]. Quant au montant des tailles, il y avait eu une réduction partielle en 1648, mais la hausse reprit en 1653 et, en 1659, lors de la paix des Pyrénées, les tailles avaient retrouvé leur niveau antérieur à 1648. D'autres taxes remises en 1648 avaient été rétablies par une déclaration du 31 décembre 1652 [54].

Les emprunts anticipant sur les tailles avaient été supprimés en 1648, ils reparurent en 1652 et ne cessèrent pas pendant toute la surintendance de Fouquet, leur maximum ayant été atteint en 1658. La Chambre de justice annoncée en juillet 1648 [55] fut abolie le 31 décembre 1652 au prix d'amendes de composition dérisoires [56]. Les hauts taux d'intérêt étaient revenus. De la sorte, le crédit fut restauré. La limitation des dépenses secrètes voulue par les Comptes fut annulée par arrêt du Conseil (16 novembre 1652). Les comptants, dès lors, se multiplièrent jusqu'à la paix des Pyrénées, s'élevant en moyenne annuelle à 54 millions de 1653 à 1659, de sorte que les financiers avaient certainement compensé leurs pertes de 1648. Du programme de la Chambre Saint-Louis plus rien ne restait.

Si les officiers connurent une revanche, ce fut peut-être une décennie plus tard avec le règne personnel de Louis XIV. Les impôts directs furent graduellement réduits. Les baux des fermes d'impôts furent révisés et des revenus bien plus importants obtenus des taxes indirectes. Colbert révoqua les emprunts, ramenant le taux d'intérêt à 7,5 %. Il dénonça aussi le volume des dépenses secrètes, et, le 24 décembre 1661, le Conseil ordonna une enquête sur les comptants depuis 1635, réalisant presque les vœux de la Chambre des Comptes en 1648. Après 1662, les comptants tombèrent à une moyenne de 12 millions, n'excédant jamais 17 millions. Le programme des officiers avait porté quelques fruits ; il avait fallu pour cela des circonstances favorables, d'abord, une période de paix, à peu près douze ans de 1660 à 1671, ensuite, un roi capable de gouverner personnellement et un ministre des finances (sans le nom) résolu à des réformes. La volonté réformatrice venait du pouvoir lui-même.

Puisque ce sont Louis XIV et Colbert qui ont mis en œuvre les propositions les plus constructives de la Chambre Saint-Louis, la perspective de la Fronde doit être modifiée. Dès la crise et la banqueroute, le débat s'était envenimé sur les buts et les moyens, sur la réforme du royaume et sur les instruments de cette réforme. Les discussions reflétaient les clivages sociaux et les oppositions économiques de l'époque. Hémery avait cherché à rogner les pensions des nobles, les gages des officiers et les revenus des rentiers, sans paraître favoriser les uns ou les autres. Moins impartiaux, ses successeurs surent diviser pour régner. Les rentes et les gages avaient été au cœur des débats en 1648, alors que les pensions nobiliaires n'étaient pas défendues. l'engagement de gentilshommes dans la Fronde, en effet, ne fut pas immédiat. Mais en 1652, la propagande royaliste pouvait affirmer que pour les gentilshommes « le premier motif est de travailler pour eux-mêmes ». Chaque ligue ou alliance nobiliaire réclamait d'être payée, mais la couronne, ainsi que le montraient les auteurs royalistes, « ne leur peut tenir parole qu'en augmentant les impôts et les charges publiques » [57].

Les doléances financières et fiscales avaient été les causes essentielles de la Fronde. Dans les débats sur les réformes, il devint vite clair qu'aucune solution n'aurait un soutien unanime et l'opposition se fractionna selon les intérêts économiques. Les mêmes motifs qui avaient provoqué la Fronde provoquaient son effondrement. Les procédés financiers du pouvoir étaient certes critiquables, mais, sans eux, aucun paiement de gages, rentes ou pensions n'était possible. Les Frondeurs dénonçaient la corruption de Mazarin, obstacle à la paix et aux réformes, mais les profits pécuniaires des uns ou des autres s'avéraient à la longue des ressorts plus puissants que la défense d'une cause commune contre la tyrannie mazarine. Les officiers s'émouvaient, en 1648, pour la défense de leurs gages, les rentiers formaient, en 1649, un syndicat, les gentilshommes après la paix de Rueil recherchaient sinon des pensions du moins des charges militaires rémunératrices dans les provinces. En même temps, le poids fiscal était réduit ; tout le monde, en principe, acceptait cette réduction et les restrictions du budget royal, mais personne ne les acceptait dans ses propres revenus. A la fin de la Fronde, il était devenu clair que les divers opposants souhaitaient un haut niveau de dépenses et par conséquent un haut niveau de taxation. Les intérêts de ces opposants étaient fort éloignés d'une guerre civile révolutionnaire et d'une rupture politique brutale.

Dans un domaine, pourtant, le programme des officiers eut quelques succès après 1653. Le recours à la vénalité des offices, aux parties casuelles, fut alors très modéré, il y eut peu de créations d'offices et de taxes sur les officiers. Mieux encore, le paiement des gages et rentes fut acquitté ponctuellement sous Fouquet. Si l'on regarde le programme de 1648 comme une défense des avantages corporatifs des officiers, on peut dans ce cas parler d'une victoire cachée et retardée de la Fronde parlementaire. Les officiers ne pouvaient pas abandonner « leurs intérêts pour travailler à ceux du public » [58]. Ils oubliaient « les considérations publiques, sitôt qu'ils avaient trouvé ce qu'ils désiraient ». Ainsi, la Fronde était beaucoup plus une rébellion pour des intérêts de corps qu'un mouvement modéré de réforme.

(Traduit par Y.-M. BERCÉ.)

NOTES

(1) E.H. KOSSMANN, *La Fronde*, Leyde, 1954, p. 56 et 259.
(2) A.L. MOOTE, *The revolt of the judges. The Parlement of Paris and the Fronde, 1643-1652*, Princeton, N.J., 1971, p. 43, 169, 171.
(3) P. ZAGORIN, *Rebels and rulers, 1500-1660*, Cambridge, 1982, t. II, p. 200.
(4) KOSSMANN, *op. cit.*, p. 55-56.
(5) Sauf exception indiquée, les éléments de cet article proviennent de : R.J. BONNEY, *Political change in France under Richelieu and Mazarin, 1624-1661*, Oxford, 1978 ; *Thl King's Debts : finance and politics in France, 1589-1661*, Oxford, 1981.
(6) R.J. BONNEY, « The French civil war, 1649-53 », *European Studies review*, VIII, 1978, p. 71-100 ; « Cardinal Mazarin and the great nobility during the Fronde », *English historical review*, XCVI, 1981, p. 818-833.
(7) MOOTE, *op. cit.*, p. 172.
(8) *Mémoires d'Omer Talon*, éd. MICHAUD et POUJOULAT, 3ᵉ série, VI, 1839, p. 251. On trouve les mêmes expressions dans la déclaration du 10 juillet 1648 portant révocation des commissions d'intendant, A.N. K 117 b, n° 37. Les propositions de la Chambre Saint-Louis sont convenablement résumées dans une note en bas de page des *Mémoires d'Omer Talon*, p. 241-245. Il existe d'autres versions avec de légères variantes. Talon n'avait pas numéroté les propositions et avait présenté à part les deux propositions émises le 2 juillet. Le total des propositions se monte à vingt-sept.
(9) MOOTE, *op. cit.*, p. 80.
(10) A.N. U 28, f° 389, 11 et 13 juillet 1648.
(11) BONNEY, *The King's Debts*, p. 203, n. 5.
(12) A.N. K 117 b, nᵒˢ 38, 39, 12 et 18 juillet 1648. La version imprimée dans les *Mémoires d'Omer Talon*, p. 252, donne la date du 16 juillet. Elle est confirmée par l'enregistrement des débats, A.N. U 28 f° 195.
(13) A.N. U 28, f° 397, 31 juillet 1648.
(14) *Mémoires de Mathieu Molé*, éd. A. CHAMPOLLION-FIGEAC, 4 vol., 1855-1857, t. III, p. 238.
(15) A.N. Z1a 163, f° 60v., 9 juillet 1648.
(16) *Mémoires d'Omer Talon*, p. 271 et 300.
(17) BONNEY, *The King's Debts*, p. 207.
(18) *Ibid.*, p. 281, n. 2.
(19) R.J. BONNEY, « The secret expenses of Richelieu and Mazarin, 1624-1661 », *English historical review*, XCI, 1976, p. 825-836. BONNEY, *The King's Debts*, p. 298, 308-309.
(20) *Histoire de la maison de Nicolay. Pièces justificatives. II. Chambre des Comptes*, éd. A.M. de BOISLISLE, Nogent-le-Rotrou, 1873, p. 427.
(21) *Mémoires d'Omer Talon*, p. 295.
(22) *Ibid.*, p. 310.
(23) *Mémoires d'Omer Talon*, p. 300.
(24) R. MOUSNIER, *La Vénalité des offices sous Henri IV et Louis XIII*, 2ᵉ éd., 1971, p. 296-301.
(25) *Journal inédit du Parlement de Paris pendant la Fronde...*, éd. H. COURTEAULT, « Annuaire-Bulletin de la Société de l'Histoire de France », 1916, p. 270-273.
(26) A.N. Z1a 163, f° 76v., 11 juillet 1648.
(27) *Mémoires d'Omer Talon*, p. 242.
(28) BONNEY, *The King's Debts*, p. 205, 211, n. 3, 217.
(29) *Ibid.*, p. 209-210. A.A.E. France 860, fᵒˢ 199-217.
(30) MOOTE, *op. cit.*, p. 181.
(31) R.J. BONNEY, « The failure of the French revenue farms, 1600-60 », *Economic history review*, 2ᵉ ser., XXXII, 1979, 11-32. BONNEY, *The King's Debts*, p. 299-300, 314.
(32) A.N. Z1a 161, f° 29 v°-30 r°, 4 décembre 1640.
(33) *Mémoires de Mathieu Molé*, t. III, p. 372.
(34) *Mémoires d'Omer Talon*, p. 228-230. De l'arrêt d'union, Séguier avait dit : « Sous le titre d'une alliance publique, c'est une espèce de ligue défensive, une société générale pour empêcher

d'exécution de la volonté du roi. » Citant Cardin Le Bret, il concluait que « l'autorité de la monarchie, qui consiste dans un certain point indivisible, seroit blessée par cette espèce de licence ». Pour Talon, l'intervention de Séguier fut « un long discours éloquent, plein d'observations et de remarques ».

(35) Gaston avait répondu aux Parlementaires : « Comme votre ressort ne compose que le tiers [du royaume], il est juste de laisser aux autres Parlements ce qui les concerne. » A.N. Z la 163, f° 91 bis, et U 28, f° 391 v°, 16 juillet 1648.

(36) S. KETTERING, « A provincial Parlement during the Fronde : the reforms proposals of the Aix magistrates », *European studies review*, XI, 1981, p. 151-169.

(37) *Mémoires de Mathieu Molé*, t. III, p. 373. La « parfaite jonction et intelligence » avec les cours de Rouen et d'Aix, annoncée le 5 février 1649, ne dura pas longtemps : A.N. U 28, f° 338 v°- 339 r°.

(38) S. KETTERING, « The causes of the judicial Fronde », *Canadian journal of history*, XVII, 1982, p. 275-306.

(39) BONNEY, *Political change*, p. 64.

(40) MOOTE, *op. cit.*, p. 219.

(41) R.J. BONNEY, « Cardinal Mazarin and his critics : the remonstrances of 1652 », *Journal of European Studies*, X, 1980, p. 15-31.

(42) A.A.E. France, 875, f° 268 v°, S.d. [24 juin 1651, environ].

(43) Madame de MOTTEVILLE, *Mémoires...*, ed. J.F. MICHAUD and J.J.F. POUJOULAT, 2ᵉ ser., X, 1838, p. 412.

(44) A.A.E. France, 881, f° 136, 24 janv. 1652.

(45) H. MAILFAIT, *Un magistrat de l'ancien régime. Omer Talon, sa vie et ses œuvres, 1595-1652* (1902), p. 41-42.

(46) MOOTE, *op. cit.*, p. 369.

(47) A.A.E. France, 890, f° 144, 1652.

(48) MOOTE, *op. cit.*, p. 354, 373, 375.

(49) S. HANLEY, *The lit de justice of the kings of France...*, Princeton, N.J., 1983, p. 322.

(50) *Mémoires d'Omer Talon*, p. 513. A.N. U 30, f° 356, 22 octobre 1652. A.A.E. France, 885, f° 226, 20 oct. 1652.

(51) BONNEY, *Political change*, p. 67.

(52) MOOTE, *op. cit.*, p. 354, 357.

(53) BONNEY, *Political change*, p. 70-71, 196-203.

(54) A.N. Xlb 8857.

(55) *Mémoires d'Omer Talon*, p. 249.

(56) A.N. Xlb 8857, p. 237 et 535-547.

(57) A.A.E. France, 883, f°ˢ 251, 253, juillet 1652.

(58) Transposition d'une citation de Talon, *Mémoires...*, p. 300.

IX

MAZARIN ET LA FRONDE :
LA QUESTION DE RESPONSABILITE

Au cours de l'histoire de France, peu d'hommes politiques ont subi, de leur vivant, des critiques aussi dures que le cardinal Jules Mazarin, premier ministre de Louis XIV. La plupart de ces critiques se sont exprimées pendant la grande crise politique de la Fronde. Un grand nombre des quelques 5400 pamphlets politiques parus pendant cette période furent écrits dans l'intention délibérée de le perdre de réputation. L'expression définitive de ces critiques se trouve en fait, plutôt que dans les *Mazarinades*, dans les remontrances du parlement de Paris du 21 janvier 1649 et du 23 mars 1652[1].

L'essentiel de leur argument portait sur sa responsabilité, ou responsabilité présumée, dans la Fronde : elles affirmaient que, si Mazarin n'était pas devenu premier ministre, la crise n'aurait pas eu lieu ; et que le seul espoir de règlement de la crise était qu'il fût exclu du gouvernement, de façon permanente, si possible mis en jugement[2] - et il y eut une tentative manquée pour le faire - du moins qu'il soit exilé hors du royaume. Les *Mazarinades* et les remontrances prétendaient que Mazarin devait être considéré comme le seul responsable des troubles. En succombant à ces pressions politiques et en s'exilant volontairement à deux reprises, le premier ministre confirma jusqu'à un certain point ces affirmations.

Le point de vue des contemporains de Mazarin a été vigoureusement réaffirmé par l'historien américain Lloyd Moote[3]. Moote ne trouve chez Mazarin rien qui rachète sa « duplicité et sa déplorable façon de gouverner ». Sa réaction à la Fronde parlementaire fut « vague », « émotive » et même celle d'un esprit « déséquilibré ». « Le fardeau de culpabilité (*sic*) résultant de la violence de 1649 doit reposer sur les épaules d'Anne (d'Autriche, la Régente) et Mazarin » puisque ce fut « la politique de duplicité » qui engendra les conflits civils. Plus tard, en 1650, Mazarin « perdit son sang-froid » et la politique de duplicité fit place à une politique d'indécision, ce qui fut « fatal » à la cause du gouvernement. Même la libération des Princes par Mazarin en 1651 fut un échec, tandis que son retour d'exil à la fin de l'année fut « une bêtise »[4]. La conclusion de Moote est que le grand responsable de la Fronde fut Mazarin, puisqu'Anne et lui avaient, en définitive, l'autorité nécessaire pour pacifier tous les éléments de la sédition[5]. Depuis les remontrances du 23 mars 1652, dont le ton - en particulier eu égard au machiavélisme de Mazarin - se retrouve dans le récit de Moote, il n'y a pas eu de réquisitoire si violent contre le premier ministre.

Cette analyse historiographique suggère le besoin d'une réévaluation de la responsabilité du cardinal Mazarin dans la Fronde. Toute révision du rôle de Mazarin pendant la Fronde doit considérer la question dans la perspective à la fois du développement chronologique de la crise[6] et de la structure de la politique contemporaine[7]. Jusqu'ici les analyses ont eu tendance à négliger cette dernière et à se concentrer sur la première et, ce faisant, sont arrivées à des conclusions sommaires et hâtives sur le rôle de Mazarin. Il semble que tout le monde soit d'accord pour dire que la responsabilité de la Fronde doit bien être attribuée à quelqu'un, et à qui de mieux qu'à un premier ministre d'origine italienne qui était sensé avoir exercé le pouvoir absolu ? Ce postulat est peut-être, lui-même, erroné ; il exclut la possibilité que la Fronde ait découlé de préconditions anciennes, ou de précipitants récents, qui n'avaient rien, ou pas grand'chose, à voir avec un individu quelconque[8].

Il ne faut pas oublier que lorsque Mazarin arriva au pouvoir en 1643, son but principal était de continuer l'oeuvre de son prédécesseur, Richelieu, et de réaliser ses plans. En fait, on pourrait avancer que Mazarin était si étroitement soucieux de pratiquer la politique traditionnelle que la responsabilité de la Fronde pourrait être attribuée à Louis XIII et à Richelieu[9]. Mais ce point de vue décharge trop Mazarin de sa responsabilité immédiate. On peut certainement faire remonter les origines de la Fronde au gouvernement précédent. Que la guerre d'Espagne ait éclaté ou non en 1635 en conséquence de l'aggression gratuite du roi de France et de son premier ministre, ils étaient en tout cas responsables de ses conséquences. Dans un célèbre aphorisme, Richelieu avait dit un jour « en matière de guerres on sçait comment et quand elles commencent, mais nul ne peut prévoir le temps et la qualité de leur fin ». Et en cas de guerre, « il faut qui(t)ter toute pensée de repos, d'espargne et de règlement du dedans du royaume »[10]. En d'autres termes, Richelieu avait prévu que la guerre serait longue et coûteuse, et qu'elle exigerait de grands sacrifices du pays : en effet, ce serait une lutte de ressources contre les Habsbourgs dans laquelle la supériorité de l'organisation, la puissance fiscale et la volonté politique joueraient un rôle primordial : gagner des batailles ne serait pas suffisant puisque la victoire avait peu de chance d'être définitive, étant donné la nature de l'art militaire de l'époque et il faudrait savoir transformer les succès militaires en règlements de paix. Louis XIII et Richelieu ne surent léguer ni une victoire définitive ni un règlement diplomatique à la nation française en retour de son sacrifice de huit années. Mazarin hérita d'un problème financier de première dimension : plus la guerre durait, plus elle coûtait cher, à cause de l'anticipation des revenus et des taux exorbitants des intérêts payés aux débiteurs de l'Etat[11]. Le royaume n'était peut-être pas tout à fait épuisé, mais ses habitants souhaitaient désespérément la paix et la réduction du fardeau des impôts[12].

La question était de savoir s'il était possible d'obtenir la paix de l'Espagne et, si oui, quel était le meilleur moyen de l'obtenir. La politique de Mazarin fut de maintenir l'alliance avec la Suède et la République Hollandaise le plus longtemps possible et d'instaurer une politique militaire agressive. Mais l'alliance était vouée à se désagréger pour des raisons internes : les Hollandais étaient en guerre depuis 1621, et la Suède depuis 1630 ; le deux pays rechignaient donc à continuer la guerre encore longtemps. En outre, le gouvernement espagnol cherchait en priorité à signer une trêve avec les Hollandais, afin de pouvoir continuer la guerre avec la France. Les Espagnols, en effet, estimaient que le gouvernement français allait inévitablement être affaibli par la minorité royale et, par conséquent, qu'il était inutile de faire des concessions politiques[13]. Or la maxime « le Fançais en tant qu'ami, non en tant que voisin » (*Gallicus amicus non vicinus*) servait souvent à justifier l'attitude ambiguë des hollandais envers leurs alliés français. Cette attitude fut soigneusement exploitée par le plénipotentiaire de Philippe IV aux négociations de la paix de Westphalie, le comte de Peñaranda, convaincu qu'il était que l'intérêt de l'Espagne était d'être en paix avec les Hollandais plutôt qu'avec les Français. Il considérait les Hollandais comme plus responsables, moins puissants, et dépourvus de la rivalité naturelle des Français à l'égard de l'Espagne[14]. Etant donné, en outre, que ni Anne d'Autriche ni Mazarin ne pouvaient autoriser une paix désavantageuse, il n'est pas surprenant que les négociations de Westphalie aient abouti à une impasse. Moote a affirmé que Mazarin « rejeta l'occasion d'une paix honorable dans sa recherche de gains territoriaux »[15]. Mais on ne peut guère le tenir responsable du désastre diplomatique qui s'abattit sur les Français lorsque la paix fut signée entre l'Espagne et la République Hollandaise en janvier 1648. La vérité est qu'une paix franco-espagnole ne pouvait être signée parce que ce n'était pas dans l'intérêt des Espagnols. La politique étrangère de Mazarin a été dénoncée, par la suite, comme inutilement belliqueuse, point de vue que certains historiens ont suivi aveuglement. Mais le pire que l'on puisse dire contre Mazarin est que sa diplomatie échoua et que cet échec affaiblit sa capacité à se défendre contre ses critiques. En France, cet échec sapa la capacité de Mazarin à gouverner efficacement. En effet pourquoi les individus et les groupes constitués tels que les officiers eussent-ils contribué à l'effort de guerre quand celle-ci avait été désastreuse ?

Le cours de la Fronde, par la suite, découla en grande partie des circonstances dans lesquelles eut lieu la réunion de la Chambre Saint-Louis, et de l'incapacité dans laquelle le gouvernement fut alors placé de refuser des concessions à ses adversaires. La politique de Mazarin a été définie comme ayant « résolu les problèmes par la duplicité et les intrigues » entraînant inévitablement des conflits civils[16]. Mais que pouvait-il faire d'autres ? Les officiers considérèrent les concessions de 1648 comme des réformes comparables aux trois grandes ordonnances du XVIe siècle[17]. Mais le gouvernement prit la position opposée. Il considéra les concessions accordées par les déclarations du 18 juillet et 22 octobre 1648 comme ayant été faites à son corps défendant et, par conséquent, révocables dès que l'occasion s'en présenterait. Les ministres ne proclamèrent pas publiquement leurs intentions parce que c'eut été politiquement désastreux, mais ils ne s'en cachaient pas en privé[18]. Sans aucun doute le souci de préserver les prérogatives royales avait compté pour beaucoup aux yeux des ministres : en effet, au lieu d'une monarchie absolue dans laquelle le roy jouissait d'une souveraineté sans partage le royaume de France risquait de devenir une monarchie limitée par le pouvoir des officiers. C'est ce que Mazarin voulait dire lorsqu'il écrivait dans les *carnets secrets* que, si elles avaient été définitivement appliquées, les déclarations de 1648 auraient aboli « la meilleure partie de la monarchie »[19]. On a vu que certains commentateurs ont jugé cette réaction excessivement émotive ou même « déséquilibrée »[20] ; mais c'est ne pas tenir compte des questions vitales qui étaient en jeu - le droit du roi à déterminer sa politique étrangère et à légiférer sans le consentement de ses sujets. Dans la situation de 1648-49, la régente et son ministre durent user de duplicité pour réserver l'avenir.

Avec l'arrestation des Princes en 1650, Mazarin franchit le Rubicon ; après cela, les événements politiques se mirent rapidement à le dépasser. L'emprisonnement des Princes agit comme un acide sur le corps politique. Désormais il devait y avoir des révoltes continuelles de leurs partisans jusqu'à leur libération - que Mazarin repoussa jusqu'en février 1651 et qui le força pour la première fois à prendre le chemin de l'exil volontaire. Cependant, il faut faire une distinction très nette entre les révoltes des nobles et la période d'exil de Mazarin à Brühl dans l'archevêché de Cologne. Evidemment Mazarin passa son exil à l'étranger à essayer de récupérer sa position. Il se servit du pot-de-vin de 400 000 livres[21] de La Vieuville pour louer 6000 mercenaires à l'électeur de Brandebourg pour envahir la France en décembre 1651[22]. Il faut noter que lorsque Concini avait recruté des troupes de mercenaires à Liège en 1617 cela avait été par la suite considéré un acte de trahison[23]. Néanmoins, ce que Mazarin ne fit pas, bien que Fuensaldaña, le représentant de Philippe IV, ait continué à négocier avec lui pendant la Fronde[24], fut de signer un traité avec l'Espagne pour se tirer de ses difficultés. Cela lui donna sur ses adversaires, un formidable avantage moral que sa propagande chercha à exploiter en décembre 1651. Son amour de la France était si grand qu'« aucun mauvais traictement n'est capable de l'esbranler... » Plus tard on n'oublia pas qu'en tant qu'ex-ministre en exil « qui en sçavoit tous les secretz » il aurait pu « facilement se vanger en les découvrant aux ennemis... »[25].

Par contraste les adversaires nobles de Mazarin s'allièrent tous tôt ou tard avec l'Espagne. Dans le cas des partisans de Condé ce fut très tôt, quelques mois seulement après l'arrestation des Princes. La duchesse de Longueville et Turenne, dont le quartier général était à Stenay sur la frontière

Mazarin et la Fronde : la question de responsabilité

nord-est de la France, signèrent un traité avec l'archiduc Léopold-Guillaume le 30 avril 1650. La princesse de Condé, Bouillon, La Rochefoucauld, Sauveboeuf et Lusignan, à Bordeaux, signèrent un traité avec Philippe IV le 26 juin 1650. Après son échec à contrôler le gouvernement après sa libération, Condé, lui aussi, entra en rébellion et fit cause commune avec l'Espagne dans un traité signé le 6 novembre 1651[26]. En termes techniques les accords entre Philippe IV ou ses représentants d'une part et les nobles français, n'étaient pas des traités de partage - bien que Mazarin et le conseil du roi les aient qualifiés de tels[27], et que Philippe IV ait bien escompté le partage[28]. Ce n'étaient pas de vrais traités de partage puisque les conquêtes des troupes espagnoles devaient être temporaires seulement : elles devaient les garder « en dépôt » jusqu'à la signature de la paix définitive. Néanmoins, le fait que les nobles français dépendaient des troupes et des subsides espagnols les mettaient dans une situation ambiguë. D'une certaine façon ils étaient politiquement naïfs et ils tombèrent certainement dans le piège de croire à leur propre propagande. Ils pensaient, qu'une fois que Mazarin aurait été chassé du pouvoir, l'Espagne accepterait de signer la paix avec le nouveau gouvernement français. En réalité les nobles français furent impuissants à obtenir un règlement de paix réaliste parce que Philippe IV et ses représentants avaient la haute main sur eux[29]. Des troupes de mercenaires furent utilisées à la fois par les Grands et par le gouvernement dans ses tentatives pour réprimer la rébellion : avec cette différence que le gouvernement français payait ses troupes alors que les nobles rebelles ne le pouvaient pas. Anne d'Autriche et son premier ministre, en exil ou non, étaient donc plus crédibles en tant que négociateurs avec l'Espagne, que leurs nobles adversaires.

Je n'ai point l'intention dans cette conférence de substituer l'hagiographie à la dénigration de la réputation de Mazarin pendant la Fronde. Mazarin et ses adversaires étaient tous aussi conscients des occasions et des possibilités qu'offrait une habile campagne de propagande : la preuve en est le manifeste qu'il publia à son retour d'exil en décembre 1651, sa réaction aux remontrances du parlement de Paris en mars 1652 ; les tentatives de ses collègues pour orchestrer son retour à Paris comme « doucement insinué dans les esprits... », et enfin son utilisation des pamphlétaires, tels que Gabriel Naudé et Jean de Silhon. De nouveaux termes furent créés pour répondre au climat politique. *Se mazariner* consistait à travailler à la victoire du ministre sur ses ennemis ; les *mazarins* étaient ses partisans, et le *mazarinisme* était son système de gouvernement[30]. Ensemble ces divers moyens de propagande réussirent à perpétuer un mythe pro-Mazarin qui était tout aussi convaincant que la légende noire. Il ne manquait plus à Mazarin que sa réputation internationale - qu'il acquit grâce aux traités de Westphalie et des Pyrénées - pour que le Cardinal soit considéré comme l'épitomé de l'homme d'État. Un pamphlet publié en Angleterre au moment de la mort de Mazarin disait[31] : « Que la France serait tombée dans les mêmes désordres que nous si elle avait perdu un Mazarin par la même violence qui nous avait fait perdre un Strafford... Je ne crois pas qu'il ait été.[...] l'ami ni l'ennemi d'aucun prince ou pays sauf dans l'intérêt de la France, dont il a été le fidèle ministre et dont il a poursuivi l'intérêt comme en vérité c'était son devoir de le faire, sans souci des alliances ou de la parenté. »

L'historien se doit naturellement de se méfier des attitudes qui acceptent le mythe pro-Mazarin. Il suffit de se rappeler sa vanité et ses efforts inlassables pour élever sa famille grâce à des mariages avec la grande noblesse[32] ; son pluralisme ecclésiastique acharné et sa chasse aux bénéfices[33] ; enfin son avarice et son mépris de la bonne conduite du gouvernement lorsqu'il se mit à reconstituer sa fortune personnelle après la Fronde[34], pour savoir que les critiques des Frondeurs n'étaient pas sans fondement. Il était devenu très riche entre 1643 et 1651, mais les attaques sur sa fortune pendant qu'il était en exil l'avaient presque mené à la banqueroute. Il est presqu'aussi difficile aux historiens qu'à ses contemporains de justifier les accusations des frondeurs sur les malversations de Mazarin : en définitive on peut considérer que tous les deniers qu'il avait reçus étaient des dons volontaires du roi à son très loyal serviteur...

Faut-il donc voir en Mazarin un grand homme d'Etat français ou un aventurier italien dont la chance ne se démentit jamais ? Qu'il ait été un aventurier tout autant qu'un homme d'Etat est indéniable et cet élément de paradoxe est au coeur de toute sa carrière[35]. L'origine italienne de Mazarin et sa naturalisation tardive (il ne reçut les lettres patentes qu'en avril 1639) formèrent la base de la « légende noire » qui s'attacha à lui. Sa personnalité était vulnérable à « toute sorte de mauvaises impressions que les peuples lui vouloient imposer... »[36.] L'équation : origine italienne - égale machiavélisme, s'imposa sans peine à ses contemporains et fut même acceptée par le parlement de Paris[37]. De plus, une vieille tradition française voulait que l'on dénonce le rôle des étrangers au gouvernement : l'exemple le plus récent en était l'arrêt du parlement de Paris du 8 août 1617 déclarant Concini et sa femme coupables de lèse-majesté et interdisant aux étrangers d'occuper des offices et des postes de gouverneurs en France[38]. Cet arrêt fut proclamé par Viole au Parlement le 22 septembre 1648[39], et fut en fait repromulgué le 7 février 1651[40]. L'un des aspects de l'héritage du régime de Concini fut que les Français qui détestaient les favoris du roi en général et contestaient le principe de la nécessité d'un premier ministre en particulier, furent désormais animés d'une horreur profonde à l'égard de la version italienne du genre.

Néanmoins, l'aventurisme italien de Mazarin présente un autre aspect qui, tout en compliquant ses difficultés à court terme avant et pendant la Fronde lui fut, en définitive, favorable. Il avait renoncé à faire carrière au service de la papauté et n'avait d'autre choix que de rester fidèle au roi de France. Pendant la Fronde on critiqua sa décision, autour de 1644, de poursuivre la guerre sur le front d'Italie. Cette décision, prétendait-on, portait atteinte aux intérêts de la France et s'expliquait par le désir de Mazarin de se constituer un fief italien où il puisse se réfugier s'il était chassé du pouvoir en France. Les événements de 1651, où Mazarin refusa absolument d'aller en

Italie pendant son exil, même avec le titre de *surintendant des affaires en Italie*, démentent les critiques des frondeurs[41]. Sa position était, en un certain sens, comparable à celle d'Anne d'Autriche, qui était la soeur de Philippe IV. Au début le gouvernement espagnol s'était flatté de pouvoir manipuler le coeur « espagnol » de la Régente ; assez rapidement, cependant, il comprit qu'Anne (contrairement à Louis XIII et Richelieu) ne pouvait même pas prendre le risque d'entrer en négociations secrètes avec l'ennemi[42]. Le gouvernement de la régence dut faire preuve de la plus grande prudence dans ses rapports avec les Habsbourgs : c'eut été un suicide politique que de signer une paix qui eut pu être attaquée, par la suite, comme contraire aux intérêts de la France. La grande noblesse française révoltée pouvait agir sans ce genre de contrainte et elle tomba dans le piège de sa propre propagande. Un Grand, tel que Conty, était convaincu qu'il était inconcevable qu'il fît quoi que ce soit qui « allast contre sa naissance et contre ce qu'il doibt à l'estat »[43]. Bien que Conty n'ait pas signé de traité avec l'Espagne et qu'à la fin de la Fronde il ait repris d'importants commandements militaires et des postes de gouverneur de province, d'autres grands nobles comme lui signèrent des accords avec les Habsbourgs qui auraient pu être considérés comme des traités de partage. Mazarin n'aurait jamais pu prendre ce risque et cela lui a permis d'assurer sa réputation posthume.

Quelles qu'aient été les erreurs de Mazarin pendant la Fronde, dans un domaine au moins, son oeuvre fut couronnée de succès. Il poursuivit la politique étrangère de Louis XIII et Richelieu en dépit de toutes les difficultés de la minorité royale auxquelles s'ajoutait le fait sans précédent pour un gouvernement de régence, d'avoir à mener une longue guerre avec l'étranger. On a vu plus haut que Richelieu admettait que c'était une chose de commencer une guerre, mais tout autre chose d'y mettre fin et que, lorsqu'on était en guerre il fallait « quitter toute pensée de repos, d'espargne et de règlement du dedans du royaume ». Le parlement de Paris croyait que Mazarin voulait continuer la guerre à la fois pour se rendre indispensable et pour s'enrichir. En réalité le Cardinal n'était pas un fauteur de guerre. Il faut être deux pour signer un traité de paix. Philippe IV et ses ministres ne voulaient pas un coup d'Etat en France, sous la direction de Condé, qui aurait permis une juste paix. Ils voulaient l'anarchie qui aurait entraîné une solution favorable à l'Espagne. Ils eurent donc tendance à soutenir la faction française la plus faible afin de faire durer la crise, tout en durcissant leurs positions dans les négociations diplomatiques[44]. On peut donc raisonnablement reprocher au gouvernement de Mazarin la série d'erreurs qui mena aux débuts de la Fronde ainsi que d'autres erreurs de jugement qui intensifièrent la crise. Ce gouvernement était aussi vénal, ce qui donna une arme puissante à ses adversaires. Néanmoins c'était avant tout un gouvernement de temps de guerre, dévoué à la cause française. L'opposition des frondeurs elle aussi commit des erreurs et sans aucun doute aurait été aussi vénale si elle avait été au pouvoir. On peut donc arguer que la Fronde parlementaire « était beaucoup plus une rébellion pour les intérêts de corps qu'un mouvement modéré de réforme »[45]. On pourrait aussi dire des Grands, comme le fit Mazarin, qu'ils ne pouvaient prétendre être « restaureurs de l'Etat » : « l'on (ne) se servoit du moyen et de l'aide du diable pour gagner le chemin du paradis... »[46]. Si l'opposition fut autre chose qu'une alliance disparate des ennemis de Mazarin, ce fut une coalition contre les conséquences fiscales de la guerre. N'empêche qu'il n'y avait que deux possibilités : accepter les dures réalités financières de la guerre ou capituler devant l'Espagne.

L'opposition même unifiée n'avait aucun espoir de succès : en effet, plutôt que de suivre les nobles jusqu'au bord de l'abîme, la plupart des officiers préférèrent, même si ce fut à contre-coeur, renoncer à leurs objectifs de 1648-49 et soutenir Anne d'Autriche et Mazarin. La lassitude engendrée par la guerre, qui avait été un tel danger pour Mazarin au début de la Fronde, se retourna finalement contre les nobles : si l'on devait faire la guerre, il valait mieux faire la guerre contre l'Espagne, sur le sol espagnol, qu'une guerre civile aux portes de Paris comme pendant l'été de 1652. Nous savons que ce fut l'un des arguments de la propagande mazariniste[47], mais dans ce cas-là du moins, il semble qu'il y ait eu une heureuse coïncidence entre la propagande, l'opinion publique et le verdict de l'histoire.

NOTES

1. R.J. Bonney, « Cardinal Mazarin and his critics : the remonstrances of 1652 », *Journal of European Studies* 10, 1980, p. 15-31.
2. Les documents préparatoires du procès sont à la Bib. nat. Ms. fr. 6888.
3. A.L. Moote, *The revolt of the judges. The Parlement of Paris and the Fronde, 1643-1652*, Princeton, NJ, 1971, p. 369.
4. *Ibid.*, p. 68, 168, 180, 228, 279, 281.
5. *Ibid.*, p. 276.
6. R.J. Bonney, « The French civil war, 1649-53 », *European studies review*, 8, 1978, p.71-100.
7. R.J. Bonney, « Cardinal Mazarin and the great nobility during the Fronde », *English historical review*, 96, 1981, p. 818-833.
8. R.E. Mousnier, « The Fronde », *Preconditions of revolution in early modern Europe*, éd. R. Forster and J.P. Greene, Baltimore, Md., 1970.
9. J.H. Elliott, *Richelieu and Olivares*, Cambridge, 1984, p. 171 : « la Fronde, tout autant que la France de Louis XIV, fut l'héritage de Richelieu ».
10. R.J. Bonney, *Political change in France under Richelieu and Mazarin, 1624-1661*, Oxford, 1978, p. 36-37. *Idem,The king's debts : finance and politics in France, 1589-1661*, Oxford, 1981, p. 152. Les citations proviennent respectivement des *Lettres, instructions diplomatiques de papiers d'état du Cardinal de Richelieu*, éd. D.L.M. Avenel, 8 vols.,1853-77, II. p. 83 et de G. Pagès, « Autour du " grand orage " Richelieu et Marillac. Deux politiques », *Revue historique*, 179, 1937, p. 66.
11. R. J. Bonney, « The secret expenses of Richelieu and Mazarin, 1624-1661 » *English Historical Review*, 91, 1976, p. 825-36. *Idem, The king's debts*, p. 309 (*comptants*, c.-à-d. essentiellement des versements pour couvrir le paiement des intérêts) ; p. 315 (revenu royal des *affaires extraordinaires*) ; et p. 317 (emprunts contractés par la monarchie française).
12. Omer Talon écrivait que « la plupart des levées ayant pour prétexte la nécessité de la guerre, chacun espéroit que la paix lui donneroit du soulagement » : Omer Talon, *Mémoires*, éd. J.F. Michaud and J.J.F. Poujoulat, 3e série VI, 1839, p. 299.
13. *Correspondance de la cour d'Espagne sur les affaires des Pays-Bas aux XVIIe siècle, 1647-1665*, éd. H. Lonchay, J. Cuvelier et J. Lefèvre, Bruxelles, 1933, n° 95, 105, 201, 215. Bonney, « The French civil war », p. 83.
14. J.I. Israel, *The Dutch republic and the Hispanic world, 1606-1661*, Oxford, 1982, p. 359. Voir aussi N.G. Parker, *Spain and the Netherlands, 1559-1659. Ten studies*, 1979, p. 58-60.
15. A. L. Moote, *Revolt of the judges*, p. 73.
16. A. L. Moote, *Revolt of the judges*, p. 180, 228.
17. Les déclarations de 1648 furent qualifiées de « règlements nécessaires sur la distribution de la justice et de l'ordre de nos finances » ce qui suggère une intention réformatrice.
18. Lionne à Servien, 6 fév. 1649, cité par P.A. Chéruel, *Histoire de France pendant la minorité de Louis XIV*, 4 vols., 1879-80, III. p. 200.
19. Chéruel, « Les carnets de Mazarin », p. 135.
20. A. L. Moote, *Revolt of the judges*, p. 168.
21. La Vieuville fut nommé surintendant des finances le 8 septembre 1651.
22. F. Desrobert, *Charles IV et Mazarin, 1643-1661*, Nancy-Paris, 1899, p. 407.
23. F. Hayem, *Le maréchal d'Ancre et Léonora Galigaï*, 1910, p. 231.Bibl. nat. 500 Colbert 221, f° 23^V.
24. *Recueil des instructions données aux ambassadeurs... XI. Espagne*, éd. A. Morel-Fatio, 1894, p. 1-19. Talon, *Mémoires*, éd. Michaud et Poujoulat, p. 452. *Lettres du Cardinal Mazarin à la reine, à la princesse palatine...*, éd. J. Ravenel, 1836, p. 237-238.
25. R. J. Bonney, « Cardinal Mazarin and his critics », p. 23. A[rchives] des A[ffaires] E[trangères], France 879, f° 188, 23 déc. 1651. A.A.E. France 888, f° 116^V, 1652.
26. R. J. Bonney, « The French civil war », p. 80-81. Bibl. nat. Ms. fr. 3855, f° 1, 26 juin 1650. Bibl. nat. Dupuy 775, f° 114, 26 juin 1650. H.E.P.L. d'Orléans, duc d'Aumale, *Histoire des princes de Condé pendant les XVIe et XVIIe siècles*, 8 vols., 1863-96, VI. p. 101-103.
27. *Lettres du Cardinal Mazarin*, éd. Ravenel, p. 26. Arch. nat. E. 1698, n° 120, 13 juillet 1652.
28. *Correspondance*, éd. Cuvelier et Lefèvre, n° 600.

29. Comme des frondeurs tels que Retz le faisaient remarquer : *Oeuvres de Retz*, éd. A. Feillet et al., 10 vols., 1870-96, II. p. 359, 428.
30. R. J. Bonney, « Cardinal Mazarin and his critics ».
31. Anon, *An impartial character of that famous politician and late admired minister of state Cardinal Mazanne (sic)* Londres, 22 mars 1660 [1661]. B.L. Collection Thomason E 1085 (4).
32. R. J. Bonney, « Cardinal Mazarin and the great nobility during the Fronde ».
33. J.A. Bergin, « Cardinal Mazarin and his benefices », *French History*, 1, 1987, p. 3-26.
34. R. J. Bonney, *The king's debts*, chap. 6. D. Dessert, *Argent, pouvoir et société au grand siècle*, 1984, p. 279-310.
35. R.J. Bonney, « The paradox of Mazarin », *History today* 32, 1982, p. 18-24.
36. Talon, *Mémoires*, éd. Michaud et Poujoulat, p. 300.
37. R. J. Bonney, « Cardinal Mazarin and his critics » p. 18.
38. R. J. Bonney, « Cardinal Mazarin and the great nobility », p. 819.
39. *Journal d'Olivier Lefèvre d'Ormesson et extrait des mémoires d'André Lefèvre d'Ormesson*, éd. P.A. Chéruel, 1860-1, I. 577.
40. A. L. Moote, *Revolt of the judges*, p. 293-294.
41. R. J. Bonney, « Cardinal Mazarin and his critics », p. 24.
42. R. Kleinman, *Anne of Austria. Queen of France*, Columbus, Ohio, 1985, p. 158, 160-161.
43. Bibl. nat. Ms. fr. 3854, f° 65, sans date [1649].
44. *Correspondance*, éd. Cuvelier et Lefèvre, n° 123, 223, 250, 299, 321, 331, 428, 432, 434, 599, 600.
45. R. J. Bonney, « La Fronde des officiers », p. 339.
46. R. J. Bonney, « The French civil war », p. 87. *Lettres du Cardinal Mazarin*, éd. Ravenel, p. 26.
47. University of London, MSS additionnel 247, f° 7, « Secret de la négociation du retour du Roy dans sa bonne ville de Paris ».

X

The secret expenses of Richelieu and Mazarin, 1624-1661

THAT the finances of the French monarchy were in a serious state of disarray at the time of Richelieu and Mazarin is now well known.[1] The reasons for the disarray are not yet fully understood, however. Was the Crown at the mercy of its financiers, and incapable of carrying out financial reform? Alternatively, were there specific, structural causes for the financial crisis, some of which were capable of reform? The secret expenses of the French monarchy provide a clear issue on which these alternative theories may be tested. Since recent discussion of the secret expenses has been inaccurate and misleading,[2] the issue should be clarified by an examination of original sources.

What were these secret expenses? They were cash payments – *ordonnances de comptant*[3] – ordered by the finance ministers (*surintendants des finances*). In theory, these payments concerned matters so secret that public knowledge of them would endanger the state. In practice, the types of payment made in this way were often not of a secret nature at all – in the sense of affecting affairs of state (*arcana imperii*) – but payments which for political reasons it was convenient to keep from public scrutiny. Colbert remarked that 'sous couleur de ce secret se cachent tous les abus et tous les malversations qui se commettent dans les finances'.[4] Recent historians have accepted Colbert's verdict, and one has judged the abuse of the *comptants* 'the most striking feature of the financial administration of the mid-seventeenth century'.[5]

The reasons why the secret payments were open to abuse are clear. All expenses of the French Crown were audited in the first instance by the council of finance (*conseil d'état et des finances*), a specialized section of the king's council. Once the accounts had been closed – often several years later – they were sent to the

---

1. J. Dent, *Crisis in finance. Crown, financiers and society in 17th-century France* (1973). *Cf.* his earlier paper, 'The collapse of the financial administration of the French monarchy. 1653-1661', *Economic History Review*, 2nd. ser., xx (1967), 241-56.

2. Dent, *Crisis in finance*, pp. 84-85. Dent asserts that the annual average for the *comptants* in the years 1630-42 was just under 5 million *livres*. The real figure was just under 32 million. His figure for 1643 – 18·2 million – is far too low. His figure for 1660 ('in the order of 80 millions') is too high. He appears not to have been aware of the statistical material cited *infra*, Table II.

3. Dent, *loc. cit.* An *ordonnance* or *arrêt de comptant* was issued by the *surintendant des finances* or by the whole council of finance. Quarterly totals of the secret expenses were called *certifications de comptant*. The document sent to the *Chambre des Comptes* of Paris was called an *acquit de comptant*.

4. *Lettres, instructions et mémoires de Colbert* . . . (ed. P. Clément, 10 vols., 1861-82), ii. pt. i, 28-29.   5. Dent, p. 84.

Chambre des Comptes of Paris for a second audit. The accounting process at the *Chambre des Comptes* was criticized by contemporaries as being too formalized, yet it did provide a check on overspending by the executive. In particular, the *Chambre des Comptes* upheld the legal interest rate of 5.55 per cent on government borrowing.[1] If it had not done its work with some degree of thoroughness, the concept of secret payments would not have been necessary. For the finance ministers of Richelieu and Mazarin used these payments as a means of circumventing the vigilance of the *Chambre des Comptes*.[2] Other items of expenditure were specified in detail, and checked by the *Chambre des Comptes* in a painstaking way. The secret expenses, however, were not. The finance ministers announced that a set figure had been paid out, about which 'il n'est pas besoing de donner plus ample et particullière cognoissance'.[3] The *Chambre des Comptes* was informed of the king's wish that the *trésorier de l'Épargne* should be allowed to claim this amount in his accounts. The *Chambre des Comptes* was thus reduced to the task of verifying the totals of *acquits de comptant* in a particular year, instead of scrutinizing the individual items.

This procedure of allowing secret expenses had certainly existed in the sixteenth century,[4] but by the time of Richelieu and Mazarin, its importance had grown almost beyond recognition. The resources of the French Crown, although greatly increased after the 1630s, were limited: expenses almost invariably exceeded income. Thus the kings of France had to borrow money – as did the king of Spain with whom they were at war between 1635 and 1659 – and at a disastrously high rate of interest, much higher than the legal limit of 5.55 per cent. The secret expenses thus offered the finance ministers a procedure whereby high interest rates could be paid to the financiers without public knowledge, and without the risk of the *Chambre des Comptes* withholding approval of these payments in the final audit of accounts. Table I demonstrates that payments to financiers through the secret expenses did in fact occur: in 1654 and 1657, respectively 67 and 79 per cent of the payments made by *comptants* went to the financiers. Moreover, a further proportion of payments – 14 and 4 per cent respectively went on a further dubious procedure, the discounting of old Treasury bills (*vieux*

---

1. *Ibid.* p. 103.
2. *Ibid.* p. 78. The specific point is made by Véron de Forbonnais, with reference to Foucquet's use of the secret payments. F. Véron de Forbonnais, *Recherches et considérations sur les finances depuis... 1595 jusqu'à... 1721* (2 vols., Liège 1758 – N.B. two different formats at this date), ii. 115.
3. B[ibliothèque] N[ationale] Pièces Originales 36, no. 127. *Certification de comptant*, amounting to 1,626,012 *livres*, signed by Aligre (Chancellor), Bochart de Champigny and Marillac (joint *surintendants*), Duret de Chevry, Tronson, Mallier de Houssay and Baudouin de Soupire (*intendants des finances*), 14 Sept. 1624.
4. Mlle. H. Michaud, 'L'ordonnancement des dépenses et le budget de la monarchie 1587–1589', *Annuaire-Bulletin de la société de l'histoire de France* (1970–1) [1972], 87–150.

billets de l'Épargne)[1] from which the financiers sometimes benefited also.

TABLE I
Types of payment made through the secret expenses in 1654 and 1657

Type of payment	Proportion of expenditure in the secret expenses	
	1654[†] %	1657[‡] %
Interest payments to financiers*	67.24	79.32
Payments to replace old Treasury bills	14.80	4.80
'Genuine' secret expenses	1.34	7.36
Miscellaneous payments	16.62	8.52
Total	100	100

* Including payments to *donneurs d'avis*, those who proposed new fiscal measures to the government.

† BN. MS. fr. 18496, which includes the *comptants* from 7 Apr. to 10 Nov. 1654. BN. 500 Colbert 106, fos. 563–81ᵛ., which includes the *comptants* from Jan. to Mar. 1654. The two lists give a total of 20,808,455 *livres* from 343 items. The total for the year was 23,950,693 *livres*.

‡ BN. n[ouvelles] a[cquisitions] f[rançaises] 170, four lists of *comptants* amounting to 63,432,193 *livres* from 518 items.

The secret expenses were acceptable to the *Chambre des Comptes* during the reign of Henry IV, because they were kept at a low level and represented a small percentage of total expenditure. Henry IV and Sully never spent more than 4 million *livres* per annum[2] by this method – out of total government expenditure which in 1609 reached 32.5 million.[3] The Regency government of Marie de Médicis was much more open-handed, however.[4] Successive finance ministers – Jeannin, Schomberg, La Vieuville, Bochart de

---

1. This problem is explained by Dent, *op. cit.* p. 83 and A. Chauleur, 'Le rôle des traitants dans l'administration financière de la France de 1643 à 1653', *XVIIè. Siècle*, lxv (1964), 30.
2. This was nevertheless a large sum of money. In 1609–10, 12.9 *livres* could buy a standard measure (*setier*) of best quality wheat at Les Halles in Paris. A family would consume about three *setiers* of inferior grain a year. Yet a day labourer might earn no more than 70 *livres* a year. Four million *livres* was more than the combined revenue of two of the largest tax farms in 1624 (2.3 million from the *aides*; 1.65 million from the *cinq grosses fermes*). It was not far short of the revenue from the largest tax farm of all, the *gabelle* (5.99 million in 1624). One of the richest men in France, Chancellor Séguier, left a fortune of 4 million *livres* on his death in 1672.
3. D. J. Buisseret, *Sully and the growth of centralized government in France 1598–1610* (1968), p. 81. Total expenditure in 1609 was 32,573,457 *livres*. BN. 500 Colbert 106 fo. 101ᵛ.
4. J. M. Hayden, *France and the Estates-General of 1614* (Cambridge, 1974), pp. 31–32.

Champigny and Marillac – were unable to halt the trend. In 1622, the secret expenses reached the record figure of 10·7 million. By the time of the Assembly of Notables held in 1626–7, the secret expenses were a source of concern[1]: Nicolay, the *premier président* of the *Chambre des Comptes* demanded a strict limitation on these payments.[2]

Richelieu, too, hoped to limit the secret expenses: 'on a vécu au siècle passé sans les comptants', he wrote, 'on y vivra bien encore'.[3] As with other projected reforms of Richelieu – such as the abolition of the sale of offices – the abolition of the secret expenses was not for him a priority, however. While he wanted reform, Richelieu believed that the requirements of French foreign policy had to take precedence over all domestic considerations. He believed the financiers to be 'une partie séparée, préjudiciable à l'état, mais pourtant nécessaire'.[4] The great struggle between Louis XIII and the Habsburgs required resources on an unprecedented scale. These resources could only be mobilized by the financiers.[5] Richelieu's finance ministers thus had to sign tax contracts with the financiers for enormous sums and at damaging rates of interest. As the war against the Habsburgs became increasingly expensive, so the gap between expenditure and resources widened, thus necessitating reliance on medium-term borrowing – that is, the anticipation of revenues two or three years in advance. At the same time, however, this 'floating debt' was itself very expensive. The longer the war went on, the more expensive was the money raised.

In 1630, the *grand tournant* of Richelieu's ministry – the year of decision after which a prolonged war with the Habsburgs became only a matter of time – overall expenditure had stood at 41·2 million, with the secret expenses accounting for only 6·3 million.[6] By 1633, the *guerre couverte* – Richelieu's subsidy policy to the enemies of the Habsburgs – had caused total expenses to rise to 65·2 million. In the meantime, the secret expenses had risen to 22·7 million.[7] By 1642, the last year of Richelieu's ministry, when the war had

1. J. Petit, *L'assemblée des notables de 1626–1627* (1936), p. 108.
2. A. D. Lublinskaya, *French absolutism: the crucial phase, 1620–1629* (Cambridge, 1968), p. 302, n. 2.
3. A. J. du Plessis, Cardinal de Richelieu [?], *Testament Politique* (ed. L. André, 1947), p. 431. 4. *Ibid.* p. 250.
5. *Cf.* A[rchives] N[ationales] E 1689 fo. 28, 9 Feb. 1645: 'L'expérience a faict cognoistre que sans les officiers de finance et de ceux qui sont entrez dans les fermes, prestz et traictez ... il eust esté difficile, voire impossible, de faire réussir si glorieusement les grands desseings et entreprises'.
6. Overall expenditure was 41,224,002 *livres*. The *comptants* were 6,311,336 *livres*. BN. MS. fr. 10410, *compte de l'Épargne* of Gaspard de Fieubet. (Where possible, the figures given for the period of Richelieu and Mazarin are the actual and not the official totals, which show some variation.)
7. Overall expenditure was 65,227,798 *livres*. The *comptants* were 22,686,604 *livres*. Same source.

already lasted seven years, overall expenditure had reached 88·7 million and the secret expenses amounted to 32 million.[1] As the war progressed, therefore, the secret expenses accelerated much faster than the overall rise in expenditure. In the years between 1635 and 1639, the secret expenses alone amounted on average to only slightly less than the total of *all* expenses in 1630 [Table II]. The war coincided with a period of relatively stable prices: thus the rise in expenditure was a real increase, and was not offset by inflation.

By 1640–2, the size of secret expenditure had come to pose an extremely serious problem for the government. From 15·3 per cent

TABLE II
Secret payments of the French monarchy 1625–1659

Date	Quinquennial totals livres	Average per annum livres
1625–9	52,416,787	10,483,357
1630–4	99,138,240	19,827,648
1635–9	207,880,836	41,576,167
1640–4	210,840,605	42,168,121
1645–9	222,103,618	44,420,723
1650–4	62,998,505	12,599,701
1655–9	334,189,875	66,837,975

Sources: (*a*) 'Les comptants employés au compte de l'Épargne montant par roole', in reality an appendix to the remonstrances of the *Chambre des Comptes* of 7 July 1648. A[rchives des] A[ffaires] E[trangères], Mémoires et Documents] France 861, fo. 225. The list ends in 1644, the last year to have been accounted at this moment. The list seems to have been fairly accurate if the years 1630, 1633, 1643 and 1644 – when direct comparison is possible with other sources – are typical.

(*b*) More reliable is the list which has been used for the years 1644–61, which was Chancellor Séguier's own ['Inventaire des Estatz de comptant qui sont ès mains de Monseigneur le Chancelier'. B[ritish] L[ibrary] Harleian 4472b, fos. 413–17]. As president of the council of finance, Séguier was in a position to know. Séguier's figures accord exactly with other sources for the years 1653, 1657, 1660 and 1661. Moreover, there is the evidence of the *Chambre de Justice* of 1661, which found 384 million in *comptants* from 1655–61 [Dent, *op. cit.* p. 85]. Séguier's figure was 385,230,984 *livres*.

1. Figures for overall expenditure:

	1636	1639	1642
(i)	108,799,019 *livres*	90,572,430	88,766,785
(ii)	96,762,070	87,364,277	

Figures for the *comptants:*

(i)	31,246,840	37,559,849	32,978,120
(ii)		37,733,223	

Source (i) BN. MS. fr. 10410, Fieubet's accounts for 1636, 1639 and 1642.
Source (ii) BN. n.a.f. 164, 165, *rôles de l'Épargne* for 1636, 1639.

of total expenses in 1630, these sums had risen to 34.8 per cent in 1633, and 37.2 per cent in 1642. In 1639, they exceeded 40 per cent of all expenses. In a memoir written shortly before his death in 1640, Bullion, the *surintendant des finances*, pointed out the need to 'abolir les comptants', but only, he added significantly, after the war had ended.[1] In the *Testament Politique*, a collection of Richelieu's writings probably compiled by his secretaries and dating from the years 1639–40, Richelieu states: 'l'abus [des comptants] est venu jusques à tel point que n'y remédier pas et perdre l'état est une même chose'.[2] The scale of government borrowing was chiefly responsible for this situation. Interest had to be paid on a 'floating debt' of 36.2 million in 1640, 35.6 million in 1641 and 25.6 million in 1642.[3] Sometimes the interest rate exceeded 33 per cent.[4]

If the situation was already serious by the time of Richelieu's death (4 December 1642), Mazarin made it much worse. With a gambler's instinct, Mazarin sought to anticipate as much future revenue as possible in the hope of gaining a conclusive military victory, and thus of imposing a decisive peace treaty on the Habsburgs. In 1645, Mazarin and D'Hémery – the *contrôleur-géneral des finances* in the years 1643–7 and *surintendant* in 1647–8 – borrowed 115 million, thus anticipating the revenues of the French Crown up to the end of the fiscal year 1647.[5] Overall expenditure in 1645 reached a record 136.2 million,[6] while the secret expenses –

---

1. BN. 500 Colbert 194 f. 273, 'ordre à préparer lorsqu'il plairra à Dieu donner la paix au Royaume'.
2. *Testament politique* (ed. André), p. 430.
3. Gross amount borrowed, including interest charges. 1640: 36,188,939 *livres* from 62 contracts. 1641: 35,619,602 *livres* from 58 contracts. 1642: 25,564,300 *livres* from 40 contracts. AN, E 154a–175, *arrêts de prêt, passim*. The author hopes to return to this subject more fully at a later date.
4. (i) Loan of Bordeaux, Bordier, Bretonvilliers and Galland under the name of Jean Levesque: 5 million at 37.33 per cent interest (2 July 1639). *Cf.* AN. E 392 fo. 5, 7 Oct. 1666; E 392 fo. 656, 30 Oct. 1666. (ii) Loan of François Sabathier under the name of François Brunet: 9 million at 33.33 per cent AN. E 154b fo. 365, 20 Feb. 1640; *cf.* AN. E 392 fo. 146, 7 Oct. 1666. (iii) 'Loan upon loan' under the name of Michel Collin: 1.8 million at 38.88 per cent. AN. E 156b fo. 654, 29 Aug. 1640; *cf.* AN. E 377b fo. 282ᵛ, 31 Mar. 1665; AN. E 393b fo. 492, 20 Dec. 1666. (iv) Loan under the name of Denis Guesdon: 506,000 *livres* at 49.40 per cent. AN. E 155a fo. 281, 28 Apr. 1640; *cf.* AN. E 392 fo. 5, 7 Oct. 1666. (v) Loan by Pierre Puget sieur de Montauronunder the name of Jacques Petit dit la Veuve: 3,054,880 *livres* at 33.32 per cent. AN. E 156a fo. 654, 30 July 1640; *cf.* AN. E 382b fo. 76, 15 Oct. 1665; AN. E 384b fo. 521, 15 Feb. 1666.
5. Gross amount borrowed, including interest charges. 1643: 55,538,565 *livres* from 103 contracts. 1644: 66,733,455 *livres* from 126 contracts. 1645: 115,750,265 *livres* from 112 contracts. 1646: 80,486,528 *livres* from 132 contracts. 1647: 39,902,012 *livres* from 77 contracts. AN. E 176a–227c, *arrêts de prêt, passim*. Supplemented by loans in BN. n.a.f. 201, 'Traités et prêts faits au Roy ès années 1643 et 1644' (*traités* discounted from calculations).
6. Overall expenditure in 1643 stood at 120,187,622 *livres*, and the *comptants* amounted to 48,453,125 *livres*. BN. n.a.f. 168, *rôles de l'Épargne*. Overall expenditure in 1645 stood at 136,181,222 *livres*, and the *comptants* amounted to 57,672,904 *livres*. BN. MS. fr. 10410, account of Nicolas Jeannin de Castille.

representing in large part the interest on government borrowing – reached the record figure of 57.7 million.[1]

The weakness of Mazarin's policy was that the gamble was far from certain of success. Certainly, no quick settlement was forthcoming at the Westphalian negotiations, while in domestic political terms this policy was disastrously unpopular. The *Parlement* of Paris became increasingly critical of the financiers during and after 1644.[2] In January 1648, hostile speeches in the *Cour des Aides* influenced adversely the negotiations between the Crown and its financiers.[3] The conflict over the *arrêt d'union* prevented the raising of new loans between 13 May and 30 June 1648.[4] When the representatives of the four Parisian sovereign courts met at the *Chambre St Louis* on 30 June, the presence of members of the *Chambre des Comptes* ensured that the secret expenses would be the object of critical and informed examination. The *Chambre des Comptes* provided a list of the annual totals of secret expenses since the reign of Henry IV.[5] Knowledge of these statistics must have had a profound effect on the members of the *Chambre St Louis* as they set about formulating their criticisms of the government. The eleventh proposal they issued compared the figures for 1609 and 1644 to demonstrate the rise in secret expenditure. There could be no public confidence in the conduct of financial administration, the *Chambre St Louis* asserted, until 'l'excedz desdits comptans' had been remedied. The members of the *Chambre St Louis* declared all loan contracts to be illegal and demanded the holding of an extraordinary tribunal (*chambre de justice*) to prosecute the financiers. These proposals, together with the dismissal of D'Hémery on 9 July 1648, brought about a collapse of confidence and the declaration of bankruptcy of the French Crown. The government renounced its debts of 80 million to the financiers.[6]

No clear decisions were taken on the question of the secret expenses, however, until the *Chambre des Comptes* enacted proposal eleven of the *Chambre St Louis* in decree form on 27 November 1648. The *Chambre des Comptes* declared that secret expenses should not exceed three million *livres* per annum – about the level of Henry

---

1. Dent, *op. cit.* p. 85, asserts that in 1644 the secret payments reached 59,457,000 *livres*. The figure of 59,457,354 *livres* was given by the *Chambre des Comptes*. However, Séguier's figure was 53,848,205 *livres*, and this lower figure has been accepted in the calculations in Table II. The figure for 1645 was 57,657,990 *livres*.

2. As a result, La Rallière, a financier, compared the *Parlement* of Paris to the Long Parliament. E. H. Kossmann, *La Fronde* (Leiden, 1954), p. 34. *Journal d'Olivier Lefèvre d'Ormesson et extraits des mémoires d'André Lefèvre d'Ormesson* (ed. A. Chéruel, 2 vols., 1860–1), i. 214. AAE. France 850 fo. 55, 10 Sept. 1644.

3. AN. ZIa 162 fo. 245, 7 Jan. 1648.

4. Omer Talon, *Mémoires* (ed. Michaud and Poujoulat, 3rd. ser., vi. 1839), p. 245. B.L. Harleian 4466 fos. 106ᵛ–107ʳ, 112.   5. This list is used as source i in Table II.

6. AN. U 28 fo. 389ᵛ, 11 July 1648. Séguier announced a deficit of 78 million. The financiers claimed *c*. 1654 that in 1648 80 million had been owed to them. AAE. France 893/2 fo. 419, remonstrances of the 'intéressés aux prêts'.

IV's reign. This decree was not binding on the government, but political weakness necessitated fiscal caution: on 22 December 1648, a royal declaration implemented the decision of the *Chambre des Comptes*.[1] Not surprisingly, the immediate effect on the government was a shortage of funds. The government lacked the means of paying the financiers an attractive rate of interest. Moreover, after the peace of Rueil (11 March 1649), when the government began anticipating revenues once more, limitations were placed on the amount that could be borrowed and the interest that could be paid.[2] As a result, the cash expenses fell: in 1650 they actually went below three million *livres*. The financiers needed a victory in the Fronde to secure compensation for their losses in 1648. In the short-term, therefore, the financiers were prepared to lend money to the government at a low rate of interest or without charging interest at all.

The royalist victory at the end of the Fronde reversed all these tendencies. Far from moderating his policies and accepting the proposals of the *Chambre St Louis*, Mazarin was determined to govern France 'comme un vainqueur absolu gouverne un pays de conquête'.[3] The defeat of the Fronde meant the continuation of war with Spain. Overall government expenditure reached 113.5 million in 1653 and 155 million in 1657.[4] At the same time, the government was strong enough to be able to borrow money on a significant scale once more: 22.9 million were borrowed in 1654, 32.8 million in 1655, 78.6 million in 1656 and 74.7 million in 1657.[5]

1. Dent, *op. cit.* p. 100.
2. A. L. Moote, *The revolt of the judges. The Parlement of Paris and the Fronde. 1643–1652* (Princeton 1971), pp. 212–13. An interest rate of 8.33 per cent was allowed in 1649 and 1650, and 10 per cent 'pendant la guerre'. AN. U 29 fo. 82ᵛ. On 1 June 1650, the council of state agreed to pay interest at 5.55 per cent with effect from 1 Jan. 1650, and set up a fund of 3 million for this purpose. AN. E 1695 fo. 153.
3. Véron de Forbonnais, *op. cit.* ii. 105. In contrast, Moote, *op. cit.* p. 357, asserts that 'the Mazarinist régime of 1653–1661 made only piecemeal attacks on specific aspects of the reforms of 1648 . . .'.
4. 113,535,651 *livres* in 1653 and 154,946,677 *livres* in 1657. BN. n.a.f. 169, 170, *rôles de l'Épargne*.
5. Gross amount borrowed, including interest charges. 1654: 22,906,375 *livres* from 31 contracts. 1655: 32,770,377 *livres* from 50 contracts. AN. E 263a–284b, *arrêts de prêt, passim*. 1656: 78,569,657 *livres* from 133 contracts. 1657: 74,722,320 *livres* from 119 contracts. For loans in the years 1656–61, the source is BN. MS. fr. 18221–7, with *traités* excluded from the calculations. The figures have to be used with caution, since the copies of the loan contracts sent to Séguier were not dated precisely. Moreover, whereas in the records of the council of finance, the loan contracts were filed according to the date of negotiation, Séguier filed them according to the years on which the revenues were anticipated. These difficulties are not insuperable, however, since in 1661 revenues were anticipated one year in advance. For 1661, the contracts on the revenues of 1662 were abrogated by Colbert and are to be found in AN. E 350, *passim*. The contracts for the same revenues in the volume for 1661 were negotiated in 1660 and are thus transposed back to the earlier date [BN. MS. fr. 18227 fos. 111–45]. A similar procedure has been adopted by working backwards through the evidence to 1656. N. B.: Dent's figures for loans in these years (*op. cit.* p. 71) are in fact inaccurate figures for *traités*.

The financiers were prepared to lend money, but only at a price. Led by Thomas Bonneau, they demanded as the price for cooperation compensation for the disaster of 1648 and interest on loans made subsequently.[1] The result was a staggering increase in the cash expenses, made possible by the fact that on 16 November 1652, immediately after the royalist victory, the government had removed the restrictions imposed in 1648.[2] Between 1655 and 1659, the cash expenses reached record levels, averaging over 66 million per annum. In the record year of 1659, Foucquet signed cash expenses to the value of 88·3 million.

The signing of the Peace of the Pyrenees on 7 November 1659 permitted a substantial reduction in government expenditure. On 31 December 1659, the council of state concluded that financial reform was not only possible in the new context of peace, but essential. It was recognized that since the declaration of the Regency in 1643 the anticipation of revenues had been a major cause of the budgetary deficit. It was considered necessary to cut expenditure to the level of Louis XIII's lifetime.[3] Foucquet reduced the secret expenses to 30·6 million in 1660 and 20·3 million in 1661. The weakness of Foucquet's position, however, was that these reforms were too little and too late. The government borrowed 40·5 million in 1660 and 44·5 million in 1661[4] – a level of borrowing that was higher than in 1654, a year of war and the last year in which Servien and not Foucquet enjoyed real control of the royal finances. On 1 October 1659, Colbert had advised Mazarin of the abuses committed by the *surintendants des finances* past and present. On 28 October, he informed Mazarin that Foucquet had 'administré les finances avec une profusion qui n'a point d'exemple'.[5] The split between Foucquet and Colbert was papered over in January 1660, but the criticisms were not forgotten. Foucquet's position was thus emperilled from the moment of Mazarin's death on 9 March 1661 and the appointment of Colbert, his severest critic, as an *intendant des finances*. On 5 September 1661, Foucquet was arrested. Ten days later the *surintendance* was abolished 'pour toujours'. Instead, a new council – the *conseil royal des finances* – was established. Louis XIV presided over this council in person, although Colbert was its driving force.

1. AN. E 263b fo. 620, 25 Feb. 1654. A.A.E. France 893/2 fo. 419, remonstrances of the 'intéressés aux prêts'.
2. AN. E 1698 fo. 183. If the annual average of the *comptants* is calculated for the period between 1650 and 1659, then the figure arrived at − 39·7 million − is actually lower than the average for the 1640s. A great deal of the exceptionally high cash expenses of the 1650s may thus be presumed to be the legacy of the Fronde. *Cf.* Dent *op. cit.* p. 89.   3. AN. E 1712 fo. 37.
4. Gross amount borrowed, including interest charges. 1658: 35,281,905 *livres* from 62 contracts. 1659: 54,164,892 *livres* from 101 contracts. 1660: 40,553,297 *livres* from 59 contracts. 1661: 44,500,039 *livres* from 66 contracts.
5. *Lettres . . . de Colbert* (ed. Clément), i. 390–4; vii. 164–83.

Colbert was determined to bring about a drastic reduction in government expenditure. One aspect of this policy was an undeclared bankruptcy: fines totalling 156.7 million were imposed on the financiers by the *chambre de justice* of 1661.[1] These were moderated in 1665 and 1666 by the *conseil royal des finances* to about 110 million.[2] Colbert also dramatically reduced the secret expenses, believing these to have been the cause of the budgetary deficit at the time of Richelieu and Mazarin: 'il ne faut chercher ailleurs la source de tous les désordres', he wrote.[3] Already by the years 1665–9, the cash expenses averaged less than eight million a year, less than at any time during the ministries of Richelieu and Mazarin [Table III]. As a result of these measures, Colbert was able to reduce overall expenditure to 42 million at its lowest point in 1663.[4] Such restraint could not be maintained, but when Colbert complained to Louis XIV in 1670 that increased expenditure was undermining his reforms,[5] the figure he was criticizing – 75 million – was lower than that of any year between 1636 and 1662 for which evidence is available.

Colbert solved the problem of the secret expenses during his own lifetime. He did not reduce them quite to the level of Henry

TABLE III

Secret payments of the French monarchy 1660–1679

Date	Quinquennial totals livres	Average per annum livres
1660–4	82,562,448	16,512,489
1665–9	38,119,164	7,623,832
1670–4	59,250,262	11,850,052
1675–9	54,238,404	10,847,680

Sources: For 1660–1, as Table II(*b*). For 1662–79, the figures are taken from the relevant years of the expenditure accounts. BN. Mélanges Colbert 264–310, forty-seven volumes of expenditure accounts verified in the *Conseil royal des finances*. BN. n.a.f. 209 is incomplete for the year 1682. BN. n.a.f. 210 provides figures for the *comptants* for the years 1678, 1679 and 1680. No complete expenditure accounts appear to survive for the years 1682 and 1683, the last years of Colbert's ministry.

1. D. Dessert, 'Finances et société au xviiè. siècle: à propos de la Chambre de Justice de 1661', *Annales E.S.C.* xxix (1974), 850; Dent, *op. cit.* pp. 107, 151.
2. Ormesson, *Journal* (ed. Chéruel), ii. 400 (18 Oct. 1665). For the reduction of fines on individual financiers, Dessert, *art. cit.* 872–81, *passim*.
3. *Lettres ... de Colbert* (ed. Clément), ii. pt. i. 28–29.
4. Overall expenditure was 76,132,346 *livres* in 1662, 42,017,738 *livres* in 1663, 63,492,355 *livres* in 1664, 77,305,847 *livres* in 1665, 66,347,009 *livres* in 1666, 70,855,046 *livres* in 1667, 67,744,957 *livres* in 1668, 74,477,796 *livres* in 1669, 77,240,235 *livres* in 1670, and 85,260,431 *livres* in 1671. With the exception of 1662, these totals are the official, not the actual totals, which show some variation.
5. *Lettres ... de Colbert* (ed. Clément), vii. 234.

IV's reign, but they were removed as an issue from politics. From 29 per cent of total expenditure in 1662, Colbert succeeded in reducing the secret expenses to 6 per cent by 1670.[1] Colbert's reforms earned both political and financial advantages for the government in the short term. They were politically advantageous in that to Louis XIV and Colbert accrued the prestige of having achieved some of the more constructive aims of the *Chambre St Louis*. They were financially advantageous in that the reduction of the secret expenses and the fines levied on the financiers facilitated the balancing of the budget and further reductions in government expenditure. To this extent at least, the reforms of Colbert suggest that the French government was capable of reform and that the financiers could be held in check – at least in peace time. There was never any suggestion that Colbert, the son of a financier,[2] either wished – or would have been able – to 'abolish' the financiers. Colbert needed the financiers to provide funds for his commercial and industrial plans.

What was not possible, however, was for reform of the financial administration to take place in time of war. This had been the great problem under Richelieu and Mazarin, as the failure to grapple with the issue of the secret expenses demonstrates. Colbert was able to deal with the problem because he enjoyed twelve years of peace (1660–71).[3] Colbert was certainly not an advocate of the Dutch war of 1672, which was decided upon by Louis XIV as punishment for the Regents having entered the Triple Alliance against him in 1668. The war was in flat contradiction to Colbert's policy of retrenchment and reform. It rapidly escalated into a German war as well. By 1674, total expenditure reached 113 million, approximately the level of 1653. The debt left by the war accounted for expenditure of over 130 million in 1679 and 1681.[4] The war revived the issue of the secret expenses, although on a much more limited scale than under Richelieu and Mazarin. The secret expenses regularly exceeded 10 per cent of total expenditure, however.[5]

---

1. 29·13 per cent in 1662, 12·43 per cent in 1663, 6·33 per cent in 1664, 10·15 per cent in 1665, 11·04 per cent in 1666, 12·09 per cent in 1667, 10·49 per cent in 1668, 9·44 per cent in 1669, 6·15 per cent in 1670 and 16·08 per cent in 1671.

2. J. L. Bourgeon, *Les Colbert avant Colbert. Destin d'une famille marchande* (1973), pp. 173–214.

3. Less than eleven in view of the fact that he did not gain power until 15 Sept. 1661. Less than ten in view of the War of Devolution of 1667–8.

4. Overall expenditure was 91,213,058 *livres* in 1672, 99,099,087 *livres* in 1673, 113,676,401 *livres* in 1674, 115,783,007 *livres* in 1675, 106,093,801 *livres* in 1676, 111,812,091 *livres* in 1677, 97,781,328 *livres* (minimum figure) in 1678, 133,186,898 *livres* in 1679, 82,770,450 *livres* (minimum figure) in 1680, and 131,579,495 *livres* (minimum figure) in 1681.

5. As a proportion of total expenses, the *comptants* were 11·19 per cent in 1672, 14·01 per cent in 1673, 14·70 per cent in 1674, 10·90 per cent in 1675, 8·72 per cent in 1676, 10·12 per cent in 1677 and 9·86 per cent in 1679. Proportions are not calculated for 1678, 1680 and 1681 because the figures are incomplete.

Loans were incurred by the government on a significant scale once more. The official rate of interest was restated as 5·55 per cent in February 1672. Nevertheless, Colbert, however reluctantly, was obliged to pass in the secret expenses interest rates that were higher than the legal limit.[1] The problem never got out of hand in Colbert's lifetime, but after his death in 1683 his reforms were completely undermined.

The evidence of the secret expenses suggests that the structural causes of the financial crisis were capable of some degree of reform but that reform required the circumstances of peace. Henry IV and Sully had kept the secret expenses in check because they enjoyed eleven years of peace between 1598 and 1610.[2] The civil disturbances during the minority of Louis XIII, and Louis XIII's wars against the Protestants had undermined their achievement. Richelieu and Bullion appreciated the need for restraint, and hoped that a firm treaty with the Habsburgs would permit financial reform and a strict limit being placed on the secret expenses. The treaty was not achieved in their lifetime. Foucquet began cutting the secret expenses after the Peace of the Pyrenees in 1659, but it was left to Colbert to reduce them to a politically acceptable level. Continued retrenchment and reform along the lines advocated by Colbert was not only possible, but essential for the continuance of financial stability. However, Louis XIV set his course along the path of war and returned to Richelieu's maxim of subordinating domestic political considerations to the demands of his foreign policy. Once Louis XIV began the first of two major struggles with the formidable financial resources of England,[3] the Crown was once more at the mercy of its financiers.[4]

---

1. 'Gratifications' and 'augmentations de remises' in the *comptants*. BN. Mélanges Colbert 298 fos. 872–905ᵛ, a list from 1676.
2. On 11 Aug. 1600, Henry IV went to war with Savoy over the marquisate of Saluzzo, but quickly made peace at Lyon on 17 Jan. 1601. Shortly before his death in 1610, Henry IV was contemplating armed intervention in the Cleves-Jülich crisis. Either of these events could have undermined Sully's achievement.
3. R. Mousnier, 'L'évolution des finances publiques en France et en Angleterre', *Revue Historique*, ccv (1951), 1–23. P. G. M. Dickson, *The financial revolution in England. A study in the development of public credit, 1688–1756* (1967).
4. I would like to express my gratitude to the Leverhulme Trust, the *Centre National de la Recherche Scientifique*, Merton College, Oxford, the Twenty-Seven Foundation and the Research Board of the University of Reading, without whose generosity the research that went into this paper could not have been undertaken. I would like to thank Professor Emmanuel Leroy-Ladurie of the *Collège de France* for his advice and encouragement. I am particularly indebted to Mrs Menna Prestwich of St Hilda's College, Oxford, both for commenting on this paper and for her seminars on seventeenth-century France which, while I was an undergraduate, stimulated my interest in this subject.

XI

The Failure of the French Revenue Farms, 1600–60[1]

WHEN Colbert established the general farm (*ferme-générale*) of indirect taxes in 1681, he set up an organization which was to endure for a hundred and ten years[2] and was to provide on average half the annual revenues of the French monarchy. The long-term success of Colbert's reform might lead one to suppose that biggest was best—that an amalgamation of leases of separate farms into a larger unit inevitably and necessarily brought with it greater profitability and efficiency. Yet the experience of the first half of the seventeenth century in France was the reverse, and tended to show that biggest was worst—that separate, smaller leases on the indirect taxes were more profitable and carried fewer risks for the lessees. "Occasionally... individual financiers made attempts to add farm to farm until they held large numbers of leases. But such combinations were ephemeral. No attempt was made to unify the holdings financially or bureaucratically. The retirement or bankruptcy of the individual left the structure to collapse into its original parts."[3] The purpose of this article is to explain why this was the case, to describe the altered circumstances in which the *ferme-générale* could be established and prosper, and where appropriate to make comparisons with the situation in England in the same period.

I

The concept of a revenue farm—the leasing by the crown of a tax to a private contractor for a set number of years in return for a fixed annual rent, any additional profits of the farm accruing to the contractor—is immediately familiar to students of English financial history in the seventeenth century.[4] The customs were leased as "the great farm" between 1604 and 1643 and again between 1662 and 1671. Between 1632 and 1640 the farms of wines and currants were linked together as a "petty farm". The English Civil War and Interregnum form a break in this tradition, however. The administration of existing revenues, and the new tax, the excise—chiefly on beer, ale, and other liquor—was handed over to parliamentary commissioners. In 1657–8 there was a move to return to full-scale revenue farming, but this was not achieved—with the exception of part of the excise—before the Restoration.[5] In France, a much greater range of commodities

---

[1] I should like to express my gratitude to the Twenty-Seven Foundation, without whose generosity the research that went into this article could not have been undertaken.
[2] With the exception of the period of direct administration (*régie*) between 1721 and 1726.
[3] G. T. Matthews, *The Royal General Farms in Eighteenth-Century France* (New York, 1958), p. 46.
[4] R. Ashton, *The Crown and the Money Market, 1603–40* (Oxford, 1960), p. 79. Cf. his earlier paper, 'Revenue Farming under the Early Stuarts', *Economic History Review*, 2nd ser. VIII (1956), 310–22.
[5] M. P. Ashley, *Financial and Commercial Policy under the Cromwellian Protectorate* (2nd edn. 1962), pp. 53–4, 65; C. D. Chandaman, *The English Public Revenue, 1660–88* (Oxford, 1975), pp. 21–3, 51–5.

was taxed indirectly, and the number of farms was accordingly larger. The three most important farms were the *gabelles de France*, the *aides*, and the *cinq grosses fermes* which produced between them about three-quarters of the total yield of the indirect taxes.¹ Yet these three farms operated in only part of the country—basically 12 *généralités* in northern France. Elsewhere, there were similar but distinct farms enjoying comparable but not necessarily identical taxes. The *gabelles*—whether of northern France (the so-called *gabelles de France*), of the Lyonnais and Languedoc, or of the Dauphiné and Provence—were basically taxes on the sale of salt, a vital commodity not especially burdened in England. Englishmen were struck by the difference. Sir George Carew, the English ambassador in France in 1609, noted that the *gabelles* were "very thick and biting; as for example so much salt as served my house for one whole year, costing but 40s. in England would have cost 30*l*. sterling."² The taxes levied together in the farm of the *aides* were chiefly taxes on drink—especially wine, beer, cider, and perry (*poiré*)—levied when it arrived at the gates of the town. However, the great wine-producing area of south-west France had its own levy on the transportation of wines which formed part of the farm known as the *convoy et comptablie* of Bordeaux. The taxes levied together within the farm known as the *cinq grosses fermes* consisted chiefly of customs duties (*traites*), both on exports and imports between France and abroad, and between the area of the farm and the rest of the kingdom.

The indirect taxes were thus heavier in France than in England and also covered a wider range of commodities. In Carew's words, "not only all kind of necessaries for man's food and raiment coming into town pay these impositions to the king, but abroad in the country also they levy to his use one kind of imposition upon cloven-footed beasts and another upon whole or round-footed, besides many other."³ The burden of indirect taxes was perhaps lighter in France than in the Netherlands,⁴ but there is little doubt that the crown sought to increase the burden. In 1597–1602 and 1640–3 attempts were made in France to introduce a 5 per cent sales tax (the *sol pour livre* or *pancarte*) on the Dutch model,⁵ which would have added substantially to the number of revenue farms.⁶ Serious rioting prevented the establishment of the *sol pour livre*, however, and the government was left with the only alternative of increasing existing taxes. It has been said of the English revenue farms that "the system did no great harm to the consumer or taxpayer except in so far as it provided the crown with an incentive to burden trade with more and more impositions."⁷ The same could scarcely be claimed for the French system, which it is tempting to view as inequitable,

¹ Appendix, Table 4, col. f.
² Sir George Carew, 'A relation of the state of France', in T. Birch, ed. *An Historical View of the Negotiations between the Courts of England, France, and Brussels, 1592–1617* (1749), p. 438. The £ sterling was equivalent to approximately 10 *livres tournois*.—A[rchives] N[ationales], P 2334, p. 1219. Treaty of 16 Aug. 1594 between Henri IV and Elizabeth I, ratified by Henri IV on 7 Nov. 1594.
³ Carew, loc. cit. p. 439. Carew refers to the tax known as the *ferme de bétail à pied fourché*. This, together with the *ferme de bétail à pied rond*, was later amalgamated into the *ferme-générale*.
⁴ C. H. Wilson, *Economic History and the Historian: Collected Essays* (1969), p. 120.
⁵ A. N. Z1a 161, fo. 29*v*–30, 4 Dec. 1640: "qu'elle étoit dans tous les états voisins les mieux policiés comme en Hollande, où il ne se levoit rien par capitation".
⁶ Separate leases were negotiated for each *généralité*. For example, Tours: A.N. E 162a, fo. 350, 8 June 1641.
⁷ L. Stone, *The Crisis of the Aristocracy, 1558–1641* (Oxford, 1965), p. 429.

difficult to administer, and economically counter-productive. If we take the example of the farm of the *gabelles de France*, it is clear that fiscal considerations led to a distortion of the market. Artificial "salt boundaries" had gradually evolved, and these were difficult to police.[1] There was a basic inequity since the price of salt was much higher in some areas than in others—the farmers had to import salt from areas in which they controlled production to fill the salt deposits (*greniers à sel*) in other areas of the farm, which might have been supplied more cheaply by direct trading across the artificial "salt boundary".[2] The variation in the price of salt led to contraband in this staple commodity from one area of the kingdom to another.[3] Contraband in turn led to high administrative costs: the farmers had to employ *gardes des gabelles* to protect their rights. By 1644, peasant riots and rebellions against the salt tax had become so common that the farmers were allowed to levy at the crown's expense two companies of fusileers—80 men in all, with two captains and two lieutenants in addition—in order to enforce payment in six provinces.[4] The monopolistic and distorting effect of the other indirect taxes was less marked, but each had its own defects. There were local immunities from the *aides* and the dues were heavier in some localities than others, while the *traites* must have positively hindered commercial expansion by taxing home-based trade between provinces as well as imports from abroad. Indeed, Sir George Carew commented that "a cup of Orléans wine, before it be bought by the stranger out of the tavern in Paris, payeth ten or twelve several duties to the king."[5]

II

Turning from the nature of the indirect taxes to the method by which they were raised, in England, the same syndicate held the customs farm through successive bids and counter-bids from 1604 until 1621, although initially the lease lasted for only seven years. A new syndicate controlled the farm from 1621 to 1625, to be displaced by another in 1625–8 and a third in 1638–9. In the years 1628–32, leases were renewed annually; thereafter the crown renewed them every three years until 1639.[6] In France, the lease on the *gabelles de France* held by Claude Josse lasted for five years (1599–1604);[7] it was then held for six years under Jean de Moisset and later Thomas Robin, whose lease did not run its full course. It was increased to seven years during Moisset's second lease (1616), but the farm was subdivided the following year and Moisset died in 1620 leaving substantial debts.[8] Antoine Feydeau's lease was to have lasted seven years, but he went bankrupt in 1626.[9] Subdivision of the farm resulted from this disaster, with the

---

[1] A.N. E 74a, fo. 140, 9 March 1623. For the "salt boundaries" see Matthews, op. cit. map facing p. 82 and *New Cambridge Modern History: Atlas* (Cambridge, 1970), p. 122(b).
[2] Matthews, op. cit. p. 91; E. P. Beaulieu, *Les Gabelles sous Louis XIV* (Paris–Nancy, 1903, repr. Geneva, 1974), pp. 12–61.
[3] Beaulieu, op. cit. pp. 149–91, and decrees of the council of finance too numerous to mention.
[4] A.N. E 191a, fo. 517, 15 June 1644. The difficulties were in the *généralités* of Orléans, Tours, Bourges, Moulins, Alençon, and Caen.
[5] Carew, op. cit. p. 438.   [6] Ashton, *The Crown and the Money Market*, pp. 87–105.
[7] A.N. P 2339, p. 37, 3 Dec. 1598.
[8] He made Pierre Payen his sole heir.—A.N. Minutier Central XCVI 8 bis, 24 Aug. 1620.
[9] Feydeau's career is traced by P. Heumann, 'Un traitant sous Louis XIII. Antoine Feydeau', in G. Pagès, ed. *Études sur l'Histoire Administrative et Sociale de l'Ancien Régime* (Paris, 1938), 183–223. Feydeau owed over one million *livres* to the crown: A.N. E 93b, fo. 114, 14 Aug. 1627.

lease being taken up jointly by Étienne Brioys, Louis Monceau, and Jean Anymé, who divided the farm geographically. On 30 March 1628, with three years remaining on Feydeau's original lease, the council of finance accepted the offers of Claude Charlot under the name of Thomas Guyot. Guyot's lease was to have run for ten years until 1637. However, in the course of 1632 Charlot began to experience increasing difficulties which were to result in his bankruptcy later that year.[1] Accordingly, the government turned to a new consortium, which in the event held the lease on the *gabelles de France*, with only relatively minor changes of personnel, from 1632 until 1655.[2] This consortium held the lease for eight years and then three years under the name of Philippe Hamel, and then for two three-year periods and one six-year period under the name of Jacques Dattin. In 1656, it joined forces with a new group in a lease under the name of Simon Le Noir. This was to have run for ten years, but in 1660 Foucquet negotiated a new seven-year contract with substantially the same syndicate but in return for a higher rent. With the fall of Foucquet and the rise of Colbert the lease was broken yet again the following year (Appendix, Table 1). Thus only six out of 14 leases on the *gabelles de France* lasted their full term: in one case, bankruptcy caused the break, but in the other five cases the government reneged on its agreements. In the case of 13 leases on the *aides*, only two ran their full term (Antoine Feydeau's first lease and Claude Bullot's) (Table 2). In the case of nine leases on the *cinq grosses fermes*, at least five failed to run for their full term: the bankruptcy of Charlot led to the dissolution of the second lease under the name of Jean de la Grange; but the government broke its faith in the other cases (Table 3).

In England, the system of farming was adopted in order to secure a settled revenue, so that the king could "know exactly how much he has"[3] and—at the moment of the renewal of the lease—to "advance [i.e. increase] the revenue".[4] The same combination of reasons applied in France, yet the order of priorities was reversed. Instead of stability being the order of the day, the finance ministers frequently broke faith with the farmers. They did so for two reasons. They feared the bankruptcy of the farmers and recognized that the surety system was ineffective.[5] Thus, they demanded loans from the farmers as a sign of their good faith and solvency:[6] the greater the lending to the crown, the wealthier (and thus more solvent) the contractor—or so it appeared. If the existing farmers were unwilling to make the loans required, the finance minister would turn to a rival consortium which would. Secondly, the prestige of the finance minister depended on his being seen to increase revenues: short-term gain was paramount, because

[1] He left debts of 1·4 million *livres*, of which one million was owed to the crown.—A.N. E 111b, fo. 222, 19 March 1633, E 114a, fo. 164, 23 Nov. 1633.
[2] D. Dessert, 'Finances et Société au xviie siècle: à propos de la Chambre de Justice de 1661', *Annales E.S.C.* XXIX (1974), app. 2.
[3] Ashton, 'Revenue Farming', 310–11.   [4] Ashley, op. cit. p. 53.
[5] The contractor had to deposit surety (*cautionnement*) for his administration of the farm—usually one-quarter of the annual lease. Guarantors were required to attest to the solvency of the farmer and to provide surety. Yet in the event of a bankruptcy, the surety usually covered only a small proportion of the total debt, even if it had not been alienated already. Moreover, the guarantors tended to be the business associates of the farmer. In some cases, they were involved in the consortium which enjoyed the lease; in other cases the guarantor was in reality the farmer himself, the nominal guarantor having merely lent his name ("il n'a ... faict que prester son nom.") A.N. Minutier Central LI 145, 29 July 1625.
[6] Jean de la Grange, the farmer of the *cinq grosses fermes*, was discharged from giving surety of 300,000 *livres* in view of loans of 600,000 *livres*.—A.N. E 67b, fo. 45, 22 May 1621.

the king's needs were pressing, especially in war time, and because all finance ministers feared dismissal. Almost immediately after a new lease was granted, the defeated rivals of the farmer presented a fresh offer to the council of finance (*conseil d'état et des finances*). Sometimes, in the first months after a new lease had been granted, the farmer (the *adjudicataire* or *adjudicataire-général*) was allowed to comment—unfavourably, of course—on these new proposals and was solemnly "confirmed" as lessee.[1] However, as the years passed, the pressure on the finance minister to break the existing lease grew, especially if the lessee was proving dilatory in fulfilling the terms of his contract. Pressure from a rival—such as the memorandum of Colbert against Foucquet in the autumn of 1659—might precipitate action, although the decision would be justified in terms of good fiscal policy.[2]

It is not surprising, therefore, that the revenue farms both in England and France showed a tendency to increase in the early years of the seventeenth century: the whole system of lease-renewals was designed to ensure a rise in the amount of revenue enjoyed from the farm at least to keep pace with inflation, the effects of which were still being felt until the 1630s and 1640s. In England the first lease of the great farm of the customs in 1604 was at an annual rent of £112,400;[3] by 1664, the figure had reached £390,000,[4] a trebling of the rent. In France, all three of the major farms increased between 1604 and 1664, with the *gabelles de France* showing a comparable rate of increase to the English customs and the other two farms showing an even faster increase.[5] A general rise in the levels of taxation in seventeenth-century France was a concomitant of stronger government: although contemporaries would have disagreed, overall tax-levels in the fifteenth and sixteenth centuries had been relatively low. The rate of increase in the farm of the *gabelles de France* between 1604 and 1664 matched the increase in overall expenditure by the French monarchy in the same period.[6] The calculations are complicated by the fact that the leases survive in manuscript form whereas the yield of the farms survives only in the form of tables compiled by J. R. Mallet, who was chief clerk of Nicolas Desmaretz,[7] and had access to materials subsequently burnt in the great fire at the *Chambre des Comptes* in 1737. Mallet's figures have the inestimable advantage of forming, with the exception of the years 1657–61, the only continuous set of financial statistics in France for

---

[1] For example, Antoine Feydeau was confirmed in his lease on the *aides* despite the counter-offers of Antoine Collot.—A.N. E 39a, fo. 101, 19 Jan. 1613. Feydeau's lease had envisaged possession for eight years from 1 Oct. 1611, so that in theory Collot's offers should not even have been considered.
[2] For Colbert's indictment of Foucquet's management of the farms (1 Oct. 1659) see P. Clément, ed. *Lettres, Instructions et Mémoires de Colbert* . . . (Paris, 1861–82), VII, 167. For Foucquet's conversion to the principle of a high yield from the farms see J. Lair, *Nicolas Foucquet. Procureur-général, Surintendant des Finances, Ministre d'état de Louis XIV* (Paris, 1890), I, 505. For Foucquet's negotiations with the farmers see A[rchives des] A[ffaires] É[trangères, Mémoires et Documents,] France, 910, fos. 3, 16, 6, 14 Jan. 1660.
[3] Ashton, *The Crown and the Money Market*, p. 87.   [4] Chandaman, op. cit. p. 303.
[5] The lowest increase (334 per cent) was that of the *gabelles de France*; next came the *cinq grosses fermes* (1,165 per cent), and finally the *aides* (3,717 per cent).
[6] Overall expenditure was 21,474,462 *livres* in 1604 (D. J. Buisseret, *Sully and the Growth of Centralized Government in France, 1598–1610* (1968), p. 81), and 63,492,355 *livres* in 1664.—R. J. Bonney, 'The Secret Expenses of Richelieu and Mazarin, 1624–61', *English Historical Review*, XCI (1976), 834, n.4. However, the rate of expenditure was much higher in the 1650s, while the yield from the revenue farms was lower.
[7] Desmaretz was an *intendant des finances* between 1678 and 1708 and *contrôleur-général des finances* between 1708 and 1715.

16

the first half of the seventeenth century. Where the overall figures for expenditure and revenues can be compared with other sources,[1] the discrepancies in Mallet's figures are relatively small. Yet it would be idle to claim that there are no difficulties about the details of Mallet's figures—for example, in his distinction between "extraordinary" and "ordinary" expenditure—quite apart from typographical mistakes[2] and errors in addition. Mallet's figures are thus the best that exist, but the best is far from perfect.[3] They have to be used to supplement evidence from other sources, not as a major source on which exclusive reliance is placed. Mallet's figures for the indirect revenues of the French monarchy, presented in quinquennial totals, form Table 4. A selected comparison with the quinquennial totals of the "secret expenses" (*comptants*) and the issues of coinage by the French crown is made in Table 5. The rate of increase in the indirect taxes, calculated in the form of index numbers, is compared in Table 6 with other revenues, expenditure, issues of coinage, and the price of grain at Paris. The calculations are based on a common index, the average of the years 1625–34 —that is to say, the decade before the beginning of the twenty-five year war against Spain in 1635. In some instances the calculations are affected by exceptional circumstances—the subsistence crisis of 1628–31 distorts the base index for the *gabelles de France* since the yield from this revenue was very low during those four years. The base index for issues of coinage was also relatively low because the major issues occurred in the 1640s and 1650s.

III

One of the crucial points to emerge from this evidence is that the yield from the indirect taxes in an average year was less than a quarter of the total revenues of the French monarchy in the first half of the seventeenth century (Table 5, col. vii). Why was this so? Why did the French revenue farms "fail" before 1660 in comparison with the later success of the *ferme-générale*? There are basically two types of answer to the problem, the one related to broad problems of the economy, the other to the institution of the farms and its manipulation by the crown. With regard to the problems of the economy, the fixed condition of the lease tended to screen the actual value of the taxes at a given moment and the extent to which they fluctuated according to economic circumstances. When rent payments were made promptly, when the farmers were ready to provide additional credit, and when their prospective successors were prepared to place a much higher valuation on the revenue of the farm, it is reasonable to assume, for example, that the English customs revenues were buoyant. It is also reasonable to assume that this buoyancy was the result of a trade revival after the conclusion of war.[4] Alternatively, in a period of sudden commercial depression such as the 1620s, the English customs revenues could become "over-rented" and the

---

[1] Such comparisons are possible from materials in Buisseret, op. cit.; J. M. Hayden, *France and the Estates-General of 1614* (Cambridge, 1974); Bonney, loc. cit.
[2] Some control on these is possible by reference to B[ibliothèque] N[ationale], MS fr. 7750, fos. 42v–51r.
[3] In the author's view they are treated too uncritically by A. Guéry, 'Les Finances de la Monarchie Française sous l'Ancien Régime', *Annales E.S.C.* xxxiii (1978), 216–39. M. Guéry does not discuss Mallet's figures for indirect revenues: but see Appendix, comments to Table 5.
[4] Cf. the example in Chandaman, op. cit. p. 24.

crown might have to accept a reduction of the lease.[1] The difficulty is to ascertain where the economic influence ended and the efficiency or otherwise of the revenue-raising machinery began.[2] In France, the policing factor and the high number of sub-leases[3] meant that the administrative costs of the farms were high. Strong-arm finance ministers such as Sully sought to ensure that the farmers, and not the government, carried these costs. Thus, according to Sir George Carew, "when Sully came first to the managing of the revenues [1597–8] ... the farms of the whole realm amounted then but to 800,000*l*. sterling, this year 1609, he had let them out for 1,000,000*l*. and that without exacting any more upon the people than was paid before, but only by reducing that to the king's coffers which was embezled [*sic*] by under-officers."[4] Carew's figures may be doubtful, but the force of his argument is not.

One of the great purposes of the revenue farming system was to obtain a settled revenue taking good and bad years together. According to Chancellor Séguier, the president of the council of finance, the farmers "devaient payer bon an, mal an".[5] The fact remains that in France—and in sharp contrast to the experience in England—this did not happen. It is reasonable to talk of the failure of the revenue farms not merely because the indirect taxes produced only a quarter of the total revenues of the monarchy, but more importantly, because the farmers rarely fulfilled their obligations to the crown. The net yield to the government from the farms was frequently much less than the ostensible value of the leases.[6] It is here that the economic situation had a direct bearing on the yield of the indirect taxes. The years 1628–31 and 1649–52 witnessed plague, subsistence crises, and high mortality rates in much of France.[7] Almost certainly there was a decline in overall population levels: there were fewer people in the 1650s and the majority of the population was poorer, too. The situation would have been quite serious enough without foreign war and internal disorder. Yet only in the years 1602–8 and 1611–13 could it be said that France was on a peace-footing in the first half of the seventeenth century. Henry IV went to war with Savoy in 1600–1 and was preparing to intervene in the Cleves–Jülich succession crisis in 1609–10. The years 1614–29 saw almost continual domestic political upheaval with revolts by the upper nobility and the Protestants. Richelieu intervened in the Valtelline crisis in 1624–6 and in the war of the Mantuan

---

[1] Ashton, *The Crown and the Money Market*, p. 95.
[2] The debate over customs administration under the Protectorate is a case in point. Cf. the contrasting views of Ashley, op. cit. pp. xi, 54, 57, and Menna Prestwich, 'Diplomacy and Trade in the Protectorate', *Journal of Modern History*, XXII (1950), 116–17.
[3] A.N. E 96a, fo. 280, 12 April 1628. Complaint of Guillaume Menant, farmer-general of the *aides*, who mentioned the high costs of renegotiating sub-leases.
[4] Carew, op. cit. p. 486.
[5] Guy Patin, *Lettres au Temps de la Fronde*, ed. A. Thérive (Paris, 1921), p. 156.
[6] The problem was most acute with the *gabelles de France* and less serious with the *aides* and the *cinq grosses fermes*.—Tables 1 to 3, figures for "average yield" compared with "net revenue payable". The salt tax reflected most closely population levels and pauperization of the peasantry.
[7] As many local studies have demonstrated, notably: P. Goubert, *Beauvais et le Beauvaisis de 1600 à 1730. Contribution à l'Histoire Sociale de France du xviième siècle* (Paris, 1960); E. Leroy-Ladurie, *Les Paysans de Languedoc* (Paris, 1966); P. Deyon, *Amiens, Capitale Provinciale: Étude sur la Société Urbaine au dix-septième siècle* (Paris and The Hague, 1967); J. Jacquart, *La Crise Rurale en Ile-de-France, 1550–1670* (Paris, 1974), and idem, 'Immobilisme et Catastrophes', in E. Leroy-Ladurie, ed. *Histoire de la France Rurale. II. L'age Classique des Paysans, 1340–1789* (Paris, 1975), 179–353.

succession between 1628 and 1631. Although officially at peace in 1631–4, France was preparing for open intervention in the Thirty Years' War, and French involvement in a protracted war with Spain lasted until 1659. By comparison, the wars of the early Stuarts before 1642 appear very small beer. The effect of these hostilities in France was devastation and dislocation in the countryside, and the interruption of trade abroad, notably with Spain but also with England. Between 1648 and 1653 France also underwent a series of political crises and civil wars known collectively as the Fronde. There were, moreover, Spanish invasions in 1596–7, 1636–7, and 1649–52.

Against this background, the revenue farmers frequently presented complaints to the council of finance about the "non-enjoyment" (*nonjouissance*) of their rights and demanded compensation. The farmers consistently referred to the state of the economy, the ravages of war, revolt or plague, the interruption of commerce, and the fall in consumption—particularly of salt. They viewed the increase in direct taxes on the peasantry, and the more effective policing of those taxes by provincial intendants and special troops, with alarm since this led to further pauperization and reduced consumption. Moreover, popular resistance to direct taxes added to the difficulties in collecting *all* revenues, including the indirect taxes. The farmers argued that the long-term profitability of the farms depended on peace, the maintenance of commercial exchange and low direct taxation which allowed for greater consumption. The evidence suggests that there was much to be said for their arguments. Thomas Guyot's difficulties in selling salt to the peasantry during the subsistence crisis of 1628–31 largely brought about the bankruptcy of Claude Charlot, the financier who held the lease.[1] In 1621, consumption of salt in the area of northern France covered by the *gabelles de France* was 11,351 *muids*.[2] In the disastrous fiscal year of 1638, following the invasion crisis of 1636–7, consumption fell to 8,221 *muids*.[3] In 1640, Philippe Hamel was convinced that the farm would become a profitable investment only with the return of peace and was accordingly reluctant to renew his lease—though he did do so in the end.[4] As late as 1664, consumption of salt in northern France was only 9,469 *muids*, substantially below the level of 1621.[5] To a considerable extent, the indirect taxes reflected the general tendencies of the economy. Indirect revenues rose in a period of economic expansion, rising prices, and rising rents until the 1640s. Yet the farms became over-rented and in the words of one contemporary, "les richesses de la France pour la plupart ont été imaginaires".[6] By the 1640s, the economy increasingly showed signs of economic depression, with substantial debasement of the coinage, a long-term trend towards price stability or even decline (although with short-term rises, notably in 1649–52 and 1661–2), more stable rents, and declining manufacturing produc-

---

[1] This despite remissions totalling 2,375,000 *livres*.—A.N. E 101a, fo. 397, 28 Jan. 1630, V6 79, no. 1, 11 Dec. 1630, E 105a, fos. 38, 129, 8, 22 Jan. 1631, E 107b, fo. 189, 20 Oct. 1631.

[2] J. Récurat and E. Leroy-Ladurie, 'Sur les Fluctuations de la Consommation taxée du Sel dans la France du Nord au xviième et xviiième siècles', *Revue du Nord*, LIV (1972), 385, 398.

[3] A.N. E 159c, fo. 27, 6 Feb. 1641.

[4] For Hamel's doubts see M. Foisil, *La Révolte des Nu-pieds et les Révoltes Normandes de 1639* (Paris, 1970), p. 154; B.N. MS fr. 18213, fo. 28, 26 June 1640, MS fr. 18215, fo. 27, 6 Feb. 1641. For the consortium represented by Hamel, see Dessert, loc. cit.

[5] Récurat and Leroy-Ladurie, loc. cit.

[6] Omer Talon, *Mémoires*, ed. J. F. Michaud and J. J. F. Poujoulat, 3rd ser. VI (1839), 270.

tion.¹ As far as the indirect revenues were concerned, the effect of the war with the Habsburgs after 1635 was immediate and far-reaching. All three major farms proved to be over-rented. Rather than risk the bankruptcy of the farmers, the abandonment of the leases, and the non-collection of revenues, the government agreed to substantial compensation and remissions.² These remissions set the pattern for the future and became a regular occurrence in the 1640s.³ Although rents envisaged in the leases increased in these years, this was largely because the government was increasing the rates of indirect tax while cutting its contractual obligations on the proceeds of the revenue such as payments of salaries to office-holders and income to *rentiers*: the real increase in the indirect revenues was therefore much smaller than might appear from the rents, since expenses were being reduced. With the outbreak of the Fronde in 1648, the difficulties of the farmers increased enormously, since they were desperately unpopular, and hostility to the fiscal system was one of the basic reasons for the political crisis. For a time in September 1649 four of the farmers of the *gabelles de France* were imprisoned;⁴ throughout the Fronde they and their colleagues were under threat (from critics of the government) of prosecution, expropriation of their possessions, or worse. The time of troubles of the French farmers was shorter than that of their English counterparts, some of whom were under a cloud from 1643 to the Restoration. The political crisis in France ended in 1652–3, but rents did not increase dramatically. The continuing war with Spain played its part. More important, perhaps, was the government's willingness to grant compensation to the financiers for their losses in the royal bankruptcy of 1648 and the difficult years which followed.⁵

IV

In the 1630s and 1640s, over-renting followed by remissions to the farmers virtually destroyed the purpose of the revenue farms in France, a situation which

---

[1] For debasements see F. C. Spooner, *The International Economy and Monetary Movements in France, 1493–1720* (Cambridge, Mass. 1972), pp. 337–9. For rents see J. Jacquart, 'La Rente Foncière, Indice Conjoncturel?', *Revue historique*, CCLIII (1975), 365–6. For manufacturing production, see Deyon, op. cit. pp. 170–1 and graph 34 at pp. 536–7.

[2] Thus Noel de Paris was remitted 1·3 million on the *cinq grosses fermes* in 1635, 1·2 million in 1636, and 969,521 *livres* in 1637.—A.N. E 134a, fo. 405, 27 Oct. 1635, E 143b, fo. 366, 15 May 1638, E 146b, fo. 137, 13 Oct. 1638. Philippe Hamel was remitted 1·7 million on the *gabelles de France* in 1634–6.—A.N. E 135a, fo. 109, 17 Jan. 1637. François Chandonnay was remitted 850,000 *livres* on the *aides* in 1637.— A.N. E 136a, fos. 183, 221, 28, 31 March 1637, E 137b, fo. 196, 21 May 1637.

[3] If we take the *gabelles de France*, there were remissions of 2,559,034 *livres* for 1638, the amount demanded; further remissions of 2,648,589 *livres* and 1,673,931 *livres* followed, respectively for 1639 and 1640; the remission for 1641 has not been found, but Hamel was remitted 1,490,808 *livres* for 1642 and 1,696,941 *livres* for 1643. Jacques Dattin, Hamel's successor, was remitted 1,941,176 *livres* for 1644 and 2,450,191 *livres* for 1645.—A.N. E 155c, fo. 476, 26 June 1640, E 159c, fo. 27, 6 Feb. 1641, E 171b, fo. 410, 28 June 1642, E 193b, fo. 366, 18 Aug. 1644, E 203a, fo. 398, 14 June 1645, E 206c, fo. 259, 13 Dec. 1645, E 217a, fo. 178, 7 Nov. 1646. Even this may not tell the full story, for it appears that on 21 Feb. 1646 Philippe Hamel was remitted a further 1,430,745 *livres* retrospectively for 1638–43. Cf. A.N. E 209c, fo. 354, 29 March 1646.

[4] Guy Patin, op. cit. p. 155.

[5] Bonney, loc. cit. 831–3. By 1656 the government recognized that remissions had been so extensive between 1630 and 1652 that they could be taxed retrospectively at 10 per cent.—A. N. E 296a, fo. 468, 16 Dec. 1656. The lease of Jacques André on the *aides* envisaged a variable rent in accordance with the state of civil and foreign war or peace. The highest rent—2·9 million *livres*—would be paid once there was general peace, and the council of finance did not enforce this rent until 1 Jan. 1659. Cf. A.N. E 317a, fo. 355, 18 Sept. 1658.

was to some extent adjusted in the 1650s by lower rents. How had this situation come about? The answer is to be found in the institution of the farms and its manipulation by the crown. One possibility was that the ministers and lesser officials in the council of finance were bribed by the farmers to accept the offer of excessive rents at the auctions (*enchères*) after secret agreements that remissions would be allowed once the farmer had taken up his post. Bribery certainly occurred in France before the auctions took place.[1] Yet it occurred in England, too, without the disastrous consequence of over-renting: Salisbury received a cash gift of £6,000 for patronizing the syndicate which gained the "great farm" of the customs in 1604.[2] Besides, bribery to over-rent would make little sense: if the finance minister was dismissed, his successor would not feel obliged by his secret undertakings. Royal policy, rather than the corruption of the finance ministers, seems the more likely reason for over-renting. In France, as in England, the government sought to anticipate as much future revenue as possible and to put pressure on the farmers to make loans which made little sense in straight financial terms. The French crown offered the farmers remissions on their rents because it wanted to secure loans.[3]

In England, the early Stuarts came to rely increasingly upon the farmers to provide them with short-term loans, that is to say advances of current rent, and later on longer-term loans, anticipating the rents two or three years in advance.[4] The last Valois king of France[5] had behaved in a similar manner: this was one reason for the amalgamation of the *cinq grosses fermes* in 1584. So too had the first Bourbon king,[6] although he acted with greater moderation after the restoration of peace in 1598. The amalgamation of the *aides* in 1604 was probably designed to increase rents rather than to secure loans. After the declaration of Louis XIII's majority in 1614, loans from the revenue farmers became once more a regular occurrence. Usually rents were anticipated by one year only, although by 1622 some of the rents were being anticipated by two years.[7] The importance of these loans was emphasized by the government in 1624 when it exempted two of the most important farmers—Antoine Feydeau and Claude Charlot—from prosecution by its extraordinary financial tribunal (*chambre de justice*),[8] which was levying fines on the other financiers. At this stage, it would appear that the French farmers were more important as long-term lenders to the crown than were their counterparts in England, even if their transactions are difficult to piece together from the surviving evidence (Table 7). However, the crash of 1626–31 altered

---

[1] Cf. the comment of Servien, the finance minister: A.A.E. France 893/2, fo. 77v, 19 June 1654. The role of the court in the marketing of concessions was particularly criticized during the Fronde. In July 1651 the farm of the *entrées* of Paris was renewed for nine years, yet at a substantially reduced rent, "ce fait crier tout le monde en ce rencontre et qui fait dire q[ue] la remise se partage entre le Chancelier [i.e. Séguier], le surintendant [i.e. Longueil de Maisons] et les fermiers . . ."—A.A.E. France 876, fo. 73, 8 July 1651.
[2] Stone, op. cit. p. 427.
[3] For example, the loans of 1·85 million on the *cinq grosses fermes* in 1638 and of one million on the *gabelles de France* in 1641.—A.N. E 146b, fo. 137, 13 Oct. 1638, E 159c, fo. 27, 6 Feb. 1641.
[4] Ashton, *The Crown and the Money Market*, pp. 97, 99. Ashton, 'Revenue Farming', 316.
[5] Henri III, *regnabat* 1574–89.   [6] Henry IV, *regnabat* 1589–1610.
[7] The rent of the *cinq grosses fermes* was anticipated two years in advance in part at least in 1617.—A.N. E 55a, fo. 115, 21 Jan. 1617. Feydeau's loan of 2·25 million in 1622 was on the rent of the *gabelles de France* in 1623–4.—A.N. E 72a, fo. 170, 12 July 1622, P 2353, p. 225, 8 April 1625.
[8] B.N. MS fr. 7583, pp. 505–6, 28 Oct. 1624.

this situation. For a number of reasons, particularly over-commitment and the economic depression, Antoine Feydeau, Pierre Payen, and Claude Charlot went bankrupt. This succession of disasters destroyed business confidence and their successors in the farms were either unwilling or unable to commit themselves to long-term lending. The late 1630s witnessed a rapid increase in government borrowing, but it appears that the economic dislocation resulting from the war against the Habsburgs after 1635 meant that there was relatively little anticipation of the rents of the farms. Perhaps only after 1643, with the regency of Anne of Austria, did the government seek to anticipate as much revenue as possible from the farms. By 1647 the rents for 1649 had been anticipated[1] and in January 1648 contracts anticipating the rents for 1650 were negotiated.[2] This policy had its origins in high politics—the desire of the crown to spend as much money as possible on the war effort in order to force the Habsburgs to make peace. It proved disastrous because peace with the emperor was not signed until 24 October 1648 while the Spanish refused to make peace at all. Meanwhile, in the face of serious domestic criticism, the French crown was forced to annul its loan contracts on 18 July 1648.[3] Thereafter, it is difficult to speak of any consistent royal policy anticipating rents of the farms until the end of the Fronde, for the *Chambre Saint-Louis* declared all loan contracts illegal, while the government, living from hand to mouth, sought to borrow where it could.[4] With the collapse of opposition to the government in 1652–3, the crown sought to borrow once more from all sources including the farmers. The difficulty was that the farmers demanded compensation for their losses in the bankruptcy in 1648 and some wanted to abandon their leases even if they received compensation. By 1655, however, it appears that the situation had been stabilized and rents were being anticipated two years in advance once again.[5]

It is tempting to argue that in France as in England the right to farm indirect revenues was "the reward of those who were prepared to meet the crown's demand for loans", and to go beyond this and argue that the consolidated revenue farms were "at least as important as instruments of government borrowing as they were ... a method of administering the revenue."[6] Yet these judgements on the English system are considerably less valid when applied to France. The early Stuarts did not have to compensate their farmers because of low yields caused by short-term economic depression. The English farmers for their part did not have to pay substantial fixed amounts to *rentiers* and office-holders, making the surplus highly vulnerable to such economic depression. A further contrast between

---

[1] For example, the loans of 1·03 million on the *aides* for 1649 and 2·46 million on the *cinq grosses fermes* for 1649.—A.N. E 222b, fo. 288, 8 May 1647, E 219a, fo. 596, 16 Jan. 1647.
[2] For example 568,734 *livres* on the *gabelles de France* and 896,000 *livres* on the *cinq grosses fermes*.—A.N. E 228b, fo. 2, 22 Jan. 1648, E 229c, fo. 208, 2 April 1648. Cf. A.N. Z1a 162, fo. 245, 7 Jan. 1648.
[3] M. Le Pesant, ed. *Arrêts du Conseil du Roi. Règne de Louis XIV: Inventaire Analytique des Arrêts en Commandement. I. 20 mai 1643—8 mars 1661* (Paris, 1976), no. 905.
[4] Ibid. no. 1495.
[5] For example, the loan of 1·9 million in 1655, anticipating the rents of the *gabelles de France* for 1656–7. —A.N. E 276a, fo. 157, 8 April 1655. Loan of 3,237,000 *livres* in 1658, anticipating the rents of the same farm for 1659–61.—A.N. E 318a, fo. 246, 6 Nov. 1658. Colbert's memorandum of 1 Oct. 1659 against Foucquet stated that "le peu qui en revient" from the farms was "consommé jusqu'en 1661".—Clément, ed. loc. cit.
[6] Ashton, 'Revenue Farming', 311, 313.

England and France is that the Stuarts tended to borrow the same sort of amounts from year to year, but relied increasingly on the farmers, while the Bourbon borrowing requirement increased rapidly in the 1630s and 1640s and was met from a much wider circle of financiers. Thus when the extraordinary financial tribunal (*chambre de justice*) of 1661 levied fines on those engaged in financial activities since 1635, the tax-farmers were a significant group among those taxed, but were far from the only group affected. Moreover, it was not just their activities within the farms that were taken into consideration (Table 8). The French revenue-farmers rarely performed this function solely: they were financiers of a general type who happened to have business interests within the farms.[1] In France, unlike England, it was not necessarily the consortium of farmers holding the lease which anticipated the rents of the farm. Sometimes the farmers holding a quite different lease might do so.[2] Sometimes the farmers might anticipate their rents too slowly for the government and another consortium was brought in to "anticipate the anticipation": such "loans upon loans" (*prêts sur prêts*) were common in the 1640s and 1650s.[3] Another contrast with England is that the French government was able to anticipate a much wider range of taxes, including the chief direct tax, the *taille*, which played a decisive part in the royal finances in the 1640s and 1650s.

Yet, almost paradoxically, it was fundamental to the difference between the English and French systems that the trend towards the consolidation of leases into a large unit had gone much further under the early Stuarts. In France, there were moments of *de facto* consolidation: for example, in the 1620s, with Antoine Feydeau's hold over the *gabelles de France* and the *aides* and Claude Charlot's later hold over the *gabelles de France* and the *cinq grosses fermes*. Yet there were also periods of fragmentation, for example, of the *gabelles de France* in 1612–22 and 1626–8,[4] of the *aides* in 1637–41,[5] and of the *gabelles* of Languedoc and the Lyonnais in 1646.[6] Sometimes the fragmentation resulted from disputes between partners;[7] on other occasions it followed a bankruptcy. In some cases it was explicitly stated that the partners refused to participate in a general lease because

[1] Thus Antoine Feydeau made payments to the government resulting from separate *traités* and he also made loans in anticipation of the revenues of the *taille*.—A.N. E 61c, fo. 174, 7 May 1619, E 67a, fo. 107, 19 April 1621, E 72a, fo. 168, 12 July 1622.

[2] Thus the consortium of financiers holding the *gabelles de France* made a loan anticipating the rents of the *convoy et comptablie of Bordeaux*.—A.N. E 126b, fo. 295, 4 Oct. 1635.

[3] For example, A.N. E 199b, fo. 311, 22 Feb. 1645, E 201b, fo. 190, 26 April 1645, E 203a, fo. 505, 14 June 1645.

[4] In 1612 Claude and Dreux Barbin and Jehan Le Prévost refused liability for seven *généralités* and the farm was divided.—A.N. E 34b–35a, fo. 143, 13 March 1612, E 35b, fo. 304, 24 May 1612, E 37a, fo. 19, 2 Aug. 1612, E 38a, fo. 4, 4 Oct. 1612. In 1616–17, when Moisset proposed to increase the rent, his partners refused to participate in a general lease because of "la solidité d'une sy grande obligation. . .".—A.N. E 55a, fo. 203, 4 Feb. 1617, E 55a, fo. 242, 11 Feb. 1617. The farm was again divided after the bankruptcy of Feydeau.

[5] The farm was divided on the withdrawal of François Chandonnay.—A.N. E 137d, fo. 152, 27 June 1637.

[6] A.N. E 218b, fo. 442, 22 Dec. 1646.

[7] Disputes between partners were widespread and could arise even between brothers, as is illustrated by the dispute between the Monnerot brothers in 1659. Although neither brother went bankrupt, and in the event the consortium survived, this incident demonstrates the way in which different business interests could impinge on the administration of the farms. The dispute was over the *parties casuelles*, but came to affect their co-operation within the consortium administering the *gabelles de France*.—A.N. E 327b, fo. 468, 21 Aug. 1659.

of the size of the liability.¹ The French revenue farms were not limited liability companies but partnerships, enforceable in the law-courts. Each partner was liable for the debts of the business in which he was engaged. In the period before the establishment of the *ferme-générale*, a financier could be involved in separate farms on different scales, each carrying its own risks and profits. If he went bankrupt, he risked bringing down not only his immediate partners in the farm in which he held his major investment but also his colleagues in farms where he was only a subsidiary partner. This was why Abel Servien, the finance minister between 1653 and 1659, viewed with disfavour the process whereby the same partnership held more than one farm.² The solvency of the partnerships was related to the general question of their sources of wealth beyond the irregular flow of funds from the indirect taxes. The active partners in England were always men of substantial means with the ability to borrow on the private market either individually or upon joint bond.³ In France, sub-farmers were sometimes forced to make loans to the general farmers⁴ but there was also a need to tap the wealth of privileged groups outside the financial community, the nobles, and the officeholders. In both countries it is probable that an element of borrowing and relending entered into most, if not all, of the large loans made by the farmers.⁵

V

It is realistic to talk of the "failure" of the French revenue farms because the yield from the indirect taxes was low in comparison with the other revenues enjoyed by the crown, and because the system of farming verged on collapse at a number of stages before 1660 and was kept going only by granting remissions which undermined the basic principle of the farm.⁶ In England, the farms were at least as important as instruments of government borrowing as they were a method of administering revenue, but in France they were uncertain and unpredictable even in this area, with the direct revenues proving much more reliable as security for loans. The yield from the indirect taxes varied so much from year to year that the anticipation of rents by two or three years was an uncertain investment. Furthermore, while there was some *de facto* consolidation of leases, there was no real attempt at their permanent amalgamation. Before 1661, the failure of the French revenue farms was in part the failure of successive finance ministers to reform an antiquated system because they were preoccupied with short-term considerations of deficit finance. The ministers lacked the means and the political will to break with the tradition of revenue-farming and to attempt the direct administration of existing revenues, or the establishment of an alternative new revenue such as the sales tax. From the point of view of the tax-farmers, the system was a lottery. A successful tax-farmer had to combine the functions of courtier, politician, banker, "investment analyst", and administrator. He had to act as a courtier, carefully bribing ministers

¹ As did Claude and Dreux Barbin and Jehan Le Prévost on the *gabelles de France* in 1612.
² A.A.E. France 894, fo. 102, 9 May 1655.   ³ Ashton, 'Revenue Farming', 320–1.
⁴ A.N. E 85a, fo. 401, 31 Jan. 1626.
⁵ Cf. Ashton, 'Revenue Farming', 322. In France, the bankruptcy of 1648 was precipitated by the closure of the subsidiary credit market due to loss of confidence.—Talon, op. cit. p. 245.
⁶ These, and other aspects of the administration of the farms, were severely criticized by the *chambre des comptes* of Paris in its remonstrances of 14 Oct. 1648.—A.A.E. France 860, fo. 210v–12r.

and lesser officials in the council in order to obtain the lease at the auction. He had to have a politician's sense of timing to know when to stick at his offer and when to concede more favourable terms to the government, when to *reculer pour mieux sauter*. As a banker, he had to act as a financial intermediary between those who had invested in his farm or held shares in his "company" and the king's council, with its voracious appetite for loans to cover the budgetary deficit. As "investment analyst", the farmer had to estimate with reasonable precision the likely yield from the farm, given the general state of the economy, the question of security, and the difficulties or otherwise of the previous farmer. As administrator, he had to manage the cumbersome administrative machinery which had been elaborated to enforce the rights of the farm. Is it any wonder, given the extent of the difficulties and the broad range of talents required, that relatively few tax-farmers were successful in the long-term, that profits were uncertain, and bankruptcies frequent? Crucial to success or failure was the strength or weakness of the French economy. Perhaps the fundamental problem with the indirect taxes resulted from the fragility of the French economy in a war situation, and the obstacles to economic development. In peace time, the indirect taxes could be levied reasonably successfully because the administrative apparatus of collection functioned smoothly, goods circulated freely for export and import, and domestic consumption was at least stable and perhaps expanded. All these trends were reversed in war time.

How was it, therefore, that the *ferme-générale* could be established in 1681? It did not happen overnight. The task of consolidating small leases into one general lease took Colbert twenty-one years (1661–81) including eleven years of peacetime administration (1661–71),[1] when the revenues were relatively easy to administer. It occurred at a time when the government sought to avoid anticipating revenue. In the early years of Colbert's ministry, royal expenditure was cut back and the budget was balanced for the first time since Sully's ministry (1598–1611).[2] At the same time, Colbert sought to alter the balance between the revenues of the French monarchy, making the crown less reliant on direct taxes while increasing the yield from indirect taxes by cutting back on standing charges such as the payment of *rentes*. Although the implementation of these objectives was delayed by the so-called Dutch War of 1672–8, the return of peace enabled Colbert to bring them to fruition. His term of office was of unparalleled length for a finance minister in seventeenth-century France. Undoubtedly it created stable conditions in which he could rely upon the co-operation of a small, tightly-knit group of financiers who came to dominate the various aspects of financial administration—men who owed everything to their patron, yet who knew that he would protect them from bankruptcy.[3] This new business confidence was essential: it encouraged smaller investors to participate and widened the credit market. The *ferme-générale* became a half-way stage towards a limited-liability

---

[1] With the exception of the short War of Devolution, 1667–8.

[2] There are objections to the statistical method of Guéry, whose calculations (loc. cit. 236–7) tend to belittle the achievements of Sully and Colbert. However, the argument—which is a technical one relating to the significance accorded to Mallet's figures for the *affaires extraordinaires*—is rather outside the scope of this article.

[3] D. Dessert and J. L. Journet, 'Le Lobby Colbert: un Royaume ou une Affaire de Famille?', *Annales E.S.C.* XXX (1975), 1310–11.

company: "the rigid form of the partnership was bent to provide some of the functional if not juridicial flexibility of a joint-stock company. The company reached beyond the restricted core of formal partners into a surrounding circle of investors".[1] As a result of these complex, and interrelated changes, the yield from the indirect taxes was increased despite the economic, and especially agrarian, depression after 1670.

The *ferme-générale* could administer the indirect taxes relatively successfully in peace time,[2] and once the structure had been securely established, the farmers-general could be expected to make loans in anticipation of rents, too. What Colbert's system could not do, however, was what was done in the England of Rochester and Sidney Godolphin. This was to increase the yield from the indirect taxes by phasing out farming—farming of the customs was abolished in 1671 and of the excise in 1683—and instead of anticipating rents, a consolidated debt was established. These changes took a long time to be put into effect, and were not a gradual or an inevitable process: they would probably have been impermanent but for the English constitutional settlement worked out between 1660 and 1702. In contrast, the strengthening of the executive in France, the absence of a national representative institution, the proliferation of the sale of offices, the much greater role of the court in the marketing of concessions, and the profits from lending meant that it was impossible politically and socially to break with the system of revenue-farming. In England in 1700 all classes of society contributed to taxation, which was levied relatively efficiently and did not fall—as it did in France—on the non-privileged classes so as to create deep and permanent grievances. The failure of the French revenue farms before 1660 had demonstrated the need for reform. When reform came, it took the form of administrative improvement without a change in the social and economic basis of the taxes themselves. The wrong solution was adopted and it endured until 1789. The belief, current in French government circles, that indirect taxes of themselves were more equitable was a chimera. It was true only because the *taille* was an inequitable tax and for political reasons it was impossible to tax the clergy and the nobility effectively. If the failure of the farms before Colbert was absolute, the success of his *ferme-générale* was relative only: the social cost was profound and enduring.

University of Reading

---

[1] Matthews, *The Royal General Farms*, p. 238.
[2] Yet only with difficulty in war time.—Ibid. pp. 54–9.

APPENDIX

Table 1. *Revenue from the gabelles de France, 1605–63*

Date of commencement of lease	Name of lessee	Net revenue payable to the crown according to the terms of the lease (livres)	Average yield p.a. during lease minimum* (livres)	Average yield p.a. during lease maximum* (livres)
1605	Jean de Moisset[1]	4,621,000	2,305,152	2,512,772
1611	Thomas Robin[2]	4,621,000	2,495,901	2,651,029
1616	Jean de Moisset[3]	6,345,140	3,403,932	3,555,918
1622	Antoine Feydeau[4]	5,988,312	1,945,954	2,061,718†
1627	Thomas Guyot[5]	8,500,000	1,020,002	1,020,237‡
1632	Philippe Hamel[6]	*12,490,600*	1,580,118	1,811,315†
1641	Philippe Hamel[7]	13,424,200	5,987,394	6,219,327
1644	Jacques Dattin[8]	13,624,200	5,914,303	6,248,482
1647	Jacques Dattin[9]	13,443,200	1,208,027	1,471,587
1650	Jacques Dattin[10]	8,200,000	1,147,953†	1,180,889
1656	Simon Le Noir[11]	8,600,000		
1660	Jacques Autruy[12]	14,750,000		
1662	Guillaume Courtial[13]	13,500,000		
1663	Jean Martinant[14]	13,800,000		

Sources:

[1] A.N. AD IX 413, no. 7, 20 Sept. 1604.   [2] A.N. AD IX 413, no. 11, 1 Oct. 1611.

[3] Originally Jean du Gonne for 5,765,140 *livres*: A.N. AD IX 413, no. 15, 7 May 1616. Lease of Jean de Moisset: A.N. AD IX 413, no. 15/2, 30 Aug. 1616; A.N. E 55a, fo. 242, 11 Feb. 1617. Subsequently subdivided: A.N. AD IX 413, no. 17, 16 March 1617.

[4] A. N. AD IX 413, no. 20, 19 March 1622. Farm subdivided on Feydeau's bankruptcy in 1626.

[5] A.N. E 94, fo. 241, 1 Dec. 1627; A.N. E 95b, fo. 324, AD IX 413 no. 33, P 2356, p. 681, 30 March 1628.

[6] Originally the lease was 6,650,000 *livres*, raised to 10·5 million in 1634, 11·9 million in 1637, and 12·4 million in 1638. A.N. E 108a, fo. 474, and AD IX 413, no. 68, 31 March 1632. Also A.N. AD IX 413, no. 105, 28 Oct. 1634, and AD IX 414, no. 2, 17 March 1637.

[7] A.N. AD IX 414, no. 10, P 2367, pp. 953–1001; B.N. MS fr. 18213, fo. 28, 26 June 1640.

[8] A.N. AD IX 414, no. 27, 31 Dec. 1642; A.N. P 2369, pp. 633–72, 23 Dec. 1643.

[9] A.N. P 2371, pp. 453–507, 19 Dec. 1646.

[10] A.N. AD IX 414, no. 40, 4 Feb. 1650; A.N. P 2372, pp. 545–621, 10 March 1650.

[11] A.N. P 2374, pp. 1179–290, 8 May 1655.   [12] A.N. AD IX 414, no. 59, 21 Jan. 1660.

[13] A.N. P 2378, pp. 457–510, AD IX 415, no. 2, 15 Oct. 1661.

[14] A.N. AD IX 415, no. 8, 25 Sept. 1663.

Comments:

* The maximum figure includes "droits et fermes dépendants de la ferme générale des gabelles", i.e. additional taxes and income paid to the crown from the redemption of alienated rights, such as *rentes*. The minimum figure excludes these items. They are listed separately in J. R. Mallet, *Comptes-rendus de l'Administration des Finances du Royaume de France* ... (1789), pp. 184–5, 198–9, 230–3, 252–3. Mallet gives no figures for 1657–60.

† One year's figures incomplete.   ‡ Four years' figures incomplete.

The figures in italics represent increases envisaged in the leases.

FRENCH REVENUE FARMS

Table 2. *Revenue from the aides, 1603–63*

Date of commencement of lease	Name of lessee	Net revenue payable to the crown according to the terms of the lease (livres)	Average yield p.a. during lease minimum* (livres)	Average yield p.a. during lease maximum* (livres)
1603	Denis Feydeau[1]	610,000	562,349	940,915
1611	Antoine Feydeau[2]	900,000	781,830	1,226,362
1619	Antoine Feydeau[3]	*1,400,000*	1,157,480	1,606,869
1623	Antoine Feydeau[4]	2,300,000	777,251	1,279,382
1625	Pierre Payen and Philippes Guerin[5]	1,900,000	1,333,187	1,864,037
1626	Philippes Guerin[6]	2,200,000	1,771,833	2,020,709
1627	Étienne Brioys[7]	2,485,000	1,577,493	2,101,868
1632	Mathieu Brabant[8]	3,135,000	1,630,418	1,993,771
1634	François Chandonnay[9]	3,985,630	923,451	1,140,545
1642	Claude Bullot[10]	3,846,571	1,412,809	1,626,054
1648	Adrian Montagne[11]	4,250,000	828,379	959,117
1653	Jacques André[12]	*3,175,000*	396,922†	591,720
1660	Claude Revol[13]	4,520,000		
1663	Jean Rouvelin[14]	13,720,000		

Sources:

[1] Lease of Jean de Moisset for 510,000 *livres*: A.N. AD IX 413, no. 2, 15 May 1604. Henri de la Ruelle, then Denis Feydeau were substituted and the lease was increased.—A.N. AD IX 413, no. 5, 20 Oct. 1605.
[2] Lease of Denis Feydeau for 820,000 *livres*: A.N. E 30, fo. 348, and AD IX 413, no. 10, 28 May 1611. Antoine Feydeau was substituted and the lease increased.—A.N. E 32a, fo. 294, 30 Aug. 1611.
[3] Originally contracted by Isaac Payot: A.N. AD IX 413, no. 16, 26 Jan. 1617.
[4] A.N. AD IX 413 nos. 12, 24, and P 2352, p. 931, 13 Dec. 1623.
[5] After Feydeau's bankruptcy: A.N. AD IX 413, no. 28, and E 85a, fo. 423, 31 Jan. 1626.
[6] Guerin died. Lease of Guillaume Menant: A.N. E 90a, fo. 261, and AD IX 413, no. 29, 23 Jan. 1627.
[7] A.N. E 96a, fo. 79, AD IX 413, no. 34, and P 2356, p. 805, 8 April 1628.
[8] A.N. AD IX 413, no. 48, 23 Jan. 1632.
[9] A.N. E 118b, fo. 11, AD IX 413, no. 104, P 2362, pp. 647–74, 19 July 1634.
[10] A.N. AD IX 414, no. 22, P 2368, pp. 391–431, 4 Dec. 1641.
[11] A.N. AD IX 414, no. 37, 30 Dec. 1645. His lease was reduced successively from 3·2 million in 1649 to 2 million at its lowest point: A.N. AD IX 414, no. 39, 24 July 1649, 22 Feb. 1653.
[12] Lease of André for 2,900,000 *livres* (peace time): A.N. AD IX 414, no. 44, and P 2373, pp. 1359–415, 2 Aug. 1653. Increased terms: P 2375, pp. 539–47, 3 July 1655; AD IX 414, no. 52, 24 March 1657.
[13] A.N. AD IX 414, no. 60, 21 Jan. 1660. [14] A.N. AD IX 415, no. 7, 25 Sept. 1663.

Comments:

* The maximum figure includes "droits annexés aux aides", i.e. additional taxes and income paid to the crown from the redemption of alienated rights, such as *rentes*. The minimum figure excludes these items. They are listed separately in Mallet, op. cit.

† Four years' figures only.

The figures in italics indicate the maximum payable according to the terms of the lease.

Table 3. *Revenue from the* cinq grosses fermes, *1604–64*

Date lease negotiated	Name of lessee	Net revenue payable to the crown according to the terms of the lease (livres)	Average yield p.a. during lease minimum* (livres)	Average yield p.a. during lease maximum* (livres)
1604	Charles du Hen[1]	670,000	431,238	1,297,072
1611	Urbain de la Mothe[2]	995,000	620,519	1,618,326
1613	Pierre de la Sablière[3]	880,000	636,957	1,505,864
1619	Jean de la Grange[4]	880,000	652,536	1,794,132
1624	Jean de la Grange[5]	1,650,000	963,743	2,675,582
1633	Noel de Paris[6]	2,450,000	1,841,283	3,732,641
1643	Toussainctz de la Ruelle[7]	2,800,000	2,392,201	3,936,740
1652	Nicolas Pinson[8]	*2,440,000*	2,323,452†	4,048,780†
1660	Sebastien Le Bar[9]	4,430,000		
1662	Jean Bourgoing[10]	5,650,000		
1664	Jean Bourgoing	*5,750,000*		

Sources:

[1] E. Frémy, 'Premières Tentatives de Centralisation des Impôts Indirects, 1584–1614', *Bibliothèque de l'École des Chartes*, LXXII (1911), 623–4; A.N. P 2342, p. 1095, 23 Sept. 1604.

[2] A.N. P 2346, p. 343, 16 June 1611, E 32b, fo. 424, 27 Sept. 1611.

[3] A.N. E 41c, fo. 191, 13 Sept. 1613, E 46b/47a, fo. 136, 26 Aug. 1614.

[4] A.N. P 2350, p. 721, 22 Aug. 1619. [5] A.N. AD IX 413, no. 27, 23 Dec. 1624.

[6] A.N. E 110b, fo. 2, 2 Feb. 1633, E 111b, fo. 266, 30 March 1633; A.N. P 2362, p. 555, 7 April 1633; A.N. AD IX, 413, no. 97, 3 Feb. 1633.

[7] A.N. P 2369, p. 527, 31 Dec. 1642; Additional leases: A.N. P 2371, pp. 1045, 1049, 18 Sept. and 15 June 1647.

[8] A.N. AD IX 414, no. 43, 5 July 1652. [9] A.N. AD IX 414, no. 58, 21 Jan. 1660.

[10] A.N. AD IX 415, no. 6, 3 May 1662.

Comments:

* The maximum figure includes "fermes et droits compris dans le bail des cinq grosses fermes", i.e. additional taxes and income paid to the crown from the redemption of alienated rights, such as *rentes*. The minimum figure excludes these items. They are listed separately in Mallet, loc. cit.

† Yield based on an average of five years only.

The figures in italics represent increases envisaged in the leases.

FRENCH REVENUE FARMS

Table 4. *Mallet's Figures for the Indirect Revenues of the French Monarchy, 1600–54*

Date	(a) Total of farms (livres)	(b) Gabelles de France (livres)	(c) Aides (livres)	(d) Cinq grosses fermes (livres)	(e) Total of three farms (b+c+d) (livres)	(f) (e) as a proportion of (a) (per cent)
1600–04	16,336,665	7,280,064	2,299,324	4,139,632	13,719,020	84·0
1605–09	28,739,947	12,657,713	5,320,017	7,269,976	25,247,706	87·8
1610–14	32,136,785	12,840,427	5,814,225	7,981,299	26,635,951	82·9
1615–19	41,209,294	18,042,543	8,394,267	7,556,644	33,993,454	82·5
1620–24	32,660,242	13,660,001	5,651,352	7,792,327	27,103,680	83·0
1625–29	38,121,844	6,830,051	10,197,383	13,835,823	30,863,257	81·0
1630–34	43,725,142	5,462,922	10,553,990	15,403,160	31,420,072	71·9
1635–39	53,637,890	9,140,246	4,802,871	18,314,546	32,257,663	60·1
1640–44	92,606,465	27,028,682	7,500,202	25,267,964	59,796,848	64·6
1645–49	67,454,713	17,534,494	5,218,974	17,879,933	40,633,401	60·2
1650–54	48,014,898	4,836,972	4,832,638	17,127,356	26,796,966	55·8

Source: Mallet, op. cit. (maximum figures).

Table 5. *Selected Comparison of Indirect Revenues with Other Revenues and Expenses of the French Monarchy*

Date	(i) Total of farms (livres)	(ii) Secret expenses (comptants) (livres)	(iii) (i) as a proportion of (ii) (per cent)	(iv) Issues of coinage (livres)	(v) (i) as a proportion of (iv) (per cent)	(vi) Total revenues (livres)	(vii) (i) as a proportion of (vi) (per cent)
1600–04	16,336,665	11,074,567		7,363,150		98,642,572	16·6
1605–09	28,739,947	15,792,443		6,976,056		150,350,218	19·1
1610–14	32,136,785	9,171,497		2,613,814		145,360,940	22·1
1615–19	41,209,294	22,180,390		5,254,402		158,383,926	26·0
1620–24	32,660,242	39,080,467	83·6	1,097,777		203,054,276	16·1
1625–29	38,121,844	52,416,787	72·7	1,552,927		231,671,321	16·5
1630–34	43,725,142	99,138,240	44·1	3,238,096		333,462,433	13·1
1635–39	53,637,890	207,880,836	25·8	10,671,172		588,137,627	9·1
1640–44	92,606,465	210,840,605	43·9	104,712,087	88·4	557,019,058	16·6
1645–49	67,454,713	222,103,618	30·4	38,528,169		589,341,343	11·4
1650–54	48,014,898	62,998,505	76·2	103,186,473	46·5	607,156,898	7·9
1655–59	—	334,189,875	—	18,109,312	—	—	—

Sources: For cols. (i), (vi): Mallet, op. cit. For col. (ii) A.N. 120 AP 10 for 1600–8; A.A.E. France 861, fo. 226, for 1609–43; British Library Harleian 4472b, fo. 413, for 1644–59. (N.B.: Mallet's figures show some variation, particularly for the years of the Fronde). For col. (iv): Spooner, op. cit.

Comment: Guéry's figures for total revenues for the years 1611–56 (loc. cit. p. 238) are too low since they fail to include the figures for the *parties casuelles*. Mallet termed the *parties casuelles* ordinary revenues between 1600 and 1610 but extraordinary revenues after 1611, a fact noted by Hayden (op. cit. p. 221), and implicitly in the table compiled by Mousnier (R. É. Mousnier, *La Vénalité des Offices sous Henri IV et Louis XIII* (2nd ed. Paris, 1971), p. 421) and which seriously affects the calculations. Thus Guéry's graph II (loc. cit. p. 226) and other calculations need modification.

In columns (iii) and (v) no proportion is given where the figure is in excess of 100 per cent, i.e. where the total of farms actually exceeds the figure for secret expenses or issues of coinage.

Table 6. *Index Numbers of Indirect Revenues and Certain Other Revenues and Expenses*

(Average of 1625–34 = 100)

A. INDIRECT REVENUES

Date	(i) Total farms	(ii) Gabelles de France*	(iii) Aides	(iv) Cinq grosses fermes
1600–04	39·9	118·4	22·2	28·3
1605–09	70·2	205·9	51·3	49·7
1610–14	78·5	208·9	56·0	54·6
1615–19	100·7	293·5	80·9	51·7
1620–24	79·8	222·2	54·5	53·3
1625–29	93·2	111·1	98·3	94·6
1630–34	106·8	88·9	101·7	105·4
1635–39	131·1	148·7	46·3	125·3
1640–44	226·3	439·7	72·3	172·8
1645–49	164·8	285·3	50·3	122·3
1650–54	117·3	78·7	46·6	117·2

* N.B. The figures for the *gabelles de France* are distorted by the subsistence crisis of 1628–31.

B. CERTAIN OTHER INDICES

Date	(v) Grain prices at Paris	(vi) Debasement	(vii) Cash expenses (comptants)	(viii) Total expenditure	(ix) Pays d'élections
1600–04	59·9	307·4	14·6	35·9	142·8
1605–09	68·1	291·2	20·8	54·4	138·5
1610–14	65·3	109·1	12·1	52·6	133·4
1615–19	73·6	219·3	29·3	58·1	136·5
1620–24	80·2	45·8	51·6	70·5	131·6
1625–29	94·5	64·8	69·2	82·8	91·9
1630–34	105·4	135·2	130·8	116·0	108·1
1635–39	87·7	445·5	274·3	162·6	174·1
1640–44	107·4	4,371·2	285·6	204·6	460·5
1645–49	100·7	1,608·3	293·0	213·0	366·2
1650–54	145·7	4,307·5	83·1	219·9	367·3
1655–59	95·5	756·0	441·0	—	—

Date	(x) Élection de Paris	(xi) Pays d'états	(xii) Diocese of Castres	(xiii) Parties casuelles
1600–04	—	61·9	—	6·9
1605–09	—	69·9	—	11·4
1610–14	—	54·2	41·3	14·0
1615–19	71·6	53·2	37·4	24·4
1620–24	95·1	55·1	48·3	72·6
1625–29	94·7	54·9	67·6	75·0
1630–34	105·3	145·1	132·4	125·0
1635–39	184·4	147·6	145·8	138·8
1640–44	272·2	124·5	131·8	79·2
1645–49	396·3	76·6	175·6	46·0
1650–54	257·3	24·8	125·4	32·2
1655–59	282·0	—	185·0	—

Sources: As Table 5 for cols. (i)–(iv), (vii). Mallet, op. cit. for cols. (viii), (ix), (xi), (xiii). For col. (v): M. Baulant, 'Le Prix des Grains à Paris de 1431 à 1788', *Annales E.S.C.* XXIII (1968), 539. For col. (vi): Spooner, op. cit. For col. (x): A.N. Z1g 281, 1–3. For col. (xii): G. Frêche, *Toulouse et la Région Midi-Pyrénées au Siècle des Lumières (vers 1670–1789)* (1974), p. 517.

Table 7. *Recorded Loans anticipating the Rents of the Revenue Farms before the Fronde*

Year loan negotiated	Gabelles de France	Loans in livres tournois Aides	Cinq grosses fermes
1614		400,000	200,000
1615		30,000	250,000
1616	900,000		
1617	1,871,000	1,822,200	400,000
1618			
1619	575,000	2,324,250	1,300,000
1620	1,000,000		223,750
1621	1,058,748	174,750	700,000
1622	2,999,000		
1623		1,300,000	
1624	1,340,001		1,200,000
1625	100,000	345,000	
1626	925,257	1,000,000	213,600
1627			100,000
1628			
1629			
1630	105,000		
1631		106,250	165,000
1632			
1633			
1634	4,035,000	55,400	
1635		540,000	
1636			1,200,000
1637	916,667		
1638			1,850,000
1639			
1640	300,000		1,856,000
1641	3,620,000		
1642	100,000		
1643	2,820,000	1,888,124	4,025,566
1644	3,209,888	131,250	2,225,000
1645	2,706,675	1,055,000	2,820,500
1646	7,897,642	814,606	738,531
1647	363,625	1,392,424	4,928,000

Comments: Unfortunately, no complete series of accounts survives from the period comparable to the English Exchequer books. The figures in this table can give only a partial view of the credit operations of the revenue farmers since they are drawn from the leases and the chance survival of loan contracts in the records of the council of finance.—A.N. E 43a–227c. Fewer contracts have survived from the years after 1648 than before and for this reason no attempt is made to present them in tabular form. The gaps in the figures do not necessarily imply that no rents were anticipated, merely that no evidence of such loans survives. All figures in this table should be regarded as minimum figures.

Table 8. *Fines Payable by Certain Revenue Farmers at the Chambre de Justice of 1661*

Name of farmer	Farm held (see key below)	Amount of fine in millions of livres tournois	Name of farmer	Farm held (see key below)	Amount of fine in millions of livres tournois
Antoine Amat	d & g	0·12	François Jacquier	a	3·0
Jacques Amat	d & g	1·0	Jacques de la Fonds	b	1·0
Jean Animé	j	0·1	Guillaume Languet	a	0·9
Pierre Aubert	a & j	3·6	Claude Le Ragois de		
Oliver Bidé d'Aganry	c	0·6	Bretonvilliers		0·8
Thomas Bonneau	a & j	3·5	Nicolas Le Vieux	e	0·2
François Bossuet	f	1·8	Étienne Macquart	b	0·8
Étienne Brioys	a & b	0·8	Ogier de Marsillac	b	0·3
Claude Chatelain	a	1·4	Guillaume Menant	b & j	0·15
Paul Chaudesolle	a	1·4	Pierre Merault	a	1·2
Cléophas Deshalus	h	1·6	Isaac Monceau	b	0·4
Jean Doublet	c	0·1	Étienne Pavillon	c	0·15
Gabriel Dumas	c	0·2	Marc-Antoine Perrachon		
Jean Faverolles	b	1·0	et al.	d & g	1·0
Jacques Forcoal	b	1·6	Bonaventure Quentin de		
Pierre Gargan	c	0·2	Richebourg	a & j	2·0
Samuel Gaudon de la			Nicolas Rambouillet	c	0·3
Rallière	b & h	0·3	Germain Rolland	a	0·4
Germain Gillot	a	0·3	Marc-Antoine Scarron	a	0·15
Claude Girardin	a	4·0	Paul and Pierre Tallemant	c	0·4
Pierre Girardin	b	4·0	Jean Terrat	e	1·0
Charles Gruyn	a	2·5	Claude Vanel	h	0·7

Total: 40 individuals taxed at 49·97 million *livres*

At the *chambre de justice* of 1661 248 individuals were taxed for a total of 156·7 million. The revenue farmers thus comprised 16·1 per cent of the financiers fined, but carried 31·9 per cent of the total amount in fines.

Key to farms:
 a—*gabelles de France*
 b—*aides*
 c—*cinq grosses fermes*
 d—*gabelles de Provence*
 e—*gabelles de Lyonnais*
 f—*gabelles de Languedoc*
 g—*gabelles de Dauphiné*
 h—*entrées*
 i—*pied fourché*
 j—*convoy et comptablie de Bordeaux*.

Sources: (i) For the farms: B.N. 500 Colbert 233, 234, register of the *chambre de justice* kept by Joseph Foucault. However, not all the farms appear in this register. For the farmers of the *gabelles de France* after 1632: Dessert, loc. cit. app. 2. For Bidé, Doublet, and Gargan: A.N. Minutier Central CXVII 515, 22 May 1643. For Bossuet: A.N. E 218b, fo. 442, 22 Dec. 1646. For Le Ragois: A.N. E 72b, fo. 288, 25 Aug. 1622. (ii) For the fines: The list supplied by Dessert, loc. cit. app. 2, has been preferred to the register kept by Foucault because it appears to be later and more complete. Cf. ibid. 849.

Comments: Only those farmers taxed at more than 100,000 *livres* are included in this list, and there may be some omissions, particularly of financiers such as the Monnerot brothers, whose main activities were outside the revenue farms listed. Not all the farmers listed were actively involved in the farms in 1661. Indeed, some were dead and their families were taxed instead. Not all those listed were primarily involved in the revenue farms: some were only occasional or minor partners in the farms. Some of these fines were later reduced. The taxes indicate the amount of illicit profits and the scale of the financiers' activities. They do not necessarily indicate the scale of activity within the farm itself.

XII

The State and its Revenues in *ancien-régime* France

THE FRENCH REVENUE SYSTEM had become very complex towards the end of the *ancien régime*.[1] The near definitive account of the system, prepared by the *intendant des finances* Moreau de Beaumont in 1769 resulted in a publication of three substantial volumes.[2] It was evident that the fiscal system was so complex that there was a serious risk of one of its elements operating against another, for example an increase in direct taxes leading to a fall in indirect taxes in a particular province. After 1642, royal commissioners in the provinces, the intendants of justice, police and finance, assumed increasing fiscal responsibilities to minimize self-contradictions with the system. In 1711, Desmaretz (controller-general of finance, 1708-15) instructed the intendants that their task was to ensure that the different aspects of taxation 'ne se croisent point et que le Roy en puisse tirer le secours dont il a besoin'.[3] Before 1630-42, there were few intendants and they had not been conferred a generalized fiscal role: the danger of competing, self-defeating fiscal measures was accordingly greater.

By the seventeenth century, the French kingdom had developed three main types of revenue: direct taxes, indirect taxes and *affaires extraordinaires*.[4] Under the category of direct taxes we may place the *taille* and *taillon* (although there were variants of these taxes within the provinces which retained provincial estates, the *pays d'états*). Prior to Richelieu's ministry (1624-42), and during his early years in power, some of these direct taxes had been alienated, that is to say the right to collect them had been sold off to private individuals who collected what were known as the *droits aliénés*: these private rights were revoked in 1634. Subsequently,

---

[1] The author wishes to thank Dr. Graham Smith for his computing advice and Dr. Margaret Bonney for the statistical work and preparation of the graphs for this article, which was first given as a paper at the Anglo-American Conference of Historians in July 1991. Research assistance from the British Academy and from the Economic and Social Research Council (Award number R000231968) for the European State Finance Database (hereafter cited as ESFDB), an international collaborative project in data collection, is gratefully acknowledged by the author. A personal research award from the Leverhulme Trust has permitted the checking of figures and the consultation of additional manuscripts. The ESFDB datasets cited in this paper may be consulted after 1993 via JANET/ERN at the ESRC Data Archive in the University of Essex.

[2] J.-L. Moreau de Beaumont, *Mémoires concernant les Impositions et Droits en Europe* (1768-9), vols. ii-iv: *Impositions et Droits en France*. The first volume concerned comparative revenue systems in Europe. All works in French are published at Paris, unless otherwise stated.

[3] Bibliothèque Nationale, Paris, MS. fr. 8896 fo. 228v, 20 Aug. 1711. Something of the intendants' role is suggested by the title of the letter, which was to 'connoistre la situa[ti]on des prouinces par rap[p]ort aux impo[siti]ons or[dinai]res et ex[traordinai]res, commerce, manufactures &a'.

[4] R. J. Bonney, *The King's Debts: Finance and Politics in France, 1589-1661* (Oxford, 1981), pp. 293-6, presents the method of collection of these taxes in the first half of the 17th century. There are also now more detailed articles by F. Bayard in *Dictionnaire du Grand Siècle*, ed. F. Bluche (1990), pp. 53 (*aides*); 585-6 (*fermes*); 593-6 (*financiers, fiscalité directe* and *fiscalité indirecte*); 631-2 (*gabelle*); 1499-1500 (*tailles*); 1529-30 (*traités*).

a number of new direct taxes were established under Louis XIII and Richelieu, most notably a new military tax called the *subsistances* (other new direct taxes were to follow under Louis XIV, chiefly the *capitation* and the *dixième*). By the end of Richelieu's ministry the revenue from these taxes was anticipated in the form of loans from financiers, on whose agents were conferred the rights of collection. This is sometimes, incorrectly, referred to as the farming of direct taxes.[5]

True revenue farming was exclusively reserved to the area of indirect taxes. The revenue farm was a fixed lease conferring exclusive rights of collection on the revenue farmer and his agents for a number of years. This system, which was largely created during Sully's ministry (1598-1611), virtually excluded royal officials from the administration of indirect taxes such as those on the consumption of salt (the various farms of the *gabelles*); drink (the *aides*); and on the circulation of goods in various parts of the kingdom allocated to particular farms (the *cinq grosses fermes* and regional variants such as the farm of the *convoy et comptablie* of Bordeaux). The third main type of revenue, the *affaires extraordinaires*, comprised virtually everything else that did not fall under the other two categories. Strictly speaking, the 'extraordinary taxes' were those raised by the method of *traités*, or one-off tax contracts with financiers: the financier undertook to raise a fixed sum of money in return for a standard rate of interest. Such contracts might concern the establishment of new offices, forced loans or new annuities (*rentes*), or any of a plethora of fiscal expedients introduced in the seventeenth century. Some 719 million *livres* were raised from this source between 1689 and 1715,[6] but the *affaires extraordinaires* were already being used more sparingly under Desmaretz's ministry (1708-15). They were abandoned altogether under Louis XV in favour of the creation of annuities and life rents which were politically less contentious and on which the rate of interest was guaranteed for the 'investor'. The concept of 'investment' in support of the French finances was itself relatively new. Before 1715, *rentiers* had seen the arbitrary withholding of interest payments in successive financial crises. Those who participated actively in financial affairs (the omnipresent financiers or *gens d'affaires*)[7] made rapid fortunes in moments of adversity for the Crown, only to undergo retrospective taxation in the form of fines levied by periodic extraordinary financial tribunals (*chambres de justice*), the last of which met in 1716.

Moreau de Beaumont's account emphasized the extent to which the fiscal system of *ancien-régime* France was a product of long-term historical developments. A prior consideration of the social structure of France is thus essential for an understanding of the revenue-raising system which it helped create and by which it

---

[5] There is much information on direct taxes in R. J. Bonney, *Political Change in France under Richelieu and Mazarin, 1624-61* (Oxford, 1978), chs. viii and ix (pp. 163-213), and J. B. Collins, *Fiscal Limits of Absolutism: Direct Taxation in early 17th-century France* (Berkeley and Los Angeles, Calif., 1988).

[6] The main criticism of this type of revenue was that it was extremely costly to administer and thus unjust. It was estimated that 891 million had actually been levied on the kingdom to raise this figure: B.N., MS. fr. 7750 fos. 110v-111. However, another estimate places the total levy at 758 million (Bonney, *King's Debts*, p. 316 after B.N., MS. fr. 7734). There are also variant calculations for the annual figures, based on the surviving tax contracts (D. Dessert, *Argent, Pouvoir et Société au Grand Siècle* (1984), p. 167).

[7] The main studies are now Dessert and F. Bayard, *Le Monde des Financiers au xviie Siècle* (1988).

was influenced. The piecemeal process by which new provinces had been acquired in the late fifteenth century left a legacy of regional privilege in the areas which, for the most part, came to be known as the provinces with estates (*pays d'états*): Languedoc had been acquired earlier on special terms, but Brittany, Provence, Dauphiné (and in the sixteenth century, though not later, Guyenne) fit this pattern. As late as 1697, even after the creation of the provincial intendancy in Brittany (which strengthened royal control), the meeting of the estates had to be carefully prepared by the ministers at Versailles and the royal officials in the province; the estates could (and in that year, did) prove troublesome; and the sessions ended as usual with a solemn 'contract' between the government and the province.[8]

The sixteenth century witnessed relative stability with regard to the privileges of the *pays d'états*, but there was significant innovation in the areas without representative institutions (known as the *pays d'élections*). The fundamental fiscal administrative division of the *ancien régime* was the *généralité*. The number of these was greatly extended in 1542, during the reign of Francis I;[9] the subdivisions (*élections*) proliferated, too, with the extension of the sale of offices in the sixteenth and early seventeenth centuries. By the seventeenth century, the French monarchy had embarked on a quest for territorial aggrandizement at the expense of Spain and the Empire. Territorial gains were still being made in the eighteenth century, and they had a considerable fiscal impact. On the eve of the French Revolution, the recently acquired provinces (*pays d'impositions*) had come to represent 14.4 per cent of the burden of direct taxes in the areas without representative institutions.[10] The long-term cost of this expansion was, however, a sustained period of foreign warfare which dominated the history of *ancien-régime* France and exacerbated the monarchy's financial problems.

The two most decisive changes in the period after 1520 were development of venality of office and a permanent debt in the form of annuities (*rentes sur l'hôtel de ville*). If it is a commonplace to state that France was dominated by social privilege and personal fiscal exemption, it is nevertheless worth stressing that French-speaking provinces seem to have been particularly prone to the lure of venality of office. La Fond, who had served as intendant of Franche-Comté before being transferred to German-speaking Alsace, noted the difference between the two regions:

ce pays est bien differend de celuy que je viens de quitter, et des autres prouinces du Royaume, ou les femmes par gloire et vanité engagent leurs maris d'achepter des charges qui ont quelque relief, ou qui leurs donnent quelque rang. Au contraire on ne sen soucie point icy, et cet usage n'est pas connu. . . .[11]

[8] Archives Nationales, Paris, G⁷ 180 no. 265, de Nointel to *contrôleur-général*, Rennes, 1 Dec. 1697, enclosing no. 266, a parchment notarized contract entitled 'Contrat des Estats passé entre Nosseigneurs les Commissaires de Sa Majesté et Messieurs des estats de la Prouince de Bretagne . . .' (11 Nov. 1697). The most detailed study of the *pays d'états* chiefly before the reign of Louis XIV is J. R. Major, *Representative Government in early modern France* (New Haven, Conn., 1980).

[9] Bonney, *Political Change*, p. 27. There were further changes in 1551, 1558, 1587, 1595, 1635, 1636, 1716 and so on. The fundamental maps of *ancien-régime* territorial boundaries are now those in *Atlas de la Révolution française*: v, *Le territoire. (2) Les limites administratives*, ed. D. Nordman and M.-V. Ozouf-Marignier (1989), cartes 3a and 3b of 'Les recettes des finances . . .' and carte 4 'les subdélégations . . .'.

[10] ESFDB dataset \rjb\frdoo1.ssd, based on AN D VI 9 (data kindly supplied by Michael Kwass).

[11] A.N., G⁷ 80 no. 114, 17 March 1698.

Offices were sold to produce new revenue, but an annual interest charge (the *gages*) had to be paid to the current holder of the office which had been alienated permanently. These offices were not bought out (that is, the debt was not redeemed) until after the French Revolution. In the sixteen-sixties, Colbert estimated the capital value held in offices at 419 million *livres* (at this time, there were over 46,000 office-holders); in 1790, the commission for the settlement of the public debt (*Comité de liquidation*) placed a figure of 200 million *livres* on the value of the offices to be redeemed at the reduced values allowable under a revolutionary regime.[12]

Henri IV and Sully tried to create a regular source of income from office-holding by taxing the right of resignation through the scheme known as the *droit annuel*, which was introduced in 1604; subsequently, at each renewal of the *droit annuel* a forced loan or *prêt* was demanded of the office-holders; and then, in the crisis of 1709–10, the office-holders were required, on a once and for all basis, to purchase exemption from both *droit annuel* and *prêt* in a new scheme known as the *droit de survivance*.[13] The overall effect of venality of office was to create an enormous (and costly) administrative apparatus which was largely outside the direct control of the Crown. On the one hand it exacerbated the revenue problems of the Crown, since a number of taxes had to be ear-marked in advance (in contemporary parlance 'assigned') to meet the annual salary bill of the office-holders; while on the other, it precluded clear administrative solutions to fiscal problems since the office-holders could block reforming measures, as both Law and Necker discovered. Venality of office and the consolidated debt consumed much of the tax revenue from the provinces: the payment of *rentes* and *gages* represented a significant burden of royal expenditure.[14] Much of the revenue was never transferred, of course, but was simply assigned locally to meet expenses;[15] for this reason, there is a practical, as well as semantic, difficulty in ascertaining the true 'net' revenue even after Colbert's accounting reforms of the sixteen-sixties.[16]

Throughout the *ancien régime*, which for the purposes of this article we will take to mean *c.* 1500–1789, taxes were paid in money rather than in kind. Such a statement requires immediate qualification. Even as late as 1725, a new tax called the *cinquantième* was established, the payment of which was to be made in kind directly from the proceeds of the harvest but although in theory more equitable than other taxes, in practice it proved unworkable as well as meeting ferocious opposition

[12] Bonney, *Political Change*, p. 450 n. 2; P.-F. Pinaud, 'The settlement of the public debt from the *ancien régime*, 1790–1810', *French Hist.*, v (1991), 414–25.

[13] A.N., G⁷ 81 no. 45, 'Declaration du Roy pour le rachat du droit annuel', 14 Jan. 1710.

[14] J.-R. Mal[l]et, *Comptes rendus de l'Administration des Finances du Royaume de France* (London [sic], 1789), pp. 49–50; A.N., G⁷ 1138–9, 'Le Roy est deuenu debiteur a tous ses suiets. Ils ne peuuent le payer que de leurs reuenus lesquels consistent en rentes, gages et droits sur le Roy. S'il ne paye point ce qu'il doit les particuliers ne seront point en etat de payer. Le seul moien d'entretenir la circulation est que le Roy reçoiue et qu'il paye ...'.

[15] W. H. Beik, *Absolutism and Society in 17th-century France: State Power and Provincial Aristocracy in Languedoc* (Cambridge, 1985), p. 266.

[16] Collins, p. 113.

STATE AND REVENUES IN *ANCIEN-RÉGIME* FRANCE   154

from clerical and aristocratic landowners.¹⁷ At this date, such a tax in kind was an aberration and it was revoked within two years. Payment in kind was reserved for wartime extremities such as 1709–10, when subsistence crises prevented the munitioning of the army on the frontier, and only special levies on the provinces could avert disaster.¹⁸ The exception was certain frontier provinces such as Alsace and Franche-Comté, where because of the predominantly agrarian economy they became the munitions base for armies operating on the frontier. The substantial payment of taxes in kind, and the requisition of peasant labour and transportation, explain why the *dixième* of 1710, for example, was not established in Alsace.¹⁹

In normal circumstances, payment in kind was inefficient in an economy which enjoyed high levels of monetization, even if there were great discrepancies between the amount of money in circulation in one province and another. Some idea of the amounts of coin issued, and thus the level of monetization at a national level, is provided by the figures for mint output (Graph 1).²⁰ Only for certain years is it possible to calculate the royal revenue derived from the total mint output. Thus, for example, we know that from 1690 the annual figures for profits from coinage alteration were 4.9 million (1690), 9.8 million (1691), 12.4 million (1692), 14.4 million (1693), and twenty-four million (1694), figures which fell sharply

---

[17] Cf. B.N., MS. fr. 7752 fo. 588: '... ce n'est point la qualité des personnes, c'est la quantité des biens qui fournira le secours. Il ne portera donc que sur ceux qui auront le moyen d'y contribuer....' The tax was introduced on 5 June 1725, but payment in kind was abolished on 21 June 1726. Final revocation came on 7 July 1727, with effect from 1 Jan. 1728 (M. Marion, *Dictionnaire des Institutions de la France aux xviie et xviiie siècles* (1923, repr. 1968), p. 93). The fundamental study of direct taxes (apart from Moreau de Beaumont) remains M. Marion, *Les impôts directs sous l'ancien régime, principalement au xviiie siècle* (1910), who, at pp. 276–83, publishes documents concerning the establishment and revocation of this tax.

[18] These levies were generalized throughout much of the kingdom: A.N., E 1945 fos. 323, 330, 17 Aug. and 15 Oct. 1709 (Champagne), fo. 326, 1 Oct. 1709 (Provence), fo. 328, 15 Oct. 1709 (Bourges), fo. 332, 15 Oct. 1709 (Brittany); E 1946 fo. 385, 28 May 1709 (Alsace), fo. 486, 1 Oct. 1709 (Dauphiné), fo. 500, 16 Oct. 1709 (maritime Flanders); E 1950 fo. 294, 17 Aug. 1709 (Picardy), fos. 335, 337, 339, 341, 343, 345, 8 Oct. and 15 Oct. 1709 (three *généralités* of Normandy), fo. 347, 15 Oct. 1709 (Tours), fo. 355, 5 Nov. 1709 (Burgundy).

[19] A.N., G⁷ 81 no. 292, 7 Sept. 1710, and unnumbered printed *mandement* of Felix Le Pelletier de la Houssaye, intendant of Alsace and the army of the Rhine, 23 Sept. 1710. On the exemption from the *dixième*, A.N., G⁷ 81 no. 39, 13 March 1711. Cf. also the intendant's earlier protests on the extent of payment in kind: A.N., G⁷ 81 no. 152, 5 Apr. 1708 (*Correspondance des Contrôleurs-Généraux des Finances avec les Intendants des Provinces, 1683–1715*, ed. A. M. de Boislisle (3 vols., 1874–9), iii. 14–17).

[20] ESFDB dataset \frindic\indg003. It should be noted that this graph is based on current values and thus makes no allowance for changes in the value of currency or inflation. It is based on the material as presented by the historians of the subject: H. A. Miskimin, *Money, Prices and Foreign Exchange in 14th-century France* (New Haven, Conn., 1963); idem, *Money and Power in 15th-century France* (New Haven, Conn., 1984); F. C. Spooner, *The International Economy and Monetary Movements in France, 1493-1725* (Cambridge, Mass., 1972); and M. Morineau, 'Les frappes monétaires françaises de 1726 à 1793: premières considérations', *Études d'histoire monétaire, xiie–xixe siècles*, ed. J. Day (Lille, 1984), pp. 72–5. It should be noted that John Day has published figures for the middle ages which differ somewhat from those of Miskimin, the chief differences being that he is prepared to extrapolate from printed sources and uses lease evidence from the farming of the mints: J. Day, 'Les frappes de monnaies en France et en Europe aux xive–xve siècles', *Rythmes de la Production Monétaire de l'Antiquité à nos Jours* ..., ed. G. Depeyrot, T. Hackens and G. Moucharte (Louvain, 1987), pp. 537–77. For the distinction between monetization and monetarization, see M. Morineau, 'Monnaie, monnayage, monétisation et monétarisation', *Histoire économique et financière de la France: Études et Documents II 1990* (1990), pp. 395–406.

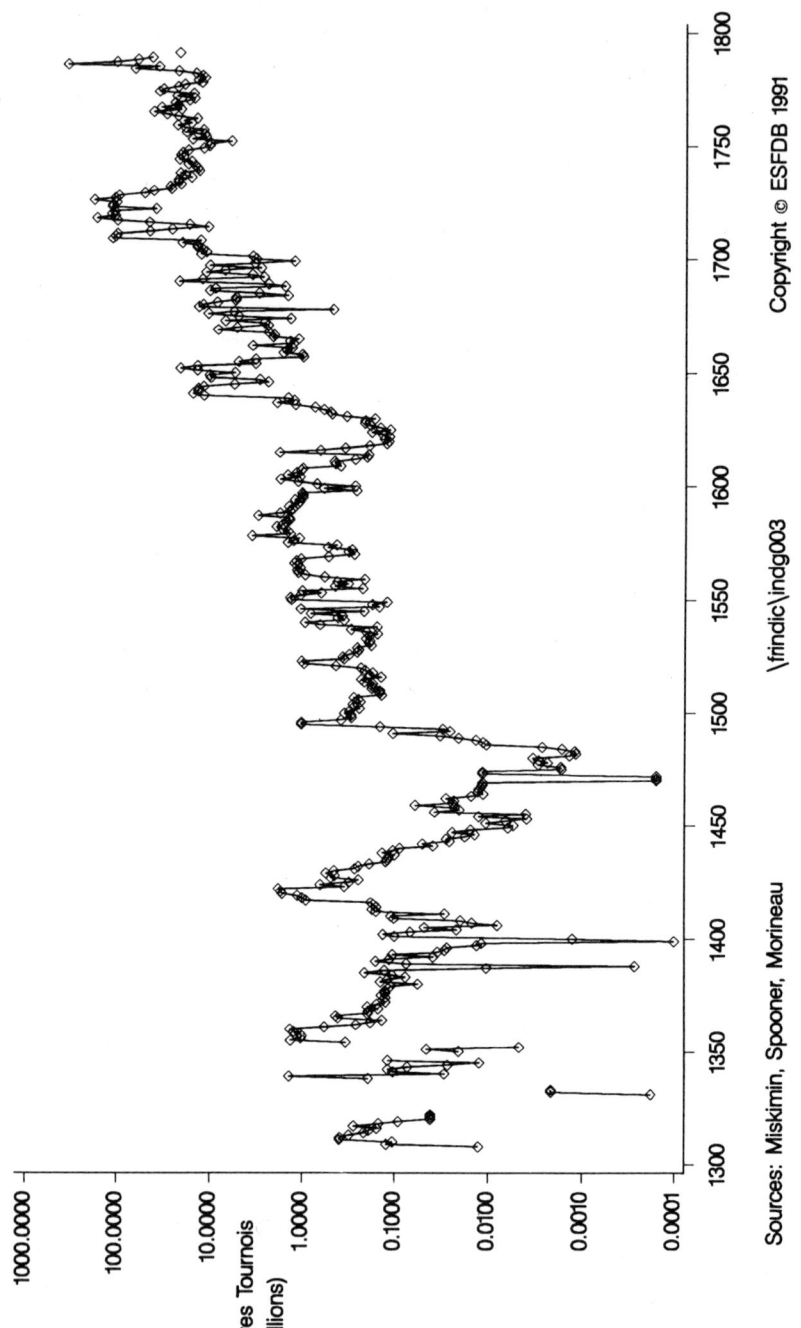

Graph 1. French mint output expressed in millions of *livres tournois*, 1308-1791 (semi-logarithmic scale)

thereafter.[21] Yet given the enormity of the Crown's financial problems in the later years of Louis XIV's reign, and the chronic monetary instability which was the consequence of the resort to frequent changes in the value of the coinage, the profits were relatively small; and, of course, after 1726 such measures were permanently dropped for the rest of the *ancien régime* since the only significant monetary reform thereafter was that undertaken by Calonne in 1785.

For the sixteenth century, there is very little in the way of overall figures for the royal revenue, and certainly no continuous series. From 1600, we are better provided with information, thanks to the efforts of the indefatigable Jean-Roland Malet, one of Desmaretz's chief clerks; we also have a manuscript summary of the contemporary accounts for the years after 1662; we have certain figures published by Boislisle; and we have the figures of Véron de Forbonnais.[22] For the eighteenth century, we may add the data published by James Riley[23] and Eugene White,[24] but there is no continuous series of figures.[25] Graph 2 presents the data in nominal terms, while in Graph 3 the data is presented in index numbers, set against the figures deflated in terms of the value of grain.[26] The index numbers are calculated on a base index of the years before France's entry into the Thirty Years' War (index 100 = 1600–30), and the figures are reworked on the basis of eleven-year centred moving averages so that the trend is more clearly discernible. By 1661, the beginning of Louis XIV's personal rule, the nominal figures had reached index 253, having risen considerably higher during the war of 1635–59; the deflated index shows a rise to only index 104. By 1702, the outbreak of the war of the Spanish Succession in terms of a war between alliances, the nominal figures had risen to index 347 and the deflated figures to index 316. By the end of the Seven Years' War in 1763, the nominal figures had reached index 962, and the deflated figures index 664. The cost of the American War (perhaps a billion *livres*)[27] led to a substantial borrowing requirement and rapid inflation in the figures for extraordinary

[21] ESFDB dataset \rjb\kk355\kkd001.ssd, based on A.N., KK 355. The most recent discussion is F. Droulers, 'Réformations et profits monétaires de Louis XIV', *Rythmes de la Production Monétaire*, pp. 639–48. The intendant of Brittany, Béchameil de Nointel, noted that only the first of the monetary measures had been particularly profitable to the Crown, since it had conferred higher profits to individuals seeking reminting of their coins: A.N., G⁷ 184 no. 246, 11 June 1704 (*Correspondance des Contrôleurs-Généraux*, ii. 186–7).

[22] The sources, and the problems they pose, are critically examined in R. J. Bonney, 'Jean-Roland Malet: historian of the finances of the French monarchy', *French Hist.*, v (1991), 180–233. The critical edition of Malet's figures in the ESFDB is forthcoming in M. M. and R. J. Bonney, *Jean-Roland Malet: Premier Historien des Finances de la Monarchie française* (Comité pour l'histoire économique et financière de la France, 1993).

[23] J. C. Riley, 'French finances, 1727–68', *Jour. Modern Hist.*, lix (1987), 226–7; idem, *The Seven Years' War and the Old Regime in France: the Economic and Financial Toll* (Princeton, N.J., 1986).

[24] E. N. White, 'Was there a solution to the ancien régime's financial dilemma?', *Jour. Econ. Hist.*, xlix (1989), 550–3.

[25] ESFDB dataset \rjb\malet\malgo34. The data appears to be more complete, but for ordinary revenues only, in M. Morineau, 'Budgets de l'État et gestion des finances royales en France au xviiie siècle', *Revue Historique*, cclxiv (1980), 333.

[26] The mean index numbers for the total revenues have been deflated by the index numbers for grain prices during the period, using the common base index of 1600–30 = index 100. The grain figures used were those of M. Baulant, 'Le prix des grains à Paris de 1431 à 1788', *Annales: Économies, Sociétés, Civilisations*, xxiii (1968), 520–40.

[27] R. D. Harris, *Necker: Reform Statesman of the Ancien Régime* (Berkeley, Calif., 1979), p. 118.

XII

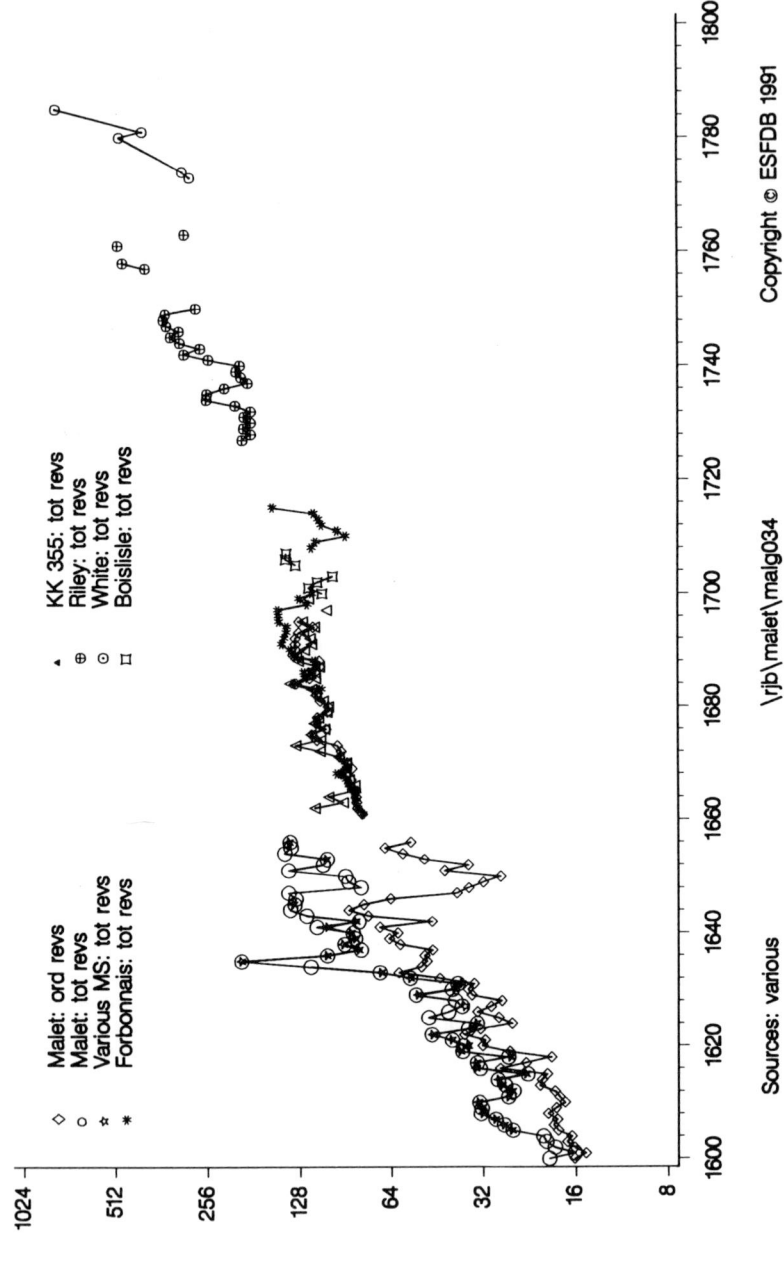

Graph 2. Semi-logarithmic graph of ordinary and total revenues of the French monarchy from various sources, 1600–1785

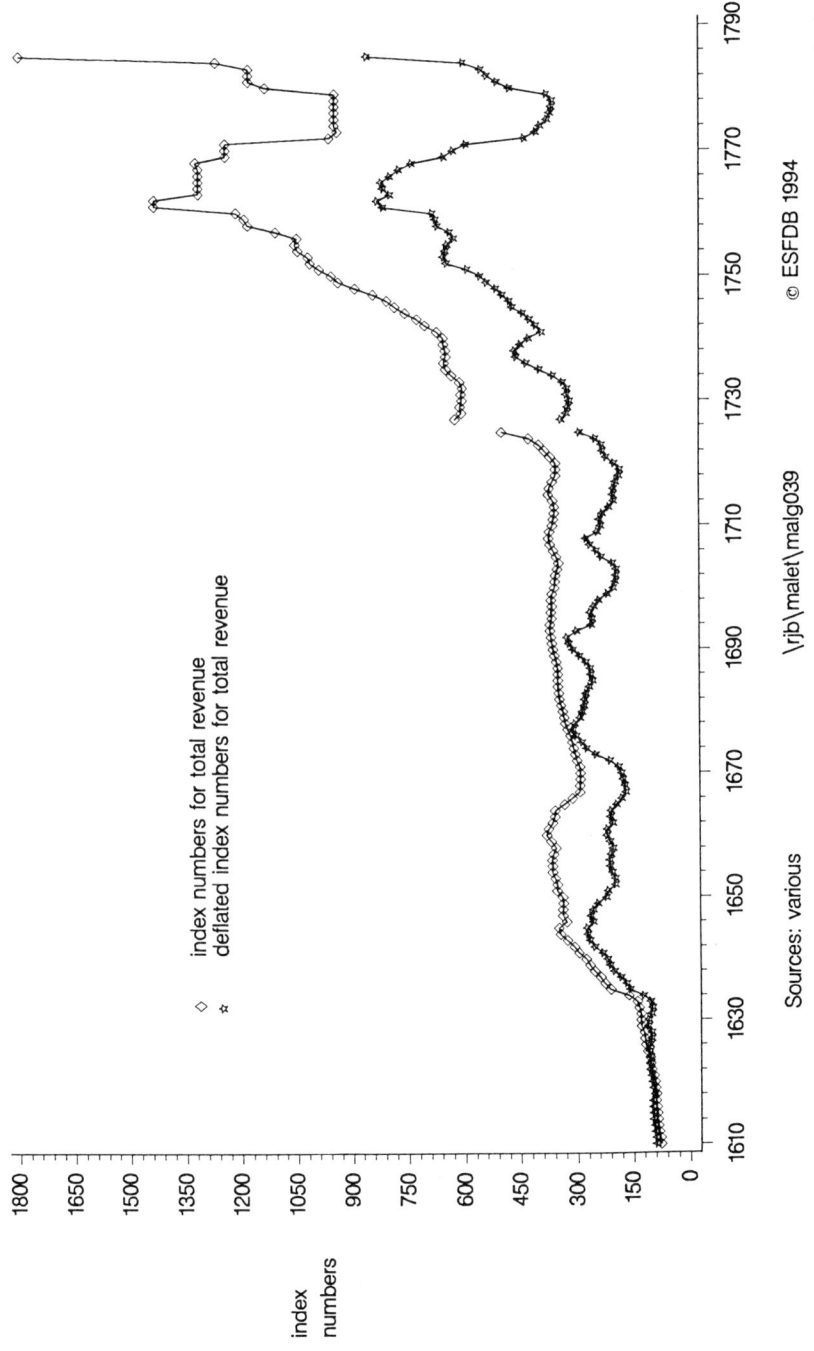

Graph 3. Eleven-year moving averages of index numbers for total royal revenue in France, 1610–1785, set against 'real' revenue index numbers (index 100 = 1600–30)

revenues. Economic growth and the increase in population were important contributory factors to the rise in the nominal figures to index 2557 (and the rise in the deflated figures to index 1126) according to the *état au vrai* of 1785.

The revenue figures present some difficulties in interpretation, leaving aside the fundamental problem caused by single-entry book-keeping until the last years of the *ancien régime*. Are the revenue figures gross or net, terms which themselves have been criticized as anachronistic? And if they are gross, do they include an element of borrowing? Of the French evidence before 1660 it is very difficult to state with certainty that borrowing is completely excluded from the total revenues; but the so-called ordinary revenues are clearly too low, and under-represent the true revenue position of the Crown. We need only to consider the significant proportion of extraordinary revenues in the total revenue before 1660 to realize that the margin for error is potentially very serious: the figure was never less than twenty-six per cent of the total per decade, and rose to forty-four per cent in the sixteen-thirties, forty-six per cent in the sixteen-forties and sixty per cent in the sixteen-fifties (Chart 1).[28] And the problem is made more significant by the fact that very considerable changes could occur in the relative importance of certain types of ordinary revenue.[29] Yet what Professor Riley calls the 'collection overhead' which he estimates at not significantly higher in France (at fourteen per cent) than England (ten per cent)[30] is equally important for us to consider; in the seventeenth century the figure was certainly higher than Riley suggests. After 1660, we can ascertain the difference between gross and net revenues payable to the Treasury:[31] but as has been seen, the process of assigning expenditure on specific revenue, which was then discharged locally, makes it virtually impossible to calculate the true overhead.

It is very difficult to discuss the 'collection overhead' for the indirect revenues because of the system of farming out the taxes. The records of the *ferme générale* in large measure were destroyed after the Revolution,[32] while the private business papers of the revenue farmers do not, for the most part, survive; nor, in many cases, do local records of the amount of revenue collected.[33] No calculation of the overhead cost is thus possible, and where a figure is available at all it is of the profit gained by the farmers and those holding an interest in the farms: under the lease of Laurent David (1774–80) this may be calculated at 21.7 million a year on a rent of 152 million (14.3 per cent).[34] For the rest, what the historian is left with is the

---

[28] ESFDB dataset \rjb\malet\malbo27. The *deniers extraordinaires* appear as 'denextra' on the chart. The other categories are direct taxes from the *pays d'élections* ('pdelec'); revenues from the *pays d'états* ('pdetat'); revenues from the farming of indirect taxes ('revfarms'); the *parties casuelles* ('partcas'); and miscellaneous revenues ('miscrev').

[29] Bonney, 'Jean-Roland Malet', pp. 203, 229.

[30] Riley, *Seven Years' War*, p. 61.

[31] Bonney, 'Jean-Roland Malet', pp. 204, 221, 222.

[32] Y. Durand, *Les Fermiers Généraux au xviiie siècle* (1971), p. 7 n. 1; J.-P. Massaloux, *La Régie de l'Enregistrement et des Domaines aux xviiie et xixe siècles: Étude historique* (Geneva, 1989), p. xiii n. 1.

[33] G. Lemarchand, *La Fin du Féodalisme dans le pays de Caux: Conjoncture Économique et Démographique et Structure Sociale dans une Région de Grande Culture de la Crise du xviie siècle à la Stabilisation de la Révolution, 1640–1795* (1989), p. 306; cf. *Le Roi, le Marchand et le Sel*, ed. J.-Cl. Hocquet (Lille, 1987).

[34] According to Lavoisier, the profit was 1,746,040 *livres* per farmer over 7 years (i.e. 249,434 *livres* multiplied by 87 farmers): Durand, pp. 104, 164. Most farmers' shares were restricted by pre-existing *croupes*, so that the calculation is a theoretical one of those holding an interest in the farm, not just the farmers.

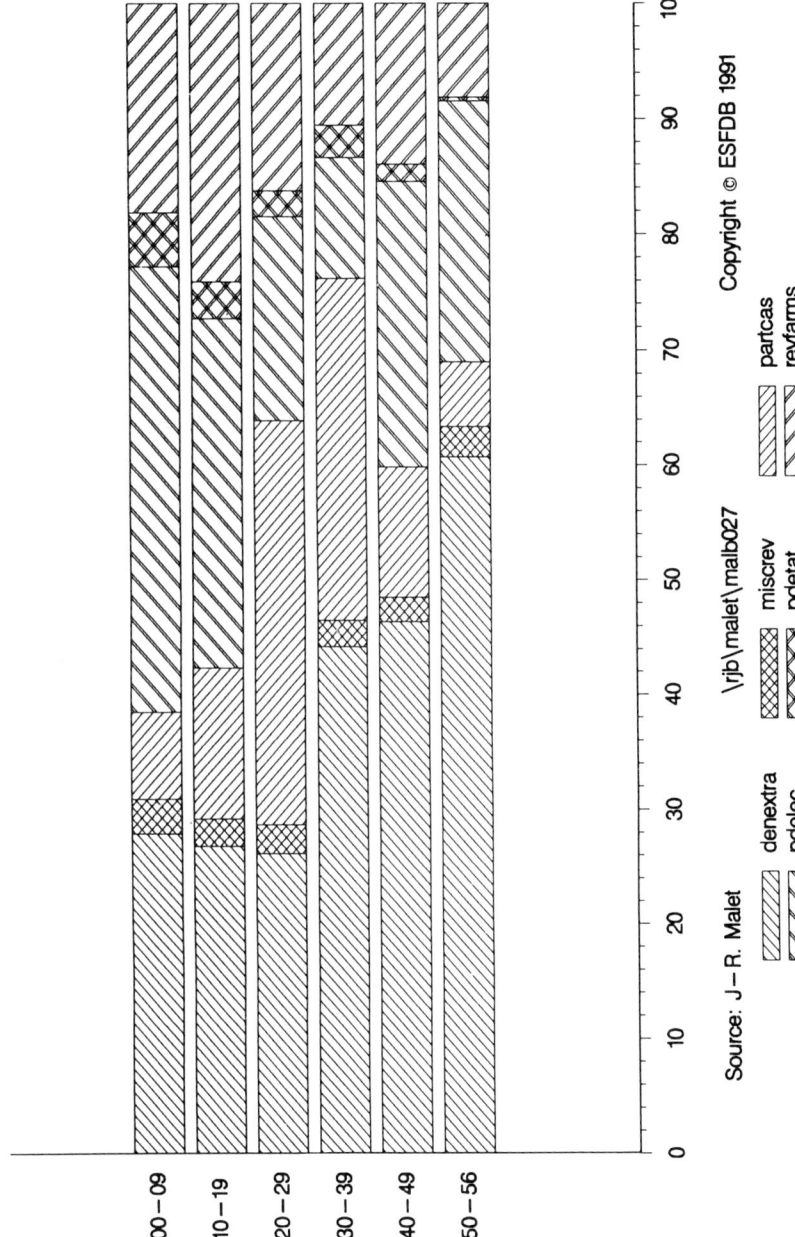

Chart 1. Categories of ordinary and extraordinary revenues of the French monarchy, 1600–56

evidence of the evolution of the rents payable by the farmers and their demands for the remission of rents in adverse circumstances, chiefly due to the fall in consumption in wartime.[35] Only for a few indirect taxes (and not necessarily those which were the most representative) do we have more details on the farming process and on the 'collection overhead'. The best example is the farm of the *devoirs* in Brittany, a province in which, uniquely in France, indirect taxes were considerably more important than direct ones, even in the late seventeenth century,[36] and where (because of the system of Estates) the information on the farming process was public knowledge. In 1706, it was argued by the farmers demanding a remission on the years 1704 and 1705 that the profitability of the revenue farm since 1693, that is mostly during wartime years, had been greatly exaggerated, and precise figures for the profit were cited; usually gains on the general farm of the *devoirs* were offset by losses on the particular farms (that is the administration of the taxes at diocesan level in the province).[37] When the provincial intendant drew up a summary in 1703 of the reasons for the farmers' refusal to contemplate a renewal of the lease of their farm with a rent of more than 3.9 million *livres* over two years, he placed most emphasis on the decline in consumption as compared with the previous war, when naval armament had been at a higher level in the province; maritime commerce had declined, as had the livestock trade, while much of the province's monetary circulation was drained off to Paris. The burden of direct taxes, above all the *capitation*, was also seen as critical in removing peasant and artisan disposable income which could have been spent in the *cabaret* and thus generated revenue for the tax farm.[38] But the general argument, that there were reduced levels of consumption and thus a decline in the profitability of the farms in wartime, seems to have been true for the indirect taxes throughout the *ancien régime*. Though overall the rents payable by the *ferme générale* rose from fifty-two million in 1697 to eighty million in 1726, this source of income was not of great assistance during the war of the Spanish Succession (the rent fluctuated around 36.6 million in 1709-11).[39] The heavy reliance on indirect taxes in the eighteenth century (on Morineau's figures, forty-eight per cent of total revenues in 1726, forty-five per cent in 1751, forty-nine per cent in 1775 and 46.5 per cent in 1788)[40] is explicable only by the fact that, relative to the *grand siècle*, there were long periods of peace in the eighteenth century; the years where there is detailed evidence available also happen to be peacetime years.

---

[35] R. J. Bonney, 'The failure of the French revenue farms, 1600-60', *Econ. Hist. Rev.*, 2nd ser., xxxii (1979), 11-32.

[36] A.N., G⁷ 181 no. 301, 4 Dec. 1699 (*Correspondance des Contrôleurs-Généraux*, ii. 16-17), which shows that direct taxes in that year were under half a million *livres*, whereas indirect taxes were over 2.77 million.

[37] A.N., G⁷ 186 no. 90, 'La demande de l'indemnité des fermiers de 1704 et 1705 est fondé sur leur perte...'.

[38] A.N., G⁷ 183 nos. 256, 257 and 277, 12 Oct. 1703; cf. also no. 305, 10 Nov. 1703.

[39] Marion, *Dictionnaire des Institutions*, pp. 232, 234; G. T. Matthews, *The Royal General Farms in 18th-Century France* (New York, 1958).

[40] Morineau, 'Budgets de l'État', p. 314; J. Meyer, *Le Poids de l'État* (1983), p. 52.

The decline in the profitability of the farms in wartime, and the inevitable demands for remission of rents and compensation for the farmers which accompanied this, meant that in the sixteenth and seventeenth centuries right up to the end of the war of the Spanish Succession, direct taxes perforce became the more important source of revenue during wartime. Until 1695, the most important direct tax was the *taille*, but this venerable source of revenue was already showing some signs of its age by the end of the seventeenth century. The principles of the *répartition* laid down in the ruling of 22 August 1642 and confirmed in the declaration of 16 April 1643 (which conferred the chief responsibility for the assessment and collection on the provincial intendants within the *pays d'élections*) remained in place throughout the *ancien régime*.[41] But the tax suffered from a stability in its repartition between *généralités*[42] and from a stability in its repartition between *élections* (Chart 2);[43] it is not surprising that since changes in economic circumstances were very difficult to reflect in changes in the repartition, the *taille* showed a tendency to decline in real terms after the reign of Louis XIV.[44] Reforming ministers and intendants showed a keen awareness of the deficiencies of the administration of the *taille* and the narrowness of its fiscal base; in wartime especially there were usually attempts to curtail fiscal privilege at a provincial level, but these were inevitably offset by the Crown's desperate need to sell new offices which conferred fiscal exemption.

The *capitation* of 1695, introduced by Pontchartrain, was the first serious attempt to broaden the fiscal base for direct taxation. The model was the tax introduced by Emperor Leopold I in his hereditary lands in 1690 (but which, unlike the case in France, included the clergy in its provisions).[45] The first *capitation* yielded net 18.3 million on a levy of 21.4 million in 1695 and 21.1 million net on a levy of 23.7 million in 1697.[46] This compares with figures for the *taille* in the *pays d'élections* of thirty-one million net on 34.5 million levy in 1695; and of about thirty million net on a levy of thirty-two million in 1697.[47] The overhead cost for the *capitation* was just under nine per cent, about the same as for the *taille* in the *pays d'élections*. Although abolished at the end of the war of the League of Augsburg, the *capitation*

---

[41] The declaration of 1643 was still cited in the last *brevets* of the *taille*: A.N., z¹ᵍ 281ᶜ, *brevet* of 21 July 1786 for 1787 in the *élection* of Paris. A recent discussion of the administration of direct taxes by one intendant is J.-P. Massaloux, 'Regards sur la fiscalité d'ancien régime: les impôts directs sous l'administration de Trudaine, intendant d'Auvergne', *Histoire économique: Études II*, pp. 183–209.

[42] Bonney, 'Jean-Roland Malet', pp. 206, 231. For a detailed discussion of the repartition of the *taille* under Henri IV see F. Bayard, 'Le poids financier des régions françaises à l'époque d'Henri IV, 1600-10', *Histoire économique: Études III 1991* (1991), pp. 39–70.

[43] ESFDB dataset \rjb\genboo1, based on *Mémoires des Intendants sur l'État des Généralités dressés pour l'Instruction du Duc de Bourgogne. I. Mémoire de la Généralité de Paris*, ed. A. M. de Boislisle (1881), pp. 530–1.

[44] ESFDB dataset \rjb\elegoo1 forthcoming as Graph 5 in R. J. Bonney, 'Louis XIII, Richelieu and the royal finances', *Richelieu and his Age*, ed. J. A. Bergin and L. W. B. Brockliss (Oxford, 1992). For the peak in real terms during the war of the Spanish Succession see Lemarchand, p. 153; but note the cautionary remark ('La taille, en 1704-1705, remonte à un niveau sans précédent dans les chiffres dont je dispose...'). There is in fact a serious gap in his documentation between 1614 and 1659, unlike the series for the *élection* of Paris in the ESFDB.

[45] J. Bérenger, *Finances et Absolutisme autrichien dans la seconde moitié du xviie siècle* (1975), p. 338.

[46] ESFDB datasets \rjb\kk355\kkd006 to kkd009 after A.N., KK 355.

[47] ESFDB datasets \rjb\kk355\kkd010 to kkd013 after A.N., KK 355.

XII

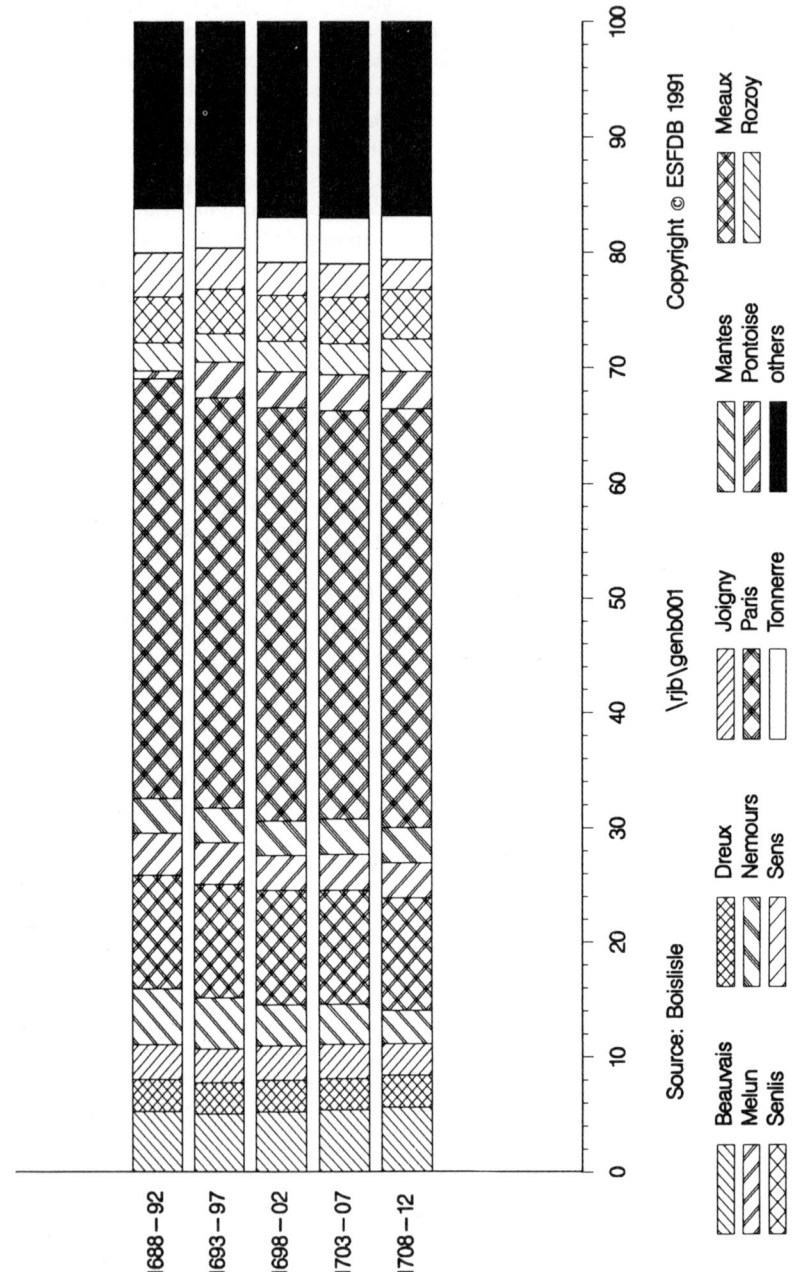

Chart 2. Repartition of the *taille* between *élections* of the *généralité* of Paris, 1688–1712

was reintroduced with the threat of war in 1701: thereafter, it became a permanent tax for the rest of the *ancien régime*, but one principally under the control of the intendants and independent of the *bureaux de finances*, the *élections* and the *Cours des Aides*.

The relative success of the new tax has to be offset by a number of considerations. Firstly, once a province came to a special arrangement with the government (*abonnement*) over the *capitation*, the regulations of the resulting decrees of the council specified conditions which might vary the original legislation. Thus in Brittany, the decree of 21 January 1696 authorized the drawing up of a new tariff for the province, while that of 21 January 1702 modified the declaration of 12 March 1701 which had reintroduced the tax shortly before the outbreak of the war of the Spanish Succession. Once the province fell into tax arrears, it inevitably demanded a reduction in the *abonnement*, particularly if another province (in this case, Languedoc), had obtained it.[48] In some provinces, and again Brittany is a good example, the *capitation* was bitterly resented, particularly by the lesser nobility, and the intendant's administration was seriously compromised by the criticism.[49] Secondly, the intendants themselves showed little enthusiasm for the new tax, because it was an administrative nightmare as a result of the multiplicity of tax rolls, with the resulting risk of a shortfall in yield: for Guyet, intendant at Lyon, it was 'cette desagreable affaire' and he only assumed responsibility for the *capitation* of the municipality of Lyon in 1703 when it was clear that its own levy in 1701 and 1702 had failed hopelessly.[50] Thirdly, after 1701 the purpose of the *capitation* changed radically: the levy was increased by half as much again, and many intendants resorted to levying it as an accessory to the *taille* ('au marc la livre de la taille'). And fourthly, the tendency increasingly was to allow individuals to purchase exemption from the *capitation*: in Desmaretz's view, these *affranchissements* (which were valued at some eight million by 1710)[51] had to be revoked if the tax was to be continued after the return of peacetime conditions.[52] Taken together these difficulties posed an administrative obstacle to a reformed fiscal system: in Forbonnais's expression, the *capitation* seemed 'plus propre à servir de ressource extraordinaire dans un tem[p]s de besoin qu'à former une branche de finance pendant la paix',[53] while Malet considered that 'tout le monde a senti & sent l'irrégularité d'un tarif qui n'a pour principes que les qualités de chaque sujet & non pas les facultés'.[54]

---

[48] A.N., G⁷ 187 nos. 213, 214, Le Peletier des Forts to Desmaretz, Paris, 4 Aug. 1707 and accompanying memorandum; G⁷ 187 no. 443, n.d., Memorandum based on a request of the estates of Brittany to Louis XIV.

[49] ESFDB dataset \rjb\capdoo1 to capdoo4.ssd, after A.N., G⁷ 180 nos. 206-9. This *état vérifié* was forwarded by Béchameil de Nointel, the intendant, to justify his administration against the criticism of the provincial estates: A.N., G⁷ 180 no. 205, 6 Nov. 1697.

[50] Le prevost des marchands et les eschevins de la ville de Lion pour auoir diminu[ti]on sur les nonvaleurs de l'année 1701 et sur la cap[itati]on de 1702: A.N., G⁷ 359 no. 28, 13 May 1702; cf. also G⁷ 359 nos. 11 and 30, 20 Feb. and 12 July 1703 (*Correspondance des Contrôleurs-Généraux*, ii. 133).

[51] A.N., G⁷ 1138-9, Untitled anon. memorandum in dossier entitled 'Memoires au sujet du dixieme des biens et autres'.

[52] *Correspondance des Contrôleurs-Généraux*, iii. 630.

[53] F. Véron de Forbonnais, *Recherches et Considérations sur les Finances de France depuis l'année 1595 jusqu'à l'année 1721* (2 vols., Basle, 1758), i. 526.

[54] Malet, p. 107 and Bonney, 'Jean-Roland Malet', p. 195.

Those intendants who showed the greatest awareness of the need to reform the *taille*, by attacking corrupt officials and eliminating needless privilege, were precisely those who recognized the injustice of the *capitation* tariff and the equally disastrous recourse to levying the tax as an adjunct to the *taille*. Thus Jubert de Bouville at Orléans praised Chamillart for recognizing that the tariff could not be followed slavishly, and that the intendants should have regard to 'les moiens et facultés de chacun'; but he also recognized that 'tous les gens riches et puissan[t]s ont crié' at this policy, and that the principal reform of the *capitation* should be to tax more heavily those who were exempt or favoured under the *taille*, in compensation.[55] However ineffective the endeavours of reformers, it is difficult to agree with the verdict that direct taxation was supposed to be 'neutral'; at least in wartime.[56] Rather, direct taxes were aimed at real wealth where it could be found and intendants expected political support from ministers when they pursued a firm policy towards privilege: in Bouville's words, '... il faut soutenir les intendan[t]s qui feront leur devoir et même les louer devant tout le monde afin d'empescher les crïeries injustes'.

By 1709–10, it was clear that the continuation of the war could no longer be financed without a new revenue. Two men dominated the intellectual debate surrounding the origins of the *dixième*: Sébastien le Prestre, maréchal de Vauban and Pierre Le Pesant, seigneur de Boisguilbert, lieutenant-general of police at Rouen; their contribution, and the way in which the new tax was introduced has been described elsewhere and is outside the scope of this article.[57] It is, however, worth stressing here that both the theoreticians behind the tax and the finance minister were greatly influenced by foreign examples and thus state competition for resources in a long and gruelling war. For Boisguilbert, it was necessary that France should model itself on its principal rivals, particularly England 'ou l'on donne le cinquieme sans murmure jusqu'aux grands seigneurs pour ataquer la France'.[58] Desmaretz was clearly influenced by Dutch models, but doubted whether they could be applied successfully to the French context ('J'avoüe qu'en France cette remise pourroit ne pas produire le mesme effect qu'en Hollande ou l'esprit d'oeconomie est plus estably qu'en France, et ou chacun concourt a soutenir les depenses de l'estat, au lieu qu'en France on n'a dautre attention qu'a se soutraire aux contributions necessaires pour les depenses publiques').[59] Desmaretz's clarity of purpose in the crisis in 1710 is particularly striking. Far from seeking to meet the revenue need with a series of expedients, he tried to impose a 'system', a set of measures which taken together amounted to a significant financial and fiscal reform.[60]

[55] A.N., G⁷ 420 nos. 106, 107 and 108, 25 Nov. and 26 Nov. 1703 (*Correspondance des Contrôleurs-Généraux*, ii. 161–2).
[56] Cf. Riley, *Seven Years' War*, p. 48. But at p. 92, Professor Riley quotes Stein's view that wartime taxation is likely to be more progressive than peacetime taxation.
[57] R. J. Bonney, 'State competition for resources and fiscal innovation under Louis XIV' forthcoming in *États, Marines et Sociétés* (essays in honour of Jean Meyer, ed. J.-P. Poussou, A. Zysberg and M. Acerra).
[58] A.N., G⁷ 721 no. 17, 27 Oct. 1703 (*Correspondance des Contrôleurs-Généraux*, ii. 534).
[59] Signed memorandum of Desmaretz to Le Rebours, Marly, 13 Oct. 1710, A.N., G⁷ 1138–9 (*Correspondance des Contrôleurs-Généraux*, iii. 608).
[60] Thus, for example, the list of 'Edits, declarations et arrests rendus au mois d'octobre 1710 pour l'arra[n]gement general des finances': A.N., G⁷ 1138–9.

It was the controller-general himself who drafted the preamble for the declaration of 14 October 1710 establishing the *dixième*, which outlined the central arguments concerning its necessity, but which (crucially) conceded its repeal three months after the peace treaty. The most effective direct tax of the *ancien régime* was thus conceived as a wartime measure only, a *subside ou imposition pour la guerre*.[61] The first *dixième* yielded twenty-eight million on a levy of 30.2 million in 1711 (including the last quarter of 1710), 22.7 million on 24.4 million in 1712, 22.5 million on 24.3 million in 1713 and 22.8 million on 24.1 in 1714, or an extra ninety-six million in total over four years.[62] The overhead cost, relatively low for a new tax in wartime, was 9.5 per cent or thereabouts. Doubtless the tax could have produced much more revenue in peacetime, had Louis XIV lived longer or had the regent possessed the political will to continue the levy. Forbonnais regarded the *dixième* as 'une taxe proportionnelle; celui qui posséde [*sic*] peu, contribue peu'.[63] But he added:

... plus on avoit tardé à employer cette ressource, plus la charge en fut pesante sur les Peuples & moins l'Etat en retira d'avantages ... tous les revenus de l'Etat étoient tombés; aussi va-t-on voir que le dixiéme [*sic*] ne rendit pas plus de vingt-quatre millions dans les meilleures années. N'est-il pas évident qu'en l'imposant dès le commencement de la guerre, lorsque tous les revenus étoient encore entiers, il eût produit beaucoup davantage?[64]

Desmaretz seems to have been disappointed with his brainchild: the declarations of the taxpayers were false, he told the regent, and thus the yield had been limited so that in the best years the levy had never exceeded twenty-four million.[65] This was, of course, far short of the 120 million which some propagandists had considered to be necessary and possible for the Crown to levy in the period before the introduction of the tax in 1710.[66] The historian cannot ascertain for certain the real shortfall between the tax yield and the notional tenth on revenue. Vauban had estimated that his *dixme royale* would produce an annual revenue of 116.8 million.[67] Interestingly, John Law, in a letter to Desmaretz dated 26 July 1715, estimated French national revenue at 1,200 million *livres*, the same capital evaluation as Vauban's, although he seems to have based his calculations on a comparison with England.[68] Modern

---

[61] Desmaretz's drafting of the preamble is in A.N., G⁷ 1138–9, in a dossier entitled 'Projets, minutes et déclaration ordonnant la levée du 10ᵉ'. Comparison with the parchment declaration in the same dossier (and also in A.N., K 2413 no. 80) shows that the wording was virtually unaltered thereafter.

[62] ESFDB dataset \rjb\dixdoo1 and dixdoo2 after A.N., G⁷ 1138–9. Malet, p. 153, stated that the yield was only 90 million in those years; Desmaretz gave the figure of 111 million in his memorandum of January 1715, but this may include an anticipation on 1715 (*Correspondance des Contrôleurs-Généraux*, iii. 619). For its impact in one locality see Lemarchand, p. 154.

[63] Forbonnais, i. 526. The remark was made in relation to the *vingtième*, the successor tax to the *dixième*.

[64] Forbonnais, ii. 221–2.

[65] *Correspondance des Contrôleurs-Généraux*, iii. 626.

[66] Apart from the memorandum quoted above, another 'Mémoire sur ce qui paroist praticable pour donner le temps au ministre de fournir a ses premʳᵉˢ depenses' in A.N., G⁷ 1138–9 stated that a *vingtième* could reach 60 million, but even if it encountered some difficulty at the outset 'l'on ne croit pas que cela monte a moins de 50 millions'.

[67] Vauban, *Projet d'une dixme royale*, ed. J.-F. Pernot (St.-Léger-Vauban, 1988), p. 66.

[68] He seems to have derived his French estimate by multiplying the English estimated national wealth by three. On an English estimate of 'entre 5 et 600 millions de livres de France', the French national revenues 'devroient monter de 15[00] à 1800 millions'. But his proposed bank 'peut augmenter les revenus généraux

estimates have tended to place the national product higher, for example at 2,700 million,[69] but these should be moderated by Forbonnais's comment on the fall in national output during the war of the Spanish Succession.[70] If John Law's may be taken as the most reliable estimate, then the *dixième* was underassessed on average by eighty per cent, although we should note that not every part of the national wealth would fall within the scope of the tax. The underassessment of the *dixième*, and its successor tax, the *vingtième*, became progressively worse in the eighteenth century.[71] Voluntary declarations were never likely to be satisfactory. The only alternative was to pitch the levy excessively high, and to allow taxpayers to obtain moderations only by presenting proof of their taxable income: but this laid the government open to the accusation of acting in an arbitrary manner in the administration of a tax that was supposed to be more equitable than those which had preceded it. The charge of despotic conduct was already levelled during Desmaretz's ministry: 'Nous serions milles fois plus heureux en Turquie quan France'. An anonymous letter to Desmaretz expressed this charge clearly in relation to the power of the intendant and the director of the *dixième* acting on the minister's instructions.[72]

In the seventeenth century, fiscal reform in wartime had often been considered by finance ministers to be impossible. The experience of the last years of Louis XIV's reign had shown that not only was it possible, it was essential as the only means of overcoming the financial crisis provoked by the duration of the war. There was perhaps a greater possibility of sustained fiscal reform under absolute monarchy than is sometimes allowed by historians. What was lacking in 1717, when the regent allowed the revocation of the *dixième*, was the political will to continue down the same path to fiscal reform in peacetime. If direct taxes declined in importance in the eighteenth century (and Morineau's figures show that they did: from forty-four per cent of total revenues in 1726 to thirty-five per cent by 1788), this was because ministers were acutely aware that the repartition and collection processes for direct revenues were inequitable and needed reform. In general, the population growth of the eighteenth century assisted the taxpayers of direct taxes since the burden was carried by more people than before. Even so, in a small parish of 100 hearths or less, the fiscal exemption gained by one or two important taxpayers could have a devastating effect on the real fiscal burden of the others.[73]

---

de la France de 1200 millions à 1800 millions': *Oeuvres complètes de John Law*, ed. P. Harsin (3 vols., Liège and Paris, 1934), ii. 50–52. The author thanks Antoin E. Murphy of Trinity College, Dublin, for this reference.

[69] Riley, *Seven Years' War*, p. 22.

[70] Forbonnais, ii. 221–2.

[71] Riley, *Seven Years' War*, p. 70, notes that the *vingtièmes* were 'avoided or evaded by some 85 per cent of the estimated national output of the 1750s'. If the calculation based on John Law's figures above is correct, then there was no real deterioration in the situation. On the phenomenon at a local level see Lemarchand, pp. 298–9.

[72] A.N., G⁷ 1138–9, anon. letter to Desmaretz, no place, 10 Oct. 1712. The letter is in the file after Desmaretz's draft of the preamble of the declaration of 14 Oct. 1710.

[73] Lemarchand, p. 156. On population growth reducing the real fiscal burden see *ibid.*, pp. 155–6, 303–5.

STATE AND REVENUES IN *ANCIEN-RÉGIME* FRANCE   168

Even if Laverdy (controller-general, 1763-8) discovered from the great comparative investigation of European public revenues launched by the French government in 1763-5 that indirect taxes were increasingly becoming the norm, it should not be forgotten that the original purpose of the enquiry had been to establish foreign models for the new *cadastre* to be introduced in France for the levy of *direct* taxes.[74] The national land register would have been very difficult to introduce, and this task would not have been eased by poor standards in the surveying profession. Yet opposition from vested interests, principally the *parlements*, was much more important, and influenced the resignation of Bertin as controller-general in 1763. The rapid changeover of controllers-general of finance in the eighteenth century (nine ministers were appointed between 1746 and the death of Louis XV in 1774, averaging just over three years per ministry) was not conducive to such a bold reform. Such instability was itself the product of political intrigue, so that the ministers frequently were held in tutelage to factions which had helped in their promotion; a succession of different interest groups to some extent captured ministerial power, and as a result the government lacked the political will to implement far-reaching structural reforms, least of all those which would damage the economic interests of the group behind the minister: Silhouette's alienation of the *fermiers généraux* caused the downfall of his ministry after only nine months in 1758-9 and there are other examples of arrivals to, and dismissals from, ministerial office being explained by this one interest group.[75] The resulting lack of continuity meant that where the *cadastre* was introduced locally, it was not as a result of the government, but on the initiative of a reforming provincial intendant, as in Alsace and the *généralité* of Paris; and by definition this could do nothing to rectify injustices in the repartition of taxes between regions.

The failure to introduce a *cadastre* was an important setback to attempts at political reform and at the creation of an efficient revenue raising system in the eighteenth century. It is true that at first the implementation of the project would have affected only direct taxes. But the French government was well aware of the Spanish attempt at introducing a *única contribución* under the marqués de Esquilache, since the minister had himself drafted the report on Spanish revenues as part of the great survey of 1763-5.[76] The Spanish government had tried (but in the event failed),[77] to shift the burden away from indirect taxes by the establishment of the *cadastre*, which had met stiff opposition from those who were privileged under the old system. And it is not inconceivable that the same sort of process could have been attempted in France. In flagrant contradiction of his reforming predecessors such as Bertin, Necker (director-general of finance, 1776-81 and again in 1788-90) denied

[74] R. J. Bonney, 'On the eve of modernity: the first enquiry on comparative fiscal systems in Europe (1763)', forthcoming in the conference proceedings of the European Science Foundation symposium on the Ottoman Empire and the European States (held at Istanbul, 1991, and to be edited in *Acta Turcica* by J.-Ph. Genet and E. Eldem). It has been demonstrated that Bertin's resignation in 1763 marked the abandonment of the attempted imposition of a national *cadastre* in France (M. Antoine, *Louis XV* (1989), pp. 792, 798-9).
[75] Durand, p. 96.
[76] A.N., K 881 no. 51, Ossun to Laverdy, 20 May 1765.
[77] R. Herr, *Rural Change and the Royal Finances in Spain at the End of the Old Regime* (Berkeley, Calif., 1989), pp. 8-10.

this. Necker was a firm believer in publicizing the state of the king's finances, in an attempt to attract public support: in 1781, he took the initiative in publishing his *compte rendu*, incurring the king's displeasure and his own temporary exile from Paris. He wanted equality in the fiscal burden, and the elimination of arbitrary tax assessments. He also supported the move towards provincial assemblies, which would have introduced an appearance of consent to taxation, while overcoming the government's ineffectiveness in the detailed execution of policy. Since Necker was critical of both the *parlements* and the intendants, he was attacked by both sides of the political spectrum when his memorandum on the establishment of provincial assemblies was published in 1781. Yet Necker was prepared to countenance two aspects of the *ancien régime*: he was no friend of uniformity at the expense of the provinces, nor did he believe that a *cadastre* could work in a complex kingdom such as France.[78] Necker wrote after his second fall from power in 1790:

... On se trompe, en présumant que toutes les difficultés inhérentes à la répartition d'un impôt territorial seroient terminées, s'il existoit dans le Royaume un cadastre général; car pour rendre utile l'application de ce cadastre, il faudroit que la masse totale de l'impôt fût divisée entre les Départemens, par somme numérique ... un pareil partage seroit une source interminable de discussions....[79]

The combined failure to resolve the problem of provincial privilege and to amalgamate the separate indirect and direct revenue systems into an *impôt unique*, or at least a consolidated revenue system applicable to all provinces, had one inevitable consequence: a gross discrepancy in the per capita fiscal burden between regions. This is an extremely difficult problem to discuss because of the paucity of accurate data. Some estimate can be made of the per capita fiscal burden in ten northern *généralités* in 1677, but for direct taxes only. The evidence from the *généralité* of Alençon suggests that depopulation occurred in those parishes which were most heavily taxed. The fiscal burden in this area was 11.52 *livres* per hearth (*feu*) in 1677 (countryside only) or 145.6 *livres* to the square kilometre. The comparable figures at Amiens were 11.07 and 125.7 respectively; at Bourges, 12.20 and 54.17; at Caen, 12.94 and 180.8; at Châlons, 12.21 and 76.8; at Orléans, 17 and 108.5; at Paris, 18.84 and 194.2; at Rouen, 15.94 and 207.72; at Soissons, 13.33 and 130.9; and at Tours, 13.80 and 130.2.[80] For the situation at the end of the *ancien régime* we

---

[78] On Necker's ideas, see Harris, pp. 84–98. The Physiocrats themselves were divided on what sort of fiscal system was desirable, and on the practicality of the *impôt unique* (G. Weulersse, *La Physiocratie sous les ministères de Turgot et de Necker, 1774–81* (1950), pp. 155, 282–5). Quesnay, the father of the Physiocratic movement, clearly believed that the *cadastre* had to follow upon, and not precede, agricultural prosperity or the Crown would be the loser (R. L. Meek, *The Economics of Physiocracy: Essays and Translations* (1962), p. 185; François Quesnay et la Physiocratie (2 vols., Institut national d'Études démographiques, 1958), ii. 613). But the inability of the Physiocrats to advise the ruler of Baden-Durlach on precisely how to implement the single-tax system suggests that there was an abstract, if not utopian, aspect to their thinking on this central fiscal issue (K. Tribe, *Governing Economy: the Reformation of German Economic Discourse, 1750–1840* (Cambridge, 1988), pp. 124–6). The controller-general closest to the Physiocrats, Turgot, was unable to introduce far-reaching reforms in office (E. Faure, *La Disgrâce de Turgot: 12 mai 1776* (1961)).

[79] *Sur l'administration de M. Necker par lui-même* (1791), pp. 159–60.

[80] J. Dupâquier, *Statistiques Démographiques du Bassin parisien, 1636–1720* (1977), pp. 60, 103, 135, 208, 316, 366, 463, 558, 597, 675. These figures are for the countryside only; the results are different if the figures for the towns are included. Note at *ibid.*, p. 6, the destruction of the original tax rolls, which removed a vital

have perforce to fall back on Necker's figures, despite the fact that he was *parti pris* on one side of the argument for financial reform. These figures suggest that total revenues imposed on the provinces in the seventeen-eighties had reached 568 million; the population of France was said to be 24.7 million; the per capita fiscal burden on average should therefore have been in the region of twenty-three *livres* per individual. But in the *généralité* of Lyon, the unfortunate taxpayer was paying thirty *livres*; in the *généralité* of Rouen he was paying almost thirty-seven *livres*; while in the *généralité* of Paris he was paying the incredible figure of over sixty-four *livres*! Some of the burden may be explained, it is true, by the proximity of the capital or other great urban conglomerations.[81] But this is only part of the story. If we leave aside the very low figure of Corsica (a mere 4 *livres* 7 *sous*), we can state with reasonable assurance that all the frontier regions or recently acquired provinces were contributing proportionately much less than the Bassin parisien: on different scales, this was true of Aix (Provence), Auch and Pau, Besançon, Dijon (Burgundy), Grenoble, Lille, Metz, Nancy (Lorraine), Perpignan (Roussillon), Rennes (Brittany), Strasbourg (Alsace) and Valenciennes (Flandres). The pattern is more complicated than this, and merits further investigation, since in the *pays d'états* a great deal of revenue was disbursed locally in expenditure and thus never arrived at the Treasury. Nevertheless, some at least of the fiscal grievances voiced in the *cahiers de doléances* of 1789 for the estates general are borne out by the evidence.[82]

Political instability and the checks on reform raise the fundamental question of what sort of monarchy, and with it what sort of revenue system, could be developed in the eighteenth century to meet the Crown's needs. Indeed, could a revenue 'system', in the sense of a coherent entity, be developed at all? The overwhelming impression gained of the eighteenth century in France is of a government which opted out of the hard decision to tax its citizens more heavily, and instead resorted to borrowing. The early years of the century under Chamillart's ministry (1699-1708) had seen the folly of using paper inflation to cover the revenue shortfall, above all in the experiment of the *billets de monnaie*. Malet contended that when Desmaretz entered office, the total debts of the French monarchy, including expenses for 1708 itself, were estimated to be in the region of 651.5 million (they became an actual total of 674.7 million once current expenses were known), of which 343.7 million was in paper. By 1710, according to Malet, 161.2 million of this paper had been redeemed, so that the total paper debt stood at 182.5 million, on which interest of 15.2 million was due up to 1 January 1710.[83] It was, of course, an attractive idea to found a bank to help get rid of this paper, doubtless one of the reasons why Law's System was at first accepted in France. Frenchmen were agreed

---

source for the historian. Cf. *idem*, *La Population rurale du Bassin parisien à l'Époque de Louis XIV* (1979), pp. 220-4.

[81] This point was made by Morineau in relation to Necker's table: Morineau, 'Budgets de l'État', p. 322 n. 93.

[82] Necker's table is usefully reprinted in *Atlas de la Révolution française*, v (2), p. 46.

[83] Malet, pp. 136-9.

on the advantages which the Bank of Amsterdam had given the Dutch, as the Bank of England had the English, and on the desirability of emulating this success. The problem was how the Crown could attempt to bring this about given its generally parlous financial position: 'c'est une maxime certaine que l'on ne peut etablir une banque sans un fond reel en especes d'or et d'argent ou sans un fond de papiers agreables au public.' The Crown lacked gold and silver reserves, so this option was ruled out; but 'faire le fond de la banque en papiers, cela ne changeroit point la prevention du public contre ce papier'.[84]

This warning, which was made in 1709, might well have been levelled against John Law's System, the revolutionary attempt in France in 1718-20 to move extremely rapidly from a specie-based system to one in which specie played no role. Law also aimed at reducing the interest payments on the national debt and removing the tax collecting powers of the financiers, who, he contended, in reality lent the king his own money (the surplus taxes that they had collected for themselves). In so doing, he was confronting head on the fundamental interest groups at work in the *ancien régime*, and it is possible to argue that for this reason alone he was predestined to fail. Yet Law's System did not fail because it was blocked by any one group or combination of interest groups, but for reasons of its own dynamic: Law expanded the market capital of his company from thirty-four million *livres* to over five billion *livres* between August 1717 and October 1719. While at first the rapid rise in the share price increased confidence in the System, capital gains rather than dividends occupied the minds of most 'investors'; shrewd operators such as Richard Cantillon were quick to exploit the advantages this bull market offered.[85] The reality, of course, was that the expansion of Law's System had greatly outstripped the growth of the real economy, and on 21 May 1720 shares were reduced by four-ninths and banknotes were to be reduced by a half between May and December. The decree was revoked on 27 May due to popular pressure, but confidence in the System never recovered from this moment. It was the excessive expansion of the scheme, rather than the resistance of vested interest groups, which brought about the final collapse of the System on 17 July 1720.[86] Confidence in financial innovation and paper money was lost for the rest of the *ancien régime*, and far from reducing the public debt, Law had in fact succeeded in increasing it.[87] When Law was once more cited with approval, it was during the Revolution, in the debates preceding the introduction of the notorious *assignats*.

Two other important aspects of the failure of the System are also worth stressing. Firstly, Law had tried to amalgamate the two main aspects of the revenue collection

---

[84] A.N., G⁷ 363 [Anon, but certainly Trudaine:] Memoire en Reponse a la propos[iti]on de l'etabliss[e]m[ent] d'une banque a Lion, n.d. [27 July 1709?].

[85] A. E. Murphy, *Richard Cantillon: Entrepreneur and Economist* (Oxford, 1986). The author is grateful to Mr. Murphy for allowing him to consult an as yet unpublished paper on John Law and the Mississippi System.

[86] For this date see: E. Faure, *17 juillet 1720: la Banqueroute de Law* (1977).

[87] Thus B.N., MS. fr. 7752, p. 578, which evaluated the debt in 1723 at 1,935.5 million as against 1,250 million in 1715. Forbonnais reached similar conclusions, citing figures of the *effets* presented to the *visa* as 2,222.6 million, with the visa annulling 521.9 million. There was thus a debt of 1,700.7 million (Forbonnais, ii. 642). The figure of 1,700 million is cited by more recent authorities (H. J. Shakespeare, *France: the Royal Loans—Les Emprunts Royaux, 1689-1789* (Dorrington, 1986), p. 89).

process within his system, that is to say, to take over both the *ferme générale* and the *receveurs généraux des finances*. Law later described his intentions in his *Histoire des Finances pendant la Régence*:

... Le projet de M. Law étoit de simplifier les revenus, afin d'y entretenir l'ordre facilement et de diminuer les frais de régie, de faire arriver dans la Banque tous les revenus du Roy, de la rendre le centre de la recette et de la dépense de l'Etat.... La régie auroit peu couté. Le Roy auroit été plus puissant et plus riche, le peuple en payant davantage auroit été soulagé, par ce que le bon ordre auroit porté la recette en entier dans la caisse générale, d'où elle seroit sortie pour se répandre rapidement partout où il étoit nécessaire, et cette circulation perpétuelle auroit empêché les amas particuliers d'argent qui mettent une obstruction léthargique dans les affaires....[88]

In short, Law was the great innovator. Law's *Compagnie des Indes* took over the lease of the general farms on 27 August 1719, with an offer to lend the Crown 1,200 million at three per cent per annum.[89] The *recettes générales* and *pays d'impositions* were added on 12 October 1719 ('... qu'il importoit au bien de ses sujets que le recouurement de ses deniers se trouuât dans les mêmes mains pour en faciliter la perception ...').[90] Only the *pays d'états* remained firmly outside the newly integrated revenue raising process. But with the collapse of Law's System, the process of amalgamation was put firmly into reverse in January 1721.[91] Only on one other occasion in the *ancien régime* was even a part of this scheme repeated: Necker's reduction of the *receveurs généraux des finances* from forty-eight to twelve in 1780 had to be rescinded the following year. Other finance ministers were prepared to concede, with Laverdy, that since the receivers and farmers-general controlled 200 million of the Crown's revenues, there was simply no choice but to do busines with them.[92] The transfer from administration by office and revenue farm to direct administration or *régie* was a European trend in the eighteenth century.[93] It is clear that France did not take on the solution adopted by the Austrian Habsburgs in some of their lands, of combining the revenue farm with an aspect of direct administration by reserving one third of the profit of the farm to the Crown and appointing administrators to ensure proper accounting. Instead, France remained (except for the years of Necker's changes) bound by the traditional forms of office, sureties, separate *caisses* and revenue farming.[94] Necker's figures for the administration of the *aides* and *domaines* under the *régie* of Jean Vincent René (six years from

---

[88] *Oeuvres complètes de John Law*, iii. 321-2.
[89] A.N., E 2007 fos. 478-86, 27 Aug. 1719.
[90] A.N., E 2008 fo. 300, 12 Oct. 1719, 'au moyen de quoy les fonctions des receueurs generaux des pays d'election, que des prouinces d'Alsace, Trois Eveschez, Franche Comté, Flandres, Hainault, et Roussillon deuenant inutils...'.
[91] A.N., E 939a fo. 53, 14 Jan. 1721, referring to the taking over of the *régie* for the general farms. Cf. Moreau de Beaumont, iv. 348: '... La chute du système entraîna celle de tous les nouueaux arrangemens qui avoient été faits dans la régie et administration des différentes branches des revenus de l'État ...'. A decree of 5 Jan. 1721 reversed the arrangements for the *recettes générales*.
[92] Durand, p. 57.
[93] P. G. M. Dickson, *Finance and Government under Maria Theresia, 1740-80* (2 vols., Oxford, 1987), ii. 51 n. 54.
[94] J. F. Bosher, *French Finances, 1770-95: from Business to Bureaucracy* (Cambridge, 1970).

1 January 1781) suggest that indirect taxes could be administered more efficiently than under the traditional system of revenue farming.[95]

The second aspect of Law's System which prompts comment was its increasing tendency towards authoritarianism.[96] It was not inevitable that financial reform in the eighteenth century would need to go down this path. Terray and Maupeou represented a later incarnation of this trend towards ministerial despotism in 1770-1; but, as has been seen, Necker differed quite markedly from Law in his view of the future shape of a reformed French monarchy and vigorously criticized Terray's policy of arbitrarily reducing the rate of interest payable to creditors of the state.[97] Even Law, who given his Scots origins was not surprisingly influenced by the Bank of England and the role played by parliament, had inclined towards concessions to the Parisian sovereign courts. *Devenir royaliste contre son inclination* was Law's only option once the Parisian courts refused to become 'les dépositaires de tout le revenu du Royaume ... en modérant le danger de l'excès du despotisme et du pouvoir arbitraire'.[98] The suspicions aroused by Law's methods as well as his ideas, and the furious opposition of the sovereign courts to the System during its last months, set a pattern for the future. Even after the collapse of the System, the reduction of the total loan debt from 2,500 million *livres* to 1,700 million after the *visa* of 1720-1 seemed an arbitrary measure. A fixed monetary value was seen as imperative if the Crown was ever to recover financial confidence and thus re-establish its credit. Not only did proponents of public credit schemes seek to limit them to a fixed quantity determined in advance (even if repeated on many occasions); there was also a tendency for corporations such as the *parlements* or representative bodies such as the estates to guarantee new loans. Above all, bold new schemes which might seem like a return to a version of the System were ruled out: the sovereign courts used their enhanced authority to block new fiscal measures.

It has been argued that the reliance on loans rather than new taxes was not in itself the cause of the financial problems of the French monarchy at the end of the *ancien régime* and that it is possible to imagine a sustainable budget deficit.[99] This point is controversial, but a comparison with England suggests that the English national debt in 1786 was higher in real terms on a revenue base that was lower. However, the French loan schemes of the eighteenth century (predominantly life rents and *tontines*) were expensive to operate, and there was an increasing tendency to accumulate new loans towards the end of the *ancien régime*: the total debt of the Crown in 1789 may have been in the region of five billion.[100] Already in 1776,

---

[95] Massaloux, p. 77. Necker gave figures for a cost of 2.34 million on 46.5 million revenue, or 5%.

[96] This theme has been developed in T. E. Kaiser, 'Money, despotism and public opinion in early 18th-century France: John Law and the debate on royal credit', *Jour. Modern Hist.*, lxiii (1991), 1-28.

[97] Necker called them 'réductions arbitraires' and advocated placing 'l'ordre des finances sous la garde de la Nation entière ...' (*Sur l'administration*, pp. 70, 73, 76). Cf. Harris, pp. 71-2, 87.

[98] *Oeuvres complètes de John Law*, iii. 321, 330.

[99] See White.

[100] A.N., AD IX 517, 'Tableau de ce que les Rentes Viagères & Tontines créées depuis 1733 ont coûté à l'Etat jusques & compris l'année 1788'. (The author thanks Claude Jollin for this reference.) The total debt of the French monarchy in 1789 is not easy to calculate. The 'Etat de la dette publique constituée au 1er janvier 1789' gives a total raised in capital of 1,861,820,258 livres (M. Marion, *Histoire financière de la France depuis 1715* (3 vols., 1914-21, repr. 1927), i. 472-3). But this was only part of the debt. C.-N. Duclos-Dufresnoy gave the

Adam Smith had noted that England had a tax burden of about ten million pounds (say 228 million *livres*) 'without it being possible to say that any particular order is oppressed'. France had a population and land area roughly three times that of England. Why should a tax burden of under fifteen million pounds sterling (Smith put the revenue at between 308 and 325 million *livres*) seem so heavy? 'The people of France... it is generally acknowledged', wrote Smith, 'are much more oppressed by taxes than the people of Great Britain.'[101] He considered that the *taille* and *capitation* should be abolished, and replaced by an increased *vingtième*; the indirect taxes and customs duties should be levied uniformly throughout the kingdom (he had earlier denounced the extent of regional privilege),[102] thus freeing the internal market from tariffs levied by one province against another; and thirdly, the profits of the revenue farmers-general should be subjected to the 'immediate inspection and direction of government'.[103] This was unlikely to be achieved, he thought, because 'the private interest of individuals' prevented it. Smith also noted that 'in France a much greater proportion of the publick debts consists in annuities for lives than in England',[104] while in general he thought that France illustrated his principle that 'the practice of funding [a debt] has gradually enfeebled every state which has adopted it.... The debts of Spain are of very long standing.... France, notwithstanding all its natural resources, languishes under an oppressive load of the same kind.'[105]

It is this context which makes the scheme for a loan of 100 million *livres* to strengthen the ministry of the hundred hours against the estates general in July 1789 so telling a death throe of the *ancien régime*.[106] And among the papers of the marquis de Bombelles, there was a plan to remodel the royal finances (undated, but probably July 1789) which aimed to suppress the main financiers and recreate them 'sous le titre d'administrateurs, desquels tous les revenus du Royaume dépendraient par une réunion de privilèges exclusifs sur tous les produits imaginables'.[107] Even

---

total debt as 4,952,145,065 *livres*, but this was at 1 Aug. 1790, which included the evaluation of offices and also 425.7 million in loans and *assignats* since 1789 (*Le calcul du capital de la dette publique* ... (1790): the author thanks Claude Jollin for this reference). Riley was inclined towards the view that French indebtedness in 1788 was 'significantly less than 5 billion *livres*' (J. C. Riley, *International Government Finance and the Amsterdam Capital Market, 1740-1815* (Cambridge, Mass., 1980), pp. 112, 289, n. 18).

[101] Adam Smith, *An Inquiry into the Nature and Causes of the Wealth of Nations*, ed. R. H. Campbell, A. S. Skinner, W. B. Todd (2 vols., Oxford, 1976), ii. 905. Also quoted in P. Mathias and P. K. O'Brien, 'Taxation in Britain and France, 1715-1810: a comparison of the social and economic incidence of taxes collected for the central governments', *Jour. European Econ. Hist.*, vii (1978), 635-6. Also quoted in Harris, p. 69.

[102] Smith, *Wealth of Nations*, ii. 900-1. Although he did note that 'such various and complicated revenue laws are not peculiar to France' (ibid., ii. 901). For the attempt to revise the customs areas see J. F. Bosher, *The Single Duty Project: a Study of the Movement for a French Customs Union in the 18th Century* (1964).

[103] Smith, *Wealth of Nations*, ii. 904-5. For Smith, 'the best and most frugal way of levying a tax can never be by farm' (ii. 902). In the case of the French duties on tobacco and salt, Smith noted that to the profit of the farmer was added 'the still more exorbitant one of the monopolist' (ii. 903).

[104] *Ibid.*, ii. 918.

[105] *Ibid.*, ii. 928.

[106] M. Price, 'The "ministry of the Hundred Hours": a reappraisal', *French Hist.*, iv (1990), 330.

[107] *Ibid.*, p. 337.

Louis XVI seems to have been convinced of the justice of the third estate's cause in 1789, and alienated by the resistance of the privileged orders to his programme of tax reform during the *révolte nobiliaire* of the previous year. His alleged reply to the queen, reported by the comtesse d'Adhémar, suggests that the future of the Bourbon monarchy was not inevitably linked with an adamant commitment to the *status quo* in fiscal matters:

> Mais, au fond, est-ce que ceux du tiers ne sont pas aussi mes enfans, et mes enfans en plus grand nombre? Ne serai-je plus leur roi lors même que la noblesse perdrait une portion de ses privilèges et le clergé quelques bribes de son revenu?[108]

Louis XVI, it seems, was prepared to become a constitutional monarch, and to accept, indeed to welcome, fiscal reform. Nevertheless, Louis XVI spectacularly failed to impress with his new credentials as a constitutional monarch and paid the price with his head. The fundamental political division of the *ancien régime*, the province, and the administrative division, the *généralité*, which had been important factors in creating differences in the per capita fiscal burden, were abolished. Instead, the countryside was divided into uniform-sized (or very nearly so) departments in order to implement the decision of 11 August 1789 that France would henceforth be a country without social, corporate or regional privilege.[109] Subsequently, the *ferme générale* was dismantled and on 8 May 1794, twenty-eight of the last group of *fermiers généraux* were guillotined for 'toutes espèces d'exactions et de concussions sur le peuple français'.[110]

Who benefited from the fiscal settlement of the French Revolution? The French population almost certainly paid heavier taxes, rather than lighter ones, as a result of the policies of the Revolution, despite some early, over-optimistic, calculations. But the repartition of taxes at local level was effected more equitably, it seems.[111] What had really changed was that the government had ceased to rely on indirect revenues, although this may not have been the initial intention of the revolutionaries. Precise figures are hard to come by, but in 1791 it was estimated that indirect taxes had fallen from 287.2 million to 133 million, while direct taxes had risen in proportion (from 171.2 million to 300 million).[112] Thereafter the reliance on direct taxes increased, and indirect taxes diminished still further.[113] The revolutionaries could agree relatively easily on the abandonment of all trace of *l'ancien régime arbitraire* and the need to avoid *l'esprit du système* of a single tax. They found it much harder to reach decisions on what to put in the place of the discredited *taille, capitation, dixième, vingtième* and *gabelles*. All they could be certain of was the need to avoid taxpayers' voluntary declarations of wealth and the general

---

[108] *Ibid.*, p. 322.
[109] M. Forsyth, *Reason and Revolution: the Political Thought of the Abbé Sieyes* (Leicester, 1987), pp. 158–9.
[110] *Gazette nationale ou le Moniteur universel*, 231, 21 Floréal l'an 2 (10 May 1794), p. 428: the execution of the farmers general took place on 19 Floréal (i.e. 8 May).
[111] Lemarchand, p. 543.
[112] Marion, *Histoire financière*, ii. 255–6.
[113] F. Hincker, 'Les finances publiques de la Révolution et de l'Empire et le développement économique', *La Révolution française et le Développement du Capitalisme*, ed. G. Gayot and J. P. Hirsch (Revue du Nord, v, hors série, 1989), p. 84.

principle of 'une contribution commune ... également répartie entre tous les citoyens en raison de leurs facultés', a principle which was enshrined in article 13 of the Declaration of the Rights of Man. It was also clear that the precious new title of *citoyen actif* would carry with it a commensurate fiscal responsibility.[114] If the reliance on direct taxes and paper *assignats*[115] in the early years of the Revolution suggests a return to some of the financial and fiscal expedients of Louis XIV's reign, something akin to the modern fiscal state was nevertheless born in the period of the Revolutionary Wars. Henceforth, Frenchmen would vote for their tax increases, however unpalatable, and in this respect 1815 (if not 1789) formed a decisive break with the *ancien régime*.[116]

---

[114] *Assemblée Nationale. Procès verbal*, xxxiv (1790), 'Rapport fait au nom du Comité de l'Imposition sur la contribution personnelle imprimé par ordre de l'Assemblée Nationale', especially pp. 1, 3-4, 5. This document refers to article 21 of the Declaration, which alludes to the version drafted by the VIe bureau of the National Assembly. This was chosen on 19 Aug. 1789 as the basis for discussion on the Declaration of the Rights of Man, and this clause was inserted without amendment as clause 13 in the final declaration on 26 Aug. (B. Schickhardt, *Die Erklärung der Menschen- und Bürgerrechte von 1789-91 in den Debatten der National Versammlung* (Berlin, 1931), pp. 85, 103, and unpaginated appendix. The author thanks Murray Forsyth for this reference.)

[115] S. E. Harris, *The Assignats* (Cambridge, Mass., 1930; repr. New York, 1969); G. Jacoud, 'La monnaie fiduciaire: d'une émission libérée au privilège de la Banque de France (26 octobre 1795-14 avril 1803)', *Histoire économique: Études III*, pp. 87-135.

[116] B. Théret, 'Le système français libéral du xixe siècle: bureaucratie ou capitalisme?', *ibid.*, pp. 137-224, who comments at p. 143: 'C'est donc dans l'apparition d'un régime parlementaire, c'est-à-dire d'un nouveau règlement de copropriété de l'État territorial dans lequel le vote de l'impôt, puis celui des dépenses publiques, occupent une place centrale, que réside la rupture révolutionnaire fondamentale'.

XIII

LOUIS XIII, RICHELIEU, AND THE ROYAL FINANCES

We need to start, perhaps, with an assertion that the subject to be studied is not simply Richelieu and the king's finances, but Louis XIII, his various ministers (including finance ministers), and the royal finances. The distinction may seem either self-evident or tautological, but it has taken the appearance of Lloyd Moote's biography of *Louis XIII, the Just* to reaffirm what should always have been evident: that from 1617, if not before, we are dealing with a king of age to rule personally, who at times sought to do so. A recognition that the king could, and did, dispose of ministers and ratify appointments, albeit under the guidance of his chief minister, is fundamental for an understanding of the development of his financial policy.[1] In 1624, 1636, and 1643, the king rid himself of the services respectively of La Vieuville, Servien, and Sublet des Noyers for reasons which had something to do with financial policy,[2] although other issues were involved; in 1636 and 1637 Bullion appealed directly to the king, when it seemed that Richelieu might

---

The author wishes to thank Dr Graham Smith for his computing advice and Dr Margaret Bonney for the statistical work and preparation of the graphs for this article. Research assistance from the British Academy and from the Economic and Social Research Council (award no. R000231968) for the E[uropean] S[tate] F[inance] D[ata]b[ase], an international collaborative project in data collection, is gratefully acknowledged by the author. A personal research award from the Leverhulme Trust has permitted the checking of figures and the consultation of additional MSS relevant both to this subject and to a projected study of the intendants of Louis XIV. The ESFDB datasets cited in this chapter may be consulted after 1993 via JANET/ERN at the ESRC Data Archive in the Univ. of Essex. A list of abbreviations used is given at the end of this chapter.

[1] A. L. Moote, *Louis XIII, the Just* (Berkeley, Calif., 1989), 105, 107–8, 167, 169, 171. One searches in vain e.g. for any real discussion of the king's control of financial policy in P. Chevallier, *Louis XIII, roi cornélien* (Paris, 1979). The title itself suggests that it is difficult to find Louis XIII at all in M. Carmona, *La France de Richelieu* (Paris, 1984), although at pp. 129–37 there is a discussion of 'le budget de la nation'.

[2] R. J. Bonney, *The King's Debts: Finance and Politics in France* (Oxford, 1981), 112, 160. Id., *Political Change in France under Richelieu and Mazarin* (Oxford, 1978), 15 n. 3.

dismiss him after the apparent failure of the war effort.³ After Bullion's death, Louis XIII noted that he missed his firmness (did he also miss his corruption?), so that it is clear that the support was indeed forthcoming:⁴ and after Bullion's death in 1640 the king also questioned Richelieu's judgement that Bouthillier was capable of managing financial affairs as sole *surintendant*.⁵

Louis XIII also discharged some royal expenditure himself and accounted to no one for it. Even if there is no evidence that he used the *comptants ès mains du roi* on anything like the scale of Louis XIV,⁶ as far as the royal finances were concerned, so-called 'absolutism' nevertheless had a direct financial implication. However, Louis XIII displayed no great understanding of financial issues. Had the king possessed any real acumen in this area, could he seriously have thought in 1634 that open intervention in the Thirty Years War would cost just a million a year more than the annual subsidy to the Swedish and Dutch allies?⁷

It is difficult to analyse a thirty-three-year reign as one long financial period. Similarly, Henri IV's reign was too short, and the reign of Louis XIV too long, for a financial comparison of the reigns, in the manner of Saint-Simon's *Parallèle des trois premiers rois Bourbons*, to make any sense. We have, perforce, to see the seventeenth century in terms of ministries, not just because they form more coherent periods for discussion but also because of the political role of the chief minister or other important political figures. Richelieu exercised rights of nomination over the position of finance minister, the significance of which was commented upon by contemporaries. Shortly before he won the battle of Castelnaudary against the forces of the rebellious duc de Montmorency in Languedoc, Schomberg (himself a former *surintendant*) remarked to Richelieu on the appointment of Bullion and Bouthillier: 'c'est un choix digne de v[ot]re prudence, et duquel il n'y aura jamais sujet de se repentir. Ils estoient desja dans les affaires[;] la confiance, la suffisance et la probité y sont, et l'[o]n sy maintiendra par la

---

³ Bonney, *Political Change*, 43. AAE France 820, fo. 258, 9 May 1636. AAE France 826, fo. 227, 25 Mar. 1637.
⁴ O. A. Ranum, *Richelieu and the Councillors of Louis XIII* (Oxford, 1963), 165.
⁵ Moote, *Louis XIII*, 171, and, ultimately, Ranum, *Councillors of Louis XIII*, 165.
⁶ Thus the expenditure accounts for 1636, which do not include *comptants par certification*, contain payments by the king (*comptants ès mains du roi*) totalling 240,000 *livres*: BN Naf 164. The figures provided by Malet (see n. 12 below) indicate much higher levels of expenditure of this type by Louis XIV, and indeed this category is not specifically identified before 1661 in his tables. For the explanation of secret expenditure, see Richard Bonney, 'The Secret Expenses of Richelieu and Mazarin', *English Historical Review*, 91 (1976), 825–36.
⁷ Bonney, *King's Debts*, 169. On the amount of the subsidy to Sweden: ibid. 163–4.

douceur de leurs humeurs et le pouvoir que vous avez sur l'un et sur l'autre....'.[8]

A brief introduction to the fiscal system inherited by Louis XIII, Richelieu, and the finance ministers in 1624 is necessary to set the context. Since the system was both complex and the product of a long period of evolution it defies simple analysis. The French kingdom had developed three main types of revenue: direct taxes, indirect taxes, and *affaires extraordinaires*. Under the category of direct taxes we place the *taille* and the *taillon* (although there were variants of these taxes within the provinces which retained provincial estates, the *pays d'états*). Prior to Richelieu's ministry, and during his early years in power, some of these direct taxes had been alienated, that is to say the right to collect them had been sold off to private individuals who collected what were known as the *droits aliénés*: these private rights were revoked in 1634. Subsequently, a number of new direct taxes were established under Louis XIII and Richelieu, most notably a new military tax called the *subsistances*. By the end of Richelieu's ministry, the revenue from these taxes was anticipated in the form of loans from financiers, on whose agents were conferred the right of collection. This is sometimes, incorrectly, referred to as the farming of direct taxes.[9] True revenue farming was exclusively reserved to the area of indirect taxes. The revenue farm was a fixed lease conferring exclusive rights of collection on the revenue farmer and his agents for a number of years. This system, which was largely created during Sully's ministry (1598–1611), virtually excluded royal officials from the administration of indirect taxes such as those on the consumption of salt (the various farms of the *gabelles*); drink (the *aides*); and on the circulation of goods in various parts of the kingdom allocated to particular farms (the *cinq grosses fermes* and the regional variants such as the farm of the *convoy et comptablie* of Bordeaux). The third main type of revenue, the *affaires extraordinaires*, comprised virtually everything else that did not fall under the other two categories. Strictly speaking, the 'extraordinary taxes' were those raised by the method of *traités*, or one-off tax contracts with financiers: the financier undertook to raise a fixed sum of money in return for a standard rate of interest. Such contracts might concern the establishment of new offices, or new annuities (*rentes*), or any of a plethora of fiscal expedients that had already been used

---

[8] AAE France 802, fo. 328, 5 Aug. 1632.
[9] There is much information on direct taxes in Bonney, *Political Change*, chs. 8 and 9 (pp. 163–213), and J. B. Collins, *Fiscal Limits of Absolutism Direct Taxation in Early Seventeenth-Century France* (Berkeley, Calif., 1988).

before 1624, and which were further developed by Louis XIII's and Richelieu's finance ministers.[10]

I

However influential the king and Richelieu might have been in the appointment or dismissal of finance ministers, once installed, the *surintendants des finances* were left to manage affairs without much in the way of direct royal supervision and only sporadic interventions by the chief minister. Louis XIII and Richelieu appointed only five *surintendants* in all: Bochart de Champigny, Marillac, d'Effiat, and Bullion and Bouthillier, of whom the last two served for the longest period, just over eight years (1632–40; Bouthillier remained sole *surintendant* until June 1643).[11] Stability rather than change was the order of the day, in marked contrast to periods of political upheaval such as the Fronde (when there were eight *surintendants* in five years). Yet though Richelieu's *surintendants* were in post longer than their successors at the time of the Fronde, the five separate changes of financial regime do not lend themselves to statistical analysis. It is therefore more appropriate to take Richelieu's ministry as a continuum and to compare it with five other ministerial periods in the seventeenth century. The ministries selected are those of Sully (here represented by the period 1600–10 only: he had been appointed *surintendant* in 1598 and was forced out of office in January 1611); the predecessors of Richelieu (the period 1611–23); Mazarin (for the years 1643–60 only: he died in March 1661); Colbert; and the successors of Colbert.

Before proceeding further, it is necessary to make some comment about the source material which permits this comparison to be made. In the absence of other manuscript sources covering a comparable period, Jean-Roland Malet (d. 1736, a chief clerk in the finance ministry whose tables of statistics were posthumously published in 1789) still remains the fundamental source for the financial history of the seventeenth century (that is, with the exception of the years 1657–61 and 1696–9 for which he provides no data). Whatever

---

[10] The system is explained in more detail in Bonney, *King's Debts*, 293–6, and in id., 'The State and its Revenues in *Ancien-Régime* France', *Historical Research*, 65 (1992), 150–76. There are also detailed articles by Françoise Bayard in *Dictionnaire du grand siècle*, ed. F. Bluche (Paris, 1990), 53 (*aides*), 585–6 (*fermes*), 593–6 (*financiers, fiscalité directe*, and *fiscalité indirecte*), 631–2 (*gabelle*), 1499–1500 (*tailles*), 1529–30 (*traités*).

[11] The list in Bonney, *King's Debts*, 285–6, has been confirmed by M. Antoine, *Le Dur Métier de roi* (Paris, 1986), 41 n. 37, and most recently by Bernard Barbiche in his contribution on the *surintendants* in *Dictionnaire du grand siècle*, ed. Bluche, 1494.

TABLE 1. Comparison of Malet's figures and the contemporary accounts for the year 1633

	Guénégaud's accounts	Malet
TOTAL REVENUE	57,450,336	57,464,923
Receptes générales (fo. 274^v)	8,376,504	8,374,393[a]
Bois (fo. 276)	580,751	580,474
Taillon (fo. 277)	1,115,794	1,115,794
Aydes (fo. 277^v)	2,179,884	2,179,893
Cinq grosses fermes (fo. 278^v)	1,618,401	1,618,401
Convoy de Bordeaux (fo. 279)	1,529,246	not itemized separately
Gabelles de France (fo. 281^v)	138,111	138,661
Other *gabelles* (fos. 282–3)[b]	1,385,392	1,464,392
Parties casuelles (fo. 293^v)[c]	28,236,934	28,231,028
Deniers extraordinaires (fo. 300^v)	11,019,968	10,418,987
TOTAL EXPENDITURE (fo. 310)	57,510,336	57,069,390
Comptants per certification (fo. 309^v)	19,127,444	29,752,935[d]

[a] Income from the *taille*, including both *pays d'élections* and *pays d'états*.
[b] Addition of separate items.
[c] Income from offices.
[d] The figure in Malet is also at variance with that compiled by the Chambre des Comptes (19,349,157 *livres*).

criticisms one may level at his figures, they form the only continuous set of financial statistics for the seventeenth century.[12] One of the few authenticated accounts from the period of Richelieu's ministry is that of Gabriel de Guénégaud for 1632.[13] This was presented to the council of finance on 30 May 1633 and was passed with the signatures of Chancellor Séguier, Bullion, Bouthillier, Mallier, and Particelli on 13 June 1633.[14] It is a relatively simple task to compare the figures in this manuscript with those presented by Malet (see table). The main problem is the breakdown of expenditure between

---

[12] J. R. Malet, *Comptes rendus de l'administration des finances du royaume de France*... (London, 1789). For his life and work, see R. J. Bonney, 'Jean-Roland Malet: Historian of the Finances of the French Monarchy', *French History*, 5 (1991), 180–233. The critical edn. of Malet's figures in the ESFDB is forthcoming in Margaret and Richard Bonney, *Jean-Roland Malet: Premier Historien des finances de la monarchie française* (Comité pour l'histoire économique et financière de la France; Paris, due out in 1993).

[13] The chief treasurer was in correspondence with Richelieu in the summer of 1632, 'afin que l'on ne me puisse imputer aucune faulte': AAE France 804, fo. 270, 19 July 1632.

[14] BI Godefroy 144, fos. 259–310. Cf. Bonney, *King's Debts*, 164 n. 4.

ordinary and extraordinary, where Malet's figures differ from those of the other sources for the period (although the figures for total expenditure are very close). In other respects, the similarity between the figures is striking.

The relative importance of different types of expenditure can be appreciated rapidly from Chart 1, which may perhaps help to overturn some preconceptions about the merits and demerits of certain ministers.[15] 'Extraordinary' expenses were higher during Richelieu's ministry, at 51 per cent of the total, than at any other time in the seventeenth century, with the exception of Mazarin's period as chief minister, when the figure reached nearly 66 per cent of the total. The much criticized predecessors of Richelieu, who used this type of expenditure for only 28 per cent of the total, were almost as prudent as the reforming Colbert, for whose period in office they comprised a mere 22 per cent of the total. The great reformer, Sully, whose reputation was secure in the eighteenth century as the last honest finance minister of the ancien régime—a reputation which, on the whole, has been reinforced by Aristide's recent study of his fortune[16]—used this type of expenditure almost as much as Richelieu and his *surintendants* did, for sums which amounted to 46 per cent of total expenditure, although in Sully's case the purpose was different.[17] In contrast, the much criticized successors of Colbert—Le Peletier and Pontchartrain (Malet's figures are complete only until 1695 and therefore do not include the whole of Pontchartrain's ministry)—used extraordinary expenditure much more sparingly, for a mere 14 per cent of the total.

The significance of this type of expenditure, chiefly *comptants par certification*, has been emphasized elsewhere[18] so that it is only necessary here to discuss its main aspects. The Chambre des Comptes audited expenditure in great detail, except for those expenses which were covered by the rules of government secrecy (*comptants*); under this category merely the total amount was presented for audit. Before Colbert's ministry, the secret expenses were abused by the government as a means of conferring excessive interest rates on financiers and of making other dubious financial transactions which it would

---

[15] ESFDB dataset \rjb\malet\malb009. Cf. chart 1 in Bonney, 'Jean-Roland Malet', 227, where the figures are calculated by decades for the entire 17th cent. A list of abbreviations used in charts and graphs is given at the end of this chapter.

[16] Isabelle Aristide, *La Fortune de Sully* (Comité pour l'histoire économique et financière de la France; Paris, 1990), who estimates (p. 92) his fortune in 1610, shortly before leaving office, at only 2.2 million *livres*.

[17] Malet characterizes such expenses under Henri IV and Sully as 'remboursements, intérêts d'avance &c' but after 1611 as 'Dépenses & gratifications par comptant'.

[18] Bonney, 'Secret Expenses'.

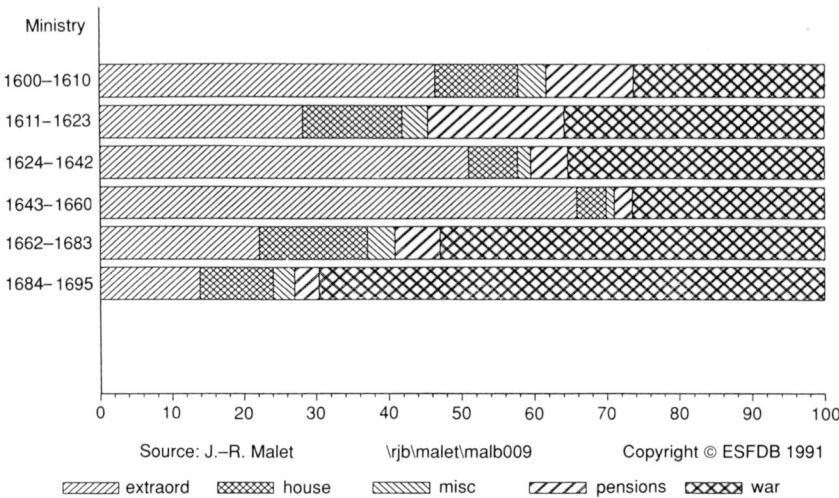

Chart 1: Categories of French royal expenditure by ministries, 1600–95

have been difficult to pass through the relatively open auditing process. In the years before 1661, much extraordinary expenditure took the form of paper transactions, including the deferring of actual payment from one accounting year to the next by the procedure known as the 'ordonnance de remise en d'autre Épargne'.[19] The greatly reduced reliance on extraordinary expenditure under Colbert reflects a conscious ministerial decision to avoid the public criticism which Foucquet's policy in the 1650s, and that of his predecessors, including Richelieu's *surintendants* (above all, Bullion),[20] had provoked. Thus the extent of reliance on extraordinary expenditure is both an index of the potential for corruption and a measurement of the autocratic nature of the ministry, of its unwillingness to submit detailed expenditure accounts to the auditing process of the Chambre des Comptes.[21]

The innovative nature of Richelieu's ministry is clearly demonstrated when extraordinary expenditure is removed from the cal-

---

[19] Bonney, *King's Debts*, 174.
[20] Ibid. 181–2.
[21] For growing unease of the Chambre des Comptes by 1631, and its later view that 1630 was the turning-point after which the abuses in financial administration reached disastrous proportions: ibid. 157–8.

culations (Chart 2).²² Never again in the seventeenth century did expenditure on war fall back to the low levels of Richelieu's predecessors, to the relatively modest 49 per cent of ordinary expenditure under Sully, and almost 50 per cent under Jeannin, Schomberg, and La Vieuville. Military expenditure during Richelieu's ministry amounted to 72 per cent of ordinary expenditure. This was exceeded only under Mazarin and Colbert's successors; under Colbert himself the decade of peace in the 1660s reduced the proportion of military expenses to 68 per cent of ordinary expenditure. Here, then, was a significant change under Louis XIII and Richelieu: in proportionate terms, expenditure on pensions and the various royal households declined in significance, and with the exception of household expenses under Colbert (which rose to 19 per cent of the total, the same figure as under Richelieu's predecessors), this became the new balance of expenditure in the seventeenth century.

Since Malet provides no figures for extraordinary revenues after 1661 it is impossible to pursue this method of analysis for total revenues after this date, except by using other sources, but ordinary revenues may be analysed under the same ministries (Chart 3).²³ Here, the striking feature of Richelieu's administration, which has been commented on elsewhere in the context of Bullion's *surintendance*,²⁴ was the extent of its reliance on income from the *parties casuelles*. It reached the record figure for the seventeenth century of 46 per cent of ordinary income. Under Mazarin, income from this source rapidly declined in importance (to a mere 17 per cent), and the proportion fell further still under Colbert and his successors. It is clear that the fall was not quite so dramatic as Malet's figures seem to suggest because part of the income drawn from the world of office-holding was redefined under Colbert and his successors as 'extraordinary revenue'.²⁵ Even so, a fundamental change in revenue-raising occurred under Richelieu which was not repeated later; and the difficulties faced by the regency government in dealing with the office-holders at the outbreak of the Fronde were at least partly a consequence of the excesses of the previous administration. The corollary of reliance on the *officiers* as a mainstay of ordinary revenue was that those two sturdy revenues of the ancien régime, the *taille* and the revenue farms of indirect revenues, reached

---

[22] ESFDB dataset \rjb\malet\malbo10. Cf. chart 2 in Bonney, 'Jean-Roland Malet', 228, where the figures are calculated by decades for the entire 17th cent.
[23] ESFDB dataset \rjb\malet\malbo11. Cf. chart 3 in Bonney, 'Jean-Roland Malet', 229, where the figures are calculated by decades for the entire 17th cent.
[24] Bonney, *King's Debts*, 177, 198.
[25] This seems clear from AN KK 355, which enumerates additional taxes on *officiers* sometimes under extraordinary and sometimes under ordinary revenues.

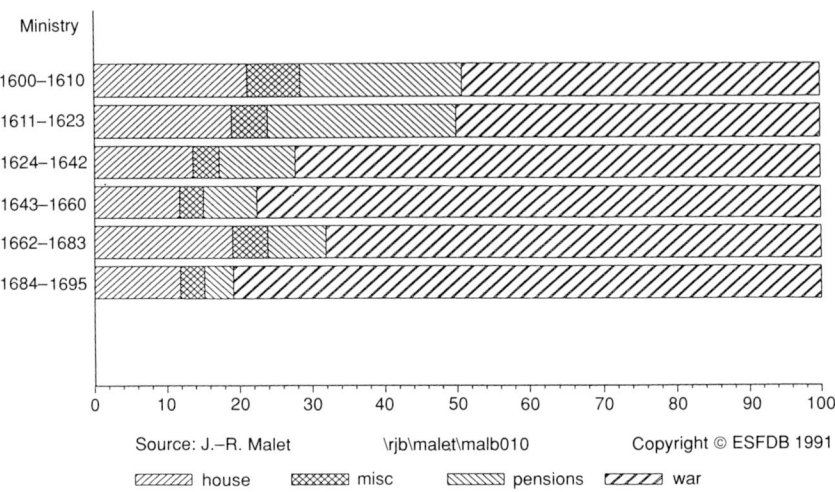

Chart 2: Categories of French royal expenditure by ministries, 1600–95 (excluding extraordinary expenditure)

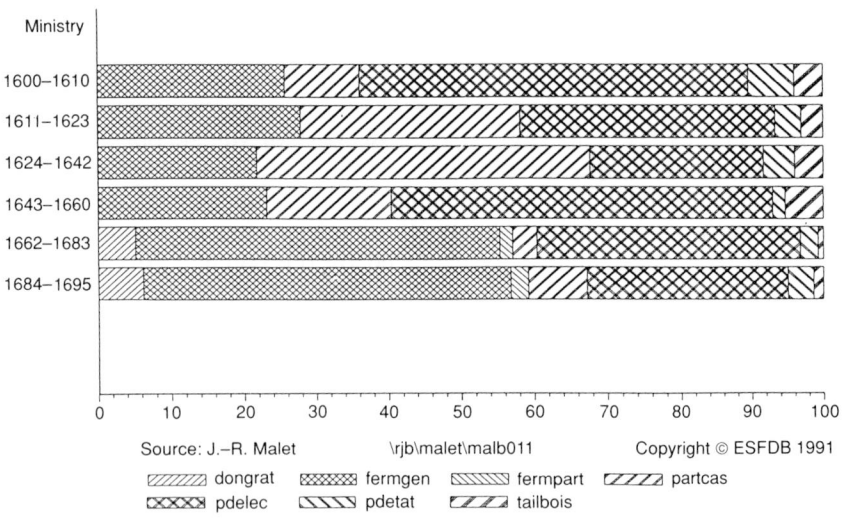

Chart 3: Categories of ordinary revenues of the French monarchy by ministries, 1600–95

an all-time low for the seventeenth century, respectively just under 24 per cent and just under 22 of the total under Richelieu. In contrast to the picture for expenditure, the balance of ordinary revenues under Richelieu is at variance with the rest of the period. Not until the war of the Spanish Succession, it seems, would the relative fiscal burden fall so heavily on the *officiers* compared to the rest of the population.

This picture is further clarified if the various categories of ordinary and extraordinary revenue are viewed in quinquennial periods before and during Richelieu's ministry (Chart 4: the base period is taken to be Louis XIII's reign, to which is added the year 1644 to maintain even divisions by quinquennia).[26] Extraordinary revenues ('denextra' on the chart, *deniers extraordinaires* in Malet's terminology) do not predominate in the first quinquennium of Louis XIII's reign (1610–14); at 31 per cent of total revenue they were on a par with the income from the *taille* from the *pays d'élections* received by the treasury (as distinct from the levy in the provinces, an important difference which will be discussed later). Nor do they predominate in the second quinquennium, the period after the Estates General (1615–19), because the *pays d'élections* and the revenue farms remained more important, even if only marginally so, at respectively 29 per cent and 26 per cent of total revenues compared to 22 per cent for extraordinary revenues. Three quinquennia followed (1620–4, 1625–9, 1630–4) in which the *parties casuelles* predominated even in comparison with extraordinary revenues and gradually squeezed out the contribution from the *pays d'élections*.[27] Only in the quinquennium after France's entry into the Thirty Years War in 1635 did the extraordinary revenues achieve the predominance which they were to retain during the remainder of Richelieu's ministry.[28]

Once extraordinary revenues are excluded from the analysis, the predominance of the *parties casuelles* between 1620 and 1639 remains clear (Chart 5).[29] Income from this source at its high point in the years 1630–4 reached 55 per cent of ordinary revenue. Before 1620 and after 1640 income from the *pays d'élections* assumed its greatest

---

[26] ESFDB dataset \rjb\malet\malbo12.

[27] R. Mousnier, *La Vénalité des offices sous Henri IV et Louis XIII* (2nd edn.; Paris, 1971), 421, where the proportions are calculated as annual figures as a % of total income (i.e. including extraordinary revenues) for the years 1600–43. Mousnier noted (p. 422), 'c'est donc de 1620 à 1633 que cette importance relative est la plus grande'.

[28] These calculations appeared in Bonney, *King's Debts*, 313, but the definition of the categories has been modified subsequently in line with those used in Bonney, 'Jean-Roland Malet', 229, which included income from the *pays d'états* in the calculations as a separate item (and thus reduced the proportion of miscellaneous revenues).

[29] ESFDB dataset \rjb\malet\malbo13.

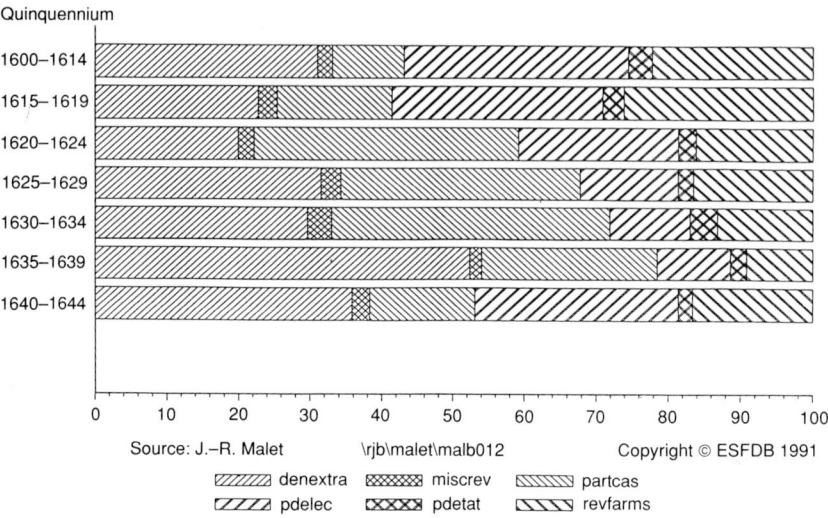

Chart 4: Categories of ordinary and extraordinary revenues of the French monarchy, 1610–44

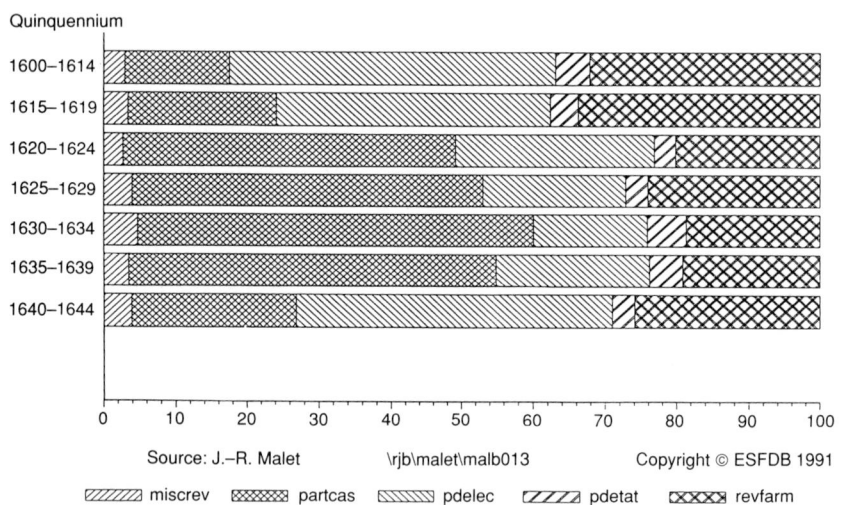

Chart 5: Categories of ordinary revenues of the French monarchy, 1610–44

proportionate significance: income from the areas without representative institutions accounted for 45 per cent of ordinary revenue in the years 1610–14, 38 per cent in the years 1615–19, and 44 per cent in the years 1640–4. Income from the revenue farms amounted to about a third of ordinary revenue in the first decade of Louis XIII's reign, but under a quarter in the second decade; it fell in the 1630s to under 20 per cent, but rose once more to just over a quarter of ordinary revenue after 1640. Consumption of salt and other commodities fell with the subsistence crisis of 1628–31 and the economic dislocation resulting from France's entry into the Thirty Years War; substantial remissions had to be accorded to the revenue farmers to prevent bankruptcy and the abandonment of their leases, and this proved to be the pattern in the 1640s.[30] Income from the *pays d'états* always averaged below 6 per cent in Louis XIII's reign.

II

There is a danger that in presenting proportions of revenue and expenditure for the seventeenth century a static impression of the overall 'budget' is given.[31] The figures were, of course, on the increase. Looking back on the reign of Louis XIII, and reflecting on the origins of the Fronde, Omer Talon concluded that more taxes had been raised by that king than all his predecessors put together. A better informed contemporary, writing in 1644, estimated that 700 million in *affaires extraordinaires* had been brought to the treasury since 1620, while the gains of the financiers on this type of transaction had amounted to 172 million.[32] The rise in secret expenditure, or expenditure by means of *comptants par certification*, in the reign of Louis XIII is clear from Graph 1, where other sources can be brought to bear on Malet's figures to establish a pattern.[33] A similar trend may be established from Malet's figures from the *pays d'élections*, the revenue farms, and the *parties casuelles* (Graph 2).[34] Wherever we look, the figures are on the increase. The treasury yield of revenues increased close to the declaration of war on Spain in

---

[30] Richard Bonney, 'The Failure of the French Revenue Farms, 1600–60', *Economic History Review*, 2nd. ser. 32 (1979), 18–19. The precise reason for the fall in income from the revenue farms in 1620–4 is less clear, except in terms of dislocation resulting from the revolts of the queen mother and the Huguenot revolt of 1621–2.
[31] On the question of the 'budget' see the sources cited in Bonney, 'Jean-Roland Malet', 208 n. 139.
[32] Both contemporaries cited by Bonney, *King's Debts*, 188–9.
[33] ESFDB dataset \rjb\malet\malgo31.   [34] ESFDB dataset \rjb\malet\malgo32.

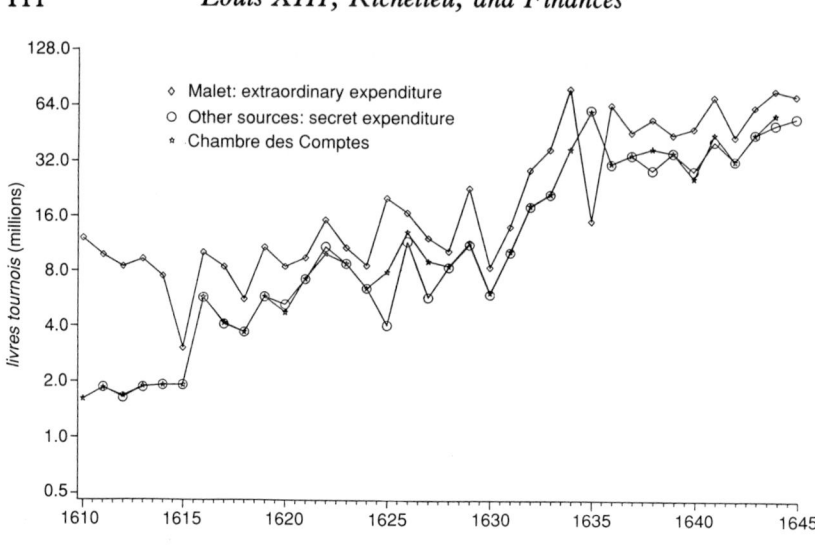

Graph 1: Malet's extraordinary expenditure totals compared with other sources, 1610–45 (semi-logarithmic scale)

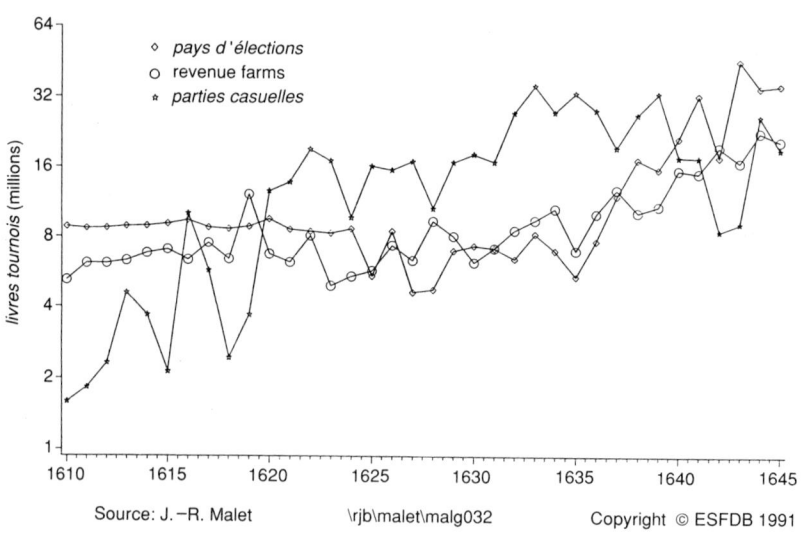

Graph 2: Semi-logarithmic graph of total receipts from the *pays d'élections*, revenue farms, and *parties casuelles*, 1610–45

1635; but as will be seen, the first real increase in taxation in the provinces had occurred earlier, before Richelieu's ministry.

Was the French intervention in the Thirty Years War financed by monetary expansion (which Bullion had hoped for in 1632)[35] or by borrowing and tax contracts—in short, by paper transactions?[36] This question can be partially resolved by setting the figures for mint output against the contracts for loans and *traités* (Graph 3).[37] There was a significant increase in mint output in the 1630s and 1640s, but on the whole this followed, rather than preceded, the revenue generated by loans and tax contracts (or more precisely, the agreement of contractors to loans and *traités*, since the actual income was often produced many months later). By 1636, Bullion was once more concerned at the lack of investment in loans and tax contracts, and the devaluation of that year was aimed at encouraging participation, since inactive cash deposits lost their value.[38]

When Malet's evidence concerning the treasury yield from the *pays d'élections* is presented according to ministries, the figures demonstrate a broad uniformity in the yield from direct taxes paid by the different regions throughout the seventeenth century (Chart 6).[39] This reflects a fiscal conservatism on the part of ministers: it was considered dangerous to meddle with the traditional allocation between one province and another. However, it also in some measure relates to the capacity to pay. Thus, the northern region (here defined as the *généralités* of Paris, Soissons, Amiens—including the Boulonnais—and Châlons) provided 15 per cent of the total income from the *pays d'élections* from the period of Sully's ministry until the end of Richelieu's ministry; from Mazarin's ministry onwards, this region provided about 20 per cent of the total. Under Richelieu, the central region (here defined as the *généralités* of Orléans, Tours, Bourges, and Moulins) provided under 18 per cent of the total income from the *pays d'élections*, its lowest proportion in the seventeenth century (under Sully the figure had reached 25 per cent of the total). In contrast, the south-east region within the *pays d'élections* (here defined as the *généralités* of Lyons, Riom, and Grenoble) provided a higher amount of revenue to the treasury than formerly

---

[35] Bonney, *King's Debts*, 171. For mint issues in France in this period: F. C. Spooner, *The International Economy and Monetary Movements in France, 1493–1725* (Cambridge, Mass., 1972).

[36] Bonney, *King's Debts*, 174–5.

[37] ESFDB dataset \rjb\kingdebt\kdg002.

[38] Bonney, *King's Debts*, 171. The devaluation of 1636 is discussed most fully in Spooner, *International Economy*, 181–2.

[39] ESFDB dataset \rjb\malet\malb015. Cf. chart 5 in Bonney, 'Jean-Roland Malet', 231, where the figures are calculated by decades for the entire 17th cent.

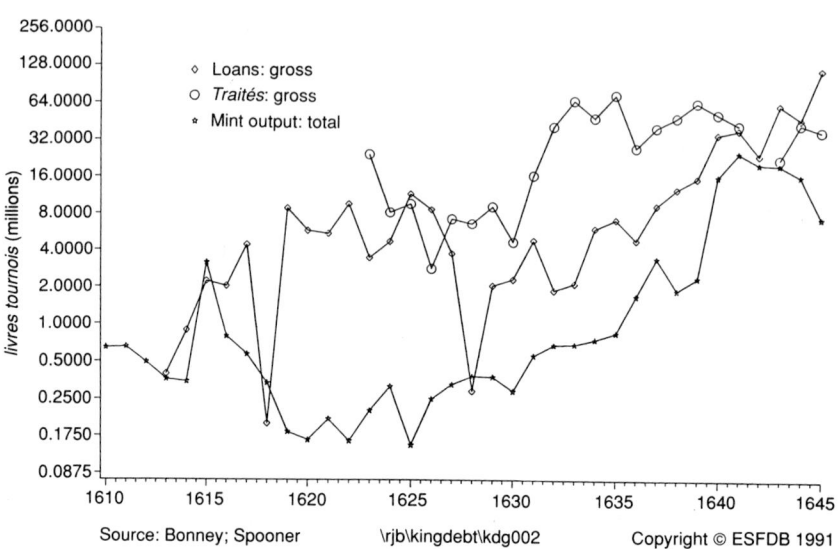

Graph 3: Royal borrowing and *affaires extraordinaires*, 1610–45, set against mint output

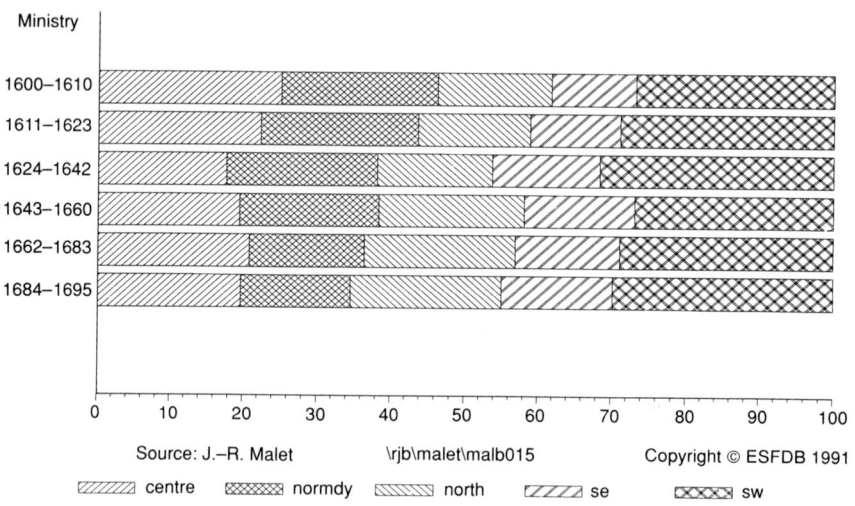

Chart 6: Receipts of direct taxes from the *pays d'élections* by region and by ministries, 1600–95

(some 14.7 per cent of the total), which remained about the level for the rest of the century. The south-west (here defined as the *généralités* of Poitiers, Limoges, Bordeaux, and Montauban—the latter established under Richelieu in 1635)[40] reached its highest point (some 31.5 per cent of the total) under Richelieu, declined markedly under Mazarin, and never rose again to the level of the first cardinal's ministry. Finally, Normandy (the *généralités* of Alençon—established under Richelieu in 1636—Caen, and Rouen) provided just over 20 per cent of the total under Richelieu, a somewhat smaller proportion than in Sully's ministry and under Richelieu's predecessors; this proportion fell consistently during the rest of the seventeenth century. When the figures are viewed in greater detail, and presented in quinquennial totals for Louis XIII's reign, the northern region within the *pays d'élections* (here defined as before) shows the greatest fluctuation, from as low as 12 per cent of the total at the beginning of Richelieu's ministry to as high as 20 per cent (Chart 7).[41] The south-eastern region within the *pays d'élections* was consistently the lowest contributor to the treasury (at between 12 and 15 per cent of the total); while the south-western region was consistently the highest (at between 27 and 32 per cent of the total).

What of the areas where provincial estates survived during Richelieu's ministry? Chart 8 takes Malet's evidence concerning the treasury yield from both the *pays d'élections* and the *pays d'états* and presents this for the whole of the seventeenth century, according to ministries.[42] The interest of this chart lies in the inclusion of the relatively small yield from the *pays d'états* ('pdetotal': the figures for the levy in the provinces themselves were much higher than was the yield to the treasury; a higher proportion of revenues was assigned to local expenses in the *pays d'états* than in the *pays d'élections*). In fact, the contribution of provinces with estates during Richelieu's ministry was the third highest for the seventeenth century: at over 15 per cent of the total, it exceeded the contribution of these areas under Sully, Richelieu's predecessors, and Mazarin (when the figure fell to a derisory 3 per cent of the total). Only under Colbert, and especially under his successors, was the contribution from the *pays d'états* significantly higher.

When these figures are viewed in greater detail for the relevant period, the rise in the contribution of the provinces with estates

---

[40] La Rochelle is added for the period after 1661.
[41] The year 1644 is added to maintain even divisions by quinquennia: ESFDB dataset \rjb\malet\malbo16.
[42] ESFDB dataset \rjb\malet\malbo17. Cf. chart 7 in Bonney, 'Jean-Roland Malet', 233, where the figures are calculated by decades for the entire 17th cent.

XIII

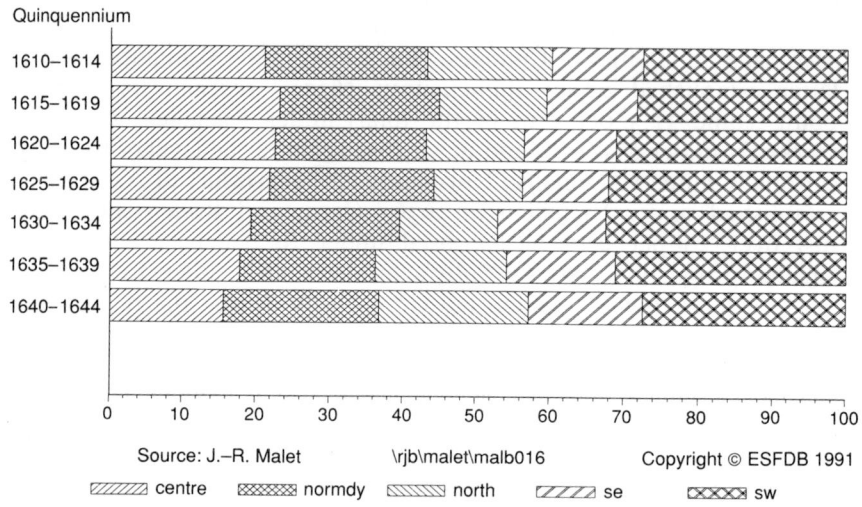

Chart 7: Receipts of direct taxes from the *pays d'élections* by region, 1610–44

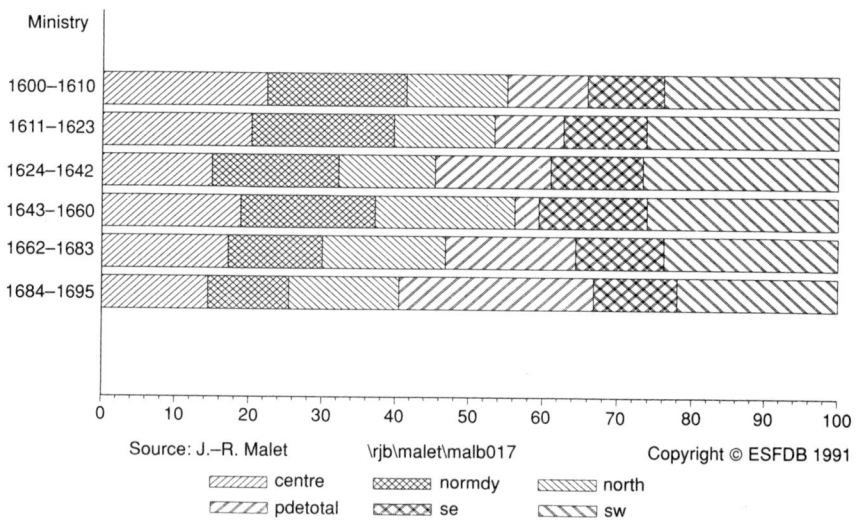

Chart 8: Receipts from the *pays d'élections* and the *pays d'états* by ministries, 1600–95 (chiefly direct taxes)

under Richelieu's ministry is confirmed (Chart 9).[43] The figures do not, however, substantiate Professor Major's view that it was Marillac who put the pressure on the *pays d'états* with the creation of *élections* in 1628.[44] Rather, the sudden increase in revenues from the *pays d'états* in the period 1630–4 can be accounted for by d'Effiat's insistence on high rates of payment by the provinces to compensate for the revocation in 1631–2 of *élections*, and the imposition on Languedoc of the regime of the edict of Béziers of 1632 (a measure which at least guaranteed a minimum amount of revenue to the crown). Revenue from this source increased from 13 per cent of the total in the years 1625–9 to 25.8 per cent in the years 1630–4. The contribution of the *pays d'états* relative to the *pays d'élections* fell back thereafter, with a dramatic fall in the last year of Richelieu's ministry. This does not necessarily imply that the fiscal burden in the *pays d'états* was reduced. It may be the case that in wartime Richelieu preferred political stability (and hence low taxes) in the frontier regions; but these areas also suffered from the billeting of troops who took what they wanted in addition to their legitimate entitlement under the levy known as winter quarter.[45]

These figures may be compared with those for the levy on the provinces (Chart 10).[46] Professor Collins provides the figures for the levy in fifteen *généralités* of the *pays d'élections* for 1597, 1599, 1600, 1607, 1609, 1620, 1634, 1640, and 1643; the years 1594, 1639, and 1647 have been added to those drawn from his table. The figures are not entirely comparable to those provided by Malet, for two reasons. One is that Malet always included a number of *généralités* omitted from Collins's list: thus the figures from eighteen *généralités* are incorporated in Charts 6–9 for the later part of Richelieu's ministry. Secondly, as Malet himself made clear, contemporary accounting practice before 1660 did not permit a detailed breakdown between the levy, the charges, and the net revenue.[47] Malet's figures therefore inform us about what, for want of a better term, we might call 'disposable treasury revenue', not the total levy on the provinces.

---

[43] ESFDB dataset \rjb\malet\malbo18.

[44] The provinces affected were Dauphiné, Burgundy, Languedoc, and Provence: J. R. Major, *Representative Government in Early Modern France* (New Haven, Conn., 1980). This thesis is discussed in Bonney, *Political Change*, 349–50, and id., 'Absolutism: What's in a Name?', *French History*, 1 (1987), 112 n. 92.

[45] For the edict of Béziers as a restriction on the levy in Languedoc: Bonney, *Political Change*, 380. The effect of military levies is discussed in W. H. Beik, *Absolutism and Society in Seventeenth-Century France* (Cambridge, 1985), 141. Since the *quartier d'hiver* was discharged locally, it affected the amount of tax revenue received by the central government.

[46] ESFDB dataset \rjb\colbo01. Collins, *Fiscal Limits of Absolutism*, 162.

[47] Malet, *Comptes rendus*, 182, quoted in Bonney, 'Jean-Roland Malet', 204.

XIII

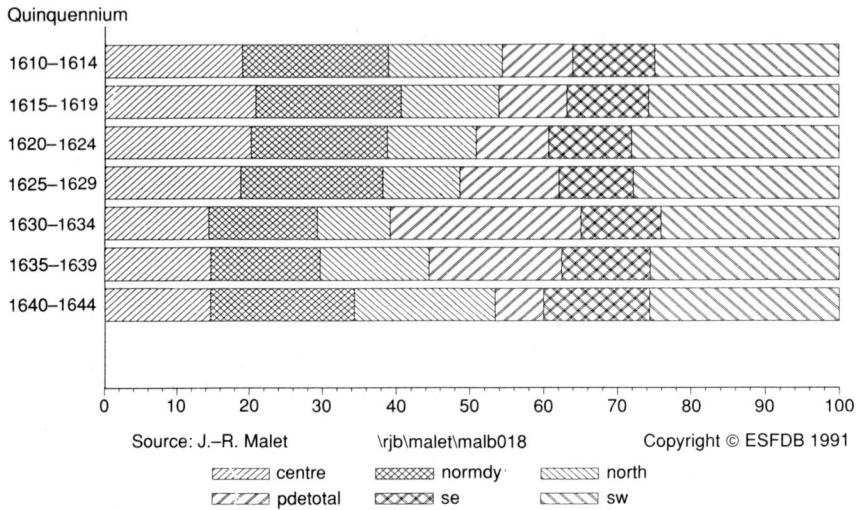

Chart 9: Receipts from the *pays d'élections* and the *pays d'états*, 1610–44 (chiefly direct taxes)

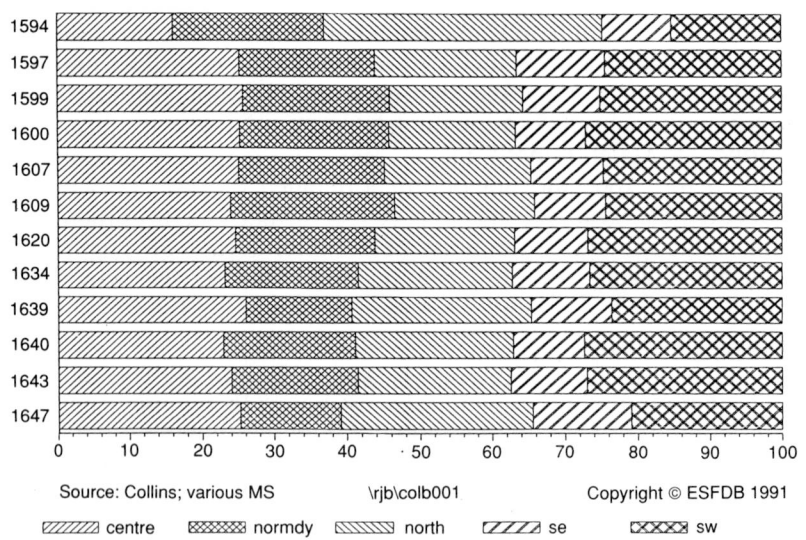

Chart 10: Direct taxes levied on the *pays d'élections* by region, 1594–1647

The figures in Chart 10, in contrast, are those for the levy. With the exception of 1594, when the Catholic League still controlled part of the kingdom, and when war taxation loomed large, the balance between the regions held reasonably steady for the levy, although less so than for payments to the treasury.[48]

The rate of tax increase in the provinces can only be ascertained from an analysis of local sources, since Malet's figures before 1660 do not enlighten us on this question. Professor Collins has provided us with two provincial series (Champagne and Normandy), respectively for the years 1602–34 and 1597–1643.[49] The series for the *élection* of Paris has been added for the years 1615–43 and the resulting graph presents the figures deflated in terms of silver value for this shorter period (Graph 4).[50] In a separate graph (Graph 5), the figures for the *élection* of Paris are presented over the longer timespan of 1615–1787, converted into index numbers to show the rate of growth from the base index of 1600–30, and recalculated on an eleven-year centred moving average so that the main trend can be seen without short-term fluctuations. The index numbers for the *taille* are also deflated by the value of grain in the same period so that the 'real' value may be perceived. The 'real' rate of increase in the period of the Thirty Years War remains impressive.[51] The figures for the *élection* of Paris show a doubling of the levy of direct taxes (including elements other than the *taille*) in the period of Richelieu's predecessors: by alienating direct taxes in the form of the *droits aliénés*, Luynes and Schomberg doubled the levy in the *élection* of Paris by 1621, to help pay for the war against the Huguenots. Shortly before the French declaration of war against Spain in 1635, the *droits aliénés* were revoked, which increased the treasury's share of the total fiscal burden to nearly a million *livres*, whereas the figure in 1625 had been under 0.4 million.[52] By the end of Louis XIII's reign, the *élection* of Paris would provide 1.4 million in direct taxes. This figure was slightly higher in nominal terms than the levy at the end of the seventeenth century. In 'real' terms, the levy actually declined in

---

[48] The figures for 1594 also include elements other than the *taille* ('a cause du domaine, aydes, impositions, tailles et crues y joinctes...'): BN MS Fr. 4680, fo. 15.

[49] Collins, *Fiscal Limits of Absolutism*, 150, 152–3.

[50] ESFDB dataset /rjb/ elego02.

[51] ESFDB dataset /rjb/ elego06. It is possible to calculate the total levy of the *taille* (i.e. *taille* plus *droits*) for only a few years in the period. For purposes of calculating the mean index numbers of the *taille*, the total levy has been used where available, with the principal of the *taille* (alone) filling in the gaps. The mean index numbers for the *taille* have also been deflated by dividing them by the index numbers for grain prices during the period, using the common base index of 1600–30 = 100. The grain figures were those of M. Baulant, 'Le Prix des grains à Paris de 1431 à 1788', *Annales: Économies, sociétés, civilisations*, 23 (1968), 539.

[52] Collins, *Fiscal Limits of Absolutism*, 136, 141.

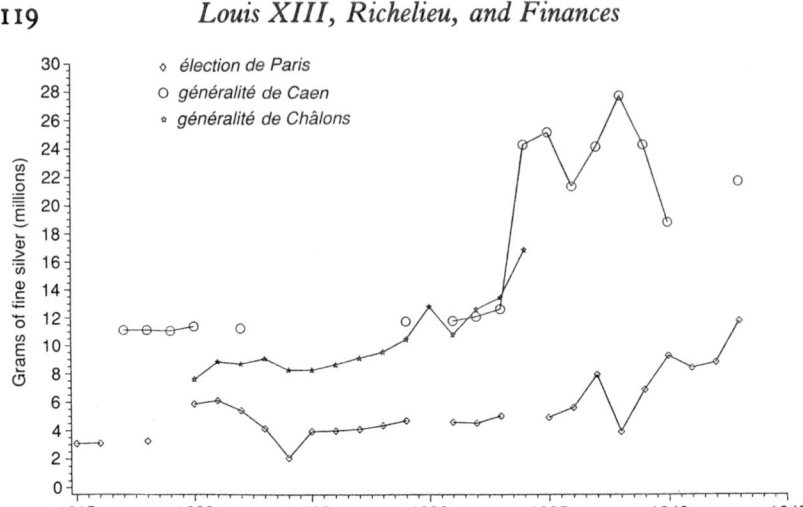

Graph 4: The value of the levy of the *taille* in the *élection* of Paris and in the *généralités* of Châlons and Caen, 1615–43, in metric tons (millions of grams of fine silver)

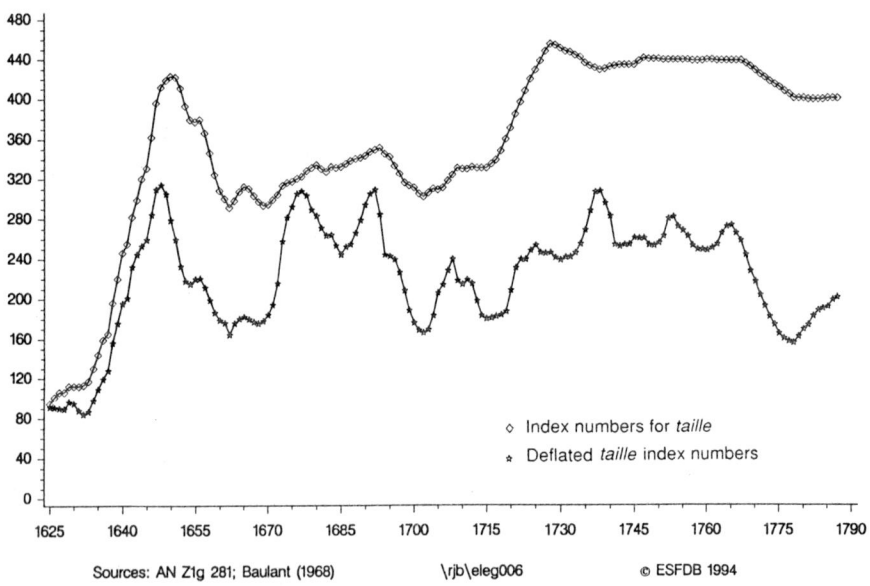

Graph 5: Eleven-year moving averages of index numbers for the *taille* in the *élection* of Paris, 1625–1787, set against 'real' *taille* index numbers (index 100 = 1600–30)

Louis XIV's reign from 1647 until the war of the Spanish Succession. The evidence from the *élection* of Paris is also of interest because it serves to test Professor Collins's argument that under Richelieu the maximum fiscal capacity of the state was reached in terms of the *taille*, at 30–35 million *livres*.[53] This argument is borne out by the accounts from Colbert's ministry onwards, where the limit of 40 million was breached only four times (in 1662, 1676, 1677, and 1678) in the seventeenth century.[54] We may estimate the fiscal burden on the *élection* of Paris at about 27.5 per cent of the *généralité* of Paris under Richelieu (it was somewhat higher at the end of the century, and may be calculated as 36 per cent of the burden on the *généralité* in the period 1688–1712)[55] and about 3.5 per cent of the total fiscal burden on the *pays d'élections*. A levy of 1.4 million on the *élection* of Paris at the end of Louis XIII's reign would thus represent a total levy in the *pays d'élections* in the region of 40 million. This was Bullion's estimate of the levy before the deduction of charges.[56]

III

By 1639–40, shortly before Bullion's death, the financial problems of the French monarchy had already become acute. In Bullion's words:[57] 'V[otre] E[minence] a raison de desirer la paix extra-ordinairement. Jamais les finances ne furent en si mauvais estat. Tous les gens de finance ne veulent entrer en aucune traitté et les peuples ne veulent rien payer...'. According to Malet's estimate, *rentes* and *gages* absorbed a total of 45.8 million by this date, and Bullion had no choice but to cut back on payments: initially he suspended a quarter of the *gages*.[58] At the same time, cash expenditure had risen because of the war effort: in peacetime, it had been usual to pay 30 million at most in cash; the limit of such expenses in practice was 40 million unless new revenues could be found. There is

---

[53] Ibid. 219. Collins states the argument as a limit on 'direct taxation'; but since this term would include the new taxes of Louis XIV's reign, the *capitation* and the *dixième*, this formulation of the argument is incorrect.

[54] ESFDB dataset \rjb\kk355\kkd004.ssd, from AN KK 355.

[55] ESFDB dataset \rjb\genb001.

[56] In 1650, the *brevet* fixed the levy at 40.2 million, of which the *élection* was to carry 1.43 million. Similiarly, in 1654, the *brevet* fixed the levy of the *taille* at 40 million; the burden on the *élection* of Paris (before reductions) was fixed at 1.43 million. For Bullion's estimate of the *taille* at '40 et tant de millions dont les charges deduictes il en revient 20 et tant de millions au Roy...': AAE France 819, fo. 97ᵛ, 'Memoire du Sr de Bullion sur les quartiers d'hiver' (1635).

[57] AAE France 834, fo. 116ᵛ, 25 Oct. (1639).

[58] Bonney, *King's Debts*, 179, and Malet, *Comptes rendus*, 94.

clear evidence that Richelieu was personally involved in establishing the priorities for expenditure.[59] The cardinal also intervened in the search for new revenues to meet such expenditure. On 2 January 1636, he met the great financier Pierre Puget de Montauron and discussed the first version of a scheme which was to become the *sol pour livre*, the 5 per cent sales tax introduced in November 1640.[60] He met Tubeuf to discuss the levy of the *subsistances* in the provinces in 1639.[61] It is also clear from Bullion's letters of the autumn of 1639 that the chief minister exercised a determining role in the main decisions (the *taxe des aisés*, the billeting of troops in Normandy after the extension of the *gabelle* into the small privileged region known as the *pays de quart bouillon*,[62] and the *affaires extraordinaires* necessary for 1640).[63]

This preoccupation of Richelieu and Bullion with the short term did not, however, preclude the hope that the war could be ended quickly and financial reforms brought about. In the last months before his death in December 1640, Bullion expressed the wish to Richelieu for 'une bonne reform[at]ion dans le royaume'.[64] Richelieu seems to have been influenced by Bullion's plans,[65] but devised his own set of proposals for restoring stability to the king's finances by creating a budgetary surplus for the first time since the ministry of Sully.[66] Royal expenditure was to be reduced drastically to 25 million 'after the peace'. All areas of royal expenditure were to be

---

[59] Bonney, *King's Debts*, 174. Bullion's last statements concerning the 40 million limit on cash expenses were shortly before his death. AAE France 835, fo. 257, 6 July (1640): 'les depenses presentes ne peuvent aller sans moyens extraordinaires et [il] faut touts les ans trouver pres de 40 millions à cause des advances pour le content'. AAE France 836, fo. 19, 9 Aug. (1640): 'l'estat que VE a ar[r]esté qui monte pour le content à 39 millions et tant de livres chose non imaginable dans le manquement des moyens extraordinaires'. AAE France 836, fo. 61, 29 Aug. (1640): 'l'ordre que VE avoit resolu pour l'année 1640 a esté excedé de plusieurs millions'.

[60] Bonney, *King's Debts*, 183–4, and AAE France 819, fos. 178, 217–18. Also AAE France 820, fos. 1, 27, and 28, 1 Jan. and 15 Jan. 1636.

[61] AAE France 833, fo. 31, 31 Jan. (1639).

[62] So-called because it enjoyed the right to free salt production, subject to paying the crown the equivalent of a quarter of the value of its production: M. Foisil, *La Révolte des Nu-Pieds et les révoltes normandes de 1639* (Paris, 1970), 152.

[63] AAE France 834, fos. 43 and 93, 1 Sept. and 11 Oct. (1639).

[64] AAE France 835, fo. 101, 7 May 1640. See Ranum, *Councillors of Louis XIII*, 146. A reform plan written in his hand was known to contemporaries and survives in the form of a copy entitled 'Ordre a préparer lors qu'il plairra à Dieu donner la paix au Royaume': BN MS 500 Colbert 194, fos. 273–4.

[65] With regard to the *rentes*, Bullion's plan was more detailed than Richelieu's although comparable figures were cited (5 million).

[66] Richelieu's own reform plan of 1639–40 is known to us under the title 'Du Card[in]al de Richelieu en 1640. Projet pour augmenter le revenu de Sa Ma[jes]té & descharger son peuple' with an accompanying 'Projet de despense après la paix': Bonney, *King's Debts*, 131 n. 1, 183. This document is transcribed for the first time in the appendix to this ch.

pruned and the need to reduce royal expenditure by abolishing the *comptants* was recognized. This was explicitly stated in Bullion's plan; Richelieu made no mention of the *comptants* except in the context of *comptants ès mains du roi*, which were envisaged at the level of a mere 300,000 *livres* per annum. The reduction in the military establishment was to be so drastic that the king's ability to fight another foreign war would have been seriously affected had the plan been implemented. On the other hand, Richelieu envisaged a total royal income of over 58 million and thus presumably a very useful war reserve of 33 million a year. This royal income would be provided from a redistribution of taxes. The chief direct tax, the *taille*, would be abolished. It would be replaced by the salt tax, which would be extended uniformly throughout the kingdom (and would raise 30 million) and the new 5 per cent sales tax (which would raise 12 million). The revenue raised from the salt tax would rise from 13 per cent to 51 per cent of the total; while the sales tax would provide 20 per cent of revenue at inception (Pie Chart 1).[67] The collapse of extraordinary expenditure in Richelieu's proposals is evident from a comparison of the figures for actual and projected expenditure under the reform plan. From 56 per cent of the total, extraordinary expenditure would fall to a mere 1.2 per cent (Pie Chart 2).[68] The budget on military expenditure rose as a proportion, but had declined in absolute terms. Household expenditure rose substantially as a proportion of the total, as did pensions, under Richelieu's reform plan.

The memoranda later edited by the *intendant des finances* Moreau de Beaumont (1713–85), which amounted, among other things, to the official history of the *gabelles* and the *aides*, explained Richelieu's intentions:[69]

Il avoit formé le projet d'une imposition uniforme dans toutes les provinces du royaume, avec une seule régie dans les marais salans dont le Roi se rendroit propriétaire. Le prix du minot, pour subvenir à toutes les dépenses, devoit être réglé, eu égard au nombre des habitants, à leur consommation dans une année. Il se proposoit par ce moyen de supprimer une grande partie des frais de régie & de ménager même des ressources qui missent en état de diminuer les autres genres d'imposition. Ce projet diffère de celui de François Ier, qui, à la vérité, avoit d'abord mis les marais salans sous sa main, mais uniquement pour en constater l'état & jusqu'à ce qu'il eût

---

[67] ESFDB dataset \rjb\malet\malio06.
[68] ESFDB dataset \rjb\malet\malio05.
[69] J.-L. Moreau de Beaumont, *Mémoires concernant les impositions et droits. Seconde partie. Impositions et droits en France* (vols. ii–iv; Paris, 1769), iii. 48.

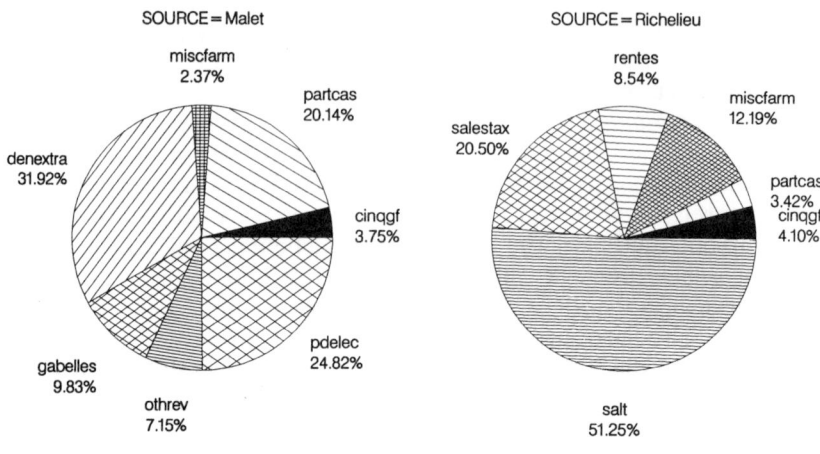

Pie chart 1: Categories of French royal revenues in 1640 according to Malet and Richelieu's reform plan

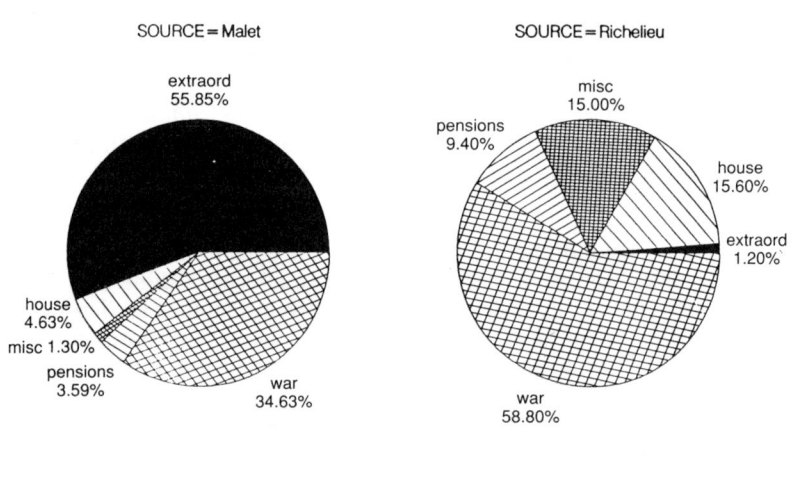

Pie chart 2: Categories of French royal expenditure in 1640 according to Malet and Richelieu's reform plan

prescrit une forme d'administration & de régie relatives à sa nouvelle opération . . .

The memorandum on the *aides* suggested that the *sol pour livre* was less radical in its purpose:[70]

Il fut crée sur la fin du règne de Louis XIII, par l'édit de novembre 1640, pour subvenir aux dépenses de la guerre, une nouvelle imposition à l'instar de l'ancien sol pour livre sur toutes les marchandises vendues, revendues & échangées, sous le nom de *subvention générale du vingtième*. La déclaration du 8 janvier suivant changea cette perception & ordonna que le nouveau droit seroit payé à l'entrée suivant des tarifs d'évaluation.

Whether or not they were feasible,[71] Richelieu's revenue proposals in his reform plan must rate with the *capitation* of 1695 and Vauban's *Projet d'une dîme royale* (written c.1697 but only published in 1707) as one of the most revolutionary fiscal ideas of the seventeenth century. They were, of course, different in nature from subsequent experiments and proposals relating to direct taxation. France and England did not rely heavily on indirect taxes (unlike Spain) in the sixteenth and seventeenth centuries. Richelieu's proposals anticipated the eighteenth-century changes in these two countries, where the greater proportionate reliance on indirect taxes tended to reinforce the social position of the upper classes.[72] To the extent that one of the revenue proposals, the sales tax or *sol pour livre*, was actually implemented, the view that Richelieu and Bullion failed to introduce any 'really new tax schemes' is perhaps not quite fair[73]

---

[70] Ibid. iii. 346.

[71] The usual judgement on the plan is that they were not, and that they showed Richelieu's ignorance of financial questions: H. Hauser, *La Pensée et l'action économiques du cardinal de Richelieu* (Paris, 1944), 178. However, this verdict in turn rests on the inaccurate (and thus incomprehensible) figures in *Test. pol.* 437–8, 441–3. André's readings for the new salt levy and the sales tax were respectively 25,000 *livres* and 12,000 *livres*! Selections from the André edn. have now been re-ed. by Daniel Dessert: see Richelieu, *Testament Politique* (Brussels, 1990). André's figures are set beside those from the document cited in n. 66 above in the appendix. Moreau de Beaumont emphasized the fact that Richelieu's plans interfered with the right of the proprietors of the *salines* to sell their salt abroad. If salt was a proper subject for taxation, 'le commerce extérieur qu'il procure est un objet digne de la plus grande attention, & qui paroit difficile à concilier avec le projet que le Cardinal de Richelieu avoit formé': *Mémoires concernant les impositions et droits*, iii. 48.

[72] 'A Tax laid upon Land seems hard to the Landholder, because it is so much Money going visibly out of his Pocket. And therefore as an Ease to himself, the Landholder is always forwarded to lay it upon Commodities . . .'. Quoted by J. V. Beckett, 'Land Tax or Excise: The Levying of Taxation in Seventeenth- and Eighteenth-Century England', *English Historical Review*, 100 (1985), 304. See also P. K. O'Brien, 'The Political Economy of British Taxation, 1660–1815', *Economic History Review*, 2nd. ser. 41 (1988), 26–7, and J. Brewer, *The Sinews of Power: War, Money and the English State, 1688–1783* (London, 1989), 95–101.

[73] Ranum, *Councillors of Louis XIII*, 137.

(although the *sol pour livre* was Henri IV's *pancarte* under another name).[74] While Sully had not opposed the establishment of the tax proposed by the Assembly of Notables of 1596, he claimed that its levy was impracticable, while its projected yield was grossly inflated; and so it had proved to be under Henri IV.[75] But whereas at the time of Sully the proponents of the *sol pour livre* had asserted that it could raise 4–5 million, by 1640 the estimated yield had risen to a minimum of 12 million.[76] There can be little doubt that, in terms of the circulation of goods, the wealth was in the kingdom waiting to be taxed, at least in peacetime. The problem was a political and an administrative one: how to organize the levy in the face of resistance. Within two months of Richelieu's death, Louis XIII succumbed to political pressure and abandoned the tax altogether.[77] In the case of Richelieu's *grand dessein du sel*, we cannot be certain that the cardinal himself would not have abandoned it in the face of opposition, given his comments and his fiscal concessions after the revolt of the Va-Nu-Pieds.[78] So we are left with a scheme on paper for the wholesale transfer of revenues—71 per cent of income was to come from the two schemes taken together, the levy on salt and the sales tax—without any political certainty that either could be levied in the kingdom at large, dominated as it was by regional privilege. Nothing came of the plan, and perhaps nothing could have come of it without a recourse to force. In this respect, perhaps, if in no other, the implications of Richelieu's plan of 1640 were akin to those in Olivares's Grand Memorandum of 1624 to reform the constitutional and fiscal structure of the Spanish Habsburg monarchy.[79]

---

[74] *Les Œconomies royales de Sully*, ed. D. J. Buisseret and B. Barbiche (vol. ii, 1595–9; Paris, 1988), 138. Sully's judgement of the scheme is worth quoting: 'l'imposition du sol pour livre qui se leveroit sur toutes sortes de vivres, denrées et marchandises, tant menues peussent-elles estre, qui seroyent vendues en detail, du revenu de laquelle les autheurs d'icelle, comme s'ilz eussent trouvé la pierre philosophale ou les mines du Perou, faisoyent une grande parade, publiant que tel revenu monteroit à plus de quatre milions de livres, faisant un certain calcul sur la despence des particuliers, lequel à l'execution se trouva ridicule et impertinent'.

[75] Ibid. 142. Sully added that the tax would be so difficult to collect that it would attract 'toutes les haines et crieries des peuples et les plainctes, reproches et importunitez des demandeurs'. See Bonney, *King's Debts*, 50.

[76] Bonney, *King's Debts*, 184.

[77] Bonney, *Political Change*, 48 n. 3 and 328–30. Moreau de Beaumont pointed out that an additional levy on drink remained within the provinces subject to the *aides*, the levy of which remained 'difficiles et dispendieuse': *Mémoires concernant les impositions et droits*, iii. 346–7.

[78] His comments are cited in Foisil, *La Révolte des Nu-Pieds*, 157, 286. The main fiscal concession was the continuing special regime of the *pays de quart bouillon*.

[79] J. H. Elliott, *The Count-Duke of Olivares* (New Haven, Conn., 1986), 197–8. Id., *Richelieu and Olivares* (Cambridge, 1984), 73–4, 77, 84.

IV

In the end, it was not Richelieu the reformer, or crypto-reformer, of the royal finances who would be remembered, but the Richelieu of the alleged *tour de vis fiscal* and the corrupt financial regime of his clients, above all Bullion. The *Mazarinades*, which may be taken as a fair reflection of popular opposition to ministerial policies at mid-century, belaboured the disastrous consequences of Richelieu's administration of the royal finances. *La Vérité toute nue...* (1652) asserted that 'On ne sçauroit penser sans horreur à la maniere dont elles ont esté administrée depuis le temps du Cardinal de Richelieu. Au lieu de choisir des homes dignes de remplir la charge de Sur-Intendant, qui est la plus importante du Royaume, principalement durant vne aussi grande guerre que celle que nous soustenous depuis tant d'années', he had appointed d'Effiat and Bullion, with Cornuel, Bordier, Galland, Lambert, Le Camus, Bretonvilliers, Bordeaux, and Tubeuf in subordinate roles: 'Ie serois trop long', the author asserted, 'si ie voulois nommer tous ceux qui ont fait comme en vn moment tant de fortunes prodigieuses....'.[80] For subsequent generations, notably Boisguilbert and Malet at the beginning of the eighteenth century, the emphasis was solely on Richelieu's *tour de vis fiscal*. Boisguilbert considered that Richelieu doubled in ten years 'tous les revenus de la Couronne; on cria extrêmement contre lui; mais c'était avec la dernière injustice que l'on faisait ces plaintes, car cette augmentation était l'effet de celle de tous les biens du Royaume, qui avait plus que doublé pareillement...'.[81] Malet, too, judged that the reign of Louis XIII saw a substantial increase in taxation, for which Richelieu's foreign policy was largely responsible ('il donna peu au soulagement des Peuples, parce qu'il donnoit tout à l'agrandissement de la Monarchie qu'il gouvernoit').[82] The Richelieu of the reform plan had largely been forgotten, despite Véron de Forbonnais's recognition that there had indeed been a plan.[83] The judgement of Voltaire, who castigated the plan as 'gibberish', has

---

[80] H. Carrier, *La Fronde: Contestation démocratique et misère paysanne* (2 vols.; Paris, 1982), i (pp. 4–5 of the *Mazarinade*, which is reproduced in its original form). For the financiers under Louis XIII, see Françoise Bayard, *Le Monde des financiers au XVIIe siècle* (Paris, 1988).

[81] *Le Détail de la France* (1695), quoted in *Pierre de Boisguilbert ou la naissance de l'économie politique*, (INED, 2 vols.; Paris, 1966), ii. 649. See also ibid. ii. 914 (*Factum de la France*, 1707): 'tous les revenus du royaume doublèrent de son temps, ainsi que ceux du Roi, auquel n'ayant trouvé que 35 millions de rente, il en laissa 70 à sa mort'.

[82] Malet, *Comptes rendus*, p. xi, and BN MS Fr. 7752, pp. 7–8, quoted by Bonney, 'Jean-Roland Malet', 191.

[83] F. Véron de Forbonnais, *Recherches et considérations sur les finances de France depuis 1595 jusqu'à l'année 1721* (2 vols.; Basle, 1758), i. 238–44.

tended to be accepted.⁸⁴ Thus the link between the reforming endeavours of the first half of the seventeenth century, chiefly the *sol pour livre* (however misguided the fiscal base of the tax), and the projects of the second half, above all the *dîme royal* of Vauban, and the new taxes of the last wars of Louis XIV's reign (the *capitation* of 1695 and the *dixième* of 1710) has been lost. The historical verdict on Richelieu has thus been narrowed;⁸⁵ and Richelieu the oppressive minister, as well as Richelieu the *affairiste*, has become the new orthodoxy.

It may seem a logical extension of the argument that Richelieu had a 'conscious and perfectly realistic ordering of priorities', in both his public and private business affairs,⁸⁶ to argue that the chief minister was properly in charge of the actions of his subordinates, the *surintendants* and *intendants des finances*. If 'the decisions which shaped the history of his wealth were his alone',⁸⁷ why should this not have been true of financial policy in general? Such an extension of the argument is not necessarily warranted, for it would assume a greater capacity to control the detailed workings of government than was possible for a chief minister in the seventeenth century. As far as is known, Richelieu never attended the *conseil d'état des finances*; Mazarin only did so in the first week of November 1643,⁸⁸ though for a few days in 1659 he contemplated becoming a joint *surintendant* with Foucquet.⁸⁹ There had been talk of Richelieu heading a group of four finance ministers in 1624;⁹⁰ but with the appointment of Bochart de Champigny and Marillac at the end of August 1624 the talk had come to nothing. It is clear that experience in managing the crown's finances was of value to a retired minister in the task of managing his private wealth, as the example of Sully demonstrates.⁹¹ But there is not a great deal of evidence that the lessons of managing a private fortune, by means of agents, helped in the task of controlling the king's finances. Bullion called Richelieu 'le meilleur mesnager en toutes fassons et pour les affaires publiques et pour les

---

⁸⁴ Voltaire commented on 'le galimatias sur les finances qu'on trouve au chapitre 9 du Testament politique' and concluded that the author was guilty of 'des fautes qu'un écolier ne commetrait pas'; either Richelieu was extraordinarily ignorant of financial questions or he was not the author of the *Testament politique*: quoted by André in *Test. pol.* 56, 495, 502.

⁸⁵ Though Carmona, it is true, has devoted a few lines to the proposed reforms: M. Carmona, *Richelieu: L'Ambition et le pouvoir* (Paris, 1983), 634–6.

⁸⁶ J. Bergin, *Cardinal Richelieu: Power and the Pursuit of Wealth* (New Haven, Conn., 1985), 67.

⁸⁷ Ibid. 68.

⁸⁸ Bonney, *Political Change*, 8 n. 2.

⁸⁹ Bonney, *King's Debts*, 1.

⁹⁰ Ibid. 114–15, and AAE France 778, fo. 196.

⁹¹ Aristide, *La Fortune de Sully*.

finances du Royaume',[92] but the cardinal always disclaimed true expertise in such matters.[93] Whether or not we accept this disclaimer must depend not merely on the evidence of the creation of Richelieu's private fortune, fundamental though this is, but on the feasibility of the reform plan of 1640. If the chief minister's scheme was more than 'gibberish', and contained (as has been argued here) not merely an internal coherence but a certain realism predicated on the idea of a return to a *status quo ante*, then we arrive not merely at a better-informed verdict on Richelieu's knowledge of the royal finances but a quite different judgement of Richelieu the 'state-builder'. The permanence of the *tour de vis fiscal* was a consequence of the continuation of the war beyond Richelieu's death. It was not something consciously willed by the cardinal, contrary to the later views of Boisguilbert and Malet. It therefore follows that as late as 1642 the state might have been 'rolled back',[94] had those famous secret peace negotiations with Philip IV (perhaps even the secret negotiations involving Cinq-Mars) led to a peace settlement in Richelieu's lifetime. This was what the public at large had hoped for on the death of Louis XIII, and it was these aspirations which the regency government so conclusively failed to meet.

Abbreviations used in charts and graphs

centre	central region within *pays d'élections*
cinqgf	*cinq grosses fermes*
denextra	*deniers extraordinaires*
dongrat	*dons gratuits* ('voluntary grants' from estates)
extraord	extraordinary income or revenue
fermgen	*fermes générales*
fermpart	*fermes particulières*
gabelles	*gabelles* (various revenue farms concerning levy of the salt tax)
house	household expenditure of the royal family
misc	miscellaneous expenditure
miscfarm	miscellaneous revenue farms
miscrev	miscellaneous revenues
normdy	Normandy
north	northern region within *pays d'élections*
othrev	other revenues

[92] AAE France 836, fo. 141, 11 Nov. 1640.
[93] Ranum, *Councillors of Louis XIII*, 136.
[94] Although the precise administrative significance of Richelieu's proposals remains elusive, the reduction in expenditure could not have failed to make its impact by restricting bureaucratic development in France.

partcas	*parties casuelles*
pdelec	direct taxes from *pays d'élections*
pdetat	*pays d'états* (chiefly direct taxes)
pensions	expenditure on gifts and pensions
pdetotal	total revenue from *pays d'états*
rentes	savings from redemption or repurchase of *rentes*
revfarms	revenue farms
salestax	sales tax (*sol pour livre*)
salt	income from salt tax after Richelieu's proposed reforms
se	south-eastern region within *pays d'élections*
sw	south-western region within *pays d'élections*
tailbois	income from *taillon* and *bois*
war	military expenditure

APPENDIX

Two Versions of Richelieu's Proposed Reform of French Finances

1. PROJECTED ROYAL REVENUE AFTER THE EXPECTED PEACE TREATY

Testament Politique, ed. André (pp. 437–8)	'Du Card^{al} de Richelieu en 1640 Projet pour augmenter le revenu de Sa Ma^{te} & descharger son peuple' (AN K 891, no. 2)
... en déchargeant entièrement le peuple de 17 millions de livres, qui reviennent maintenant aux Coffres du Roi des levées de la taille, la recette peut monter jusques à 50 millions, ainsi que l'état suivant le justifie clairement:	
De l'imposition à mettre sur le sel sur les marais ou autrement en toutes les provinces du Royaume. Il en peut revenir au Roi, tous frais faits ... 25,000	De l'imposition à mettre sur le scel soit sur les marais ou autrement en toutes les provinces du Royaume, il en peult revenir à Sa Ma^{te} ... 30,000,000 de lt
Du sol pour livre de toutes les marchandises et denrées du Royaume ... 12,000	Du sol pour livre sur toutes les marchandises et denrées ... 12,000,000 de lt
Des aides ... 400,000	De la ferme des Aydes par estimaon 2,000,000 de lt
De la réduction du rachat des rentes Constituées sur l'hôtel de ville ... 5,000,000	De la réduction ou rachapt des rentes constituées en l'hostel de ville de Paris il en reviendra à Sa Ma^{te} à déduire sur les charges la somme de ... 5,000,000 de lt
Des parties casuelles ... 2,000,000	De l'ord^{re} des parties casuelles par estimaon 2,000,000 de lt
De la ferme de Bordeaux ... 1,800,000	De la ferme du Convoy de Bordeaux & du nouveau subside imposé à Blaye & depuis transferé aud. Bordeaux ... 1,800,000 lt

Des 3 livres pour muid de vin entrant à Paris, nouvelle imposition . . . 750,000	Des trois livres pour muid de vin entrant à Paris de nouvelle imposion . . . 750,000 lt
Des 30 sols anciens et nouveaux, dix sols pour chacun muid de vin entrant à Paris . . . 580,000	Des XXXs antiens & nouveaux, X s. d'entrée sur chascun muid de vin entrant à Paris . . . 580,000 lt
De la ferme des 45 sols au lieu des péages et octrois, ci . . . 530,000	De la ferme des XLVs au lieu des péages & octroys de la rivière de Seine . . . 530,000 lt
De la ferme de Brouage . . . 254,000	De la ferme de Brouage . . . 254,000 lt
De la traité foraine de Languedoc, épiceries et drogueries de Marseille et 2 pour cent d'Arles . . . 380,000	De la traitte foraine de Languedoc, espiceries drogueries de Marseille & pour cent [sic] d'Arles . . . 380,000 lt
Des Surtaux de Lyon . . . 60,000	De la ferme du tiers surtault de la douanne de Lion . . . 60,000 lt
Des Cinq grosses fermes . . . 2,400,000	Des Cinq grosses fermes . . . 2,400,000 lt
Des nouvelles impositions de Normandie . . . 150,000	Des nouvelles imposions de Normandie dont bail a esté nouvellem. ft . . . 150,000 lt
De la Ferme du fer . . . 80,000	De la ferme du fer . . . 80,000 lt
Des ventes des bois ordinaires des Domaines . . . 550,000	Des ventes des bois ordinaires . . . 550,000 lt
TOTAL 50,483,000[a]	59,483,000[b] Sans y comprendre ce qui revient des imposions des Tailles

[a] In fact, the total was 14,971,000 livres.

[b] In fact, the total was 58,534,000 livres, including 9 lt 13 s 'pour tonneau de Picardie' (174,000 lt) and the farm of revenues from the river Loire (225,000).

2. PROJECTED ROYAL EXPENDITURE AFTER THE EXPECTED PEACE TREATY

Testament Politique, ed. André (pp. 441–3)	'Projet de despense après la paix' (AN K 891, no. 2)
	La paye de 10,000 chevaux soubz le tiltre de cent compagnies de gens d'armes qui n'estans enrollez que pour servir en cas de besoing ne recevront par an qu'un quar^{er} ... 1,300,000 lt
	La paye de 50,000 hommes du p^{er} ordre des legionnaires qui estoient enrollez dans les provinces & XXV regimens pour servir seullemt pour lors q. la nécessité le requerra ne recevront qu'une monstre pour les soldatz & quatre pour les officiers revenant à ... 1,200,000 lt
	La paye de 40,000 hommes de second ordre de gens de guerre actuellement servans qui recevront tous les jours leur pain & IIIIs de prest revenant à ... 6,000,000 de lt
	La paye de 4,000 chevaux legers payez de neuf mois au lieu qu'à présent ilz ne recoivent que 4 monstres de deux mois chascune revenans ... 1,600,000 lt
	La paye des garnisons extraord^{res} ... 1,000,000 de lt
La dépense de la [marine] de Ponant et de Levant ne sauroit être moindre que de 2 millions, ainsi qu'il paraît par les États particuliers qui en sont dressés ... 2,600,000 livres	La despense de la marine du ponant & Levant ... 2,000,000 de lt
Celle de l'artillerie reviendra à ... 600,000	Celle de l'artillerie à ... 600,000 lt
Celle des Maisons du Roi, de la Reine et de Monsieur à ci ... 3,600,000	La despense des maisons du Roy, de la Royne, de Monsieur le Dauphin & de M^r frère unique ... 3,500,000 lt

Les pensions des Suisses, dont on ne peut honorable s'exempter, sont de . . .	Les pensions des Suisses . . .
400,000	400,000 lt
Les bâtiments coûteront . . .	Les bastimens . . .
300,000	400,000 lt
Les ambassadeurs . . .	Les ambassadeurs . . .
250,000	250,000 lt
Les fortifications . . .	Les fortificaons . . .
600,000	600,000 lt
. . . les pensions et les appointements ne seront employés à l'avenir que pour . . .	Les pensions & apointemens . . .
2,000,000	2,000,000 de lt
Les [ordinaires] du Roy . . .	Les ordinaires du Roy . . .
50,000	50,000 lt
Les acquits patents . . .	Les acquits patents . . .
400,000	300,000 lt
Les parties inopinées & voyages . . .	Les parties inopinées & voyages . . .
2,000,000	2,000,000 de lt
Les nonvaleurs . . .	Nonvalleurs par estimaon . . .
150,000	1,500,000 lt
Les Comptants du Roy . . .	Les Comptans du Roy . . .
300,000	300,000 lt
Toutes ces dépenses ne reviendront qu'à 25 millions[c]	Somme de ce que dessus
	22,650,000 lt[d]

[c] In fact, the total was 13,250,000 livres.
[d] In fact, the total was 25 million livres.

XIV

'LE SECRET DE LEURS FAMILLES': THE FISCAL AND SOCIAL LIMITS OF LOUIS XIV'S *DIXIÈME*

One of the great issues in European fiscal history, indeed in the history of the state, is the relationship of the needs of government to the tax base. To what extent could the taxable capacity of a state be computed by contemporaries? What were the perceived or actual limits to a governing system's ability to extract revenue from its subjects? It has recently been argued persuasively that there was a 'fiscal limit' of some 30 to 35 million *livres* for the levy of the *taille* in seventeenth-century France, and that this restriction was imposed by the nature of the tax and the productive wealth upon which it rested.[1] This 'fiscal limit' on direct taxation was in part removed with the introduction of two new taxes, the *capitation* of 1695 and the *dixième* of 1710, which were directed at other forms of wealth and partially removed earlier fiscal exemptions. These taxes were the most important fiscal innovations of the reign of Louis XIV, and arguably in the entire history of the *ancien régime*. Scholars have been particularly interested in the *capitation*, focusing on the extent to which its tariff of taxpayers reflected the reality of the social structure of late seventeenth-century France.[2] With only a few exceptions,[3] the *dixième* of 1710 has received little scholarly attention since the studies of Marion and others at the turn

---

The author wishes to thank Dr Graham Smith for his computing advice and Dr Margaret Bonney for the statistical work and preparation of the charts for this article. Research assistance from the British Academy and from the Economic and Social Research Council (award no. R000231968) for the E[uropean] S[tate] F[inance] D[ata]b[ase], an international project in data collection, is gratefully acknowledged by the author. The ESFDB datasets cited in this chapter may be consulted after 1993 via JANET at the ESRC Data Archive in the University of Essex. The author undertook most of the research for this paper between 1989 and 1991 while in Paris as Leverhulme Research Fellow. The author is grateful to Professors Doyle and Knecht for their comments upon the draft version. Modern accentuation, and to some extent spelling, has been added to contemporary orthography.

[1] J. B. Collins, *Fiscal limits of absolutism: direct taxation in early seventeenth-century France* (Berkeley, Los Angeles and London, 1988), p. 219. R. J. Bonney, 'Louis XIII, Richelieu and the royal finances', *Richelieu and his age*, ed. J. A. Bergin and L. W. B. Brockliss (Oxford, 1992), p. 120 n. 53.

[2] F. Bluche and J-F. Solnon, *La véritable hiérarchie sociale de l'ancienne France: le tarif de la première capitation, 1695* (Geneva, 1983). A. Guery, 'État, classification sociale et compromis sous Louis XIV: la capitation de 1695', *Annales ESC*, 41 (1986), 1041-60. Further work is in progress by Michael Kwass.

[3] *Histoire économique et sociale de la France. II. Des derniers temps de l'âge seigneurial aux préludes de l'âge industriel, 1660-1789*, ed. F. Braudel and E. Labrousse (1970), p. 275. F. Bluche, *Louis XIV*, trans. M. Greengrass (1990; orig. French edn 1984), pp. 554-7. R. J. Bonney, 'Jean-Roland Malet: historian of the finances of the French monarchy', *Fr Hist*, 5

© Oxford University Press 1993

of the century.⁴ Yet the *capitation* was not in practice a particularly progressive tax, at least during the reign of Louis XIV (though there may well have been significant changes of practice in the later eighteenth century) because it proved to be excessively rigid. In some provinces, such as the Lyonnais, the tariff had in large measure to be abandoned by 1703 in the interests of bringing in the amount of taxation that the crown required. There were substantial variations in the tax burdens of members of the same 'classes' under the tax, depending on the *généralité* in which they were taxed.⁵

In contrast, the *dixième*, which sought to tax wealth rather than status, proved to be the greater innovation. It was more 'progressive' in its social implications, it yielded its revenue surprisingly easily in the most inauspicious circumstances (towards the end of a long period of warfare and after the great subsistence crisis of 1709-10, the *grand hiver*), and indeed it provoked such a fierce resistance from the privileged classes that it had to be revoked in the aristocratic reaction following Louis XIV's death. Not the least of the reasons for its revocation were the extensive powers granted to the officials responsible for collecting the tax – the provincial intendants, their subdelegates, and the directors and controllers of the *dixième* – which marked a substantial increase in the powers of the state to interfere with its subjects. The story of the introduction of the *dixième* may even prompt a reassessment of the last years of Louis XIV's reign: can the state machinery be considered quite such a shambles, and the king quite so imprisoned by powerful vested interests, especially those of financiers, when such a wide-ranging new scheme of taxation could be 'invented' relatively fast and, moreover, be made to work? Can *ancien régime* France be considered quite so reactionary in what Schumpeter might have termed its 'fiscal sociology' if there could be set in place, albeit in wartime,⁶ measures to enforce a strong commitment towards a fairer redistribution of taxes? Even Chamillart, not noted for his reforming intent as controller-

---

(1991), 196-7. Bonney, 'The state and its revenues in *ancien-régime* France', *Hist Research*, 65 (1992), 165-7. M. M. and R. J. Bonney, *Jean-Roland Malet: premier historien des finances de la monarchie française* (Comité pour l'histoire économique et financière de la France, Paris, 1993), pp. 74-81. See also the unpublished doctoral dissertation of G. McCollim, 'The formation of fiscal policy in the reign of Louis XIV: the example of Nicolas Desmaretz, controller-general of finances, 1708-15' (Ohio State University, 1979), ch. 5 ('The establishment of the *dixième*').

⁴ A. M. de Boislisle, 'L'impôt du dixième', *Mémoires de Saint-Simon*, ed. Boislisle (41 vols., 1879-1928), xx. 447-80. M. Houques-Fourcade, *Les impôts sur le revenu en France au xviiie siècle. Histoire du dixième et du cinquantième: leur application dans la généralité de Guyenne* (Paris and Bordeaux, 1889). M. Marion, *L'impôt sur le revenu au dix-huitième siècle, principalement en Guyenne* (Toulouse, 1901; repr. Geneva, 1976). Marion, *Les impôts directs sous l'ancien régime principalement au xviiie siècle* (1910). Marion, *Histoire financière de la France. I. 1715-1789* (repr. 1927), pp. 15, 36, 88.

⁵ Bonney, 'The state and its revenues', pp. 162, 164.

⁶ R. J. Bonney, 'State competition for resources and fiscal innovation under Louis XIV', forthcoming in *États, marines et sociétés (essays in honour of Jean Meyer)*, edited by J-P. Poussou, A. Zysberg and M. Acerra.

general of finance, remarked that 'il seroit à désirer que l'on pust changer la forme des impositions . . .'.[7] It was his successor Desmaretz who achieved reform – notwithstanding the fact that he has been castigated for his alleged 'failure to distinguish his private purse from that of the king'.[8] This in turn suggests the need for a re-examination of Desmaretz's ministry, although it falls outside the scope of this paper.[9] Instead the focus here is on the intellectual debate preceding the introduction of the tax, the way in which it was introduced, the fiscal results in terms of the net revenue generated, and above all, the social and fiscal limitations of the tax. What a study of the *dixième* offers us is a test case in the relationship of the state and society. Saint-Simon denounced the tax as 'une exaction si monstrueuse': 'on compta pour rien la désolation de l'impôt même dans une multitude d'hommes et de tous les états, si prodigieuse, et leur désespoir d'être forcés à révéler eux-mêmes le secret de leurs familles . . .'[10] This was not a subsequent re-reading of history. Saint-Simon's argument had been pre-empted by the longest-serving intendant of the reign of Louis XIV, Lamoignon de Basville, as early as 1705, when a precursor of the tax was first mooted in a serious way: how could a Frenchman be expected to reveal 'le secret de sa famille'? Such an expectation, in the intendant's view was 'contraire au génie de la nation'. In Languedoc troops had to be used to collect the *taille* and the *capitation*: the new tax would be 'encore bien plus désagréable'.[11] Basville made proposals of his own to avoid the need for the *dixième*; when the tax was finally introduced in 1710 he had to defend himself from criticism that he was an opponent of it.[12] The purpose of this article is therefore to ascertain what there was about the *dixième* which made it so controversial a tax even in wartime, and which helped ensure its revocation under the Regency in 1717.

I

The introduction of the *dixième* has to be understood both in terms of an intellectual debate started by Vauban and Boisguilbert at the beginning of

---

[7] A[rchives] N[ationales] G[7] 721 no. 35, note of Chamillart on a letter from Le Camus, first president of the *Cour des Aides* of Paris, September 1705 [*Correspondance des contrôleurs généraux avec les intendants des provinces, 1683–1715*, ed. A. M. de Boislisle (3 vols., 1874–9), ii. 563; also in *Pierre de Boisguilbert ou la naissance de l'économie politique* (2 vols., INED edn, Paris, 1966), i. 404].

[8] H. L. Root, 'Institutions, interest groups and authority in *ancien régime* France', *Fr Hist*, 6 (1992), 414–15.

[9] Bonney and Bonney, *Jean-Roland Malet*, pp. 49–88.

[10] Saint-Simon, *Mémoires*, ed. Boislisle, xx. 165–6. Marion, *L'impôt sur le revenu*, p. 109. Bluche, *Louis XIV*, p. 556, comments that 'Saint-Simon's lack of foresight appears extraordinary'.

[11] AN G[7] 307 no. 16 [miscatalogued in 1704]. *Correspondance des contrôleurs généraux*, ed. Boislisle, ii. 277–8 (no. 891). *Pierre de Boisguilbert ou la naissance de l'économie politique*, i. 406–8.

[12] AN G[7] 314 no. 251, 21 Nov. 1710 [*Correspondance des contrôleurs généraux*, ed. Boislisle, iii. 331 (no. 895)]. Basville took the unusual step of writing the letter in his own hand,

the new century and of a short-term fiscal crisis resulting from the unexpectedly long duration of the war and the failure of the peace negotiations of 1709-10. The one is inseparable from the other:[13] without an overwhelming need to do something, it is unlikely that the government would have risked such a controversial fiscal measure; without a preceding intellectual debate it is questionable whether such a potentially far-reaching measure could have been adopted so quickly. Average annual royal expenditure rose in nominal terms in more or less steady steps throughout the seventeenth century, including the period of the personal rule of Louis XIV (1661-1715), with the exception of the largely peacetime years of Colbert's ministry:[14] the direct and indirect costs of war predominated (Figure 1). The last two wars, of course, proved most expensive of all: the War of the League of Augsburg had seen expenditure of under 200 million *livres* per annum (Figure 2); but this rose rapidly with the scale of new commitments in Spain and Italy during the War of the Spanish Succession. Expenditure peaked first at 258 million in 1707, the last year of Chamillart's ministry, and was unquestionably a factor prompting his resignation as controller-general of finance in February 1708. But the highest expenditure of all (264 million) was in 1711, after the introduction of the *dixième* (Figure 3); expenditure remained very high (at 240 million) the following year. Indeed, it may be argued that the new tax created new revenues which alone permitted the scale of expenditure necessary to win the battle of Denain in 1712, and thus to bring the war to a conclusion[15] less disastrous than that which France might otherwise have suffered. The declaration of October 1710 stated the necessity for the tax, and outlined the fiscal context in which the decision had been reached: 'la levée du dixième nous mettra en estat de pourvoir aux dépenses extraordinaires ausquelles la continuation de la guerre nous engage'.[16]

---

not that of his secretary. Saint-Simon's contention that Basville was the author of the scheme is thus erroneous: *Mémoires de Saint-Simon*, ed. Boislisle, vi. 287, xx. 447-8.

[13] The components of the fiscal crisis are discussed in Bonney and Bonney, *Jean-Roland Malet*, pp. 49-88. McCollim concluded ('The formation of fiscal policy', p. 325) that 'the new tax was an expedient, not a reform, that was adopted at the last possible moment causing each of the . . . decisions to be made hastily'. Yet there is no evidence to suggest that any of previous fiscal reforms, including the *capitation*, had been debated for such a long period of time. McCollim's account of the intellectual origins of the tax (pp. 279-83) ignores the evidence presented here as to the earlier discussion of a precursor of the *dixième*, and is excessively reliant on the memoirs of Saint-Simon, Dangeau and de Sourches. Nor do the instructions to the intendants at the end of October 1710 suggest a lack of preparation.

[14] The definition of ministries is that given in Bonney, 'Louis XIII, Richelieu and the royal finances', p. 102, but completing the data for Pontchartrain's ministry and adding the ministries of Chamillart and Desmaretz.

[15] Bonney, 'Jean-Roland Malet', p. 197. Bonney and Bonney, *Jean-Roland Malet*, pp. 80-1.

[16] The preamble of the declaration was drafted by Desmaretz himself: Bonney and Bonney, *Jean-Roland Malet*, pp. 78-9. AN K 2413 no. 80, parchment version of the declaration, whose orthography has been followed here except where there is a divergence between contemporary and modern use of accents. Boislisle, 'L'impôt du dixième', pp. 453-9, published a complete version of the twelve clauses of the declaration after AN AD + 699 no. 46. Marion,

XIV

In May 1705, Boisguilbert presented to the government his 'Mémoire sur l'assiette de la taille et de la capitation', which had proposed that the *taille* should be fixed 'au dixième du revenu des fonds', with temporary arrangements for its levy 'en attendant un règlement général et uniforme après la paix'. He proposed that the *capitation* should in effect be doubled so as to be the equivalent of a 'vingtième du revenu des fonds'.[17] Boisguilbert talked of 'une révolution entière' in the levy of taxes,[18] and met Desmaretz's brother-in-law, Joubert de Bouville, the intendant of Orléans. Subsequently, at Rambouillet on 23 September 1705, the two of them met d'Armenonville, the director of finance,[19] and the marquis de Chamlay, Chamillart's right-hand man.[20] Despite the fact that Joubert de Bouville was interested in fiscal reform,[21] and that an experiment was carried out in the *élection* of Chartres in 1705 under his supervision, Boisguilbert's direct role came to an end, and the fiscal reform proved abortive.

Two reasons may be adduced for this failure. Boisguilbert later dissociated himself from the *dixième* because, as a precursor of the Physiocrats, he believed in allowing free rein for grain price increases to secure the economic growth which alone would generate more revenue to the crown: 'On regarde cet article comme le principal de tous, et celui qui peut seul causer l'opulence ou la misère d'un royaume.'[22] This was a crucial obstacle to reform, since in 1705 it aroused the hostility of powerful vested interests, most notably Harlay, the first president of the *Parlement* of Paris,[23] whom Boisguilbert blamed for blocking his reform proposals. Yet the government itself must have had doubts about the wisdom of freeing grain prices even in 1705, while after the great subsistence crisis of 1709–10, there could be no question of freeing grain prices and allowing them to find their natural level. Thus in the autumn of 1710 Boisguilbert was not consulted about the introduction of the *dixième*.[24]

Les impôts directs, pp. 269–73, also published a complete version of the declaration after AN AD IX 400 no. 84, which we have consulted.

[17] *Pierre de Boisguilbert ou la naissance de l'économie politique*, ii. 688, 697, 735–6.
[18] Ibid. i. 410.
[19] Ibid. i. 402. A. M. de Boislisle, 'Boisguilbert et les contrôleurs généraux', *Mémoires de Saint-Simon*, ed. Boislisle, xiv. 592. It was this meeting to which Basville alluded in his letter of 11 October 1705, 'Réponse de M de Basville sur une lettre escrite par Monseigneur pour se consulter sur les vues de MM de Bouville et d'Armenonville en conséquence des conversations qu'ils ont eues avec M de Boisguilbert'.
[20] Ibid. i. 187, 431. AN G^7 721 no. 80 [*Correspondance des contrôleurs généraux*, ed. Boislisle, iii. 653–4]: 'le modèle d'édit que Monsieur de Chamillart me fist composer il y a trois ans avec Monsieur de Chanlais [= Chamlay] qui travailla pendant trois mois sans discontinuation sur mes mémoires [et] en a gardé les pièces . . .'
[21] R. J. Bonney, review of *L'intendance d'Orléans à la fin du xviie siècle. Edition critique du Mémoire 'pour l'instruction du duc de Bourgogne'*, ed. J. Boissière and C. Michaud (1989), in *French History*, 5 (1991), 379–81.
[22] *Pierre de Boisguilbert ou la naissance de l'économie politique*, ii. 731.
[23] Ibid. i. 189–90.
[24] Ibid. i. 211–12 (Saint-Simon on 'le pauvre Boisguilbert' and his reaction to being regarded as 'l'innocent donneur d'avis d'un si exécrable monopole').

A second reason for the failure of Boisguilbert's proposals in 1705 was alluded to in Basville's letter of condemnation. This was that it was 'contraire au génie de la nation' for a Frenchman to reveal 'le secret de sa famille'. At face value, there should have been no problem since Boisguilbert argued that 'il faut en laisser la répartition au peuple, qui ne s'y trompera pas . . .'[25] However, a closer inspection of the scheme, such as Basville had clearly undertaken, would have revealed a very different philosophy and more intrusive mechanism for the levy proposed by Boisguilbert. In the case of the *taille*, the intendants were to ensure that beside each individual's entry on the tax roll there would be details of his wealth ('le prix auquel la terre ou ferme est baillée, la contenance des terres, bois, prés, rentes, droits, etc., ce rôle certifié véritable par les collecteurs, syndics, et six des principaux habitants; et en cas qu'il ne le fût pas, condamner sur-le-champ à un doublement de taille'). To propose this was to undermine a Frenchman's freedom to indulge in fiscal fraud, but there was worse to come. Boisguilbert proposed that there should be a system of paid informers to police the declarations on the tax rolls ('les frais . . . d'espions employés à découvrir le véritable état des biens de ceux qui voudraient se soustraire à la connaissance des intendants').[26] These paid informers would also operate to investigate the declarations of wealth relating to the *capitation*. The intrusion of the state into the 'secret de la famille' was even greater here. Boisguilbert distinguished three types of taxable wealth. The first type we might call capital assets ('revenus en fonds, comme terres, rentes, charges, et même billets courants'). This form of wealth was inherited, or arose from purchase or gift. It would be possible to discover the origins of such wealth from *partages*, *dots* and *douaires*, estimates of household expenditure: 'un homme habile ne se trompera pas sur les valeurs de toutes ces espèces de biens'. '[R]ien ne peut échapper aux lumières d'un homme entendu et appliqué', in Boisguilbert's view. 'Il n'y aura qu'à Paris où l'on ne pourra perfectionner les choses qu'en partie la première année.'[27] A second type of wealth arose from commerce. Similar evidence of wealth would be displayed as in the case of those holding capital assets: 'Il n'est pas plus difficile de connaître leur trafic . . .' In the case of *marchands en gros*, their houses and shops could be listed, and their account books and the local customs registers could be consulted. For *marchands en détail* or *fabricants*, such as *tisserands*, *drapiers*, *sergiers*, *rubaniers* and other master craftsmen, there was the evidence of the number of looms (*métiers*) they controlled; in the case of butchers, the number of cattle slaughtered would be known; in the case of candlemakers, the amount of candle-grease consumed would need to be accounted for, and in all cases the number of journeymen or other workers employed could be established. The third type of wealth was 'le travail

---

[25] Ibid. i. 385; ii. 727.
[26] Ibid. ii. 724, 726.
[27] Ibid. ii. 727.

manuel des simples journaliers'. With regard to workers in the cloth industry, Boisguilbert assumed that they would be required by their contracts of employment to make a contribution towards the employer's tax costs. It was important to respect freedom of contract ('laisser agir la nature dans une entière liberté'), and in general Boisguilbert proposed to leave the status quo with regard to manual labour.

An extract of Basville's denunciation of the scheme is worth quoting because it responded directly to the estimation of wealth in Boisguilbert's scheme:

> Après avoir bien examiné la proposition d'abolir la capitation et de faire payer le dixième des revenus aux particuliers, il m'a paru qu'il sera très dangereux de se servir de cet expédient, et qu'on ne pourroit pas s'en promettre aucun succès. Il est dangereux, parce que les peuples sont accoutumés à la capitation, et ne le seroient de longtemps à ce dixième, qui sera très difficile à établir. Il faudra des années entières pour vaincre les difficultés: on a besoin d'un secours prompt et facile, et l'on ne doit pas croire que l'on n'ait pas une extrême répugnance a déclarer son bien et à réveler le secret de sa famille. C'est la dernière des extrémités, et si contraire au génie de la nation, qu'il ne peut lui arriver rien de plus insupportable. Ainsi, l'on doit s'attendre a des déclarations qui ne seront point sincères. Comment obliger un marchand, un homme d'affaires, un usurier à déclarer ce qu'il a d'argent? S'il faut faire sur cela une inquisition pour les condamner au quadruple, elle sera d'une longueur infinie; et vouloir présumer que l'on déclarera de bonne foi et sincèrement ce qu'on possède, c'est présumer que les hommes seront justes et raisonnables dans leur propre interest; ce que l'on ne doit pas attendre de la pluspart . . . L'estimation des biens inconnus est très difficile à faire, car on ne peut estimer ce qu'on ne connaît pas . . .

II

Nothing was done about the prototype of the *dixième* in 1705. In the crisis atmosphere prevailing after the failure of the Gertruydenberg peace negotiations five years later, a secret government committee packed with Desmaretz's relatives and friends met at La Marche on 23 September,[28] at which the minister 'fit lecture de différens Mémoires qui lui avoit été donnés . . .' The final proposal for the new tax emanated from Jean Orry, a *munitionnaire du roi*, but this has not survived as far as is known.[29] We

---

[28] Bonney and Bonney, *Jean-Roland Malet*, p. 77 nn. 91, 92.
[29] Ibid. *Mémoires concernant les impositions et droits. Seconde partie. Impositions et droits en France*, ed. J-L. Moreau de Beaumont (1769), ii. 445.

have to assume that it was more or less the basis of the tax as it appears in the initial legislation, except that a crucial aspect of the tax, the *dixième de retenue*, 'un sistème général, que le 10ᵉ sera retenu sur tous les paiemens de toute nature pendᵗ le quartier d'octobre et l'année 1711', seems to have been Desmaretz's own idea.[30] The king and the controller-general were in consultation on 14 October, when the declaration was issued, and thus we may appropriately call the tax Louis XIV's *dixième*.[31]

Instead of Jean Orry's memorandum, we have at least two, and possibly three, of the documents which were in all likelihood discussed by the committee on 23 September. (In *ancien régime* France, it is notoriously difficult to ascertain definitively what was actually discussed in a committee of the council.) The first is an extremely interesting document, which commented that 'Il faut un sistème et des moiens nouueaux.' It seems to have been written in the summer of 1710, when the rumour of the *dixième* was common currency, although it was based on Vauban's 'false' estimates of a likely yield (120 million): 'on s'imagine trouver dans cet expédient tous les fonds nécessaires'. The memorandum had very telling comments on the likely yield of such a revenue based upon the Dutch experience.[32] A second document entitled 'Mémoire pour faire l'imposition du 20ᵐᵉ 15ᵐᵉ ou 10ᵐᵉ' considered the issues arising from the establishment of a tax – seen primarily in this memorandum as a tax on property. The taxation of *rentes* was seen as particularly dangerous: 'cela pouroit faire craindre au public que l'on ne voulut pénétrer l'intérieure des familles, qui est un secret dont il est infiniment jaloux, et qui est une question depuis longtemps en controverse . . .' As one might expect, here in one of the preparatory documents for the new tax the sort of criticism which was later voiced by Saint-Simon and others is anticipated: the sanctity of family property rights, and especially the contentious issue of the access to family papers. The *dixième de retenue* scheme, a withholding tax of a tenth on the payment of *gages*, *rentes* and other government salaries was Desmaretz's solution to this particular objection on 27 December 1710.[33]

A third document, entitled 'Subside ou Imposition pour la guerre, sur les Terres et les Maisons', appears more heavily influenced by Vauban than the others:[34] 'La taxe des arpents est naturelle et conforme à ce qui s'est pratiqué pendant longtemps en France . . .' Leaving aside the realism of the tax

---

[30] Ibid. pp. 78–9. AN G⁷ 1138–9. In a letter of 23 January 1711, ibid., Daguesseau described it as 'la retention du dixiesme sur les gages, appointements, pensions et rentes que le Roy paye . . .' AN K 2413 no. 111, Déclaration pour la retenue du dixième, 27 Dec. 1710. The system is described by Houques-Fourcade, *Les impôts sur le revenu en France au xviiiᵉ siècle*, pp. 204–5, 219–23.

[31] Bonney and Bonney, *Jean-Roland Malet*, p. 79 n. 97.

[32] It may be this document to which Desmaretz alluded on 13 October 1710 in a letter to Le Rebours, in which case it had only come to the minister's attention after the meeting at La Marche: ibid. p. 78 n. 96. The document itself is an untitled anon. memorandum in a dossier entitled 'Mémoires au sujet du dixième des biens et autres': AN G⁷ 1138–9.

[33] AN G⁷ 1138–9.

[34] Ibid.

proposed, the mechanism for its implementation included onerous declarations of wealth, enforceable only by the penalty (subsequently used in the declaration of 14 October 1710) of quadruple payment in case of false disclosure: 'Il faut dans ces déclarations que ces terres soient libellées, sçavoir tant d'arpents de vignes, tant de bois, tant de préz, tant de grains &ᵃ, et que les limites des terres soient désignées, en marquant autant qu'il sera possible le nom de ceux à qui apartiennent les terres voisines.' The result would have been a national *cadastre*, or land survey, such as was proposed in 1763 but not established until the First Empire. This indeed was exactly what was proposed in a fourth memorandum, written after the implementation of the *dixième*, the 'Moyen proposé pour faire un denombrement exact de tout le Royaume'.[35] This argued that 'Le dixième qui se lève à present dans le Royaume seroit un subside moins onereux, plus aizé à lever, et d'un plus grand rapport qua la taille si le denombrem et l'estimation des biens étoit faite avec la justesse, et la précision qu'elle se peut faire.' The memorandum considered that the intendants did not have time to do the job properly; but the directors of the *dixième* would have become extraordinarily powerful had the proposed *cadastre* been implemented during the War of the Spanish Succession. The author contended that this was preferable rather than to have recourse to 'des déclarations forcées, bien souvent fausses qui diminuent le profit au lieu de l'augmenter'.

The 'Déclaration pour la levée du Dixieme du revenu des biens du Royaume' was issued on 14 October 1710. The future Chancellor Daguesseau noted that it was extraordinary to have such an important fiscal measure established by a declaration rather than an edict; for the *procureur général* of the *Parlement* of Paris, as he was in 1710, the procedure of using a declaration seemed to demonstrate 'qu'il ne s'agist que d'une levée passagère et qui doit cesser avec la guerre'.[36] The declaration specified that the new tax would provide the crown with 'les moyens d'accorder à nos peuples un cinquième de diminution sur la Taille de l'année prochaine [1711], et nous dispensera d'avoir recours dans la suite aux af[f]aires extraordinaires, dont le recouvrement est toujours à charge de nos peuples'. The element of fiscal competition with the Maritime Powers was clearly stated in the preamble: 'nos ennemis par les imposts établis sur les biens fonds lèvent des sommes plus considérables par chacune année, que le dixième que nous nous sommes determiné à demander'. The allusion was to the English land tax, levied since 1692 at a wartime rate of four shillings in the pound; it was thus in principle a levy of a fifth of rental income, although because of underassessment the amount collected was much lower. If the tax rate was lower in France, the definition of taxable

---

[35] Ibid. and edited in Boislisle, 'L'impôt du dixième', pp. 479–80.
[36] AN G⁷ 437 fo. 483, 22 Oct. 1710. This may account for why there were no protests from either the *Parlement* of Paris or the *Cour des Aides* of Paris: AN Z¹ᵃ 182 pp. 965–6, 27 Nov. 1710.

income under the *dixième* of 1710 was more comprehensive than under the English land tax, and it seems that models in Artois and Flanders were more influential; Desmaretz had also read a memorandum concerning taxation in Holland prior to formulating the declaration for the establishment of the tax.[37] All forms of income from landed property (defined as broadly as possible),[38] whether farmed out or not, were subject to the tenth with effect from 1 October 1710 for the duration of the war.[39] So too were the 'maisons de toutes les villes et fauxbourgs du Royaume', whether leased or not. Income from office, again broadly defined,[40] was also subject to the tax, as were *rentes* and various other forms of royal income or extraordinary payments.[41] There were to be special tax rolls to levy a tenth on the profits of financiers and others who had made exceptional gains during the war after 1689. This clause, which was akin to a *chambre de justice*, proved difficult to enforce, since the services of the financiers were still needed;[42] Daguesseau for one wondered whether it did not demonstrate 'trop hautement l'extrême besoin où l'on est . . .'[43] Tenants were obliged not to pay their rents unless there was evidence that their masters had actually paid their *dixième*.[44] Ecclesiastical wealth was at first subject to the tax, but after remonstrances from the Assembly of the Clergy of 1711, a subsequent declaration was issued on 27 October 1711 which removed any fiscal liability: this was a significant setback in moves towards a more general form of taxation which paid less attention to special privileges.[45]

The *dixième* was intended as a personal tax on income[46] which was to be evaluated by self-assessment. In his instructions to the intendants,

---

[37] *Mémoires concernant les impositions et droits*, ed. Moreau de Beaumont, ii. 299, 316. Bonney and Bonney, *Jean-Roland Malet*, p. 78.

[38] 'tous les fons, terres, prez, bois, vignes, marais, pascages, usages, estangs, rivières, moulins, forges, fourneaux et autres uzines, cens, rentes, dixmes, champarts, droits seigneuriaux, péages, passages, droits de ponts, bacs et rivières . . .'

[39] Except for Languedoc, Navarre and Béarn, where the levy started on 1 January 1711, and Franche-Comté, where it started on 1 October 1711: AN G^7 1138-9.

[40] 'toutes les charges, employs et commissions, soit d'épée, de robe, des Maisons royales, villes, police, ou de finances, compris leurs appointmenents, gages, remises, taxations et droits y attribuez, de quelque nature qu'ils soient'.

[41] 'des augmentations de gages, pensions, gratifications ordinaires et extraordinaires, dons et acquits patents . . .'

[42] *Mémoires concernant les impositions et droits*, ed. Moreau de Beaumont, ii. 458-9. The difficulties in its implementation are most clearly evident in the case of Provence: BN MS Fr. 8894 fos. 354, 442, 27 Oct. and 5 Nov. 1710. MS Fr. 8895 fos. 114, 117, 475, 20 Jan., 29 Apr. and 26 June 1711. MS Fr. 8896 fos. 443, 445, 485^v, 530, 16 Nov., 23 Nov., 14 Dec. and 22 Dec. 1711.

[43] AN G^7 438 fos. 9-11, 6 Jan. 1711.

[44] This clause required subsequent enforcement. Cf. AN K 2413 no. 109, Arrest du Conseil d'Estat du Roy, 20 Dec. 1710 (printed), 'portant que faute par les Fermiers & Locataires & autres jouïssans de Biens sujets au Dixième, de justifier des Quittances du Dixième payé par les Proprietaires des mesmes Biens, ils seront contraints en leurs propres et privez noms au payement du Dixième à leurs frais sans repetition'. *Mémoires concernant les impositions et droits*, ed. Moreau de Beaumont, ii. 453. Marion, *L'impôt sur le revenu*, pp. 111-12: 'Du coup, une considérable partie des fonds du royaume se trouva affranchie du dixième . . .'

[45] Ibid. ii. 465-9. BN MS Fr. 8896 fo. 420.

[46] AN G^7 1138-9, 'Mémoire seruant de reponse aux raisons de M. le duc de Bouillon, par lesquelles il pretend être exempt de la taxe du dixième du revenu de ses terres et seigneuries':

Desmaretz had no doubt that implementation would not be easy, and that there would arise 'plusieurs difficultés non seulement lors de la confection des rôles, mais encore dans leur exécution'.[47] The minister envisaged that proprietors who farmed out their lands should show to the intendant's subdelegate a certified copy of the lease passed before the notary or other legal document, and in the case of those lands which were not farmed out, they were to provide an estimate of their revenues ('fournir leurs déclarations estimatives du produit qu'ilz en tirent . . .'). In cases of counterfeit leases ('contrelettres pour les baux') or the non-disclosure of wealth, quadruple rates of tax were to be charged, 'dont il faudra faire des exemples dans les premières rôles qui se feront afin d'obliger les autres qui seroient tombez en pareille contravention de venir promptement rectifier leurs déclarations . . .' The intendants were responsible for drawing up lists of taxpayers of the *dixième* for each town and parish, and for including at double their 'normal' rate those who had failed to provide a declaration of wealth. Desmaretz warned the intendants:

> il est d'une très grande conséquence de ne se pas fier absolument aux estim^{ons} des faisans valoir, qu'ainsi il sera très à propos de se faire secrètement informer de la verité surtout dans les pays de vignobles, et dans les provinces où les bestiaux font le principal revenu dans lesquelles il ne faut pas obmettre de comprendre les cheptels dans les rôles pour le dixième du produit qui en revient au bailleur.

Desmaretz's memorandum of 20 August 1711 further instructed the intendants to verify the declarations of wealth 'pour tâcher de porter le produit du dix^e à sa juste valleur': 'comme l'établissement de cette imp^{oon} ne fait que commencer il est nécessaire d'en suivre le recouvrement journellement'. Fortnightly statements of tax income were to be sent to the minister.[48] Desmaretz had already established a procedure for the weekly accounting of the proceeds of the tax in a form of double-entry bookkeeping[49] which distinguished the various components in the mechanism of receipts and payment (whether in paper or coin, or by the process of assignment).[50] It is certain that in the provinces, too, very detailed ac-

---

'Ainsi on peut dire qu'on le demande personnellement sans avoir égard à la nature des biens qui produisent leur revenus, c'est du produit du revenu dont on demande le dixième, et s'il est question de terres, de maisons et d'autres immeubles, ce n'est que pour prendre des précautions pour la sûreté et la facilité du payement.'

[47] Ibid., 'Copie de la lettre circulaire de Monseigneur Desmaretz, envoyée à Messieurs les intendants les 30 et 31 octobre 1710'.

[48] BN MS Fr. 8896 fo. 228.

[49] AN G^7 1140, 16 May 1711, 'caisse du dixième, Bordereau de la recette et dépense'. This has the income from the tax on the left-hand page and the expenditure of the proceeds on the right-hand page. There is a sum of the difference between receipts and expenses which is the amount which 'Reste en caisse'.

[50] For income, it was specificied whether 'en argent'; 'en billets de monnaie'; 'en assignations'; or 'en rescriptions'. For expenditure the name of the beneficiary was specified, and

counts were kept including details of the process of assigning the revenues, although for the most part these have not survived;[51] indeed the local survival of evidence for the first *dixième* is very patchy.[52] The intendants were to be assisted by controllers and directors of the *dixième*, both types of official receiving separate instructions drafted by members of the council and approved by Desmaretz.[53] Not all of these officials were equally competent. In Guyenne, Lamoignon de Courson commented that there were controllers 'qui m'ont donné des mémoires si extravagants que je n'ai pas jugé à propos d'y ajouter aucune foi, parce que cela n'eût fait que soulever les esprits'. Out of his ten controllers, six or seven had done nothing and were 'même incapables de pouvoir rien faire de bien'.[54]

What form were the declarations of wealth to take? Marion described the *dixième* as an 'impôt cédulaire sur toutes les différentes sources de revenus'. In effect there was a *dixième* (and later, *vingtième*) *des biensfonds, mobilier, d'industrie* and *des offices et droits*.[55] For Louis XIV's *dixième* we know most about the declarations concerning landed wealth. Three proposals were drafted, one for *seigneurs des paroisses*, another for *particuliers possédants biens de campagne*, and a third for *propriétaires des maisons*. The first two declarations specified the quantity and type of land held and the unit of measurement; the dues payable by the land ('desquelles redevances ces héritages sont chargez'; the names of those who worked the land ('qui laboure, exploitte ou fait valoir ces heritages'); and finally the amount of revenue of the land in question. There was a significant distinction between landholdings and rented property: in the case of the latter, the names of the occupiers, the date of the lease, the amount of the lease, and above all the name of the notary who had dealt with the contract ('nom du notaire qui a passé le bail') were to be specified. It is probable, but not certain, that Desmaretz sent these draft declarations to the intendants in late October 1710.[56] We cannot be sure how the declarations

whether the payment was 'en argent'; 'billets de monnaie'; 'billets' or 'rescriptions' of the *receveurs généraux*; or 'assignations sur les pays d'états'.

[51] AN G⁷ 164 nos. 1, 2, details of the amounts of the *rôles arrêtés* by Trudaine for 1711 and 1712 and twenty-one assignments to named individuals on the revenues for 1712.

[52] Thus only one tax roll in the pays de Caux: G. Lemarchand, *La fin du féodalisme dans le pays de Caux: conjoncture économique et démographique et structure sociale dans une région de grande culture de la crise du xviie siècle à la stabilisation de la Révolution, 1640–1795* (1989), p. 152.

[53] AN G⁷ 1138-9. The distinction was that the *contrôleurs* were responsible for the money actually levied, and that the royal declaration and ordinances of the intendant were enforced, whereas the *directeurs* were concerned with the drawing up of the tax rolls and were in effect secretaries of the intendant for the *dixième*.

[54] Houques-Fourcade, *Les impôts sur le revenu en France au xviiie siècle*, p. 275. Marion, *L'impôt sur le revenu*, p. 118.

[55] Marion, *Les impôts directs*, pp. 64–5. This follows the analysis in Houques-Fourcade, *Les impôts sur le revenu en France au xviiie siècle*, pp. 149–71.

[56] AN G⁷ 17, Projet de lettre pour Messieurs les intendants, n.d. [Oct. 1710], except that this draft referred to the declaration as an edict: it is thus probable that this draft letter was replaced by the instructions of 30 and 31 October 1710, which were less specific about draft

of wealth were drawn up for the large landowners, but it is unlikely that they assumed personal responsibility for the task. We know from the example of the *capitation* on the estates of Harlay, first president of the *Parlement* of Paris, that the task of drawing up the tax rolls was delegated to Paul Testard, *bailli* at Beaune, and an *avocat* in the *Parlement*: he had dealt with all tax matters concerning the Harlay estates for thirty-six years.[57] It is unlikely that he or his successor would have surrendered control of the declarations of wealth necessary for the *dixième*, since these required greater knowledge of the financial affairs of his master than had preceding taxes. The provincial intendant seems to have been happy to leave Harlay to have tax matters sorted out on his estates by his preferred manager.[58]

For urban property, we are well informed about the type of wealth declarations required in the provincial capital and port of Bordeaux.[59] Lamoignon de Courson's printed ordinance of 15 January 1711 and his 'Mémoire instructif pour Messieurs les commissaires nommez en conséquence de l'ordonnance' both survive.[60] Appended to the ordinance were four specimen declarations of wealth. The first was 'pour une maison louée', which required the owner to specify that the stated property had been leased for x number of years at y rent a year; he was to append a copy of the lease or an extract certified by a notary. The second type of declaration was by the owner of 'une maison occupée par le propriétaire, par lui acquise ou qui lui vient de succession'. An estimated capital value and a rental value of y rent a year were to be specified, and the title deed of the property with its value, or an extract certified by a notary, was to be appended. The third type of declaration was by the owner of 'une maison occupée en partie par le propriétaire, & louée en partie'. The rental value of y rent a year and the estimated rental value of the part of the property occupied by the landowner were to be specified, who was to append a copy of the lease as well as the title deeds or extracts certified by a notary. Finally, in the case of a 'maison d'où dépend quelque héritage', the extent of the land and rental value was to be specified and justified as with the other types of property. Courson's memorandum specified that there would be one declaration for each house although there could be composite returns in order to 'comprendre plusieurs quoy qu'appartenantes à un

---

declarations of wealth. Cf. G⁷ 365, 30 Dec. 1710. The allusion of Méliand, intendant at Lyon, was unspecific as to the origin of the declarations of wealth: 'Les modèles de déclarations de toutes sortes d'espèces de biens que j'ay fait imprimer, et que fais distribuer dans touttes les parroisses.'

[57] AN G⁷ 435 fo. 190, 23 Mar. 1708.
[58] AN G⁷ 435 fo. 197, 20 May 1701, Harlay to Testard: 'Monsieur Phélypeaux intendant de la généralité de Paris ayant trouvé à propos que vous fissies la répartition de la capitation dans touttes nos terres je vous prie d'y travailler incessamment et par préférence à toute autre sorte de chose . . .'
[59] Houques-Fourcade, *Les impôts sur le revenu en France au xviiie siècle*, pp. 189–90.
[60] AN G⁷ 1138–9.

mesme propriétaire et dans la mesme rue'. The agent acting on behalf of the intendant was to inspect the register of leases and rents for the properties concerned 'ou un extrait pardevant notaire pour vérifier si le prix du loyer se rapporte aux déclarations'. Denunciations of false returns would be received: 'Ceux qui desnonçeront les personnes qui auront fait de fausses déclarations auront le tiers de la peine réglée par la déclaration du Roy.' The fiscal state could hardly have become more intrusive than in the proposed arrangments for the levy of the *dixième* at Bordeaux.

On the other hand, within the *généralité* of Bordeaux the measures taken by the intendant were much less intrusive. Lamoignon de Courson's proposal to reduce by almost a third the tax liability of those who returned their declarations of wealth promptly was overruled by Desmaretz.[61] The intendant recognized that the declarations were 'presque toutes fausses', and used the tithe rolls as a crude basis of comparison.[62] The intendant's proposals to subcontract the collection of the tax throughout the province and to seek a composition with individuals over their tax liability were both rejected; but in the areas of land tax, Lamoignon de Courson made the *dixième* in effect an adjunct to the *taille* (as it was to become also in Languedoc): it ceased to be a tax on revenues and became one of repartition.[63] However, the tax always had something of this aspect about it, since the minister wished to obtain a secure sum of money from each *généralité* on which to base his war estimates, or (in the case of the *pays d'élections*) to borrow money from the financiers.[64] Desmaretz required Saint-Contest, intendant at Metz, to send 'une estimation de ce que vous croyéz en pouvoir retirer affin que je fasse quelques arrangements sur toute cette affaire en général. . .'[65] The figures for the *pays d'élections* for 1711 contain an *estimation du produit par Mrs les intendants* and a *projet d'avance* on the revenues.[66]

III

The subdelegates (*subdélégués*), who were venal office-holders during the War of the Spanish Succession, became the linchpins in the administration of the tax as it applied to the income from landed wealth. Desmaretz was exceedingly suspicious of their motives: 'presque tous ont favorisé leurs parents et amis et ont vexé leurs ennemis, que quelques-uns même ont ex-

---

[61] Houques-Fourcade, *Les impôts sur le revenu en France au xviiie siècle*, pp. 257–8. Marion, *L'impôt sur le revenu*, p. 116.
[62] Ibid. p. 258.
[63] Ibid. pp. 260–4. Marion, *Les impôts directs*, pp. 335–9.
[64] Bonney and Bonney, *Jean-Roland Malet*, p. 76.
[65] AN G^7 18, 19 Feb. 1711 [*Correspondance des contrôleurs généraux*, ed. Boislisle, iii. 356–7].
[66] AN G^7 1138–9, 'Dixième 1711. Bordereau général du dixième jusqu'au 6e decembre 1713'.

igé de l'argent pour répondre aux requêtes tendantes à modérations ou décharge qui leur ont été envoyées . . . La plupart ont préféré leurs intérêts particuliers et ceux de leurs amis à ceux de SM.'[67] The survival of copies of personal correspondence between one intendant (Le Gendre, intendant at Montauban) and his subdelegate at Cahors (Pousargues, who copied the correspondence to the minister in justification of his appeal against dismissal) shows how seriously the intendant took the administration of the new tax. The subdelegate, too, was required to appoint persons responsible to him to receive the declarations of wealth:[68] 'je vous prie de redoubler vos soins, et vostre vigilance, et de ne pas perdre de même un moment dans cette affaire. Je vous envoyerai incessamment une nouvelle instruction, avec des modèles des déclarations que les particuliers doivent fournir . . .'[69] 'Sil y a quelque communauté qui ne veuille pas obéir aux ordres du Roy, vous n'avez qu'à me le mander, afin que je puisse y envoyer une compagnie de cavalerie, pour les punir de leur désobeissance, mais j'espere que je ne seray pas obligé d'en venir à cette dure extrémité . . .'[70] 'Vous avez bien fait, de prendre le party d'envoyer des billets aux particuliers, pour les engager à fournir leurs déclarations, estant persuadé que cela produira un aussi bon effet, qu'à Montauban, où j'en ay usé de mesme . . .'[71] The subdelegates were not always impartial administrators, however. Desmaretz received a report from Rennes warning of the difficulty of verifying the declarations of wealth: 'Il faudra une grande précaution et une extrême délicatesse pour ne pas se laisser surprendre dans ces sortes d'opérations, car la pluspart de ces M^{rs} subdélégués et autres pourront se porter à cette affaire par differents motifs ou parce qu'ils appréhendront de désobliger leurs parents ou amis ou qu'ils appréhendront de déplaire aux grands . . .'[72] In other cases, it was not the weakness of the subdelegates but their power which was criticized. Jean-Baptiste Bosc, *procureur général* of the *Cour des Aides* of Paris, called them 'gens très dangereux et maîtres absolus dans les provinces . . .' in a case relating to the obduracy of a collector pursuing his appeal against the decision of a director of the *dixième*.[73]

On the other hand, members of the superior courts usually self-assessed their liability for the *dixième*. The process was inevitably slow. The tax

---

[67] Houques-Fourcade, *Les impôts sur le revenu en France au xviiie siècle*, p. 275. Marion, *Les impôts directs*, p. 77. Marion, *L'impôt sur le revenu*, pp. 118–19. Cf. AN G^7 721, undated memorandum c. 1713 against the subdelegates: 'Si la politique du Conseil est de faire changer de département Messieurs les intendants tous les deux ou trois ans la conséquence n'est pas moins grande à l'égard des subdélégués en charges . . .'

[68] AN G^7 398, Le Gendre-Pousargues correspondence, 13 Dec. 1710.

[69] Ibid., 29 Dec. 1710.

[70] Ibid., 12 Jan. 1711.

[71] Ibid., 20 Jan. 1711.

[72] AN G^7 193 no. 210, 10 June 1712. This argument was used to justify the proposal for increasing the number of clerks for the controllers.

[73] AN G^7 442 fo. 367, 26 Jan. 1715.

rates for the subordinate officials of the *Parlement* of Paris had not been settled by the first president as late as January 1713, 'qui tient en suspens celuy de touttes les autres compagnies de Paris'.⁷⁴ Members of the *Parlement* of Grenoble also self-assessed their liability for the *dixième*. The nonpayment of their *gages* by the government placed them in difficulties in discharging their tax liability: 'dans toutes les occasions le Parlement s'est distingué en s'épuisant pour payer les premiers les finances que Sa Majesté a souhaité et que si vous n'avés la bonté de pourvoir au payement de nos gages nous nous voyons à la veille d'estre dépossedés de nos immeubles par nos créanciers'.⁷⁵ On the other hand, practice clearly varied between one provincial *Parlement* and another. The *Parlement* of Dijon had not been paid its *gages* for 1709 and 1710 and therefore hoped in March 1711 for a delay in payment of its *dixième*; by November 1712, it had not been paid its *gages* for 1711 and 1712 and was complaining of having to pay 'sans ménagements et par la force des contraintes un dixième excessif et outré'.⁷⁶ The tax roll on the *Parlement* seems to have been settled by Trudaine, the intendant, to judge from the remark of Bouchu, the first president.⁷⁷ The *procureur général* blamed the director for the tax being levied in Burgundy 'avec plus de dureté que dans les autres provinces . . .': 'le directeur a pris grand soin d'augmenter sans discernement l'estimation des fonds; il y en à qui rendront à peine dans une année ce qui à quoi il a réglé le 10ᵉ du revenu. Ces excèz rebute le particuliers et par ce que l'on exige d'eux ce qu'ils ne doivent pas, tous refusent de paier ce qu'ils doivent . . .'⁷⁸ Although the *Parlement* was paid its *gages* for 1713 by February 1715, its members remained aggrieved at the fall in their incomes 'diminués par le dixième ou retardés par la difficulté du temps . . .'⁷⁹ In August, the court presented remonstrances at the continuation of the *dixième* and the *capitation* in the new circumstances of international peace, 'regardant la continuation comme une surcharge qui renverse le reste de leur fortune et anéantit toutes leurs espérances . . .'⁸⁰ Other courts were less intransigent but uncooperative. Ferrand, intendant of Brittany, encountered difficulties with the *Parlement* of Rennes concerning the inadequate disclosure of wealth by one of its *conseillers*, de la Nuit; Desmaretz had to write to the first president to ensure compliance.⁸¹ Other privileged groups, such as the professors of the Sorbonne, sought exemption.⁸²

---

⁷⁴ AN G⁷ 1138-9, 28 Jan. 1713.
⁷⁵ AN G⁷ 249 no. 118, n.d. (July 1711). See also no. 119, 'Estat du dixième du revenu des biens immeubles des officiers du Parlement de Grenoble', which shows a total liability of under 30,000 *livres* for the five *quartiers* from October 1710 to the end of 1711.
⁷⁶ AN G⁷ 163 no. 289, 12 Mar. 1711. G⁷ 164 no. 98, 28 Nov. 1712.
⁷⁷ AN G⁷ 163 no. 377, 21 Dec. 1711.
⁷⁸ AN G⁷ 163 no. 379, 24 Dec. 1711.
⁷⁹ AN G⁷ 165 no. 184, 3 Feb. 1715.
⁸⁰ AN G⁷ 165 no. 273, 22 Aug. 1715.
⁸¹ AN G⁷ 193 no. 376, 25 Nov. 1712. Marion, *Les impôts directs*, p. 342.
⁸² AN G⁷ 442 fo. 575, 15 May 1715.

Special dispensations were needed to protect the commercial secrets of merchants and financial wealth at Lyon:

> l'établissement de cette levée à l'égard des biens qui ne consistent pas en immeubles ne pouvoit se faire dans la ville de Lyon sans exposer le commerce en quoy consiste la fortune, et tous les biens de la plus grande partie de ses habitants, à une perte certaine. Ce commerce qui dépend ordinairement d'un grand secret ne pouvant subsister après les declarations exactes que les marchands et négociants auroient esté obligez de donner de leurs facultés . . .

The solution of a *rôle d'évaluation* was adopted, with six subcommittees set up for this purpose, responsible for the thirty-five *quartiers* of the city. The effect was akin to a composition or *abonnement*,[83] which was also the norm in the *pays d'états*.[84] Provence had entered into such an agreement for half a million *livres* before the end of May 1711.[85] Languedoc did so, too, at the rate of a tenth 'de toutes les impositions', initially estimated at 9 million; the *abonnement* of the *dixième* was thus at first 900,000 *livres*, but it was set to fall if direct taxes were reduced, or to rise if they were increased: by 1712, Basville was estimating total taxes at 11 million.[86] Brittany proved problematic. As late as November 1711, declarations of wealth were extremely difficult to obtain from the nobility, because they hoped that there would be an *abonnement*, and the intendant was reluctant to coerce recalcitrant taxpayers during a meeting of the estates.[87] New *abonnements* were entered into even after the end of the War of the Spanish Succession: Burgundy agreed in May 1715 to an *abonnement* of the *dixième* and the *capitation* for a three-year period.[88] At first, the offer of 50,000 *livres* from the estates of Béarn was considered derisory by Desmaretz, but it was later accepted.[89] In French-held Savoy, an increase in the *capitation* was agreed to rather than the levy of the *dix-*

---

[83] *Mémoires concernant les impositions et droits*, ed. Moreau de Beaumont, ii. 471, specifies the sum of 650,000 *livres* as a one-off payment. Boislisle, 'L'impôt du dixième', pp. 463-4. AN G⁷ 365, 28 Dec. 1710. Marion, *Les impôts directs*, p. 334.

[84] Boislisle, 'L'impôt du dixième', p. 465.

[85] BN MS Fr. 8895 fo. 389, 29 May 1711. Marion, *L'impôt sur le revenu*, p. 112.

[86] AN G⁷ 316 no. 299, 20 Nov. 1711. G⁷ 317 nos. 181, 203, 4 Mar., 13 Mar. 1712. AN G⁷ 1138-9, 'Produit du dixième des provinces et diocèses abonnez': 'Par arrest du 28 mars 1711 le Languedoc fut abonné pour le dixième des biens fonds sur le pied des 2s pour livre des impositions pendant les années 1711 et 1712. On a estimé le montant de ces 2s pour livre à 1.100.000^{lt} par an et par autre arrest du 24 octobre cette imposition a esté réduite a 780.000^{lt} à commencer du 1er janvier 1713. Le dixième n'eut lieu qu'à commencer du 1er janvier 1711.'

[87] AN G⁷ 192 no. 237, 26 Nov. 1711.

[88] AN G⁷ 165 nos. 215, 220, ? and 20 May 1715. This was subsequently amended to an *abonnement* for the *capitation* alone: G⁷ 166/170 no. 8, *c*. 1718 (which mentions an *abonnement* for the *capitation* of 600,000 *livres* per annum as a result of a decree of 5 June 1717).

[89] AN G⁷ 18, 25 June and 22 July 1711. R. J. Bonney, 'Was there a Bourbon style of monarchy?', *From Valois to Bourbon: dynasty, state and society in early modern France*, ed. K. Cameron (Exeter, 1989), p. 167.

ième,⁹⁰ while Alsace was exempted from the new tax because of the burden of its grain requisitions for the army.⁹¹

IV

With the exception of Sauveterre in Béarn, where there was an *émotion*, the tax met with no overt rioting.⁹² However, there was a more pacific form of resistance from several quarters. Local financiers and tax-contractors resisted the forced distribution of *rentes*, which replaced their liability under the *dixième*, though they were allowed to assess themselves if they could reach agreement.⁹³ At Lyon, Méliand was authorized to imprison the sieur Chol, *contrôleur de la monnaie*; there was also resistance from the sieur Laisné, *directeur de la monnaie*: 'ce sont de ces sortes de gens qui après avoir fait une fortune qu'on peut dire immense en servant le Roy s'oublient entièrement . . .'⁹⁴ Remissions to individuals for political reasons might be proposed by the intendant,⁹⁵ while in Languedoc Basville was openly sympathetic to their plight, 'les uns par des banqueroutes, les autres par des taxes excessives et réiterées qu'ils ont paié, ou enfin par le mauvais état de leurs affaires . . .' He proposed a general reduction in the tax liability of *gens d'affaires*, because they still had to pay the *dixième de l'industrie*.⁹⁶ Remissions of this aspect of the tax for special interest groups whose commerce had suffered might be proposed by the intendant.⁹⁷ In Guyenne as late as May 1712, Lamoignon de Courson had still not levied the *dixième de l'industrie* 'par la difficulté que je croyais de pouvoir le lever'; he proposed an *abonnement*.⁹⁸ At Lyon we know that at first 'le recouvrement du dixième de l'industrie va assez lentement, peu de personnes sont disposéz a le payer de bon gré . . .',⁹⁹ while at Paris coercion was used at least for a short time for the levy of the *dixième de l'industrie*.¹⁰⁰

It was clear that the nobility were likely to prove the biggest obstacle to an equitable levy of the *dixième*, as they had demonstrated over the levy-

---

⁹⁰ AN G⁷ 18, 23 Apr. 1711, Desmaretz specifying an increase of the *capitation* by 200.000 *livres*. G⁷ 249 no. 98, 31 May 1711. But cf. G⁷ 249 no. 199, 4 Oct. 1711, which refers to this as an *abonnement* of 150,000 *livres*. The tax, which was imposed by an ordinance of the intendant on 12 May 1711, led to a *placet* from the Senate and *Chambre des Comptes* of Savoy, but the intendant's suggestion on 31 December 1711 that the existing arrangements continue received Desmaretz's approval: G⁷ 249 nos. 236, 237, 239.
⁹¹ Bonney, 'The state and its revenues', p. 154.
⁹² AN G⁷ 19, 25 Jan. 1712.
⁹³ AN G⁷ 18, 19 Feb. 1711 [*Correspondance des contrôleurs généraux*, ed. Boislisle, iii. 356-7]. Marion, *Les impôts directs*, pp. 336-7.
⁹⁴ AN G⁷ 365, 3 Oct. 1711.
⁹⁵ AN G⁷ 366, 11 May 1713.
⁹⁶ AN G⁷ 316 nos. 217, 312, 331, 27 Sept., 25 Nov. and 4 Dec. 1711.
⁹⁷ AN G⁷ 323 no. 212, 28 June 1715.
⁹⁸ Marion, *Les impôts directs*, p. 341.
⁹⁹ AN G⁷ 365, 17 Oct. 1711.
¹⁰⁰ AN G⁷ 1138-9, 18 Mar. 1713.

ing of the *capitation*. Desmaretz informed the intendants on 20 August 1711:[101]

> L'on prétend qu'il est deub des sommes considérables de cette imposition et particulièrement par la noblesse qui en doit plusieurs années. Envoyez moy un état séparé et en détail de ces restes et marquez moy ceux des gentilishommes qui ne payent point par impuissance ou par mauvaise volonté afin d'y aporter le remède convenable.

One obvious strategy with the *dixième*, which was adopted by the nobility of Auvergne, was simply not to supply the necessary declarations of wealth.[102] Just before his departure from the province, Turgot noted that work on the tax for 1713 had been 'presque doublé par le défaut des déclarations, le nombre infiny de requêtes que l'on présente journellement rend l'ouvrage de la réforme du 10ᵉ de 1713 nécessaire mais d'une longueur infinie . . .'[103] His successor, Béchameil de Nointel, continued to experience difficulties with the nobility of Auvergne in the summer of 1715: 'Il semble même qu'ils agissent tous dans le même esprit lorsqu'on leur demande le payement . . .' The intendant stressed 'la nécessité qu'il y a de se servir des remèdes qui puissent obliger la noblesse a montrer l'exemple, et a se soumettre à payer régulièrement les impositions qui leur sont demandées'.[104] When the sieur Degoincourt arrived at Limoges in December 1711, he found that three-quarters of the landed proprietors of the province had still not supplied their declarations of wealth, while most of those who had done so had given fraudulent evaluations ('si peu sincères, et si éloignées de la juste valeur des biens, et de leur revenu . . .').[105]

Lamoignon de Courson noted similar difficulties in the *généralité* of Bordeaux in December 1711:[106]

> Plusieurs s'estoient imaginé qu'ils ne devoient rien payer, et ils s'estoient assemblés pour vous faire une députation prétendant qu'en Saintonge et en Limousin on ne l'exigeoit pas; le principal mobil de tout cela est un gentilhomme appelé M. de la Coste qui

---

[101] BN MS Fr. 8896 fo. 227ᵛ.

[102] This was a general problem, as is evident from the renewal of the legislation on 1 March 1712 concerning the failure to declare wealth (double payment of the tax was due in such cases) and false declarations (quadruple payment of the tax was due in such cases): *Mémoires concernant les impositions et droits*, ed. Moreau de Beaumont, ii. 470.

[103] AN G⁷ 108–11 no. 74, 20 Dec. 1713.

[104] AN G⁷ 108–11 no. 127, 9 Aug. 1715.

[105] AN G⁷ 1138–9, 'Mémoire présenté par Mr Pernet à Nosseigneurs les commissaires généraux du dixième,et qui a operé la révocation du Sr Degoincourt'.

[106] AN G⁷ 144 nos. 191, 193, 15 and 19 Dec. 1711 [*Correspondance des contrôleurs généraux*, ed. Boislisle, iii. 417–18]. Marion, *Les impôts directs*, pp. 339–40. The sieur de Gardonne, *conseiller au sénéchal*, was also imprisoned to assist the collection of taxes at Périgueux. La Coste paid his taxes before 19 January 1712: G⁷ 144 no. 226.

s'estoit donné beaucoup de mouvement et avoit déjà gagné plusieurs gentilshommes . . . il commençoit à se répandre un bruit dans tout le reste de la généralité que la noblesse du Périgord se feroit exempter de payer le dixième, ce qui arrestoit en ce pays cy les recouvrements . . .

At first the intendant seems to have prevailed over opposition to the tax, but the death of the king led 'les esprits mutins et séditieux de Périgueux' to talk of re-establishing 'leur ancienne independance', which suggests that fiscal resistance had returned by September 1715.[107] The opposition to the tax was led by members of the *Parlement* of Bordeaux, especially Dudon, the *avocat général*: 'Je ne l'ai taxé que suivant la déclaration qu'il m'a faite, et je suis prêt de justifier qu'il s'en faut de plus du tiers qu'il ne paie ce qu'il devrait payer dans la rigueur . . . Il a dit publiquement depuis deux ans qu'on ne l'obligerait jamais de payer et qu'il fallait être fou pour payer . . .' 'Les officiers des compagnies supérieures', he added on a subsequent occasion in August 1716, 'sont encore plus difficiles que les autres, parce qu'on ne peut les attaquer sans offenser en même temps tout le corps.'[108] As late as March 1718, the intendant was still talking of 'une grande union' among the nobility of the Périgord aimed at preventing the payment of arrears of the tax.[109]

The neighbouring *généralité* of Montauban experienced similar difficulties. Le Gendre informed Desmaretz on 31 March 1711 that 'ce travail est d'une si grande discussion, et il est si difficile dans les élections éloignées d'avoir les éclaircissements nécessaires, et même de trouver des copistes pour y travailler, dans la crainte de se faire des ennemis . . .' '[L]e grand embarras', he continued, 'sera de faire payer ce dixième à une infinité de gentilhommes, qui ont à peine de quoy vivre, ou qui ont leurs enfants au service. Il n'y en aura pas le quart qui paye volontairement, le reste ne le faira que par la contrainte et les saisies, et en accordant quelque diminution à ceux que l'on connoîtra dans l'impuissance de payer. Ainsy il faudra sur cet article diminuer au moins un sixième pour les nonvaleurs.' If the minister continued to insist on declarations from individuals, 'cest un ouvrage d'un an. Presque toutes les déclarations des particuliers seront infidèles, et sur le pied de celles que j'ay déjà reçu, le dixième du revenu des biens nobles, et des biens ruraux n'iroit pas a 200.000^{lt} dans toute la généralité'. Estimates of wealth by the intendant or his agents would have to allow individuals a right of appeal, which would cause 'des frais immenses, qui iroient plus loin que le dixième, fairoit crier les peuples, causeroit peut estre pis, et arrêteroit non seulement ce recouvrement, mais même celuy de la taille'.[110] Desmaretz denounced the intendant's conduct:

---

[107] AN G^7 146 no. 347, 17 Sept. 1715.
[108] Marion, *Les impôts directs*, pp. 343-4. Marion, *L'impôt sur le revenu*, p. 123.
[109] Marion, *L'impôt sur le revenu*, pp. 121-2.
[110] AN G^7 398, 31 Mar. 1711.

'Vôtre sistème est entièrement contraire aux intentions de Sa Majesté qui veut que la déclaration soit exécutée . . .'[111] Le Gendre was fearful of the consequences of the *dixième*, and used his twelve years' experience in the province to try to dilute the declaration of 14 October 1710, so as to make the new tax an adjunct of the *taille*. 'Les impositions sont déjà si fortes et le dixième donne tant de peine à lever qu'il est à craindre que cela ne fasse murmurer le peuple . . .', he warned Desmaretz the following year.[112] However, the intendant's capacity for dealing with the nobility was hampered by the fact that his own house was not in order. Le Gendre had to write to Desmaretz in November 1713 'au sujet de son dixième' because he had not paid any tax 'depuis l'établissement, ce qui fait 5940^{lt} que je suis bien éloigné d'avoir en mon pouvoir'.[113] By late December, the attempt to justify his conduct[114] seems to have failed, and the suggestion is that he was recalled because of his non-payment of the *dixième* and for altering the *dixième* rolls. The 'Plainte de M. Le Gendre sur sa destitution' boasted of 'la confiance que la noblesse avoit en moy m'avoit rendu le dépositaire de ce qu'il avoit de plus secret dans les principales familles'. Yet it is clear that the intendant had made many enemies in the province, and not merely through his administration of the new tax.[115] Difficulties remained in the *généralité* of Montauban after Le Gendre's recall. His successor, Laugeois d'Imbercourt, found that the marquis de Giscaro 'ne vouloit point payer ses tailles et son dixième'. De Parrade, whose grandfather had been a *président à mortier* in the *Parlement* of Toulouse, was preventing the sequestration of his property for non-payment. The intendant confessed that 'La naissance et la considération de ces deux personnes m'a empesché d'y envoyer des cavalliers en garnison, . . . ayan crû plus convenable de vous en informer Monsieur et d'attendre vos ordres.' Desmaretz provided him with the authorization for the use of force which he sought.[116]

Similar difficulties were experienced by Beauharnais de Beauville, intendant at La Rochelle, 'plusieurs gentilshommes ayant eu la témérité de menacer les huissiers et même les receveurs, prétendant se garantir par cette voye de leurs poursuites'. Desmaretz instructed the intendant that 'une conduite semblable ne devant point estre tolérée, l'intention de Sa Majesté est d'en punir ceux qui en seront coupables, et sur lesquels vous estimerez le plus convenable d'en faire des exemples'.[117] In Brittany, Ferrand, the intendant, demanded a *lettre de cachet* from the minister to discipline two noblemen, the marquis de Carman and the marquis de Bresal, who refused to pay the tax and whose obduracy served as pretext

---

[111] AN G⁷ 18, 11 Apr. 1711.
[112] AN G⁷ 398, 22 Mar. 1712.
[113] AN G⁷ 398, 1 Nov. 1713.
[114] AN G⁷ 398, 21 Dec. 1713.
[115] AN G⁷ 399, 29 May 1714. Though, after the fall of Desmaretz, Le Gendre was appointed as intendant at Pau.
[116] AN G⁷ 399, 18 Oct. 1714.
[117] AN G⁷ 20, 20 Jan. 1713.

for non-compliance by others: 'Deux ou trois exemples mettront les autres en règle.'[118] In Béarn, the leader of resistance to the tax, the baron d'Arros, was debarred from entering the estates for four years; subsequently the intendant persuaded the ministers that news of his exclusion was sufficient punishment and that he could safely be readmitted subject to good conduct.[119] Coercion by troops was used in the *généralité* of Paris,[120] but privileged persons such as the marquis d'Auray, lieutenant-general in the army, received suspension orders.[121] Appeals frequently went to the council, and for relatively trivial sums: the marquis de Chamron opposed his 800 *livres* of tax imposed by La Briffe, intendant of Burgundy, in 1714, and sent the papers to the council: the great interest of this case lies in the fact that he supported his case with extracts from notarial acts.[122] The marquise of Sailli tried to oppose the intendant's coercion order for her properties in the *élection* of Péronne on the grounds that the farmers of her properties elsewhere (in the *élections* of Doullens, Amiens and Montdidier) had already settled their due.[123]

Elsewhere, the nobility was more compliant. In the Lyonnais, Méliand had no difficulties except with the comtesse de Viruille, who told him 'qu'il ne convenoit pas à un commissaire du Roy de la mettre au rang de ceux qui dans cette affaire n'ont pas donné leurs déclarations, quoy qu'elle soit peut estre la seulle dans la noblesse qui n'ayt pas obey de bonne grâce . . .'[124] Only with the advent of the Regency did the intendant warn of impending difficulties in tax collection due to the hopes of 'un soulagement dans les impositions'.[125] In Picardy, because of the operations of the army on the frontier, the real fiscal burden was already oppressive before the introduction of the *dixième*. In September 1710, Bernage, the intendant, warned that 'cette province qui est déjà dans une misère au dessus de toute expression tombera sans ressource' without a remission of taxes, 'et vous voyez assez combien sa chute influeroit sur l'estat . . .'[126] However, the *dixième* was introduced, which resulted in the summer of 1711 in a petition presented to the king from 'des gentilshommes privilegiez et taillables' subject to the contributions exacted by the rival armies.[127] Elsewhere, the tax does not seem to have caused particular difficulties, and some intendants used the prompt levy of the *dixième* as part of their justification for the

---

[118] AN G⁷ 193 nos. 279, 311, 10 Aug. and 7 Sept. 1712. Marion, *Les impôts directs*, pp. 341-2.
[119] Bonney, 'Was there a Bourbon style of monarchy?', p. 167.
[120] AN G⁷ 440 fos. 151-2, 13 Mar. 1713.
[121] AN G⁷ 442-4, 11 Mar. 1713 (Orléans).
[122] AN G⁷ 1138-9, 'Estat des biens de Monsieur le marquis de Chamron . . .', and letter from Chamron to Desmaretz, 22 August 1714, claiming that 'Mr l'intendant a été mal informé de la situation des biens que j'ay dans son département . . .'
[123] AN G⁷ 1138-9, Sept. 1712, and accompanying printed coercion order of the intendant.
[124] AN G⁷ 365, 11 Mar. 1711.
[125] AN G⁷ 367, 7 Sept. 1715.
[126] AN G⁷ 92, 18 Sept. 1710.
[127] AN G⁷ 93, 2 Aug. 1711.

payment of a pension: thus Foullé de Montargis claimed that the *dixième* in Berry was 'plus tôt perçu et plus tôt en règle que dans les autres généralités'.[128]

V

The combined impact of concessions and fiscal resistance, whether overt or covert, clearly limited the effectiveness of the *dixième*.[129] The first *dixième* yielded 28 million on a levy of 30.2 million in 1711 (including the last quarter of 1710), 22.7 million on 24.4 million in 1712, 22.5 million on 24.3 million in 1713 and 22.8 million on 24.1 in 1714, or an extra 96 million in total over four years (Figure 4).[130] Figure 5 presents (somewhat higher) figures than those in the previous chart, with a somewhat different categories of revenue. The contribution of the *pays d'élections* loomed much larger than that of the *pays d'états*, and again the figures are gross. There are no figures for 1715 in this table.[131] The overhead cost, relatively low for a new tax in wartime, was 9.5 per cent or thereabouts. Desmaretz considered that in the best years the levy had never exceeded 24 million.[132] This was, of course, far short of the 120 million which some propagandists had considered necessary and possible for the crown to levy in the period before the introduction of the tax in 1710.[133] The historian cannot ascertain the real shortfall between the tax yield and the notional tenth on revenue. Vauban had estimated that his *dixme royale* would produce an annual revenue of 116.8 million.[134] John Law, in a letter to Desmaretz dated 26 July 1715, estimated French national revenue at 1,200 million

---

[128] AN G⁷ 128-30, 22 Jan. 1715. Though there were arrears of taxes, and tax resistance, at Bourges: G⁷ 128-30, 10 Dec. 1714.

[129] This paragraph draws, in a modified form, on material which first appeared in Bonney, 'The state and its revenues', pp. 166-7. Figure 4 includes the charges and thus gives the gross figures.

[130] ESFDB \rjb\dixb003 based on dataset \dixd001.ssd (after AN G⁷ 1138-9, 'Récapitulation du Bordereau général du produit du dixième dans le Royaume'). In the chart, 'charges' include the *Dixième des charges* and *Dixième des charges de Bourgogne*. 'Other' includes the *Dixième des Communautés du Châtelet*; *Dixième des communautés de la ville de Paris*; *Dixième des 12 & 25 privilegiez maîtres de vin, et des officiers et archers de la ville de Paris*; *Dixième des États des Trésoriers*; *Dixième des appointements des commis*; *Dixième des droits attribuez à plusieurs offices et droits aliénés*; *des rentes dûs par des ecclésiastiques à des laiques et des rentes*; *des communautés d'arts et métiers et du recouvrement du Sr Goujon*. For the impact of the *dixième* in the localities: Lemarchand, *La fin du féodalisme dans le pays de Caux*, p. 154. Houques-Fourcade, *Les impôts sur le revenu en France au xviiie siècle*, pp. 238-9.

[131] ESFDB \rjb\dixb004 based on dataset \dixd002.ssd (after AN G⁷ 1138-9, 'Montant du dixième des 19 généralités, des Pays d'États, de la ville de Paris, des charges, et des employez pour les années 1711, 1712, 1713 et 1714').

[132] *Correspondance des contrôleurs-généraux des finances*, ed. Boislisle, iii. 626.

[133] Apart from the memorandum quoted above, another 'Mémoire sur ce qui paroist praticable pour donner le temps au ministre de fournir à ses premières dépenses' in AN G⁷ 1138-9 stated that a *vingtième* could reach 60 million, but even if it encountered some difficulty at the outset 'l'on ne croit pas que cela monte à moins de 50 millions'.

[134] Vauban, *Projet d'une dixme royale*, ed. J-F. Pernot (Saint-Léger-Vauban, 1988), p. 66.

'LE SECRET DE LEURS FAMILLES'

livres, the same capital evaluation as Vauban's, although he seems to have based his calculations on a comparison with England.[135] Modern estimates have tended to place the national product higher,[136] but these should be moderated by Forbonnais's comment on the fall in national output during the War of the Spanish Succession. Forbonnais regarded the *dixième* as 'une taxe proportionnelle; celui qui possède peu, contribue peu'.[137] But he added: 'plus on avoit tardé à employer cette ressource, plus la charge en fut pesante sur les Peuples & moins l'État en retira d'avantages . . . tous les revenus de l'État étoient tombés; aussi va-t-on voir que le dixième ne rendit pas plus de vingt-quatre millions dans les meilleures années. N'est-il pas évident qu'en l'imposant dès le commencement de la guerre, lorsque tous les revenus étoient encore entiers, il eût produit beaucoup davantage?'[138] If John Law's may be taken as the most reliable estimate, then the *dixième* was underassessed on average by 80 per cent, although we should note that not every part of the national wealth would fall within the scope of the tax. The underassessment of the *dixième*, and its successor tax, the *vingtième*, became progressively worse in the eighteenth century.[139] Voluntary declarations were never likely to be satisfactory. The only alternative was to pitch the levy excessively high, and to allow taxpayers to obtain moderations only by presenting proof of their taxable income: but this laid the government open to the accusation of acting in an arbitrary manner in the administration of a tax that was supposed to be more equitable than those which had preceded it. The charge of despotic conduct was already levelled during Desmaretz's ministry: 'Nous serions mille fois plus heureux en Turquie qu'en France.' An anonymous letter to Desmaretz expressed this charge clearly in relation to the power of the intendant and the director of the *dixième* acting on the minister's instructions.[140]

On the other hand, the government clearly sought to act with moderation, which explains the numerous concessions to corporate and provincial interests.[141] These concessions, in turn, are reflected in the different

---

[135] He seems to have derived his French estimate by multiplying the English estimated national wealth by three. On an English estimate of 'entre 5 et 600 millions de livres de France', the French national revenues 'devroient monter de 15[00] à 1800 millions'. But his proposed bank 'peut augmenter les revenus généraux de la France de 1200 millions à 1800 millions': *Oeuvres complètes de John Law*, ed. P. Harsin (3 vols., Liège and Paris, 1934), ii. 50–2.

[136] J. C. Riley, *The Seven Years' War and the Old Regime in France: the economic and financial toll* (Princeton, N.J., 1986), p. 22.

[137] F. Véron de Forbonnais, *Recherches et considérations sur les finances de France depuis l'année 1595 jusqu'à l'année 1721* (2 vols., Basle, 1758), i. 526. The remark was made in relation to the *vingtième*, the successor tax to the *dixième*.

[138] Ibid. ii. 221–2.

[139] Riley, *The Seven Years' War*, p. 70, notes that the *vingtièmes* were 'avoided or evaded by some 85 per cent of the estimated national output of the 1750s'. If the calculation based on John Law's figures above is correct, then there was no real deterioration in the situation. On the phenomenon at a local level: Lemarchand, *La fin du féodalisme dans le pays de Caux*, pp. 298–9.

[140] AN G⁷ 1138–9, anon. letter to Desmaretz, no place, 10 Oct. 1712.

[141] Cf. Houques-Fourcade, *Les impôts sur le revenu en France au xviiie siècle*, p. 234: 'La levée du dixième fut certainement partout faite avec une grande douceur.'

types of record surviving for the levy of the *dixième*. The *pays d'élections* were the only areas where the original objectives of the declaration of 14 October 1710 were carried out with relatively little modification, and as with the *taille*, there was a substantial measure of stability in the yield from the different *généralités* from one year to the next,[142] the greatest variations being caused by the fact that the figures for 1711 included the last quarter for 1710, while those for 1717 lack the returns from Paris, Soissons, Limoges, Moulins, Riom, Lyon and Grenoble (Figure 6).[143] The figures for the *pays d'états* which settled their *dixième* liability by composition (*abonnement*) are incomplete and too much should not be read into them; the total contribution of Languedoc was greater than that of Franche-Comté or Provence, as one would expect (Figure 7).[144]

VI

French taxpayers were obsessed by fears of 'une inquisition fascheuse qui mettra tous les sujets du Roy à la discrétion des secrétaires et des subdélégués de Messieurs les intendants'.[145] The threat posed by the *dixième* to taxpayers, and the difficulties faced by the government in trying to implement the tax, were perhaps greater in kind than with other taxes (in the case of the *taille*, for example, intendants rarely entered into detailed discussion of the case of *particuliers contribuables*),[146] but they were by no means unique. Nor were the difficulties faced by the government in 1710-17 unique to France. The English land tax of 1692 had originally been devised as a levy on all forms of incomes, but its incidence fell mainly on rents which, unlike other sources, could be more or less readily assessed. Valuations of landed property were reasonably acceptable because land could be seen, and there was much local knowledge regarding its relative value; but to place a value on personal and moveable wealth

---

[142] On this point, Bonney, 'Jean-Roland Malet', pp. 206, 231 and Bonney, 'The state and its revenues', p. 162.

[143] ESFDB \rjb\dixb001 based on dataset \dixm001.ssd (after AN G⁷ 1138-9, 'Dixième 1711', 'Dixième 1712', 'Dixième 1713' - in each case the 'Montant des rôles'; 'Estat du montant des rôles du dixième des années 1715, 1716 et 1717'.). These are gross figures; net figures only survive for 1711, 1712 and 1713. No detailed breakdown of figures appears to survive for the year 1714, while for 1717 the returns were affected by the revocation of the tax in August 1717. There were also reductions, amounting to 244,744 *livres* for 1716 and 38,872 *livres* for 1717 (an incomplete figure). On the chart the category 'other' represents Soissons, Bourges, Moulins, Lyon, Riom, Limoges, La Rochelle, Auch and Grenoble.

[144] ESFDB \rjb\dixb002 based on dataset \dixd004.ssd (after AN G⁷ 1138-9, 'Produit du dixième des provinces et diocèses abonnez'). The distinction between the two figures for Languedoc is that one represents the composition of the tax instead of the tax on landed wealth, while the other the levy of the *dixième* on other sources of wealth than land.

[145] AN G⁷ 437 fos. 361-4, 3 Apr. 1710 [*Correspondance des contrôleurs généraux*, ed. Boislisle, iii. 281]. Le Peletier, the first president of the *Parlement* of Paris, was writing on the question of the *taxe des aisés*.

[146] AN G⁷ 440 fos. 340-1, 22 Aug. 1713.

required an institutional structure which smacked of French 'despotism'.[147] Thirty years earlier, Sir William Petty's *Treatise of taxes and contributions* (1662) had been written with the practical purpose of justifying the hearth tax; but the author also publicized his ideas on the need for 'exact computation' so as to avoid fiscal fraud:[148]

> The . . . objection against this so exact computation of the Rents and wor[th] of lands, &c. is, that the Sovereign would know too exactly every man's Estate; to which I answer, that if the Charge of the Nation be brought as low as it may be, . . . and if the people be willing and ready to pay, and if care be taken, that although they have not ready money, the credit of their Lands and Goods shall be as good; and lastly, that it would be a great discommodity to the Prince to take more then he needs . . . where is the evil of so exact knowledge? And as for the proportion of every Contributor, why should any man hope or accept to ease himself by his craft and interest in a confusion? or why should he not fear, though he may be advantaged this time, to suffer in the next?

A letter from Petty to Arlington, secretary of state and a prominent member of the Cabal, in September 1671 reveals that at the king's 'command' he had considered how any new levy might be 'equally and proportionably taxed upon all persons and things' as well as 'speedily, safely and inexpensively collected'. A second consideration was not merely how the new fiscal system might be established for the current needs ('some single emergency') but subsequently so that the crown could judge what 'real effect and value' there might be in any tax proposals. The king must be in a position to know 'the wealth and other efficiencies of his subjects', as might be estimated by their expenditure and income from land, labour and personal estate: he would then be able to judge 'what part or proportion his subjects are able to spare in case of the greatest extremity and [that] which will suffice in the most serene and secure tymes'. 'An exact accompt' must be taken of the population 'in a conspic[u]ous and examinable man[n]er soe as to prevent all imaginary and arbitrary proceedings in this great poynt'. It was proposed that this investigation was to take place over a year between September 1671 and December 1672, and should comprise a census of the population, according to age, trade, office, title, religious status or other qualifications; the value of lands in each parish, their quan-

---

[147] D. E. Ginter, *A measure of wealth: the English land tax in historical analysis* (1992), pp. 21-2. J. Brewer, *The sinews of power: war, money and the English state, 1688-1783* (London, Boston, Sydney, Wellington, 1989), pp. 99-100. D. W. Jones, *War and economy in the age of William III and Marlborough* (Oxford, 1988), pp. 70-3. W. A. Speck, 'England in the 1690s. The emergence of the fiscal-military state', *Historian*, 38 (1993), 4.

[148] *The economic writings of Sir William Petty*, ed. C. H. Hull (2 vols., 1899; repr. New York, 1963), i. 53-4.

tity, quality, situation, rentable value, and so on would be enumerated; so too would the external measurement of every house in the kingdom, its location whether in city, market town or village, and the rent and value of each building; a property valuation of each inhabitant (including furniture, clothes and utensils as well as an estimate for 'ye ware and tare of ye same') would be carried out; and finally other forms of wealth ('goods out of doors'), including shipping and exports, the cost of poor relief, and so on, would be evaluated. The purpose of the investigation, declared Petty, was not to enable the king to 'take one pen[n]y more than is necessary but only to levy with ease, certainty and equality what ye reason of his affaires requires'. In one sense, Petty failed. He proposed to Arlington a scheme which was far too ambitious for the needs of the moment (the eve of the third Anglo-Dutch war), and far too costly in its implementation, apart from risking recreating the intrusive state which Englishmen felt had been laid to rest at the end of the Commonwealth.[149]

Petty certainly influenced Boisguilbert,[150] and though there is no evidence that the Frenchman had any idea of Petty's unpublished plans for 'exact accompts', he, too, was pushed in a similar direction in 1705, proposing the revelation of wealth on which an accurate estimate of tax liability might be formulated. The same considerations that in the England of Charles II had led to the abandonment of Petty's plans prevailed in France, which also lacked one of his prior conditions ('if the people be willing and ready to pay . . .'). The future Chancellor Daguesseau summed up prevailing attitudes with his comment that 'il est bien dur d'obliger des [particuliers] . . . à produire des titres contre eux mesmes . . .'[151] We have seen that Desmaretz's plans for the *dixième de retenue* were designed to prevent the alarm which a more elaborate scheme might have aroused; this was the one aspect of the reform which was not revoked in 1717, but remained permanently in place until the end of the *ancien régime*. Taxation at the source of payment of *gages* and *rentes* did not arouse the same degree of hostility because it did not lead to an estimation or verification of wealth. One contemporary, who proposed a more extensive measure of fiscal reform, concluded on the enforcement arrangements for the declarations of wealth arising from the *dixième*: 'il semble qu'on n'a pas voulu alarmer les peuples par une recherche trop scrupuleuse'. The weakness of the French administrative system was the impossibility of finding impartial evidence for evaluating wealth and landed property; there was also an inadequate training of 'experts', who were mostly private enterprise financiers, or relatively poorly trained *arpenteurs*: 'Il faut non seulement de

---

[149] British Library, Petty Papers box c, item 23.
[150] *Pierre de Boisguilbert ou la naissance de l'économie politique*, i. 160–1.
[151] AN G⁷ 438 fos. 9–11, 6 Jan. 1711. Daguesseau's remarks were specifically concerned with a clause concerning the tax payable by financiers, and the extent to which successors of the financiers might be concerned, but this raised questions concerning 'les personnes de la première consideration qui ont épousé des filles des gens d'affaires . . .'

l'expérience et une connoissance des terres et de l'état des provinces, mais une grande capacité et de jugement, surtout un grand fonds de probité et de désintéressement, voir tout par soi même si cela se peut, ou ne s'en rapporter qu'à des gens fidèles et expérimentés, sçavoir la géometrie pour suppléer et pour se garantir de l'ignorance et des fraudes des arpenteurs.'[152] What might be just tolerated in wartime was likely to prove unacceptable in time of peace.

The judgement of two contemporaries provides a final verdict on the success of the evaluation of wealth. The first is that of the true author, though not the original proposer,[153] of the scheme, Desmaretz. The most effective direct tax of the *ancien régime* was conceived by him as a wartime measure only, a *subside ou imposition pour la guerre*.[154] In a memorandum of January 1715 to the king, he outlined four alternatives for financing the deficit after the war including the continuation of the tax. In a second memorandum of 20 February 1715, he tried to calculate the cost of these four options.[155] The proposal to continue the *dixième* and the *capitation* suffered from two disadvantages: 'il faudroit ordonner la levée de ces impositions extraordinaires à perpétuité, et il ne paroit pas possible d'établir pour un revenu ordinaire du Roi des levées extraordinaires qui n'ont été ordonnées que par rapport aux besoins pressants de la guerre'. Though the *dixième* was supposed to be rescindé within three months of the peace, it was continued by a declaration of 9 July 1715 shortly before the king's death, on the grounds of the pressing debts resulting from the war and the alienation of revenues since 1689.[156] Of equal importance for Desmaretz was a second objection: 'à l'égard du dixième, une grande partie des déclarations sont fausses, et il est bien difficile d'entrer dans l'examen de toutes les terres pour constater le revenu d'un chacun. On le pourroit; mais ce seroit la voie de rigueur.' Thus when Philibert Orry reintroduced the tax in 1733,[157] at the outbreak of the War of the Polish Succession, he specified that though there might be recourse to wealth declarations from 1710 as general guidance, no great reliance could be placed on them since

---

[152] AN G⁷ 1138–9, 'Moyen proposé pour faire un dénombrement exact de tout le Royaume'.

[153] At the end of August 1710, Boisguilbert's latest proposals were brutally rejected: 'en finance les principes doivent être fondés sur des faits réels et indubitables, et un projet dont toutes les parties ne répondent pas parfaitement à l'état du royaume ne peut avoir de succès . . .' AN G⁷ 17 [*Correspondance des contrôleurs généraux*, ed. Boislisle, iii. 310–11]. Desmaretz rejected on 22 June 1711 a request from the sieur de Malon, *commissaire provincial des guerres* at Auteuil, that he had 'donné l'avis pour l'establissement du dixième. Lequel n'auroit pû estre executé sans la clause de retenue': AN G⁷ 1138–9.

[154] Desmaretz's drafting of the preamble is in AN G⁷ 1138–9, in a dossier entitled 'projets, minutes et déclaration ordonnant la levée du 10ᵉ'. Comparison with the parchment declaration in the same dossier [and also in AN K 2413 no. 80] shows that the wording was virtually unaltered thereafter.

[155] Ibid. iii. 622–9.

[156] *Mémoires concernant les impositions et droits*, ed. Moreau de Beaumont, ii. 472. Marion, *Les impôts directs*, pp. 274–5.

[157] The fact that the controller-general chose his father's scheme may, of course, indicate a family commitment to this type of fiscal solution.

'les déclarations ayant été inférieures de plus de moitié aux revenus réels; les états donnés à cette date ne devront servir que d'indications . . .' The earlier declarations had been too generalized; in future, they should be more detailed so that their accuracy could be checked.[158]

John Law arrived at similar conclusions to those of Desmaretz when evaluating the success of the tax. He emphasized the difficulty of enforcing the royal declaration concerning the levy of the *dixième*:[159]

> 1° la moitié des déclarations ne fut pas fournie; 2° celles qui furent fournies le furent sur le pied de moitié moins que leur véritable valeur; on ne doit pas en être surpris, les ministres du Roy n'ayant pas voulu poursuivre à la rigueur le recouvrement d'une nouvelle imposition, qui étoit une augmentation à plusieurs autres ordinaires et extraordinaires déjà établies, en sorte que toutes jointes ensemble, elles excédoient peut-être le 25ᵉ denier. C'est pourquoy les ministres se contentèrent alors de tirer ce qu'ils purent du dixième.

The Physiocrats would later criticize the successor tax of the *dixième*, the *vingtième*, for its failure to tax net income.[160] Boisguilbert already saw clearly that it was a tax on gross income in the countryside, and argued that the tax on industry should be increased threefold to counterbalance this.[161] To what extent were contemporaries aware of this criticism? That it was a tax on gross income seems clear from the remark of La Briffe, intendant of Burgundy, that a reduction in the *capitation des taillables* would 'donner moyen aux fermiers de payer leurs maîtres qui seront en estat de payer le dixième'.[162] In Guyenne, Lamoignon de Courson specified that under his preferred solution, taxpayers 'ne payeront que le 17ᵉ ou le 18ᵉ de la valeur des revenus des fonds', whereas under the terms of the declaration they were to pay a 'dixième effectif . . . sans déduction des charges . . .'[163] In Languedoc, Basville, who had been sceptical about the tax from the outset, tried to dispel doubts about his commitment to it by pressing for prompt declarations of wealth, without allowing moderations or appeals until this had been done. But were the costs of cultivation

---

[158] Marion, *Les impôts directs*, pp. 345-6. Cf. ibid. p. 347: 'un fait certain, c'est que toutes les déclarations sont plus ou moins infidèles et que le sujet a cherché à tromper le prince . . .'
[159] *Oeuvres de Law*, ed. Harsin, iii. 55
[160] There is an old scholarly controversy on this point. Houques-Fourcade, *Les impôts sur le revenu en France au xviiiᵉ siècle*, pp. 152-3, claimed it was a tax on gross income. This was vigorously refuted by Marion, *L'impôt sur le revenu*, p. 94 n. 1, and Marion, *Les impôts directs*, pp. 65-6. However, all Marion's evidence on this point comes from the later *dixième* or its successor, the *vingtième*, so his point remains unproven for Louis XIV's *dixième*.
[161] Boislisle, 'L'impôt du dixième', p. 467. *Pierre de Boisguilbert ou la naissance de l'économie politique*, i. 473-4. *Correspondance des contrôleurs généraux*, ed. Boislisle, iii. 662. AN G⁷ 721 no. 95, 29 Jan. 1713.
[162] AN G⁷ 165 no. 183, 1 Feb. [1716]. Cf. G⁷ 166-70 no. 3, 27 Jan. 1716.
[163] Marion, *Les impôts directs*, p. 336 (evidence which seems to contradict categorically his assertion made ibid. pp. 65-6).

allowable, he asked, and if not, 'si l'on n'admet pas des imputations, comment feront-ils pour payer?' And what would be the consequences for agriculture? 'Il ne faut point entrer dans ces détails' was Desmaretz's answer.[164] The tax was far from the Physiocratic ideal of a single tax on net income. Reflecting on the idea that there should be fiscal reform at the beginning of the Regency, Basville commented that new tax schemes such as Vauban's had always seemed to him 'trop difficile et d'une dangereuse conséquence'. Taxpayers paid by habit, he asserted, and also because they were forced to pay, the question being how best to moderate the use of force 'et de ne la faire que bien à propos'. The problem with new tax schemes was that they risked creating the impression that the old taxes would no longer have to be paid, while everyone sought to evade payment under the new scheme, 'ce qui jetterait les affaires dans une grande confusion'. The *dixième* had not been acceptable in Languedoc until there had been an *abonnement*, which led to its being confused with other taxes and thus no longer contentious.[165] The longest-serving intendant, a covert opponent of Louis XIV's *dixième* ('révéler le secret de sa famille . . . C'est la dernière des extrémités, et si contraire au génie de la nation'), saw his view confirmed when the tax was revoked in August 1717.[166] Collective resistance and significant concessions to individuals had damaged the viability of a tax which could only have been countered by a much more authoritarian government than existed under the regency of Philippe d'Orléans.[167] The 'fiscal limits' of the tax were in fact restrictions on what was permissible which were imposed by prevailing political conditions and social attitudes. In this respect we may speak of the 'fiscal and social limits' of Louis XIV's *dixième*.

[164] AN G⁷ 314 no. 243, 17 Nov. 1710 [*Correspondance des contrôleurs généraux*, ed. Boislisle, iii. 330-1].
[165] *Mémoires des intendants sur l'état des généralités pour l'instruction du duc de Bourgogne. I. Mémoire de la généralité de Paris*, ed. A. M. de Boislisle (1881), pp. 486-7.
[166] Marion, *Les impôts directs*, pp. 275-6.
[167] Ibid. p. 348, for Orry's judgement on the concessions in 1717. Houques-Fourcade, *Les impôts sur le revenu en France au xviiie siècle*, pp. 73-4, on collective resistance.
Since this paper went to press, an extremely interesting discussion of the issues of progressive taxation in France has appeared: J-P. Gross, 'Progressive taxation and social justice in eighteenth-century France', *Past and P*, 140 (1993), 79-126. However, at pp. 87-8, Gross devotes only a paragraph to the *dixième*.

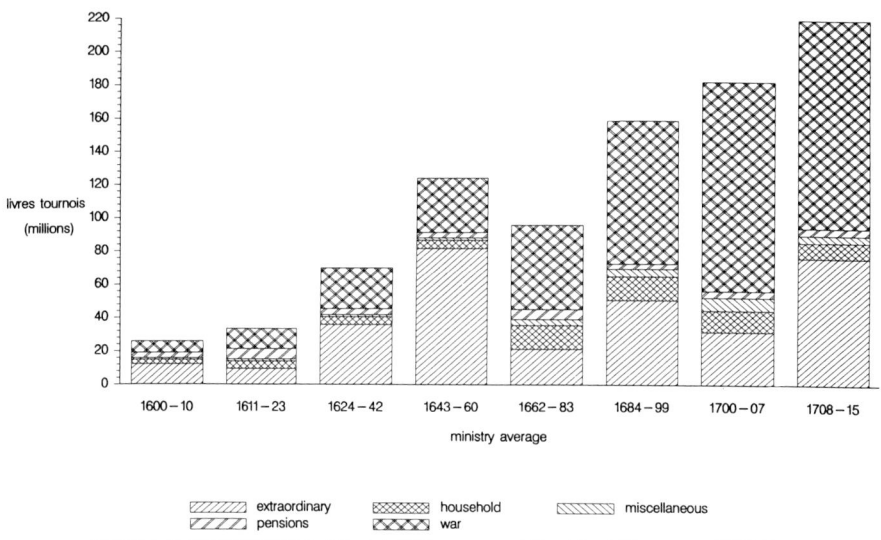

Figure 1: Categories of French royal expenditure averaged by ministry, 1600–1715.

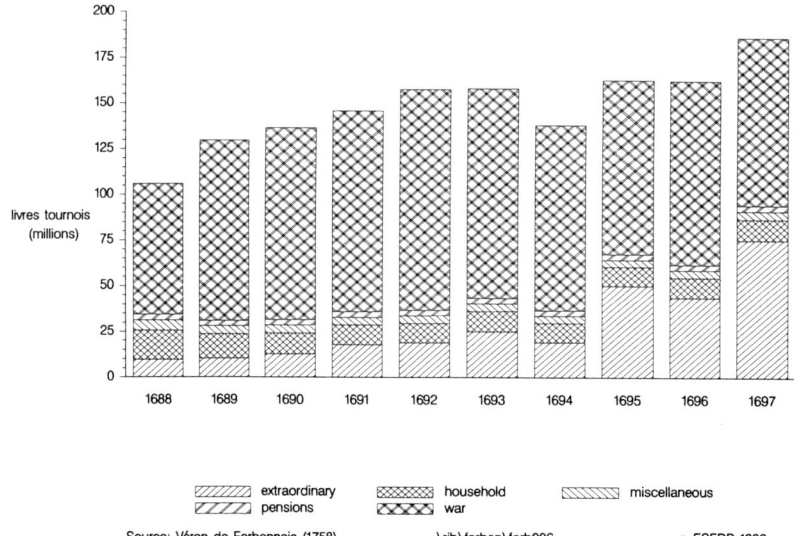

Figure 2: French royal expenditure during the war of the League of Augsburg, 1688–1697.

414 'LE SECRET DE LEURS FAMILLES'

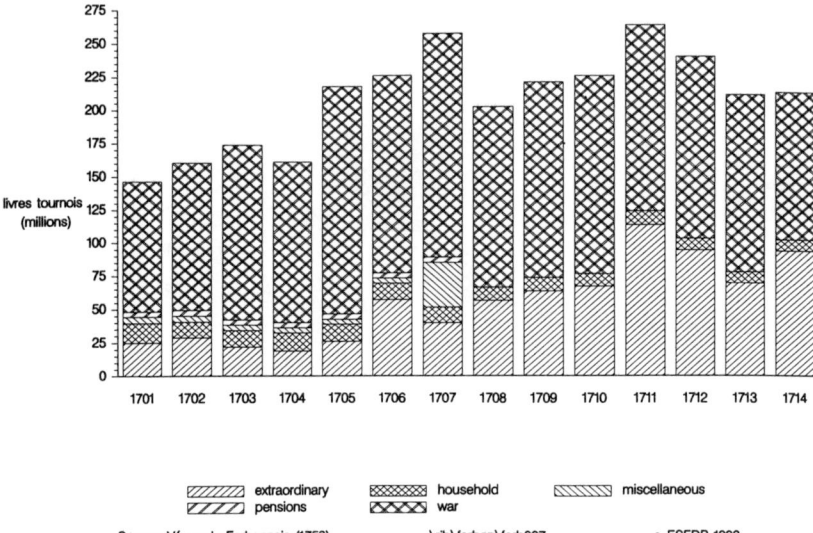

Figure 3: French royal expenditure during the war of the Spanish succession, 1701–1714.

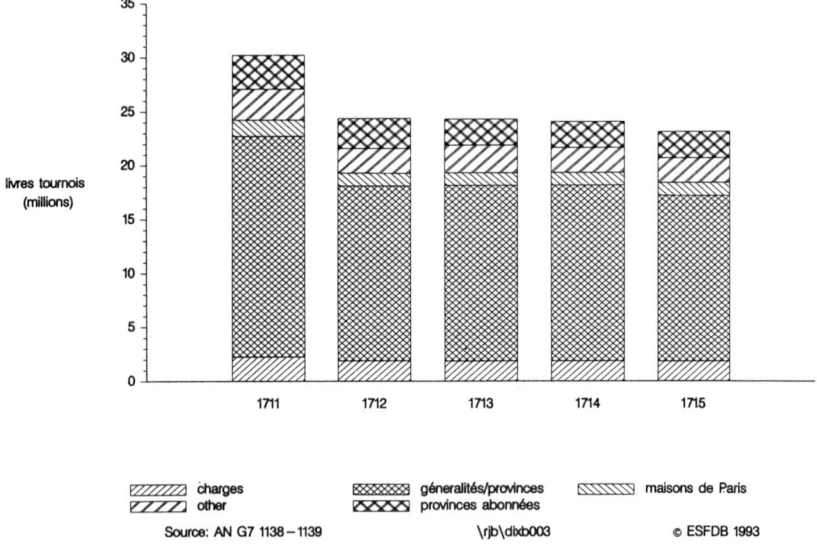

Figure 4: Total levy of the *dixième* in France, 1711–1715.

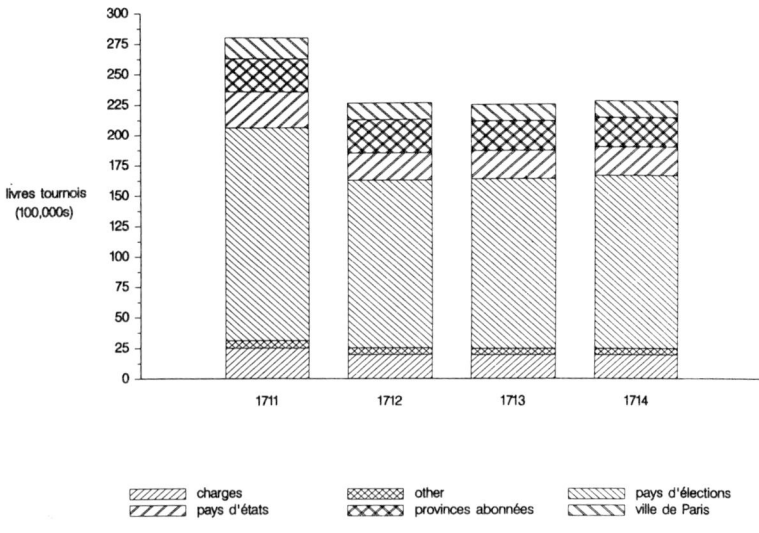

Figure 5: Gross revenue from the *dixième* in France, 1711–1714.

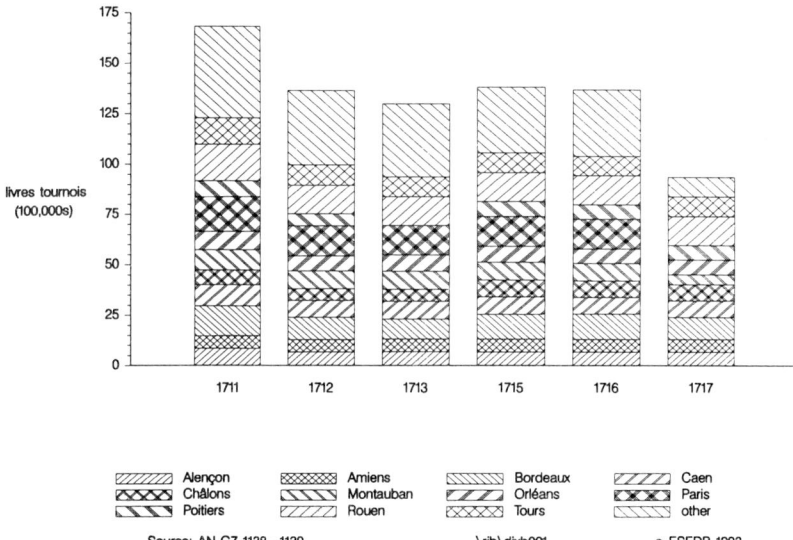

Figure 6: Total levy of the *dixième* in the *pays d'élections*, 1711–1717.

416 'LE SECRET DE LEURS FAMILLES'

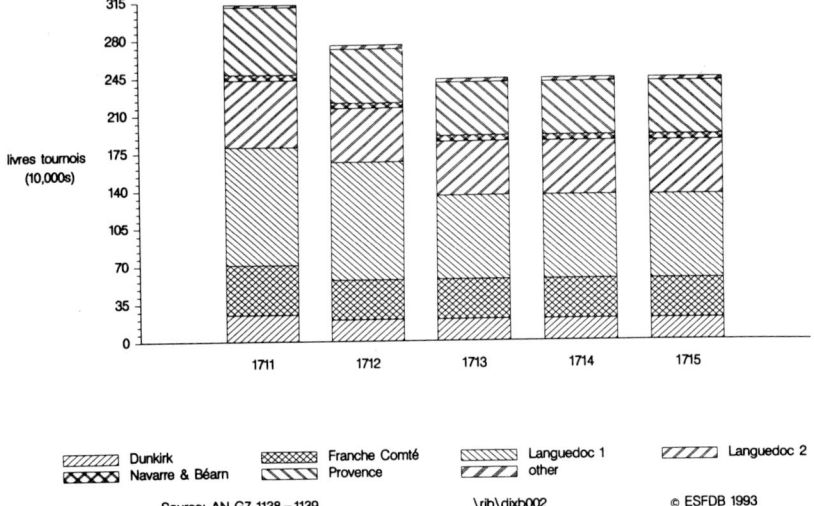

Figure 7: Revenue from the *dixième* in the provinces abonnées et diocèses abonnés, 1711–1715.

XV

COMPARATIVE FISCAL SYSTEMS ON THE EVE OF MODERNITY: THE FRENCH ENQUIRY OF 1763*

A paper delivered at Istanbul on comparative fiscal systems has perforce to start not in 1763, but in 1576 with Jean Bodin and his celebrated distinction between monarchies. In a *monarchie seigneuriale*, he wrote, the ruler :

> est faict seigneur des biens & des personnes par le droit des armes & de bonne guerre, gouvernant ses subiects comme le père de famille ses esclaves.[1]

According to Bodin, there was no seigneurial monarchy in Europe except in Muscovy and the Ottoman empire. Elsewhere, entrenched property rights precluded such a system of rule :[2]

> les hommes qui sont francs, & seigneurs des biens, si on veut les asseruir, ou s'empieter de ce qui leur appartient, se ressentent, & se rebellent aisement, ayant le coeur genereux, nourri en liberté, & non abastardi de seruitude.

Of course, Bodin was not the only European commentator to make such a distinction between *monarchie royale*, which protected private property rights, and *monarchie seigneuriale* which did not. François Bernier, a distinguished traveller of Egypt, Palestine and India in the reign of Louis XIV, made substantially the same differentiation and drew essentially the same conclusion :[3]

> ... supprimez le droit à la propriété privée de la terre et vous introduisez inévitablement la tyrannie, l'esclavage, l'injustice, la mendicité et le barbarisme.

By the time of Montesquieu's *De l'esprit des lois* (1748), the difference between state systems had become enunciated into a general rule on the re-

---

*) A personal research award from the Leverhulme Trust has permitted the consultation of additional manuscripts relevant both to this subject and to a projected study of the intendants of Louis XIV.
1) Jean BODIN, *Les six livres de la république*, Paris, 1583, repr. Darmstadt, 1977, p. 273.
2) *Ibid.*, p. 279.
3) François BERNIER, *Voyages* (2 vols., 1699), I, p. 319. P. ANDERSON, *Lineages of the Absolutist State* (repr. 1974), p. 399. R.J. BONNEY, *L'absolutisme*, Paris, 1989, p. 68.

lation between the amount of taxes paid and political liberty. Montesquieu's 'general rule' was that the freer the country in political terms the greater the public revenue that could be extracted. Thus England and Holland were heavily taxed. As political liberty declined, he postulated, so the fiscal burden fell, with Ottoman Turkey the least oppressively taxed of all. Moderate taxes were thus the compensation for a loss of political liberty. Poll taxes, or per capita direct taxes, were common to political regimes without political liberty, whereas taxes on commodities, which were less directly related to the person, were more common in states which enjoyed such freedom. But in any case fewer taxes were levied in so-called tyrannical states than in the western European states, and there was, according to Montesquieu, a preponderance of payment in kind (via the distribution of lands) rather than in money.[4] In England, Montesquieu wrote, because of the prevalence of indirect taxation, a merchant in effect lent the state fifty to sixty pounds sterling for every barrel of wine he received. What merchant, he asked, would dare to do such a thing in a country gqverned like Turkey ? And if he dared to do it, how would he be able to do so, with a suspect, uncertain, and ruined fortune ?

Montesquieu thus forms a continuum with Bernier back to Bodin, and modern historiography has tended to accept the view of the fiscal implications of *monarchie seigneuriale* as compared to *monarchie royale*.[5] From our point of view the interest of the great European enquiry into comparative revenue systems launched by the French government in 1763-6 is that it enables us to test some of these hypotheses. Not, regrettably, by a direct analysis of the east European states because Ottoman Turkey, Muscovy, and Poland were all omitted from the investigation. Internal political dissension was the reason subsequently given for omitting Poland, ostensibly the easiest of the three to incorporate into the enquiry :[6]

> il n'est fait aucune mention de ce royaume ... sans doute parce qu'il n'a pas été possible de se procurer des renseignemens sur les finances de cet Etat, longtems agité par des dissensions intestines, & dont le gouvernement aristocratique laissoit difficilement reconnoître le principe de ses finances & la forme des impositions.

As for Muscovy, the French ambassador was apparently written to for information but no report survives,[7] and the Ottoman lands were apparent-

---

4) MONTESQUIEU, *The Spirit of the Laws*, ed. A.M. COHLER, B.C. MILLER and H.M. STONE, Cambridge, 1989, pp. 220-2, extracts from Part 2, chapters 12 ("The relation of the size of taxes to liberty"), 13 ("In which government taxes are susceptible to increase") and 14 ("That the nature of taxes is relative to the government").
5) Thus, for Muscovy, R. PIPES, *Russia Under the Old Regime*, New York, 1974, pp. 22-3, 65-6. For the Ottoman lands, H. İNALCIK, "Ottoman methods of conquest", *Studia Islamica*, 2, 1954, p. 103-129 at p. 112.
6) *Encyclopédie méthodique. Finances*, ed. J. Rousselot de SURGY, 3 vols., 1784, III, p. 341.
7) *Das Steuersystem der Europäischen Staaten am ende des Ancien Régime. Eine offizielle französische Enquête (1763-8). Dokumente, Analyse und Auswertung. England und die Staaten Nord- und Mitteleuropas*, ed. P. C. HARTMANN, Munich, 1979, p. 29. As the title sug-

THE FRENCH FISCAL ENQUIRY OF 1763   63

ly not considered at all. Notwithstanding these deficiencies, the enquiry launched by controller-general Bertin, and continued by his successor L'Averdy, comprised 31 states (or perhaps one should say 31 returns, because some of the areas covered by several reports were ruled by a single ruler)[8] thus making it by far the most comprehensive survey in the *ancien régime*. Most of the reports were reprinted in extenso by Jean-Louis Moreau de Beaumont, who as *intendant* des finances was in charge of the detailed investigation;[9] but crucial details are sometimes only extant in the manuscript evidence concerning the enquiry; and in one case, Prussia, the full report does not even survive among the manuscripts, but in a subsequent printed edition, the *Encyclopédie Méthodique* edited by Rousselot de Surgy, who himself was a *commis des finances*.[10] It is clear that some of the reports were not compiled until 1766, while Moreau de Beaumont did not publish the findings until two years later.

I

The immediate issues raised by the French enquiry into comparative revenue systems were firstly, the intentions of the government in launching the enquiry; secondly, the quality of the information gathered; and thirdly, whether or not the evidence gained bore out Montesquieu's argument on the relationship between political freedom and the fiscal burden. The reforming intent of the French government at the end of the Seven Years' War is clear. The return to peacetime forms of administration in 1763 provided what in modern parlance we would call a 'window of opportunity' to reform the French fiscal system. Correctly or incorrectly, the reform of direct taxation was seen as synonymous with the establishment of a *cadastre*, a national land register which, it was believed, would remove the twin vices of arbitrary and unjust fiscal burdens. The edict of April 1763 and declaration of 21 November 1763 committed the government to establish a "*cadastre général de tous les biens fonds du Roïaume, afin d'exclure toute*

---

gests, Hartmann's excellent edition concerns only part of the enquiry. The Russian data does not provide any reliable figure for revenues in the 1760s, there being an estimate of 9.3 million roubles in 1764, but 19.9 million in 1769: J.P. LeDONNE, *Ruling Russia. Politics and administration in the age of absolutism, 1762-1796*, Princeton, NJ, 1984, p. 245.

8) These were: *Angleterre; Suède; Danemark et Norvège; Villes Hanséatiques (Hambourg, Brême, Lubeck, Danzig); Bohême; Autriche; Hongrie; Transylvanie; Prusse; Silésie; Saxe; Hanovre; Bavière; Mayence; Suisse; Liège; Pays-bas autrichiens; Hollande; Tirol; Venise; Mantoue; Modène; Milanois; Sardaigne; Gênes; Toscane; Parme, Plaisance, Guastalle; État ecclésiastique; Naples; Espagne; Portugal.*

9) *Mémoires concernant les impositions et droits en Europe. Première partie contenant les droits qui ont lieu dans les Isles Britanniques, les Couronnes du Nord, les États d'Allemagne, ceux d'Italie, d'Espagne et de Portugal*, ed. J-L MOREAU DE BEAUMONT (1768). This work has not been greatly utilized, but see the comments in G. ARDANT, *Histoire de l'impôt*, 2 vols., 1971-2, II, pp. 49-54.

10) *Encyclopédie méthodique*, III, pp. 405-9; the rest of the report on Prussia (III, pp. 409-17) was subsequent to the enquiry. This evidence was missed by HARTMANN in his edition in 1979: cf. HARTMANN, *Das Steuersystem*, pp. 219-22.

inégalité dans la répartition des impositions..."[11] Bertin, the controller-general, wrote to the provincial *intendants* in June 1763 to ask for their opinions on the feasibility of the *cadastre*.

Thus, from the outset, the French government had a distinctly pragmatic and practical viewpoint. It associated the *cadastre* with reform, and wished to learn practical lessons on how to proceed from the leading reformers of other states. For this purpose, Harvoin, the *receveur-général des finances* of Alençon, was sent to visit a number of Italian states to investigate *cadastres* that had recently been introduced. He talked to the king of Sardinia, and to the abbé Pompeo Neri, who had presided over the Milanese commission for the *censimento* for nine years and was regarded as the great European authority on land registers and the reform of direct taxes.[12] At first, Neri was inclined to doubt whether a comparable reform could be introduced in France *"parce que les auteurs françois qui ont ecrit sur cette matiere, pénétrés vivement des désordres de la taille arbitraire n'ont pas osé proposer le cadastre..."* After an analysis with Harvoin, Neri eventually concluded that there was no fundamental obstacle to the *cadastre* in France, *"puisqu'il reduira les privilèges dans leur limites, en ôtant tout ce qu'il peut y avoir d'abusif..."*[13]

Given the immediate preoccupations of the French government, the practice of certain states virtually disqualified them from any relevance to the enquiry. The Ottoman practice of collective responsibility for taxation and revenue farming which had developed since the seventeenth century placed the community at the mercy of the notables who controlled the system. It increased the arbitrary incidence of taxation and aggravated precisely those abuses which the proposed French reform was intended to correct. The irony, of course, was that the Ottoman state had developed complex and sophisticated land registers (*defter*) earlier than much of western Europe.[14] Originally, these had been updated at thirty- or forty-year intervals,

---

11) Edict of Apr. 1763 and declaration of 21 Nov. 1763 both in M. MARION, *Les impôts directs sous l'ancien régime, principalement au XVIIIe siècle*, 1910, pp. 297-302. A[rchives] N[ationales, Paris] K 891 n5/1, Mémoire. HARTMANN, *Das Steuersystem*, p. 24. J.C. RILEY, *The Seven Years' War and the Old Regime in France. The Economic and Financial Toll*, Princeton, NJ, 1986, p. 48 (on the *taille arbitraire*).
12) For Neri : J.-Cl. WAQUET, *Le grand-duché de Toscane sous les derniers Médicis. Essai sur le système des finances et la stabilité des institutions dans les anciens États italiens*, (École française de Rome), 1990, pp. 30-1, 333, 544-5. M.S. ANDERSON, "The Italian reformers", in *Enlightened Absolutism. Reform and Reformers in Later Eighteenth-Century Europe*, ed. H.M. SCOTT, 1990, p. 64. There is a chapter on him in D.M. KLANG, *Tax Reform in Eighteenth-Century Lombardy*, New York, 1977, pp. 24-32.
13) AN K 880 n60, *Extrait du journal envoyé a Monsieur d'Ormesson par le Sr Harvoin, depuis le 9 juillet, jour de son départ de Paris, pour aller en Italie, à l'effet d'y prendre des renseignemens sur les cadastres...* The full journal is in AN 114 ap Dr. 2 [156 mi 72].
14) There were both detailed census and tax registers (*mufassal defter*) and synoptic registers (*icmal defter*), which drew upon the detailed ones : P. K. Dooern, "Population and settlements in central Greece: computer analysis of Ottoman registers of the fifteenth and sixteenth centuries", *History and computing II*, ed. P. DENLEY, S. FOGELVIK and C. HARVEY, Manchester and New York, 1989, p. 195.

THE FRENCH FISCAL ENQUIRY OF 1763   65

but the system had not applied to the whole range of taxation and had been abandoned after the sixteenth century in favour of tax-farming (*iltizam*); after 1695, the tax farms were in turn subject to lifetime grants (*malikane*). The result was a decline of revenue in real terms, apart from the fall in the value of the Ottoman currency in relation to its European rivals and the penetration of the Spanish *real* into the Ottoman market.[15] Elsewhere, the agents of the French government commented on the doubtful relevance of local administrative practice to the concerns of Bertin and L'Averdy. The fiscal practices of Sweden, for example, were considered "*aussi fort compliquées que peu appliquables à votre administration*",[16] while of the Papal States it was said :

> Ce pays est pauvre et misérable, destitué de presque tout commerce, peu peuplé et la plus grande partie des terres sont en friche... il n'y a rien de bon à trouver dans un tel pays relativement à l'administration...[17]

The second consideration raised by the French enquiry into comparative revenue systems is the quality of the information supplied. Apart from the intelligence of the French ambassador or French representative, much depended on the co-operation of the foreign government and the complexity of its fiscal system. The Chevalier de St-Priest met with great difficulties in Portugal, where the government was dominated by the autocratic (but reforming) marquês de Pombal and memories of the Third Family Compact between France and Spain, and the subsequent Spanish invasion of 1762, were very recent. St-Priest recognized :

> combien j'ay rencontré d'obstacles pour remplir cet objet. Ce gouuernement, loin de donner les facilités que vous esperiés, auroit pris les soupcons les plus violens quoique les plus mal fondé...

Thus he had been forced to rely for his information on the *sieur abbé* Garnier, *chapelain de l'église de St-Louis* at Lisbon :

> Je sens combien ce mémoire vous laissera de choses à désirer mais... il seroit presque impossible de traiter méthodiquement l'assemblage informe qui compose le sistème des finances du Portugal. C'est une masse produite des revenus des domaines royaux de droits et d'impositions établies en différentes circonstances par des principes souvent très irréguliers...[18]

Thus there was no clear account of Pombal's attempt to revive and ex-

---

15) H. İSLAMOĞLU-İNAN and Ç. KEYDER, "Agenda for Ottoman history", *The Ottoman Empire and the World-Economy*, ed. H. İSLAMOĞLU-İNAN, Cambridge, 1987, pp. 57-8 and p. 396 n.49. On the erosion of revenues under tax-farming: İ. SUNAR, "State and economy in the Ottoman empire", *ibid.*, pp. 70-1. See also *Histoire de l'Empire ottoman*, ed. R. MANTRAN, 1989, p. 330. Contrast with *ibid.*, p. 198.
16) HARTMANN, *Das Steuersystem*, p. 69. On Sweden, there is a fundamental study by K. Åmark, *Sveriges statsfinanser, 1719-1809*, Stockholm, 1961, who publishes an almost complete run of statistics for the period.
17) AN K 881 n21, 25 Oct. 1764.
18) AN K 881 n57, 8 Jan. 1766.

tend the *décima*, a tax granted in the mid-seventeenth century to the Portuguese monarch by the Cortes in a time of national emergency, and to convert this into a comprehensive tax on all income and production.[19] What a contrast with Spain! There, the French representative, the marquis d'Ossun, consulted the Spanish finance minister directly. The marqués d'Esquilache was flattered by the approach from the representative of Louis XV and promised in time a full memorandum. The resulting document was announced nine months later as having been

> dressé sous les yeux de M. le marquis d'Esquilace, surintdt général des finances, et je l'ai traduit moi même en françois avec beaucoup d'attention. Ainsi, Monsieur, vous pouvés le regarder comme l'ouvrage le plus exact qu'il soit possible de se procurer sur cette matiere.[20]

There can be no doubt about the accuracy of the report, which would seem to confirm Esquilache's supervision: the figures produced for the evaluation of wealth in 22 provinces by the *junta de única contribución* exactly accord with those given in the report to the French government.[21]

Similarly, the king of Sardinia offered close collaboration with the French envoy, Harvoin, the *receveur-général des finances* of Alençon.[22] Elsewhere, the complexity of the fiscal structure sometimes defied a simple return. Thus d'Harincourt informed L'Averdy in August 1765 that he had not attempted to write a full report on the United Provinces, because to do so would be

> un ouvrage de fort longue haleine, trés volumineux, et d'autant plus difficile dans l'éxécution, que je ne pense pas qu'il existe un seul homme en ce pais cy qui soit instruit des détails de l'administration de toutes les provinces; il s'en trouve même trés peu dans chacunne d'elles qui soit exactement au fait de toutes les parties de l'administration de la province dont il est sujet...[23]

Thus Holland was preferred to the other six provinces of the United Provinces for the description of its financial system, as was Brabant for the report on the Austrian Netherlands.

The third issue raised by the French enquiry into comparative revenue systems is whether or not the reports received bore out Montesquieu's views on the relationship between political freedom and the fiscal burden. Montesquieu had used both the Swiss Confederation and the Ottoman

---

19) Though there was a discussion of the *dixième* (*sic*): MOREAU DE BEAUMONT, I, p. 503 and AN K 881 n54. Cf. K. MAXWELL, "Pombal: the paradox of enlightenment and despotism", in *Enlightened absolutism*, ed. SCOTT, p. 75-118 at p. 106.
20) AN K 881 n51, 20 May 1765. Cf. AN K 881, n48, 20 Aug. 1764.
21) MOREAU DE BEAUMONT. I, p. 493-4. These figures have been compared with those of the *junta*, dated 30 April 1756: A. Matilla TASCÓN, *La única contribución y el catastro de la Ensenada*, Madrid, 1947. pp. 92-3.
22) MOREAU DE BEAUMONT. I, pp. 286-7. AN K 880 n59.
23) AN K 879 n126, 13 Aug. 1765. In this and other quotations contemporary orthography is respected.

lands as examples; but the evidence from the *enquête* regarding the Swiss Confederation and Transylvania was less clear cut. For Montesquieu the Swiss Confederation showed how little some land could be taxed, due to its poverty and the desire of its inhabitants to enjoy freedom.[24] The report to L'Averdy, which was very detailed on the differences between the cantons, agreed that "*On ne connoit point de peuple en Europe chéz lequel les impositions soient moins multipliées et plus modiques que chéz les Suisses*", but nevertheless showed that the reality was much more complex and diverse than Montesquieu had suggested.

> Quelques cantons de la Suisse ont été forcés par la nature du sol et du climat qu'ils habitent de conserver leur ancienne maniere d'etre, et avec elle se sont perpétués l'amour de la liberté et l'eloignement invincible pour toute espèce d'impôt au moins fixe et permanent.

But elsewhere in the Swiss Confederation :

> De petites conquêtes, un sol moins ingrat, l'espoir enfin de se civiliser qui entraine toujours avec lui une sorte de luxe, ont raproché quelques autres cantons des moeurs européens, ont mis quelques entraves à leur indépendance et ont enfin conduit à la nécessité d'etablir parmi eux quelques impôts.

Finally, there was a group of cantons which had moved furthest from the mythical Swiss liberty,

> ... et qui par cette raison ont établi et levé plus d'impositions et de droits dans l'etendüe de leur territoire. Tels sont les cantons de Berne, Lucerne, Fribourg et Soleure que l'on pouroit dire qui forment des Etats presque aristocratiques ...[25]

The second example, the Transylvanian border with the Ottoman lands, seemed to give clearer support to Montesquieu's rule because the local peasantry was prepared to emigrate rather than suffer an arbitrary and oppressive military rule under the Austrian Habsburgs :

> ... la population a beaucoup souffert, les habitans ont passé par milliers sous la domination des Turcs ou ils n'eprouuent pas les memes vexations; differentes peuplades ont mis le feu a leurs habitations la les quittant. Il est constant en effet que cet assujetissement seroit très pezant puisqu'independamment d'un service très dur, les frais d'habillement et d'entretien de la milice seroient très considerable.[26]

If this evidence is to be believed, then in the choice between political

---

24) MONTESQUIEU, *The Spirit of the Laws*, ed. COHLER, MILLER and STONE, p. 221 : "Switzerland does not seem to conform to this [rule] because no taxes are paid there, but the particular reason is known... In those barren mountains, food is so dear and the country so heavily populated that a Swiss pays four times more to nature than a Turk pays to the sultan."
25) MOREAU DE BEAUMONT, I, p. 149-150. AN K 879 no. 107.
26) AN K 879 n80/9, a version of the text that was not reprinted in MOREAU DE BEAUMONT, I, p. 111-113. The memorandum commenced with the comment "*C'est un gouvernement purement militaire; le souverain peut y etablir tels impôts qu'il juge convenable. L'administration de ce pays a eprouvé depuis quelques années des variations si fréquentes qu'il n'y a actuellement rien de fixe que la contribution...*"

freedom and arbitrary taxation, the peasantry preferred lower taxes and the nominal loss of political freedom.

II

Modernity depends on perspective, and to some extent is in the eye of the beholder. Montesquieu's views were representative of ideas of modernity in a fiscal system in the mid-eighteenth century and three of his theses bear careful examination in the context of the French enquiry. Firstly, on the relationship between indirect taxes and direct taxes: Montesquieu asserted the principle that the nature of taxation was relative to the government of the state; indirect taxes, or commodity taxes, were thus more natural than direct ones in free political states since they were related less directly to the person.[27] Secondly, Montesquieu was clear in his preference for direct administration (*régie*) rather than revenue farming, which carried with it fatal abuses.[28] Thirdly, on the subject of the relationship between war finance and the consequent development of credit, Montesquieu showed himself to be studiously behind the times: he lamented the development of large standing armies and thus the permanent increase in taxes that resulted.[29] He knew of no advantages in a large public debt, except when (as in the case of England) a large amount of specie was simultaneously attracted into the kingdom by trade so that credit was not jeopardized and the just proportion between the state as creditor and state as debtor was maintained.[30]

First, then, we will examine the evidence of the French enquiry into comparative revenue systems concerning the balance between indirect taxes and direct taxes, and the relation of both to the real economy. Montesquieu asserted the principle that there was no harm in some people not paying sufficient in taxation since their plenty always reverted to the public; on the contrary, if individuals paid too much in taxes their ruin turned against the public interest. The desirable form of fiscal regime was therefore one which developed at the pace of the real economy.[31] Montesquieu was suspicious of direct taxation, since he regarded land taxes as inherently inequitable if they rested on the assessment of landed wealth; yet they were not necessarily oppressive if the amount levied was reasonable. Indirect taxes he considered to be least damaging, if two prior conditions were fulfilled: the tax should be levied at the point of production rather than consumption, since it was less noticeable there; and the balance between the price of the commodity and the amount of tax levied must be respected. A

---

27) MONTESQUIEU, *The Spirit of the Laws*, ed. COHLER, MILLER and STONE, p. 222.
28) *Ibid.*, p. 226.
29) *Ibid.*, pp. 224-5.
30) *Ibid.*, pp. 418-19.
31) *Ibid.*, p. 217.

disproportionate levy on a particular item required a royal or governmental monopoly, which Montesquieu regarded as inherently disadvantageous.[32] It has been argued that the French enquiry into comparative revenue systems demonstrated that indirect taxes were increasingly the 'modern' trend in taxation.[33] But this is to oversimplify its findings. Most states, even the United Provinces —often seen as *par excellence* the home of excessive indirect taxation— maintained a balance between the two types of revenue[34] and it was rare for a state consciously to eschew one source of revenue in favour of another. Indeed, rather than pronounce in favour of indirect taxes, a number of the French ambassadors and representatives reported on the disadvantages of an excessive reliance on taxes on consumption. Thus for Holland it was stated that

> Les impots sont extrêmement multipliées... Le nombre et la nature de ces différentes impôts paroissent même difficiles à concilier avec ce que sembleroient exiger l'industrie et le commerce.[35]

The burden of indirect taxes on the countryside was not considered oppressive in Holland:

> Les cultivateurs et autres gens de la campagne, quoique les impôts soient extremement multipliés, sont en général très aisés, parce que les droits qui se perçoivent portant presque tous sur la consommation, les denrées se vendent à proportion, de maniere que le cultivateur paye l'impot et les droits avec l'argent des consommateurs.

But in the towns the reverse was true:

> Les droits d'accises sont en général trop mulitipliés et trop considérables. Il en résulte de jour en jour la chute des manufactures qui ne peuvent soutenir la concurrence avec l'etranger, parce que la main d'oeuvre y est portée à un prix excessif. Ainsi les habitans des villes qui sont eloignées du commerce maritime sont pauvres, les marchands même ne s'y soutiennent qu'à peine. Cette même circonstance de la cherté de la main d'oeuvre pour tous les ouvrages qui tiennent au commerce et à la marine, affecte aussi les principales branches du commerce, et notamment la pêche du hareng et de la baleine, et la construction des vaisseaux, ce qui inflüe nécessairement sur le commerce en général.

But it was Spain that offered the clearest example of a state in which

---

32) *Ibid.*, pp. 217-18.
33) "*La conclusion qui s'imposait aux bureaux de Versailles est que la puissance d'un Etat est directement liée à l'importance de ses revenus provenant des impôts indirects. La «modernité» est en faveur de l'impôt indirect*": Jean MEYER, *Le poids de l'État*, Paris, 1983, p. 62.
34) W. FRITSCHY, "Taxation in Britain, France and the Netherlands in the Eighteenth Century", *Economic and Social History in the Netherlands*, II, 1990, p. 66. Though the balance between direct and indirect taxes may have been largely accidental and is true chiefly of Holland.
35) MOREAU DE BEAUMONT, I, p. 202. AN K 879 n123. However, the significance of the impact of taxation on wages and that of high wages on economic development remains contentious. Moreover, external changes may have been more important than internal developments in determining the economic fate of the Dutch Republic.

the necessary balance between indirect and direct taxes had been lost. The marquis d'Ossun commented to L'Averdy in May 1765:[36]

> les terres ne payent rien dans ce royaume, et que la pluspart des impôts portent sur les consommations; cette methode destructive de l'industrie a produit le mauvais effet qu'on en devoit attendre, puisque le com[m]erce intérieur de l'Espagne est tombé dans un état déplorable, et que l'agriculture y est extremement negligée; en effet des particuliers qui doivent payer à proportion des terres qu'ils possedent s'efforcent à les faire valoir, affin qu'elles produisent de quoi satisfaire aux charges, et ils y trouvent en outre un bénéfice personnel plus ou moins considérable; d'où il résulte que comme une taxe trop forte sur les terres en ralentit la culture, une taxe raison[n]able et bien combiné, doit au contraire l'accroître; mais ce véhicule manquant en Espagne, le propriétaire des terres prend le parti de les laisser en pâturages rustiques, parce qu'elles lui raportent environ deux pour cent par an, soit par le bétail qu'il en tient dessus pour son compte, soit parce qu'il louë ces pâturages à ceux qui ont des troupeaux et qui ne possedent pas de terres...

Yet the balance between indirect and direct taxes was not the only consideration; the nature of the items taxed indirectly was of fundamental importance. Bread, flour and grain were not taxed in France. But in Holland, flour was taxed so that it doubled in price. The cities enjoyed the freedom to produce bread for both towns and countryside, but producers in the countryside had to pay an entry tax when their bread was brought into the city.[37] The administration of indirect taxes on bread at Milan was considered disastrous :[38]

> ... ces objets universels si précieux et si necessaires en souffrent, [ce qui] blesse tout le monde, mais beaucoup plus le pauvre que le riche. Il ruine précisement la main d'oeuvre, et il gêne l'agriculture, et par là toutes les sources du bien public qui y ont rapport et connexion.

There was a limit to the number of indirect taxes that could be levied efficiently, as was commented upon in the context of Tuscany:[39]

> ... il faut que ces impositions soient plutôt fortes que nombreuses parce que les petites occasionnent plus de vexations qu'elles ne valent. Il faut qu'elles soient générales, tant parce qu'elles sont plus justes, que par ce qu'elles sont moins sensibles... la levée des impositions en cet Etat est fort sujete aux fraudes et fort onereuse au Peuple autant qu'elle est peu utile au souverain en egard a ce que paye le même peuple. Les causes de ces inconvenients arrivent de la petitesse et consequemment de la multiplicité des imposi[ti]on[s].

Even more damning was the report on Castilian indirect taxation drawn up by the Spanish minister of finance himself :[40]

---

36) AN K 881 n51, 20 May 1765.
37) MOREAU DE BEAUMONT, I, p. 211-12. AN K 879 n123.
38) AN K 880 n13.
39) AN K 880 n6, 14 June 1765.
40) MOREAU DE BEAUMONT, I, p. 489-901. AN K 881 n44.

> ... L'etablissement de ces impositions est si vicieux dans le fond et dans la forme, qu'il n'a pas été possible, malgré l'attention suivie qui a été donnée à cet objet, d'en reformer les abus... Ces impositions sont portée si haut qu'elles sont intolerables. Le seul droit d'alcavala [sic: alcabala], qu'on exige sur tous les meubles et immeubles, et sur toutes les denrées qui se vendent, est porté depuis 8 jusqu'à 14 %. Ce droit se reproduit sur les mêmes objets à chaque fois qu'ils changent de main, de façon qu'il arrive souvent que les droits d'alcavala emportent en peu de temps le valeur intrinseque de la chose, ce qui occasione des ventes frauduleuses, des compositions secretes avec les employés au préjudice du fisc, des emprisonnemens, des faux sermen[t]s... Toutes ces charges detruisent et découragent tellement les cultivateurs, les trafiquants et les proprietaires, qu'ils preferent souvent de s'adonner à l'oisiveté plutot que d'être exposés aux recherches avides des exacteurs.

It was precisely to counteract these abuses that under the marqués d'Esquilache a *junta* was established to impose a *única contribución* or *contribution unique*, which would ensure greater freedom of commerce and limit the vexations caused by the agents of the old fiscal system :

> ... le peuple ne sera plus exposé aux vexations des employés, qui ne seront plus à même d'apliquer à leur profit particulier les contributions arbitraires qu'ils exigeoient à la faveur du désordre qui regne dans les rentes provinciales.

The Spanish government had tried (but in the event failed, due to aristocratic and popular opposition to Esquilache, which culminated in the riots of 1766)[41] to shift the burden away from indirect taxes by the establishment of the *cadastre*. In other parts of Europe, however, revenue farmers were seen as more corrupt than government agents. Where customs revenues and excises were farmed in Norway and Denmark, royal administrators or controllers were seen as essential to prevent fraud; but it was believed that indirect revenues *en régie* were underassessed by perhaps as much as a third.[42] The fiscal administration of Prussia was viewed as the most advanced in the Holy Roman Empire, particularly after the reforms of 1766; at first, control of the excise, tolls and tobacco monopoly was conferred on French revenue farmers, but subsequently a *régie* was established.[43] Within the Austrian Habsburg lands, which also underwent financial reform in the mid-eighteenth century under the influence of the Prussian example,[44] the abuses of revenue farming were limited by the prac-

---

41) R. HERR, *Rural Change and the Royal Finances in Spain at the End of the Old Regime*, Berkeley-Los Angeles-London, 1989, pp. 8-10. C.C. NOEL, "Charles III of Spain", *Enlightened Absolutism*, ed. SCOTT, p. 134. The *única contribución* was reenacted in 1770, but "was in practice dropped a few years later": *ibid.*, p. 142.
42) MOREAU DE BEAUMONT, I, p. 65-7. HARTMANN, *Das Steuersystem*, p. 98.
43) *Encyclopédie méthodique*, III, p. 406. The administration of these taxes was further reformed in 1766 : *ibid.*, III, p. 411.
44) H.M. SCOTT, "The Problem of Enlightened Absolutism", in *Enlightened Absolutism*, ed. SCOTT, p. 24 and *idem*, "Reform in the Habsburg Monarchy, 1740-90", *ibid.*, pp. 152-4. The influence of Prussian reforms in Silesia was seminal. On this, see the report in

tice of reserving one third of the profit of the farm to the crown and appointing royal administrators to ensure proper accounting.[45] Doubtless the report exaggerated the profiteering made by the revenue farmers in the United Provinces, but it was correct in stressing that the greatest change from revenue farming to *régie* occurred there in 1748, which was tantamount to a political revolution :[46]

> La perception des impots a été en ferme jusqu'a l'avénement de Guillaume 4 au stathouderat. Il fut reconnu et constaté par les recherches que ce prince fit faire que d'un florin d'impot [le florin d'Hollande revient à 42s de notre monnoye] il n'entroit pas 5s dans la caisse du receveur général. Il proposa la suppression des fermes, et cette proposition n'ayant point eté reçüe il la fit imprimer et répandre dans le public, les esprits s'echaufferent, les maisons et les bureaux des fermiers furent pillés et détruits dans toutes les villes de la Hollande, et depuis cette révolution, on compte que la régie fait rentrer un peu plus de la moitié de l'impôt dans la caisse publique.

III

However important the analysis of indirect taxes in the various European states, the French government was highly unlikely to consider the abandonment of revenue farming and it was not particularly concerned with applying the lessons from other countries to the administration of the *ferme générale*. In contrast, it was deeply involved in the intricacies of the administration of direct taxes and the European movement of reform to establish modern land registers. The unreformed Saxon land register was considered to be "*une source de disproportion et d'injustices*".[47] The report on the electorate of Mainz said of the Holy Roman Empire in general that "*il est peu de pays en Europe ou l'administration des impots et des finances ait des aparences plus simples et plus œconomes... et ou dans l'execution elle soit plus vicieuse et plus destructiue*" with Prussia, Saxony and the Austrian Habsburg lands the chief exceptions.[48] The Bohemian *cadastre* was reported on, but this was not particularly influential since it was the product of a gradual

---

MOREAU DE BEAUMONT, I, p. 117-23 and the documents published by HARTMANN, *Das Steuersystem*, pp. 203-14. P. Baumgart, "The Annexation and Integration of Silesia into the Prussian State of Frederick the Great", *Conquest and Coalesence. The Shaping of the State in Early Modern Europe*, ed. M. GREENGRASS, London, 1991, pp. 164-6. The importance of the Prussian acquisition of Silesia in general European history is stressed in J. MEYER, *Le despotisme éclairé*, Paris, 1991, pp. 56-8, 86-7.

45) For Milan: MOREAU DE BEAUMONT, I, p. 275-6. AN K 880 n10 : "*...de maniere que la conduite de ces fermiers est continuellement eclairée, et que le montant du produit des droits est exactement connu.*" For Bohemia : MOREAU DE BEAUMONT, I, p. 98. AN K 879 n70.
46) MOREAU DE BEAUMONT, I, p. 203. AN K 879 n123. On the opposition to the tax-farmers in the riots of 1747-8 : H.H. ROWEN, *The Princes of Orange. The Stadholders in the Dutch Republic*, Cambridge, 1988, pp. 174-6. However, the changes were largely confined to Holland and the increased revenue which was achieved was largely a consequence of the rise in tariffs on certain goods, for instance on the milling of the grain.
47) HARTMANN, *Das Steuersystem*, p. 237.
48) *Ibid.*, p. 312.

THE FRENCH FISCAL ENQUIRY OF 1763   73

evolution over a century.[49] In Austria, the land register was old, but the nature of the levy had changed dramatically with the reforms of 1748 when royal and clerical wealth were subjected to the contribution for the first time.[50] Prussia introduced a new *cadastre* in occupied Silesia, which received a special report of its own;[51] of Prussia generally it was said that "*on a pris... toutes les précautions qu'on a cru propres à prévenir l'inégalité dans la répartition du droit de contribution*".[52] Outside the Holy Roman Empire, the evidence was not clearcut, and there was no single example to follow. One of the Italian experts rated the English land tax highest, and attributed the success of the agricultural revolution to it;[53] but the report on England made it clear that there were the greatest discrepancies in the self-evaluation of wealth by landed proprietors. Jacobites underassessed their wealth while Whigs paid up loyally to their government. If the agricultural prosperity of England had anything to do with the land tax, it was not a result of its fiscal justice but of its relatively light burden. From 20% of the landed revenue, it fell to 15% in 1767; and as a proportion of total government revenue it declined in the eighteenth century. In contrast, in Prussian Silesia the nobles paid 20-25% of their revenues, while the clergy were required to pay 40-45%.[54] The proposed Castilian reformed land register, although reported on in detail, was not in place by the time of the French investigation into comparative revenue systems (and in the end because of political opposition it was not established until 1845). The chief models for any French reform to establish a modern land register thus had to be those from Italy. In June 1765, Lorenzy informed L'Averdy of the Italian experience:[55]

> ... Dans tous les administrations de finances dont j'ai pris connoissance il y a partout un *cadastre*, mais ils sont presque tous differents dans la forme, ce qui montre la necessité, l'utilité, la justice de cette methode, et la difficulté de son execution.

In Italy, the Florentine *catasto* of 1427 was a precocious example of a sophisticated land register, which had subsequently been amended in the late seventeenth and early eighteenth century. But it was not regarded as an acceptable model:[56]

> ...Ces regles pour la repartition peuvent avoir été justes dans chaque communauté en particulier pour la repartition interieure et locale,

---

49) MOREAU DE BEAUMONT, I, p. 183. AN K 879 n70. For the Bohemian cadastre of 1747 and subsequent reforms: P.G.M. DICKSON, *Finance and Government under Maria Theresia, 1740-1780*, 2 vols., Oxford, 1987, II, p. 224ff.
50) MOREAU DE BEAUMONT, I, p. 100-1. DICKSON, *Maria Theresia*, II, p. 252.
51) MOREAU DE BEAUMONT, I, p. 117-23. AN K 879 n81. HARTMANN reprinted detailed classifications of types of cultivation and the distribution of taxes: HARTMANN, *Das Steuersystem*, pp. 203-13.
52) *Encyclopédie méthodique*, III, p. 407.
53) AN K 881 n3. The expert was the Florentine Pagnini.
54) HARTMANN, *Das Steuersystem*, pp. 50, 52, 59-60, 222.
55) AN K 880 n6.
56) AN K 881 n3, *Mémoire sur le cadastre de Toscane et l'imposition qui en resulte* (in Lorenzy's hand).

> puisque les communautés n'ont pas reclamé, mais elles sont contraires aux regles générales, et a la justice comparative, c'est a dire celle qui proportione la force actuelle oeconomique de chaque contribuable avec la force de la contribution...

Neri's Milanese *censimento* was regarded as distinctly preferable; Bertin was sent a copy of his learned treatise on the reform of land registers; and Neri's views on the applicability of this sort of reform to the French context have been quoted above. But it was above all the king of Sardinia and his officials who provided the model, because they claimed to have avoided Charles VI's (and Neri's) mistakes in the Milanese *censimento*:[57]

> ...Ce prince en a relevé les deffauts en faisant remarquer combien il etoit important que toutes les opérations d'un même Etat se fissent en même têms, sur les mêmes principes et par une meme direction, puisque la différence des tems, comme celle des opinions de ceux chargés d'une semblable administration, changeoient les proportions entre les différentes provinces, comme entre les communautés, ce qui dérangeoit et privoit de la balance d'une juste répartition dans les tributs, objet principal, qu'il ne falloit jamais perdre de vuë dans la formation d'une péréquation.

As to the long-term benefits for the state from such a reform, it was claimed of the reform in Savoy and Piedmont that a just balance of taxes was obtainable for the first time from the detailed estimate of production and the potential taxable revenue. The government was also better informed about relative population levels and consumption, and thus able to anticipate and prevent food shortages. Even landlords benefited from the reform, because of the improved capacity of their peasants to pay their rents since they were no longer oppressed by excessive direct taxation.[58]

IV

One of the interesting aspects of the French enquiry was that it enabled a rough and ready ranking of some of the European fiscal systems to be made. A previous French investigation of exchange rates ordered by Bertin provided a reasonable basis of equivalence of the other currencies to the *livre tournois*.[59] In terms of fiscal resources alone (that is, excluding credit), France still dominated in 1764, with a revenue of 321 million livres.[60] Next came England with 224 million.[61] No evaluation was placed on Spanish revenues by the Spanish finance minister, but we may estimate these at between 90.6 and 103 million.[62] Thus, according to the evidence of

---

57) AN K 880 n60.
58) MOREAU DE BEAUMONT, I, p. 312-15. AN K 880 n59.
59) HARTMANN, *Das Steuersystem*, p. 22.
60) J.C. RILEY, "French finances, 1727-1768", *Journal of Modern History*, 59, 1987, p. 227.
61) HARTMANN, *Das Steuersystem*, p. 49. Cf. *ibid.*, p. 328.
62) MEYER, *Le poids de l'État*, p. 61, evaluates Spanish revenues at around 140 million. However, the two figures suggested for 1759-60 by Ozanam are 39.250.641 and 34.543.062 *es-*

the French enquiry, the United Provinces came third, with a revenue of 120 million, but this represented the total fiscal burden (that is, *"le revenu total des Etats Généraux et des villes"*); disposable state revenue may have been as low as 85 million.[63] The Austrian Habsburgs were close behind with 92 million excluding Lombardy and the Austrian Netherlands.[64] The rising state was Prussia, whose revenues were not evaluated by the French enquiry, but which are thought to have been the equivalent of only 49 million.[65] Prussian revenues were increasing so rapidly, however, that they were estimated at nearly 166 million before the end of the *ancien régime*, while Dutch revenues had remained virtually static.[66] Portugal, with a revenue of perhaps 50 million,[67] Sweden and Finland with 40 million,[68] Naples with 27 million,[69] and Denmark and Norway with 24 million[70] were some considerable way behind, as were the Papal States (with perhaps 13 million)[71] and other German states such as Saxony,[72] Hanover[73] and Bavaria. Though their reports attested to the permanent increase in taxes, relatively few of the French representatives abroad attempted an analysis of the per capita fiscal burden because of the lack of reliable population data.[74]

cudos : D. OZANAM, "Notas para un estudio de los presupuestos de la monarquía española a mediados del siglo XVIII", *Dinero y Crédito, siglos XVI al XIX*, ed. A. OTAZU, Madrid, 1978, pp. 51, 54. One *escudo* was equivalent to 10 *reales*, and although in the War of Succession the exchange rate had been 1 *livre tournois* to 5 *reales* of vellon, by 1764 the rate had further declined to 3.80 *reales* to the *livre* (1 *real* = 5 *sous* 3 *deniers*): H. KAMEN, *The War of Succession in Spain, 1700-15*, 1969, p. 398. MOREAU DE BEAUMONT, I, p. 483. This calculator reduces the Spanish revenue figures to a maximum of 103.032.933 and a minimum of 90.675.538 *livres tournois*.

63) These figures are based on the same exchange rate as in the enquiry. The lower figure is based on revenues of 22.2 million florins for Holland in 1754, which comes from a detailed listing in F. VÉRON DE FORBONNAIS, *Recherches et considérations sur les finances de France depuis l'année 1595 jusqu'à l'année 1721*, 2 vols., Basle, 1758, II, 337. A similar figure of 22.8 million florins comes from the calculation of a per capita fiscal burden of 29 guilders per person for Holland in 1761, when the population was 786.000 : FRITSCHY, "Taxation in Britain, France and the Netherlands", p. 64.
64) HARTMANN, *Das Steuersystem*, p. 196 using an exchange rate of 1 florin = 45 *sous* : MOREAU DE BEAUMONT, I, p. 79 and AN K 879 n70.
65) HARTMANN, *Das Steuersystem*, p. 222.
66) *Encyclopédie méthodique*, III, p. 417. For the decline in Dutch revenue: FRITSCHY, "Taxation in Britain, France and the Netherlands", p. 61.
67) MOREAU DE BEAUMONT, I, p. 504. AN K 881 n54.
68) HARTMANN, *Das Steuersystem*, p. 92, adjusted by Åmark, *Sveriges statsfinanser*, p. 151.
69) MOREAU DE BEAUMONT, I, p. 453. AN K 881 n25 at f67.
70) HARTMANN, *Das Steuersystem*, p. 123.
71) MOREAU DE BEAUMONT, I, p. 384 and AN K 881 n20 refer to 2.5 million *écus romains* or 13.1 million *livres*.
72) Saxon revenues were estimated as likely to reach 18 million only after the *cadastre* had been reformed : HARTMANN, *Das Steuersystem*, p. 239. MOREAU DE BEAUMONT, I, p. 127.
73) Estimated at 7 million : HARTMANN, *Das Steuersystem*, p. 248. MOREAU DE BEAUMONT, I, p. 128.
74) An exception was AN K 881 n23, *Plan abrégé du gouvernement économique de l'Etat ecclésiastique*. This discussed the population level in the Papal States (2 million inhabitants *"suivant le tableau avoué par le gouvernement, calcul que je crois porté trop haut"*) in comparison with France's 18 million (sic). France paid 300 million in taxes. *"Pour que le rapport fut gardé dans le nombre des habitants des Etats du Pape en le comparant avec ceux de la France, il faudroit que les premiers eussent près de trois millions d'habitants"*. This, how-

A clear relationship emerged from the enquiry between high rates of monetary circulation and sophisticated and highly developed fiscal systems. Montesquieu had noted that in Muscovy Peter the Great had required payment of taxation in silver, thus adopting German practice.[75] The French enquiry revealed that the trend was firmly away from payment of taxes in kind elsewhere in Europe. The commutation to money payments was enacted in Denmark in October 1763,[76] although Sweden still practised mixed payment. The result was that the evaluation of Swedish revenues was difficult because of the survival of payments in kind.[77] The trend away from payment in kind reinforced the evolution from a demesne state towards a tax state: France itself had been a precocious example with virtually all demesne revenues farmed out by the seventeenth century.[78] Only in relatively exceptional circumstances, such as the prevalence of (unsuccessful) aristocratic revolt in Hungary, was a growth of the royal demesne recorded.[79] In the predominantly pastoral areas of the kingdom of Naples the royal demesne also remained extensive.[80]

In some states, monetary circulation was depicted as so low as to be almost non existent: "... *a Rome la monnoye de papier est celle qui circule le plus, et qu'on a beaucoup de peine a trouver à la changer contre l'espece.*"[81] There were similar comments on the lack of monetary circulation in Sweden:[82]

> La Suède... auroit grand besoin d'imaginer quelques moyens de ramener... la circulation de l'espèce numéraire, car, depuis plusieurs années, elle a totalement disparu, et ce royaume est réduit á une monnoye représentative en papiers, dont le crédit porte sur une banque anciennement établie et qui avoit toujours soutenu et mérité la confiance publique jusques à l'année 1761, ou le prétexte des besoins de l'Etat et de fausses spéculations ont engagé à multiplier, sans mesures, les billets de banque.

In contrast, the high levels of monetary circulation in England and the United Provinces assisted the growth of enormous funded debts (estimated respectively at 2,964 million[83] and 2,100 million).[84] Even some of the smaller Italian principalities such as Tuscany had significant public debts. In a

---

ever, assumed a higher fiscal burden within the Papal States than at the time of the enquiry.
75) MONTESQUIEU, *The Spirit of the Laws*, ed. COHLER, MILLER and STONE, p. 216.
76) HARTMANN, *Das Steuersystem*, p. 119. MOREAU DE BEAUMONT, I, p. 63, noted that the reform was "*à la grande satisfaction des peuples*".
77) *Ibid.*, p. 71, 73. MOREAU DE BEAUMONT, I, p. 27, 29.
78) MOREAU DE BEAUMONT's fourth volume contains a detailed analysis of legislation concerning the royal demesne in France.
79) MOREAU DE BEAUMONT, I, p. 109. AN K 881 n7.
80) MOREAU DE BEAUMONT, I, p. 429. AN K 881 n25.
81) AN K 881 n23.
82) HARTMANN, *Das Steuersystem*, p. 69. On this problem, see L. JÖRBERG, *A History of Prices in Sweden, 1734-1914*, 2 vols., Lund, 1972, I, p. 78-82.
83) HARTMANN, *Das Steuersystem*, p. 56.
84) MOREAU DE BEAUMONT, I, p. 202. AN K 879 n123.

THE FRENCH FISCAL ENQUIRY OF 1763

letter to L'Averdy in June 1765, Lorenzy tried to establish a principle concerning the size of the public debt in relation to the available amount of silver and gold coins in a state :[85]

> Je suppose que le Roi ne veut pas payer entierement mais seulement reduire les dettes de l'Etat puisqu'elles rapportent beaucoup plus d'avantages que le prejudice de la necessité d'augmenter les impôts pour payer les interêts, pourvu que les dettes soient proportionnées a l'effectif du païs. Ceux qui ont examiné cette proportion ont eu differentes opinions a ce sujet et les plus éclairés ont fixé cette proportion comme d'un a dix, c'est a dire, que dans un Etat ou il y a un milion d'effectif l'on peut contracter jusques a dix millions de dettes... [E]n Toscane il y a environ 16 millions d'écus qui sont le double des écus de France, de dettes, et l'effectif ne vas pas certainement a 3 millions. Tellement que ladite proportion peut être fixée comme d'un a 5. L'on ne considere ici les dettes publiques que comme un mal qui produit beaucoup de bien, puisque par le commerce continuel et facile qu'on fait de ces dettes et par les payements de leurs interêts, elles sont devenues un instrument qui fait circuler perpetuellement et rapidem[en]t l'argent.

V

Considerations of space preclude more detailed discussion of other aspects of the French enquiry into comparative revenue systems, but sufficient extracts have been cited to demonstrate that it was serious in purpose and in some cases conducted with considerable thoroughness, although much depended on the degree of co-operation offered by the authorities within the state under investigation. What did the French government make of the results of the enquiry? Moreau de Beaumont published the *résumés* of the reports as the first tome of his four-volume study, the other three being exclusively concerned with the evolution of the French revenue structure.[86] Since there was a full report by Moreau de Beaumont, at least the enquiry had some permanency. Within his report, Moreau de Beaumont alluded to the projected reform of both direct and indirect taxes in France. There were to be reforms of direct taxes within the *pays d'élections* both at regional and parish level.[87] And, with regard to indirect taxes, there was to be a root and branch reform of the *traites* so that all internal customs barriers would be removed, thus freeing commerce from one of the great impediments of the *ancien-régime* political structure. Significantly, however, there was nothing in Moreau de Beaumont's extensive and detailed study on how to overcome the likely resistance of the sovereign courts and

---

85) AN K 880 n6, 14 June 1765.
86) *Mémoires concernant les impositions et droits. Seconde partie. Impositions et droits en France*, ed. J.-L. MOREAU DE BEAUMONT, II-IV, 1769.
87) MOREAU DE BEAUMONT, II, p. 81-83 (need for detailed information on each parish); II, p. 105-113 (citing instructions to the *intendants* of 4 Aug. 1767).

of the provinces to the proposed changes.[88]

On the central reason for the French enquiry, the establishment of a *cadastre*, nothing was achieved at all under the *ancien régime*, except by one or two reforming *intendants* on a piecemeal basis.[89] Poor standards in the surveying profession would have made it difficult to introduce nationally. The king of Sardinia had told Harvoin that it was essential for the survey to be carried out everywhere in the state at the same time and on the same principles. The *intendant* in the *généralité* of Paris estimated the work would require three to four years of continuous effort;[90] and there remained the problem of updating the land registers. There was also clearly a shortage of qualified personnel: by the mid-eighteenth century landlords were able to find *arpenteurs* who could perform the job properly, surveying the estate with precise measurements and drawing relatively accurate maps; but there was still the thorny difficulty of the investigation of ancient titles to the property, and without precise enquiry of this sort, the *terrier* was always found to have been misdrawn.[91]

These technical deficiencies do not in themselves provide the whole answer as to why no national *cadastre* was attempted in the eighteenth century, when it had been possible to undertake an impressive enquiry into comparative revenue systems in Europe. Opposition from vested interests, principally the *Parlements*, was much more important,[92] and influenced the resignation of Bertin as controller-general in 1763.[93] The rapid changeover of controllers-general of finance in the eighteenth century was not conducive to such a bold reform. Nine ministers were appointed between 1746 and the death of Louis XV in 1774, averaging just over three years per ministry. Though in many respects his appointment was a concession to the sovereign courts, L'Averdy himself left office in 1768, the year that Moreau de Beaumont commenced publication of the French enquiry. Such insta-

---

88) *Ibid.*, III, p. 585-588. On the failure of the single duty project: J.F. BOSHER, *The Single Duty Project. A Study of the Movement for a French Customs Union in the Eighteenth Century*, 1964.
89) Above all in the *généralité* of Paris under the *intendant* Bertier de Sauvigny: MARION, *Les impôts directs*, pp. 43-5, 168-171.
90) AN 144 ap 12 [156 mi 72]. The author thanks Joël Félix for this reference. It was a weakness of the Napoleonic *cadastre* that "an exact cross section in time can never be achieved for more than a limited group of *communes*" : H.D. CLOUT and K. SUTTON, "The Cadastre as a Source for French Rural Studies", *Agricultural History*, 43, 1969, pp. 215-23 at p. 219.
91) J. BASTIER. *La féodalité au siècle des lumières dans la région de Toulouse, 1730-1790*, 1975, pp. 250-3.
92) The opposition of the *Parlements* is stressed by M. ANTOINE, *Louis XV*, Paris, 1989, pp. 794-5. For the opposition of the *Cours des Aides* see, for example, MARION, *Les impôts directs*, pp. 215-16 : "*...les principes d'après lesquels on veut l'établir sont encore inconnus, et l'exécution d'un si grand projet est toujours incertaine; ainsi on est fondé à craindre que la nouvelle déclaration... ne servît à augmenter l'imposition de quelques particuliers sans soulager les autres contribuables et sans avancer la confection du cadastre.*"
93) It has been demonstrated that Bertin's resignation in 1763 marked the abandonment of the attempted imposition of a national *cadastre* in France : ANTOINE, *Louis XV*, pp. 792, 798-9.

THE FRENCH FISCAL ENQUIRY OF 1763

bility was itself the product of political intrigue, so that the ministers frequently were held in tutelage to factions which had helped in their promotion; a succession of different interest groups to some extent captured ministerial power, and as a result the government lacked the political will to implement far-reaching structural reforms, least of all those which would damage the economic interests of the group behind the minister: Silhouette's alienation of the *fermiers généraux* caused the downfall of his ministry after only nine months in 1758-9. The resulting lack of continuity meant that where the *cadastre* was introduced locally, it was not as a result of the government, but on the initiative of a reforming provincial *intendant*, as in Alsace and the *généralité* of Paris; and by definition this could do nothing to rectify injustices in the repartition of taxes between regions. The failure to introduce a national *cadastre* was a decisive setback to attempts at political reform and to the creation of an efficient revenue raising system in eighteenth-century France.

At first, it appeared that the issue had simply been deferred. At the end of the Seven Years' War in 1763, France seemed in need of drastic reform. Ministerial reformers such as Bertin, and to a more limited extent L'Averdy, were heavily influenced by the ideas of the Physiocratic movement. Yet the Physiocrats themselves were divided on what sort of fiscal system was desirable, and on the practicality of their *impôt unique*.[94] Quesnay, the father of the Physiocratic movement, clearly believed that the *cadastre* had to follow upon, and not precede, agricultural prosperity or the Crown would be the loser.[95] But the inability of the Physiocrats to advise the ruler of Baden-Durlach on precisely how to implement the single-tax system suggests that there was an abstract, if not utopian, aspect to their thinking on this central fiscal issue,[96] while even in French-controlled Corsica the implantation of a new administrative structure did not in the end lead to the introduction of the single tax on land.[97] Yet it is possible to argue that the Physiocrats' influence over government reached its greatest extent at precisely the moment that the implementation of the *cadastre* was abandoned, that it is to say with the fall of Bertin in 1763. It was Bertin who had drafted the reform measures for the liberalization of the grain trade, measures which his successor L'Averdy implemented in full.[98] Originally

---

94) G. WUELERSSE, *La Physiocratie sous les ministères de Turgot et de Necker, 1774-81*, 1950, pp. 155, 282-5.
95) R. L. MEEK, *The Economics of Physiocracy. Essays and Translations*, 1962, p. 185. François Quesnay et la Physiocratie, 2 vols., Institut national d'Études démographiques, 1958, II, p. 613.
96) K. TRIBE, *Governing Economy. The Reformation of German Economic Discourse, 1750-1840*, Cambridge, 1988, pp. 124-6 and especially H.P. LIEBEL, *Enlightened Bureaucracy versus Enlightened Despotism in Baden, 1750-1792*, Proceedings of the American Philosophical Society, 55, Philadelphia, 1965, pp. 47-51.
97) T.E. HALL, "Thought and Practice of Enlightened Government in French Corsica", *American Historical Review*, 74, 1969, p. 880-905, especially pp. 885, 893-4 and 901-2 for the contrast between reforming ideas and actual achievement.
98) S.L. KAPLAN, *Bread, Politics and Political Economy in the Reign of Louis XV*, 2 vols., The

conceived as a measure to be introduced simultaneously with the implementation of the national *cadastre*, grain liberalization could be interpreted as a surrogate for, or prelude to, fundamental fiscal reform.[99] Moreover, unlike the *cadastre*, the policy of grain liberalization received a measure of support in the *Parlements*, who in the aftermath of the fall of Bertin appeared to be in control of public affairs.[100] Success in the area of economic reform might thus help clear the way for later fiscal and institutional reforms. Conversely, the failure of grain liberalization -which began with the subsistence crisis of 1765 and was evident with the reversal of policy under Terray- foreclosed the possibility of any consequential fiscal reform. Thus when he arrived in office in 1774 after the fall of Terray, and under a new king who was committed in turn to reverse Terray's policies, Turgot, the controller-general closest to the Physiocrats, was unable to introduce far-reaching reforms since by this date the ideas of the reform movement were largely discredited.[101]

The *enquête* published by Moreau de Beaumont was thus a testimony to the strength of Physiocratic influence in Europe at a time when the movement failed in its purpose within France itself. Adam Smith, whose *Wealth of Nations* (1776) is usually seen as an attack on Physiocratic ideas,[102] was nevertheless heavily influenced by their doctrine and drew almost all his examples for his discussion "Of the Sources of the general or publick Revenue of the Society" (Book V, chapter II of the *Wealth of Nations*) from Moreau de Beaumont's *Mémoires concernant les impositions et droits en Europe*.[103] It has not been noticed that a number of Smith's views (or prejudices) concerning the administration of public revenues were formulated on the basis of the evidence presented in the printed version of the *enquête*; some of them, indeed, may have been a misreading of the situation prevailing in the country concerned.[104] All Smith's observations on the land tax, for example, were drawn from historical examples of reforming cadas-

---

Hague, 1976, I, p. 90-6, 136-7, 142. And for Physiocratic influence over the drafting of the measures: *ibid.*, I, p. 146-9.
99) *Ibid.*, I, p. 158-9.
100) *Ibid.*, I, p. 180; II, p. 448. ANTOINE, *Louis XV*, p. 799.
101) KAPLAN, *Bread, Politics and Political Economy*, II, p. 661-2. E. FAURE, *La disgrâce de Turgot. 12 mai 1776*, Paris, 1961.
102) Smith denounced "the capital error" of the Physiocratic system, which in his view was to represent "the class of artificers, manufacturers and merchants, as altogether barren and unproductive": Adam SMITH. *An Inquiry into the Nature and Causes of the Wealth of Nations*, ed. R.H. CAMPBELL, A.S. SKINNER, W.B. TODD, 2 vols., Oxford, 1976, II, p. 674.
103) In a letter dated 24 Nov. 1778, Smith stated that he had had frequent occasion to study this book, a copy of which he had obtained through Turgot's favour. He was unwilling to lend it, since "if any accident should happen to my book, the loss is perfectly irreparable". Smith believed that there were as few as three copies in Britain at that date: *ibid.*, II, p. 816 n.
104) Thus for Smith, "the best and most frugal way of levying a tax can never be by farm" (*Ibid.*, II, p. 902). Here he may have been influenced by the accusation of excessive profits by Dutch revenue farmers in the *enquête*, which were certainly exaggerated. His comments on the fiscal burden in Holland (*ibid.*, II, pp. 845, 851-2, 861, 905) reflected the wording of the *enquête*.

THE FRENCH FISCAL ENQUIRY OF 1763   81

tral surveys mentioned in the *enquête*.[105] And it may well have been indirectly through Smith's *Wealth of Nations* that the eighteenth-century tradition of cadastral surveys was passed on to the Napoleonic period. When we reach the period of the *cadastre* introduced under Gaudin, it was the French experience which was imported to other European countries, along with the metric system and the Napoleonic Code[106] -the reverse of the European influence on French reforming endeavour intended by Bertin when he launched the first enquiry into comparative revenue systems shortly before his resignation as controller-general in 1763.[107]

---

105) *Ibid.*, II, p. 833-6, 934. KLANG, *Tax Reform in Eighteenth-Century Lombardy*, pp. 1, 83 n. 1, notes Smith's "warm praise" for the Milanese *censimento*, but also that he "conveyed some misinformation about the tax".
106) ARDANT, *Histoire de l'impôt*, II, p. 197-209 and *idem*, *Théorie sociologique de l'impôt*, 2 vols., 1965, I, p. 227-9, 456-7. J. Pro RUIZ argued in "The Cadaster: the Struggle against Tax Fraud in Modern Spain, 1715-1982" (unpublished paper to the International Economic History Congress at Leuven in August 1990, p. 8) that "the Napoleonic cadaster was to be the model on which all cadasters of Continental Europe would be worked out, making allowances for the autochthonous traditions of each region, inherited from the seventeenth century".
107) Bertin launched the enquiry in November 1763, but was replaced by L'Averdy on 13 Dec. 1763 as controller-general although he remained a minister : HARTMANN, *Das Steuersystem*, p. 22. ANTOINE, *Louis XV*, p. 799.

ADDITIONAL NOTES

I   Absolutism: what's in a name?

Since this article was published in 1987 a number of publications have appeared which affect the value judgements as to whether one reign or another has received scholarly attention. Firstly, there are the three relevant volumes of *A History of France* (Blackwell): Emmanuel Le Roy Ladurie, *The French Royal State, 1460–1610*, trans. Juliet Vale (Oxford, 1994); Emmanuel Le Roy Ladurie, *The Ancien Régime. France, 1610–1774*, trans. Mark Greengrass (Oxford, 1995); François Furet, *Revolutionary France, 1774–1880*, trans. Antonia Nevill (Oxford, 1992). Francis I's reign has now been re-examined by R. J. Knecht, *Renaissance Warrior and Patron: The Reign of Francis I* (Cambridge, 1994). Henri II's relatively short reign was revised by F. J. Baumgartner, *Henri II, King of France, 1547–1559* (Durham and London, 1988). Mark Greengrass has revised his study of Henri IV's reign: *France in the Age of Henri IV* (London, 1995), while the key event in the creation of a Catholic Bourbon dynasty is reviewed by Michael Wolfe, *The Conversion of Henri IV. Politics, Power and Religious Belief in Early Modern France* (Cambridge, Mass. 1993). The youth of Louis XIII is interpreted in controversial fashion by Elizabeth Wirth Marvick, *Louis XIII. The Making of a King* (New Haven and London, 1986) while the story is taken up for the rest of the reign by A. Lloyd Moote, *Louis XIII. The Just* (Berkeley and Los Angeles, 1989). The most famous king of France has received an excessively adulatory portrait from F. Bluche, *Louis XIV*, trans. Mark Greengrass (Oxford, 1990), while the visual propaganda of the reign has been studied by Peter Burke, *The Fabrication of Louis XIV* (New Haven and London, 1992). Louis XIV's mediocre brother is considered by Nancy Nichols Barker, *Brother to the Sun King: Philippe, Duke of Orléans* (Baltimore and London, 1989). The long reign of Louis XV is considered in a magisterial volume, although one with prejudices, by Michel Antoine, *Louis XV* (Paris, 1989). The same author's two essays on absolutism need also to be included here: M. Antoine, 'La monarchie absolue', *The French Revolution and the Creation of Modern Political Culture. I. The political culture of the old regime*, ed. K. M. Baker (Oxford–New York, 1987); and 'La monarchie française de François Ier à Louis XVI', *Les monarchies*, ed. E. Le Roy Ladurie (Paris, 1986), 185–208. Louis XVI has been reassessed by J. Hardman, *Louis XVI* (New Haven and London, 1993), while his period as a constitutional monarch is considered by P. R. Campbell, 'Louis XVI, King of the French', *The French Revolution and* the *Creation of Modern Political Culture. II. The Political Culture of the French Revolution*, ed. C. R. Lucas (Oxford–New York, 1988), 161–82. Two ministerial fortunes have received full-scale studies since the article was published: I. Aristide, *La fortune de Sully* (Paris, 1990); J. Villain, *La fortune de Colbert* (Paris, 1994).

II   Bodin and the development of the French monarchy
p. 45, line 6: post-Bodin jurists (not post-Bodin jurist).

III   Was there a Bourbon style of monarchy?
On the history of Protestant Béarn before 1620 see now M. Greengrass, 'The Calvinist experiment in Béarn', *Calvinism in Europe, 1540-1620*, ed. A. Pettegree, A. C. Duke and G. Lewis (Cambridge, 1994), 119–42.

IV   The French civil war, 1649–53
Note that the orthography in the references respects that of the original documents consulted, not the modern spelling of the names concerned.

VIII   La Fronde des officiers: mouvement réformiste ou rébellion corporatiste?
p. 338, line 10 should read 'pas défendues, l'engagement de gentilshommes dans la Fronde, en effet, ne fut pas immédiat'.

XII   The state and its revenues in *ancien régime* France
Graph 3 has been slightly altered since the original publication in 1992, and now covers the dates 1610–1785 and provides revenue figures deflated by a mean of index numbers for grain prices. As a result of this change, the deflated index numbers cited at pp. 156, 159 should read 220 (1661), 196 (1702), 796 (1763) and 858 (1785).

p. 153: it should be noted that the once and for all exemption from the *droit annuel* was reversed in 1722. The *droit annuel* then lasted until 1771, when it was replaced by the *centième denier*.

p. 171 n. 87: the public debt in 1715 has now been estimated as 1,739 million *livres* (or 1,977 million if non interest-bearing debts are included): J. M. Félix, 'Les dettes de l'État à la mort de Louis XIV', *Comité pour l'histoire économique et financière de la France. Études et documents*, 6 (1994), 603–8.

p. 172: the *Histoire des Finances pendant la Régence* is now considered to have been written by a supporter of Law rather than by Law himself.

XIII   Louis XIII, Richelieu and the royal finances
Graph 5 has been slightly altered since the original publication in 1992. At p. 118 n. 51 should read 'by dividing them by the mean index numbers for grain

prices'. At p. 118, line 15, the text should read 'over the long timespan of 1625–1787, converted into index numbers to show the rate of growth from the base index of 1600–30, and recalculated on an eleven-year moving average so that the main trend can be seen without short-term fluctuations'. The change has been made to take account of missing data, to remove centring and to provide a mean of index numbers for grain prices.

XV   Comparative fiscal systems on the eve of modernity

At p. 75 Åmark's deflator was not incorporated into the proofs of the paper. The nominal figure for Sweden and Finland is correct; the deflated figure should be 23 million, but is open to dispute.

INDEX

abonnements: XII 164; XIV 399–400, 412
absolutism
  as a relative phenomenon: I 94
  charge of despotic conduct: XII 167, 173; XIV 406
  development of: IV 92
  fiscal implications: XIII 100
  lack of blueprint for: I 115
affaires extraordinaires: XI 24 n 2; XII 150, 151; XIII 101, 108, 110, 121
affranchissements: XII 164
aides: XI 12, 20, 22, 27; XII 151; XIII 101, 122, 124
Aix-en-Provence: XII 170
Alais, Louis-Emmanuel de Valois, comte d': VII 825; VIII 334
Alençon: XII 169; XIII 114
Alençon, duc d': III 177
Aligre family: I 116
Alsace: IV 88; V 372; VII 826–7, 832; XII 152, 154, 168; XIV 400; XV 79
Amiens: XII 169; XIII 112
Angers: IV 90
Anjou: IV 88; VII 825
Anne of Austria: I 105; IV 71, 74, 83–4, 92; V 369; VI 18, 26; VII 829, 833; XI 21
  foreign origins and foreign policy: IX 331, 335
  full powers as Regent: IV 85; V 375
  governor of Brittany: VII 824
Antoine, Michel: III 161–2
Armenonville, Joseph-Jean-Baptiste Fleuriàu d', director of finance: XIV 387
arpenteurs: XIV 409–10; XV 78

arrears, tax: VIII 327
arrêt d'union: IV 72; V 369; VIII 325; X 831
Artois: XIV 392
Assembly of Notables: III 174; IV 85; X 828; XIII 125
assignats: XII 171, 174 n.100, 176
Auch: III 166; XII 170
Austrian Habsburg lands: XV 67, 71–2, 73
Auvergne: IV 88; XIV 401
Avaux, Claude Mesmes, comte d': IV 78

banks and banknotes: XII 171, 173
'bankruptcy' (debt rescheduling): IV 72–3; VI 21; VIII 329; X 831; XI 21
Barillon, president of the *Parlement* of Paris: VI 24–5
Barillon, intendant: III 168, 170–71
Bastille: V 370; VII 821
Basville, Nicolas de Lamoignon de, intendant: II 52; XIV 385, 387 n.19, 388, 389, 399, 400, 411, 412
Bazin de Bezons, intendant: III 165
Béarn: II 162–72; XIV 399, 400, 404
Beauharnais de Beauville, intendant at La Rochelle: XIV 403
Beaufort, François de Vendôme, duc de: IV 81, 85, 88; VI 25
Beauvillier, Paul, duc de: III 175
Beik, William H.: I 112–13
Bercé, Yves-Marie: I 98–9
Bernage, intendant of Picardy: XIV 404
Bernier, François: XV 61
Bertin, Henri Léonard, comte de Bourdeille: XII 168; XV 63, 64, 65, 74, 78, 79, 80,81

Besançon: XII 170
Béziers, edict of: XIII 116
billets de monnaie: XII 170
Birague, René de, Chancellor: VII 819
Biron, Charles de Gontaut, duc de: III 174; VII 818
Bochart de Champigny, Jean, finance minister: X 827–8; XIII 102, 127
Bodin, Jean: I 96; II 43–4, 46–8, 60; III 161; XV 61
Boisguilbert, Pierre Le Pesant de: XII 165; XIII 126, 128; XIV 385, 387–9, 409, 411
Bombelles, marquis de: XII 174
Bonneau, Thomas, financier: X 833
Bordeaux: IV 86, 91; V 373; VI 25; XIII 114
Botero, Giovanni: II 59
Bouillon, Frédéric-Maurice de la Tour d'Auvergne, duc de: IV 78, 80, 86; VII 827–8, 833
Boulonnais: XIII 112
Bourges: XII 169; XIII 112
Bouthillier, Claude le, finance minister: XIII 100, 102, 103
Bouville, Michel-André Jubert de, intendant at Orléans: XII 165; XIV 387
Brittany: IV 88; V 368; VI 25; VII 824, 825, 831; XII 152, 164; XIV 399, 403–4
Broussel, Pierre: IV 85; VI 21, 26
  arrest of as a factor in precipitating the Fronde: V 371; VI, 25; VIII 330
  demands tax remissions: VIII 328
Bullion, Claude de, finance minister: X 830; XIII 99–100, 102, 103, 106, 112, 126, 127
  criticism of: XIII 105
  reform plan: X 836; XIII 120–21
Burgundy: IV 88; V 368; VII 824, 825, 826; VIII 326; XIV 399, 404, 411
Burke, Peter: I 103

cadastre: XII 168, 169; XIV 391; XV 63–4, 73, 78, 79, 80, 81
cahiers de doléances: XII 170
Caen: XII 169; XIII 114

Calonne, Charles Alexandre de: XII 156
Cantarini, Thomas: VI 21; VII 822
capitation: III 167; XII 151, 162, 164–5, 174, 175; XIII 124, 127; XIV 383–4, 385, 387, 388, 389, 399, 410, 411
Carew, Sir George: XI 12, 13, 17
Carr, de Montgeron, intendant: II 56
Catalonia: IV 79; VI 23, 24
catasto: XV 73
Catherine de Médicis: I 105
censorship: VI 15, 27
centralization: I 94
chambre de justice: IV 73; V 371; VIII 329, 333; X 834; XI 20, 22, 32; XII 151; XIV 392
Chambre des Comptes: VIII 331–3; X 826–8, 831–2; XI 15; XIII 103, 104–5
Chambre St Louis: IV 73–4, 76, 90; V 369–70, 371; VIII 325, 331, 336, 337; X 831, 832; XI 21
Chamillart, Michel de: XII 165, 170; XIV 384–5, 386, 387
Chamlay, Jean-Louis Bolé, marquis de: XIV 387
Champagne: IV 88; VII 826; VIII 326; XIII 118
Châlons: XII 169; XIII 112
Chancellor: III 171, 173
Charles I: IV 92
  Mazarin on the structural weakness of English constitution: V 370
  personal rule: V 366, 368–9
Charles VIII: I 100
Charlot, Claude, financier: XI 14, 18, 20, 21, 22
Chartres: XIV 387
Châteauneuf, Charles de l'Aubespine, marquis de: IV 85; VI 18, 27
Chaulnes, Honoré d'Albert, duc de: VII 826
Chavigny, Léon le Bouthillier, comte de: IV 85; VI 27
China: I 115
cinq grosses fermes: XI 12, 20, 28; XII 151; XIII 101
Cinq-Mars: IV 77, 78; XIII 128
cinquantième: XII 153–4

clergy, French: VI 19; XIV 392
clientage: V 378; VI 22–3
coinage, issues of: *see* debasement
Colbert, Jean-Baptiste, controller-general of fianance: I 101–2;
  II 52–3, 55; III 164; VI 21;
  VIII 337; X 825, 833–6; XI 11,
  14, 15, 24–5; XII 153; XIII 102,
  104, 105, 106, 114; XIV 386
'collection overhead': XII 159, 162,
  166; XIV 405
Collins, James B.: XIII 116, 118, 120
Comité de liquidation: XII 153
commissaires: II 47–8; VIII 337
comptants (secret expenses): VIII 331,
  337; X *passim*; XI 16, 29;
  XIII 104–5, 120, 121 n.59, 122
Concini, Concino: VII 819, 820, 822–3,
  824, 829, 831; IX 332, 334
contrôleur général des finances:
  XII 168
convoy et comptablie of Bordeaux:
  XI 12; XII 151; XIII 101
Condé, Henri II de Bourbon, prince de:
  IV 85; V 379; VII 820, 829
Condé, Louis II de Bourbon, prince de:
  III 175; IV 80, 81–6; V 372, 373,
  374, 379; VI 19, 20, 22, 24;
  VII 820, 823, 826, 829, 830,
  831–2
  seeks dismissal of Servien, Le Tellier
    and Lionne: VIII 335
  treaty with Philip IV: IV 81; VI 26;
    VIII 335; IX 333
Condéen: IV 76
Conty, Armand de Bourbon, prince de:
  IV 79, 80, 88; V 373; VII 820,
  826, 830, 832, 833; VIII 335
Corbie, année de: V 372
coronation, royal: I 96–7
Corsica: II 50; XII 170; XV 79
council, king's: II 55; III 172, 173–5;
  X 825, 833; XI 15
Courson, Lamoignon de, intendant of
  Bordeaux: XIV 394, 395–6, 400,
  401–2, 411

Daguesseau (d'Aguesseau), Henri-François, *procureur général* of the
  Parlement of Paris and later
    Chancellor: XIV 391, 392, 409
Dauphiné: I 110–11; III 167; VII 825;
  XII 152
debasement: XI 16, 29; XII 154–6;
  XIII 112
debt, public: X 831, 832, 835;
  XI 20–21, 31; XII 170–71, 173,
  174; XIII 112; XIV 410; XV 68
  comparative size of English and
    Dutch debt: XV 76
prêts sur prêts: XI 22
declarations of wealth: XII 167, 175;
  XIV 389, 391, 393–6, 397, 411
departments, creation of: XII 175
Desmaretz, Nicolas, finance minister:
  III 167; XI 15; XII 150, 151, 156,
  164, 165–6, 170; XIV 385,
  389–90, 392, 393, 394, 396, 397,
  402–3, 405, 406, 409, 410, 411,
  412
Dessert, Daniel, historian: I 109–10;
  XIII 124 n.71
devoirs, farm of in Brittany: XII 161
dixième: III 167; XII 151, 154, 165–7,
  175; XIII 127; XIV *passim*
dixième de retenue: XIV 390, 409
donneur d'avis (projector): IV 100
  n.111; VIII 333; X 827
Doyle, William: I 103
droits aliénés: XII 150; XIII 101, 118
droit annuel: I 102; III 173, 175; IV
  72, 89; XII 153
du Bois du Baillet, intendant: II 53;
  III 166
Dubosc-Montandré: VI 16
Dupes, Day of: IV 74, 77

Effiat, Antoine Coiffier de Ruzé,
  marquis d', finance minister:
  III 174; XIII 102, 116
élections: I 111–12; II 51, 52; XII 152,
  162; XIII 116, 118, 120; XIV 404
élus: IV 73; V 368; VIII 326
Elias, Norbert: I 103–4
Elbeuf, Charles II de Lorraine, duc d':
  VII 826
Emperor, Holy Roman: IV 74; VIII 324;
  XI 21

Emperor, Holy Roman cont.
  in his kingdom: I 94
England: XV 62
Épernon, Bernard de Nogaret de la
  Valette duc d': VII 825; VIII 334
Épernon, Jean-Louis de Nogaret de la
  Valette duc d': VII 818, 824
Esquilache, marqués d': XII 168;
  XV 66, 71
'estate states': I 94
Estates General: I 97, 101, 102, 105;
  III 173; XIII 108
  abortive during the Fronde: IV 76,
    81, 82; V 367–8, 380
  lack of legislative power: V 380
estates, provincial: I 112; III 166–9;
  XIII 116
exemption, fiscal: XII 167
expenditure
  distinction between ordinary and
    extraordinary: XIII 102–3, 105–6
  proposed peacetime reduction in:
    XIII 121–2
  war: VIII 333; X 828–30, 832, 835;
    XIII 106, 122; XIV 386, 413–14

Fabert, Abraham de: VII 828
Faucon de Ris, intendant: III 164–5, 166
ferme générale: XI 11, 16, 23, 24–5;
  XII 159, 161; XV 72; *see also*
  revenue farming
Ferrand, intendant of Brittany:
  XIV 398, 403
Feydeau, Antoine, financier: XI 13, 20,
  21, 22
Feydeau, intendant: III 166
Fiesque, comte de: IV 81
financiers (*gens d'affaires*): I 109–10;
  IV 73, 92; VI 20–21; VIII 329;
  X 826–7, 828, 831, 835; XII 151,
  172; XIV 392, 400, 409 n.151
fiscal base: XIV 383–4
fiscal burden
  of Britain and France compared:
    XII 174
  per capita: XII 169–70; XV 72
  under the Revolution: XII 175
fiscal limit, of direct taxes: XIII 120;
  XIV 383

Flanders: XIV 392
Fontrailles, Louis d'Astarac, marquis
  de: IV 77–8
Foucquet, Antoine, sr. de Croissy: IV 81
Foucquet, Nicolas, vicomte de Melun
  and marquis de Belle-Ile, finance
  minister: I 115; V 376; VII 821,
  831; VIII 337, 338; X 826 n.2,
  833; XI 14, 15; XIII 105, 127
Foullé de Montargis, intendant:
  II 56 n.66
Franche-Comté: XII 152, 154
Francis I: I 100–101; XII 152
Fronde: II 49–50; IV *passim*
  and revenue farmers: XI 19
  as defence of corporate interests of
    officiers: VIII 338–9
  as disparate grouping of Mazarin's
    enemies: VII 15; IX 336
  as *révolution manquée* Introduction;
    IV 90–91; V 365
  contrasted with English Civil War:
    V 374
  fiscal origins: VIII 338; IX 336;
    XIII 110
  foreign war preferable to civil war:
    V 373–4; IX 336; X 832
  general causation balanced against
    Mazarin's responsibility: IX 330;
    XIII 106
  military course of: V 373
  ministerial instability during:
    XIII 102
Frondeurs: IV 76, 78, 79–81, 88;
  VII 826, 830
Fuensaldaña, comte de: IV 83; IX 332

gabelles de France and other *gabelles*:
  XI 12–13, 22, 26; XII 151, 175;
  XIII 101
  breaking of leases: XI 13–14
  Richelieu's proposed reform of salt
    tax: XIII 122, 125
  salt consumption: XI 18–19; XIII 110
gages: VIII 325, 330, 332, 338;
  XII 153; XIII 120; XIV 398, 409
Gallicus amicus non vicinus: IX 331
Garrisson, Janine: I 102–3
Gaston d'Orléans: III 175, 176; IV 77,

81–6, 88; V 373; VI 20, 24, 26; VII 826, 829, 830, 832; VIII 328, 335
Gaudin, Martin Michel Charles, duc de Gaëte: XV 81
généralités: XII 152, 162, 169, 170, 175; XIII 112, 114, 116, 120; XIV 404
government: III 162
governors, provincial: I 113; III 172; IV 77, 88–9; VI 22; VII *passim*
grain liberalization: XIV 387; XV 79–80
Grand Remonstrance: V 370
Greengrass, Mark: I 102; III 173
greniers à sel (salt deposits): XI 13
Grenoble: XII, 170; XIII 112
Guénégaud, Gabriel de, *trésorier de l'Épargne*: XIII 103
Guise family: I 101
Guyenne: IV 75, 81, 88; VII 825, 829; XII 152; XIV 396, 411
Guyet, intendant: XII 164

habeas corpus: VIII 332
Hanley, Sarah: I 97–8
Harcourt, Henri de Lorraine, comte d': VII 826–7, 829; VIII 334
Harlay, Achille III de, comte de Beaumont: XIV 387
Harlay de Champvallon, François de, archbishop of Rouen: VI 19
Harlay, intendant: III 171
Haro, Don Luis de: IV 83
Harvoin, receiver-general at Alençon: XV 64, 66
Hémery, Michelle Particelle, sieur d', finance minister: IV 71, 72, 73; V 369; VI 22; VII 824; VIII 324–5, 330, 338; X 830, 831; XIII 103
Henri II: I 100; VII 818
Henri III: I 101–2; III 172, 177; V 377; VII 818
Henri IV: I 101–2; III 162–3, 173; VI 22, 27; VII 823, 829; VIII 331, 336; X 827, 834–5, 836; XIII 100, 125
Héroard, Jean: I 103
Hickey, Daniel: I 110–11

Hintze, Otto: II 46
hôtel de ville, 'massacre at' Parisian: IV 86
Huguenots: III 165, 173; V 376; XIII 110 n.30, 118
Hurepoix: IV 77

Importants, Cabale des: IV 77; VI 24
impôt unique: XII 169 n.78; XV 79
Ile-de-France: VII 825
intendants of justice, police and finance: I 114, 115; II 45, 50–52; III 161
  and *dixième*: XIV 393, 395, 397
  careers: VIII 327
  contrasted with English Major-Generals: V 368
  drafting of decrees: II 55
  tax powers: III 171; VIII 337; XII 150
  recalled in 1648: IV 73; V 368; VIII 326, 328–9
  reinstated in 1652–53: IV 92; V 368, 380; VIII 337
interest, rate of: VIII 333–4, 337; IX 330; X 826, 836; XIII 104–5

Jackson, Richard: I 96–7
Jansenism: I 99; V 377
Jeannin, Pierre, finance minister: X 827; XIII 106
Joly, Claude: VI 16
Joly, Guy: IV 80
Joyeuse, Anne, duc de: VII 818, 824

Keohane, Nannerl O.: I 95; II 46
Kettering, Sharon: I 113–14
Knecht, Robert: I 100, 102–3
Kossmann, E.H.: VIII 323, 328, 333, 336

La Briffe, intendant of Burgundy: XIV 404, 411
La Ferté-Senectère, Henri, marquis de: VII 828
La Fond, intendant: XII 152
La Meilleraye, Charles de la Porte, duc de: IV 88; VII 824–5, 831–2, 833; VIII 331, 333
La Mothe-Houdancourt, viceroy of Catalonia: VI 24

land tax in England: XIV 391–2, 407; XV 73
Languedoc: I 112–13; IV 88; V 368; VII 826, 832; VIII 326; XII 152, 164; XIII 116; XIV 385, 396, 399, 411, 412
La Rochefoucauld, François, duc de: IV 80, 88
La Rochelle: XIII 116 n.114; XIV 403
La Trémouille, Henri-Charles, duc de: IV 88
Laugeois d'Imbercourt, intendant at Montauban: XIV 403
L'Averdy, Clément Charles F. de: XII 168, 172; XV 63, 65, 66, 73, 78, 79
La Vieuville, Charles duc de, finance minister: III 174; IV 376; VI 22; VII 826; VIII 331, 335; IX 332; X 827; XIII 99, 106
Law, John: I 116; VIII 328; XII 153, 166–7, 171–2; XIV 405–6, 411
League, Catholic: I 97; III 173; V 373; VII 829; XIII 118
Le Bret, Cardin: II 45, 49–51
Le Gendre, intendant at Montauban: XIV 397, 402–3
Leopold I, Emperor: XII 162
Le Peletier, Claude, finance minister: XIII 104
Le Roy Ladurie, Emmanuel: I 103
Lesdiguières, Constable of France: III 173
Lille: XII 170
Limoges: XIII 114
Limousin: IV 88; VII 828
Lionne, Hugues de: VI 23
Lipsius, Justus: II 59
lit de justice: I 97–8; IV 72; VIII 330, 336
loans, reliance on revenue from: VIII 328
Longueville, Henri II d'Orléans, duc de: IV 78, 80, 88; VII 820, 823, 826, 829; VIII 335
Longueville, Anne-Geneviève de Bourbon, duchesse de: IV 80
Loricards: IV 90
Lorraine, Charles IV, duc de: IV 82, 86; VI 23

Louis XI: II 48
Louis XII: I 100
Louis XIII: I 103; III 163–4, 174–5; IV 74, 79; X 833, 836; XI 20; XII 151
   fiscal policy: XIII 99–101, 106, 114, 118, 120, 125, 126, 128
   foreign policy: IX 330–31
   last will and testament: V 375; VI 20
   revenue compared with that of Charles I: V 367
Louis XIV: I 103; III 164, 171, 175; IV 74, 84, 91; V 375; VI 20, 27; VII 828; VIII 336; X 833–6; XII 156, 162, 166; XIII 100, 120, 127; XIV 383–4, 386, 412
Louis XV: I 104
Louis XVI: I 104; XII 175
Louvois: I 108
Loyseau, Charles: I 96; II 44, 48–9
Luynes, Charles I, marquis d'Albert, duc de: VII 819, 822; XIII 118
Luynes, Louis-Charles, marquis d'Albert, duc de: IV 88
Lyon: XII 164, 170; XIII 112; XIV 399, 400
Lyonnais: VII 825; VIII 326; XIV 384, 404

Machiavelli, Niccolò: VI 18
maîtres des requêtes: VIII 327, 331
Major, J. Russell: I 100–101, 111–12; XIII 118
Mal(l)et, Jean-Roland, finance ministry clerk and financial historian: XI 15–16, 24 n.2; XII 156, 164, 170; XIII 102–4, 106, 108, 110, 112, 114, 116, 118, 120, 126, 128
Mallier, Claude sr. du Houssay: XIII 103
Marie de Médicis: I 105; III 173; VI 26; X 827
Marillac, Michel de, finance minister and Keeper of the Seals: I 111–12, 115; X 828; XIII 102, 116, 127
Marle, intendant: II 53
Maupeou 'revolution': I 99
Mazarin, Cardinal Jules: IV 71, 72, 74, 80; VIII 324; XIII 102

adventurer or statesman: IX 334
alleged duplicity during the Fronde:
    IX 329
alleged Machiavellianism: VI 18;
    IX 334
and *comptants*: X 830-32
and English constitution: V 370
and king's council: XIII 127
and provincial governorships: IV 88;
    VII *passim*
and royal declarations during the
    Fronde: IV 74-5, 76; IX 332
champion of rentiers: VIII 331
criticism of foreign policy during the
    Fronde: IV 78-9; VI 18; IX 335
fiscal policy during ministry:
    XIII 104, 106, 114
fortune: VI 21; VII 821
governor of Auvergne: VII 825
'held Louis XIV in captivity': IV 91;
    V 375; VI 19
invasion of 1651: IV 81, 84; VI 17,
    24; VII 828, 831; IX 332
Italian birth: VI 19
library: VI 18
loyalty during the Fronde: IX 333
nieces (*Mazarinettes*): IV 88;
    VII 822-3, 828, 832
orders arrest of princes: IV 80; VI 25;
    VII 820-21; VIII 335; IX 332
perceived parallel with Strafford:
    V 376; VI 26; IX 333
political acceptability in 1652:
    IV 89; V 376; VIII 336
relationship with Anne of Austria:
    VI 16
supposed place of exile in Italy:
    VI 24; IX 334-5
unpopularity: VI 15; VII 819;
    VIII 334, 335
Mazarinades: V 376; VI 15-16, 21, 26;
    VII 819, 832; IX 329; XIII 126
Mazarini, Michele: VII 822
Mercoeur, Philip-Emmanuel de
    Lorraine, duc de: IV 88;
    VII 823-4
Méliand, intendant at Pau and later
    Lyon: II 54, 55; III 169;
    XIV 404

Metz: XII 170
ministériat: VI 19; XIII 102
minorities, royal: III 177
Molé, Mathieu: IV 76; VIII 330, 333,
    334
Montauban: XIII 114; XIV 397, 402-3
Montesquieu, Charles Louis de
    Secondat, baron de: XV 61-2, 63,
    66-7, 68
Montmorency-Damville, Henri de,
    Constable: VII 819
Moote, A. Lloyd: IV 71-7, 90;
    VIII 323-4, 333, 335; IX 329-30,
    331; X 832, n. 3; XIII 99
Moreau de Beaumont, Jean-Louis:
    XII 150, 151; XIII 122, 124;
    XV 63, 77, 78, 80
Morgues, Mathieu de: VI 18, 26
Morineau, Michel, historian:
    XII 154 n. 20, 161, 167, 170 n. 81
Motteville, Madame de: IV 86-7
Moulins: XIII 112

Nancy: XII 170
Napoleon Bonaparte: I 93; XV 81
Naudé, Gabriel: VI 17; IX 333
Necker, Jacques: XII 153, 168-70, 172
Neri, Pompeo: XV 64, 74
Nicolay, Antoine II: X 828
nobility
    distinctions: V 379
    during the Fronde: IV 76-87;
        VII *passim*; VIII 338
Nointel, Louis Béchameil de: XIV 401
Normandy: I 110; IV 82, 87, 88; VI 25;
    VII 820, 824, 826; XIII 114, 118

officier(s): II 46-7; III 176; IV 72;
    V 368-9; VIII 324 and *passim*;
    XIV 392
    sale of offices: XII 152-3; XIII 106,
        108, 110
Olivares, Gaspar de Guzmán, count-duke
    of: I 115; II 58; XIII 125
Orléans: XII 165; XIII 112
Ormée: IV 89, 90; V 373
Orry, Jean: XIV 389-90
Orry, Philibert: XIV 410
Ottoman Turks: XV 61, 62, 64-5

Papacy: II 44 n.6, 48
Paris: VI 25; VIII 328, 332–3;
    XII 168, 169, 170; XIII 112, 118,
    120; XIV 400, 404; XV 79
Parker, David: I 95; II 43, 45
Parlement(s): V 381; XV 78, 80
    and religious pacification: III 172
    Louis XIV curtails powers of: III 176
    of Aix: V 382; VIII 331, 334
    of Bordeaux: IV 86, 89; V 382;
    VIII 334
    of Dijon: XIV 398
    of Grenoble: XIV 398
    of Paris: IV 71, 75, 79, 82, 86, 90,
    91; V 371, 375, 382; VI 15, 17,
    20, 23, 24, 27, 30 n. 63;
    VII 819–20, 822, 830; VIII 325–7,
    332, 334–5, 336; IX 334; XIV 398
    of Pau: III 168–71
    of Rennes: IV 88; XIV 398
    of Rouen: V 382; VIII 331, 334
    of Toulouse: VIII 334
parties casuelles: see *officier(s)*
Patin, Guy: V 375 n.36; VI 16, 19;
    VII 819, 823
Pau: XII 170
Payen, Pierre, financier: XI 21
pays d'élections: XII 152, 162, 172;
    XIII 108, 110, 112, 114, 116, 120;
    XIV 405, 407; XV 77
pays d'états: XII 152, 172;
    XIII 101, 108 n.28, 110, 114, 116;
    XIV 399
pays d'impositions: XII 152, 172
Pellot, Claude, intendant: II 51–2
Peñaranda, count of: II 60; IX 331
Perpignan: XII 170
personal rule of king: III 177
Petty, Sir William: XIV 408–9
Philip IV of Spain: II 59, 60; IV 79, 80,
    83; VI 23–4, 26; VII 826–7;
    VIII 328; IX 331, 332, 333, 335;
    XIII 128
Philippe d'Orléans, brother of Louis
    XIV: IV 78
Philippe d'Orléans, Regent: I 106;
    III 175; XII 166, 167; XIV 412
Physiocracy: XII 169 n. 78; XIV 387,
    411, 412; XV 79–80

Picardy: VII 824, 826; VIII 326;
    XIV 404
Poitiers: XIII 114
Poitou: IV 88; VII 825
Poland: XV 62
Pombal: XV 65
Poncet de la Rivière, intendant: II 53
Pontchartrain, Louis Phélypeaux, comte
    de: XII 162; XIII 104
Portugal: VI 23; XV 65–6
princeps legibus solutus: I 93
Provence: IV 75, 88; VII 824, 825, 829;
    VIII 326; XII 152; XIV 399
Prussia: XV 63, 71, 73
Puget de Montauron, Pierre, financier:
    XIII 121
Pyrenees, Peace of: IV 82

Quesnay, François: XII 169 n. 78
quod principi placuit: I 93

rebellion, popular: I 98; IV 90
receveurs généraux des finances:
    XII 172
regency council: IV 80, 83–5
regents: I 105–6; V 377
remonstrances: VI 16–17, 25–6;
    VIII 335
Rennes: XII 170
rentes: IV 89; VIII 330–31, 332, 338;
    XI 19, 21, 24; XII 151, 152;
    XIII 120; XIV 392, 400, 409
    rachat des rentes: VIII 333
representation: XII 175–6
republicanism: IV 91, 99 n.108; V 375;
    VI 27
Retz, Jean-François-Paul de Gondi,
    Cardinal de: IV 81; V 375 n.35,
    377; VI 16, 27
revenue farming: XI 11; XIII 106
    Adam Smith on: XII 174 n.103
    amount of revenues from: XI 15;
    XII 161; XIII 110
    and economic crisis: XI 17–19
    auctions: XI 20
    de facto consolidation of leases:
    XI 22–3
    direct administration (*régie*): XII 172;
    XV 68

England and France compared: XI 13,
    20, 21–2, 25
  farms leased by the *Compagnie des
    Indes*: XII 172
  last revenue farmers guillotined:
    XII 175
  over-renting: XI 16
  political role of farmers: XII 168,
    172; XV 79
  remissions: XI 19
  security of revenue from: XI 17
  sub-farmers: XI 23; *see also ferme
    générale*
revenues
  anticipation of: XI 20–21; XIII 101
  balance between direct and indirect:
    XII 161, 175; XV 68
  distinction between ordinary and
    extraordinary: XIII 106, 108
  evolution of: XII 156–8
  gross and net: XII 159
  proposed reform in peacetime:
    XIII 122
  regressive character of indirect taxes:
    XIII 124
  structure of: XII 150–51
  unification of: XII 172
Richelieu, Armand-Jean du Plessis,
    Cardinal de: IV 77–8
  alleged Machiavellianism: VI 18–19
  and *comptants*: X 830
  and financiers: X 828
  and internal reform in time of war:
    IX 330
  and king's council: XIII 127
  as affairiste: XIII 127
  fiscal policies during his ministry:
    XII 150–51; XIII 99–101, 104,
    106, 110, 114
  fortune: I 106–7; VII 821 n. 2
  governor of Brittany: VII 824
  judgement on Richelieu as
    'state-builder': XIII 128
  reform plan: X 836; XIII 121–5,
    130–33
  subordination of domestic to foreign
    policy: X 836
Riley, James C.: XII 156, 159,
    173 n.100

Riom: XIII 112
Rohan, Henri Chabot, duc de: IV 88;
    VII 833
Rohan, Louis, chevalier de: VII 818
Rouen: XII 169, 170; XIII 114
Rousseau, Jean-Jacques: I 95–6
Rousselot de Surgy, Jacques Philibert:
    XV 63
Roussillon: IV 88
Rowen, Herbert: I 95
Rueil, Treaty of: IV 80, 87, 90;
    VI 16–17; VII 820; VIII 333–4,
    335, 338; X 832
Russia: XV 62, 76

Saint-Contest, de, intendant at Metz:
    XIV 396
Saint-Macary, acting intendant: II 54–5;
    III 169–70
Saint-Simon, Louis de Rouvroy, duc de:
    I 103; III 162; XIII 100; XIV 385
salines (salt works): XIII 124 n. 71
Savoy: XIV 399–400; XV 74
Schomberg, Henri de, finance minister:
    III 174; X 827; XIII 100, 106, 118
Sedan: IV 78; VII 827–8
Séguier, Pierre, Chancellor of France:
    IV 75, 85; VII 833; VIII 326, 332;
    XI 17; XIII 103
semestres, creation of in sovereign
    courts: VIII 334
Servien, Abel, finance minister: IV 78;
    X 833; XI 23; XIII 99
Ship Money: V 366
Silhon, Jean de: VI 23; IX 333
Silhouette, Étienne de: XII 168; XV 79
Skinner, Quentin: II 43, 61
Smith, Adam: XII 174; XV 80–81
Soissons: XII 169; XIII 112
Soissons, comte de: IV 77
sol pour livre or *pancarte* (5 per cent
    sales tax): XI 12; XIII 121, 124–5
sovereign courts: III 176; IV 73, 86;
    V 381; XII 173; XV 77–8
sovereignty: II 43, 45, 49, 53
Spain: II 57–60; III 177; IV 72, 74,
    78–9, 86; V 368, 373–4, 377;
    VI 24; VII 830–1; VIII 324;
    XI 21

Spain cont.
  balance between direct and indirect taxes: XV 69–70
  fiscal reform in the eighteenth century: XII 168; XV 66, 70–1
  peace negotiations as a political issue during the Fronde: IV 76–83, 91–2
  única contribución: XII 168; XV 66, 71
Strasbourg: XII 170
Suárez, Francisco: II 59
subdélégués: II 51–3; XIV 393, 396–7
subdélégués-généraux: II 53, 54–5
Sublet des Noyers, François, intendant of finance and secretary of state for war: XIII 99
subsistances: XII 151; XIII 101, 121
Sully, Maximilien de Béthune, duc de: I 111; III 173–4; VII 821, 830; X 827; XI 17, 24; XII 151; XIII 104, 106, 114, 125 n.74, 127
surintendance des finances: III 173, 174; X 833
Sweden: XIII 100; XV 65, 76
Swiss Confederation: XV 67

taille: IV 73, 77, 92; V 368; VIII 326–9; XI 25; XII 150, 162, 164, 165, 174, 175; XIII 101, 106; XIV 385, 388, 396, 407
  distinction between levy, *charges* and net revenue: XIII 116, 120 n. 56
taillon: XII 150; XIII 101
Talon, Omer: VI 17, 22; VII 818, 832; VIII 330, 332; XIII 110
taxe des aisés: XIII 121
Touraine: IV 88
Tours: XII 169; XIII 112
traites (customs duties): XI 12, 13; XII 174 n.102; XV 77
traités: see *affaires extraordinaires*
trésorier de l'Épargne: X 826
trésoriers de France: IV 73; V 368; VIII 326

Tubeuf, Jacques, intendant of finance: XIII 121, 126
Turenne, Henri de la Tour d'Auvergne, vicomte de: IV 80, 82, 84, 88; V 372, 373; VII 827–8, 829
Turgot, Anne Robert Jacques: XII 169 n.78
Turgot, intendant of Auvergne: XIV 401
Tuscany: XV 73–4, 77

United Provinces: IV 72; IX 331; XI 12; XV 75
  balance between direct and indirect taxes: XV 69
  French subsidies: XIII 100
  provincial fiscal structure: XV 66
  role of Dutch models in taxation: XI 12; XII 165; XIV 392
  shift away from revenue farming: XV 72

Valenciennes: XII 170
Vauban, Sébastien Le Prestre, Maréchal de: XII 165, 166; XIII 124, 127; XIV 385, 390, 405, 406, 412
Vendôme, César de Bourbon, duc de: IV 88; VII 823–4
Véron de Forbonnais, F.: X 826 n.2; XII 156, 164, 166, 167; XIII 126; XIV 406
Versailles: I 104
Villeroy, Nicolas II de Neufville, duc de: III 175; VI 18; VII 825 n.3
vingtième(s): XII 167, 175; XIV 411
visa: XII 173
Voltaire, François-Marie Arouet, known as: XIII 126
Voyer d'Argenson, intendant: II 52

Westphalia, peace negotiations at: IV 72; VI 23

Zagorin, Perez: VIII 323